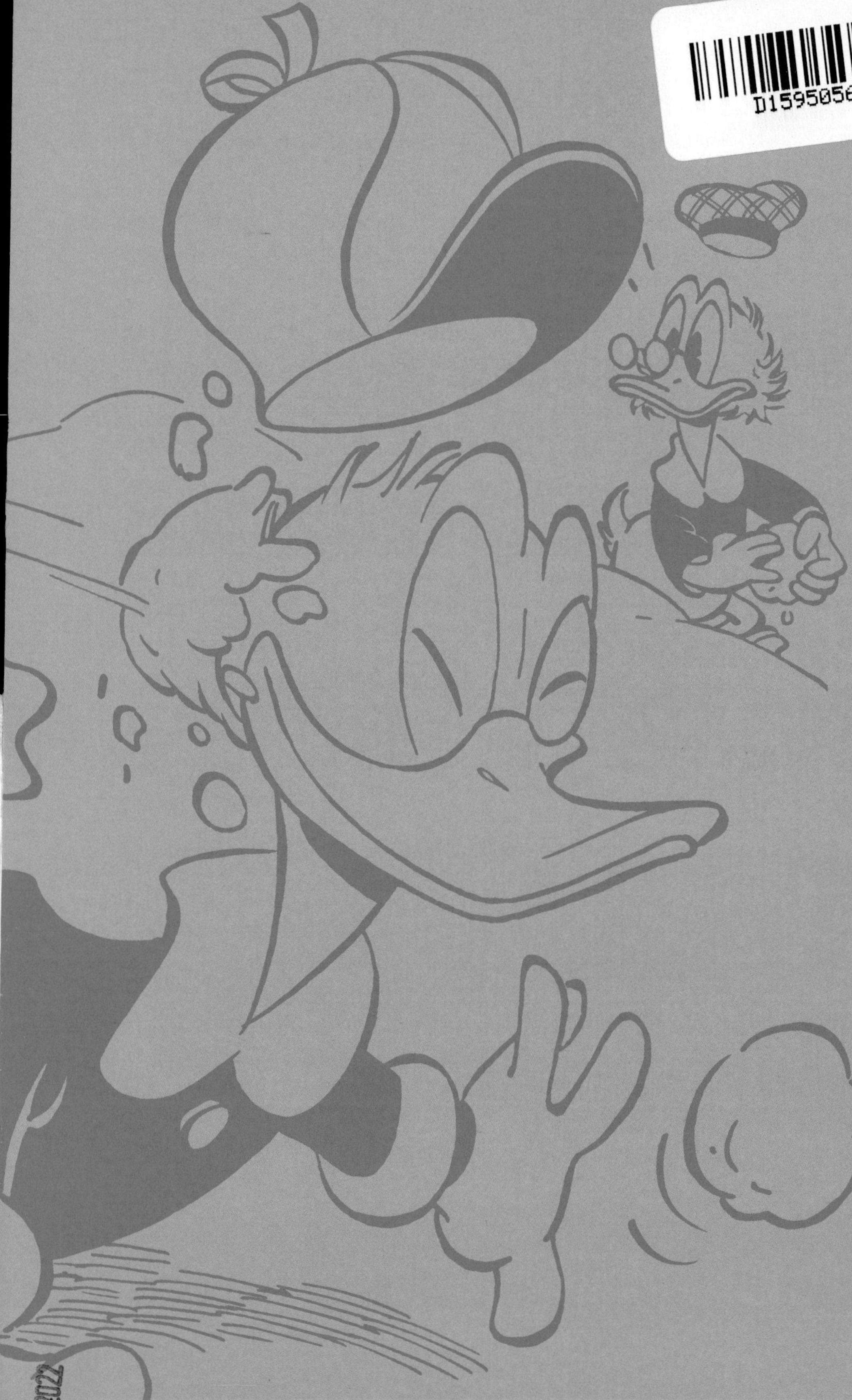

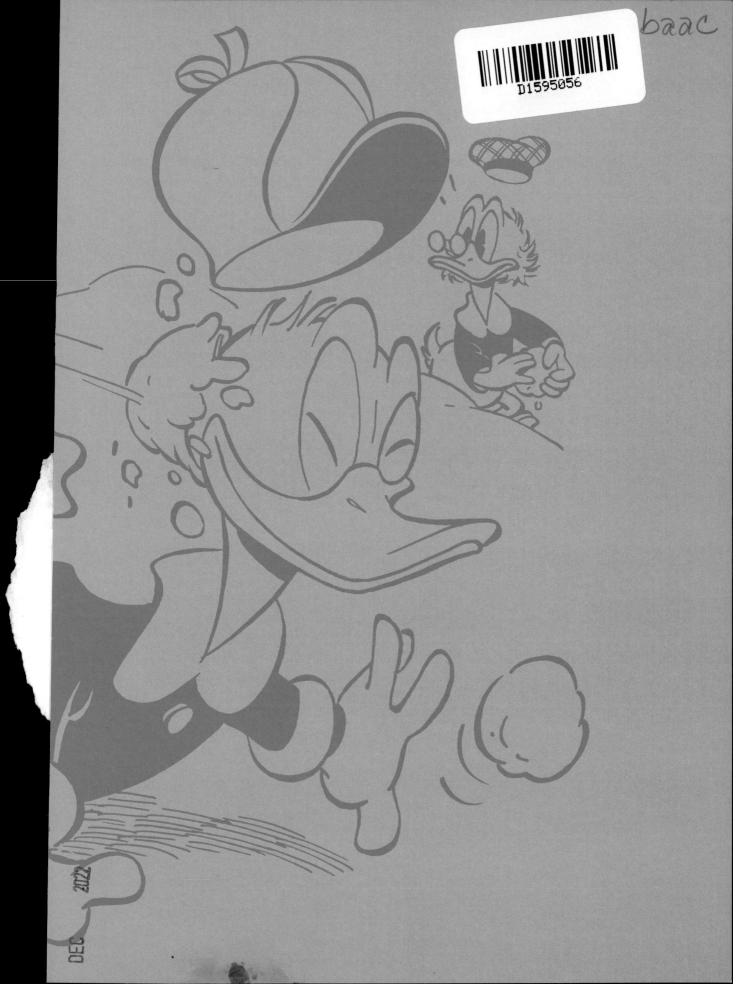

Walt Disney

Uncle $crooge and Donald Duck

Bear Mountain Tales

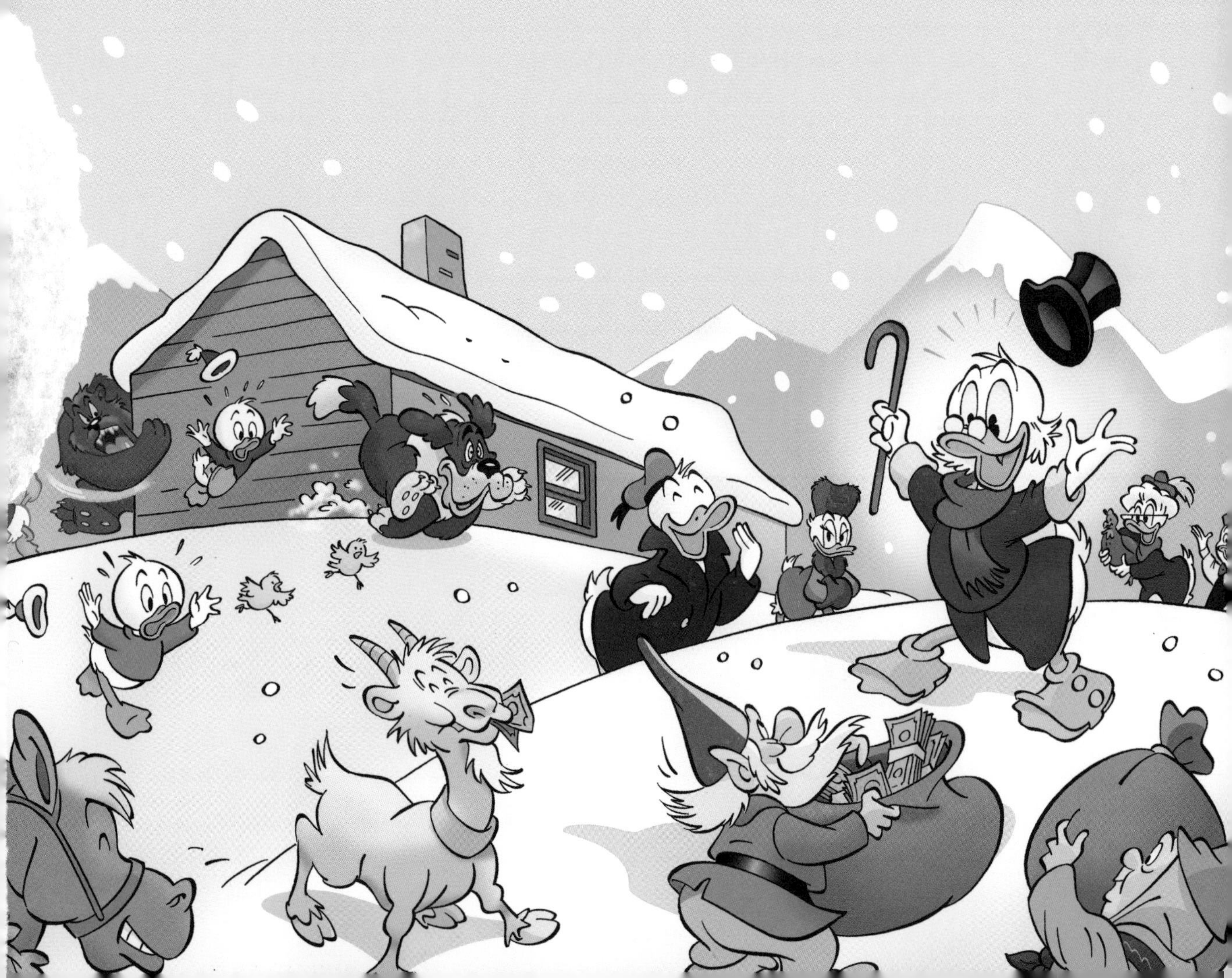

PUBLISHER: Gary Groth
EDITOR: David Gerstein
DESIGN: Kayla E.
PRODUCTION: Paul Baresh and Christina Hwang
ASSOCIATE PUBLISHER: Eric Reynolds

Fantagraphics Books, Inc. | 7563 Lake City Way NE | Seattle WA 98115 | (800) 657-1100

Visit us at fantagraphics.com. Follow us on Twitter at @fantagraphics and on Facebook at facebook.com/fantagraphics.

Thanks to Monty Bali, Diego Ceresa, John Clark, Ferdi Felderhof, Thomas Jensen, Iliana Lopez, Carol McGreal, and Ken Shue.

First printing: October 2022 • ISBN 978-1-68396-661-6
Printed in China • Library of Congress Control Number: 2022935199

The stories in this volume were originally published in the following magazines:

"Christmas on Bear Mountain" in American Donald Duck *Four Color* 178, November 1947 (W OS 178-02)
"Ducking Out" in American *Donald Duck* 77, May 1961 (W DD 77-01)
"Bear Right" in American *Donald Duck* Sunday comic strip, November 4, 1962 (ZD 62-11-04)
"Return to Bear Mountain" in German *Disney-Sonderalbum* 5, 1987 (D 9614)
"Growf!" in Danish *Anders And & Co.* 1978-52, December 23, 1978 (D 4034)
"When Christmas Went Cuckoo" in Danish *Anders And & Co.* 1991-52, December 23, 1991 (D 91139)
"Bolivar's Job" in Danish *Anders And & Co.* 1989-52, December 18, 1989 (D 88121)
"The Man Who Drew Ducks" in Italian *Topolino* 1919, September 6, 1992 (I TL 1919-C)
"Missing Mogul Mystery" in Dutch *Donald Duck Weekblad* 1995-22, June 2, 1995 (H 95007)
"The Richest Duck in the World" in Danish *Anders And & Co.* 1994-22, June 2, 1994 (D 93488)
"Lost on Bear Mountain" in Danish *Anders And & Co.* 2013-50, December 13, 2013 (D 99099)
"New Year's Daze" in Swedish *Kalle Anka & C:o* 1994-51, December 19, 1994 (D 94039)
"Another Christmas on Bear Mountain" in Italian *Topolino* 2717, December 25, 2007 (I TL 2717-1)
"Christmas Magic" in Danish *Anders And & Co.* 2003-51, December 18, 2003 (D 2003-121)
"The Snow Duck of Bear Mountain" in Italian *Topolino* 3032, January 7, 2014 (I TL 3032-2)
"Holiday Hideaway on Bear Mountain" in Danish *Anders And & Co.* 2017-49, December 7, 2017 (D 2016-347)
"Scaredy Showdown" in supplement to Dutch *Donald Duck Weekblad* 2017-52, December 19, 2017 (H 2017-043)
"Nightmare on Bear Mountain!" in American *DuckTales* (series III) 11, August 2018 (XPW DTT CP 5-2)
"The Wonderful Wishing Crown" in Italian *Topolino* 3238, December 13, 2017 (I TL 3238-1)

Cover art by Marco Rota originally published in Italian *Zio Paperone* 75, December 1995 (IC ZP 75B).

Endpaper drawings by Daan Jippes originally published in Dutch *Oom Dagobert* 29, October 1985
(HC OD 29) and *De Beste Verhalen van Donald Duck* 97, November 1998 (HC BV 97).

Pretitle page art by Kari Korhonen originally published in supplement to Finnish
Aku Ankka 2007-51, December 19, 2007 (D/SAN 2007-065). Color by Sanoma.

Title page art by Carl Barks originally published in Finnish *Aku Ankka* 1997-48,
November 26, 1997 (CB OIL 145); image courtesy Sanoma.

Back cover art by Daan Jippes (top) and Ulrich Schroeder (bottom), originally published in American *Walt Disney's Christmas Parade*
[series II] 2, 1989 (ARC CPG 2) and *Uncle Scrooge* 336, December 2004 (D 18303). Color by Digikore Studios (top) and Sanoma (bottom).

Walt Disney

UNCLE $CROOGE
and
Donald Duck
BEAR MOUNTAIN TALES

CONTENTS

Trouble Bruin 6
David Gerstein

Christmas on Bear Mountain . . 7
First published in American Donald Duck
Four Color 178, November 1947 • Story,
Art and Lettering by Carl Barks • Color
by Rich Tommaso

Ducking Out 27
First published truncated in American *Donald
Duck* 77, May 1961; first published more
complete in Swedish *Kalle Anka Klassiker*
2020-02, April 21, 2020 • Story by Carl Fallberg
Pencils by Tony Strobl • Inks by John Liggera
Lettering by Rome Siemon • Color by
Digikore Studios

Bear Right 38
First published in American *Donald Duck*
Sunday comic strip, November 4, 1962
Story by Bob Karp • Art and Lettering by Al
Taliaferro • Color by Digikore Studios

Return to Bear Mountain 39
First published in German *Disney-
Sonderalbum* 5, 1987; first American printing
in *Donald Duck Adventures* [series II] 32-33,
January and February 1993 • Plot by Lars
Bergström • Script by Stefan Printz-Påhlson
Art by Daniel Branca • Translation and
Dialogue by Gary Leach • Lettering by John
Clark • Color by Digikore Studios

Growf! 68
First published in Danish *Anders And & Co.*
1978-52, December 23, 1978 • Story by Tom
Anderson • Art by Santiago Scalabroni
Translation, Dialogue and Lettering by David
Gerstein • Color by Digikore Studios

**When Christmas
Went Cuckoo** 69
First published in Danish *Anders And &
Co.* 1991-52, December 23, 1991 • Story by
Stefan Printz-Påhlson • Art by Victor "Vicar"
Arriagada Rios • Translation and Dialogue
by Jonathan H. Gray • Lettering by Christina
Hwang • Color by Sanoma

Bolivar's Job 79
First published in Danish *Anders And & Co.*
1989-52, December 18, 1989 • Plot by Mike
Sharland and Stefan Printz-Påhlson • Script
by Unn Printz-Påhlson • Art by Daniel Branca
Translation, Dialogue, and Lettering by David
Gerstein • Color by Sarah Flanagan and
Digikore Studios

The Man Who Drew Ducks . . . 87
First published in Italian *Topolino* 1919,
September 6, 1992; first American printing
in *Uncle Scrooge* 400, February 2011 • Story
by Rudy Salvagnini • Pencils by Giorgio
Cavazzano • Inks by Sandro Zemolin
Translation, Dialogue, and Lettering by David
Gerstein • Color by Disney Italia

Missing Mogul Mystery **108**
First published in Dutch *Donald Duck Weekblad* 1995-22, June 2, 1995 • Story by Evert Geradts • Pencils by Freddy Milton Inks by Jaap Stavenuiter • Translation, Dialogue, and Lettering by David Gerstein Color by Sanoma

The Life and Times of Scrooge McDuck: The Richest Duck in the World **109**
First published in Danish *Anders And & Co.* 1994-22, June 2, 1994; first American printing in *Uncle Scrooge* 296, February 1996 Story and Art by Don Rosa • Lettering by Todd Klein with Scott Rockwell and David Gerstein • Color by Susan Daigle-Leach and Scott Rockwell

Lost on Bear Mountain **128**
First published in Danish *Anders And & Co.* 2013-50, December 13, 2013 • Story by Per Hedman • Art by Tino Santanach • Translation, Dialogue, and Lettering by David Gerstein • Color by Digikore Studios

New Year's Daze **129**
First published in Swedish *Kalle Anka & C:o* 1994-51, December 19, 1994; first American printing in *Uncle Scrooge* 349, January 2006 Plot by Stefan Printz-Påhlson • Script by Unn Printz-Påhlson • Art by Victor "Vicar" Arriagada Rios • Translation and Dialogue by David Gerstein • Lettering by Willie Schubert • Color by Barry Englin Grossman

Another Christmas on Bear Mountain **139**
First published in Italian *Topolino* 2717, December 25, 2007; first American printing in *Uncle Scrooge* 413, December 2015 Story by Tito Faraci • Pencils by Giorgio Cavazzano • Inks by Sandro Zemolin Translation and Dialogue by Gary Leach Lettering by Nicole and Travis Seitler Color by Disney Italia with Nicole and Travis Seitler

Christmas Magic **171**
First published in Danish *Anders And & Co.* 2003-51, December 18, 2003; first American printing in *Uncle Scrooge* 336, December 2004 • Story by Per Hedman • Art by Victor "Vicar" Arriagada Rios • Lettering by Willie Schubert • Color by Egmont and Susan Daigle-Leach

The Snow Duck of Bear Mountain **183**
First published in Italian *Topolino* 3032, January 7, 2014 • Story by Ricardo Pesce Art by Nicolino Picone • Translation and Dialogue by Joe Torcivia • Lettering by Paul Baresh and Christina Hwang • Color by Disney Italia

Holiday Hideaway on Bear Mountain **215**
First published in Danish *Anders And & Co.* 2017-49, December 7, 2017 • Story by Pat and Carol McGreal • Art by Francisco Rodriguez Peinado • Lettering by David Gerstein • Color by Digikore Studios

Scaredy Showdown **205**
First published in supplement to Dutch *Donald Duck Weekblad* 2017-52, December 19, 2017 • Story by Frank Jonker and Paul Hoogma • Pencils by Daniel Perez • Inks by Comicup Studio • Translation and Dialogue by Thad Komorowski • Lettering by David Gerstein • Color by Sanoma

Nightmare on Bear Mountain! **227**
First published in American *DuckTales* (series III) 11, August 2018 • Story by Steve Behling • Layouts by Antonello Dalena Pencils by Danilo Loizedda • Inks by Cristina Stella • Lettering by Tom B. Long Color by Kawaii Creative Studio

The Wonderful Wishing Crown **237**
First published in Italian *Topolino* 3238, December 13, 2017; first American printing in *Uncle Scrooge* 438, April 2018 Story by Vito Stabile • Art by Alessandro Perina • Translation and Dialogue by Joe Torcivia • Lettering by Nicole and Travis Seitler • Color by Disney Italia

Cover Gallery **273**
Color by Comicup Studios, Susan Daigle-Leach, Digikore Studios, David Gerstein, and Ronda Pattison

Opposite top: watercolor by Carl Barks illustrating "Christmas on Bear Mountain." Image courtesy The Walt Disney Company Italia.

This content in this volume was first created in 1947-2018.

TROUBLE BRUIN!

by **DAVID GERSTEIN**

TODAY WE KNOW SCROOGE McDUCK as the richest duck in the world—as the Klondike sourdough who parlayed a Number One Dime into a Money Bin. But as conceived in 1947 for the story "Christmas on Bear Mountain," Scrooge was little more than a miserly plot device. "I thought of [Donald] getting involved with a bear up in the mountains," creator Carl Barks later recalled. "Somebody had to own this cabin he was going to."[1]

In execution, of course, the plot device became a striking new character. When Barks realized he "kind of liked old Scrooge," he brought McDuck back for ever-richer adventures. But what of Bear Mountain itself—the first locale ever connected with Scrooge McDuck? For decades, only an occasional story featured it again.

Then Disney fandom's awareness of comics history took its course. In the 1980s Stefan Printz-Påhlson and Lars Bergström, Swedish Barks-fan editors working at the Danish comics studio Egmont, turned Bear Mountain into an ongoing location for new stories. And why not? It held ornery animals to battle, wilderness to camp in, and amazing secrets to find. Before long, Italian and Dutch Disney talents were hatching new Bear Mountain tales, too.

Soon stories not entirely set on Bear Mountain were making the location pivotal to their plotlines. "The Richest Duck in the World," a chapter of Don Rosa's *Life and Times of Scrooge McDuck*, fleshes out Donald's first adult meeting with Scrooge, taking place *between* the Ducks' Bear Mountain fracas and the next day's dinner at McDuck Manor. Rudy Salvagnini's "The Man Who Drew Ducks" portrays Barks himself visiting Duckburg, basing his "Bear Mountain" comic on Donald's and Scrooge's direct memories. And Vito Stabile's birthday story, "The Wonderful Wishing Crown," mostly takes place on a pirate island—but relocates to Scrooge's famous cabin for an emotional finish.

Even more ordinary Bear Mountain stories can take on an extraordinary feel, with everyone from Santa Claus to Magica De Spell visiting Scrooge's cabin. At Fantagraphics, we long ago realized that our readers might like to explore all of these sagas. This comprehensive collection is the result.

We advise, however, that no one cave can contain every grizzly. There will always be more Bear Mountain tales to find and tell.

[1] Both quotes: Carl Barks to Malcolm Willits and Don and Maggie Thompson, 1962, transcribed in Donald Ault (ed.), *Carl Barks: Conversations* (Jackson: University Press of Mississippi, 2003), p. 13.

Walt Disney's
DONALD DUCK
MMM! DINNER SMELLS GOOD, DAISY!

Donald and the gang have been happy—and unhappy—campers since the start of their careers. Gag strip first published in German *Donald Duck Sonderheft* 231 (2006); story, art, and lettering by William Van Horn. Image courtesy Disney Publishing Worldwide.

NOTHING LIKE GETTING AWAY FROM IT ALL FOR A FEW DAYS!
WE'LL HAVE TO DO IT AGAIN REAL SOON!
I CAN HARDLY WAIT!

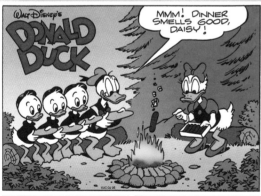

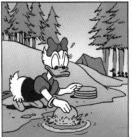

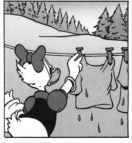

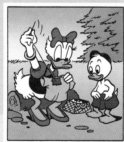

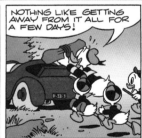

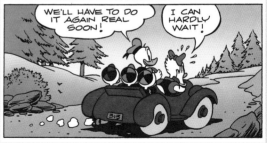

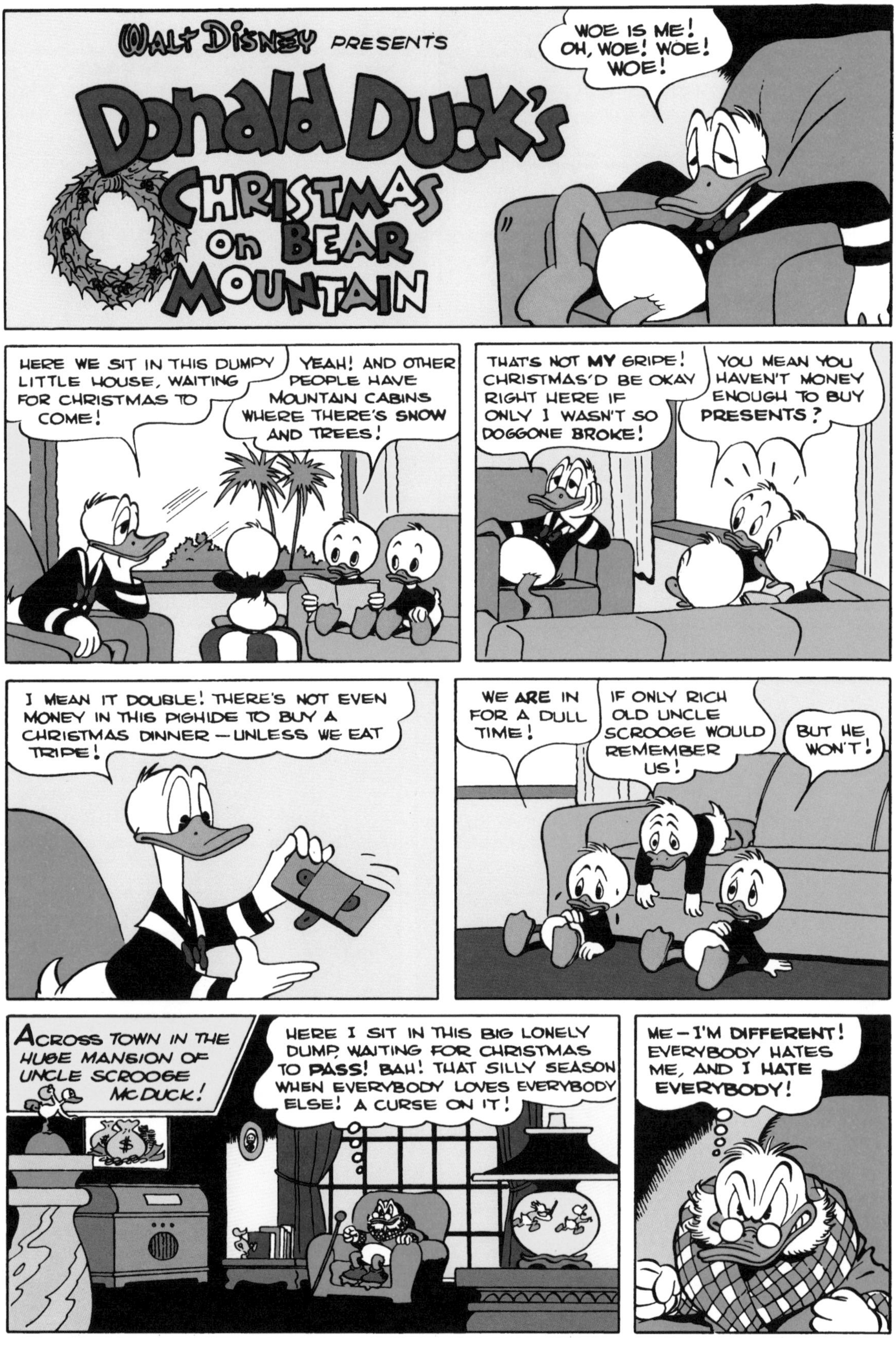
WALT DISNEY PRESENTS
Donald Duck's CHRISTMAS on BEAR MOUNTAIN
WOE IS ME! OH, WOE! WOE! WOE!
HERE WE SIT IN THIS DUMPY LITTLE HOUSE, WAITING FOR CHRISTMAS TO COME!
YEAH! AND OTHER PEOPLE HAVE MOUNTAIN CABINS WHERE THERE'S SNOW AND TREES!
THAT'S NOT MY GRIPE! CHRISTMAS'D BE OKAY RIGHT HERE IF ONLY I WASN'T SO DOGGONE BROKE!
YOU MEAN YOU HAVEN'T MONEY ENOUGH TO BUY PRESENTS?
I MEAN IT DOUBLE! THERE'S NOT EVEN MONEY IN THIS PIGHIDE TO BUY A CHRISTMAS DINNER — UNLESS WE EAT TRIPE!
WE ARE IN FOR A DULL TIME!
IF ONLY RICH OLD UNCLE SCROOGE WOULD REMEMBER US!
BUT HE WON'T!
ACROSS TOWN IN THE HUGE MANSION OF UNCLE SCROOGE McDUCK!
HERE I SIT IN THIS BIG LONELY DUMP, WAITING FOR CHRISTMAS TO PASS! BAH! THAT SILLY SEASON WHEN EVERYBODY LOVES EVERYBODY ELSE! A CURSE ON IT!
ME — I'M DIFFERENT! EVERYBODY HATES ME, AND I HATE EVERYBODY!

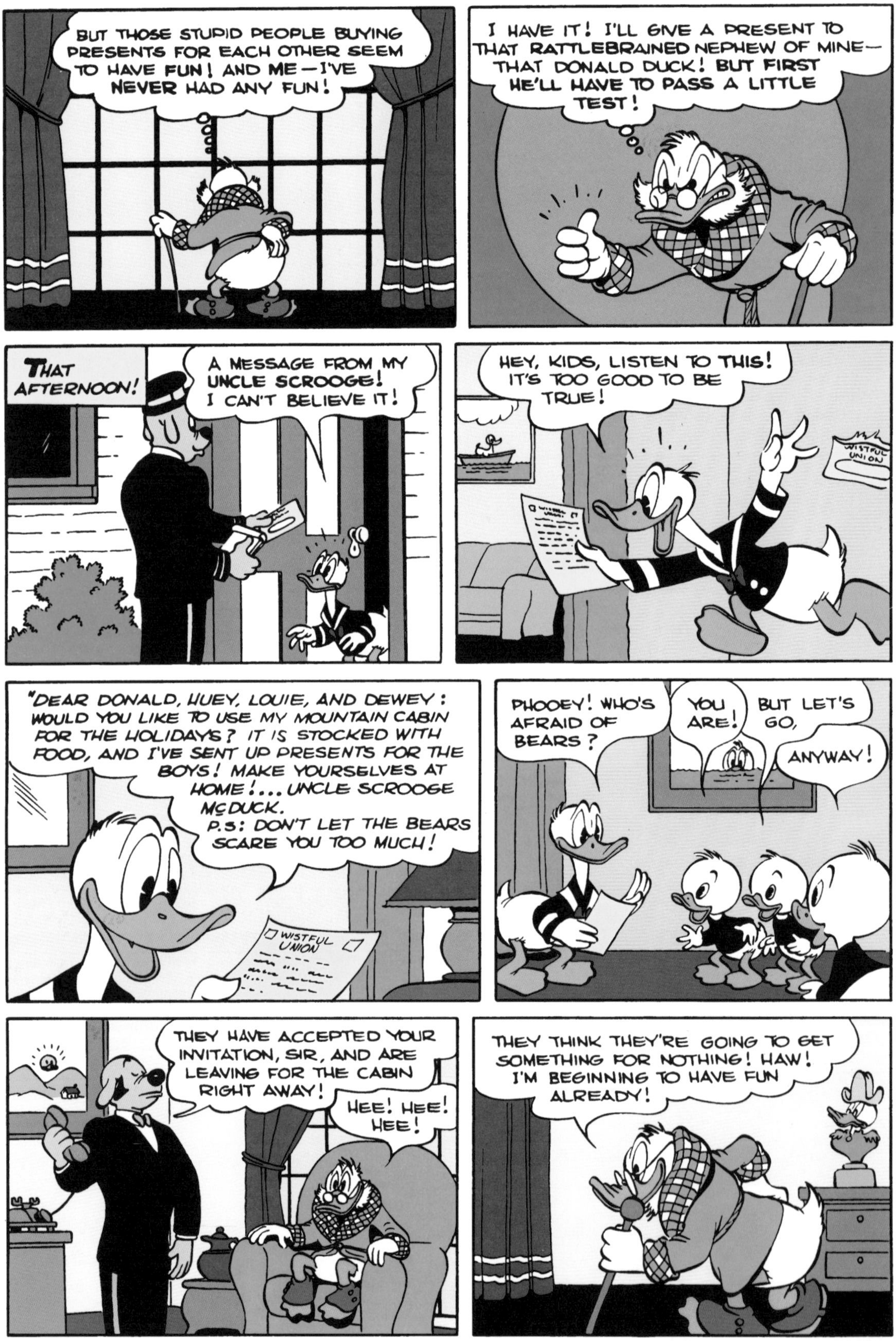
BUT THOSE STUPID PEOPLE BUYING PRESENTS FOR EACH OTHER SEEM TO HAVE FUN! AND ME—I'VE NEVER HAD ANY FUN!
I HAVE IT! I'LL GIVE A PRESENT TO THAT RATTLEBRAINED NEPHEW OF MINE— THAT DONALD DUCK! BUT FIRST HE'LL HAVE TO PASS A LITTLE TEST!
THAT AFTERNOON!
A MESSAGE FROM MY UNCLE SCROOGE! I CAN'T BELIEVE IT!
HEY, KIDS, LISTEN TO THIS! IT'S TOO GOOD TO BE TRUE!
WISTFUL UNION
"DEAR DONALD, HUEY, LOUIE, AND DEWEY: WOULD YOU LIKE TO USE MY MOUNTAIN CABIN FOR THE HOLIDAYS? IT IS STOCKED WITH FOOD, AND I'VE SENT UP PRESENTS FOR THE BOYS! MAKE YOURSELVES AT HOME!... UNCLE SCROOGE McDUCK.
P.S: DON'T LET THE BEARS SCARE YOU TOO MUCH!
WISTFUL UNION
PHOOEY! WHO'S AFRAID OF BEARS?
YOU ARE!
BUT LET'S GO,
ANYWAY!
THEY HAVE ACCEPTED YOUR INVITATION, SIR, AND ARE LEAVING FOR THE CABIN RIGHT AWAY!
HEE! HEE! HEE!
THEY THINK THEY'RE GOING TO GET SOMETHING FOR NOTHING! HAW! I'M BEGINNING TO HAVE FUN ALREADY!

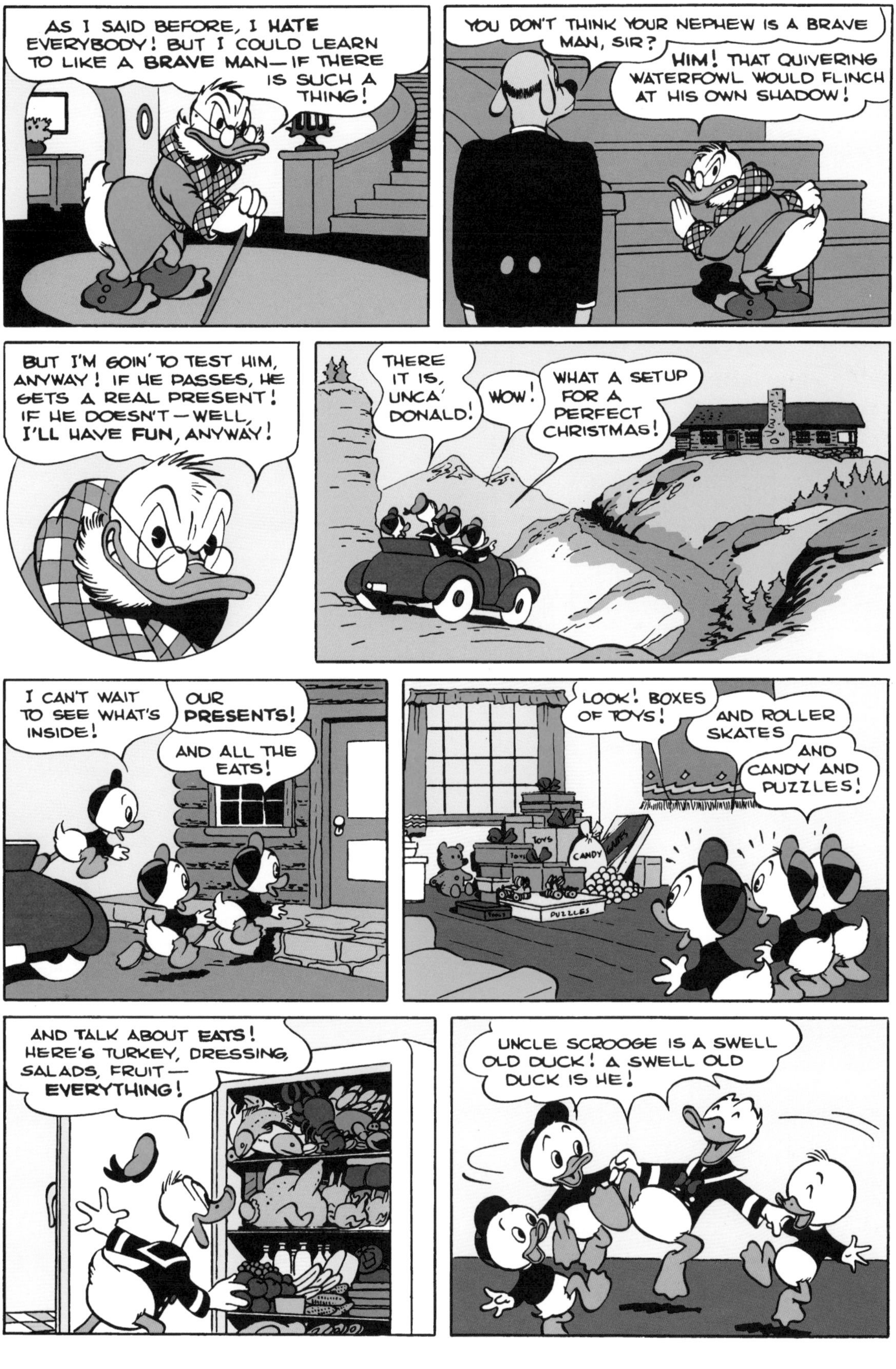

AS I SAID BEFORE, I HATE EVERYBODY! BUT I COULD LEARN TO LIKE A BRAVE MAN—IF THERE IS SUCH A THING!
YOU DON'T THINK YOUR NEPHEW IS A BRAVE MAN, SIR?
HIM! THAT QUIVERING WATERFOWL WOULD FLINCH AT HIS OWN SHADOW!
BUT I'M GOIN' TO TEST HIM, ANYWAY! IF HE PASSES, HE GETS A REAL PRESENT! IF HE DOESN'T—WELL, I'LL HAVE FUN, ANYWAY!
THERE IT IS, UNCA' DONALD!
WOW!
WHAT A SETUP FOR A PERFECT CHRISTMAS!
I CAN'T WAIT TO SEE WHAT'S INSIDE!
OUR PRESENTS!
AND ALL THE EATS!
LOOK! BOXES OF TOYS!
AND ROLLER SKATES
AND CANDY AND PUZZLES!
TOYS
CANDY
PUZZLES
AND TALK ABOUT EATS! HERE'S TURKEY, DRESSING, SALADS, FRUIT—EVERYTHING!
UNCLE SCROOGE IS A SWELL OLD DUCK! A SWELL OLD DUCK IS HE!

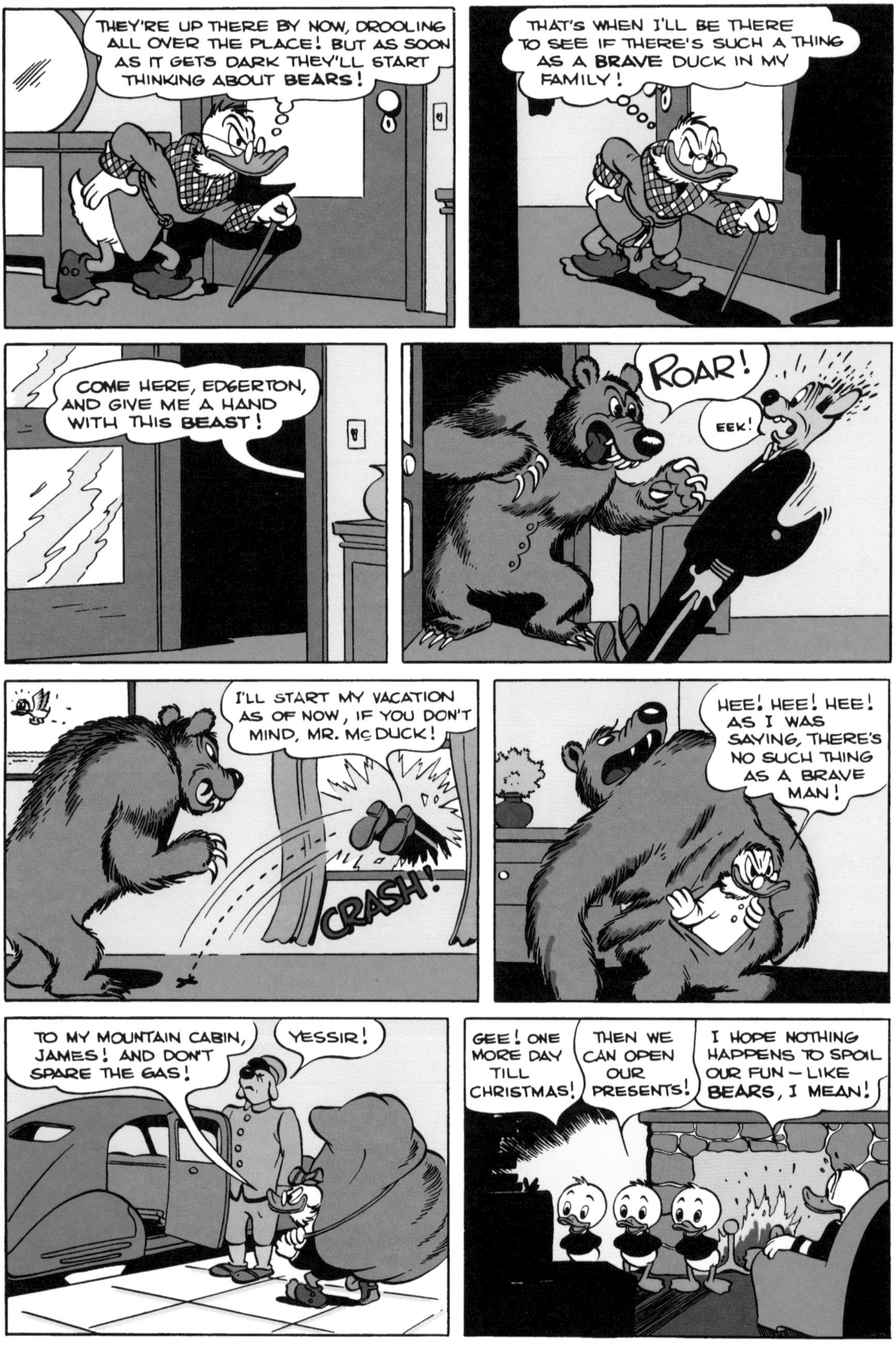
THEY'RE UP THERE BY NOW, DROOLING ALL OVER THE PLACE! BUT AS SOON AS IT GETS DARK THEY'LL START THINKING ABOUT BEARS!
THAT'S WHEN I'LL BE THERE TO SEE IF THERE'S SUCH A THING AS A BRAVE DUCK IN MY FAMILY!
COME HERE, EDGERTON, AND GIVE ME A HAND WITH THIS BEAST!
ROAR!
EEK!
I'LL START MY VACATION AS OF NOW, IF YOU DON'T MIND, MR. McDUCK!
CRASH!
HEE! HEE! HEE! AS I WAS SAYING, THERE'S NO SUCH THING AS A BRAVE MAN!
TO MY MOUNTAIN CABIN, JAMES! AND DON'T SPARE THE GAS!
YESSIR!
GEE! ONE MORE DAY TILL CHRISTMAS!
THEN WE CAN OPEN OUR PRESENTS!
I HOPE NOTHING HAPPENS TO SPOIL OUR FUN—LIKE BEARS, I MEAN!

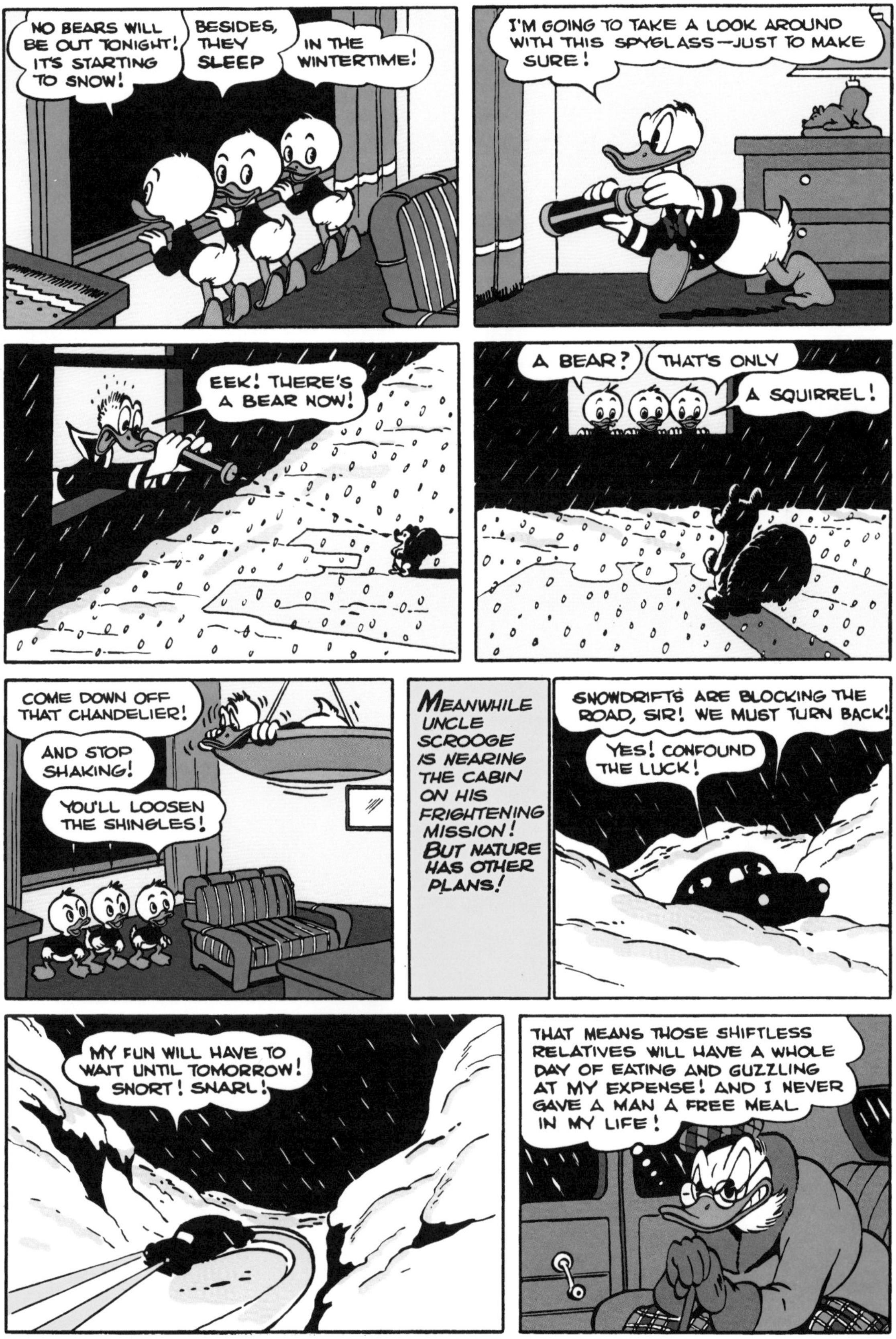
NO BEARS WILL BE OUT TONIGHT! IT'S STARTING TO SNOW!
BESIDES, THEY SLEEP
IN THE WINTERTIME!
I'M GOING TO TAKE A LOOK AROUND WITH THIS SPYGLASS—JUST TO MAKE SURE!
EEK! THERE'S A BEAR NOW!
A BEAR?
THAT'S ONLY
A SQUIRREL!
COME DOWN OFF THAT CHANDELIER!
AND STOP SHAKING!
YOU'LL LOOSEN THE SHINGLES!
MEANWHILE UNCLE SCROOGE IS NEARING THE CABIN ON HIS FRIGHTENING MISSION! BUT NATURE HAS OTHER PLANS!
SNOWDRIFTS ARE BLOCKING THE ROAD, SIR! WE MUST TURN BACK!
YES! CONFOUND THE LUCK!
MY FUN WILL HAVE TO WAIT UNTIL TOMORROW! SNORT! SNARL!
THAT MEANS THOSE SHIFTLESS RELATIVES WILL HAVE A WHOLE DAY OF EATING AND GUZZLING AT MY EXPENSE! AND I NEVER GAVE A MAN A FREE MEAL IN MY LIFE!

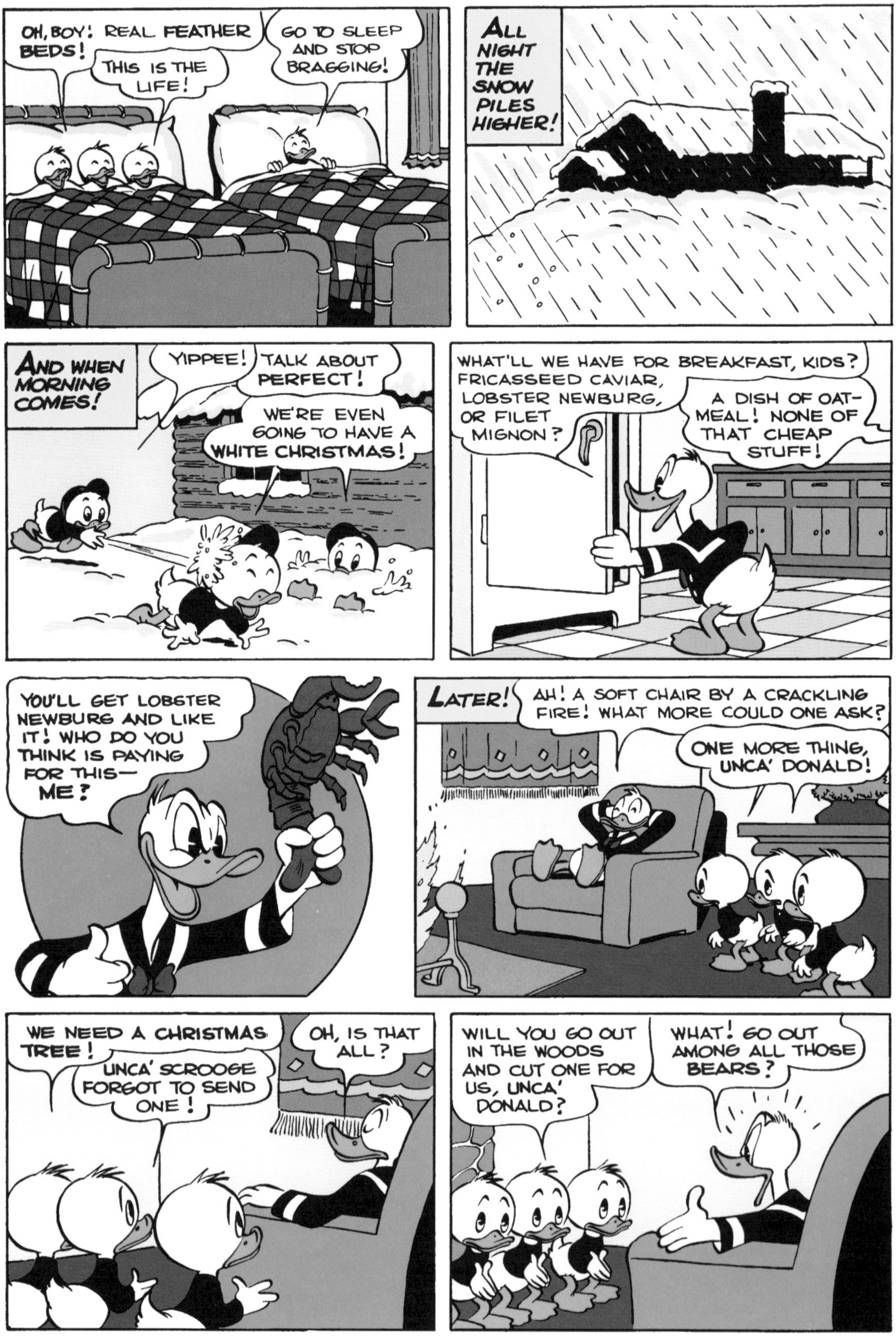
OH, BOY! REAL FEATHER BEDS!
THIS IS THE LIFE!
GO TO SLEEP AND STOP BRAGGING!
ALL NIGHT THE SNOW PILES HIGHER!
AND WHEN MORNING COMES!
YIPPEE!
TALK ABOUT PERFECT!
WE'RE EVEN GOING TO HAVE A WHITE CHRISTMAS!
WHAT'LL WE HAVE FOR BREAKFAST, KIDS? FRICASSEED CAVIAR, LOBSTER NEWBURG, OR FILET MIGNON?
A DISH OF OATMEAL! NONE OF THAT CHEAP STUFF!
YOU'LL GET LOBSTER NEWBURG AND LIKE IT! WHO DO YOU THINK IS PAYING FOR THIS— ME?
LATER!
AH! A SOFT CHAIR BY A CRACKLING FIRE! WHAT MORE COULD ONE ASK?
ONE MORE THING, UNCA' DONALD!
WE NEED A CHRISTMAS TREE!
UNCA' SCROOGE FORGOT TO SEND ONE!
OH, IS THAT ALL?
WILL YOU GO OUT IN THE WOODS AND CUT ONE FOR US, UNCA' DONALD?
WHAT! GO OUT AMONG ALL THOSE BEARS?

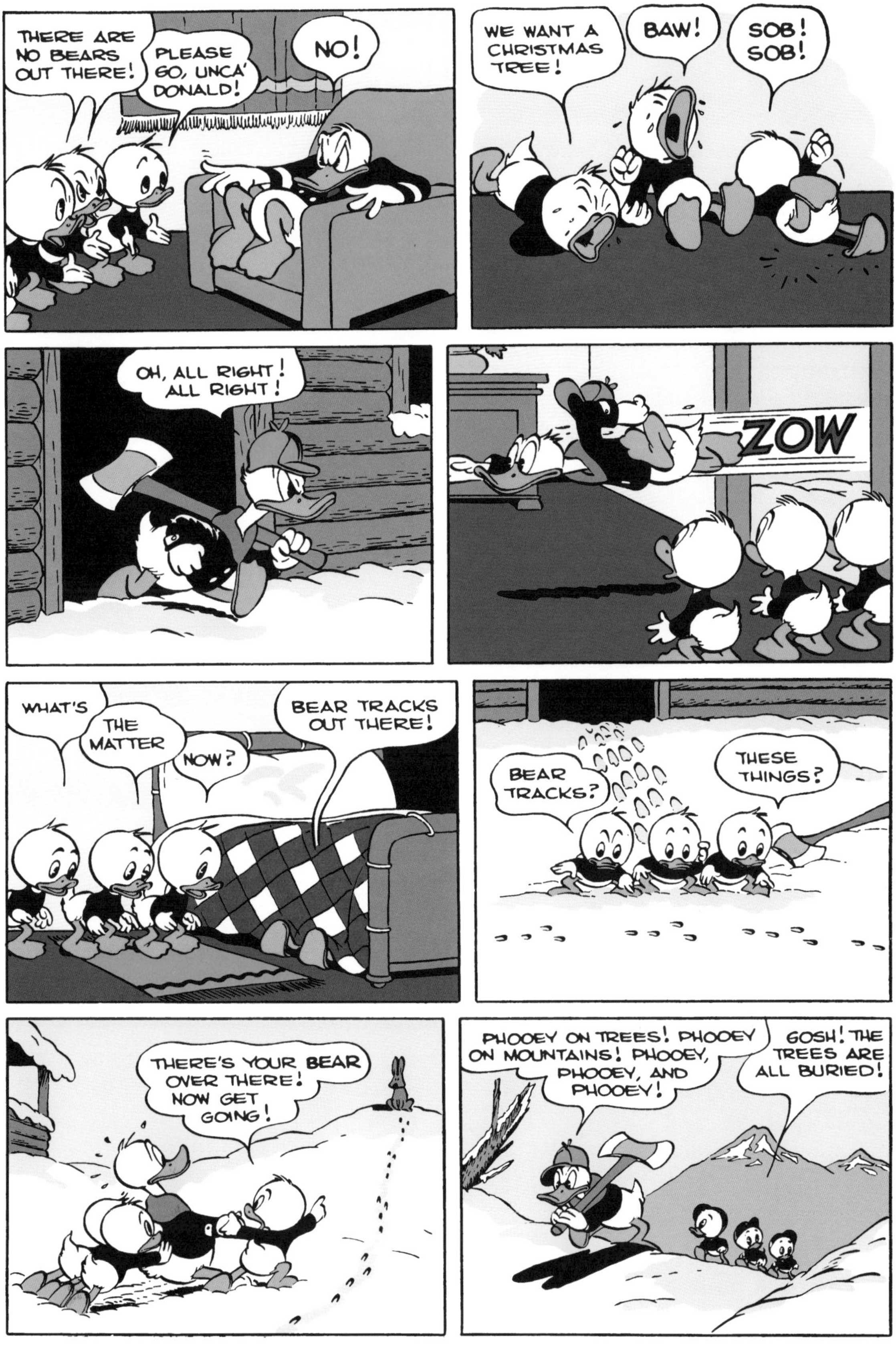

THERE ARE NO BEARS OUT THERE!
PLEASE GO, UNCA' DONALD!
NO!
WE WANT A CHRISTMAS TREE!
BAW!
SOB! SOB!
OH, ALL RIGHT! ALL RIGHT!
ZOW
WHAT'S
THE MATTER
NOW?
BEAR TRACKS OUT THERE!
BEAR TRACKS?
THESE THINGS?
THERE'S YOUR BEAR OVER THERE! NOW GET GOING!
PHOOEY ON TREES! PHOOEY ON MOUNTAINS! PHOOEY, PHOOEY, AND PHOOEY!
GOSH! THE TREES ARE ALL BURIED!

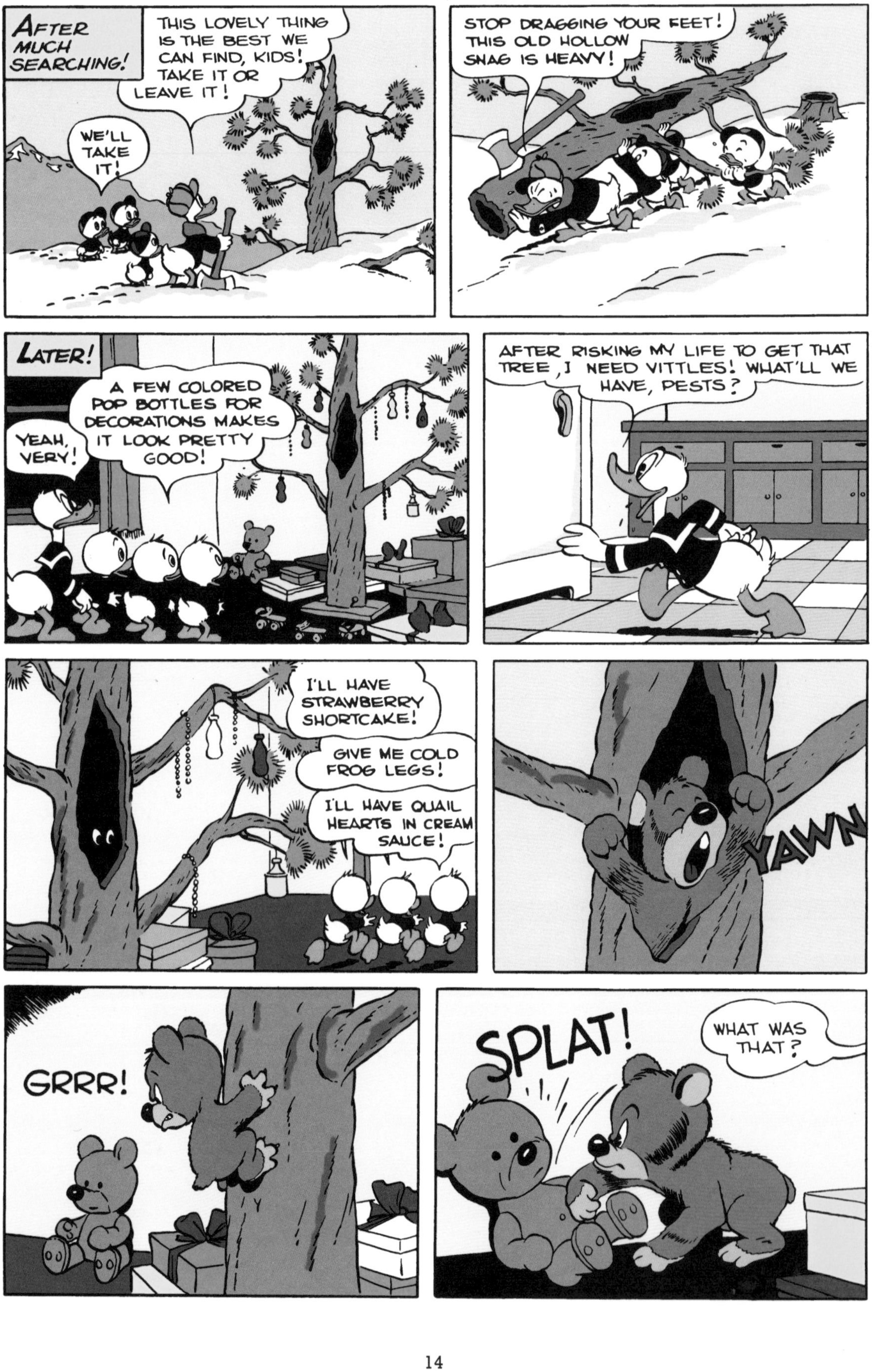
AFTER MUCH SEARCHING!
THIS LOVELY THING IS THE BEST WE CAN FIND, KIDS! TAKE IT OR LEAVE IT!
WE'LL TAKE IT!
STOP DRAGGING YOUR FEET! THIS OLD HOLLOW SNAG IS HEAVY!
LATER!
A FEW COLORED POP BOTTLES FOR DECORATIONS MAKES IT LOOK PRETTY GOOD!
YEAH, VERY!
AFTER RISKING MY LIFE TO GET THAT TREE, I NEED VITTLES! WHAT'LL WE HAVE, PESTS?
I'LL HAVE STRAWBERRY SHORTCAKE!
GIVE ME COLD FROG LEGS!
I'LL HAVE QUAIL HEARTS IN CREAM SAUCE!
YAWN
GRRR!
SPLAT!
WHAT WAS THAT?

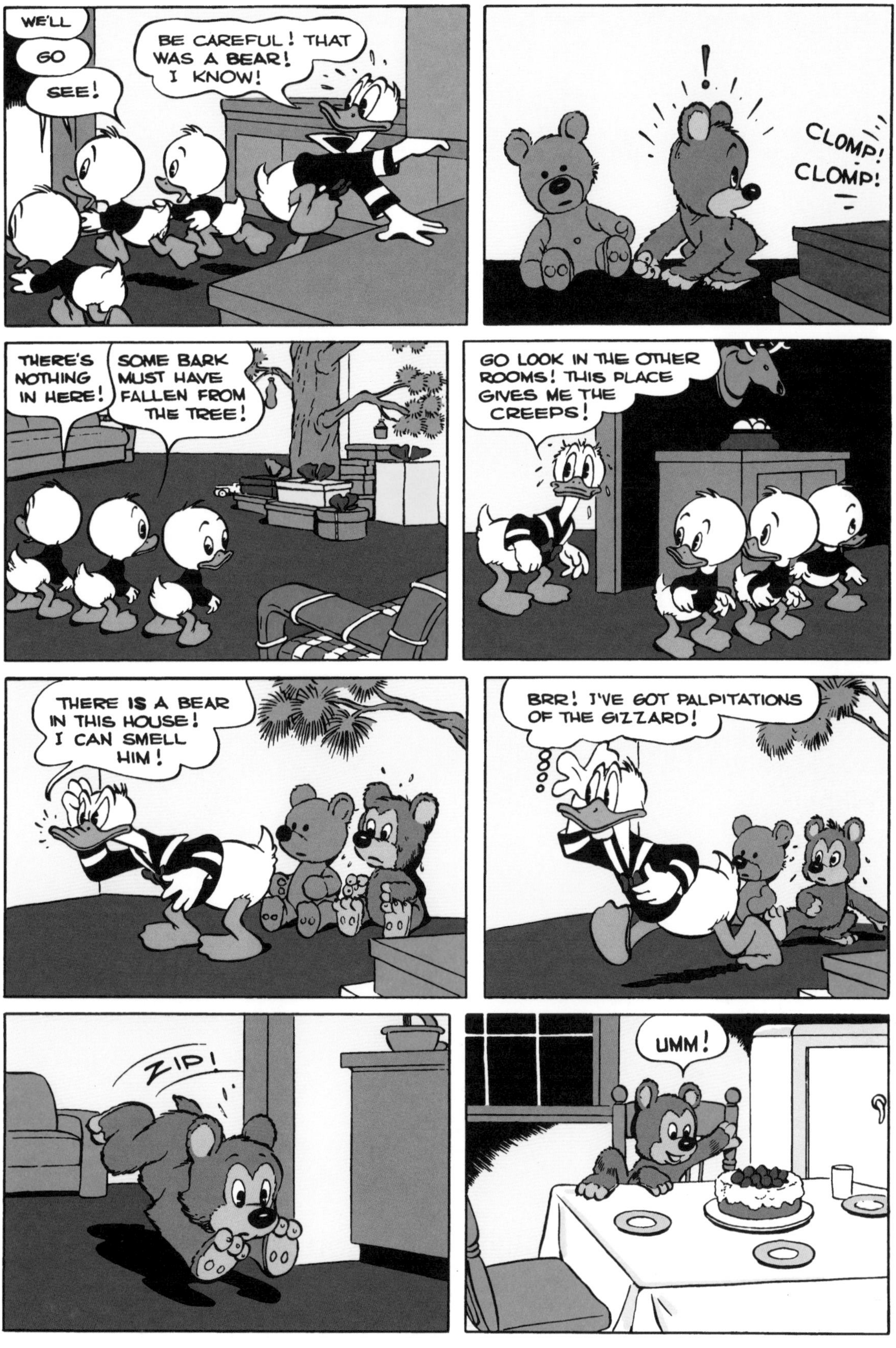
WE'LL
GO
SEE!
BE CAREFUL! THAT WAS A BEAR! I KNOW!
!
CLOMP! CLOMP!
THERE'S NOTHING IN HERE!
SOME BARK MUST HAVE FALLEN FROM THE TREE!
GO LOOK IN THE OTHER ROOMS! THIS PLACE GIVES ME THE CREEPS!
THERE IS A BEAR IN THIS HOUSE! I CAN SMELL HIM!
BRR! I'VE GOT PALPITATIONS OF THE GIZZARD!
ZIP!
UMM!

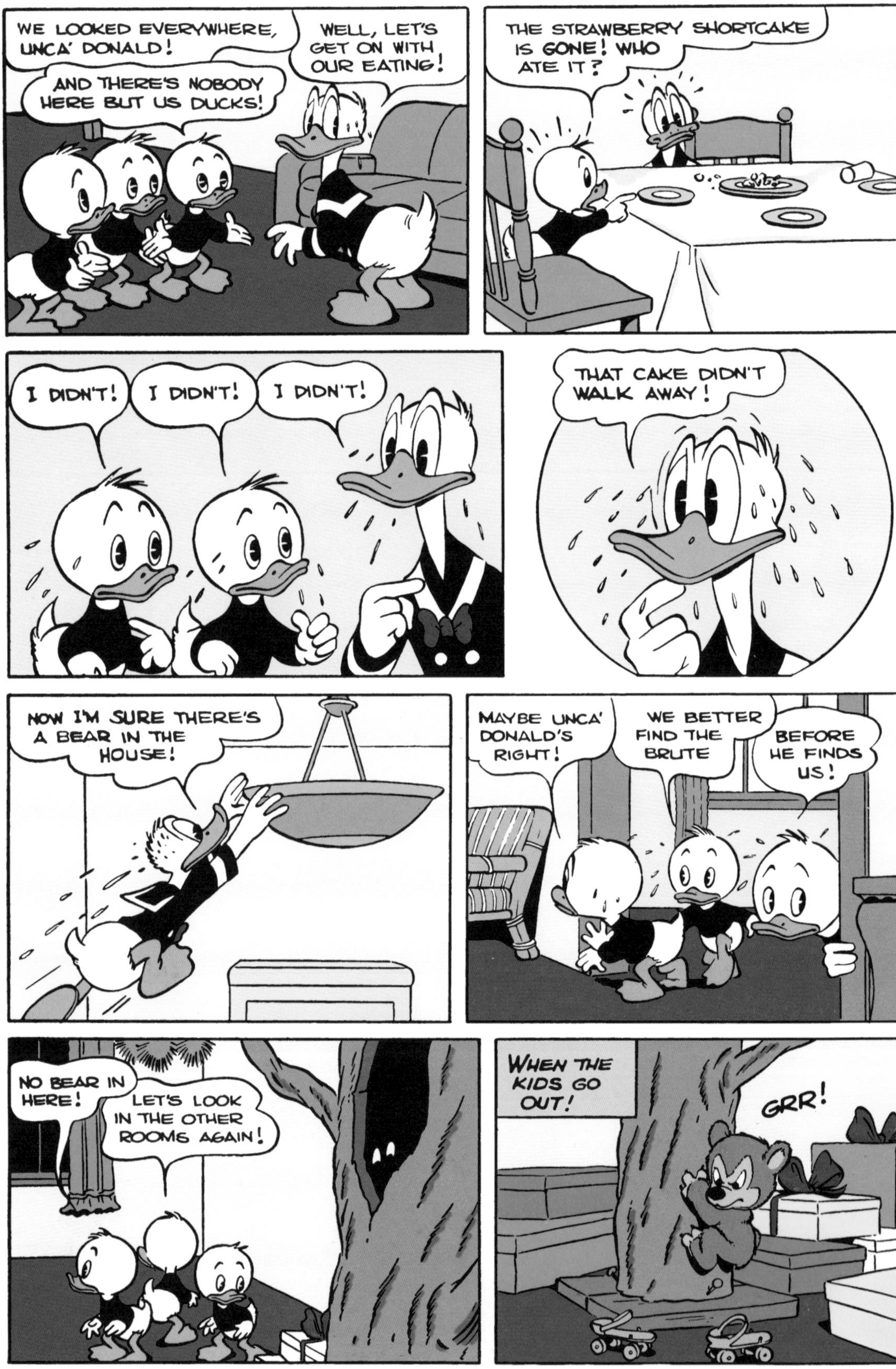
WE LOOKED EVERYWHERE, UNCA' DONALD!
AND THERE'S NOBODY HERE BUT US DUCKS!
WELL, LET'S GET ON WITH OUR EATING!
THE STRAWBERRY SHORTCAKE IS GONE! WHO ATE IT?
I DIDN'T!
I DIDN'T!
I DIDN'T!
THAT CAKE DIDN'T WALK AWAY!
NOW I'M SURE THERE'S A BEAR IN THE HOUSE!
MAYBE UNCA' DONALD'S RIGHT!
WE BETTER FIND THE BRUTE
BEFORE HE FINDS US!
NO BEAR IN HERE!
LET'S LOOK IN THE OTHER ROOMS AGAIN!
WHEN THE KIDS GO OUT!
GRR!

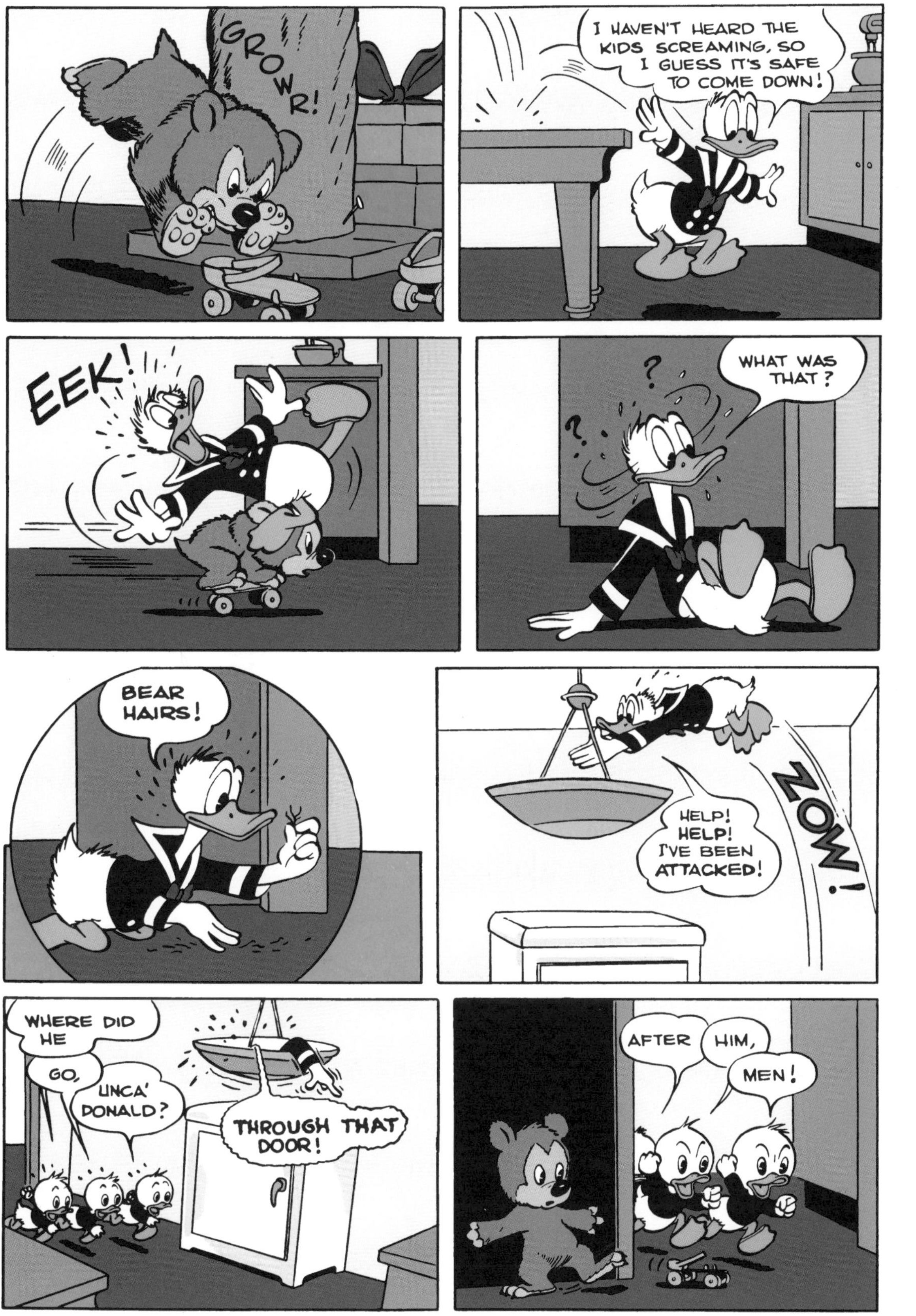
GROWR!
I HAVEN'T HEARD THE KIDS SCREAMING, SO I GUESS IT'S SAFE TO COME DOWN!
EEK!
WHAT WAS THAT?
BEAR HAIRS!
HELP! HELP! I'VE BEEN ATTACKED!
ZOW!
WHERE DID HE
GO,
UNCA' DONALD?
THROUGH THAT DOOR!
AFTER
HIM,
MEN!

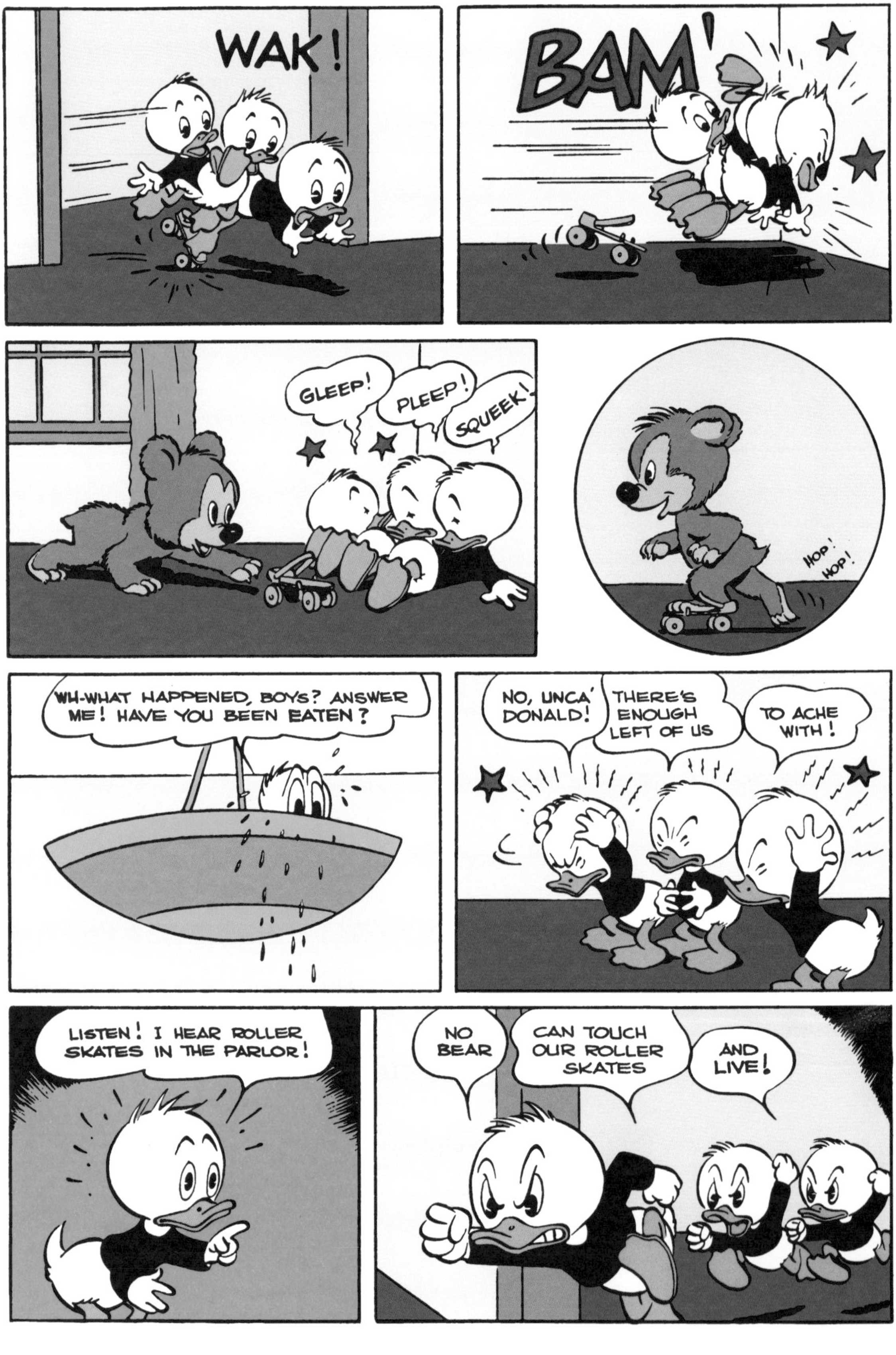
WAK!
BAM!
GLEEP!
PLEEP!
SQUEEK!
HOP! HOP!
WH-WHAT HAPPENED, BOYS? ANSWER ME! HAVE YOU BEEN EATEN?
NO, UNCA' DONALD!
THERE'S ENOUGH LEFT OF US
TO ACHE WITH!
LISTEN! I HEAR ROLLER SKATES IN THE PARLOR!
NO BEAR
CAN TOUCH OUR ROLLER SKATES
AND LIVE!

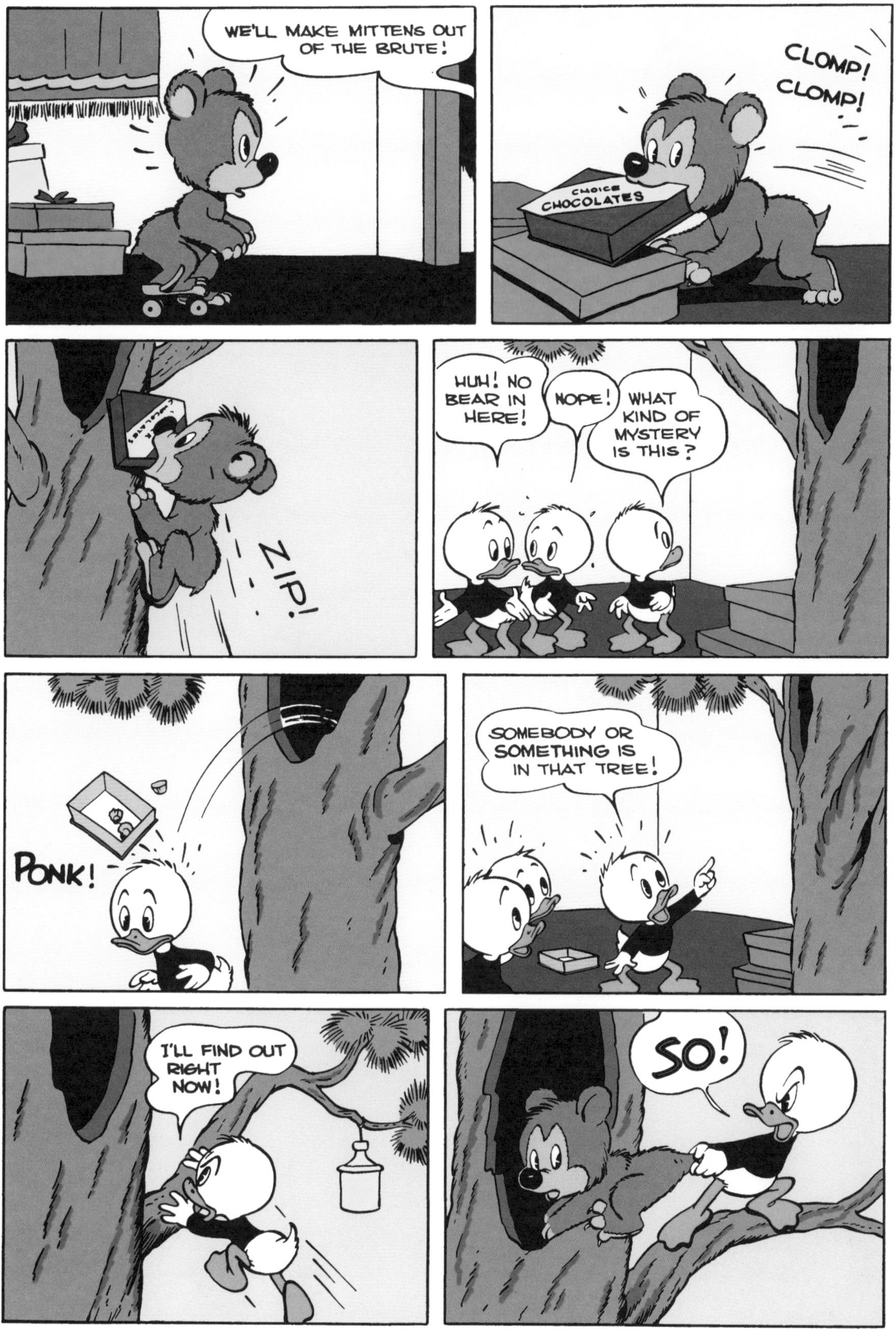
WE'LL MAKE MITTENS OUT OF THE BRUTE!
CLOMP! CLOMP!
CHOICE CHOCOLATES
ZIP!
HUH! NO BEAR IN HERE!
NOPE!
WHAT KIND OF MYSTERY IS THIS?
PONK!
SOMEBODY OR SOMETHING IS IN THAT TREE!
I'LL FIND OUT RIGHT NOW!
SO!

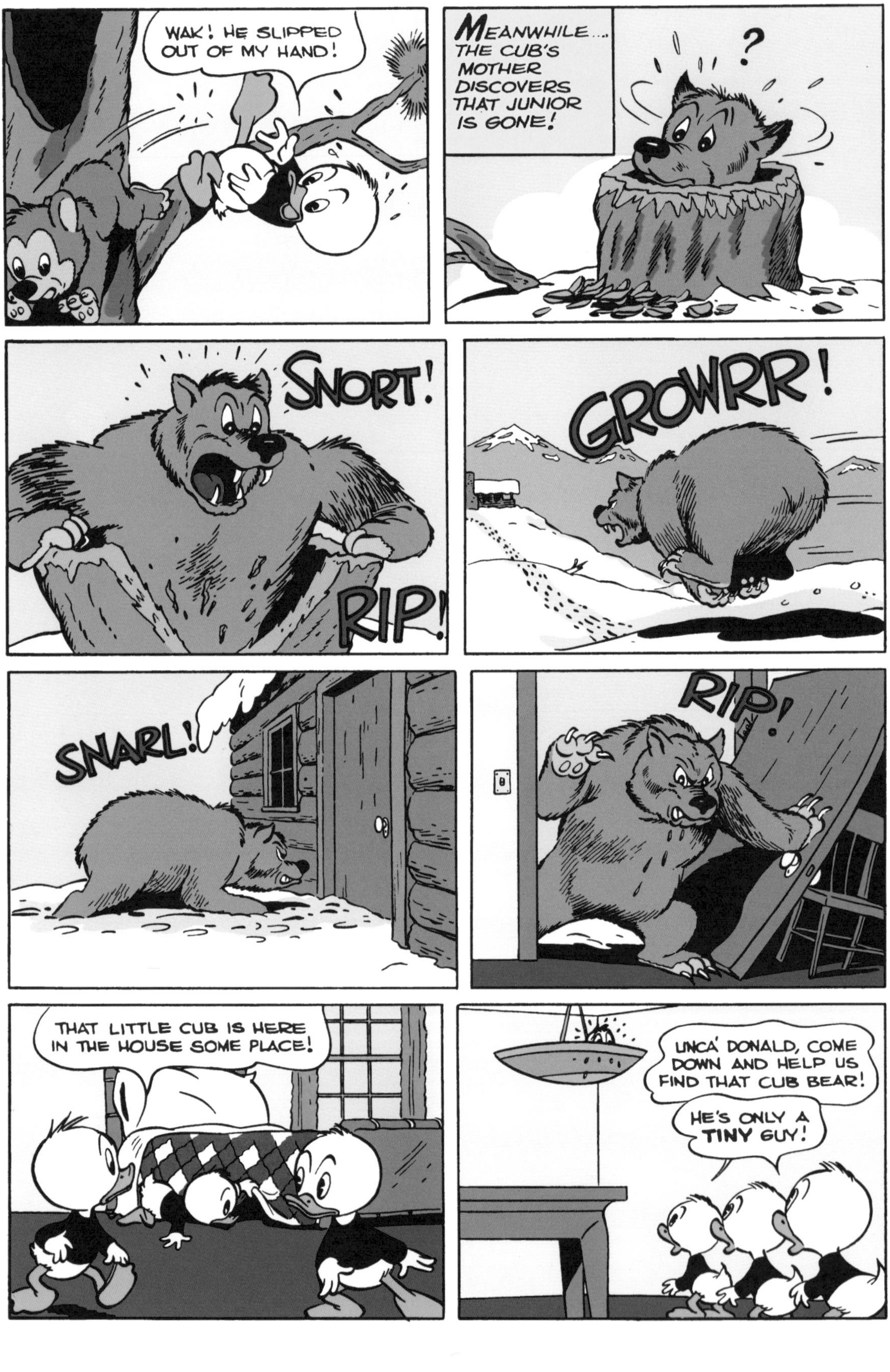
WAK! HE SLIPPED OUT OF MY HAND!
MEANWHILE.... THE CUB'S MOTHER DISCOVERS THAT JUNIOR IS GONE!
?
SNORT!
RIP!
GROWRR!
SNARL!
RIP!
THAT LITTLE CUB IS HERE IN THE HOUSE SOME PLACE!
UNCA' DONALD, COME DOWN AND HELP US FIND THAT CUB BEAR!
HE'S ONLY A **TINY** GUY!

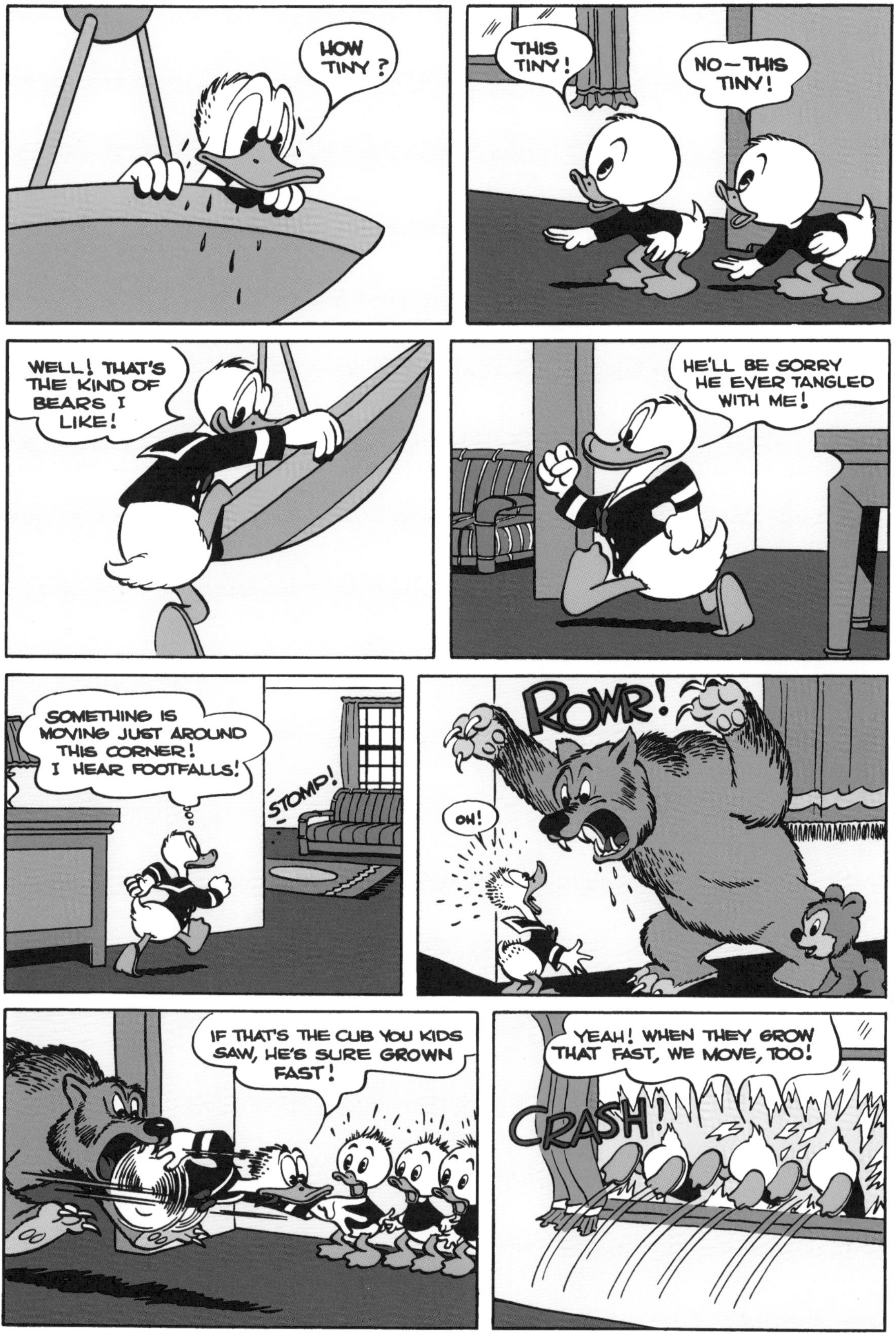
HOW TINY ?
THIS TINY!
NO—THIS TINY!
WELL! THAT'S THE KIND OF BEARS I LIKE!
HE'LL BE SORRY HE EVER TANGLED WITH ME!
SOMETHING IS MOVING JUST AROUND THIS CORNER! I HEAR FOOTFALLS!
STOMP!
ROWR!
OH!
IF THAT'S THE CUB YOU KIDS SAW, HE'S SURE GROWN FAST!
YEAH! WHEN THEY GROW THAT FAST, WE MOVE, TOO!
CRASH!

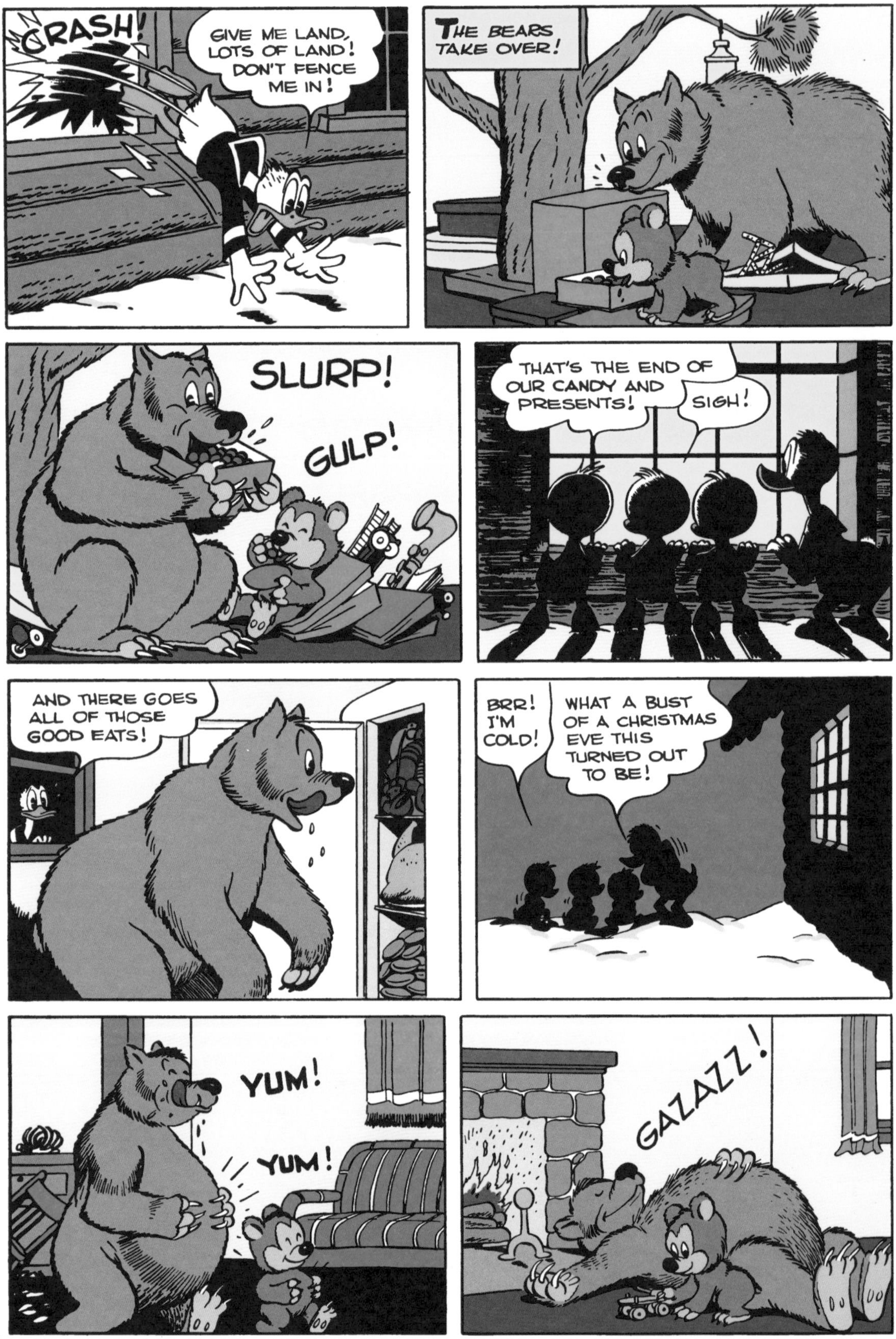
CRASH!
GIVE ME LAND, LOTS OF LAND! DON'T FENCE ME IN!
THE BEARS TAKE OVER!
SLURP!
GULP!
THAT'S THE END OF OUR CANDY AND PRESENTS!
SIGH!
AND THERE GOES ALL OF THOSE GOOD EATS!
BRR! I'M COLD!
WHAT A BUST OF A CHRISTMAS EVE THIS TURNED OUT TO BE!
YUM!
YUM!
GAZAZZ!

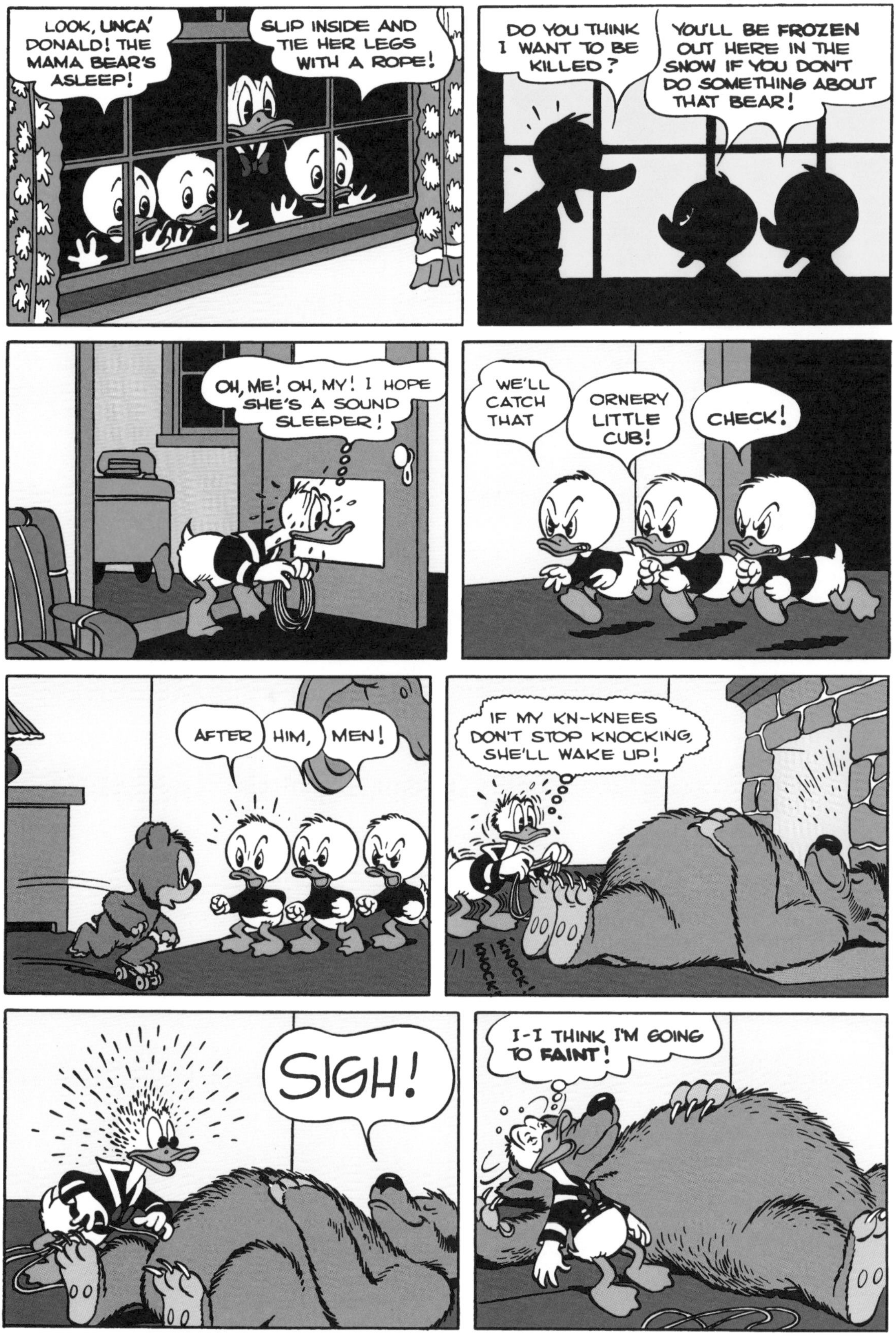

LOOK, UNCA' DONALD! THE MAMA BEAR'S ASLEEP!
SLIP INSIDE AND TIE HER LEGS WITH A ROPE!
DO YOU THINK I WANT TO BE KILLED?
YOU'LL BE FROZEN OUT HERE IN THE SNOW IF YOU DON'T DO SOMETHING ABOUT THAT BEAR!
OH, ME! OH, MY! I HOPE SHE'S A SOUND SLEEPER!
WE'LL CATCH THAT
ORNERY LITTLE CUB!
CHECK!
AFTER
HIM,
MEN!
IF MY KN-KNEES DON'T STOP KNOCKING, SHE'LL WAKE UP!
KNOCK!
KNOCK!
SIGH!
I-I THINK I'M GOING TO FAINT!

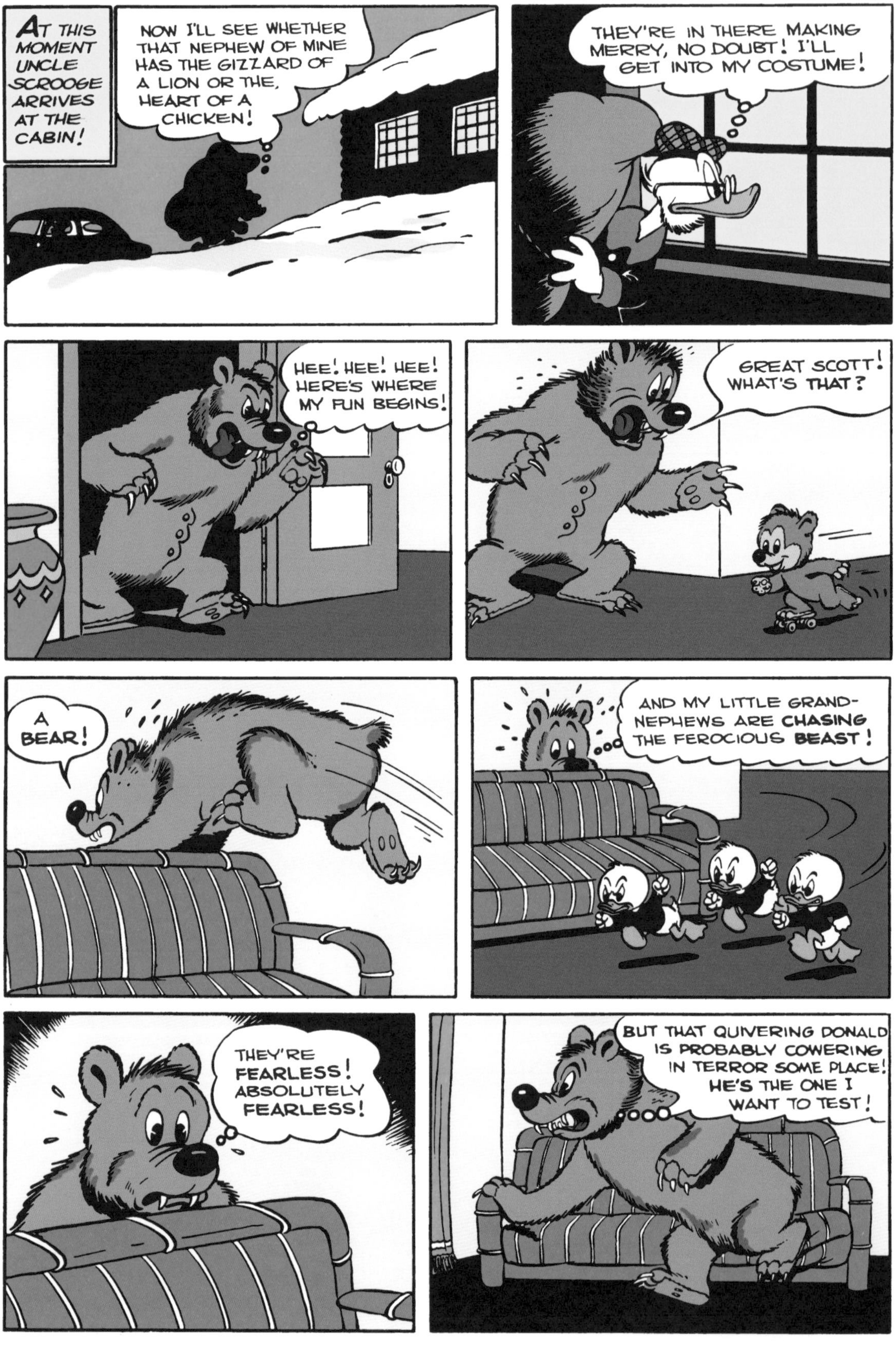
AT THIS MOMENT UNCLE SCROOGE ARRIVES AT THE CABIN!
NOW I'LL SEE WHETHER THAT NEPHEW OF MINE HAS THE GIZZARD OF A LION OR THE, HEART OF A CHICKEN!
THEY'RE IN THERE MAKING MERRY, NO DOUBT! I'LL GET INTO MY COSTUME!
HEE! HEE! HEE! HERE'S WHERE MY FUN BEGINS!
GREAT SCOTT! WHAT'S **THAT**?
A BEAR!
AND MY LITTLE GRAND-NEPHEWS ARE **CHASING** THE FEROCIOUS **BEAST**!
THEY'RE **FEARLESS**! ABSOLUTELY **FEARLESS**!
BUT THAT QUIVERING DONALD IS **PROBABLY** COWERING IN TERROR SOME PLACE! **HE'S** THE ONE I WANT TO TEST!

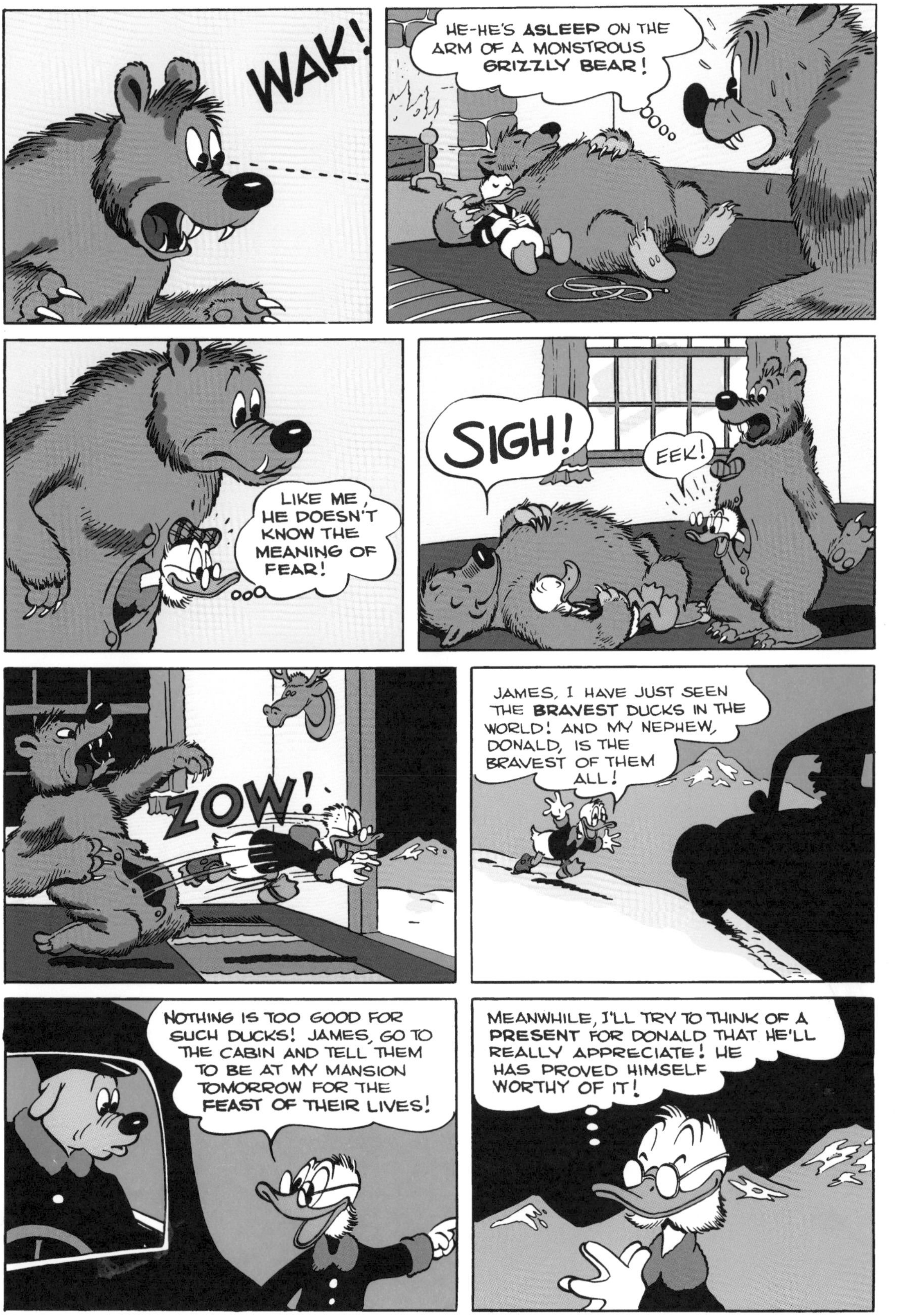
WAK!
HE-HE'S ASLEEP ON THE ARM OF A MONSTROUS GRIZZLY BEAR!
LIKE ME, HE DOESN'T KNOW THE MEANING OF FEAR!
SIGH!
EEK!
ZOW!
JAMES, I HAVE JUST SEEN THE BRAVEST DUCKS IN THE WORLD! AND MY NEPHEW, DONALD, IS THE BRAVEST OF THEM ALL!
NOTHING IS TOO GOOD FOR SUCH DUCKS! JAMES, GO TO THE CABIN AND TELL THEM TO BE AT MY MANSION TOMORROW FOR THE FEAST OF THEIR LIVES!
MEANWHILE, I'LL TRY TO THINK OF A PRESENT FOR DONALD THAT HE'LL REALLY APPRECIATE! HE HAS PROVED HIMSELF WORTHY OF IT!

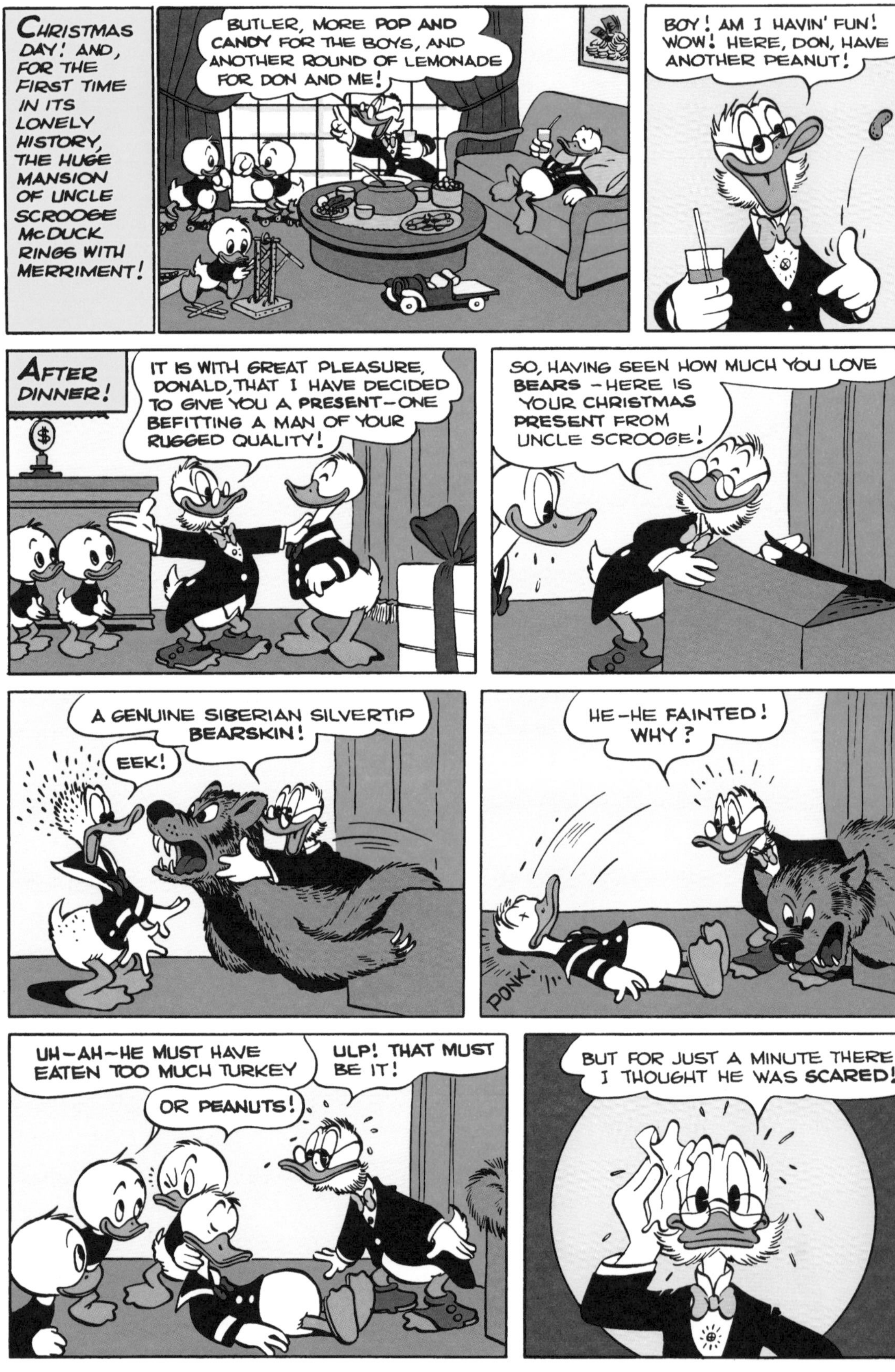

CHRISTMAS DAY! AND, FOR THE FIRST TIME IN ITS LONELY HISTORY, THE HUGE MANSION OF UNCLE SCROOGE McDUCK RINGS WITH MERRIMENT!
BUTLER, MORE POP AND CANDY FOR THE BOYS, AND ANOTHER ROUND OF LEMONADE FOR DON AND ME!
BOY! AM I HAVIN' FUN! WOW! HERE, DON, HAVE ANOTHER PEANUT!
AFTER DINNER!
IT IS WITH GREAT PLEASURE, DONALD, THAT I HAVE DECIDED TO GIVE YOU A PRESENT—ONE BEFITTING A MAN OF YOUR RUGGED QUALITY!
SO, HAVING SEEN HOW MUCH YOU LOVE BEARS—HERE IS YOUR CHRISTMAS PRESENT FROM UNCLE SCROOGE!
A GENUINE SIBERIAN SILVERTIP BEARSKIN!
EEK!
HE—HE FAINTED! WHY?
PONK!
UH—AH—HE MUST HAVE EATEN TOO MUCH TURKEY
ULP! THAT MUST BE IT!
OR PEANUTS!
BUT FOR JUST A MINUTE THERE I THOUGHT HE WAS SCARED!

Walt Disney Donald Duck

DUCKING OUT

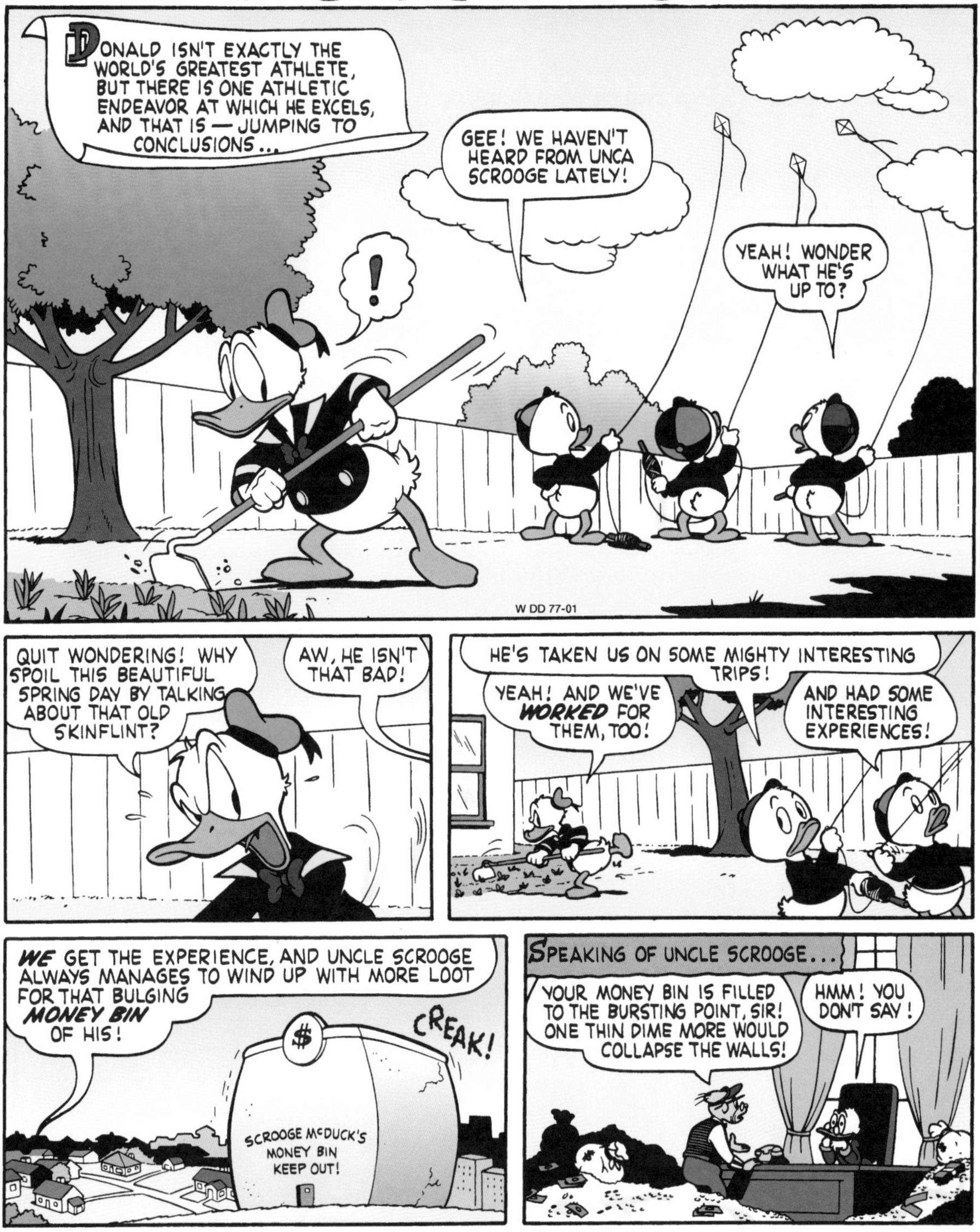
DONALD ISN'T EXACTLY THE WORLD'S GREATEST ATHLETE, BUT THERE IS ONE ATHLETIC ENDEAVOR AT WHICH HE EXCELS, AND THAT IS — JUMPING TO CONCLUSIONS...
GEE! WE HAVEN'T HEARD FROM UNCA SCROOGE LATELY!
!
YEAH! WONDER WHAT HE'S UP TO?
W DD 77-01
QUIT WONDERING! WHY SPOIL THIS BEAUTIFUL SPRING DAY BY TALKING ABOUT THAT OLD SKINFLINT?
AW, HE ISN'T THAT BAD!
HE'S TAKEN US ON SOME MIGHTY INTERESTING TRIPS!
YEAH! AND WE'VE WORKED FOR THEM, TOO!
AND HAD SOME INTERESTING EXPERIENCES!
WE GET THE EXPERIENCE, AND UNCLE SCROOGE ALWAYS MANAGES TO WIND UP WITH MORE LOOT FOR THAT BULGING MONEY BIN OF HIS!
CREAK!
$
SCROOGE McDUCK'S MONEY BIN KEEP OUT!
SPEAKING OF UNCLE SCROOGE...
YOUR MONEY BIN IS FILLED TO THE BURSTING POINT, SIR! ONE THIN DIME MORE WOULD COLLAPSE THE WALLS!
HMM! YOU DON'T SAY!

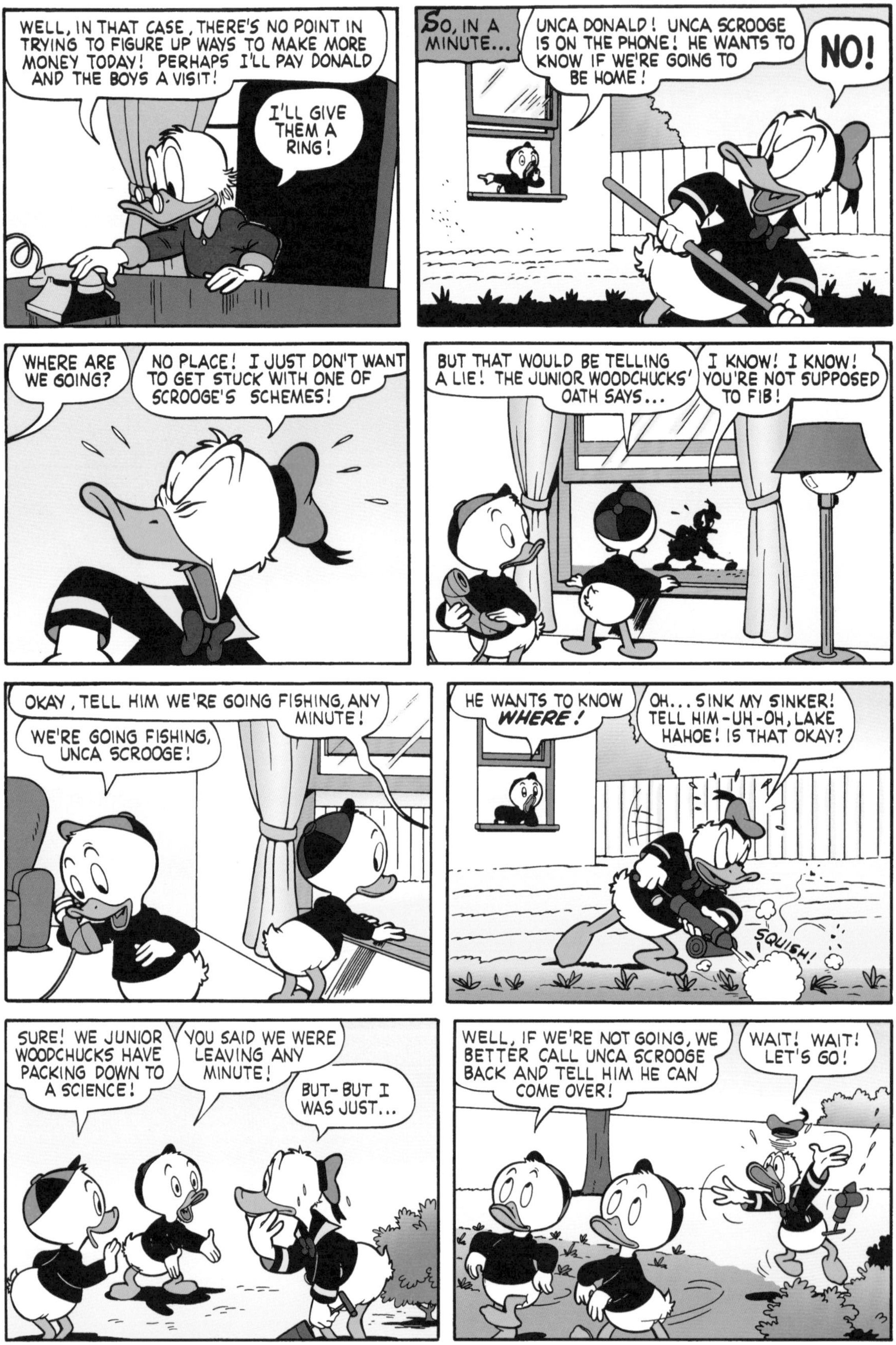

WELL, IN THAT CASE, THERE'S NO POINT IN TRYING TO FIGURE UP WAYS TO MAKE MORE MONEY TODAY! PERHAPS I'LL PAY DONALD AND THE BOYS A VISIT!
I'LL GIVE THEM A RING!
SO, IN A MINUTE...
UNCA DONALD! UNCA SCROOGE IS ON THE PHONE! HE WANTS TO KNOW IF WE'RE GOING TO BE HOME!
NO!
WHERE ARE WE GOING?
NO PLACE! I JUST DON'T WANT TO GET STUCK WITH ONE OF SCROOGE'S SCHEMES!
BUT THAT WOULD BE TELLING A LIE! THE JUNIOR WOODCHUCKS' OATH SAYS...
I KNOW! I KNOW! YOU'RE NOT SUPPOSED TO FIB!
OKAY, TELL HIM WE'RE GOING FISHING, ANY MINUTE!
WE'RE GOING FISHING, UNCA SCROOGE!
HE WANTS TO KNOW WHERE!
OH... SINK MY SINKER! TELL HIM-UH-OH, LAKE HAHOE! IS THAT OKAY?
SQUISH!
SURE! WE JUNIOR WOODCHUCKS HAVE PACKING DOWN TO A SCIENCE!
YOU SAID WE WERE LEAVING ANY MINUTE!
BUT-BUT I WAS JUST...
WELL, IF WE'RE NOT GOING, WE BETTER CALL UNCA SCROOGE BACK AND TELL HIM HE CAN COME OVER!
WAIT! WAIT! LET'S GO!

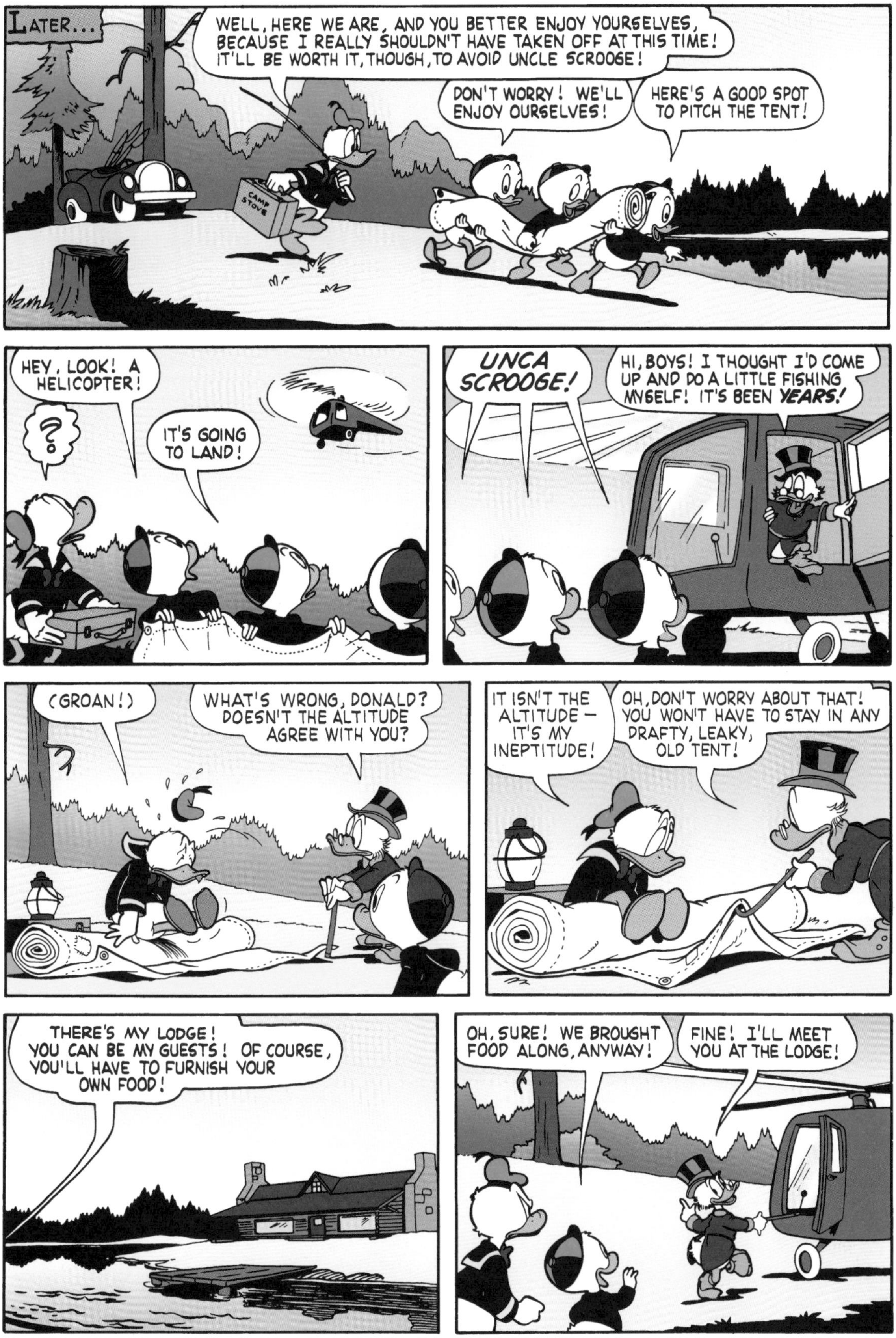
LATER...
WELL, HERE WE ARE, AND YOU BETTER ENJOY YOURSELVES, BECAUSE I REALLY SHOULDN'T HAVE TAKEN OFF AT THIS TIME! IT'LL BE WORTH IT, THOUGH, TO AVOID UNCLE SCROOGE!
DON'T WORRY! WE'LL ENJOY OURSELVES!
HERE'S A GOOD SPOT TO PITCH THE TENT!
CAMP STOVE
HEY, LOOK! A HELICOPTER!
?
IT'S GOING TO LAND!
UNCA SCROOGE!
HI, BOYS! I THOUGHT I'D COME UP AND DO A LITTLE FISHING MYSELF! IT'S BEEN YEARS!
(GROAN!)
WHAT'S WRONG, DONALD? DOESN'T THE ALTITUDE AGREE WITH YOU?
IT ISN'T THE ALTITUDE — IT'S MY INEPTITUDE!
OH, DON'T WORRY ABOUT THAT! YOU WON'T HAVE TO STAY IN ANY DRAFTY, LEAKY, OLD TENT!
THERE'S MY LODGE! YOU CAN BE MY GUESTS! OF COURSE, YOU'LL HAVE TO FURNISH YOUR OWN FOOD!
OH, SURE! WE BROUGHT FOOD ALONG, ANYWAY!
FINE! I'LL MEET YOU AT THE LODGE!

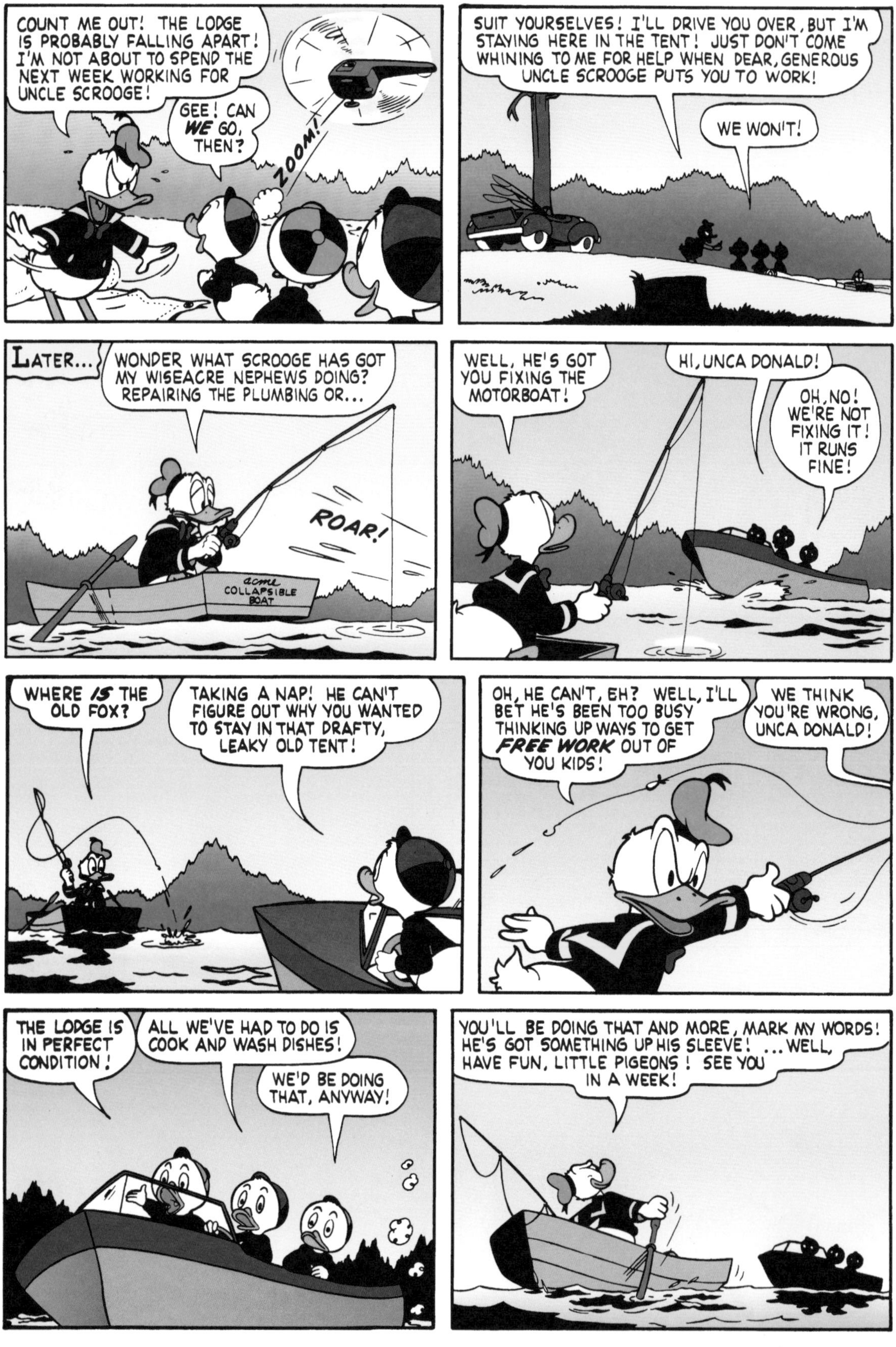
COUNT ME OUT! THE LODGE IS PROBABLY FALLING APART! I'M NOT ABOUT TO SPEND THE NEXT WEEK WORKING FOR UNCLE SCROOGE!
GEE! CAN WE GO, THEN?
ZOOM!
SUIT YOURSELVES! I'LL DRIVE YOU OVER, BUT I'M STAYING HERE IN THE TENT! JUST DON'T COME WHINING TO ME FOR HELP WHEN DEAR, GENEROUS UNCLE SCROOGE PUTS YOU TO WORK!
WE WON'T!
LATER...
WONDER WHAT SCROOGE HAS GOT MY WISEACRE NEPHEWS DOING? REPAIRING THE PLUMBING OR...
ROAR!
acme COLLAPSIBLE BOAT
WELL, HE'S GOT YOU FIXING THE MOTORBOAT!
HI, UNCA DONALD!
OH, NO! WE'RE NOT FIXING IT! IT RUNS FINE!
WHERE IS THE OLD FOX?
TAKING A NAP! HE CAN'T FIGURE OUT WHY YOU WANTED TO STAY IN THAT DRAFTY, LEAKY OLD TENT!
OH, HE CAN'T, EH? WELL, I'LL BET HE'S BEEN TOO BUSY THINKING UP WAYS TO GET FREE WORK OUT OF YOU KIDS!
WE THINK YOU'RE WRONG, UNCA DONALD!
THE LODGE IS IN PERFECT CONDITION!
ALL WE'VE HAD TO DO IS COOK AND WASH DISHES!
WE'D BE DOING THAT, ANYWAY!
YOU'LL BE DOING THAT AND MORE, MARK MY WORDS! HE'S GOT SOMETHING UP HIS SLEEVE! ...WELL, HAVE FUN, LITTLE PIGEONS! SEE YOU IN A WEEK!

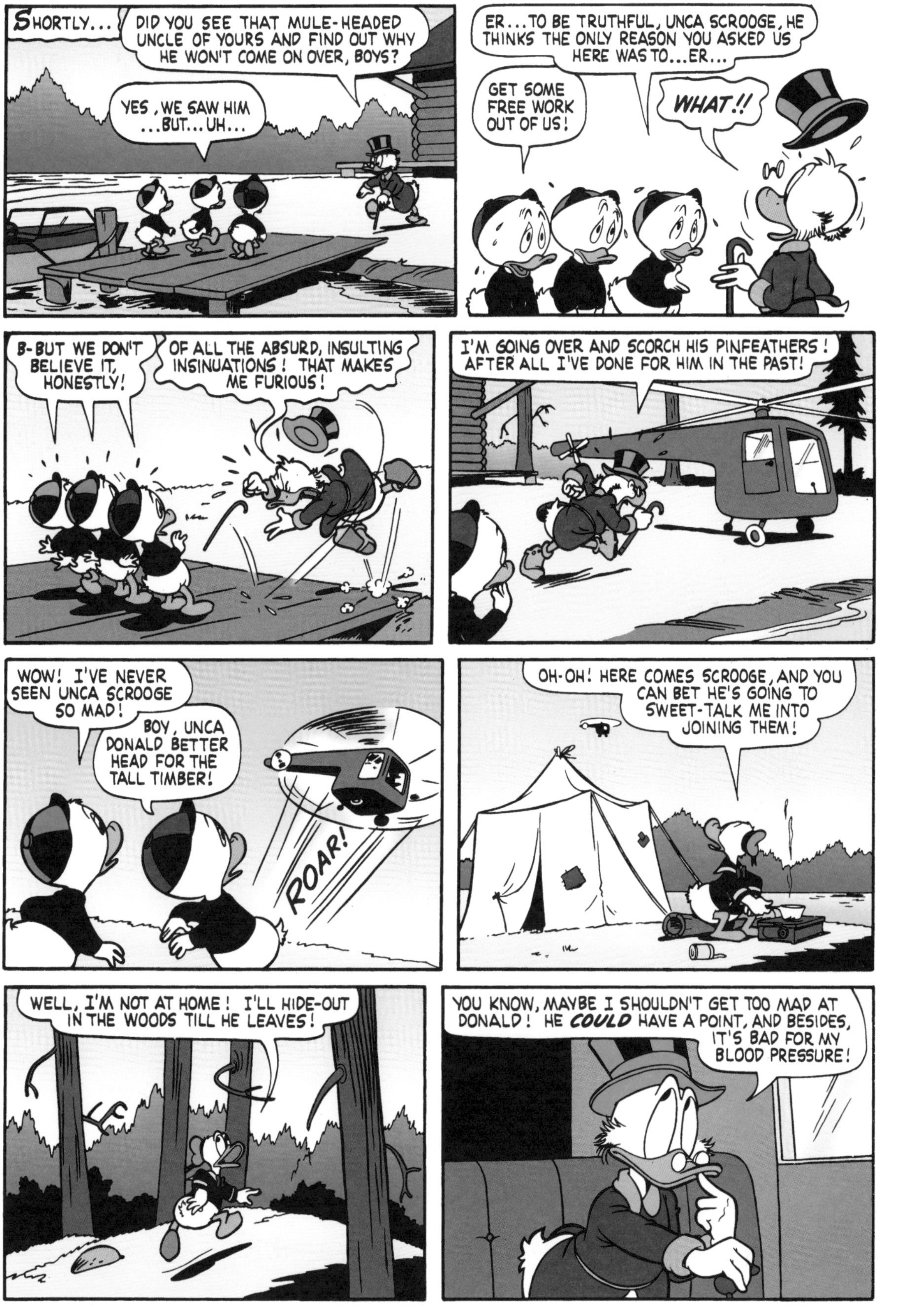
SHORTLY...
DID YOU SEE THAT MULE-HEADED UNCLE OF YOURS AND FIND OUT WHY HE WON'T COME ON OVER, BOYS?
YES, WE SAW HIM ...BUT...UH...
ER...TO BE TRUTHFUL, UNCA SCROOGE, HE THINKS THE ONLY REASON YOU ASKED US HERE WAS TO...ER...
GET SOME FREE WORK OUT OF US!
WHAT!!
B-BUT WE DON'T BELIEVE IT, HONESTLY!
OF ALL THE ABSURD, INSULTING INSINUATIONS! THAT MAKES ME FURIOUS!
I'M GOING OVER AND SCORCH HIS PINFEATHERS! AFTER ALL I'VE DONE FOR HIM IN THE PAST!
WOW! I'VE NEVER SEEN UNCA SCROOGE SO MAD!
BOY, UNCA DONALD BETTER HEAD FOR THE TALL TIMBER!
ROAR!
OH-OH! HERE COMES SCROOGE, AND YOU CAN BET HE'S GOING TO SWEET-TALK ME INTO JOINING THEM!
WELL, I'M NOT AT HOME! I'LL HIDE-OUT IN THE WOODS TILL HE LEAVES!
YOU KNOW, MAYBE I SHOULDN'T GET TOO MAD AT DONALD! HE COULD HAVE A POINT, AND BESIDES, IT'S BAD FOR MY BLOOD PRESSURE!

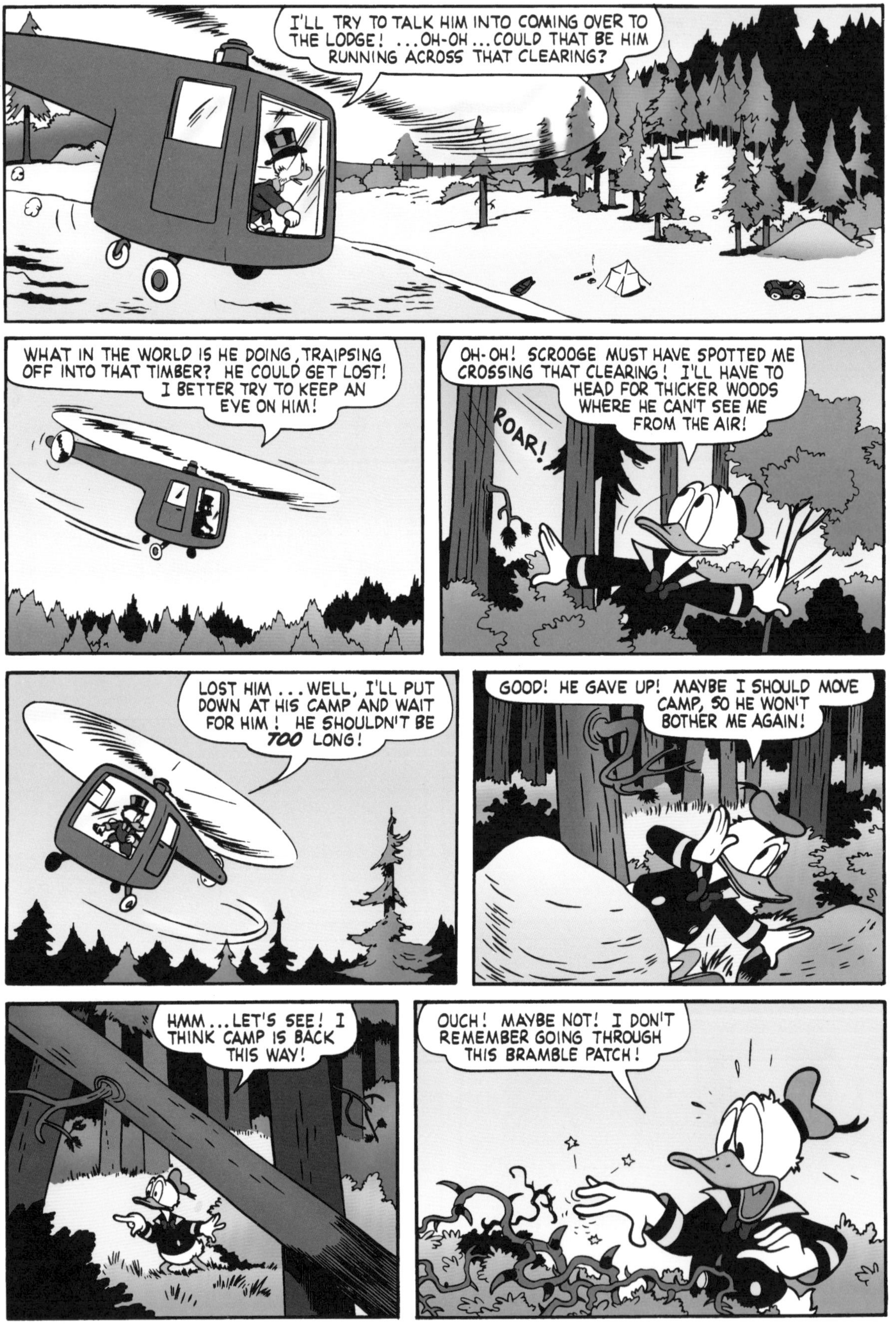
I'LL TRY TO TALK HIM INTO COMING OVER TO THE LODGE! ...OH-OH ... COULD THAT BE HIM RUNNING ACROSS THAT CLEARING?
WHAT IN THE WORLD IS HE DOING, TRAIPSING OFF INTO THAT TIMBER? HE COULD GET LOST! I BETTER TRY TO KEEP AN EYE ON HIM!
OH-OH! SCROOGE MUST HAVE SPOTTED ME CROSSING THAT CLEARING! I'LL HAVE TO HEAD FOR THICKER WOODS WHERE HE CAN'T SEE ME FROM THE AIR!
ROAR!
LOST HIM ... WELL, I'LL PUT DOWN AT HIS CAMP AND WAIT FOR HIM! HE SHOULDN'T BE TOO LONG!
GOOD! HE GAVE UP! MAYBE I SHOULD MOVE CAMP, SO HE WON'T BOTHER ME AGAIN!
HMM ... LET'S SEE! I THINK CAMP IS BACK THIS WAY!
OUCH! MAYBE NOT! I DON'T REMEMBER GOING THROUGH THIS BRAMBLE PATCH!

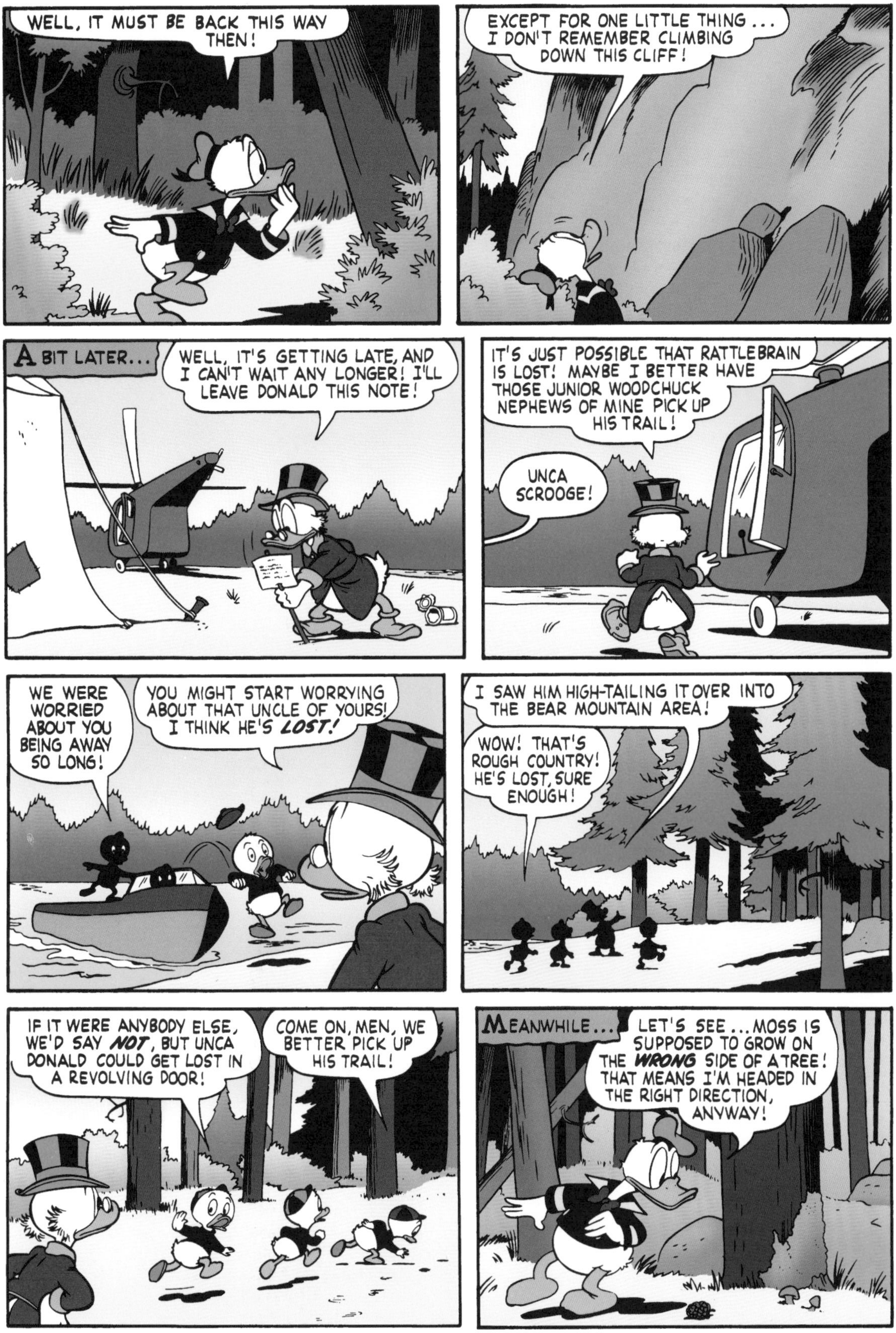
WELL, IT MUST BE BACK THIS WAY THEN!
EXCEPT FOR ONE LITTLE THING ... I DON'T REMEMBER CLIMBING DOWN THIS CLIFF!
A BIT LATER...
WELL, IT'S GETTING LATE, AND I CAN'T WAIT ANY LONGER! I'LL LEAVE DONALD THIS NOTE!
IT'S JUST POSSIBLE THAT RATTLEBRAIN IS LOST! MAYBE I BETTER HAVE THOSE JUNIOR WOODCHUCK NEPHEWS OF MINE PICK UP HIS TRAIL!
UNCA SCROOGE!
WE WERE WORRIED ABOUT YOU BEING AWAY SO LONG!
YOU MIGHT START WORRYING ABOUT THAT UNCLE OF YOURS! I THINK HE'S *LOST!*
I SAW HIM HIGH-TAILING IT OVER INTO THE BEAR MOUNTAIN AREA!
WOW! THAT'S ROUGH COUNTRY! HE'S LOST, SURE ENOUGH!
IF IT WERE ANYBODY ELSE, WE'D SAY *NOT*, BUT UNCA DONALD COULD GET LOST IN A REVOLVING DOOR!
COME ON, MEN, WE BETTER PICK UP HIS TRAIL!
MEANWHILE...
LET'S SEE... MOSS IS SUPPOSED TO GROW ON THE *WRONG* SIDE OF A TREE! THAT MEANS I'M HEADED IN THE RIGHT DIRECTION, ANYWAY!

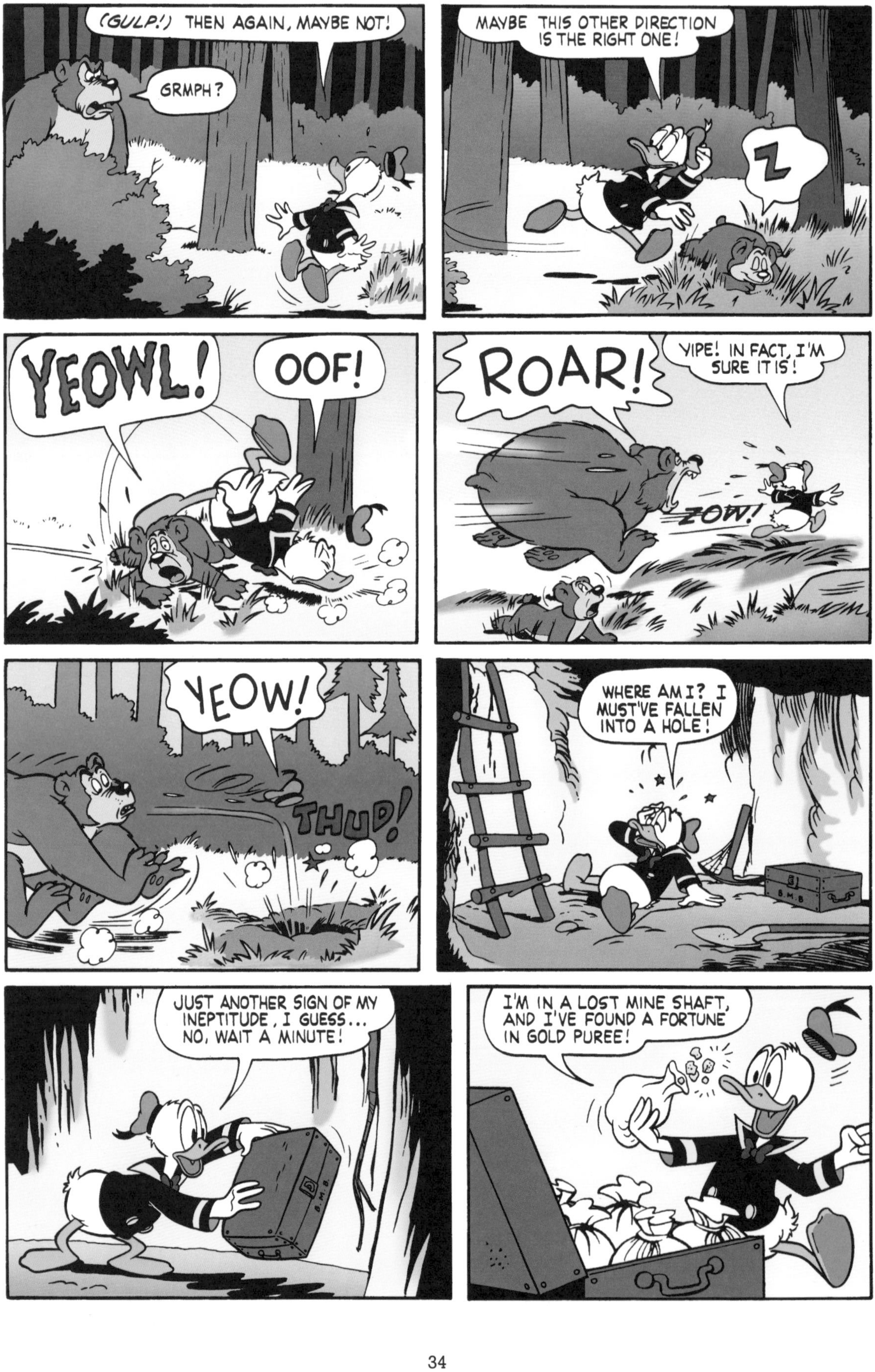
(GULP!) THEN AGAIN, MAYBE NOT!
GRMPH?
MAYBE THIS OTHER DIRECTION IS THE RIGHT ONE!
Z
YEOWL!
OOF!
ROAR!
YIPE! IN FACT, I'M SURE IT IS!
ZOW!
YEOW!
THUD!
WHERE AM I? I MUST'VE FALLEN INTO A HOLE!
B.M.B.
JUST ANOTHER SIGN OF MY INEPTITUDE, I GUESS... NO, WAIT A MINUTE!
B.M.B.
I'M IN A LOST MINE SHAFT, AND I'VE FOUND A FORTUNE IN GOLD PUREE!

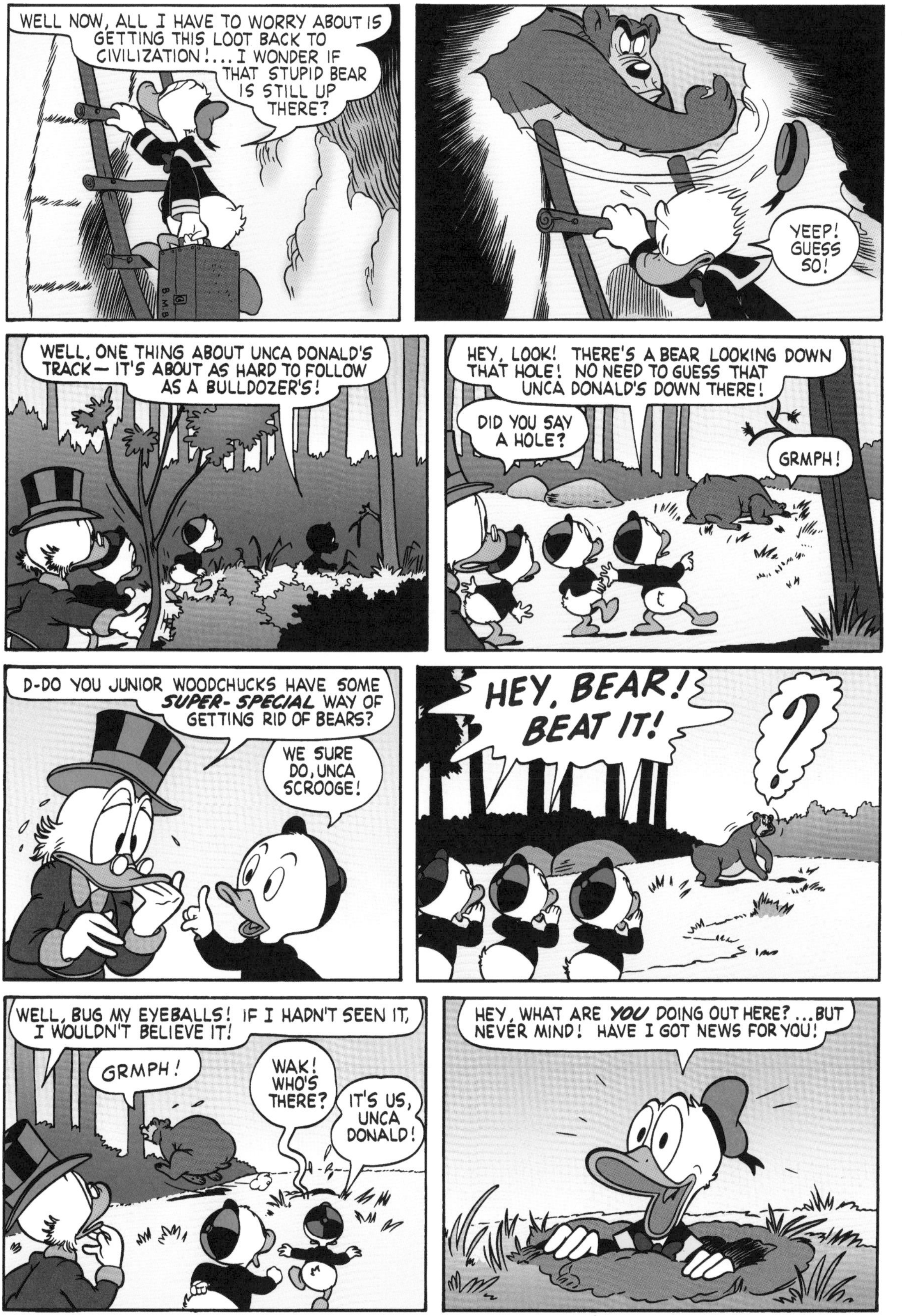
WELL NOW, ALL I HAVE TO WORRY ABOUT IS GETTING THIS LOOT BACK TO CIVILIZATION!... I WONDER IF THAT STUPID BEAR IS STILL UP THERE?
B.M.B.
YEEP! GUESS SO!
WELL, ONE THING ABOUT UNCA DONALD'S TRACK— IT'S ABOUT AS HARD TO FOLLOW AS A BULLDOZER'S!
HEY, LOOK! THERE'S A BEAR LOOKING DOWN THAT HOLE! NO NEED TO GUESS THAT UNCA DONALD'S DOWN THERE!
DID YOU SAY A HOLE?
GRMPH!
D-DO YOU JUNIOR WOODCHUCKS HAVE SOME SUPER-SPECIAL WAY OF GETTING RID OF BEARS?
WE SURE DO, UNCA SCROOGE!
HEY, BEAR! BEAT IT!
?
WELL, BUG MY EYEBALLS! IF I HADN'T SEEN IT, I WOULDN'T BELIEVE IT!
GRMPH!
WAK! WHO'S THERE?
IT'S US, UNCA DONALD!
HEY, WHAT ARE YOU DOING OUT HERE?...BUT NEVER MIND! HAVE I GOT NEWS FOR YOU!

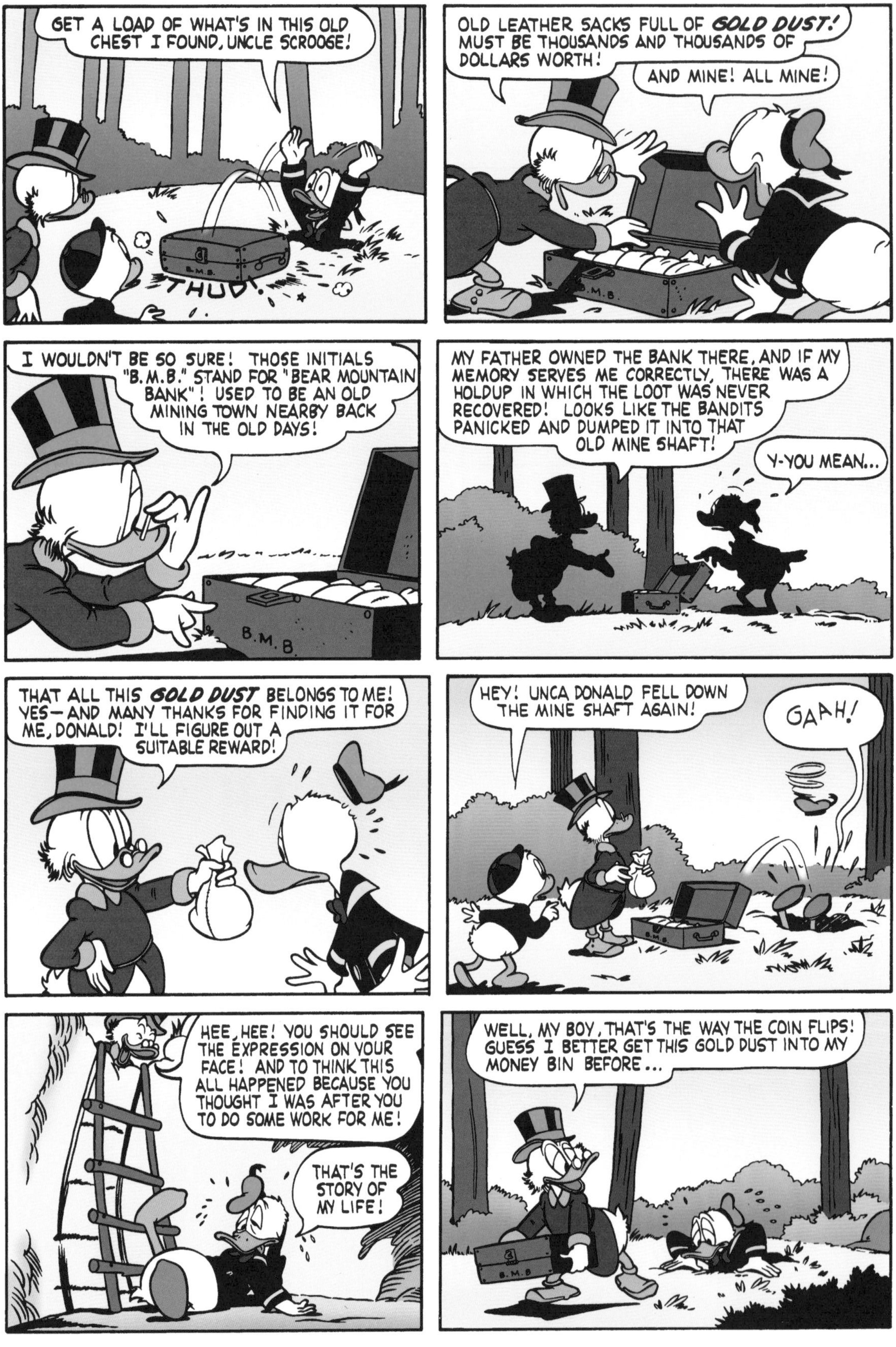
GET A LOAD OF WHAT'S IN THIS OLD CHEST I FOUND, UNCLE SCROOGE!
THUD!
OLD LEATHER SACKS FULL OF GOLD DUST! MUST BE THOUSANDS AND THOUSANDS OF DOLLARS WORTH!
AND MINE! ALL MINE!
I WOULDN'T BE SO SURE! THOSE INITIALS "B.M.B." STAND FOR "BEAR MOUNTAIN BANK"! USED TO BE AN OLD MINING TOWN NEARBY BACK IN THE OLD DAYS!
B.M.B.
MY FATHER OWNED THE BANK THERE, AND IF MY MEMORY SERVES ME CORRECTLY, THERE WAS A HOLDUP IN WHICH THE LOOT WAS NEVER RECOVERED! LOOKS LIKE THE BANDITS PANICKED AND DUMPED IT INTO THAT OLD MINE SHAFT!
Y-YOU MEAN...
THAT ALL THIS GOLD DUST BELONGS TO ME! YES—AND MANY THANKS FOR FINDING IT FOR ME, DONALD! I'LL FIGURE OUT A SUITABLE REWARD!
HEY! UNCA DONALD FELL DOWN THE MINE SHAFT AGAIN!
GAAH!
HEE, HEE! YOU SHOULD SEE THE EXPRESSION ON YOUR FACE! AND TO THINK THIS ALL HAPPENED BECAUSE YOU THOUGHT I WAS AFTER YOU TO DO SOME WORK FOR ME!
THAT'S THE STORY OF MY LIFE!
WELL, MY BOY, THAT'S THE WAY THE COIN FLIPS! GUESS I BETTER GET THIS GOLD DUST INTO MY MONEY BIN BEFORE...
B.M.B

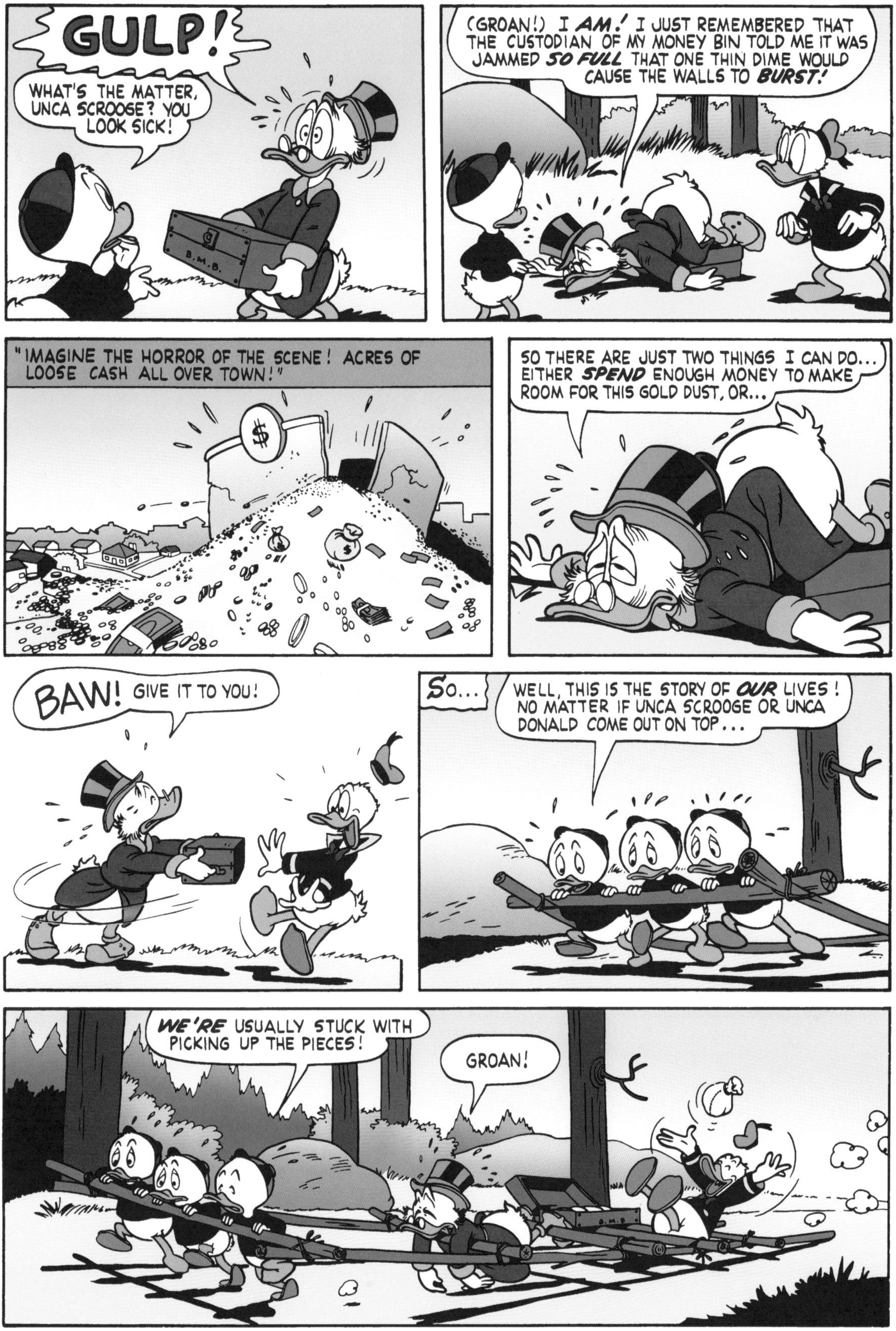
GULP!
WHAT'S THE MATTER, UNCA SCROOGE? YOU LOOK SICK!
(GROAN!) I AM! I JUST REMEMBERED THAT THE CUSTODIAN OF MY MONEY BIN TOLD ME IT WAS JAMMED SO FULL THAT ONE THIN DIME WOULD CAUSE THE WALLS TO BURST!
B.M.B.
"IMAGINE THE HORROR OF THE SCENE! ACRES OF LOOSE CASH ALL OVER TOWN!"
SO THERE ARE JUST TWO THINGS I CAN DO... EITHER SPEND ENOUGH MONEY TO MAKE ROOM FOR THIS GOLD DUST, OR...
BAW! GIVE IT TO YOU!
SO...
WELL, THIS IS THE STORY OF OUR LIVES! NO MATTER IF UNCA SCROOGE OR UNCA DONALD COME OUT ON TOP...
WE'RE USUALLY STUCK WITH PICKING UP THE PIECES!
GROAN!

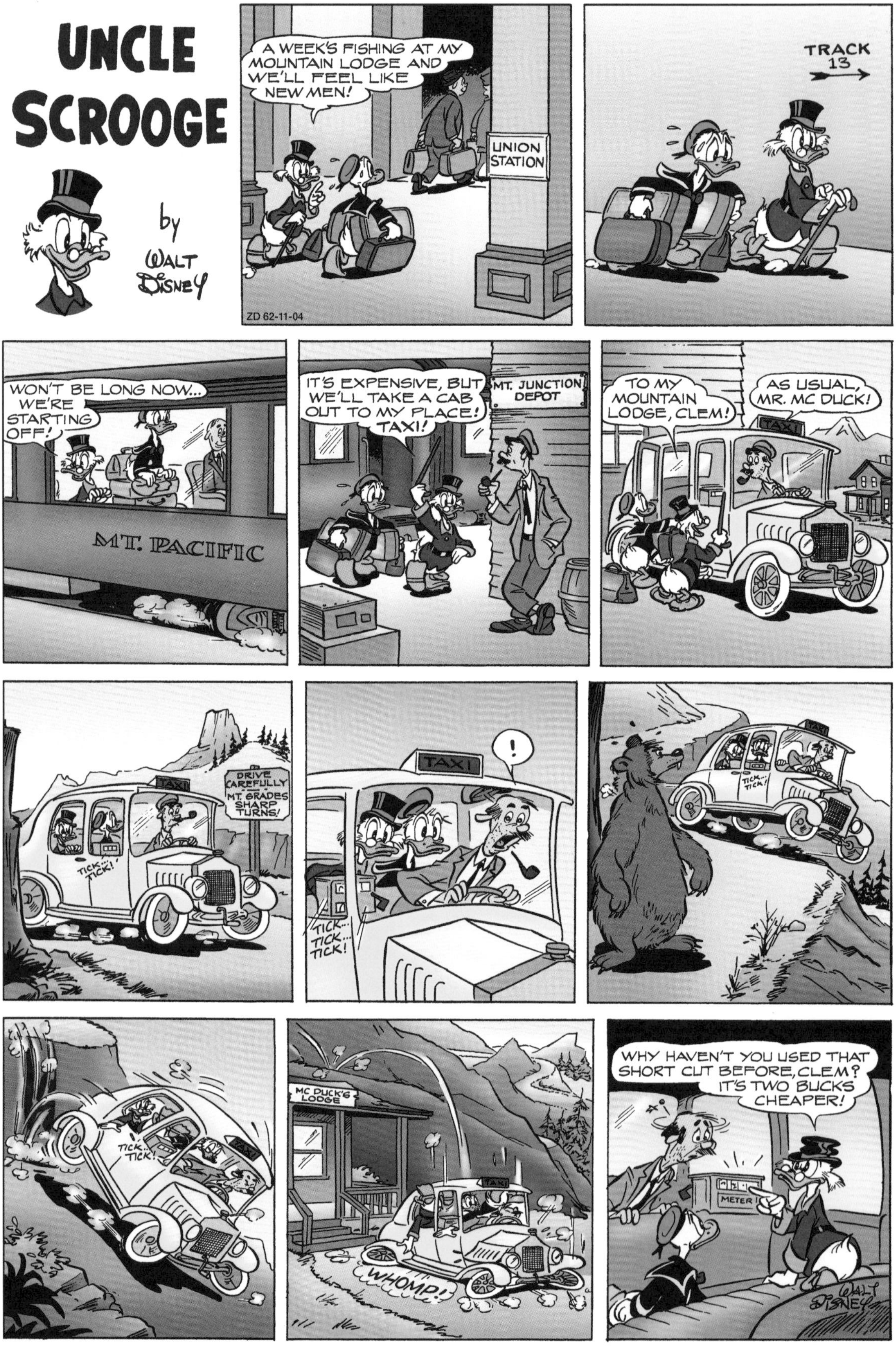
UNCLE SCROOGE
by WALT DISNEY
A WEEK'S FISHING AT MY MOUNTAIN LODGE AND WE'LL FEEL LIKE NEW MEN!
UNION STATION
ZD 62-11-04
TRACK 13
WON'T BE LONG NOW... WE'RE STARTING OFF!
MT. PACIFIC
IT'S EXPENSIVE, BUT WE'LL TAKE A CAB OUT TO MY PLACE! TAXI!
MT. JUNCTION DEPOT
TO MY MOUNTAIN LODGE, CLEM!
AS USUAL, MR. MC DUCK!
TAXI
DRIVE CAREFULLY MT. GRADES SHARP TURNS!
TICK... TICK!
TAXI
!
TICK... TICK... TICK!
TICK... TICK!
TICK... TICK!
MC DUCK'S LODGE
WHOMP!
WHY HAVEN'T YOU USED THAT SHORT CUT BEFORE, CLEM? IT'S TWO BUCKS CHEAPER!
METER
WALT DISNEY

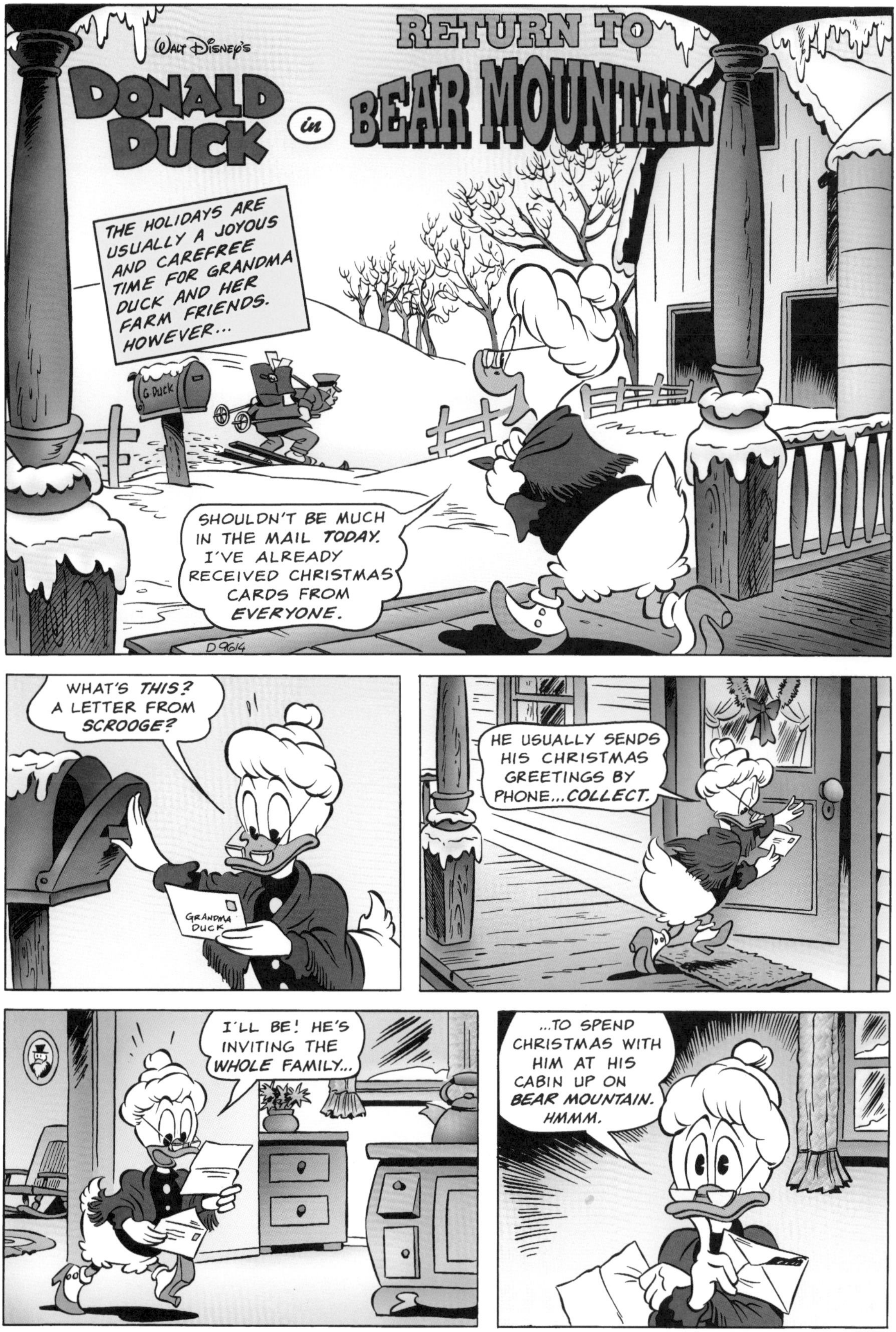
Walt Disney's
DONALD DUCK in
RETURN TO BEAR MOUNTAIN
THE HOLIDAYS ARE USUALLY A JOYOUS AND CAREFREE TIME FOR GRANDMA DUCK AND HER FARM FRIENDS. HOWEVER...
G. DUCK
SHOULDN'T BE MUCH IN THE MAIL TODAY. I'VE ALREADY RECEIVED CHRISTMAS CARDS FROM EVERYONE.
D 9614
WHAT'S THIS? A LETTER FROM SCROOGE?
GRANDMA DUCK
HE USUALLY SENDS HIS CHRISTMAS GREETINGS BY PHONE...COLLECT.
I'LL BE! HE'S INVITING THE WHOLE FAMILY...
...TO SPEND CHRISTMAS WITH HIM AT HIS CABIN UP ON BEAR MOUNTAIN. HMMM.

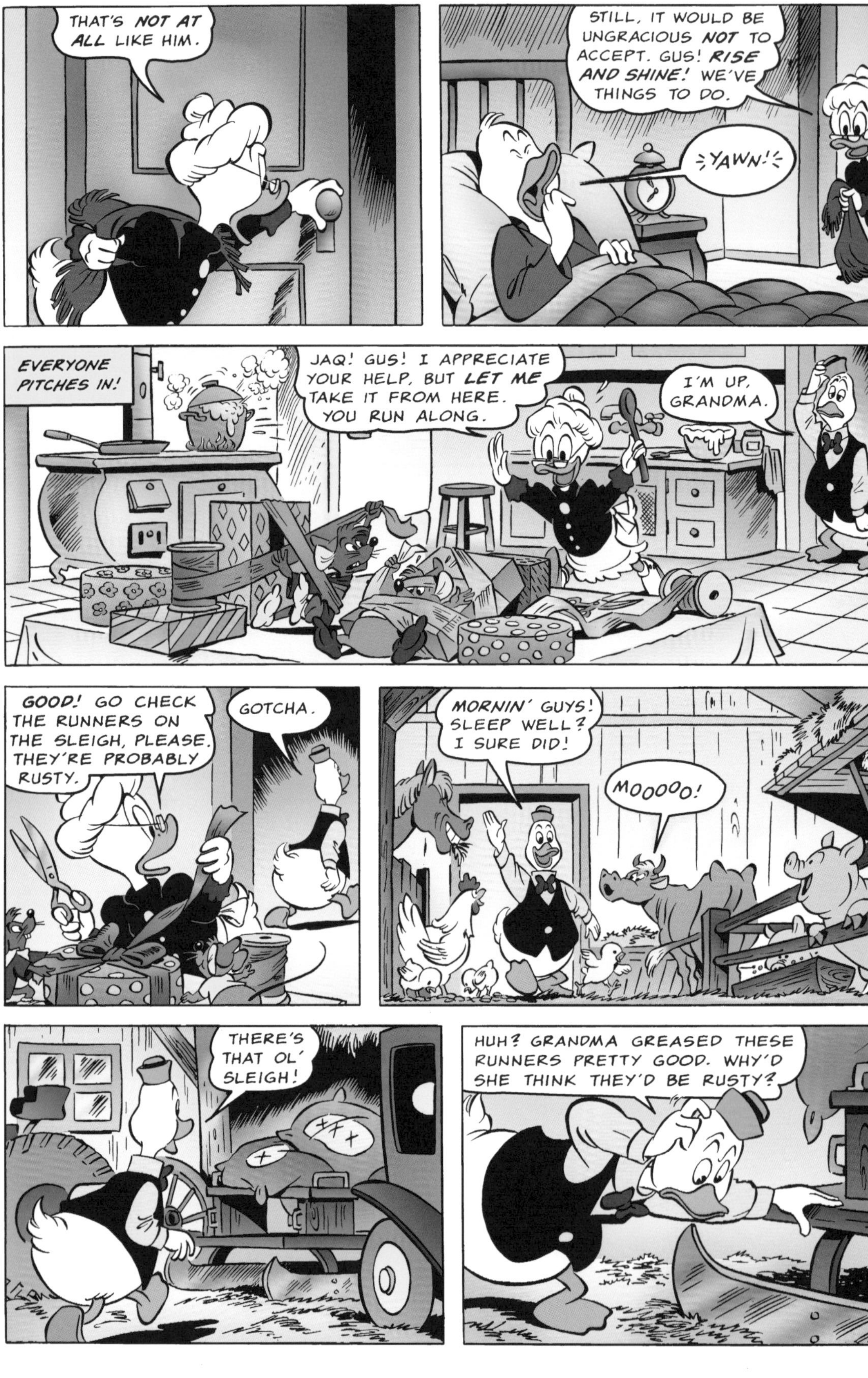
THAT'S NOT AT ALL LIKE HIM.
STILL, IT WOULD BE UNGRACIOUS NOT TO ACCEPT. GUS! RISE AND SHINE! WE'VE THINGS TO DO.
YAWN!
EVERYONE PITCHES IN!
JAQ! GUS! I APPRECIATE YOUR HELP, BUT LET ME TAKE IT FROM HERE. YOU RUN ALONG.
I'M UP, GRANDMA.
GOOD! GO CHECK THE RUNNERS ON THE SLEIGH, PLEASE. THEY'RE PROBABLY RUSTY.
GOTCHA.
MORNIN' GUYS! SLEEP WELL? I SURE DID!
MOOOOO!
THERE'S THAT OL' SLEIGH!
HUH? GRANDMA GREASED THESE RUNNERS PRETTY GOOD. WHY'D SHE THINK THEY'D BE RUSTY?

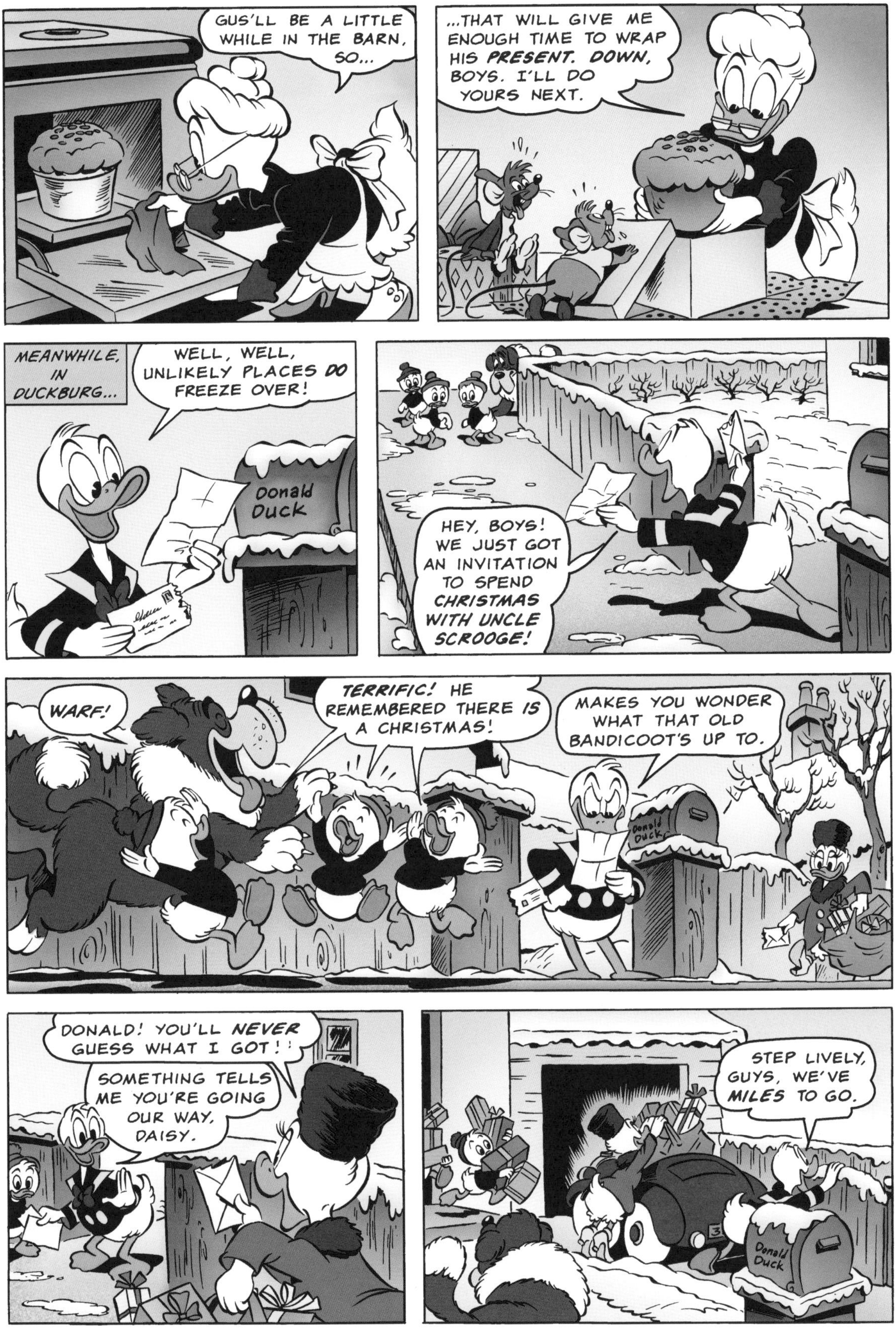
GUS'LL BE A LITTLE WHILE IN THE BARN, SO...
...THAT WILL GIVE ME ENOUGH TIME TO WRAP HIS PRESENT. DOWN, BOYS. I'LL DO YOURS NEXT.
MEANWHILE, IN DUCKBURG...
WELL, WELL, UNLIKELY PLACES DO FREEZE OVER!
Donald Duck
HEY, BOYS! WE JUST GOT AN INVITATION TO SPEND CHRISTMAS WITH UNCLE SCROOGE!
WARF!
TERRIFIC! HE REMEMBERED THERE IS A CHRISTMAS!
MAKES YOU WONDER WHAT THAT OLD BANDICOOT'S UP TO.
DONALD! YOU'LL NEVER GUESS WHAT I GOT!
SOMETHING TELLS ME YOU'RE GOING OUR WAY, DAISY.
STEP LIVELY, GUYS, WE'VE MILES TO GO.
Donald Duck

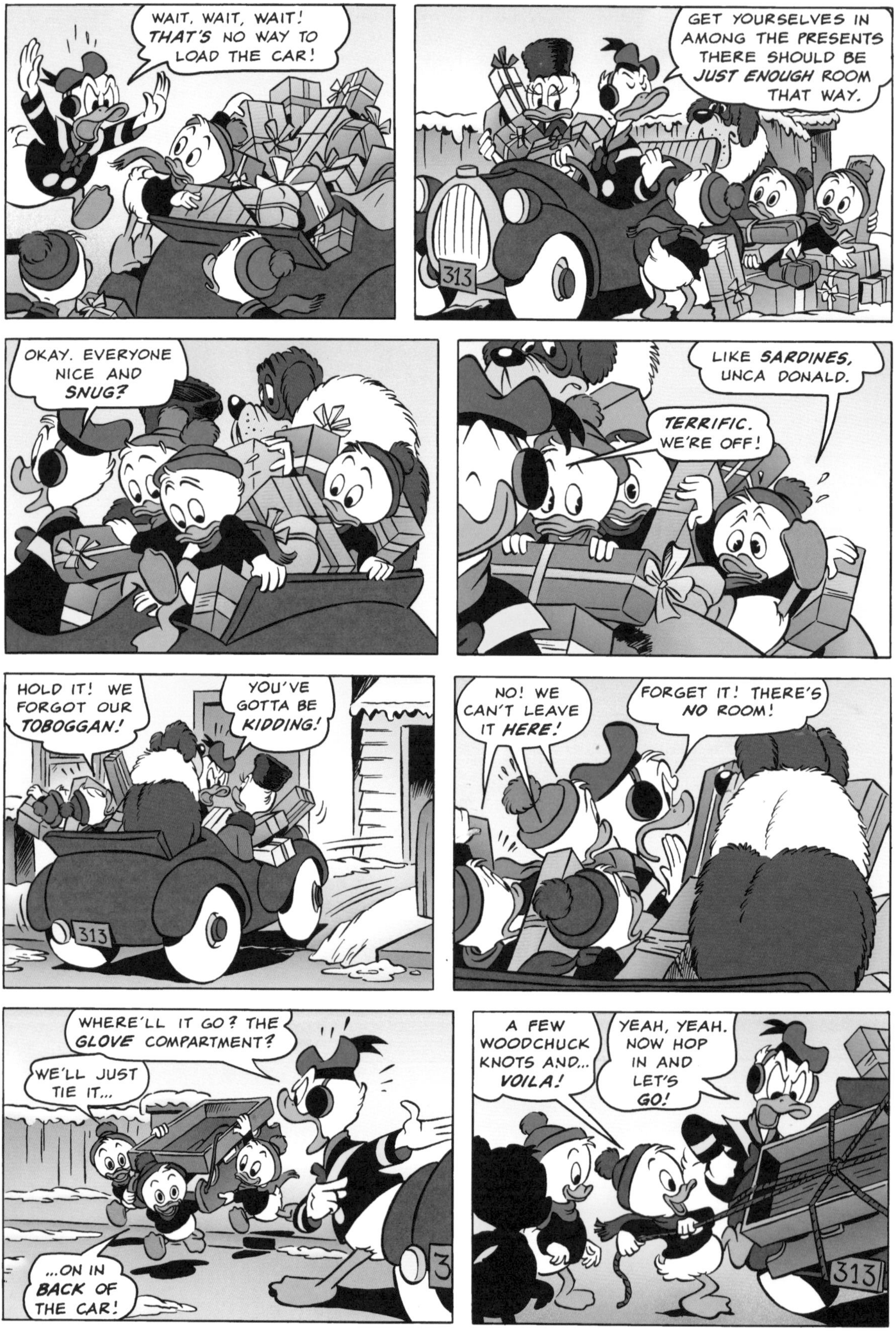

WAIT, WAIT, WAIT! THAT'S NO WAY TO LOAD THE CAR!
GET YOURSELVES IN AMONG THE PRESENTS THERE SHOULD BE JUST ENOUGH ROOM THAT WAY.
313
OKAY. EVERYONE NICE AND SNUG?
LIKE SARDINES, UNCA DONALD.
TERRIFIC. WE'RE OFF!
HOLD IT! WE FORGOT OUR TOBOGGAN!
YOU'VE GOTTA BE KIDDING!
313
NO! WE CAN'T LEAVE IT HERE!
FORGET IT! THERE'S NO ROOM!
WHERE'LL IT GO? THE GLOVE COMPARTMENT?
WE'LL JUST TIE IT...
...ON IN BACK OF THE CAR!
A FEW WOODCHUCK KNOTS AND... VOILA!
YEAH, YEAH. NOW HOP IN AND LET'S GO!
313

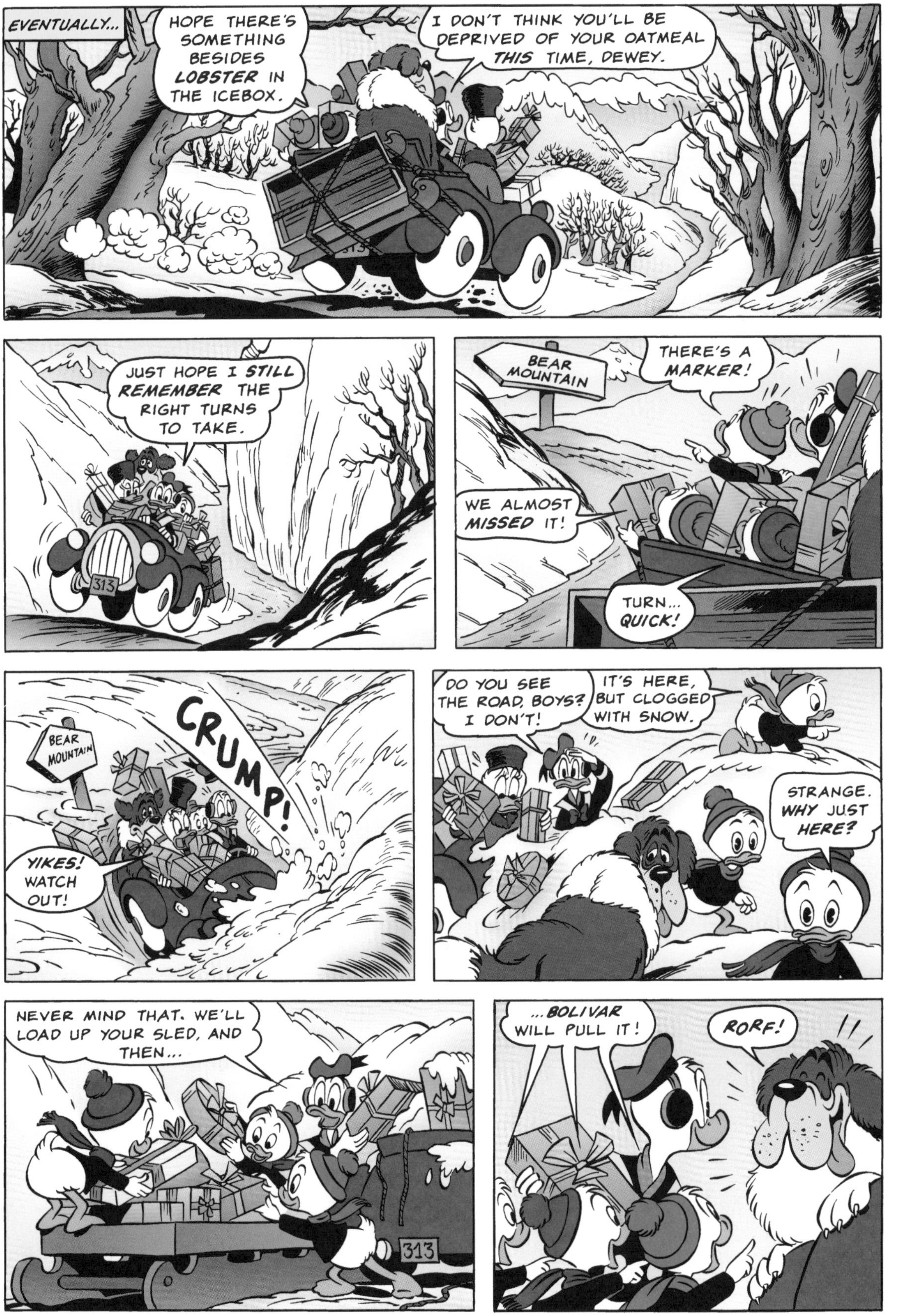
EVENTUALLY...
HOPE THERE'S SOMETHING BESIDES LOBSTER IN THE ICEBOX.
I DON'T THINK YOU'LL BE DEPRIVED OF YOUR OATMEAL THIS TIME, DEWEY.
JUST HOPE I STILL REMEMBER THE RIGHT TURNS TO TAKE.
BEAR MOUNTAIN
THERE'S A MARKER!
WE ALMOST MISSED IT!
TURN... QUICK!
BEAR MOUNTAIN
CRUMP!
YIKES! WATCH OUT!
DO YOU SEE THE ROAD, BOYS? I DON'T!
IT'S HERE, BUT CLOGGED WITH SNOW.
STRANGE. WHY JUST HERE?
NEVER MIND THAT. WE'LL LOAD UP YOUR SLED, AND THEN...
...BOLIVAR WILL PULL IT!
RORF!

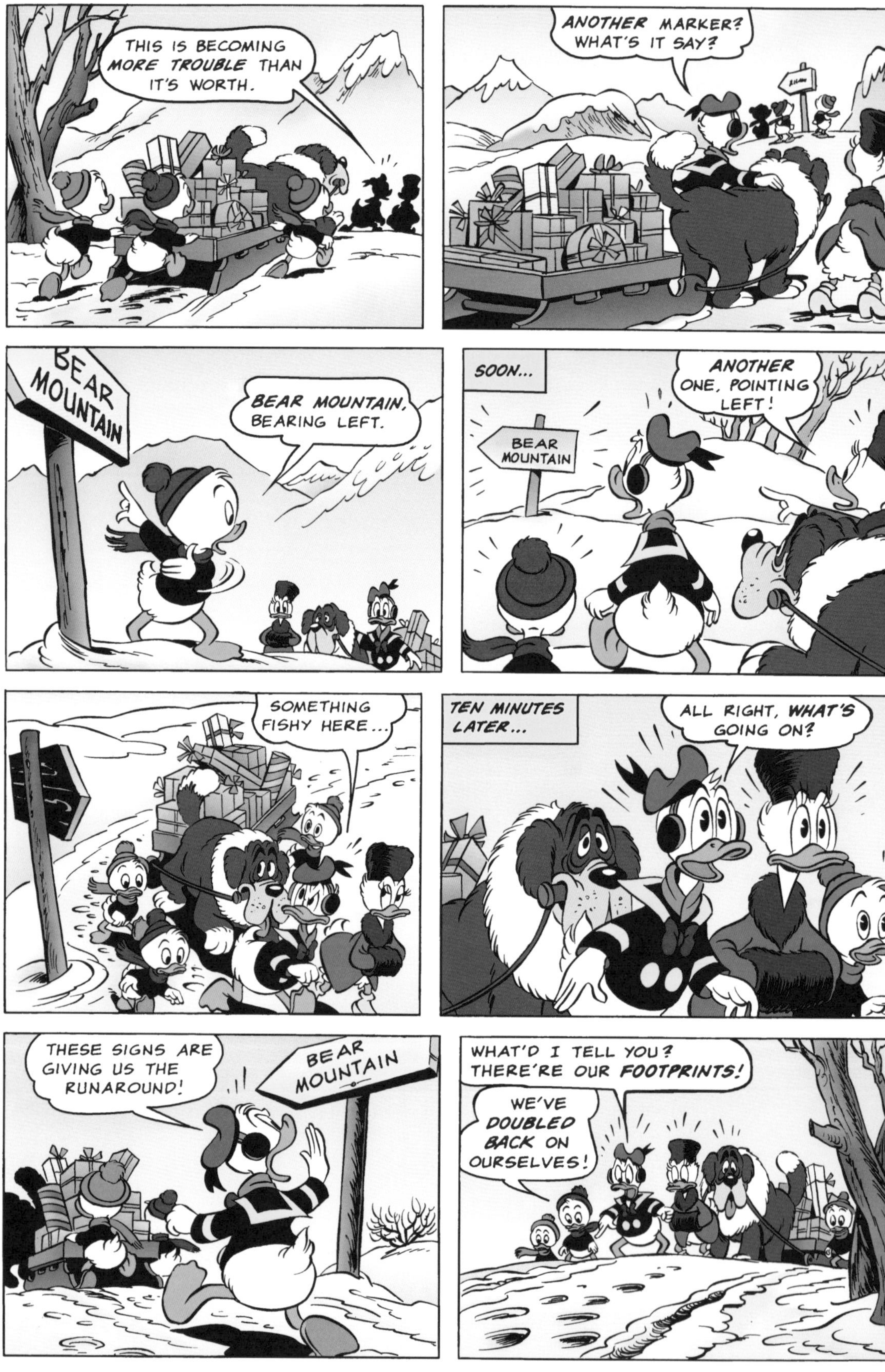
THIS IS BECOMING MORE TROUBLE THAN IT'S WORTH.
ANOTHER MARKER? WHAT'S IT SAY?
BEAR MOUNTAIN
BEAR MOUNTAIN, BEARING LEFT.
SOON...
ANOTHER ONE, POINTING LEFT!
BEAR MOUNTAIN
SOMETHING FISHY HERE...
TEN MINUTES LATER...
ALL RIGHT, WHAT'S GOING ON?
THESE SIGNS ARE GIVING US THE RUNAROUND!
BEAR MOUNTAIN
WHAT'D I TELL YOU? THERE'RE OUR FOOTPRINTS!
WE'VE DOUBLED BACK ON OURSELVES!

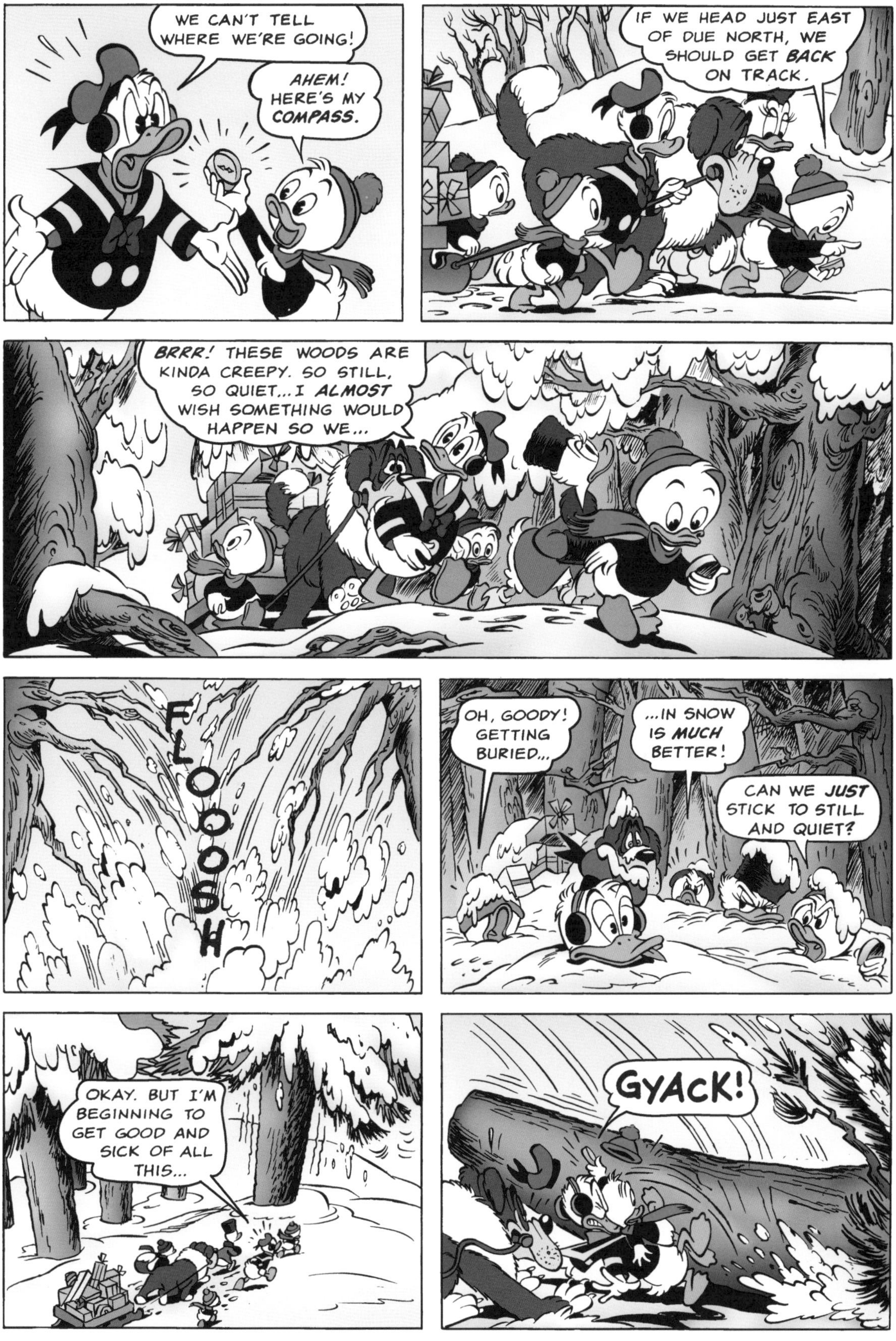
WE CAN'T TELL WHERE WE'RE GOING!
AHEM! HERE'S MY COMPASS.
IF WE HEAD JUST EAST OF DUE NORTH, WE SHOULD GET BACK ON TRACK.
BRRR! THESE WOODS ARE KINDA CREEPY. SO STILL, SO QUIET... I ALMOST WISH SOMETHING WOULD HAPPEN SO WE...
FLOOOOSH
OH, GOODY! GETTING BURIED...
...IN SNOW IS MUCH BETTER!
CAN WE JUST STICK TO STILL AND QUIET?
OKAY. BUT I'M BEGINNING TO GET GOOD AND SICK OF ALL THIS...
GYACK!

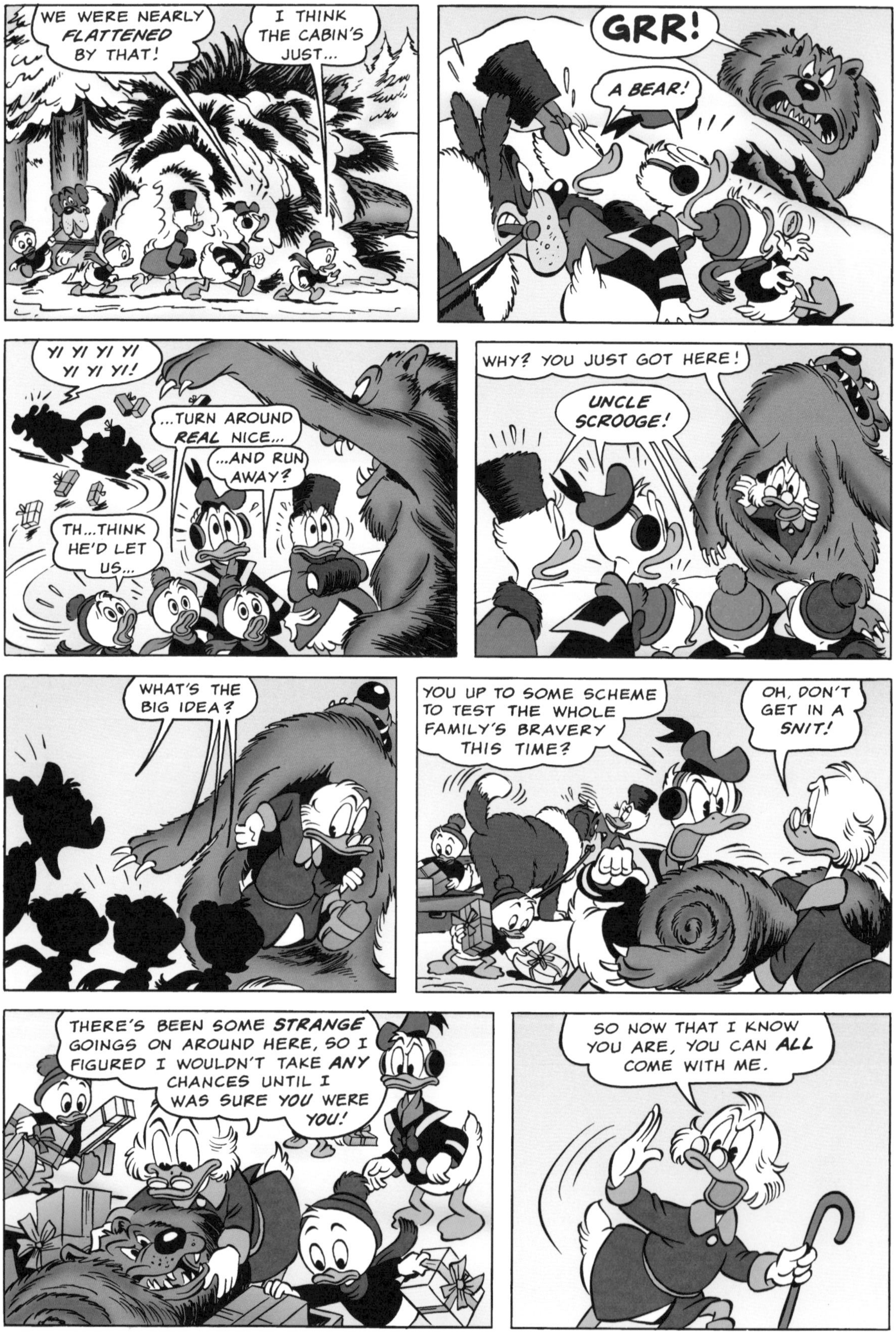
WE WERE NEARLY FLATTENED BY THAT!
I THINK THE CABIN'S JUST...
GRR!
A BEAR!
YI YI YI YI YI YI YI!
...TURN AROUND REAL NICE...
...AND RUN AWAY?
TH...THINK HE'D LET US...
WHY? YOU JUST GOT HERE!
UNCLE SCROOGE!
WHAT'S THE BIG IDEA?
YOU UP TO SOME SCHEME TO TEST THE WHOLE FAMILY'S BRAVERY THIS TIME?
OH, DON'T GET IN A SNIT!
THERE'S BEEN SOME STRANGE GOINGS ON AROUND HERE, SO I FIGURED I WOULDN'T TAKE ANY CHANCES UNTIL I WAS SURE YOU WERE YOU!
SO NOW THAT I KNOW YOU ARE, YOU CAN ALL COME WITH ME.

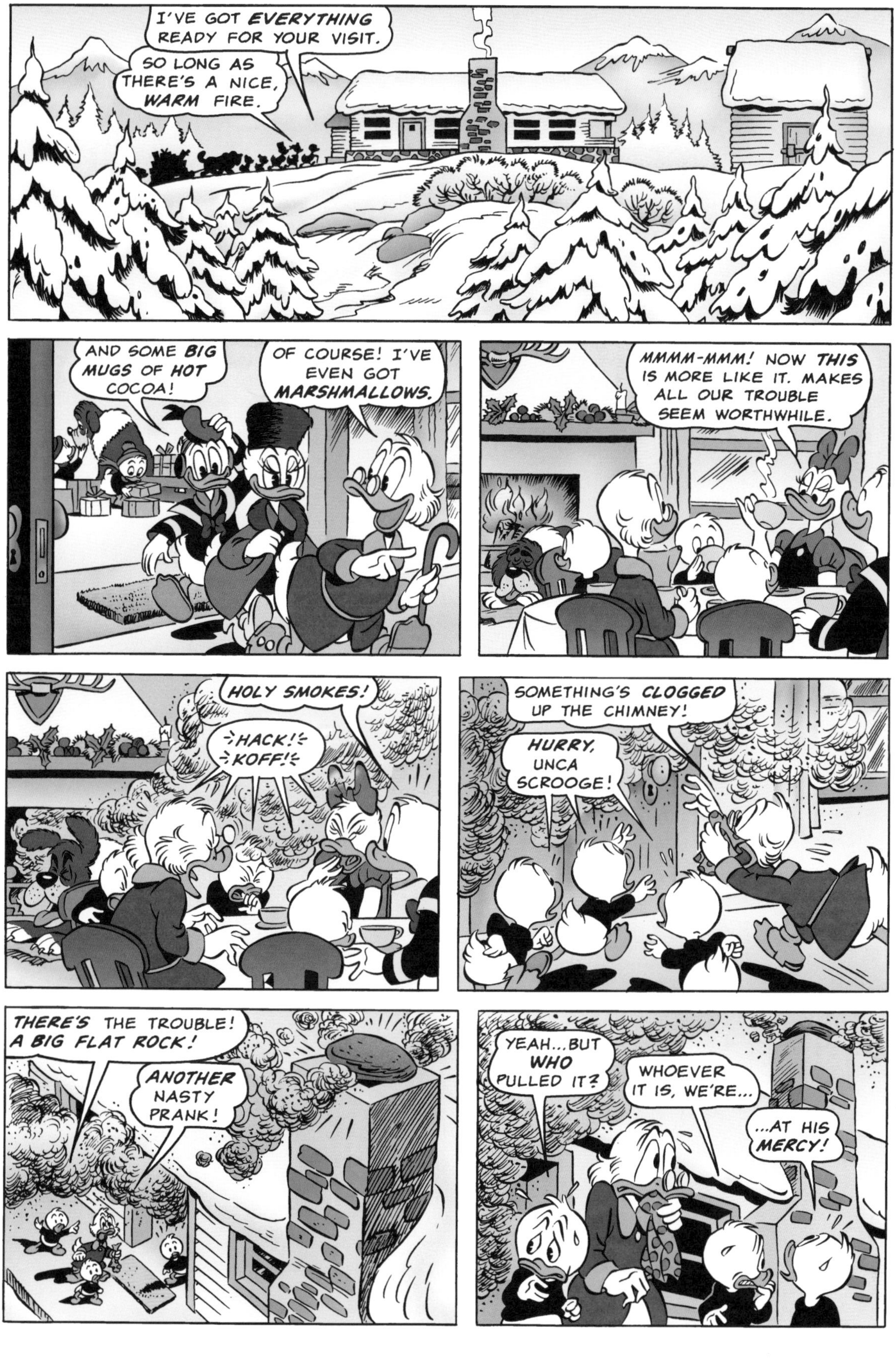

I'VE GOT EVERYTHING READY FOR YOUR VISIT.
SO LONG AS THERE'S A NICE, WARM FIRE.
AND SOME BIG MUGS OF HOT COCOA!
OF COURSE! I'VE EVEN GOT MARSHMALLOWS.
MMMM-MMM! NOW THIS IS MORE LIKE IT. MAKES ALL OUR TROUBLE SEEM WORTHWHILE.
HOLY SMOKES!
HACK! KOFF!
SOMETHING'S CLOGGED UP THE CHIMNEY!
HURRY, UNCA SCROOGE!
THERE'S THE TROUBLE! A BIG FLAT ROCK!
ANOTHER NASTY PRANK!
YEAH...BUT WHO PULLED IT?
WHOEVER IT IS, WE'RE...
...AT HIS MERCY!

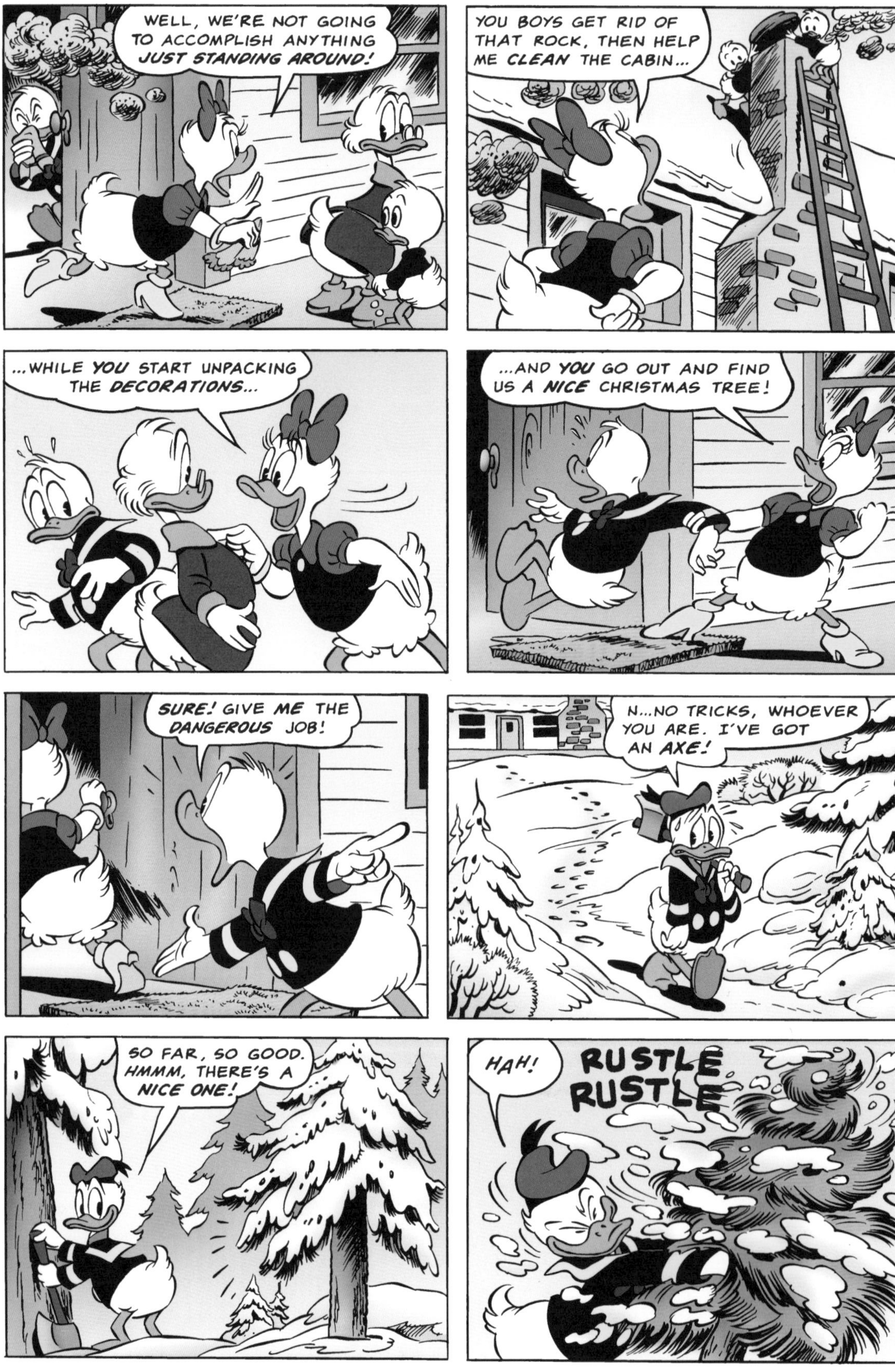
WELL, WE'RE NOT GOING TO ACCOMPLISH ANYTHING JUST STANDING AROUND!
YOU BOYS GET RID OF THAT ROCK, THEN HELP ME CLEAN THE CABIN...
...WHILE YOU START UNPACKING THE DECORATIONS...
...AND YOU GO OUT AND FIND US A NICE CHRISTMAS TREE!
SURE! GIVE ME THE DANGEROUS JOB!
N...NO TRICKS, WHOEVER YOU ARE. I'VE GOT AN AXE!
SO FAR, SO GOOD. HMMM, THERE'S A NICE ONE!
HAH!
RUSTLE RUSTLE

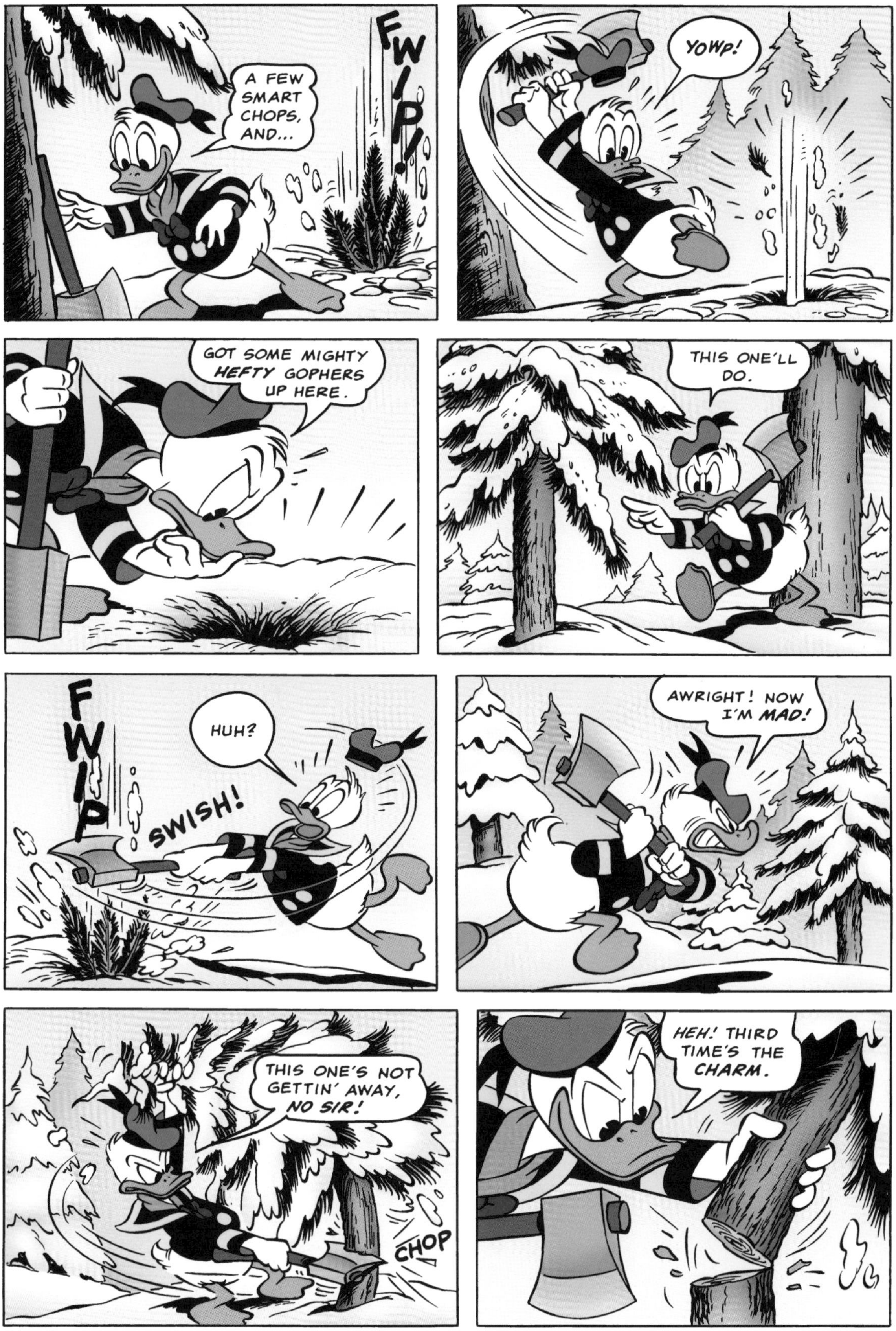
A FEW SMART CHOPS, AND...
FWIP!
YOWP!
GOT SOME MIGHTY HEFTY GOPHERS UP HERE.
THIS ONE'LL DO.
FWIP
HUH?
SWISH!
AWRIGHT! NOW I'M MAD!
THIS ONE'S NOT GETTIN' AWAY, NO SIR!
CHOP
HEH! THIRD TIME'S THE CHARM.

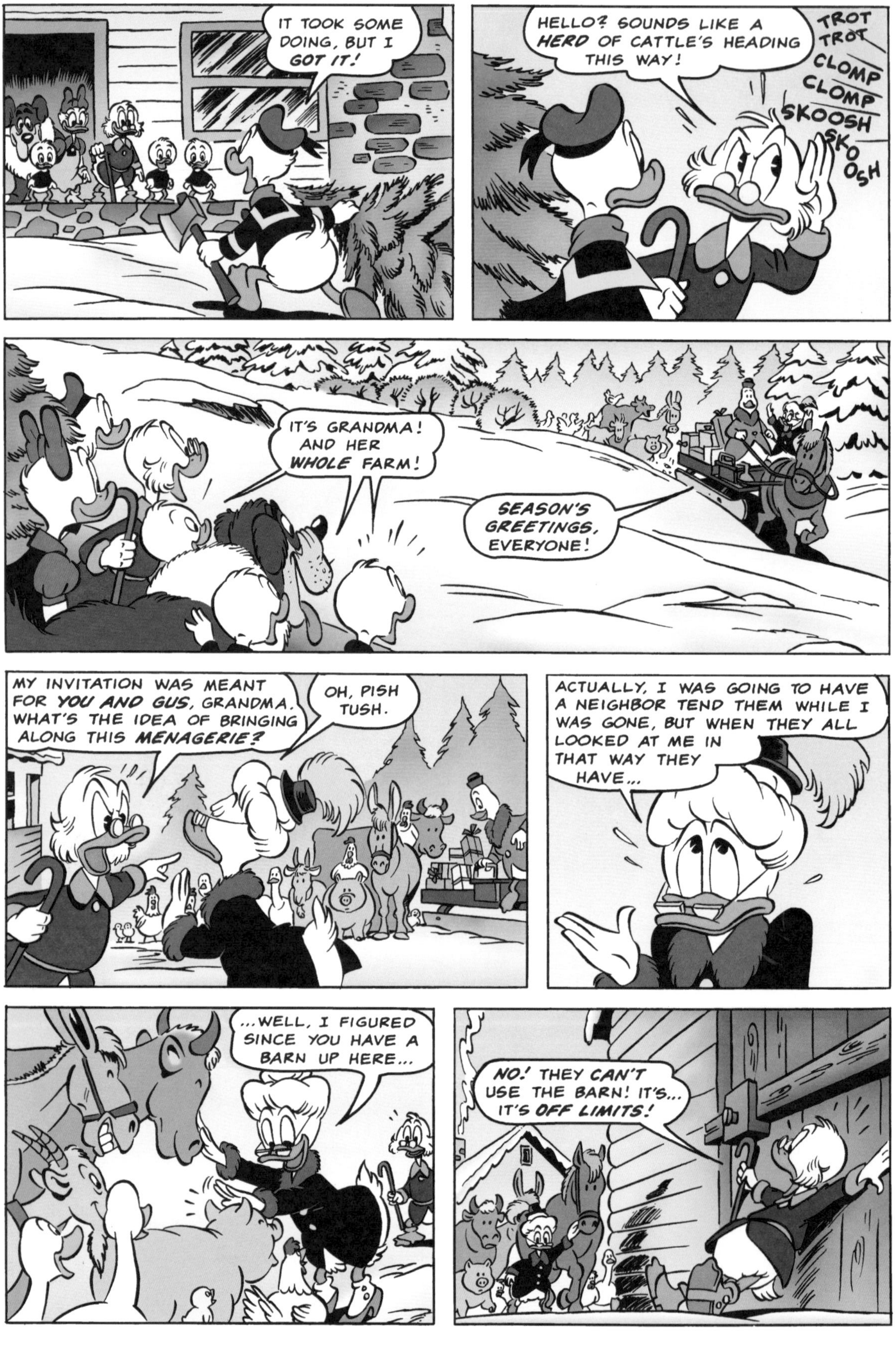

IT TOOK SOME DOING, BUT I GOT IT!
HELLO? SOUNDS LIKE A HERD OF CATTLE'S HEADING THIS WAY!
TROT TROT
CLOMP CLOMP
SKOOSH SKOOSH
IT'S GRANDMA! AND HER WHOLE FARM!
SEASON'S GREETINGS, EVERYONE!
MY INVITATION WAS MEANT FOR YOU AND GUS, GRANDMA. WHAT'S THE IDEA OF BRINGING ALONG THIS MENAGERIE?
OH, PISH TUSH.
ACTUALLY, I WAS GOING TO HAVE A NEIGHBOR TEND THEM WHILE I WAS GONE, BUT WHEN THEY ALL LOOKED AT ME IN THAT WAY THEY HAVE...
...WELL, I FIGURED SINCE YOU HAVE A BARN UP HERE...
NO! THEY CAN'T USE THE BARN! IT'S... IT'S OFF LIMITS!

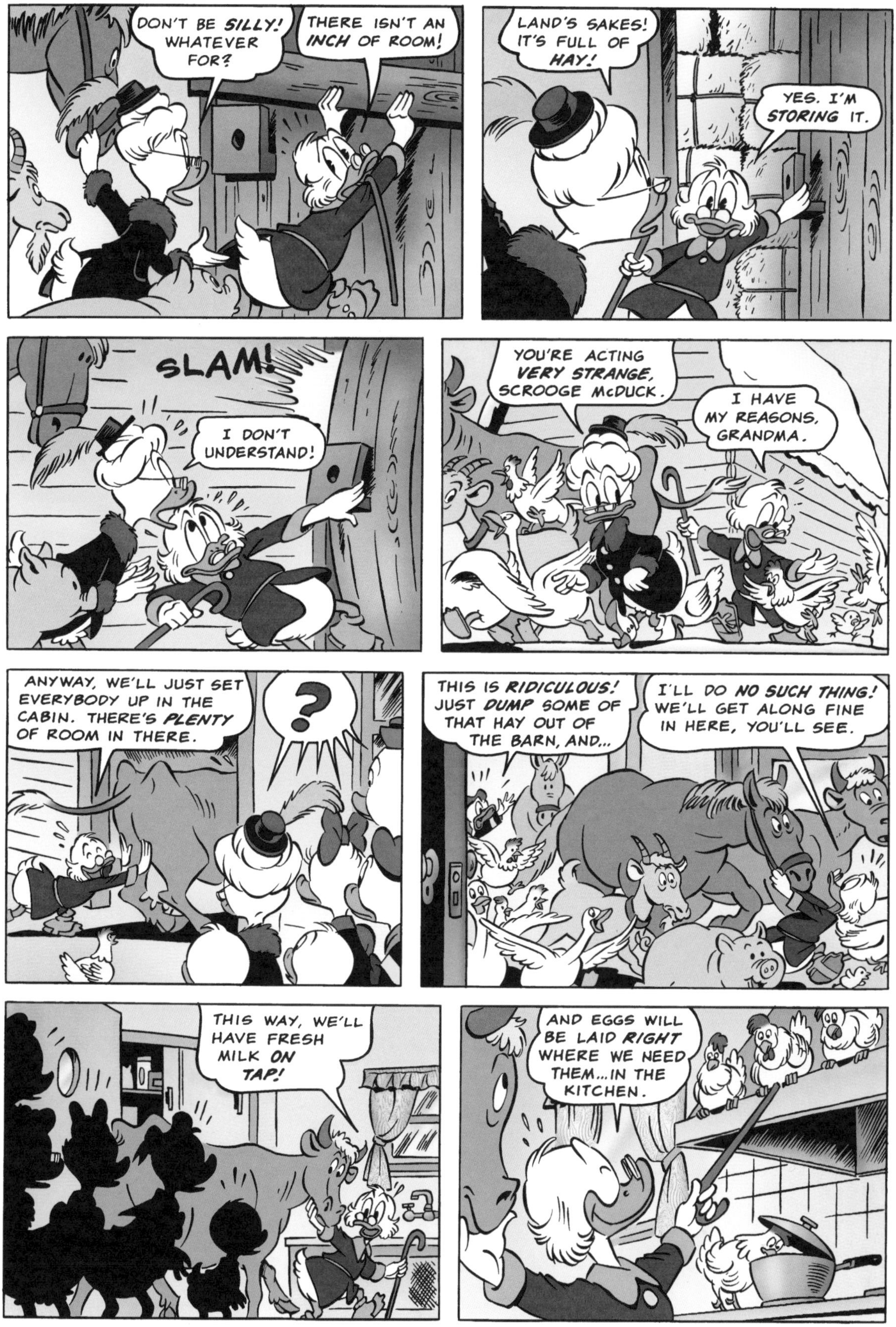
DON'T BE SILLY! WHATEVER FOR?
THERE ISN'T AN INCH OF ROOM!
LAND'S SAKES! IT'S FULL OF HAY!
YES. I'M STORING IT.
SLAM!
I DON'T UNDERSTAND!
YOU'RE ACTING VERY STRANGE, SCROOGE McDUCK.
I HAVE MY REASONS, GRANDMA.
ANYWAY, WE'LL JUST SET EVERYBODY UP IN THE CABIN. THERE'S PLENTY OF ROOM IN THERE.
?
THIS IS RIDICULOUS! JUST DUMP SOME OF THAT HAY OUT OF THE BARN, AND...
I'LL DO NO SUCH THING! WE'LL GET ALONG FINE IN HERE, YOU'LL SEE.
THIS WAY, WE'LL HAVE FRESH MILK ON TAP!
AND EGGS WILL BE LAID RIGHT WHERE WE NEED THEM...IN THE KITCHEN.

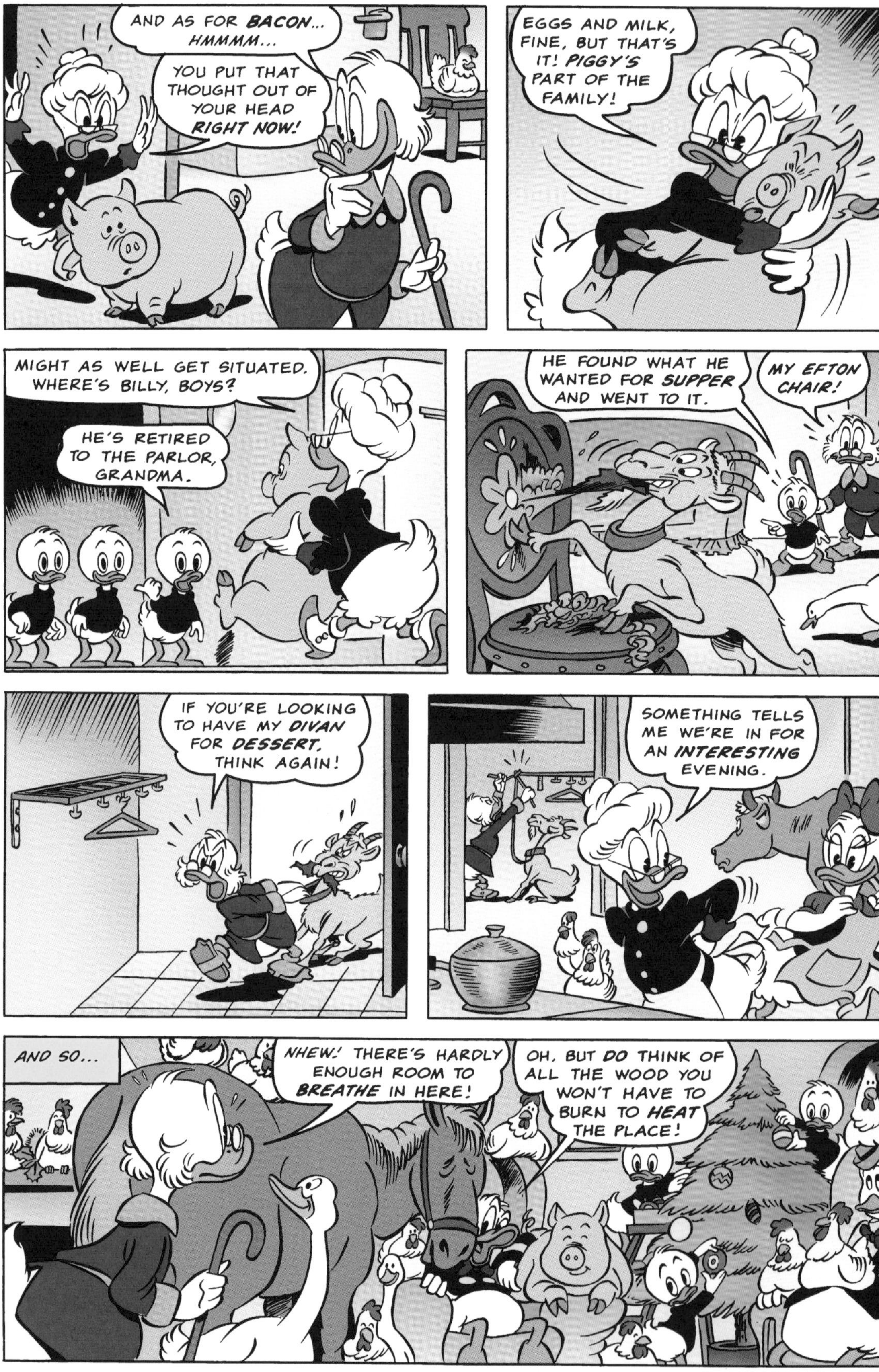
AND AS FOR BACON... HMMMM...
YOU PUT THAT THOUGHT OUT OF YOUR HEAD RIGHT NOW!
EGGS AND MILK, FINE, BUT THAT'S IT! PIGGY'S PART OF THE FAMILY!
MIGHT AS WELL GET SITUATED. WHERE'S BILLY, BOYS?
HE'S RETIRED TO THE PARLOR, GRANDMA.
HE FOUND WHAT HE WANTED FOR SUPPER AND WENT TO IT.
MY EFTON CHAIR!
IF YOU'RE LOOKING TO HAVE MY DIVAN FOR DESSERT, THINK AGAIN!
SOMETHING TELLS ME WE'RE IN FOR AN INTERESTING EVENING.
AND SO...
NHEW! THERE'S HARDLY ENOUGH ROOM TO BREATHE IN HERE!
OH, BUT DO THINK OF ALL THE WOOD YOU WON'T HAVE TO BURN TO HEAT THE PLACE!

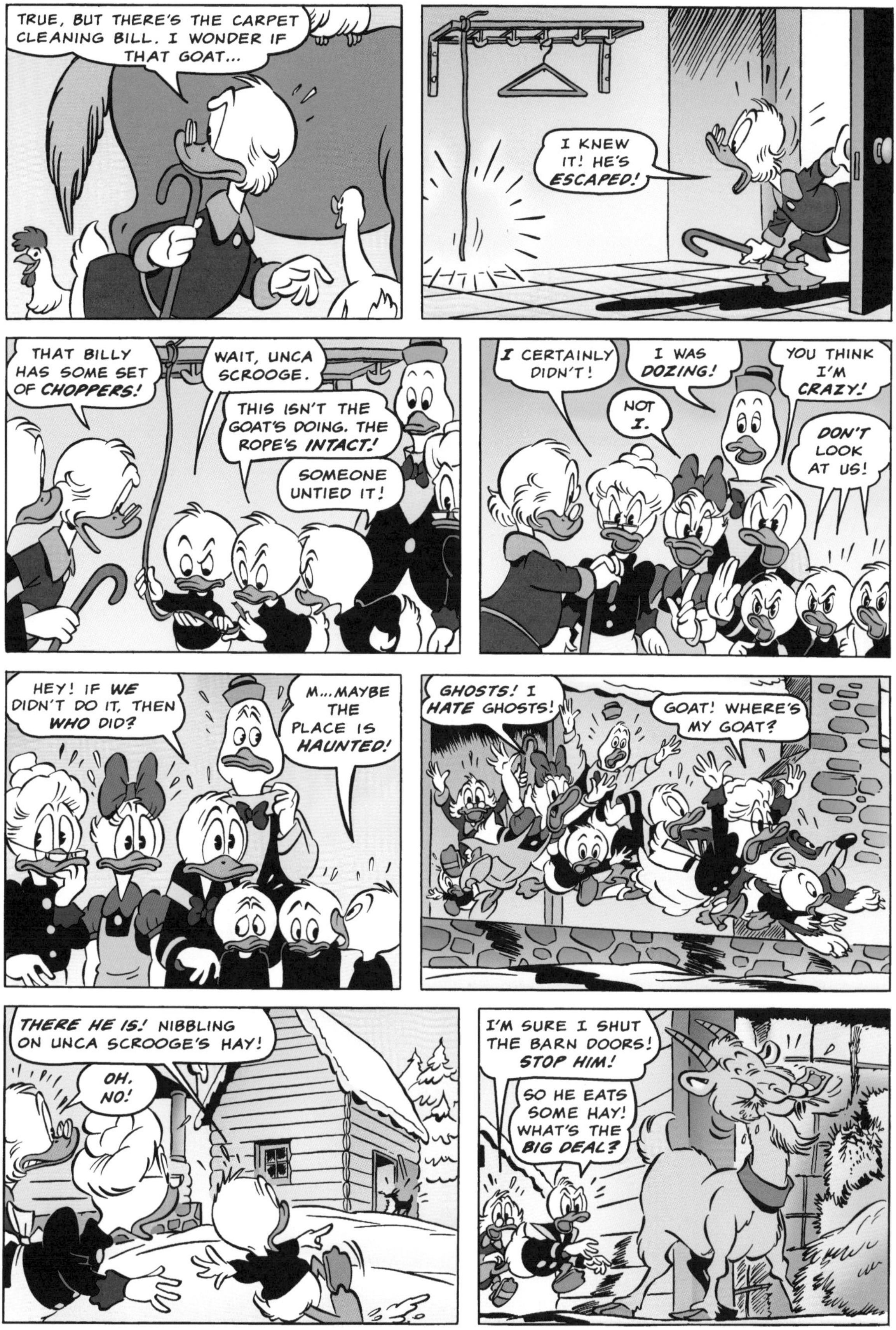
TRUE, BUT THERE'S THE CARPET CLEANING BILL. I WONDER IF THAT GOAT...
I KNEW IT! HE'S ESCAPED!
THAT BILLY HAS SOME SET OF CHOPPERS!
WAIT, UNCA SCROOGE.
THIS ISN'T THE GOAT'S DOING. THE ROPE'S INTACT!
SOMEONE UNTIED IT!
I CERTAINLY DIDN'T!
I WAS DOZING!
NOT I.
YOU THINK I'M CRAZY!
DON'T LOOK AT US!
HEY! IF WE DIDN'T DO IT, THEN WHO DID?
M...MAYBE THE PLACE IS HAUNTED!
GHOSTS! I HATE GHOSTS!
GOAT! WHERE'S MY GOAT?
THERE HE IS! NIBBLING ON UNCA SCROOGE'S HAY!
OH. NO!
I'M SURE I SHUT THE BARN DOORS! STOP HIM!
SO HE EATS SOME HAY! WHAT'S THE BIG DEAL?

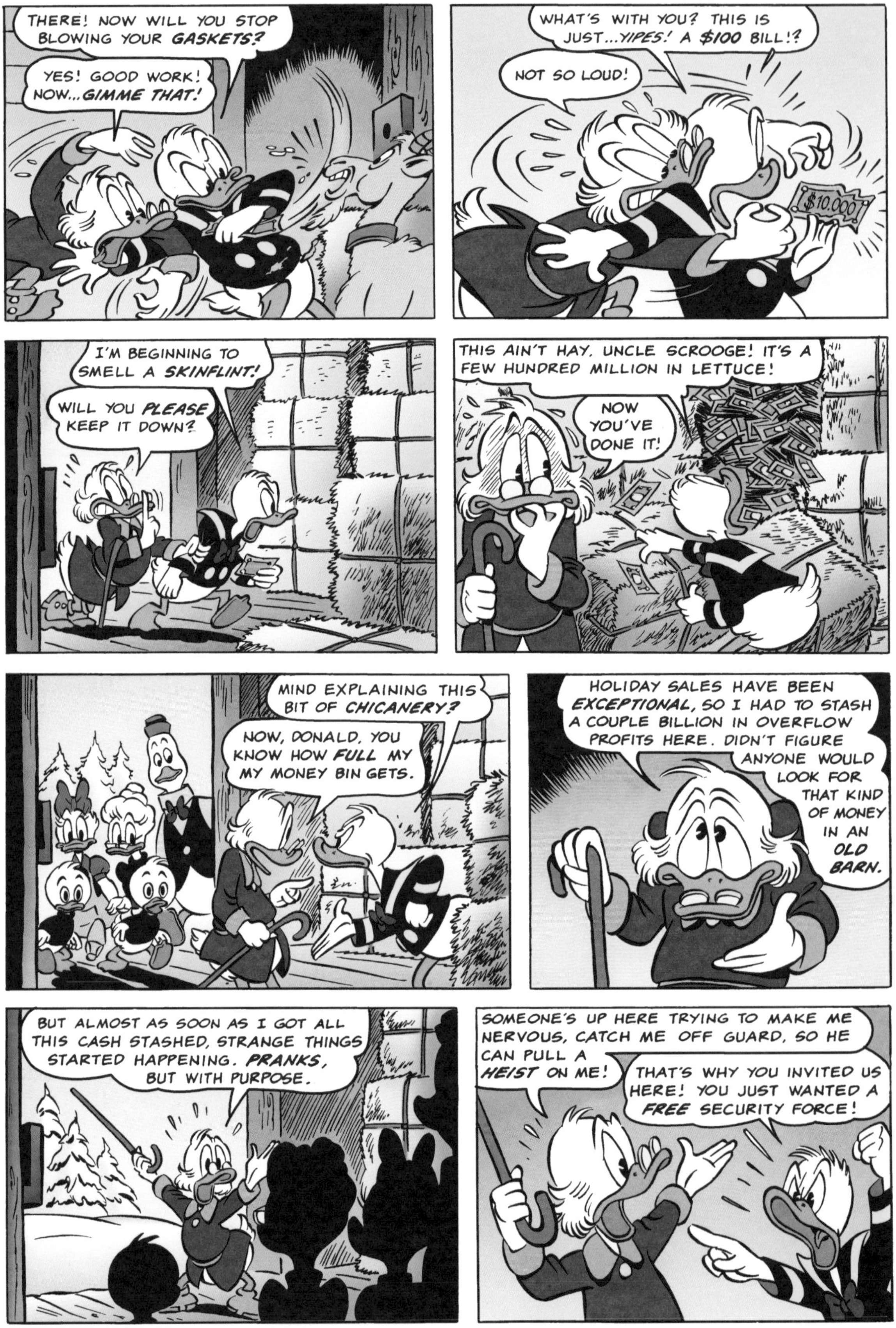
THERE! NOW WILL YOU STOP BLOWING YOUR GASKETS?
YES! GOOD WORK! NOW... GIMME THAT!
WHAT'S WITH YOU? THIS IS JUST... YIPES! A $100 BILL!?
NOT SO LOUD!
$10,000
I'M BEGINNING TO SMELL A SKINFLINT!
WILL YOU PLEASE KEEP IT DOWN?
THIS AIN'T HAY, UNCLE SCROOGE! IT'S A FEW HUNDRED MILLION IN LETTUCE!
NOW YOU'VE DONE IT!
MIND EXPLAINING THIS BIT OF CHICANERY?
NOW, DONALD, YOU KNOW HOW FULL MY MY MONEY BIN GETS.
HOLIDAY SALES HAVE BEEN EXCEPTIONAL, SO I HAD TO STASH A COUPLE BILLION IN OVERFLOW PROFITS HERE. DIDN'T FIGURE ANYONE WOULD LOOK FOR THAT KIND OF MONEY IN AN OLD BARN.
BUT ALMOST AS SOON AS I GOT ALL THIS CASH STASHED, STRANGE THINGS STARTED HAPPENING. PRANKS, BUT WITH PURPOSE.
SOMEONE'S UP HERE TRYING TO MAKE ME NERVOUS, CATCH ME OFF GUARD, SO HE CAN PULL A HEIST ON ME!
THAT'S WHY YOU INVITED US HERE! YOU JUST WANTED A FREE SECURITY FORCE!

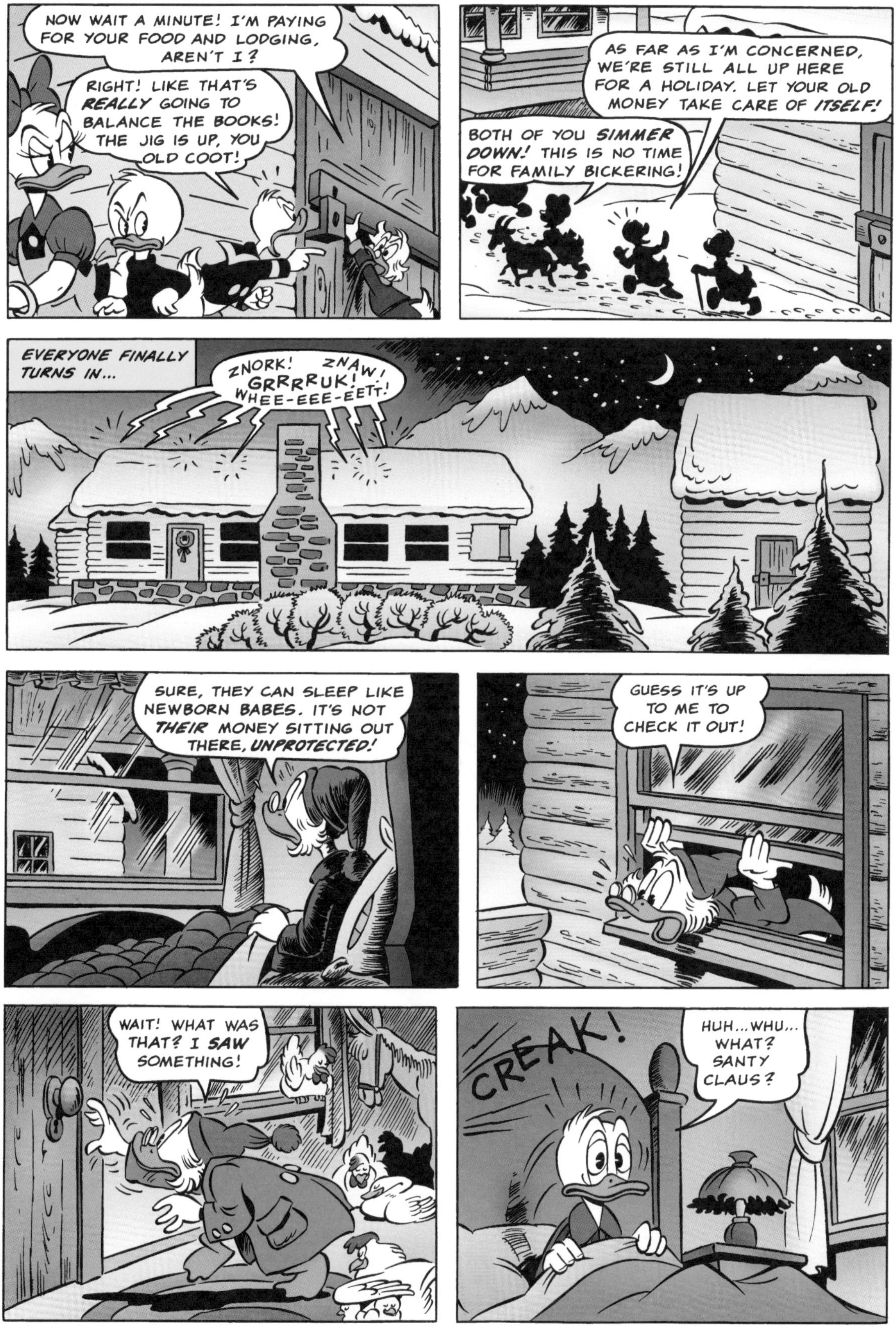
NOW WAIT A MINUTE! I'M PAYING FOR YOUR FOOD AND LODGING, AREN'T I?
RIGHT! LIKE THAT'S REALLY GOING TO BALANCE THE BOOKS! THE JIG IS UP, YOU OLD COOT!
AS FAR AS I'M CONCERNED, WE'RE STILL ALL UP HERE FOR A HOLIDAY. LET YOUR OLD MONEY TAKE CARE OF ITSELF!
BOTH OF YOU SIMMER DOWN! THIS IS NO TIME FOR FAMILY BICKERING!
EVERYONE FINALLY TURNS IN...
ZNORK! ZNAW! GRRRRUK! WHEE-EEE-EETT!
SURE, THEY CAN SLEEP LIKE NEWBORN BABES. IT'S NOT THEIR MONEY SITTING OUT THERE, UNPROTECTED!
GUESS IT'S UP TO ME TO CHECK IT OUT!
WAIT! WHAT WAS THAT? I SAW SOMETHING!
CREAK!
HUH...WHU... WHAT? SANTY CLAUS?

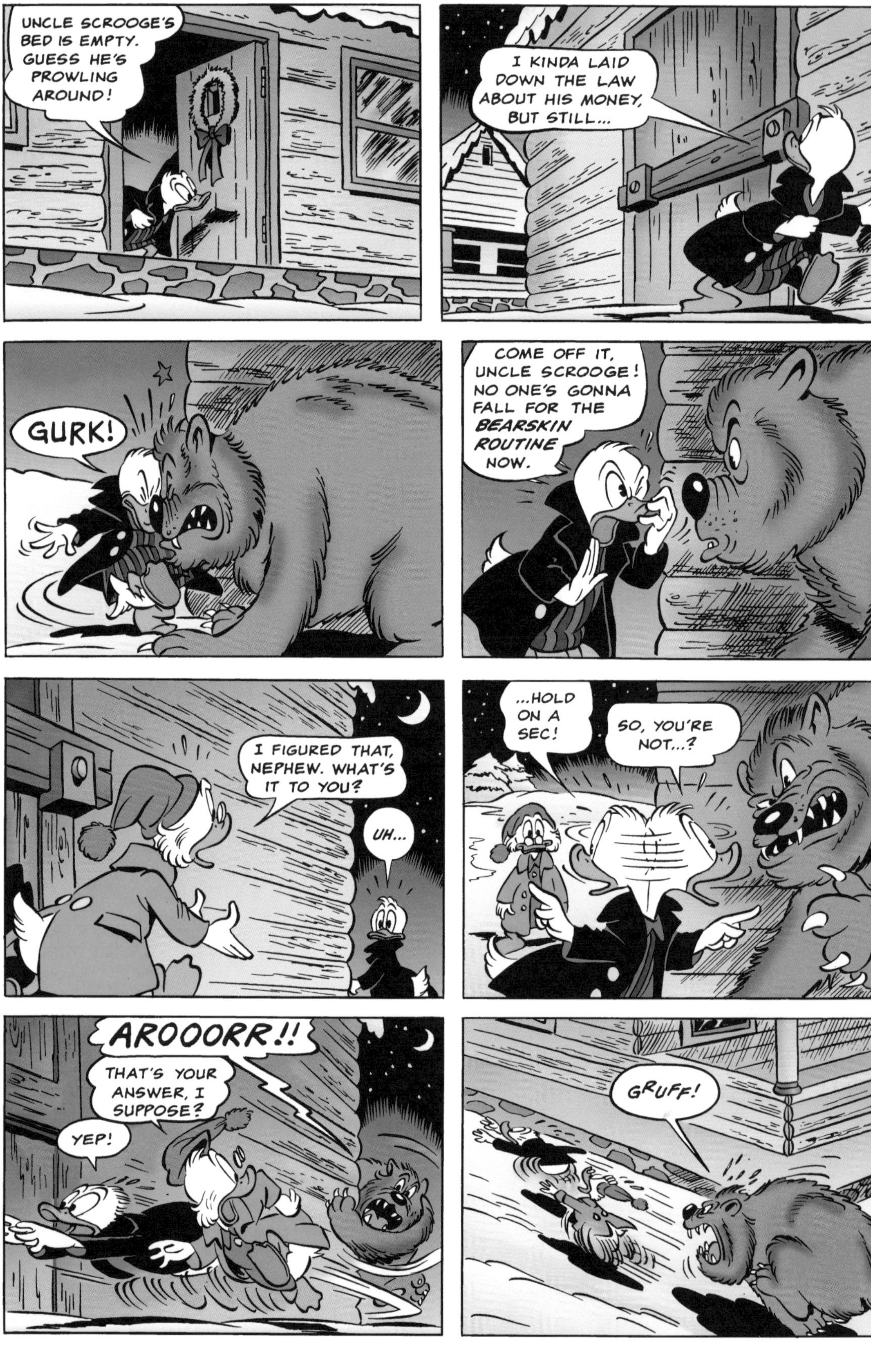
UNCLE SCROOGE'S BED IS EMPTY. GUESS HE'S PROWLING AROUND!
I KINDA LAID DOWN THE LAW ABOUT HIS MONEY, BUT STILL...
GURK!
COME OFF IT, UNCLE SCROOGE! NO ONE'S GONNA FALL FOR THE *BEARSKIN ROUTINE* NOW.
I FIGURED THAT, NEPHEW. WHAT'S IT TO YOU?
UH...
...HOLD ON A SEC!
SO, YOU'RE NOT...?
AROOORR!!
THAT'S YOUR ANSWER, I SUPPOSE?
YEP!
GRUFF!

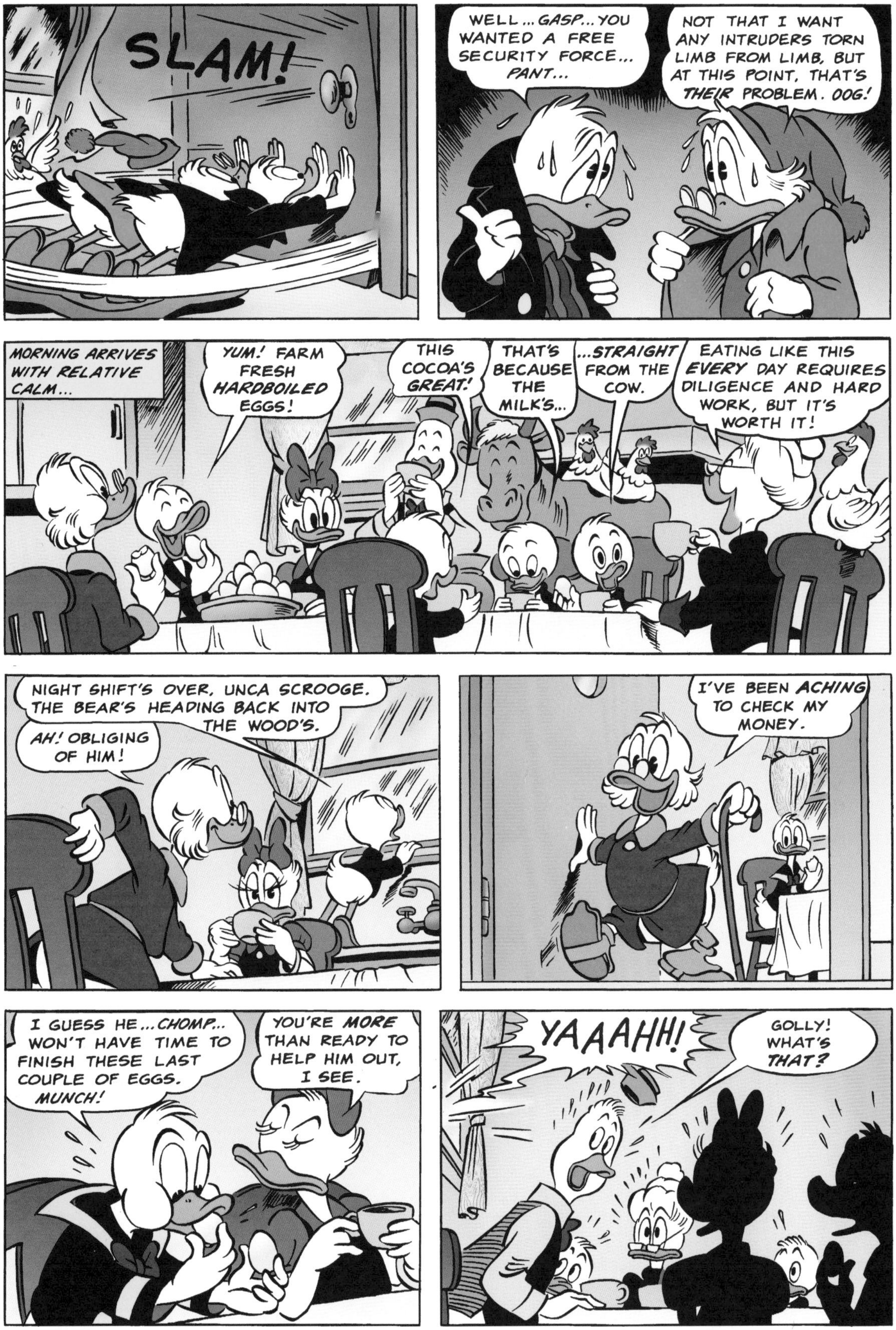
SLAM!
WELL ...GASP... YOU WANTED A FREE SECURITY FORCE... PANT...
NOT THAT I WANT ANY INTRUDERS TORN LIMB FROM LIMB, BUT AT THIS POINT, THAT'S THEIR PROBLEM. OOG!
MORNING ARRIVES WITH RELATIVE CALM...
YUM! FARM FRESH HARDBOILED EGGS!
THIS COCOA'S GREAT!
THAT'S BECAUSE THE MILK'S...
...STRAIGHT FROM THE COW.
EATING LIKE THIS EVERY DAY REQUIRES DILIGENCE AND HARD WORK, BUT IT'S WORTH IT!
NIGHT SHIFT'S OVER, UNCA SCROOGE. THE BEAR'S HEADING BACK INTO THE WOOD'S.
AH! OBLIGING OF HIM!
I'VE BEEN ACHING TO CHECK MY MONEY.
I GUESS HE ...CHOMP... WON'T HAVE TIME TO FINISH THESE LAST COUPLE OF EGGS. MUNCH!
YOU'RE MORE THAN READY TO HELP HIM OUT, I SEE.
YAAAHH!
GOLLY! WHAT'S THAT?

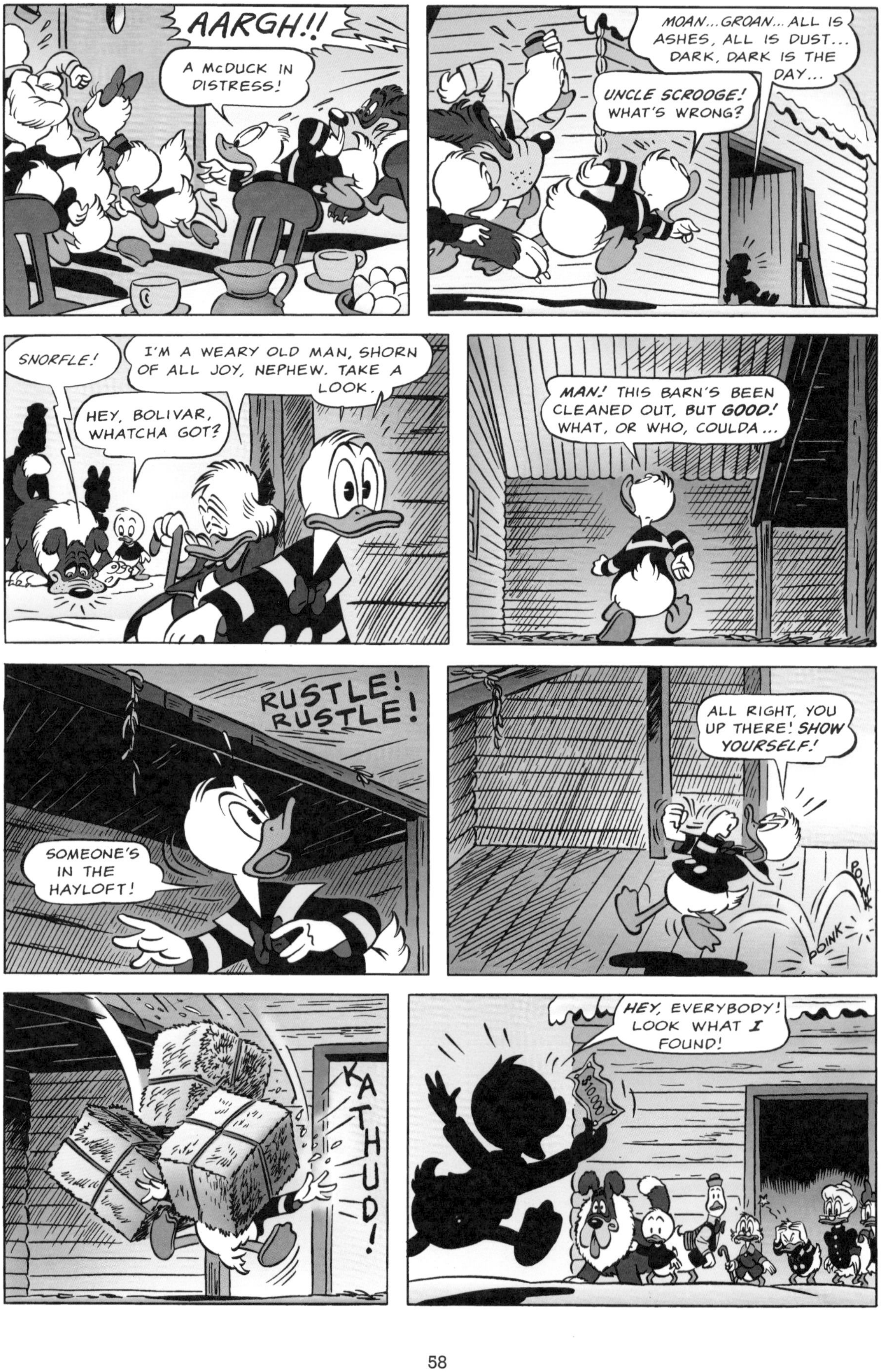
AARGH!!
A McDUCK IN DISTRESS!
MOAN...GROAN...ALL IS ASHES, ALL IS DUST... DARK, DARK IS THE DAY...
UNCLE SCROOGE! WHAT'S WRONG?
SNORFLE!
I'M A WEARY OLD MAN, SHORN OF ALL JOY, NEPHEW. TAKE A LOOK.
HEY, BOLIVAR, WHATCHA GOT?
MAN! THIS BARN'S BEEN CLEANED OUT, BUT GOOD! WHAT, OR WHO, COULDA...
RUSTLE! RUSTLE!
SOMEONE'S IN THE HAYLOFT!
ALL RIGHT, YOU UP THERE! SHOW YOURSELF!
POINK
POINK
KATHUD!
HEY, EVERYBODY! LOOK WHAT I FOUND!
$10,000

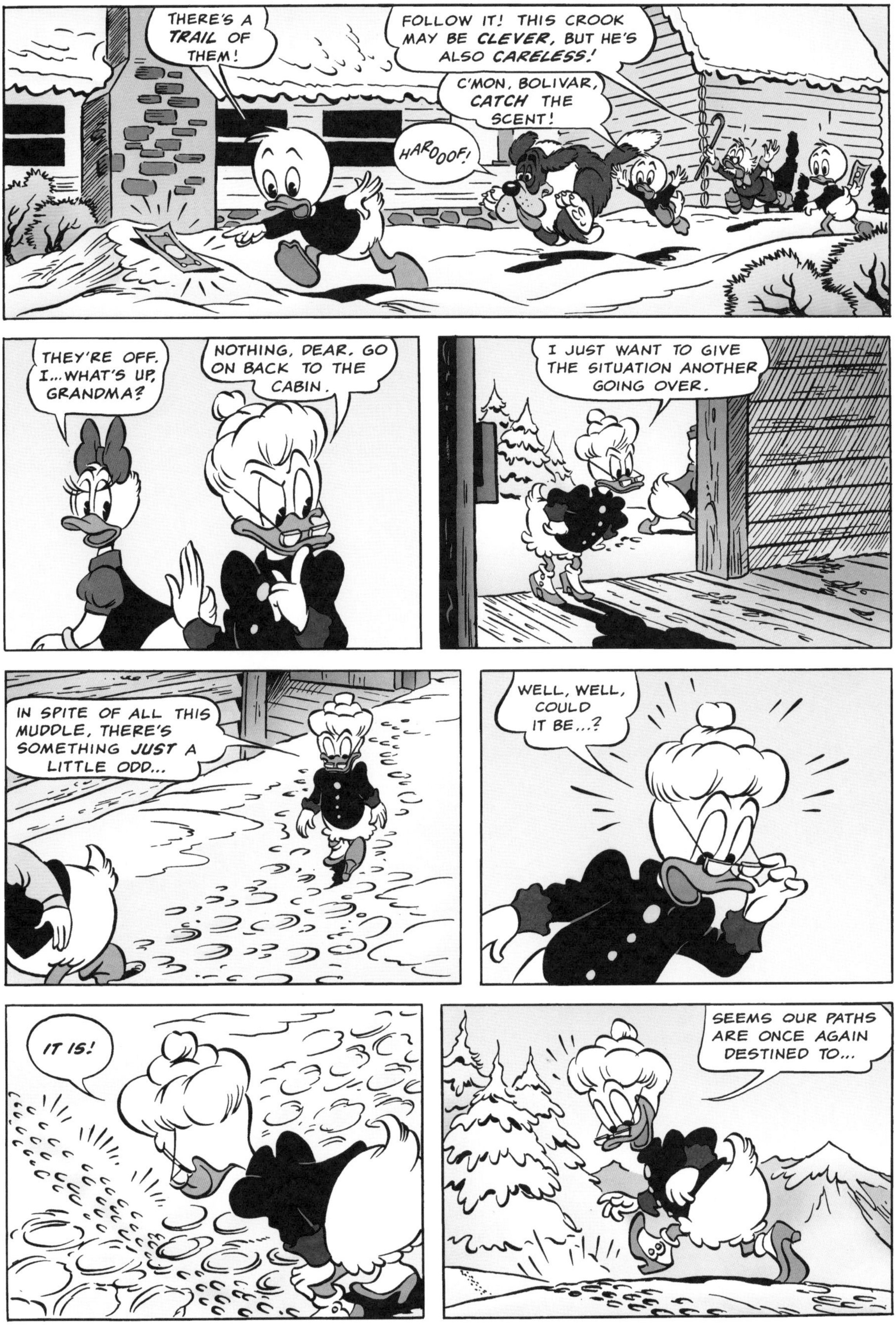
THERE'S A TRAIL OF THEM!
FOLLOW IT! THIS CROOK MAY BE CLEVER, BUT HE'S ALSO CARELESS!
C'MON, BOLIVAR, CATCH THE SCENT!
HAROOOF!
THEY'RE OFF. I...WHAT'S UP, GRANDMA?
NOTHING, DEAR. GO ON BACK TO THE CABIN.
I JUST WANT TO GIVE THE SITUATION ANOTHER GOING OVER.
IN SPITE OF ALL THIS MUDDLE, THERE'S SOMETHING JUST A LITTLE ODD...
WELL, WELL, COULD IT BE...?
IT IS!
SEEMS OUR PATHS ARE ONCE AGAIN DESTINED TO...

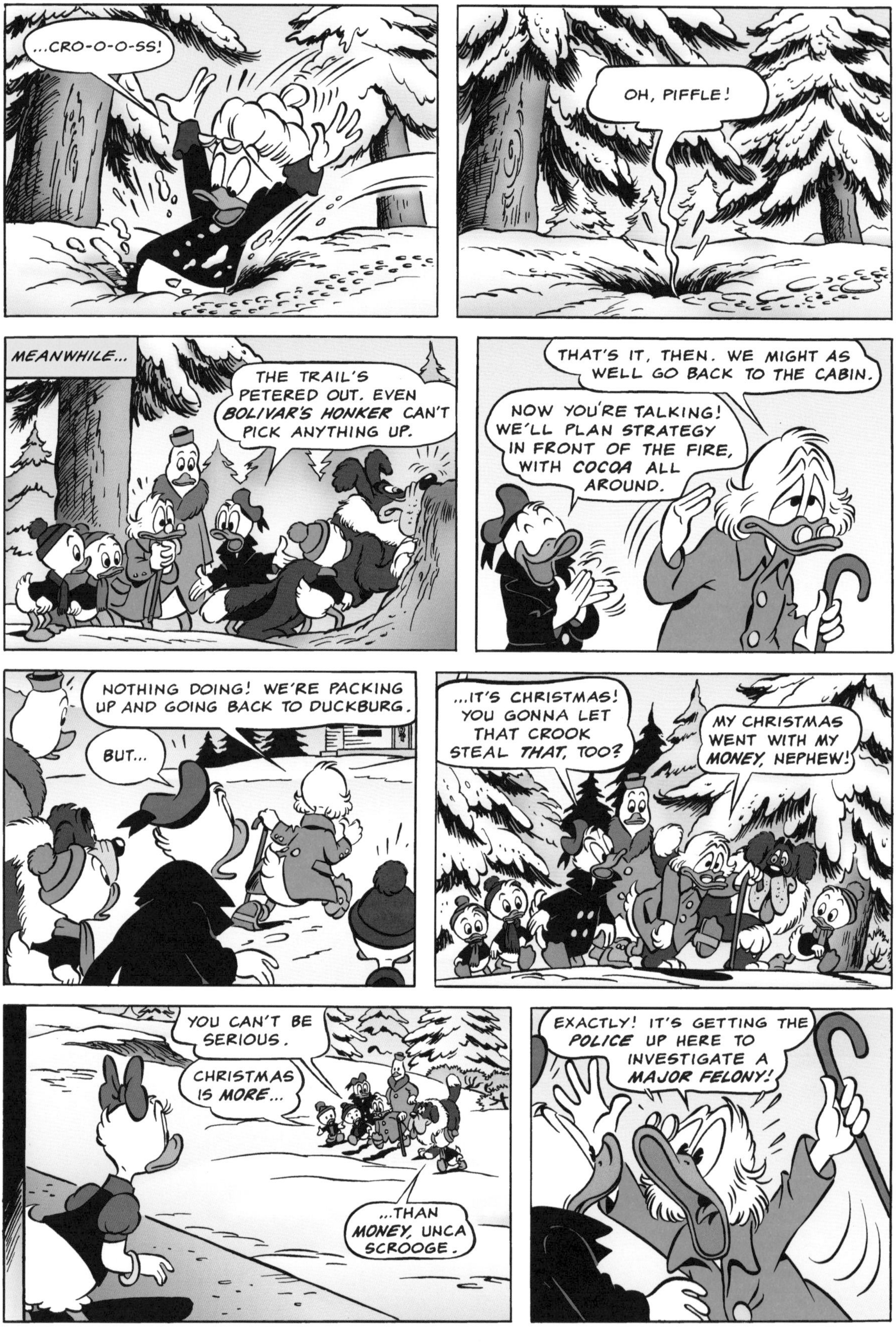
...CRO-O-O-SS!
OH, PIFFLE!
MEANWHILE...
THE TRAIL'S PETERED OUT. EVEN BOLIVAR'S HONKER CAN'T PICK ANYTHING UP.
THAT'S IT, THEN. WE MIGHT AS WELL GO BACK TO THE CABIN.
NOW YOU'RE TALKING! WE'LL PLAN STRATEGY IN FRONT OF THE FIRE, WITH COCOA ALL AROUND.
NOTHING DOING! WE'RE PACKING UP AND GOING BACK TO DUCKBURG.
BUT...
...IT'S CHRISTMAS! YOU GONNA LET THAT CROOK STEAL THAT, TOO?
MY CHRISTMAS WENT WITH MY MONEY, NEPHEW!
YOU CAN'T BE SERIOUS.
CHRISTMAS IS MORE...
...THAN MONEY, UNCA SCROOGE.
EXACTLY! IT'S GETTING THE POLICE UP HERE TO INVESTIGATE A MAJOR FELONY!

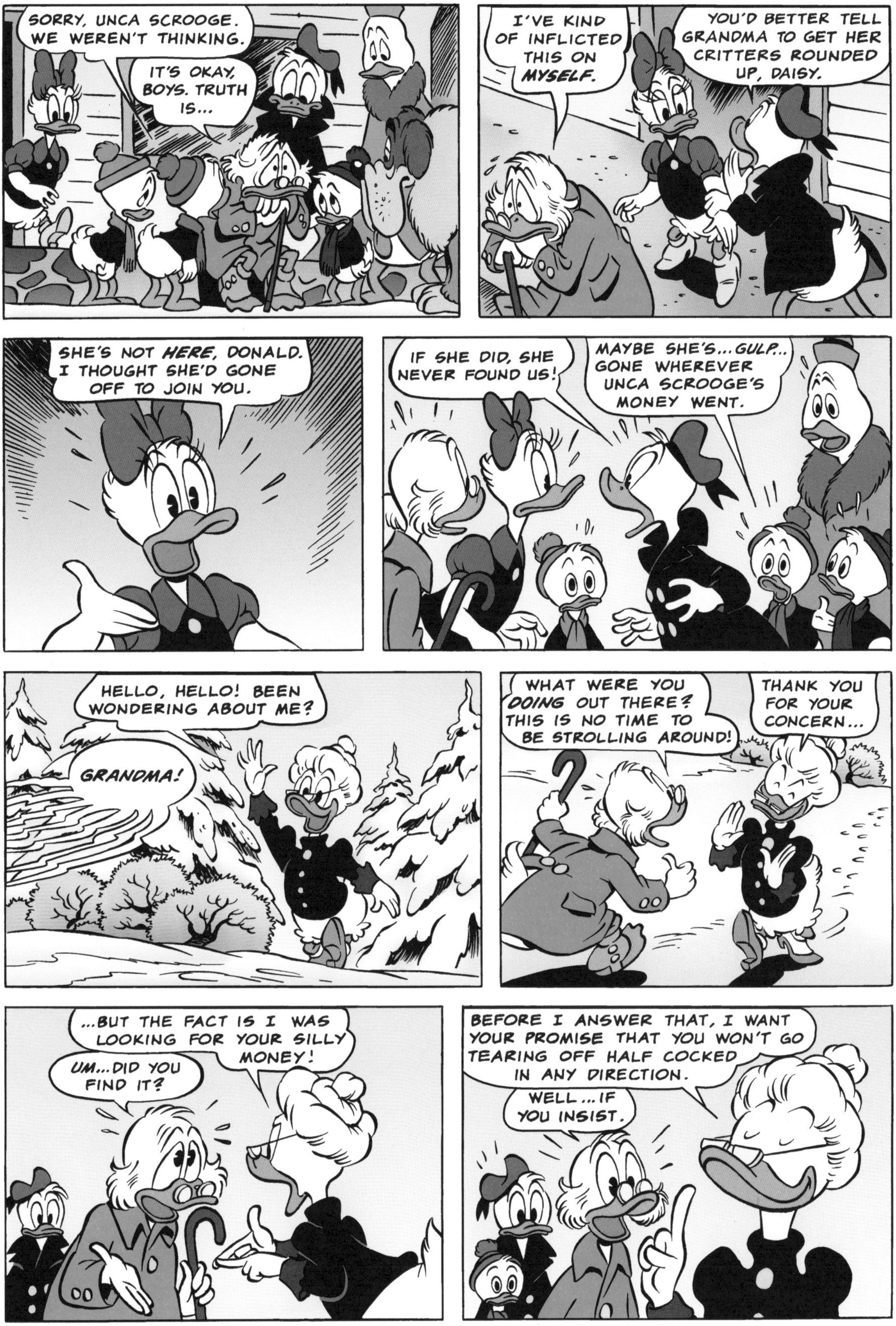
SORRY, UNCA SCROOGE. WE WEREN'T THINKING.
IT'S OKAY, BOYS. TRUTH IS...
I'VE KIND OF INFLICTED THIS ON MYSELF.
YOU'D BETTER TELL GRANDMA TO GET HER CRITTERS ROUNDED UP, DAISY.
SHE'S NOT HERE, DONALD. I THOUGHT SHE'D GONE OFF TO JOIN YOU.
IF SHE DID, SHE NEVER FOUND US!
MAYBE SHE'S...GULP... GONE WHEREVER UNCA SCROOGE'S MONEY WENT.
HELLO, HELLO! BEEN WONDERING ABOUT ME?
GRANDMA!
WHAT WERE YOU DOING OUT THERE? THIS IS NO TIME TO BE STROLLING AROUND!
THANK YOU FOR YOUR CONCERN...
...BUT THE FACT IS I WAS LOOKING FOR YOUR SILLY MONEY!
UM...DID YOU FIND IT?
BEFORE I ANSWER THAT, I WANT YOUR PROMISE THAT YOU WON'T GO TEARING OFF HALF COCKED IN ANY DIRECTION.
WELL...IF YOU INSIST.

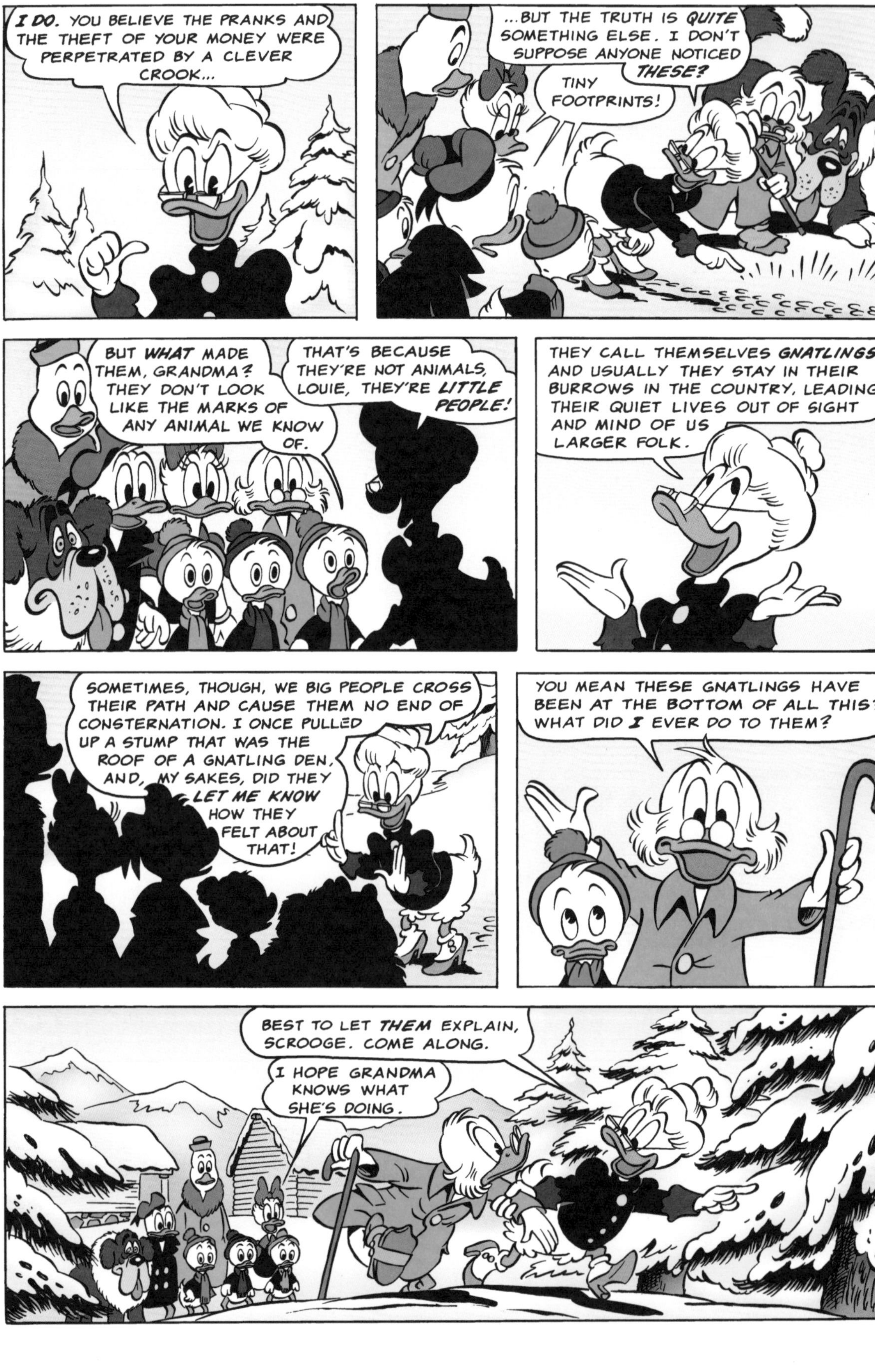
I DO. YOU BELIEVE THE PRANKS AND THE THEFT OF YOUR MONEY WERE PERPETRATED BY A CLEVER CROOK...
...BUT THE TRUTH IS QUITE SOMETHING ELSE. I DON'T SUPPOSE ANYONE NOTICED THESE?
TINY FOOTPRINTS!
BUT WHAT MADE THEM, GRANDMA? THEY DON'T LOOK LIKE THE MARKS OF ANY ANIMAL WE KNOW OF.
THAT'S BECAUSE THEY'RE NOT ANIMALS, LOUIE, THEY'RE LITTLE PEOPLE!
THEY CALL THEMSELVES GNATLINGS, AND USUALLY THEY STAY IN THEIR BURROWS IN THE COUNTRY, LEADING THEIR QUIET LIVES OUT OF SIGHT AND MIND OF US LARGER FOLK.
SOMETIMES, THOUGH, WE BIG PEOPLE CROSS THEIR PATH AND CAUSE THEM NO END OF CONSTERNATION. I ONCE PULLED UP A STUMP THAT WAS THE ROOF OF A GNATLING DEN, AND, MY SAKES, DID THEY LET ME KNOW HOW THEY FELT ABOUT THAT!
YOU MEAN THESE GNATLINGS HAVE BEEN AT THE BOTTOM OF ALL THIS? WHAT DID I EVER DO TO THEM?
BEST TO LET THEM EXPLAIN, SCROOGE. COME ALONG.
I HOPE GRANDMA KNOWS WHAT SHE'S DOING.

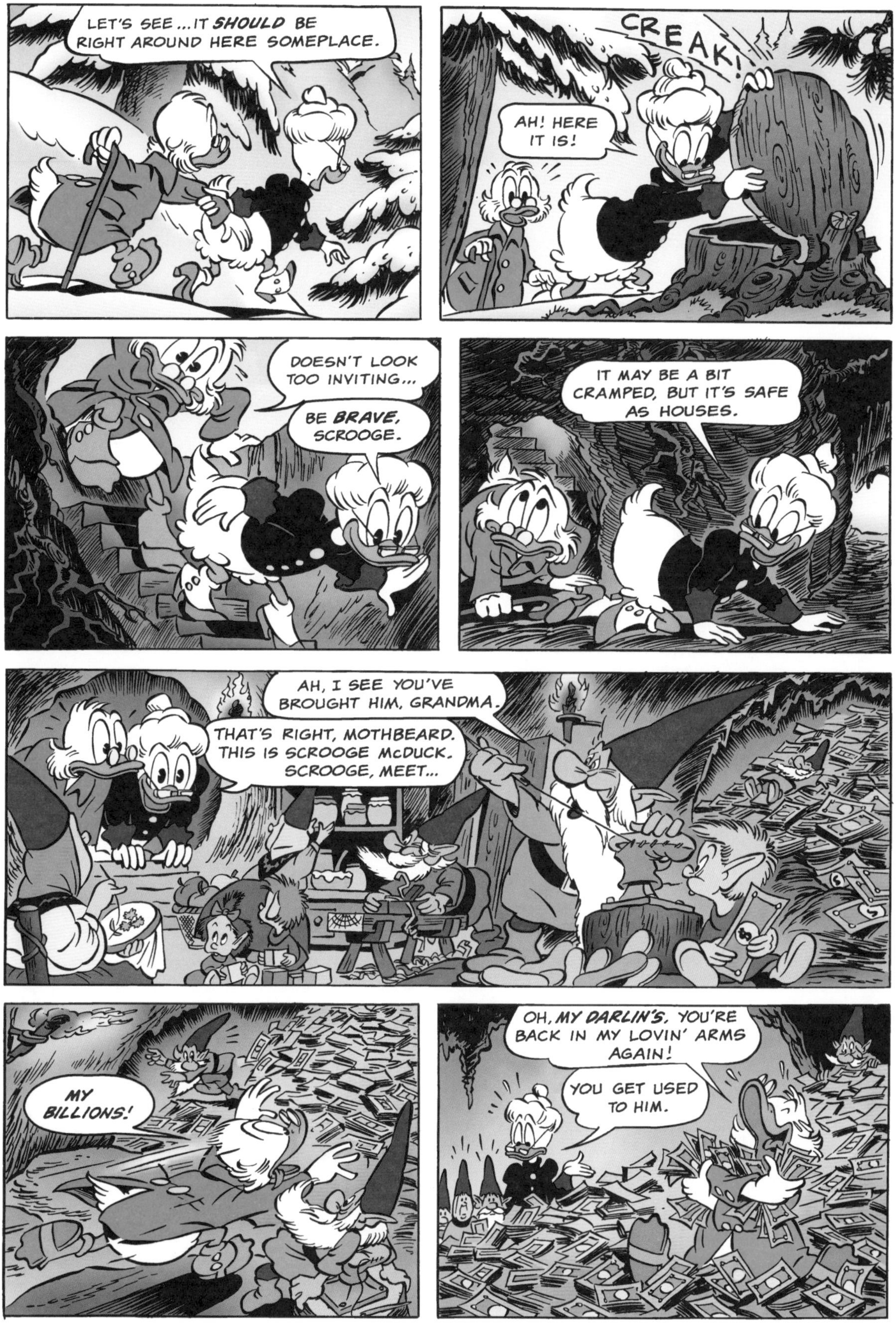
LET'S SEE ...IT SHOULD BE RIGHT AROUND HERE SOMEPLACE.
CREAK!
AH! HERE IT IS!
DOESN'T LOOK TOO INVITING...
BE BRAVE, SCROOGE.
IT MAY BE A BIT CRAMPED, BUT IT'S SAFE AS HOUSES.
AH, I SEE YOU'VE BROUGHT HIM, GRANDMA.
THAT'S RIGHT, MOTHBEARD. THIS IS SCROOGE McDUCK. SCROOGE, MEET...
MY BILLIONS!
OH, MY DARLIN'S, YOU'RE BACK IN MY LOVIN' ARMS AGAIN!
YOU GET USED TO HIM.

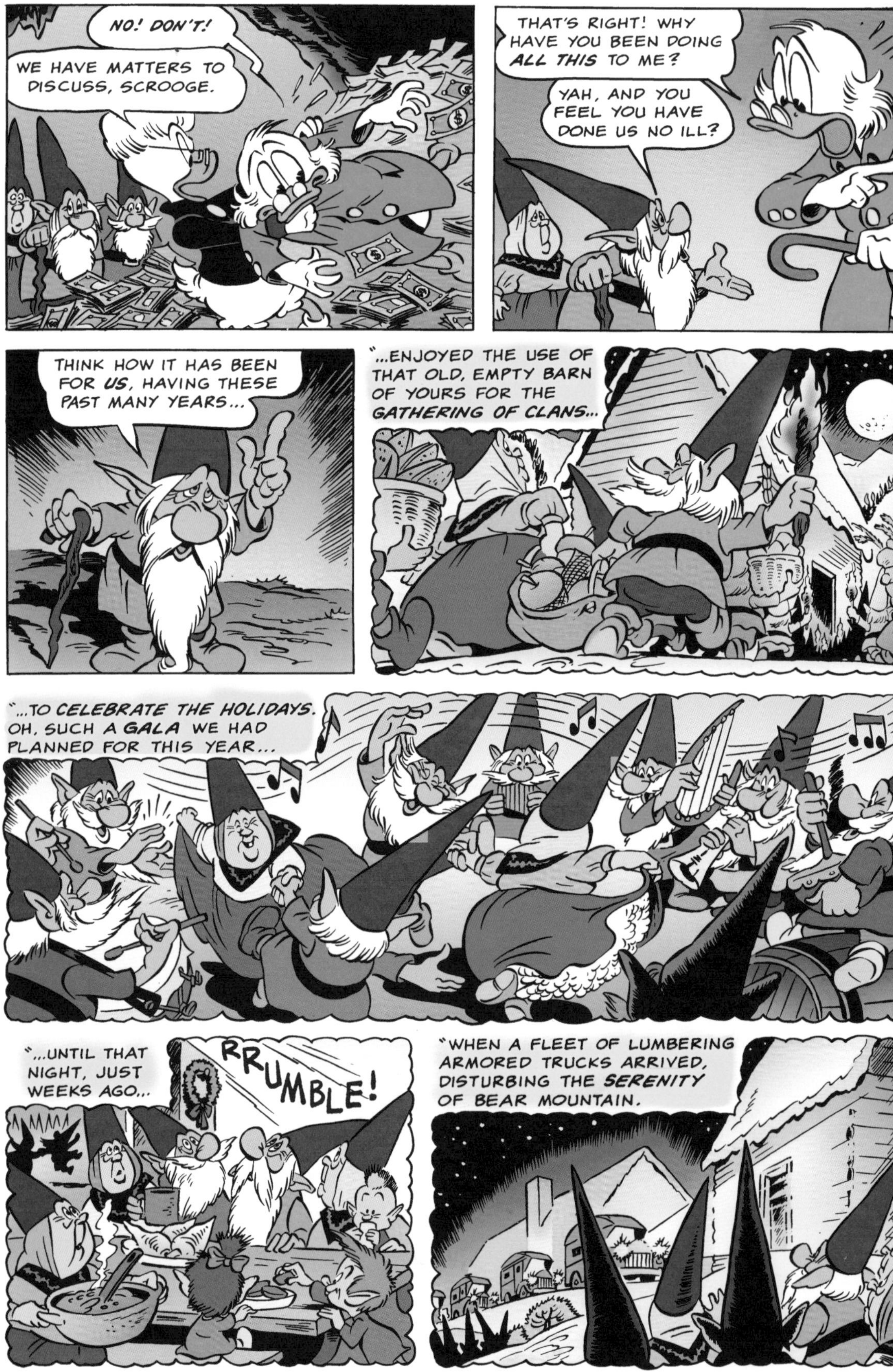
NO! DON'T!
WE HAVE MATTERS TO DISCUSS, SCROOGE.
THAT'S RIGHT! WHY HAVE YOU BEEN DOING ALL THIS TO ME?
YAH, AND YOU FEEL YOU HAVE DONE US NO ILL?
THINK HOW IT HAS BEEN FOR US, HAVING THESE PAST MANY YEARS...
"...ENJOYED THE USE OF THAT OLD, EMPTY BARN OF YOURS FOR THE GATHERING OF CLANS...
"...TO CELEBRATE THE HOLIDAYS. OH, SUCH A GALA WE HAD PLANNED FOR THIS YEAR...
"...UNTIL THAT NIGHT, JUST WEEKS AGO...
RRUMBLE!
"WHEN A FLEET OF LUMBERING ARMORED TRUCKS ARRIVED, DISTURBING THE SERENITY OF BEAR MOUNTAIN.

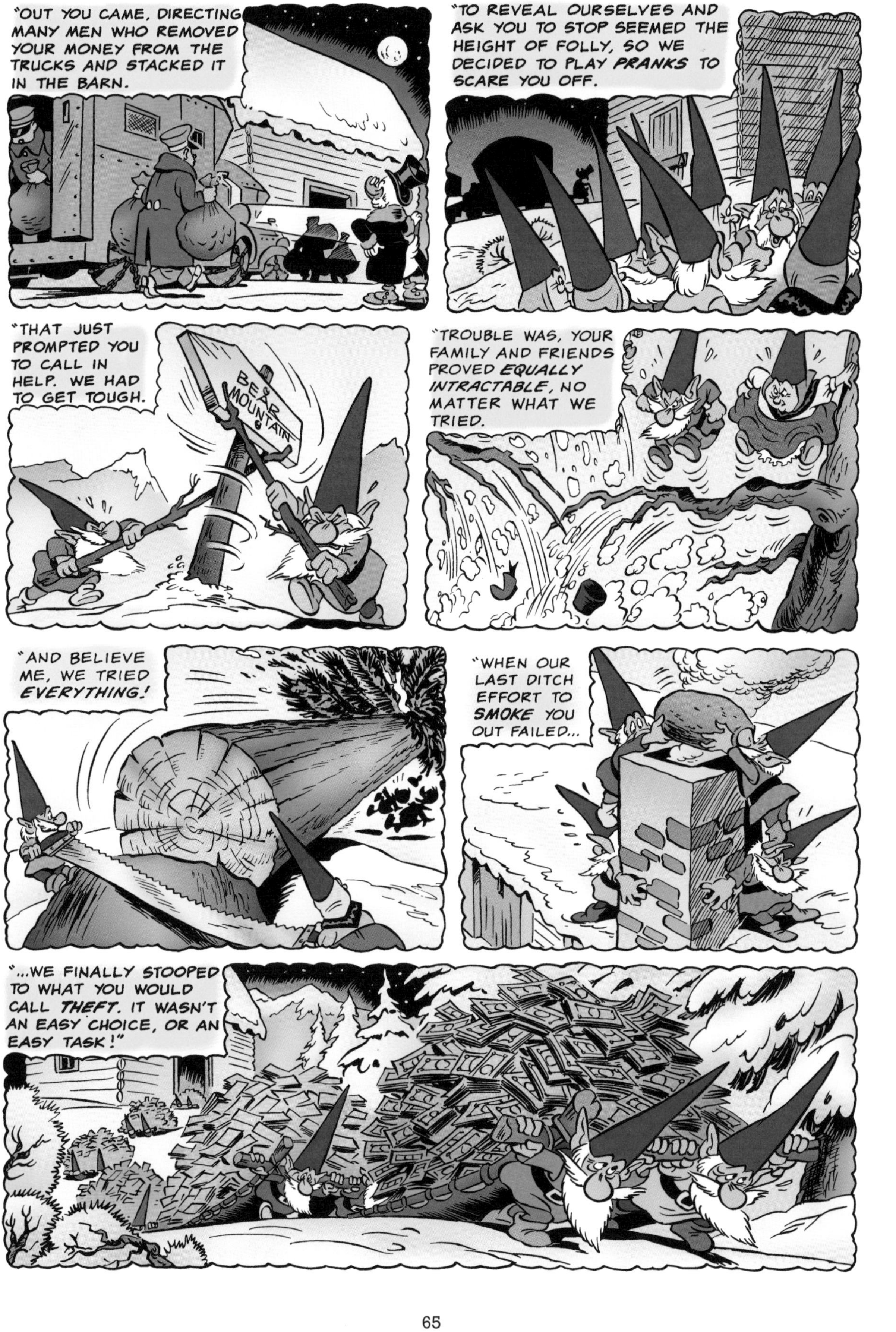
"OUT YOU CAME, DIRECTING MANY MEN WHO REMOVED YOUR MONEY FROM THE TRUCKS AND STACKED IT IN THE BARN.
"TO REVEAL OURSELVES AND ASK YOU TO STOP SEEMED THE HEIGHT OF FOLLY, SO WE DECIDED TO PLAY PRANKS TO SCARE YOU OFF.
"THAT JUST PROMPTED YOU TO CALL IN HELP. WE HAD TO GET TOUGH.
BEAR MOUNTAIN
"TROUBLE WAS, YOUR FAMILY AND FRIENDS PROVED EQUALLY INTRACTABLE, NO MATTER WHAT WE TRIED.
"AND BELIEVE ME, WE TRIED EVERYTHING!
"WHEN OUR LAST DITCH EFFORT TO SMOKE YOU OUT FAILED...
"...WE FINALLY STOOPED TO WHAT YOU WOULD CALL THEFT. IT WASN'T AN EASY CHOICE, OR AN EASY TASK!"

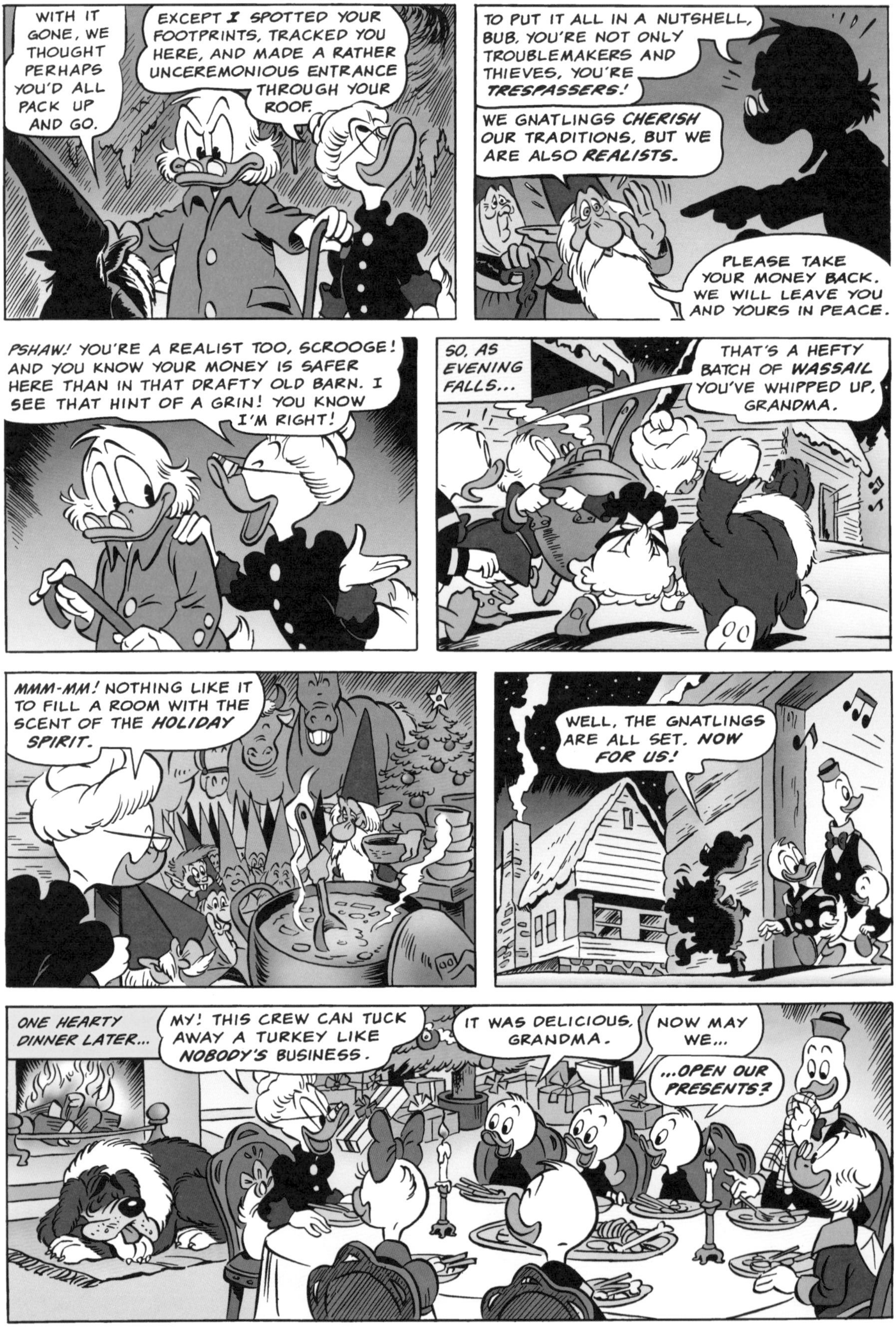
WITH IT GONE, WE THOUGHT PERHAPS YOU'D ALL PACK UP AND GO.
EXCEPT I SPOTTED YOUR FOOTPRINTS, TRACKED YOU HERE, AND MADE A RATHER UNCEREMONIOUS ENTRANCE THROUGH YOUR ROOF.
TO PUT IT ALL IN A NUTSHELL, BUB, YOU'RE NOT ONLY TROUBLEMAKERS AND THIEVES, YOU'RE TRESPASSERS!
WE GNATLINGS CHERISH OUR TRADITIONS, BUT WE ARE ALSO REALISTS.
PLEASE TAKE YOUR MONEY BACK. WE WILL LEAVE YOU AND YOURS IN PEACE.
PSHAW! YOU'RE A REALIST TOO, SCROOGE! AND YOU KNOW YOUR MONEY IS SAFER HERE THAN IN THAT DRAFTY OLD BARN. I SEE THAT HINT OF A GRIN! YOU KNOW I'M RIGHT!
SO, AS EVENING FALLS...
THAT'S A HEFTY BATCH OF WASSAIL YOU'VE WHIPPED UP, GRANDMA.
MMM-MM! NOTHING LIKE IT TO FILL A ROOM WITH THE SCENT OF THE HOLIDAY SPIRIT.
WELL, THE GNATLINGS ARE ALL SET. NOW FOR US!
ONE HEARTY DINNER LATER...
MY! THIS CREW CAN TUCK AWAY A TURKEY LIKE NOBODY'S BUSINESS.
IT WAS DELICIOUS, GRANDMA.
NOW MAY WE...
...OPEN OUR PRESENTS?

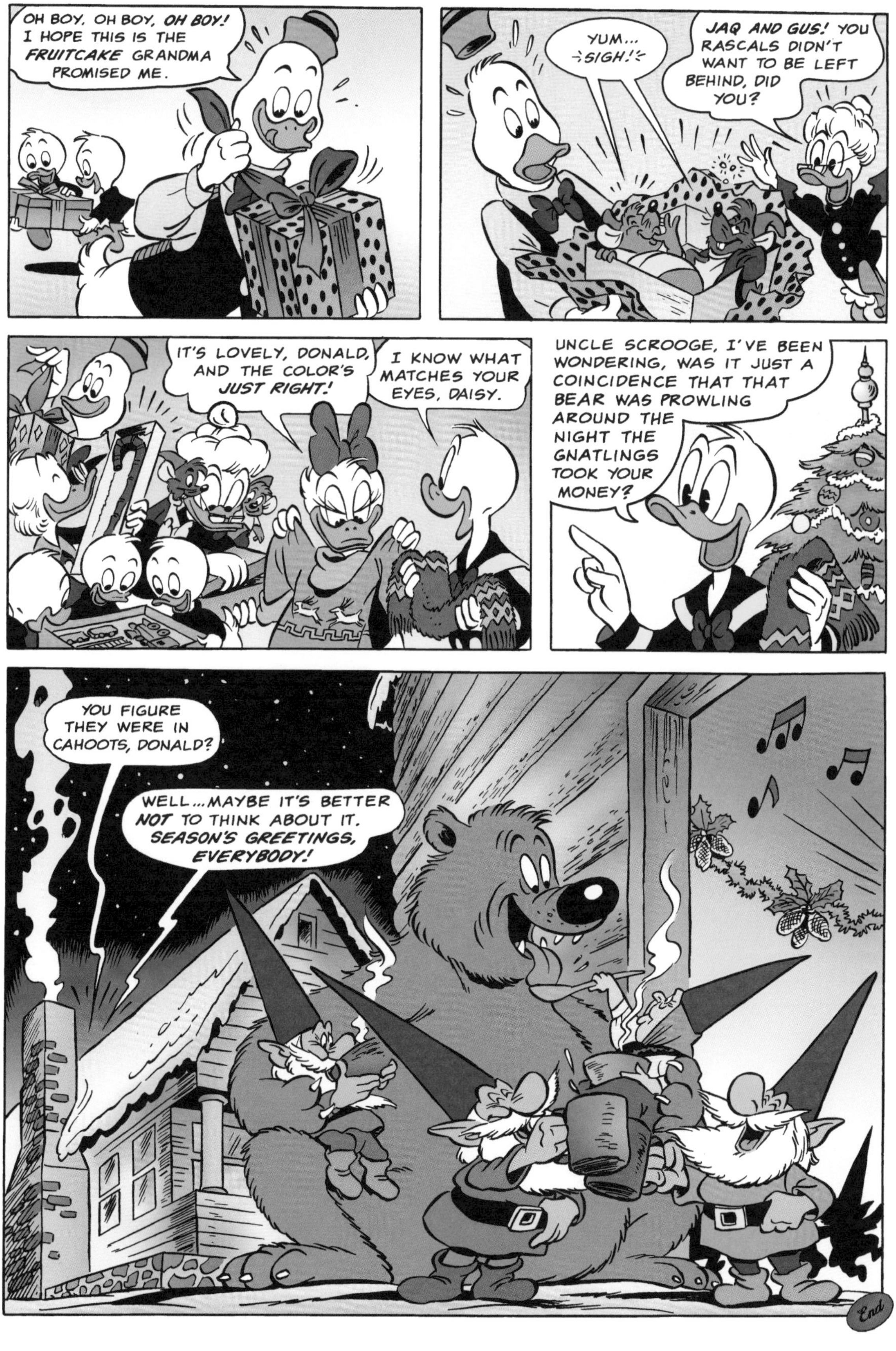
OH BOY, OH BOY, OH BOY! I HOPE THIS IS THE FRUITCAKE GRANDMA PROMISED ME.
YUM... SIGH!
JAQ AND GUS! YOU RASCALS DIDN'T WANT TO BE LEFT BEHIND, DID YOU?
IT'S LOVELY, DONALD, AND THE COLOR'S JUST RIGHT!
I KNOW WHAT MATCHES YOUR EYES, DAISY.
UNCLE SCROOGE, I'VE BEEN WONDERING, WAS IT JUST A COINCIDENCE THAT THAT BEAR WAS PROWLING AROUND THE NIGHT THE GNATLINGS TOOK YOUR MONEY?
YOU FIGURE THEY WERE IN CAHOOTS, DONALD?
WELL...MAYBE IT'S BETTER NOT TO THINK ABOUT IT. SEASON'S GREETINGS, EVERYBODY!
End

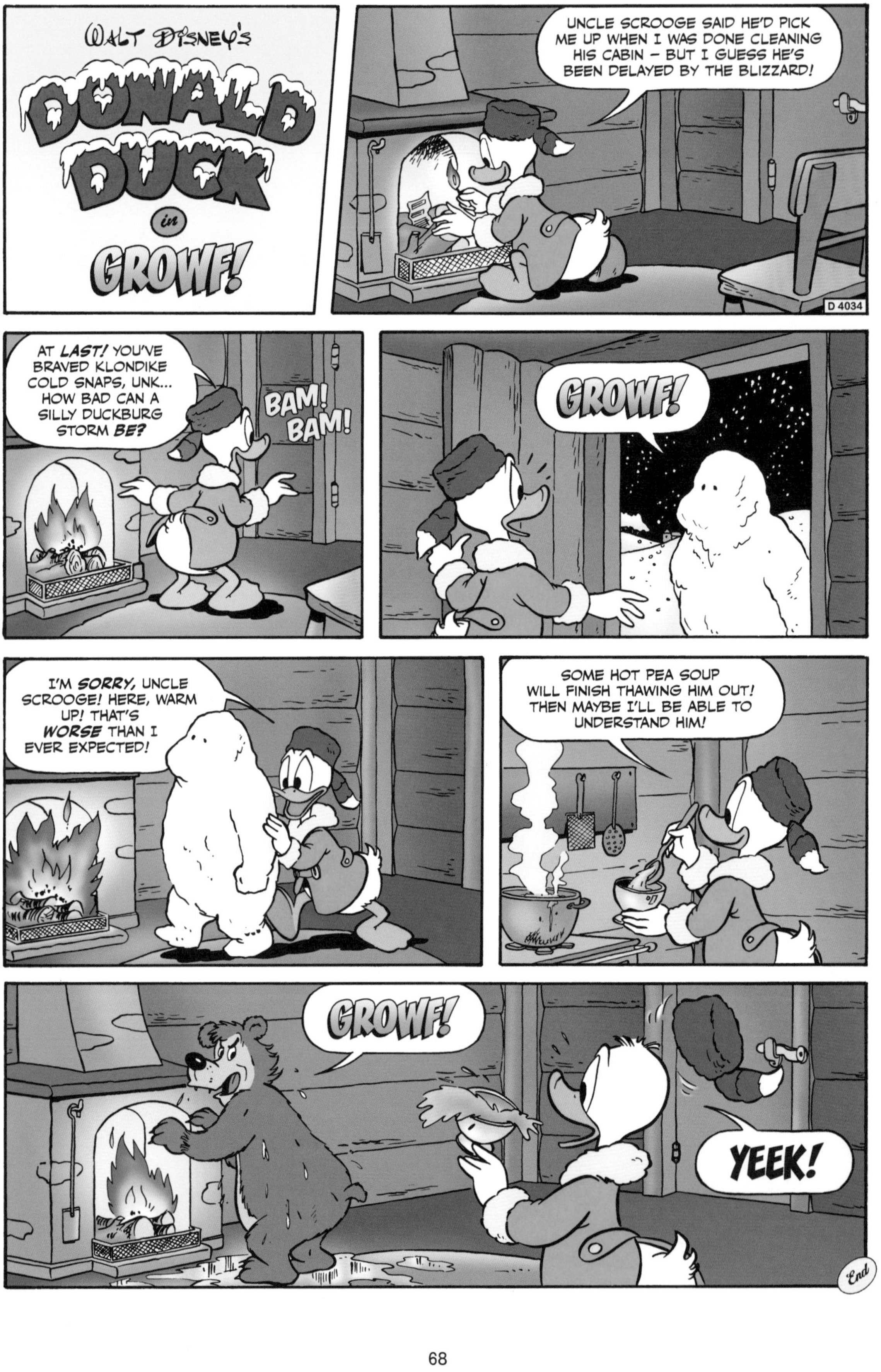
Walt Disney's
DONALD DUCK
in
GROWF!
UNCLE SCROOGE SAID HE'D PICK ME UP WHEN I WAS DONE CLEANING HIS CABIN – BUT I GUESS HE'S BEEN DELAYED BY THE BLIZZARD!
D 4034
BAM! BAM!
AT LAST! YOU'VE BRAVED KLONDIKE COLD SNAPS, UNK... HOW BAD CAN A SILLY DUCKBURG STORM BE?
GROWF!
I'M SORRY, UNCLE SCROOGE! HERE, WARM UP! THAT'S WORSE THAN I EVER EXPECTED!
SOME HOT PEA SOUP WILL FINISH THAWING HIM OUT! THEN MAYBE I'LL BE ABLE TO UNDERSTAND HIM!
GROWF!
YEEK!
End

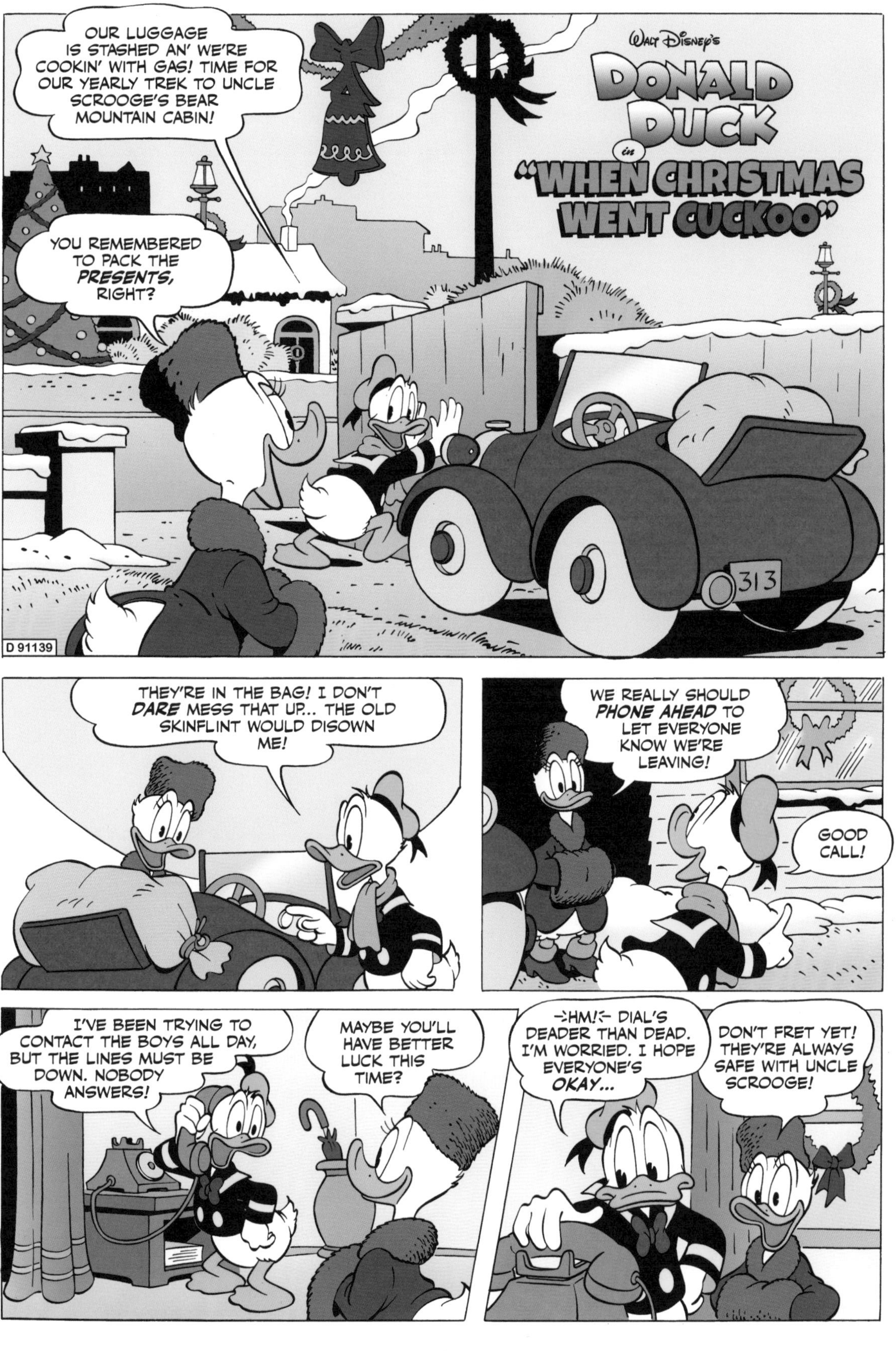

Walt Disney's
DONALD DUCK in "WHEN CHRISTMAS WENT CUCKOO"
OUR LUGGAGE IS STASHED AN' WE'RE COOKIN' WITH GAS! TIME FOR OUR YEARLY TREK TO UNCLE SCROOGE'S BEAR MOUNTAIN CABIN!
YOU REMEMBERED TO PACK THE PRESENTS, RIGHT?
313
D 91139
THEY'RE IN THE BAG! I DON'T DARE MESS THAT UP... THE OLD SKINFLINT WOULD DISOWN ME!
WE REALLY SHOULD PHONE AHEAD TO LET EVERYONE KNOW WE'RE LEAVING!
GOOD CALL!
I'VE BEEN TRYING TO CONTACT THE BOYS ALL DAY, BUT THE LINES MUST BE DOWN. NOBODY ANSWERS!
MAYBE YOU'LL HAVE BETTER LUCK THIS TIME?
HM! DIAL'S DEADER THAN DEAD. I'M WORRIED. I HOPE EVERYONE'S OKAY...
DON'T FRET YET! THEY'RE ALWAYS SAFE WITH UNCLE SCROOGE!

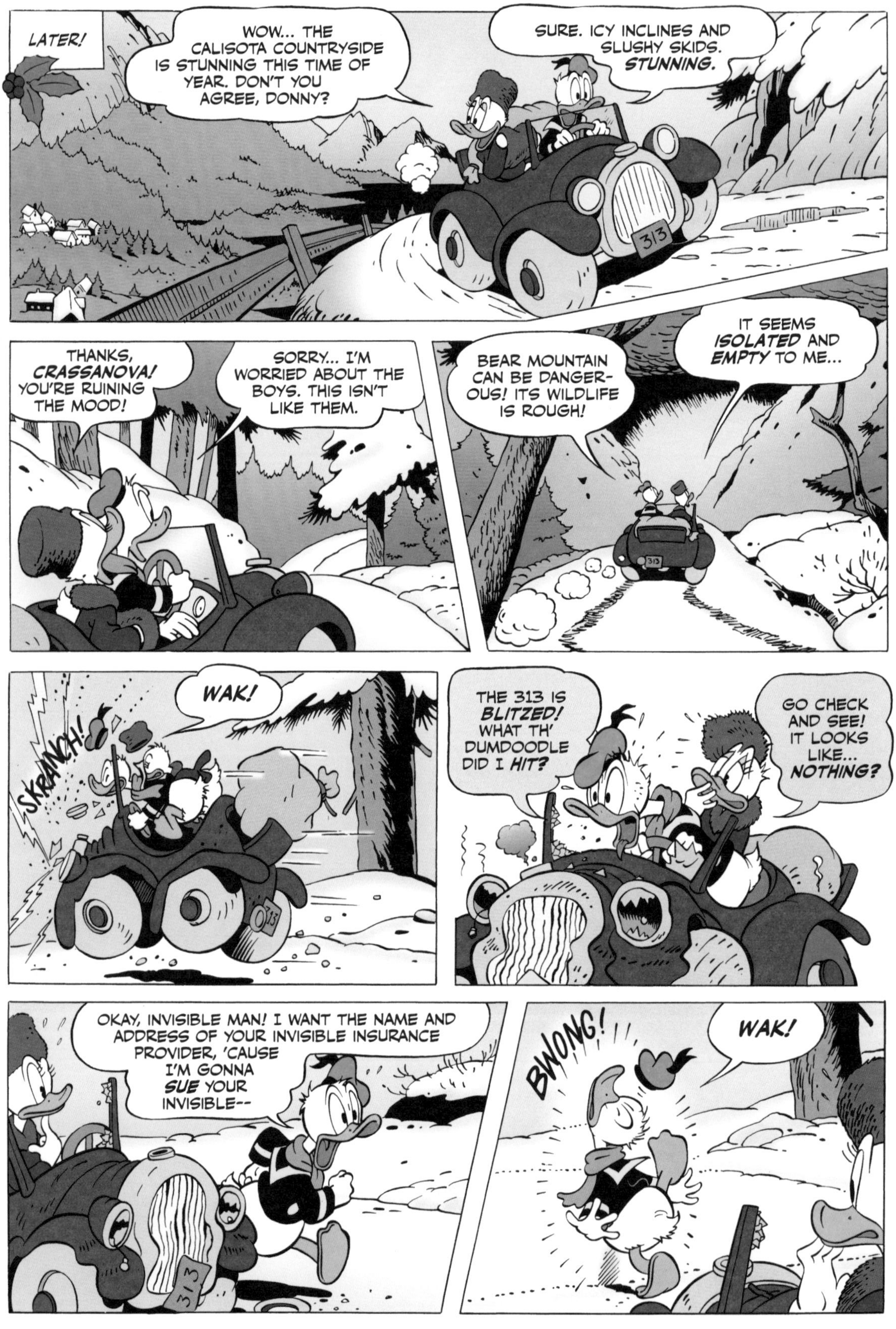
LATER!
WOW... THE CALISOTA COUNTRYSIDE IS STUNNING THIS TIME OF YEAR. DON'T YOU AGREE, DONNY?
SURE. ICY INCLINES AND SLUSHY SKIDS. ***STUNNING.***
313
THANKS, ***CRASSANOVA!*** YOU'RE RUINING THE MOOD!
SORRY... I'M WORRIED ABOUT THE BOYS. THIS ISN'T LIKE THEM.
BEAR MOUNTAIN CAN BE DANGEROUS! ITS WILDLIFE IS ROUGH!
IT SEEMS ***ISOLATED*** AND ***EMPTY*** TO ME...
WAK!
SKRANCH!
THE 313 IS ***BLITZED!*** WHAT TH' DUMDOODLE DID I ***HIT?***
GO CHECK AND SEE! IT LOOKS LIKE... ***NOTHING?***
OKAY, INVISIBLE MAN! I WANT THE NAME AND ADDRESS OF YOUR INVISIBLE INSURANCE PROVIDER, 'CAUSE I'M GONNA ***SUE*** YOUR INVISIBLE--
313
BWONG!
WAK!

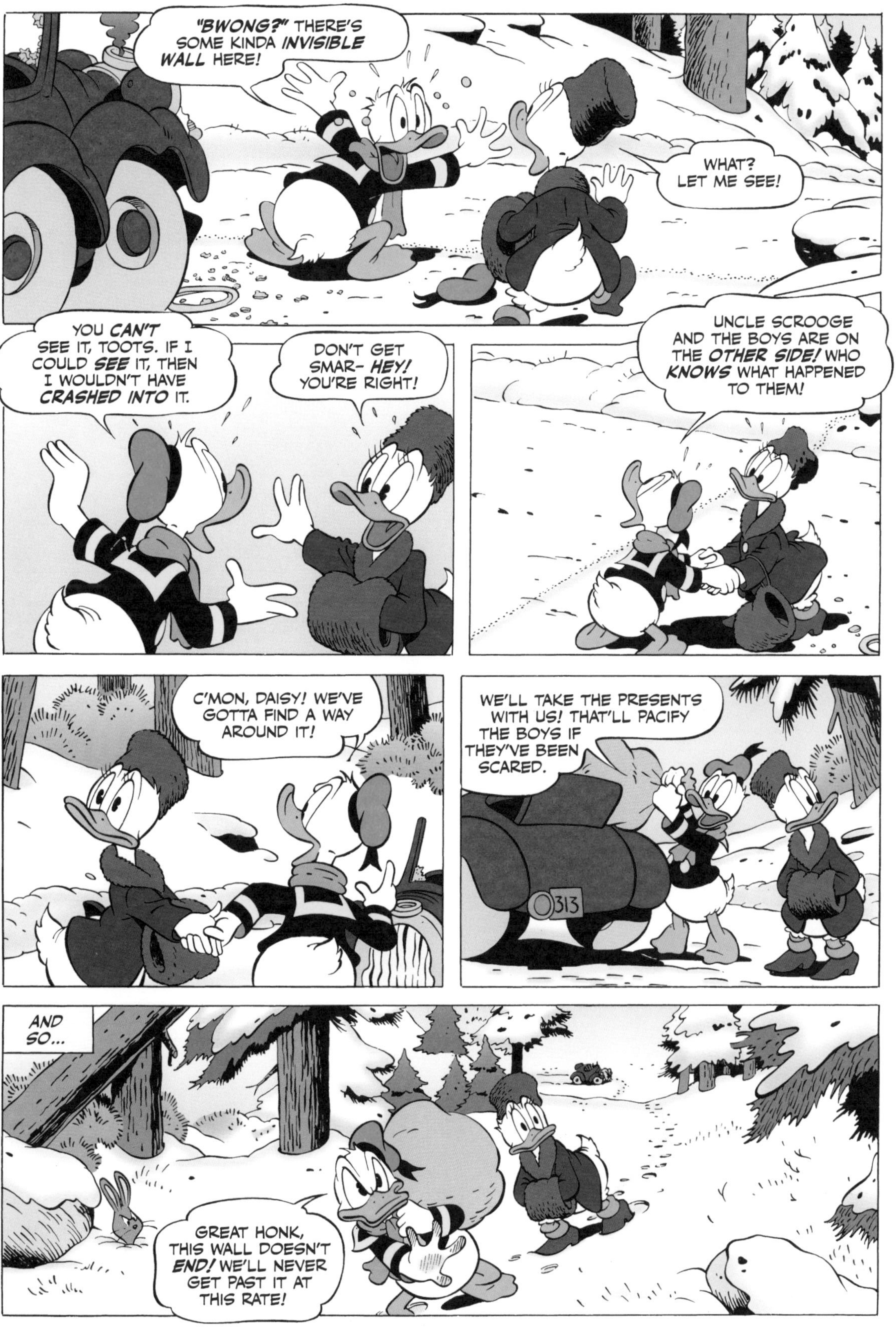
"BWONG?" THERE'S SOME KINDA INVISIBLE WALL HERE!
WHAT? LET ME SEE!
YOU CAN'T SEE IT, TOOTS. IF I COULD SEE IT, THEN I WOULDN'T HAVE CRASHED INTO IT.
DON'T GET SMAR– HEY! YOU'RE RIGHT!
UNCLE SCROOGE AND THE BOYS ARE ON THE OTHER SIDE! WHO KNOWS WHAT HAPPENED TO THEM!
C'MON, DAISY! WE'VE GOTTA FIND A WAY AROUND IT!
WE'LL TAKE THE PRESENTS WITH US! THAT'LL PACIFY THE BOYS IF THEY'VE BEEN SCARED.
313
AND SO...
GREAT HONK, THIS WALL DOESN'T END! WE'LL NEVER GET PAST IT AT THIS RATE!

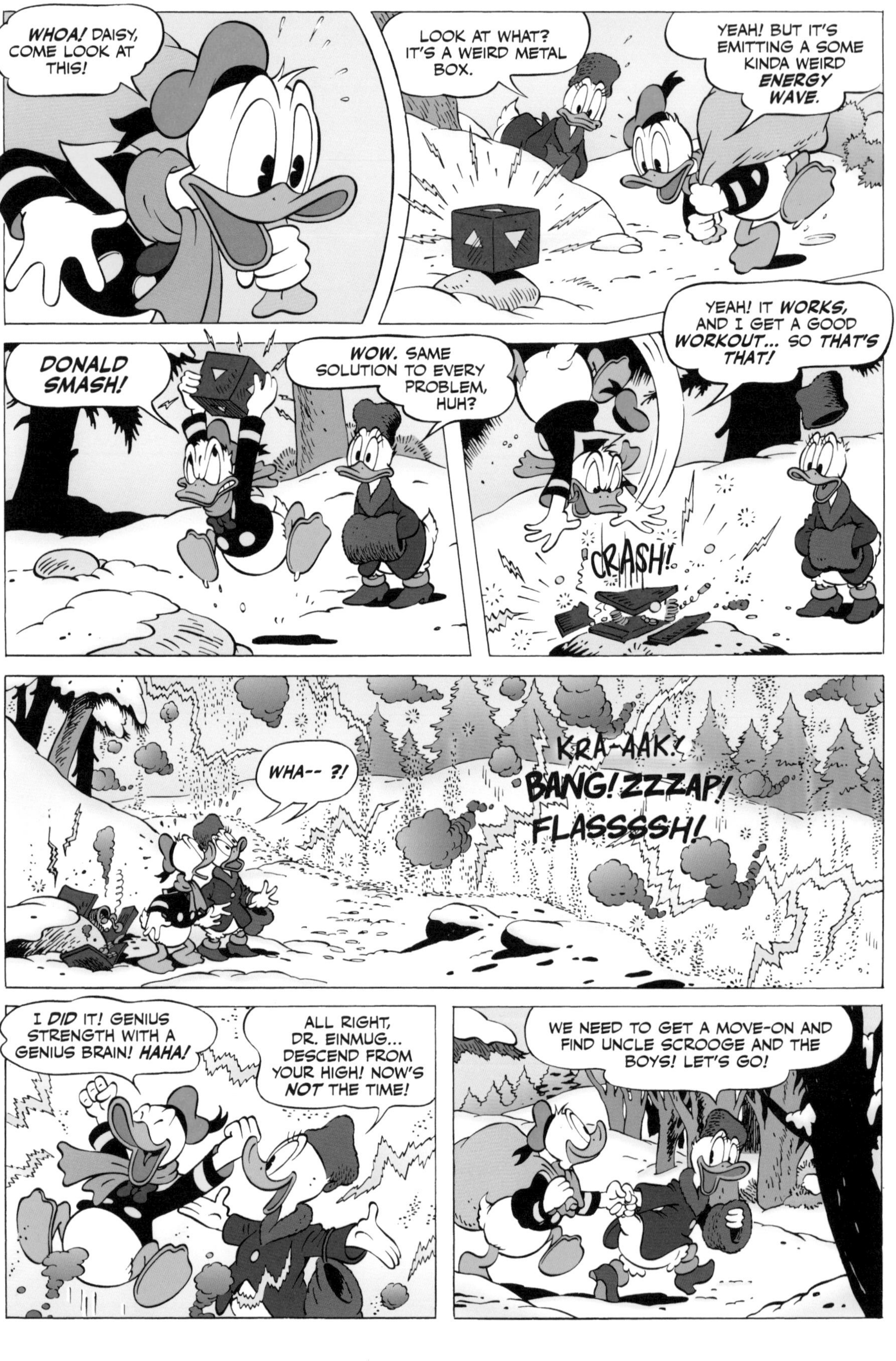
WHOA! DAISY, COME LOOK AT THIS!
LOOK AT WHAT? IT'S A WEIRD METAL BOX.
YEAH! BUT IT'S EMITTING A SOME KINDA WEIRD ENERGY WAVE.
DONALD SMASH!
WOW. SAME SOLUTION TO EVERY PROBLEM, HUH?
YEAH! IT WORKS, AND I GET A GOOD WORKOUT... SO THAT'S THAT!
CRASH!
WHA-- ?!
KRA-AAK!
BANG! ZZZAP!
FLASSSSH!
I DID IT! GENIUS STRENGTH WITH A GENIUS BRAIN! HAHA!
ALL RIGHT, DR. EINMUG... DESCEND FROM YOUR HIGH! NOW'S NOT THE TIME!
WE NEED TO GET A MOVE-ON AND FIND UNCLE SCROOGE AND THE BOYS! LET'S GO!

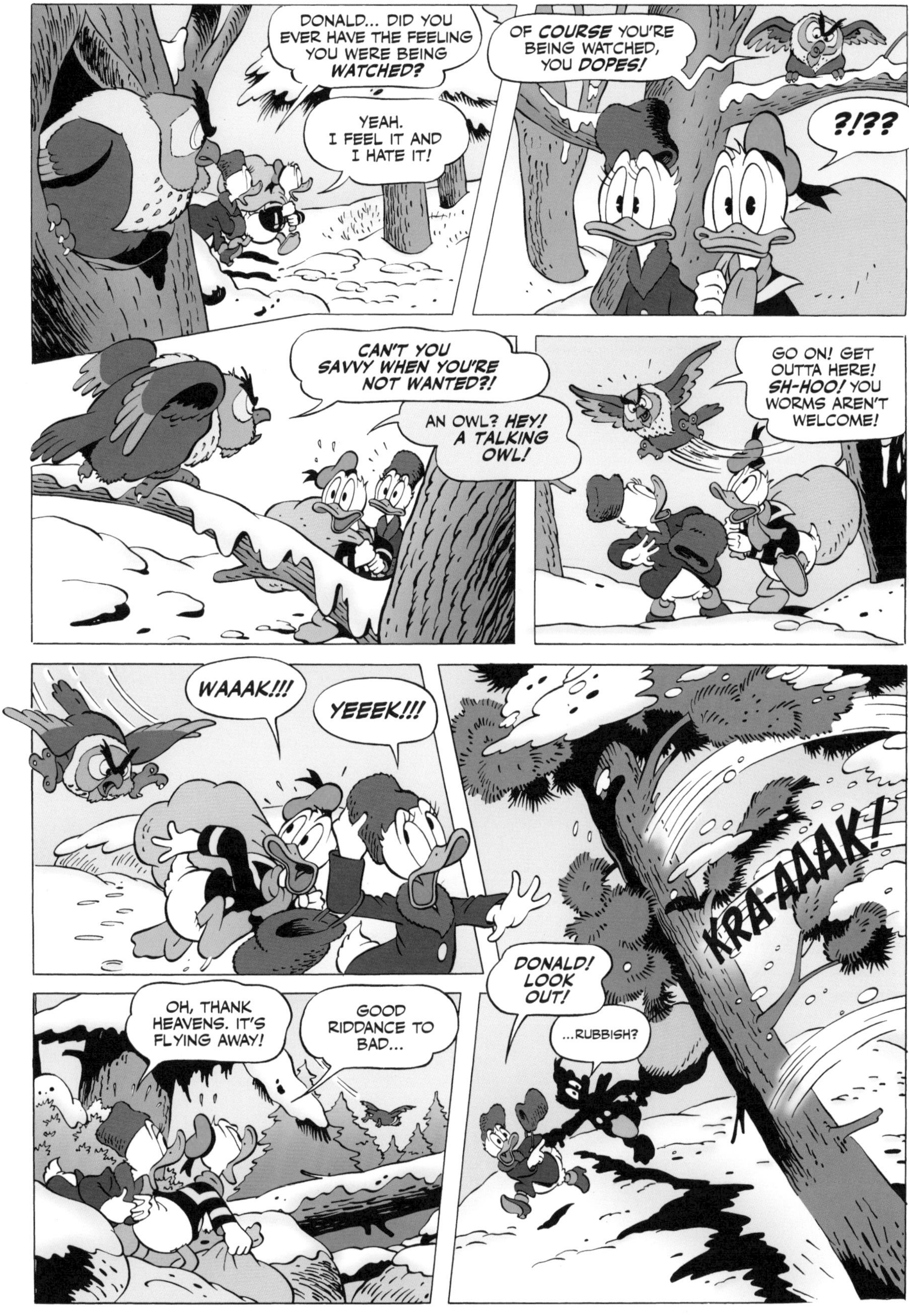
DONALD... DID YOU EVER HAVE THE FEELING YOU WERE BEING WATCHED?
YEAH. I FEEL IT AND I HATE IT!
OF COURSE YOU'RE BEING WATCHED, YOU DOPES!
?!??
CAN'T YOU SAVVY WHEN YOU'RE NOT WANTED?!
AN OWL? HEY! A TALKING OWL!
GO ON! GET OUTTA HERE! SH-HOO! YOU WORMS AREN'T WELCOME!
WAAAK!!!
YEEEK!!!
KRA-AAAK!
OH, THANK HEAVENS. IT'S FLYING AWAY!
GOOD RIDDANCE TO BAD...
DONALD! LOOK OUT!
...RUBBISH?

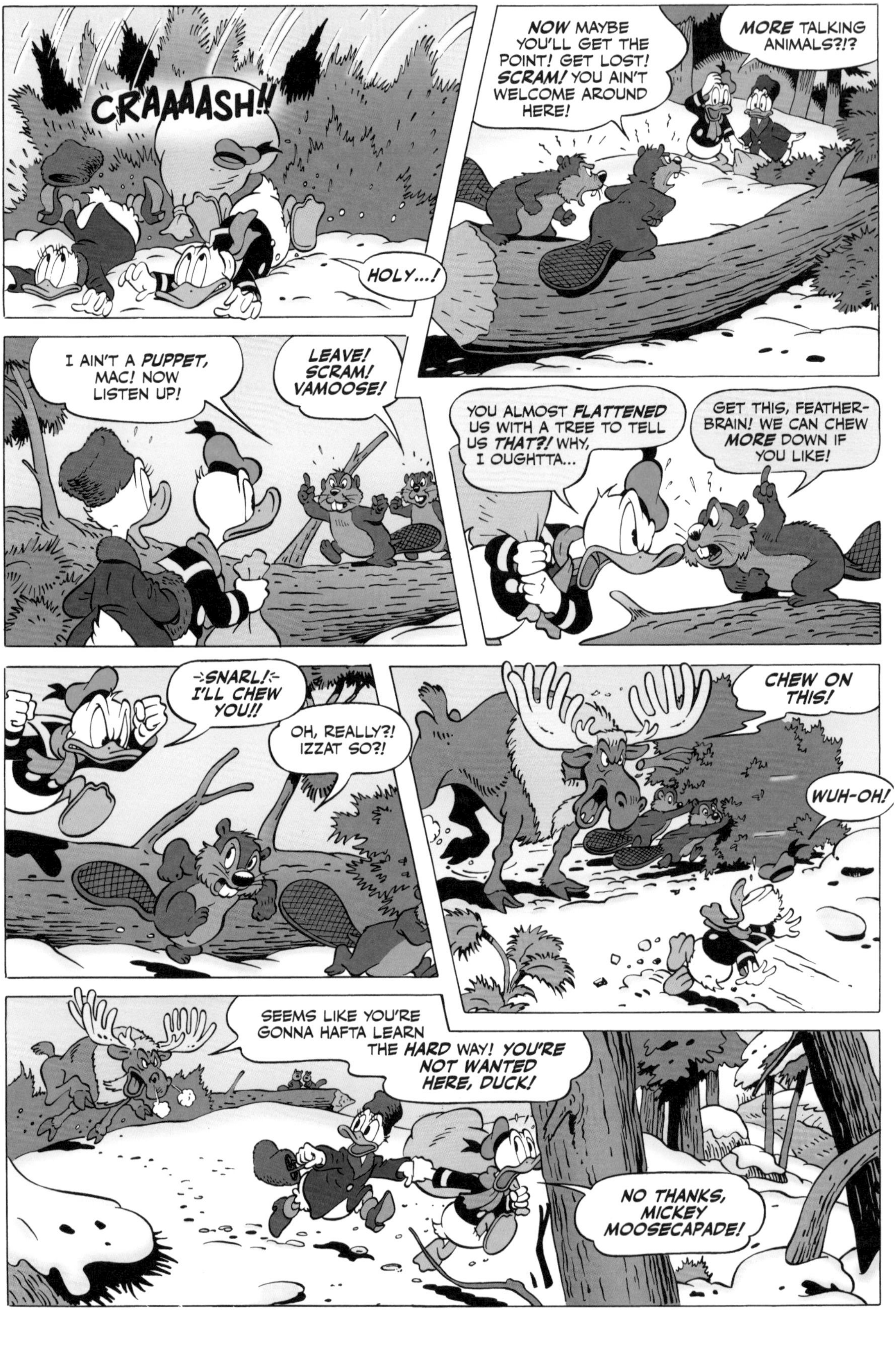
CRAAAASH!!
HOLY...!
NOW MAYBE YOU'LL GET THE POINT! GET LOST! SCRAM! YOU AIN'T WELCOME AROUND HERE!
MORE TALKING ANIMALS?!?
I AIN'T A PUPPET, MAC! NOW LISTEN UP!
LEAVE! SCRAM! VAMOOSE!
YOU ALMOST FLATTENED US WITH A TREE TO TELL US THAT?! WHY, I OUGHTTA...
GET THIS, FEATHER-BRAIN! WE CAN CHEW MORE DOWN IF YOU LIKE!
SNARL! I'LL CHEW YOU!!
OH, REALLY?! IZZAT SO?!
CHEW ON THIS!
WUH-OH!
SEEMS LIKE YOU'RE GONNA HAFTA LEARN THE HARD WAY! YOU'RE NOT WANTED HERE, DUCK!
NO THANKS, MICKEY MOOSECAPADE!

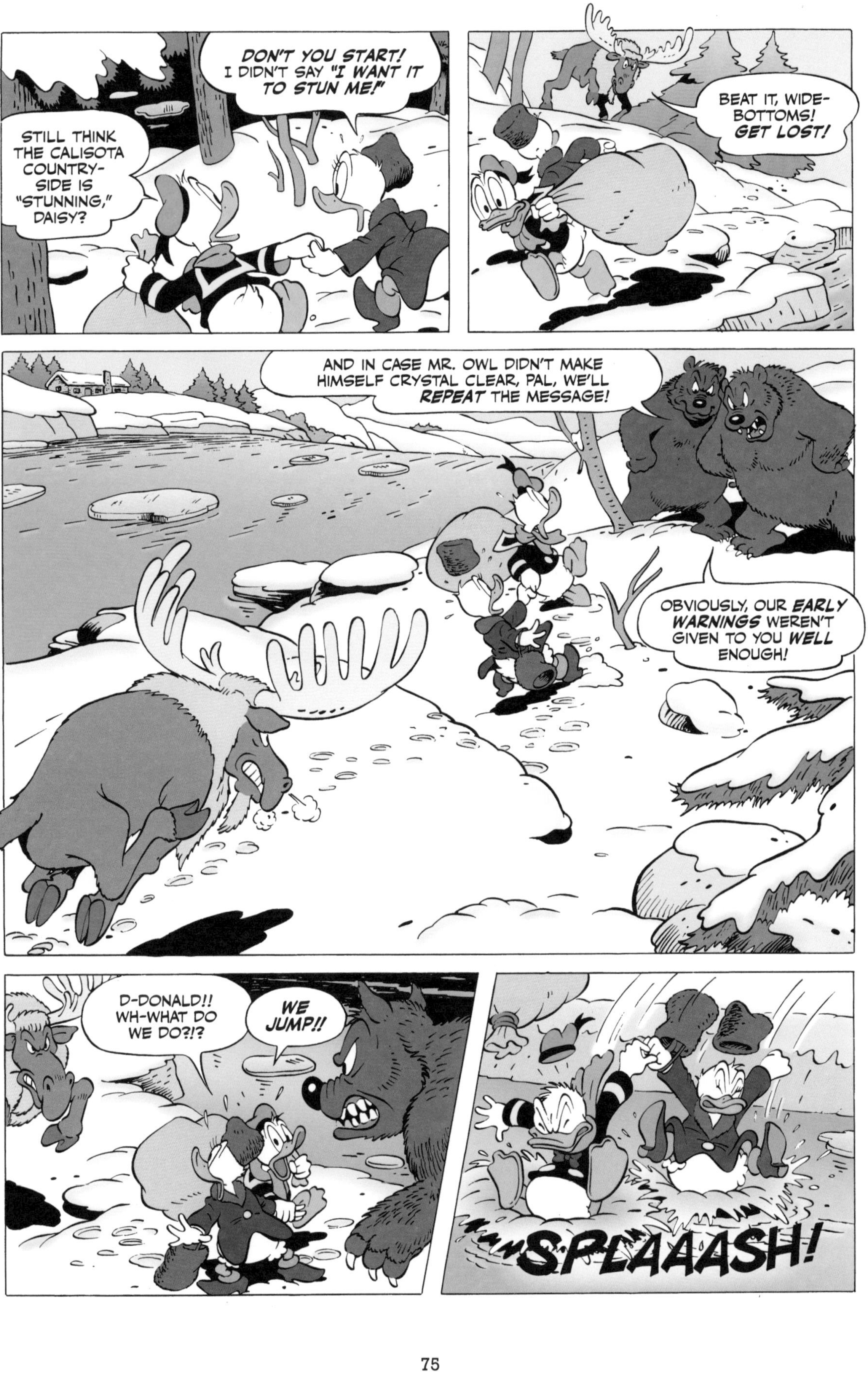

STILL THINK THE CALISOTA COUNTRY-SIDE IS "STUNNING," DAISY?
DON'T YOU START! I DIDN'T SAY "I WANT IT TO STUN ME!"
BEAT IT, WIDE-BOTTOMS! GET LOST!
AND IN CASE MR. OWL DIDN'T MAKE HIMSELF CRYSTAL CLEAR, PAL, WE'LL REPEAT THE MESSAGE!
OBVIOUSLY, OUR EARLY WARNINGS WEREN'T GIVEN TO YOU WELL ENOUGH!
D-DONALD!! WH-WHAT DO WE DO?!?
WE JUMP!!
SPLAAASH!

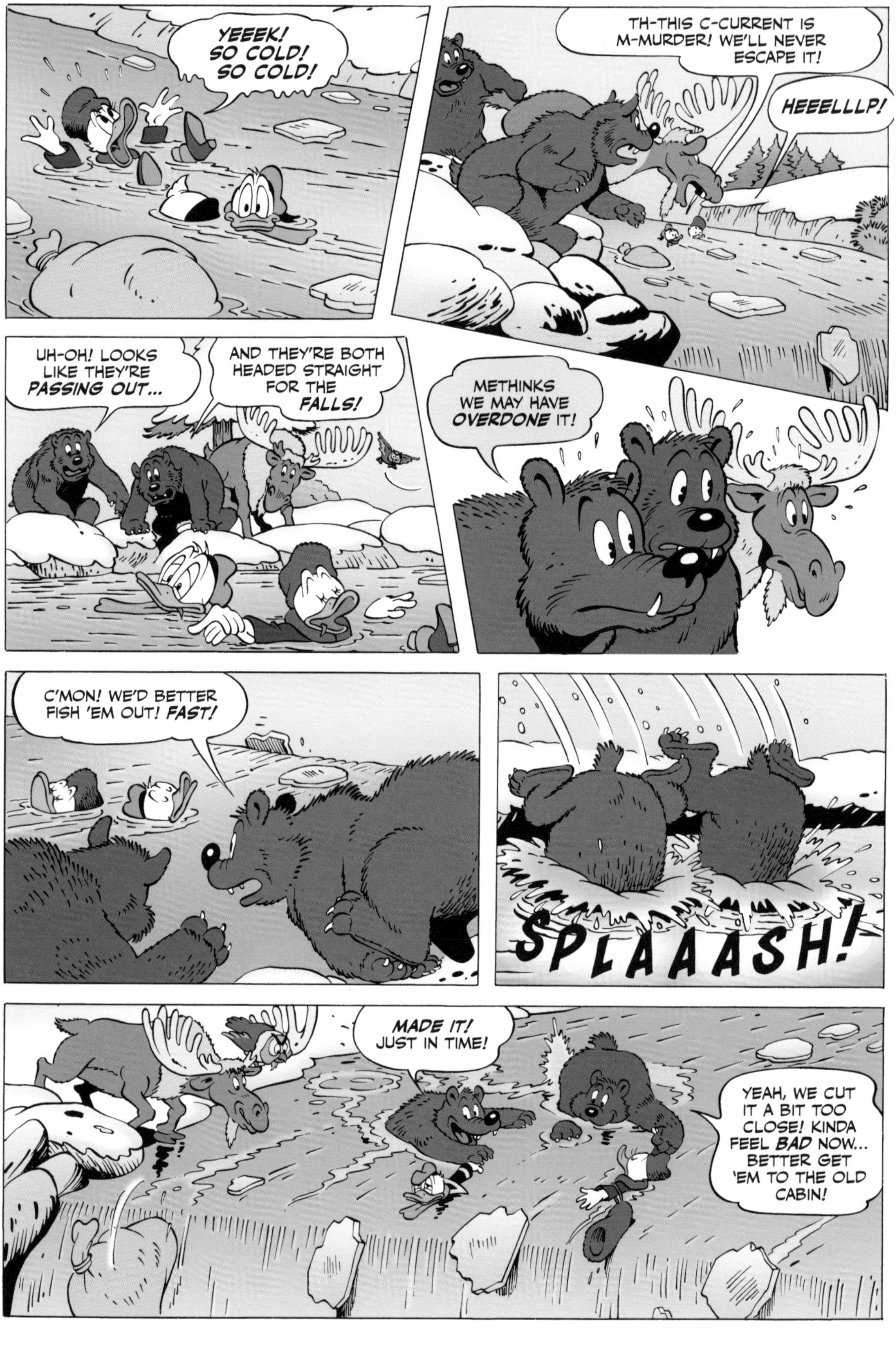
YEEEK! SO COLD! SO COLD!
TH-THIS C-CURRENT IS M-MURDER! WE'LL NEVER ESCAPE IT!
HEEELLLP!
UH-OH! LOOKS LIKE THEY'RE PASSING OUT...
AND THEY'RE BOTH HEADED STRAIGHT FOR THE FALLS!
METHINKS WE MAY HAVE OVERDONE IT!
C'MON! WE'D BETTER FISH 'EM OUT! FAST!
SPLAAASH!
MADE IT! JUST IN TIME!
YEAH, WE CUT IT A BIT TOO CLOSE! KINDA FEEL BAD NOW... BETTER GET 'EM TO THE OLD CABIN!

SORRY! WE RAN INTO TROUBLE!

OUR BLOCKADE DIDN'T WORK THE WAY WE PLANNED!

glxblt!

OH, MY POPPIN' EYEBULBS! WE AVOIDED GETTING EATEN BY A FURBALL MENAGERIE... ONLY TO BE DRAGGED INTO SPACE BY LITTLE GREEN MEN?!

WAIT... UNCLE SCROOGE! BOYS! ARE... ARE YOU ALL OKAY?!

UNCA DONALD! MEET MR. AND MRS. ᔕᗷᗝᗝᑎᕵ! THEY'LL EXPLAIN EVERYTHING!

♪ WE'RE SO SORRY! ᔕᗷᗝ AFTER WE SET UP A FORCEFIELD AROUND THE AREA, WE TOLD THE WILDLIFE TO KEEP EARTHIANS AWAY... ☺

♪ BUT ONLY WHILE WE RECHARGED OUR SHIP! ᔕᗷᗝ THEY GOT A TAD OVERZEALOUS! ☺

♪ SEE, WE SPENT TOO LONG SPACEMAS SHOPPING... ᔕᗷᗝ OUR BATTERY BLEW A FUSE! ☺

SPACEMAS? YOU HAVE A SPACE CHRISTMAS?

♪ DOESN'T EVERYONE? ᔕᗷᗝ BUT IT WON'T BE HAPPY... ☺

♪ NO PRESENTS FOR WOWIE, ZOWIE, AND POWIE! ᔕᗷᗝ

PRESENTS? OUR PRESENTS WENT OVER THE FALLS!

PARENTS! ᔕᗷᗝ THEY'RE THE ABSOLUTE LIMIT... FROM GALAXY A TO GALAXY B!

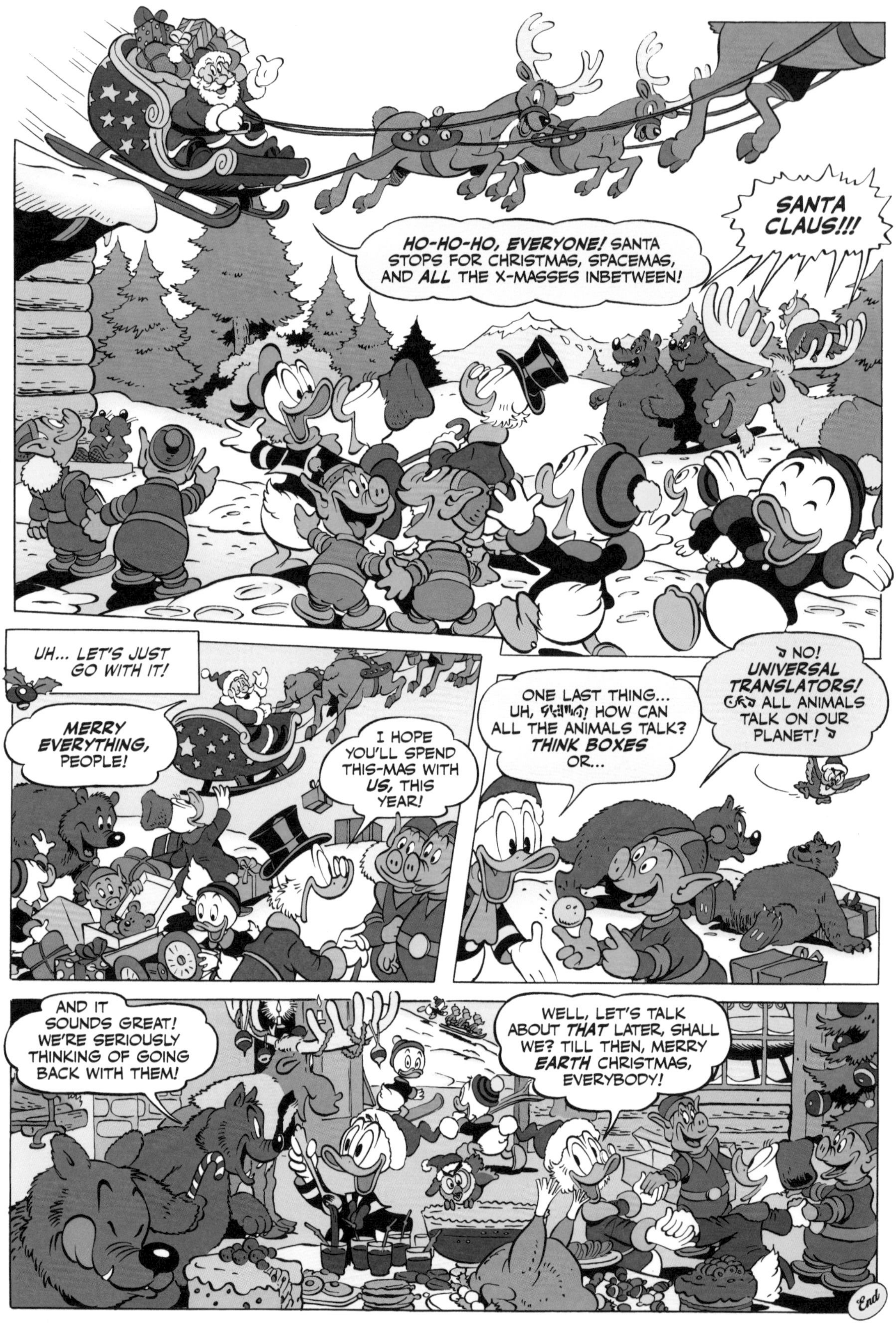
HO-HO-HO, EVERYONE! SANTA STOPS FOR CHRISTMAS, SPACEMAS, AND ALL THE X-MASSES INBETWEEN!
SANTA CLAUS!!!
UH... LET'S JUST GO WITH IT!
MERRY EVERYTHING, PEOPLE!
I HOPE YOU'LL SPEND THIS-MAS WITH US, THIS YEAR!
ONE LAST THING... UH, HOW CAN ALL THE ANIMALS TALK? THINK BOXES OR...
NO! UNIVERSAL TRANSLATORS! ALL ANIMALS TALK ON OUR PLANET!
AND IT SOUNDS GREAT! WE'RE SERIOUSLY THINKING OF GOING BACK WITH THEM!
WELL, LET'S TALK ABOUT THAT LATER, SHALL WE? TILL THEN, MERRY EARTH CHRISTMAS, EVERYBODY!
End

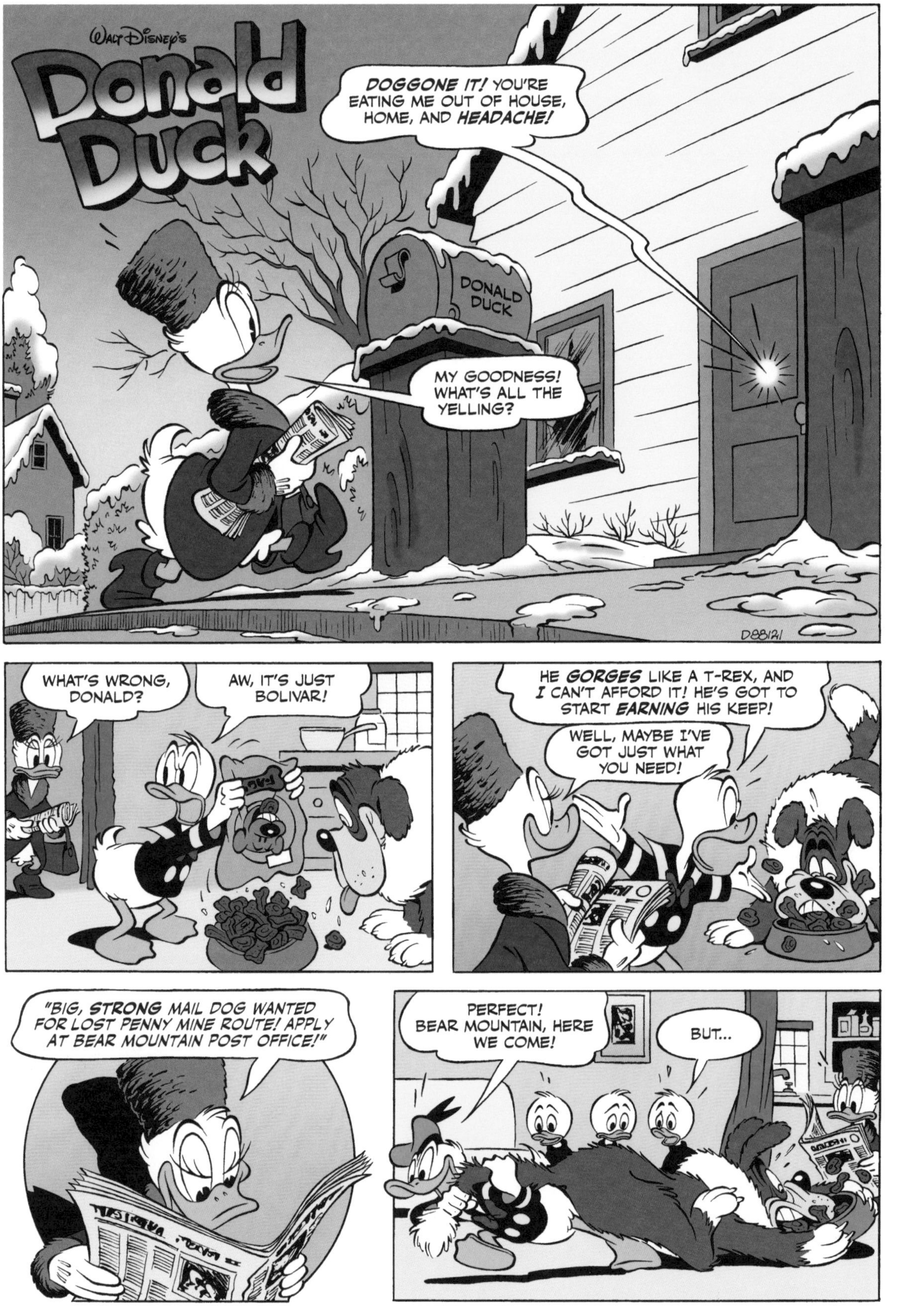
WALT DISNEY'S
Donald Duck
DOGGONE IT! YOU'RE EATING ME OUT OF HOUSE, HOME, AND HEADACHE!
DONALD DUCK
MY GOODNESS! WHAT'S ALL THE YELLING?
D88121
WHAT'S WRONG, DONALD?
AW, IT'S JUST BOLIVAR!
HE GORGES LIKE A T-REX, AND I CAN'T AFFORD IT! HE'S GOT TO START EARNING HIS KEEP!
WELL, MAYBE I'VE GOT JUST WHAT YOU NEED!
"BIG, STRONG MAIL DOG WANTED FOR LOST PENNY MINE ROUTE! APPLY AT BEAR MOUNTAIN POST OFFICE!"
PERFECT! BEAR MOUNTAIN, HERE WE COME!
BUT...

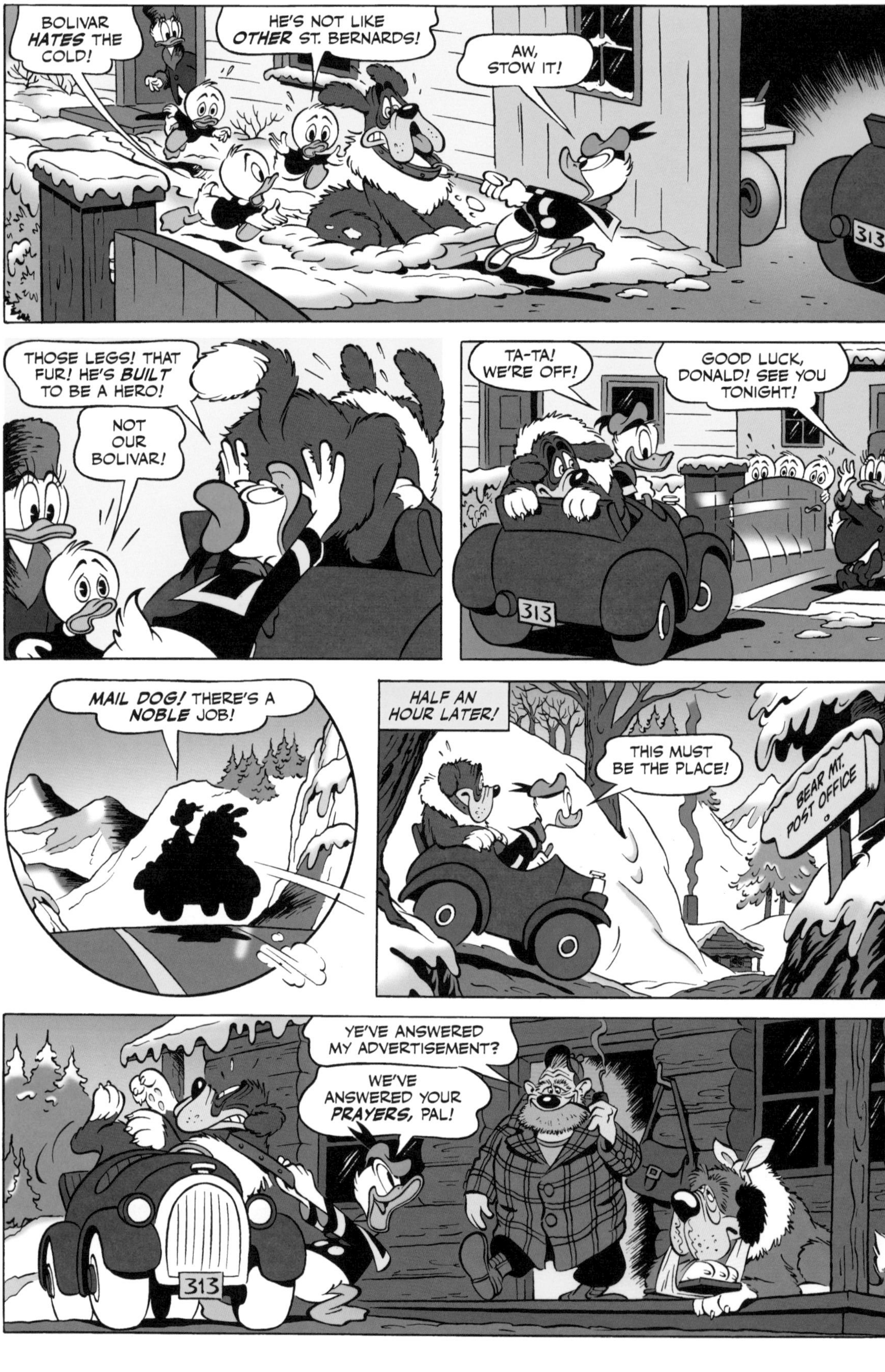
BOLIVAR HATES THE COLD!
HE'S NOT LIKE OTHER ST. BERNARDS!
AW, STOW IT!
313
THOSE LEGS! THAT FUR! HE'S BUILT TO BE A HERO!
NOT OUR BOLIVAR!
TA-TA! WE'RE OFF!
GOOD LUCK, DONALD! SEE YOU TONIGHT!
313
MAIL DOG! THERE'S A NOBLE JOB!
HALF AN HOUR LATER!
THIS MUST BE THE PLACE!
BEAR MT. POST OFFICE
YE'VE ANSWERED MY ADVERTISEMENT?
WE'VE ANSWERED YOUR PRAYERS, PAL!
313

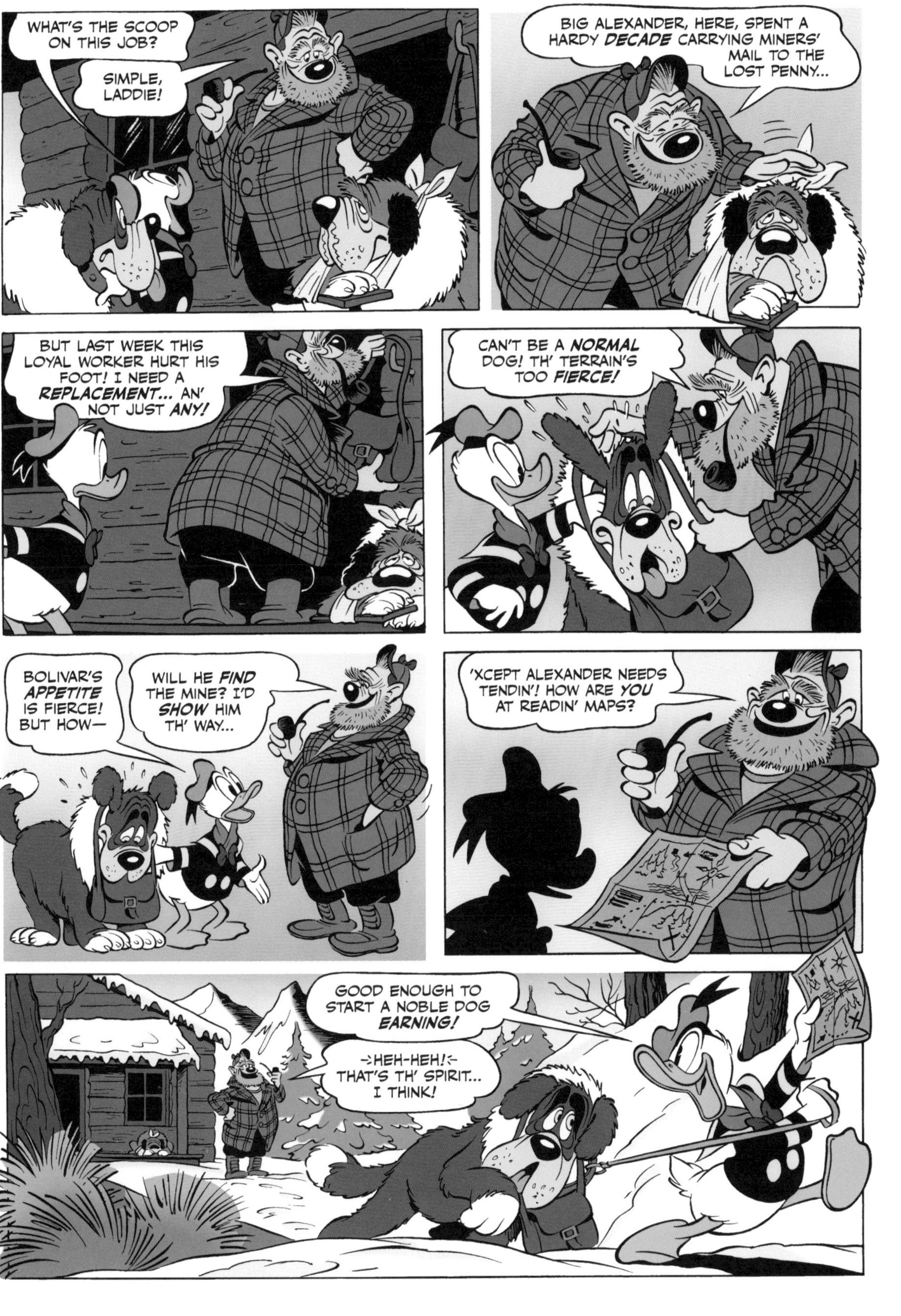
WHAT'S THE SCOOP ON THIS JOB?
SIMPLE, LADDIE!
BIG ALEXANDER, HERE, SPENT A HARDY *DECADE* CARRYING MINERS' MAIL TO THE LOST PENNY...
BUT LAST WEEK THIS LOYAL WORKER HURT HIS FOOT! I NEED A *REPLACEMENT...* AN' NOT JUST *ANY!*
CAN'T BE A *NORMAL* DOG! TH' TERRAIN'S TOO *FIERCE!*
BOLIVAR'S *APPETITE* IS FIERCE! BUT HOW—
WILL HE *FIND* THE MINE? I'D *SHOW* HIM TH' WAY...
'XCEPT ALEXANDER NEEDS TENDIN'! HOW ARE *YOU* AT READIN' MAPS?
GOOD ENOUGH TO START A NOBLE DOG *EARNING!*
HEH-HEH! THAT'S TH' SPIRIT... I THINK!

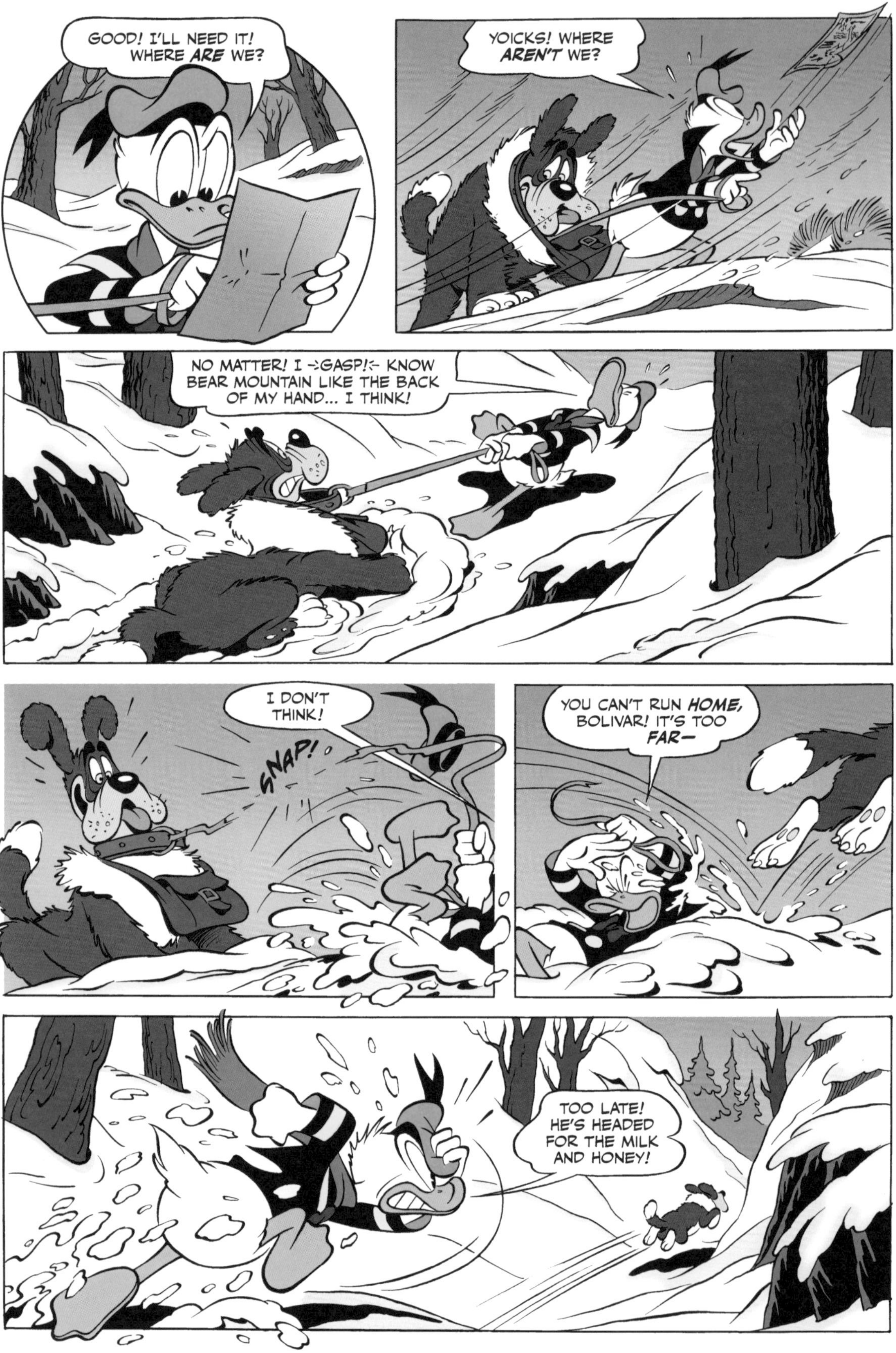
GOOD! I'LL NEED IT! WHERE ARE WE?
YOICKS! WHERE AREN'T WE?
NO MATTER! I →GASP!← KNOW BEAR MOUNTAIN LIKE THE BACK OF MY HAND... I THINK!
I DON'T THINK!
SNAP!
YOU CAN'T RUN HOME, BOLIVAR! IT'S TOO FAR—
TOO LATE! HE'S HEADED FOR THE MILK AND HONEY!

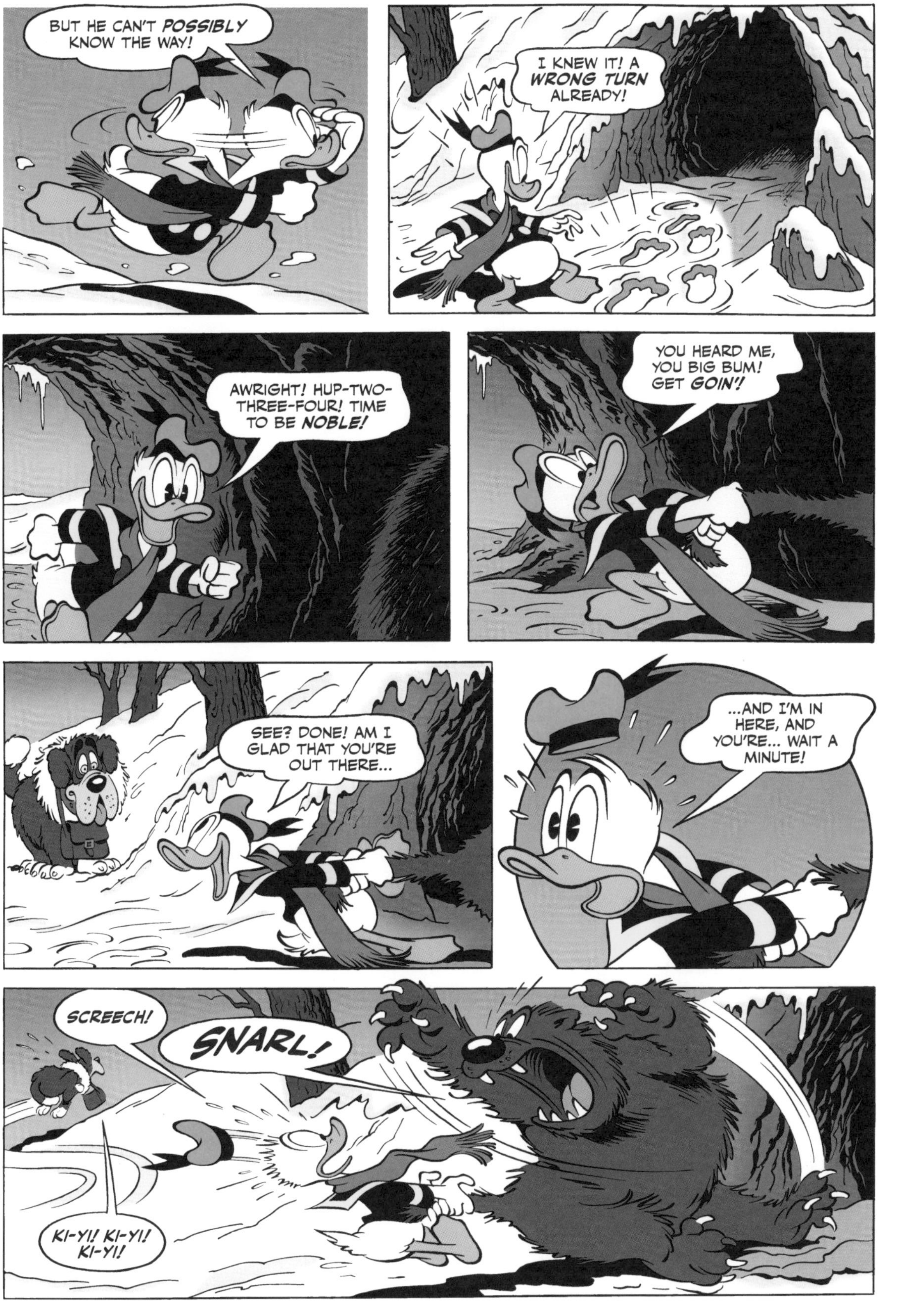
BUT HE CAN'T POSSIBLY KNOW THE WAY!
I KNEW IT! A WRONG TURN ALREADY!
AWRIGHT! HUP-TWO-THREE-FOUR! TIME TO BE NOBLE!
YOU HEARD ME, YOU BIG BUM! GET GOIN'!
SEE? DONE! AM I GLAD THAT YOU'RE OUT THERE...
...AND I'M IN HERE, AND YOU'RE... WAIT A MINUTE!
SCREECH!
SNARL!
KI-YI! KI-YI! KI-YI!

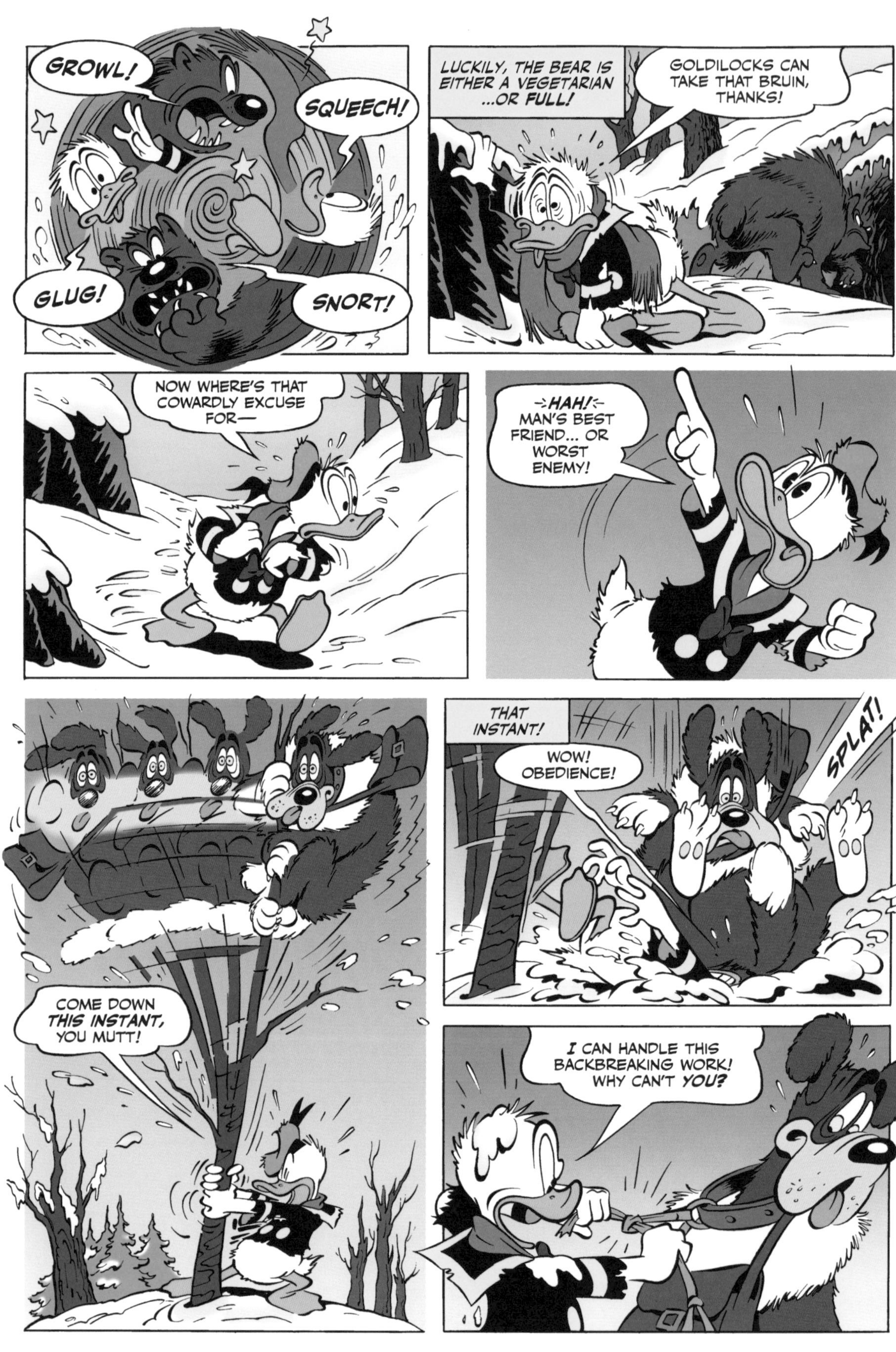
GROWL!
SQUEECH!
GLUG!
SNORT!
LUCKILY, THE BEAR IS EITHER A VEGETARIAN ...OR FULL!
GOLDILOCKS CAN TAKE THAT BRUIN, THANKS!
NOW WHERE'S THAT COWARDLY EXCUSE FOR—
HAH! MAN'S BEST FRIEND... OR WORST ENEMY!
COME DOWN THIS INSTANT, YOU MUTT!
THAT INSTANT!
WOW! OBEDIENCE!
SPLAT!
I CAN HANDLE THIS BACKBREAKING WORK! WHY CAN'T YOU?

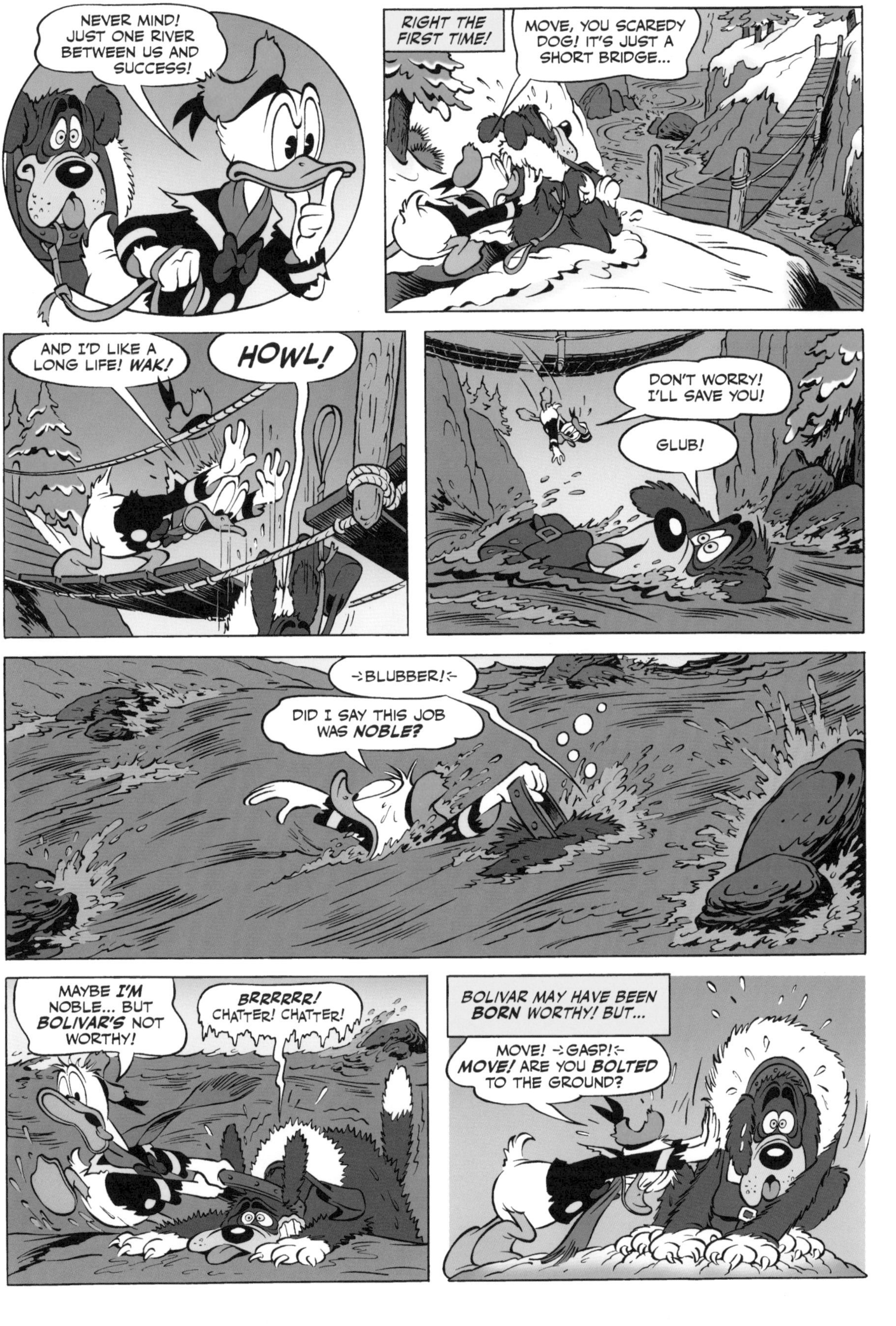
NEVER MIND! JUST ONE RIVER BETWEEN US AND SUCCESS!
RIGHT THE FIRST TIME!
MOVE, YOU SCAREDY DOG! IT'S JUST A SHORT BRIDGE...
AND I'D LIKE A LONG LIFE! WAK!
HOWL!
DON'T WORRY! I'LL SAVE YOU!
GLUB!
-BLUBBER!-
DID I SAY THIS JOB WAS NOBLE?
MAYBE I'M NOBLE... BUT BOLIVAR'S NOT WORTHY!
BRRRRRR! CHATTER! CHATTER!
BOLIVAR MAY HAVE BEEN BORN WORTHY! BUT...
MOVE! -GASP!- MOVE! ARE YOU BOLTED TO THE GROUND?

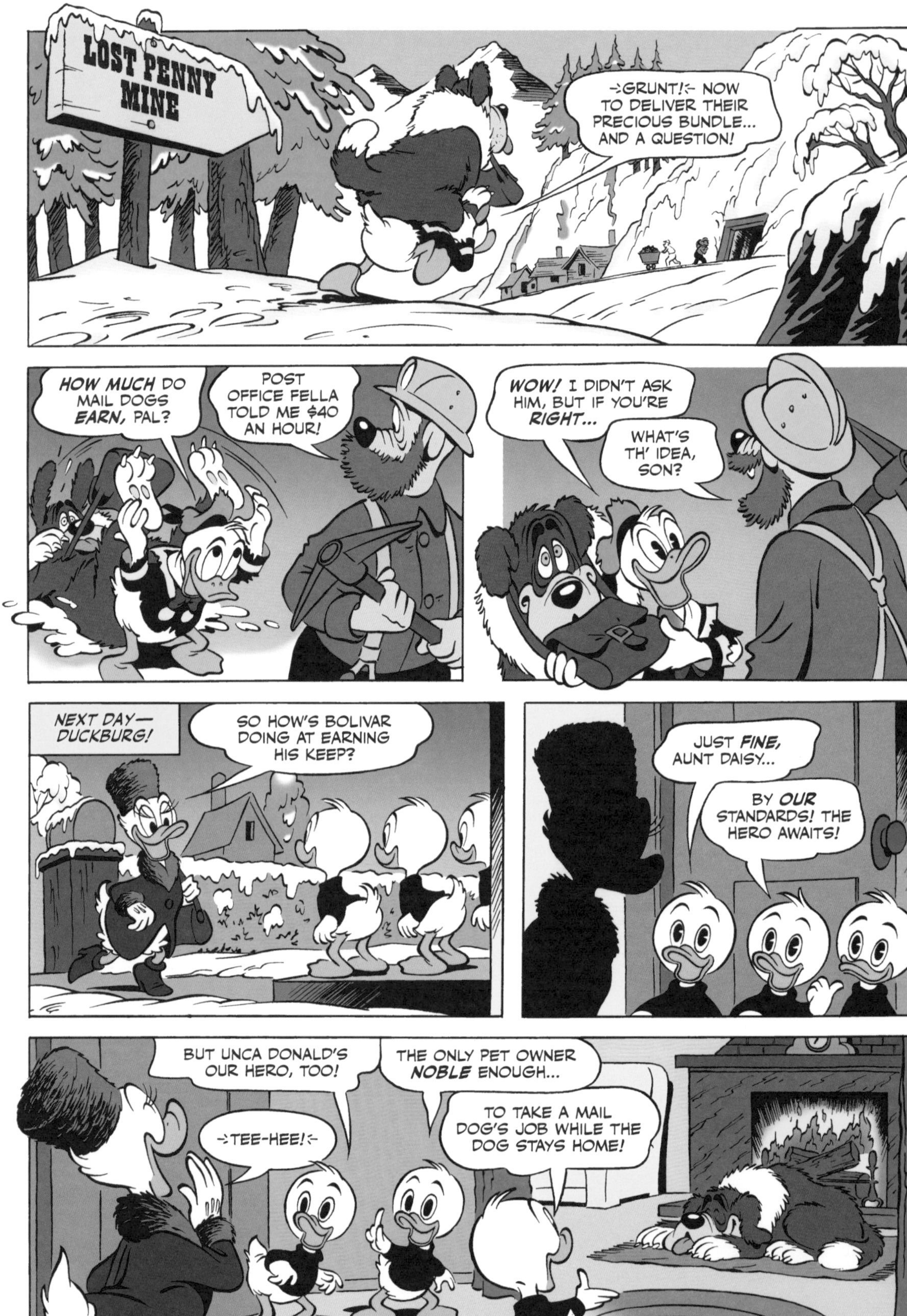
LOST PENNY MINE
-GRUNT!- NOW TO DELIVER THEIR PRECIOUS BUNDLE... AND A QUESTION!
HOW MUCH DO MAIL DOGS EARN, PAL?
POST OFFICE FELLA TOLD ME $40 AN HOUR!
WOW! I DIDN'T ASK HIM, BUT IF YOU'RE RIGHT...
WHAT'S TH' IDEA, SON?
NEXT DAY— DUCKBURG!
SO HOW'S BOLIVAR DOING AT EARNING HIS KEEP?
JUST FINE, AUNT DAISY...
BY OUR STANDARDS! THE HERO AWAITS!
BUT UNCA DONALD'S OUR HERO, TOO!
-TEE-HEE!-
THE ONLY PET OWNER NOBLE ENOUGH...
TO TAKE A MAIL DOG'S JOB WHILE THE DOG STAYS HOME!

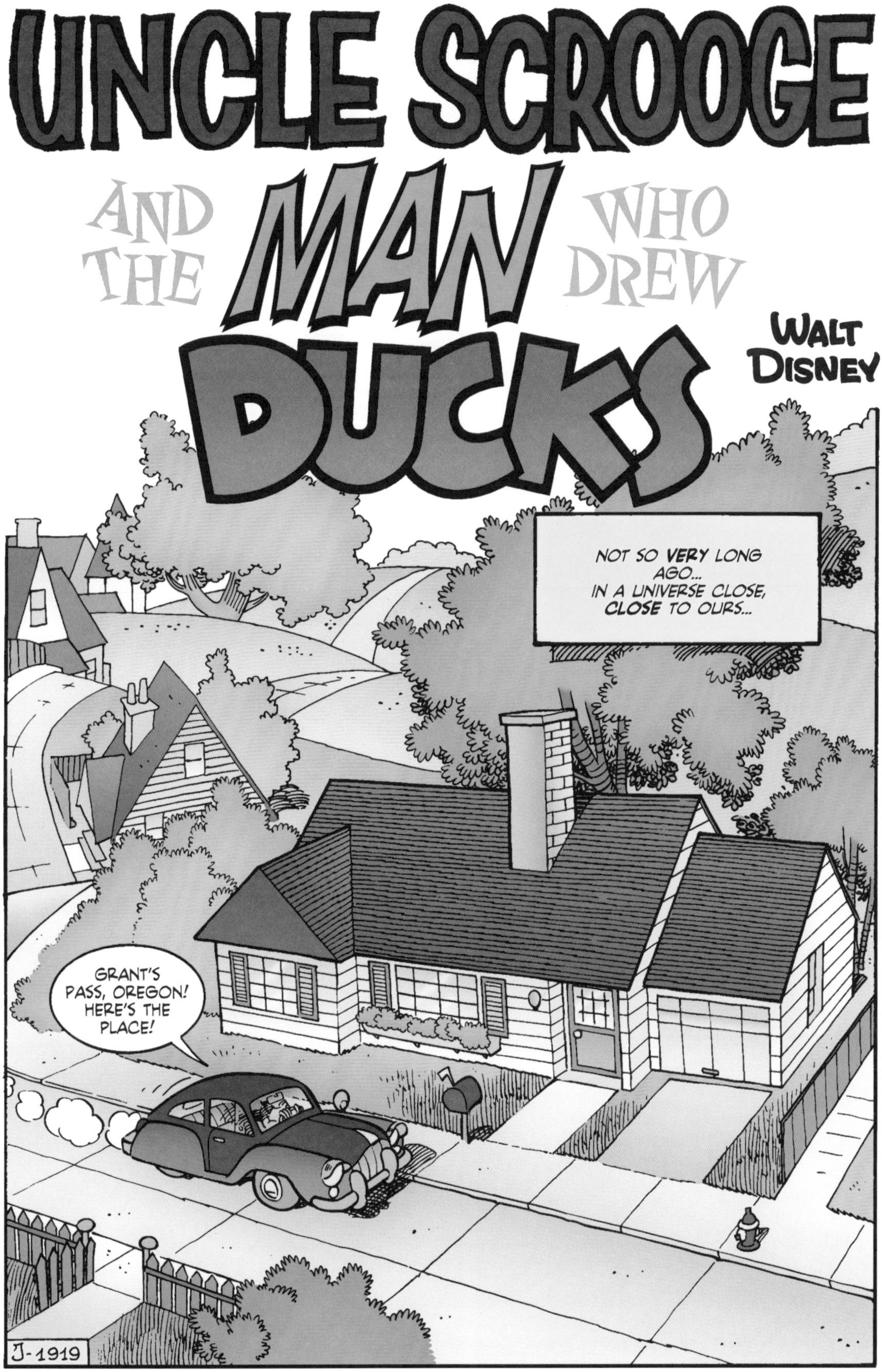
UNCLE SCROOGE
AND THE MAN WHO DREW DUCKS
WALT DISNEY
NOT SO VERY LONG AGO... IN A UNIVERSE CLOSE, CLOSE TO OURS...
GRANT'S PASS, OREGON! HERE'S THE PLACE!
J-1919

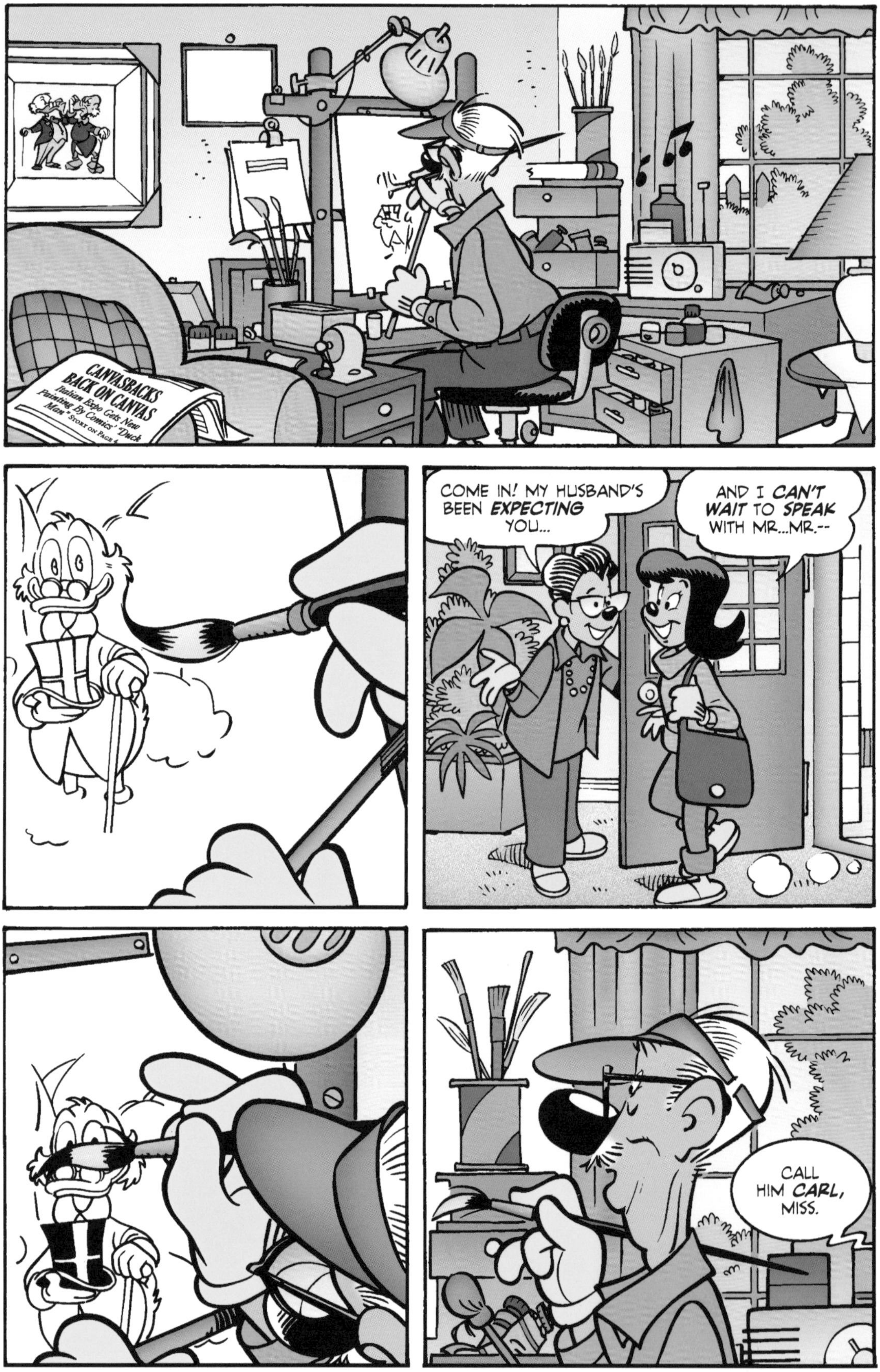
CANVASBACKS BACK ON CANVAS
Italian Expo Gets New Painting By Comics' "Duck Man" Story on Page 4
COME IN! MY HUSBAND'S BEEN EXPECTING YOU...
AND I CAN'T WAIT TO SPEAK WITH MR...MR.--
CALL HIM CARL, MISS.

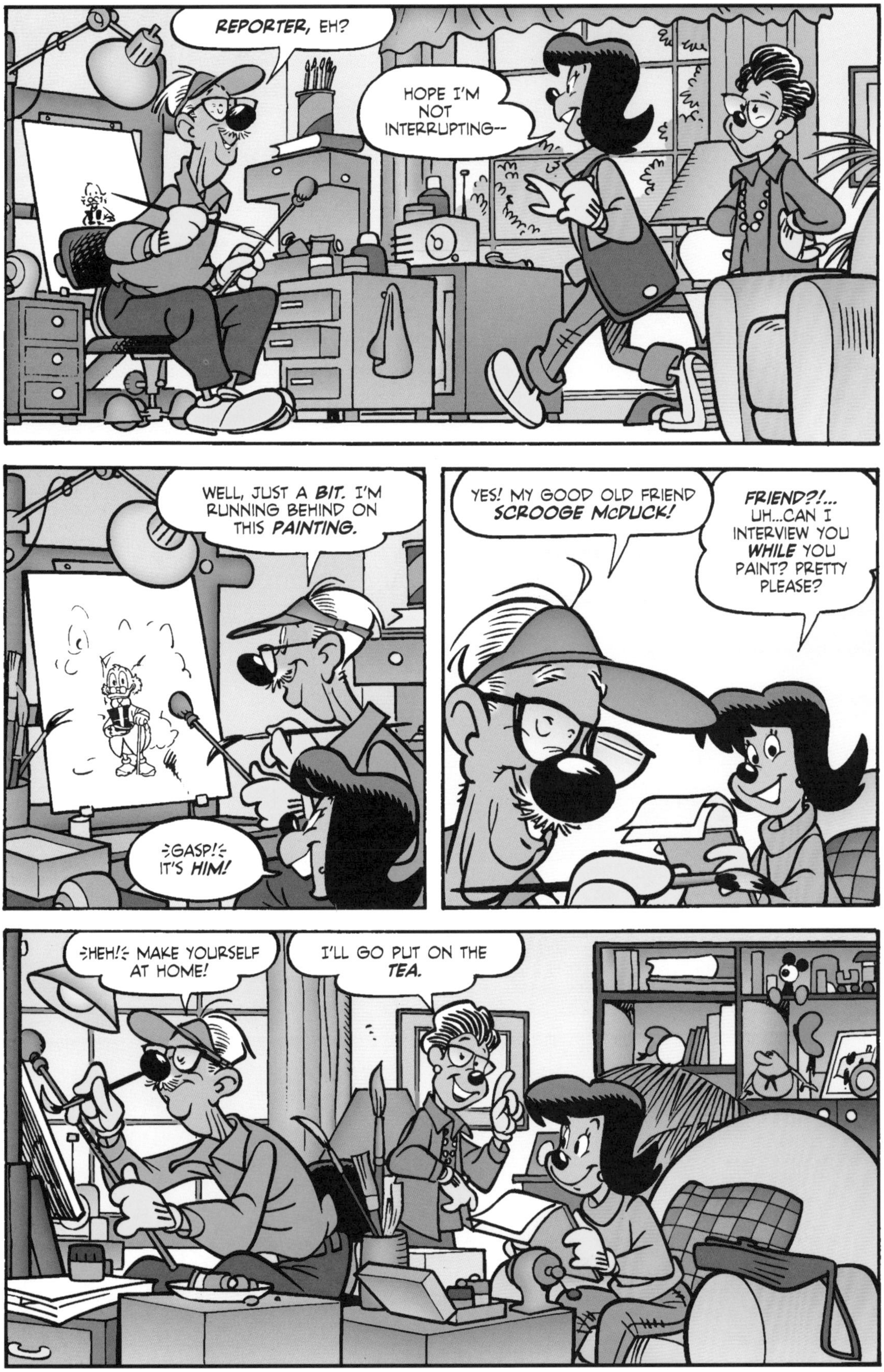
REPORTER, EH?
HOPE I'M NOT INTERRUPTING--
WELL, JUST A BIT. I'M RUNNING BEHIND ON THIS PAINTING.
GASP! IT'S HIM!
YES! MY GOOD OLD FRIEND SCROOGE McDUCK!
FRIEND?!... UH...CAN I INTERVIEW YOU WHILE YOU PAINT? PRETTY PLEASE?
HEH! MAKE YOURSELF AT HOME!
I'LL GO PUT ON THE TEA.

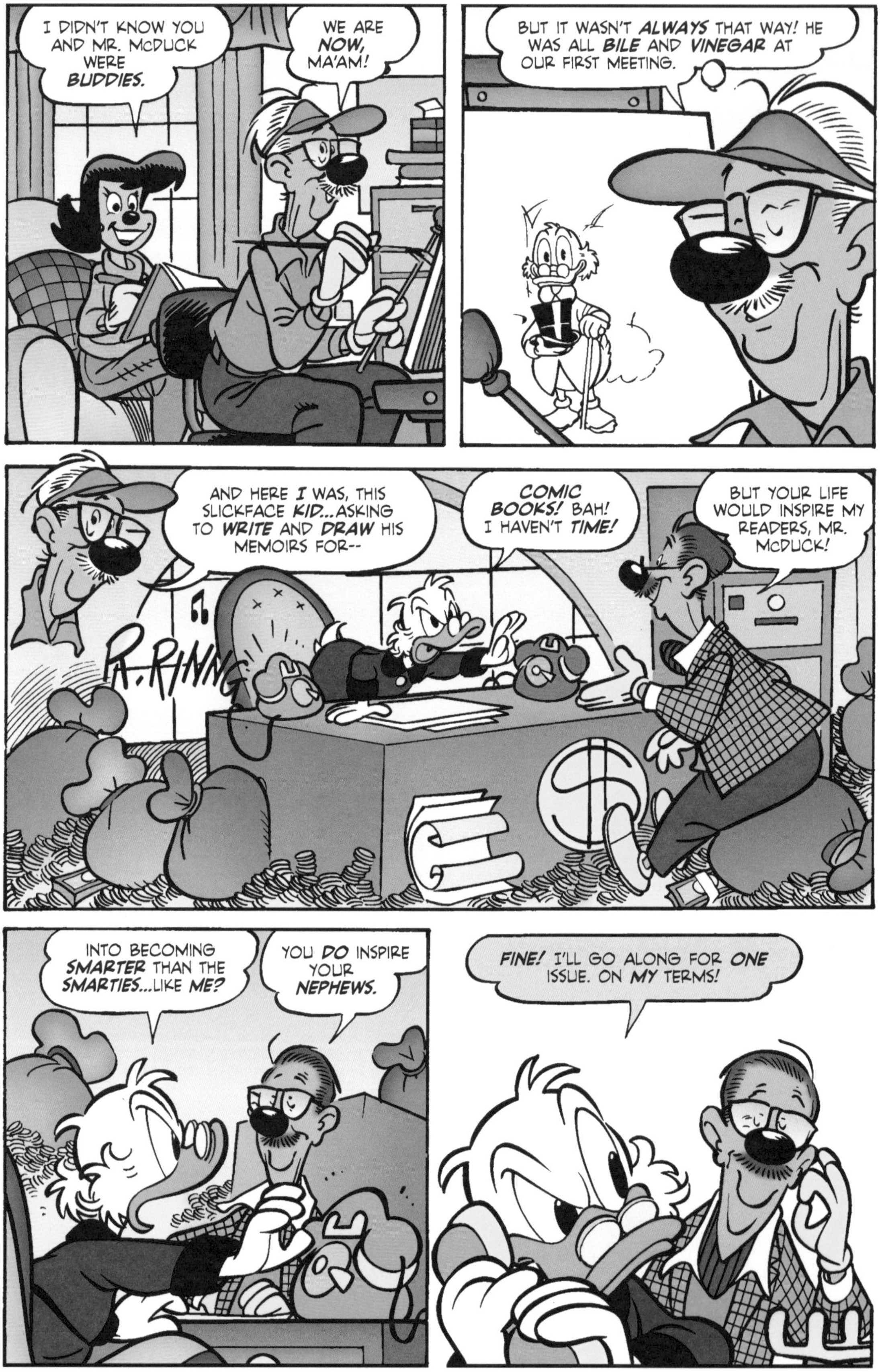

I DIDN'T KNOW YOU AND MR. McDUCK WERE BUDDIES.
WE ARE NOW, MA'AM!
BUT IT WASN'T ALWAYS THAT WAY! HE WAS ALL BILE AND VINEGAR AT OUR FIRST MEETING.
AND HERE I WAS, THIS SLICKFACE KID...ASKING TO WRITE AND DRAW HIS MEMOIRS FOR--
COMIC BOOKS! BAH! I HAVEN'T TIME!
BUT YOUR LIFE WOULD INSPIRE MY READERS, MR. McDUCK!
R-RINNG
INTO BECOMING SMARTER THAN THE SMARTIES...LIKE ME?
YOU DO INSPIRE YOUR NEPHEWS.
FINE! I'LL GO ALONG FOR ONE ISSUE. ON MY TERMS!

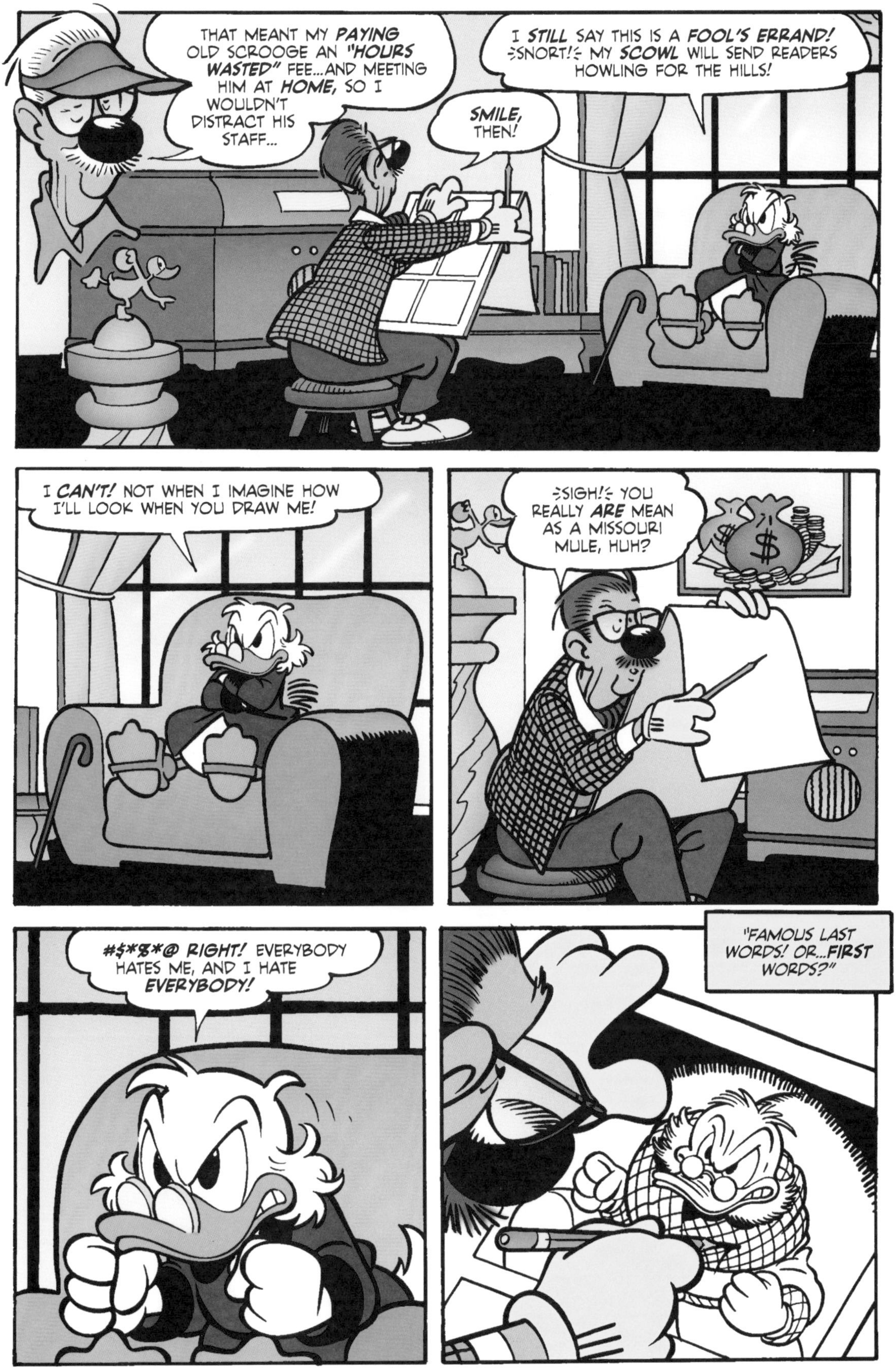

THAT MEANT MY PAYING OLD SCROOGE AN "HOURS WASTED" FEE...AND MEETING HIM AT HOME, SO I WOULDN'T DISTRACT HIS STAFF...
I STILL SAY THIS IS A FOOL'S ERRAND! ≈SNORT!≈ MY SCOWL WILL SEND READERS HOWLING FOR THE HILLS!
SMILE, THEN!
I CAN'T! NOT WHEN I IMAGINE HOW I'LL LOOK WHEN YOU DRAW ME!
≈SIGH!≈ YOU REALLY ARE MEAN AS A MISSOURI MULE, HUH?
$
#$*&*@ RIGHT! EVERYBODY HATES ME, AND I HATE EVERYBODY!
"FAMOUS LAST WORDS! OR...FIRST WORDS?"

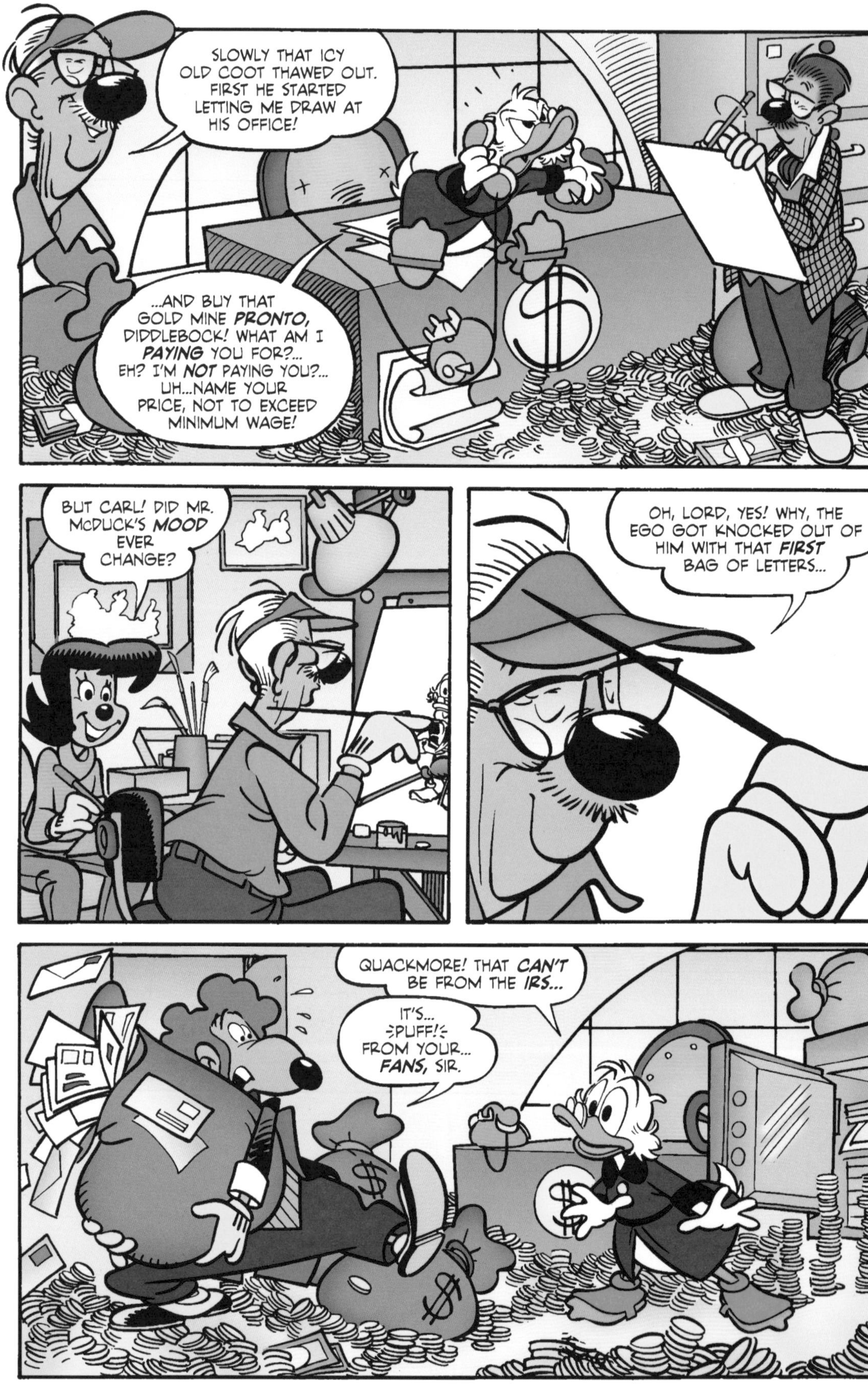
SLOWLY THAT ICY OLD COOT THAWED OUT. FIRST HE STARTED LETTING ME DRAW AT HIS OFFICE!
...AND BUY THAT GOLD MINE **PRONTO,** DIDDLEBOCK! WHAT AM I **PAYING** YOU FOR?... EH? I'M **NOT** PAYING YOU?... UH...NAME YOUR PRICE, NOT TO EXCEED MINIMUM WAGE!
BUT CARL! DID MR. McDUCK'S **MOOD** EVER CHANGE?
OH, LORD, YES! WHY, THE EGO GOT KNOCKED OUT OF HIM WITH THAT **FIRST** BAG OF LETTERS...
QUACKMORE! THAT **CAN'T** BE FROM THE **IRS...**
IT'S... PUFF! FROM YOUR... **FANS,** SIR.

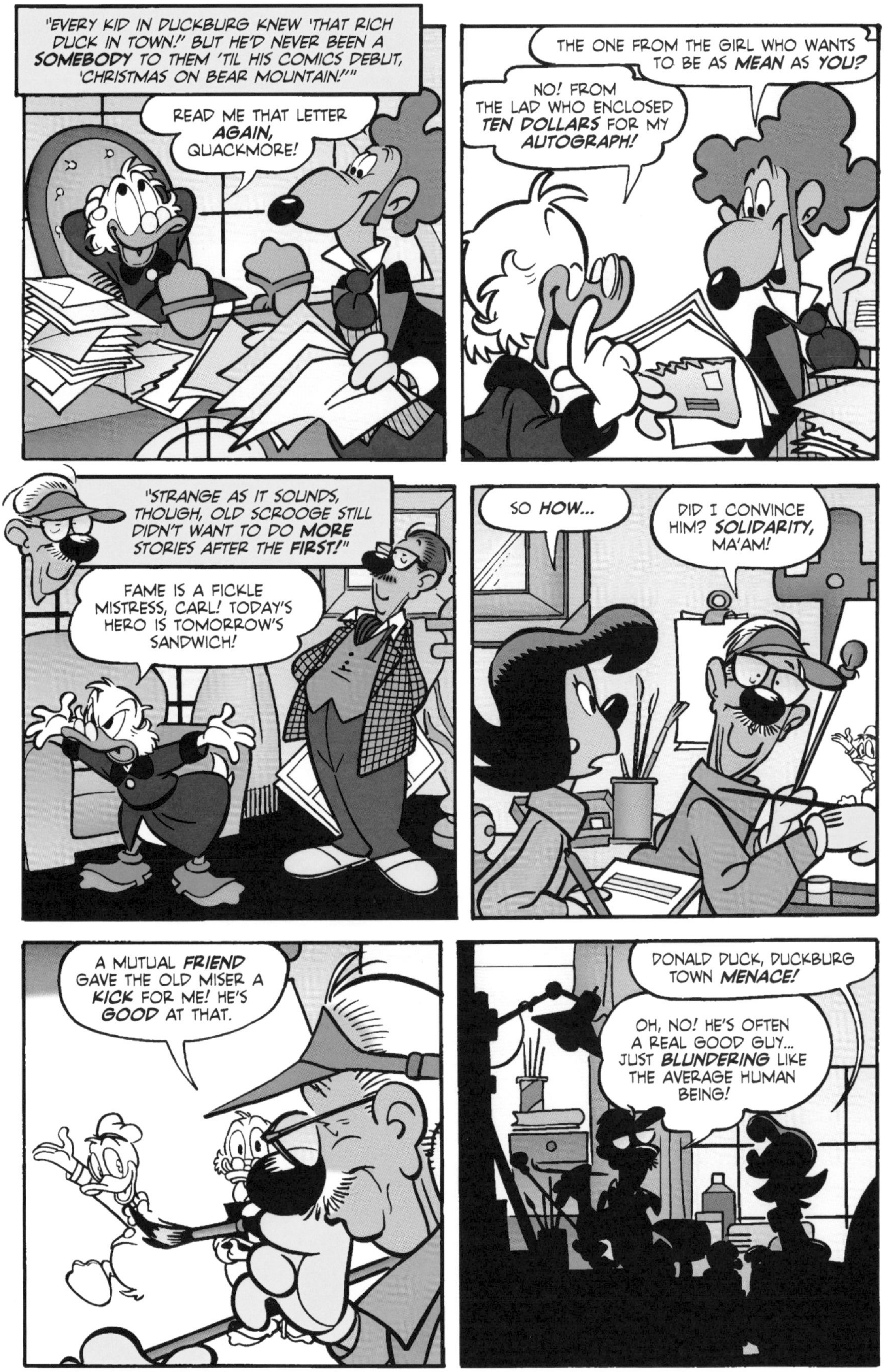
"EVERY KID IN DUCKBURG KNEW 'THAT RICH DUCK IN TOWN!' BUT HE'D NEVER BEEN A **SOMEBODY** TO THEM 'TIL HIS COMICS DEBUT, 'CHRISTMAS ON BEAR MOUNTAIN!'"
READ ME THAT LETTER **AGAIN,** QUACKMORE!
THE ONE FROM THE GIRL WHO WANTS TO BE AS **MEAN** AS **YOU?**
NO! FROM THE LAD WHO ENCLOSED **TEN DOLLARS** FOR MY **AUTOGRAPH!**
"STRANGE AS IT SOUNDS, THOUGH, OLD SCROOGE STILL DIDN'T WANT TO DO **MORE** STORIES AFTER THE **FIRST!**"
FAME IS A FICKLE MISTRESS, CARL! TODAY'S HERO IS TOMORROW'S SANDWICH!
SO **HOW...**
DID I CONVINCE HIM? **SOLIDARITY,** MA'AM!
A MUTUAL **FRIEND** GAVE THE OLD MISER A **KICK** FOR ME! HE'S **GOOD** AT THAT.
DONALD DUCK, DUCKBURG TOWN **MENACE!**
OH, NO! HE'S OFTEN A REAL GOOD GUY... JUST **BLUNDERING** LIKE THE AVERAGE HUMAN BEING!

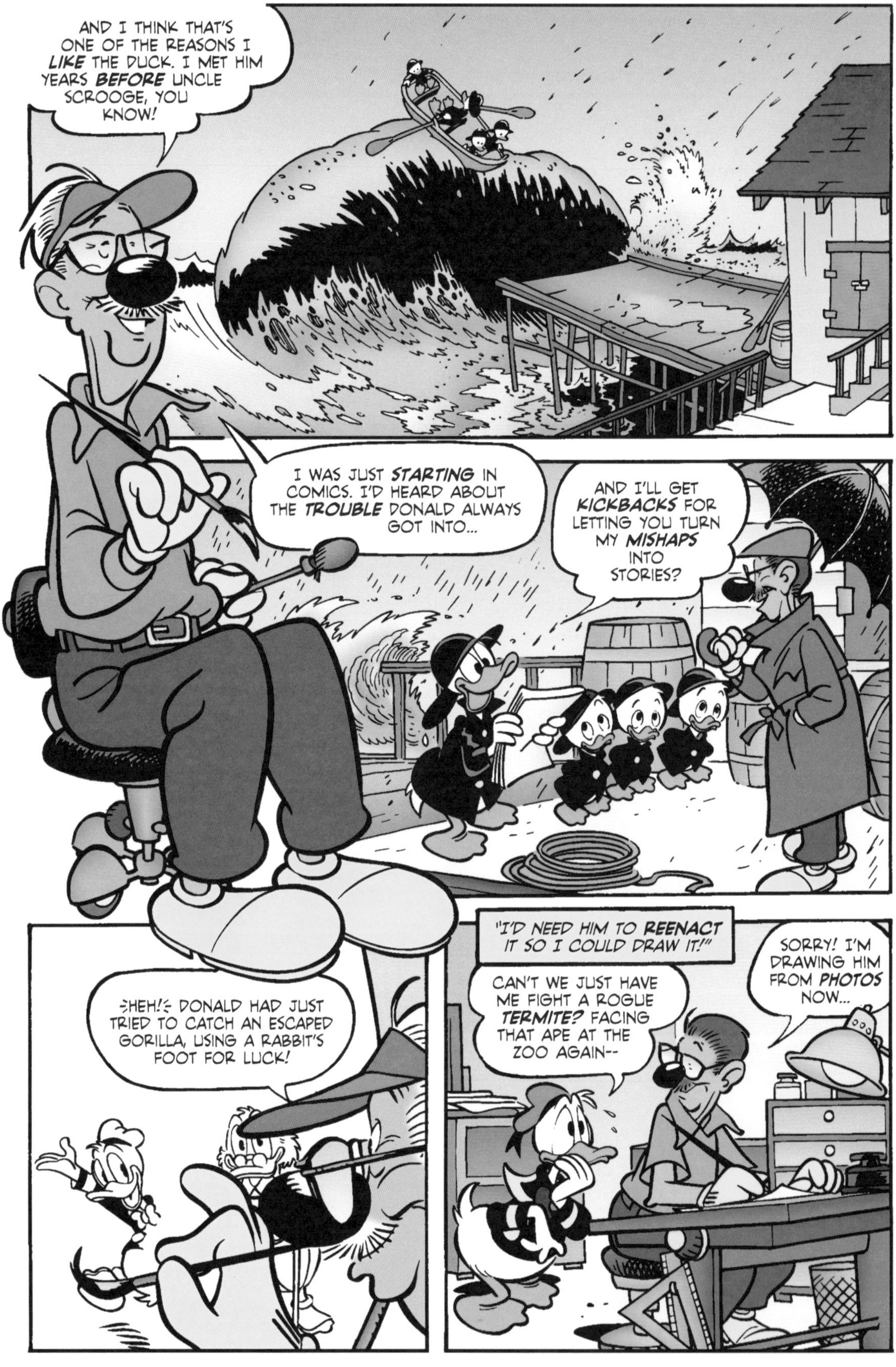
AND I THINK THAT'S ONE OF THE REASONS I LIKE THE DUCK. I MET HIM YEARS BEFORE UNCLE SCROOGE, YOU KNOW!
I WAS JUST STARTING IN COMICS. I'D HEARD ABOUT THE TROUBLE DONALD ALWAYS GOT INTO...
AND I'LL GET KICKBACKS FOR LETTING YOU TURN MY MISHAPS INTO STORIES?
HEH! DONALD HAD JUST TRIED TO CATCH AN ESCAPED GORILLA, USING A RABBIT'S FOOT FOR LUCK!
"I'D NEED HIM TO REENACT IT SO I COULD DRAW IT!"
CAN'T WE JUST HAVE ME FIGHT A ROGUE TERMITE? FACING THAT APE AT THE ZOO AGAIN--
SORRY! I'M DRAWING HIM FROM PHOTOS NOW...

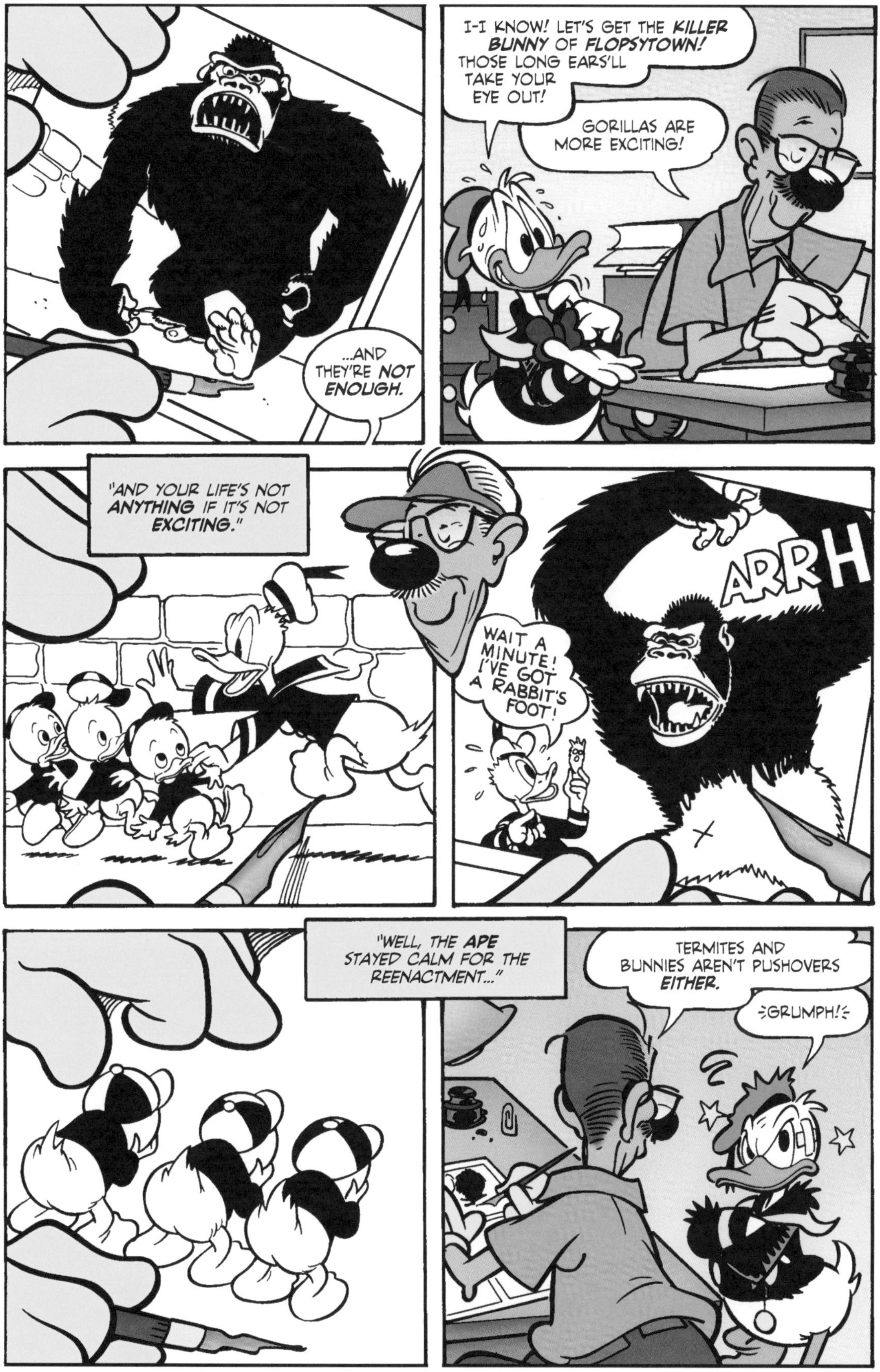
...AND THEY'RE NOT ENOUGH.
I-I KNOW! LET'S GET THE KILLER BUNNY OF FLOPSYTOWN! THOSE LONG EARS'LL TAKE YOUR EYE OUT!
GORILLAS ARE MORE EXCITING!
"AND YOUR LIFE'S NOT ANYTHING IF IT'S NOT EXCITING."
ARRH
WAIT A MINUTE! I'VE GOT A RABBIT'S FOOT!
"WELL, THE APE STAYED CALM FOR THE REENACTMENT..."
TERMITES AND BUNNIES AREN'T PUSHOVERS EITHER.
GRUMPH!

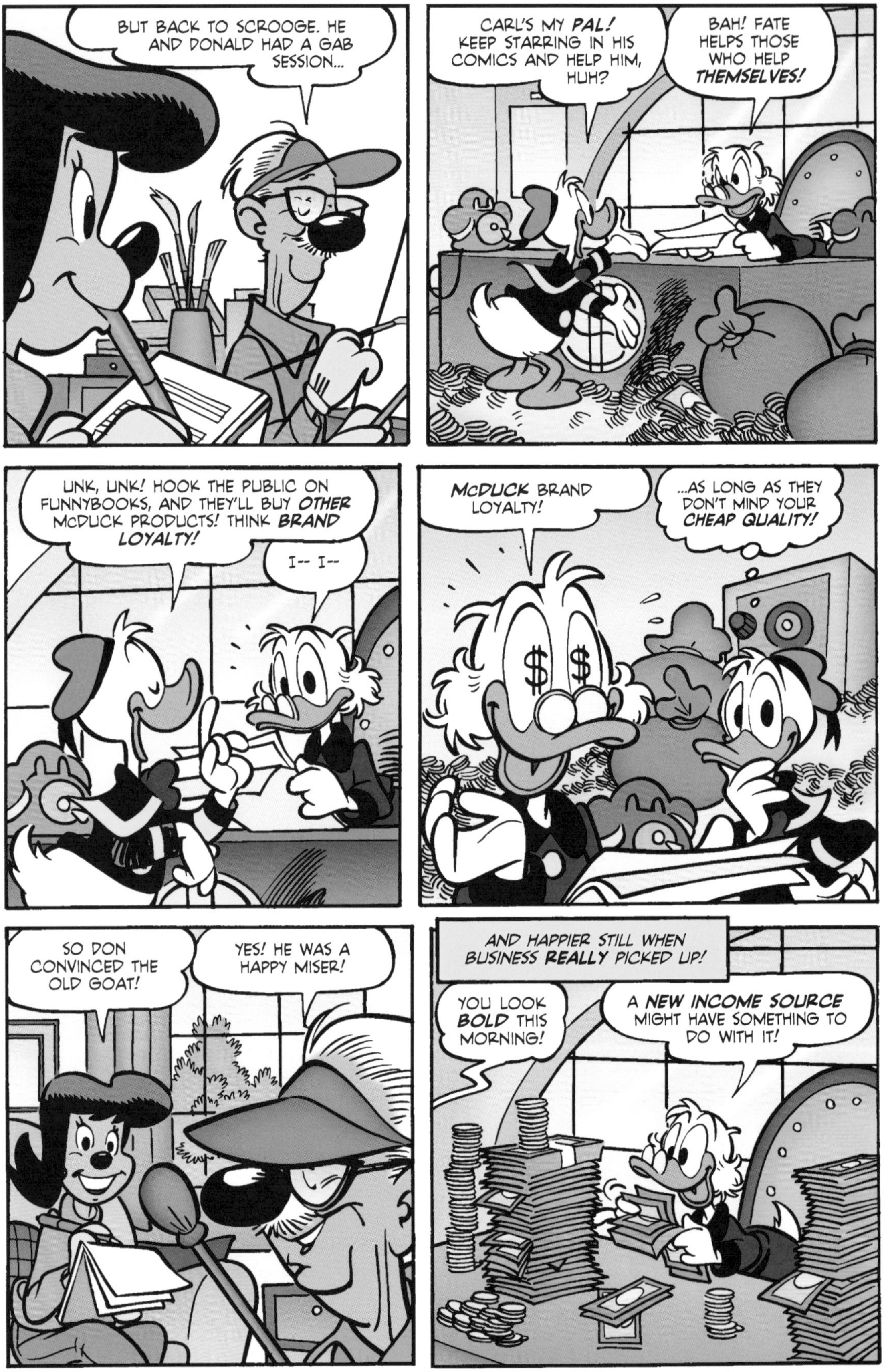
BUT BACK TO SCROOGE. HE AND DONALD HAD A GAB SESSION...
CARL'S MY PAL! KEEP STARRING IN HIS COMICS AND HELP HIM, HUH?
BAH! FATE HELPS THOSE WHO HELP THEMSELVES!
UNK, UNK! HOOK THE PUBLIC ON FUNNYBOOKS, AND THEY'LL BUY OTHER McDUCK PRODUCTS! THINK BRAND LOYALTY!
I-- I--
McDUCK BRAND LOYALTY!
...AS LONG AS THEY DON'T MIND YOUR CHEAP QUALITY!
SO DON CONVINCED THE OLD GOAT!
YES! HE WAS A HAPPY MISER!
AND HAPPIER STILL WHEN BUSINESS REALLY PICKED UP!
YOU LOOK BOLD THIS MORNING!
A NEW INCOME SOURCE MIGHT HAVE SOMETHING TO DO WITH IT!

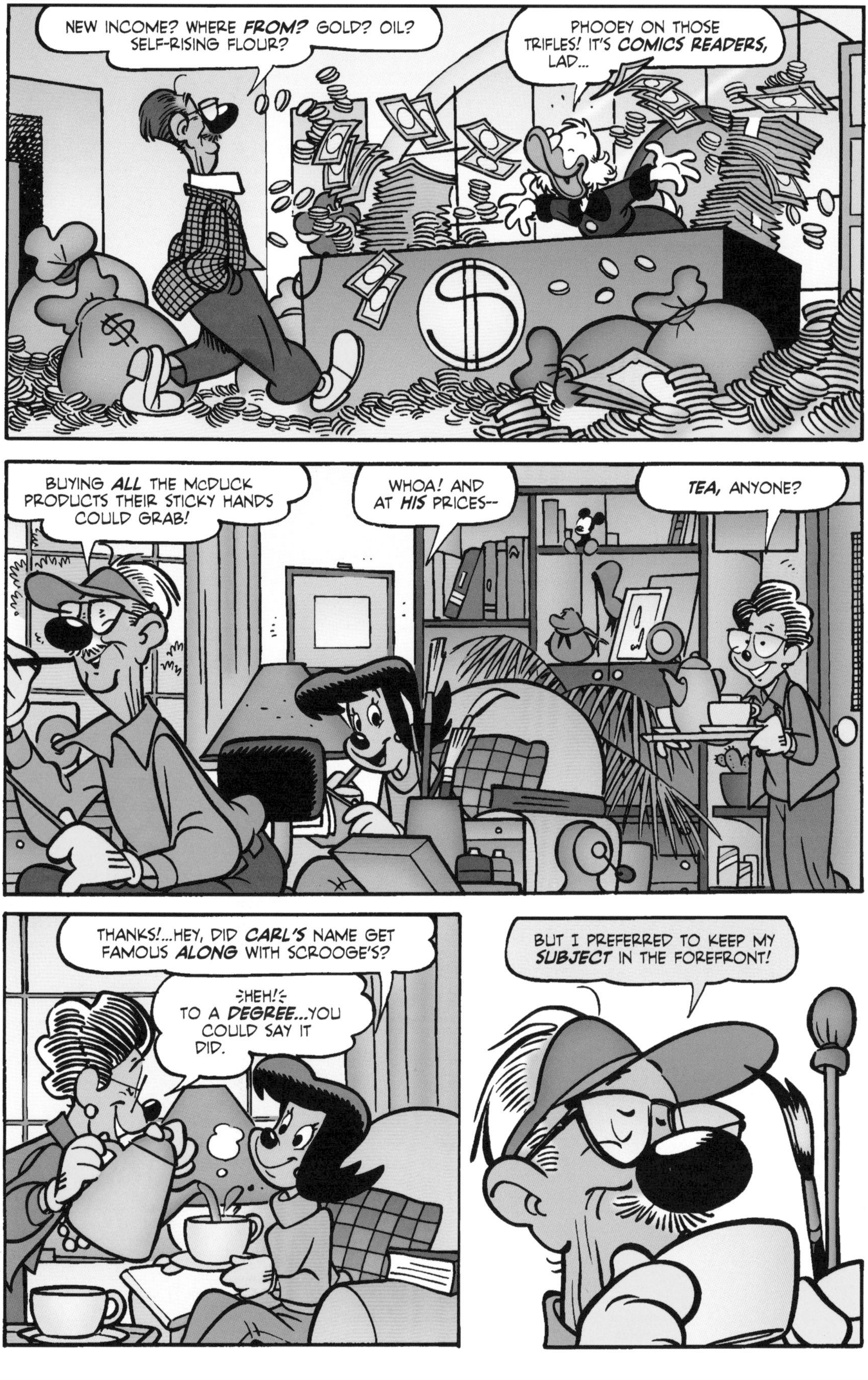
NEW INCOME? WHERE FROM? GOLD? OIL? SELF-RISING FLOUR?
PHOOEY ON THOSE TRIFLES! IT'S COMICS READERS, LAD...
BUYING ALL THE McDUCK PRODUCTS THEIR STICKY HANDS COULD GRAB!
WHOA! AND AT HIS PRICES--
TEA, ANYONE?
THANKS!...HEY, DID CARL'S NAME GET FAMOUS ALONG WITH SCROOGE'S?
HEH! TO A DEGREE...YOU COULD SAY IT DID.
BUT I PREFERRED TO KEEP MY SUBJECT IN THE FOREFRONT!

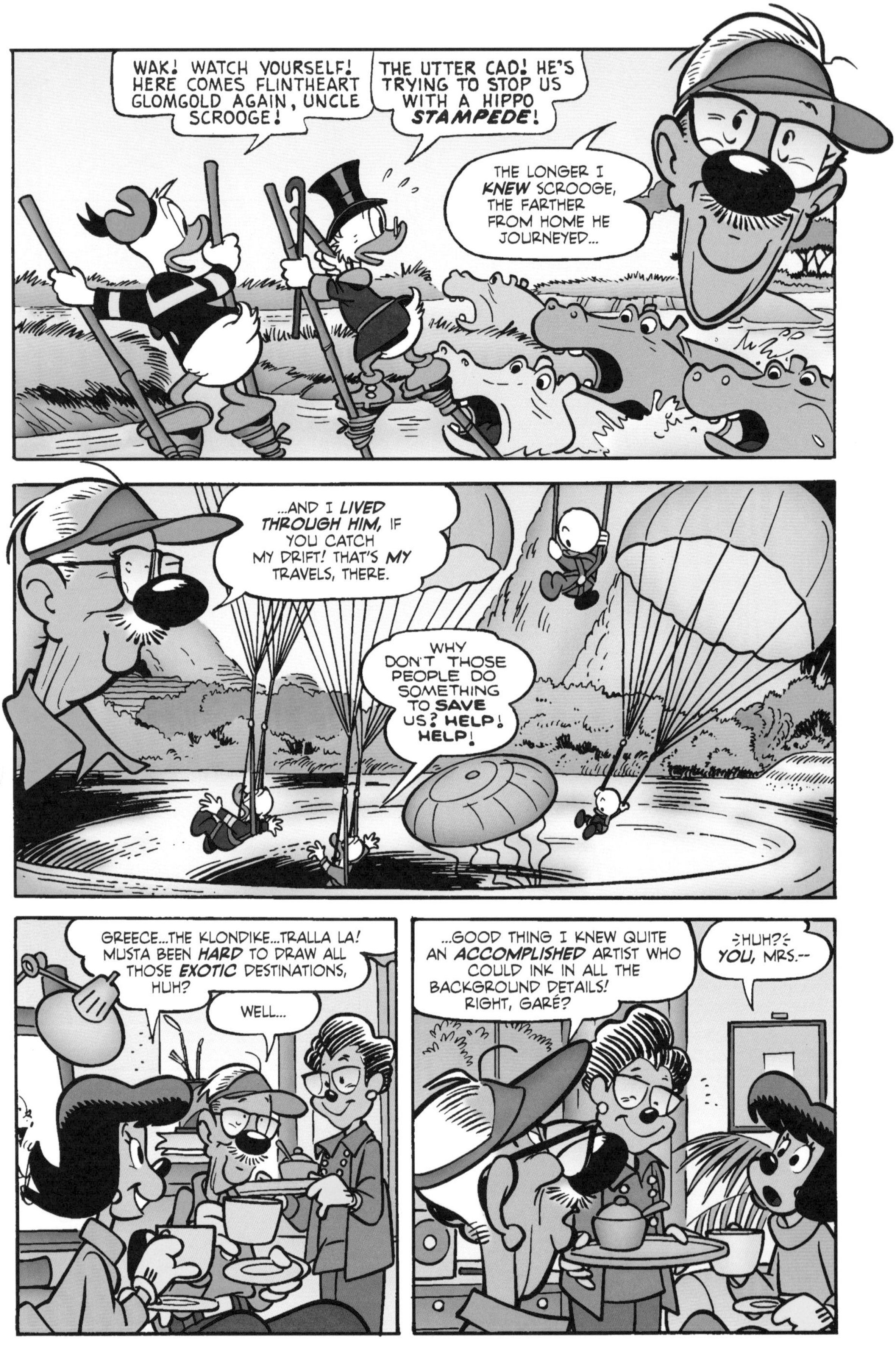
WAK! WATCH YOURSELF! HERE COMES FLINTHEART GLOMGOLD AGAIN, UNCLE SCROOGE!
THE UTTER CAD! HE'S TRYING TO STOP US WITH A HIPPO STAMPEDE!
THE LONGER I KNEW SCROOGE, THE FARTHER FROM HOME HE JOURNEYED...
...AND I LIVED THROUGH HIM, IF YOU CATCH MY DRIFT! THAT'S MY TRAVELS, THERE.
WHY DON'T THOSE PEOPLE DO SOMETHING TO SAVE US? HELP! HELP!
GREECE...THE KLONDIKE...TRALLA LA! MUSTA BEEN HARD TO DRAW ALL THOSE EXOTIC DESTINATIONS, HUH?
WELL...
...GOOD THING I KNEW QUITE AN ACCOMPLISHED ARTIST WHO COULD INK IN ALL THE BACKGROUND DETAILS! RIGHT, GARÉ?
HUH? YOU, MRS.--

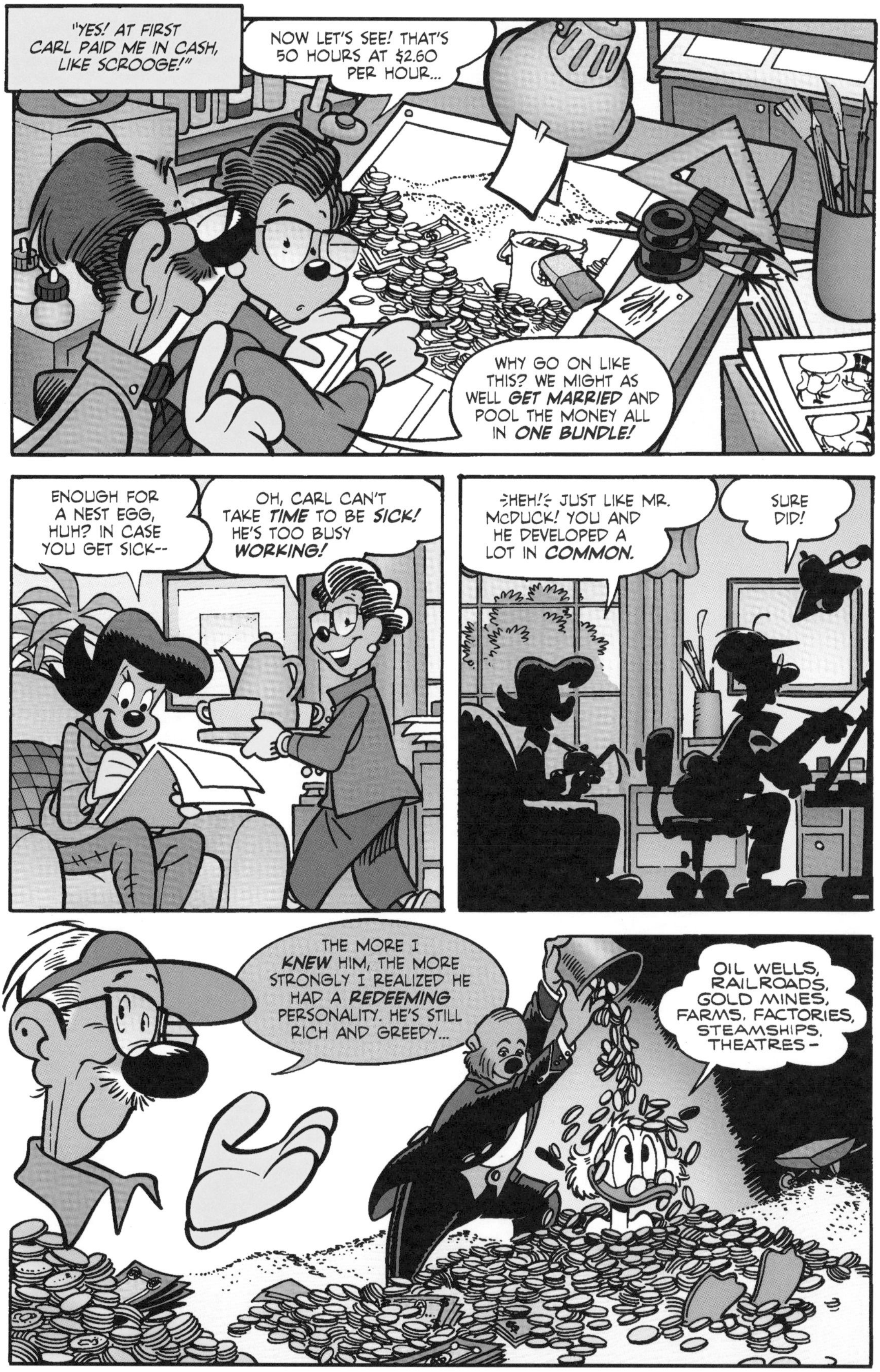
"YES! AT FIRST CARL PAID ME IN CASH, LIKE SCROOGE!"
NOW LET'S SEE! THAT'S 50 HOURS AT $2.60 PER HOUR...
WHY GO ON LIKE THIS? WE MIGHT AS WELL GET MARRIED AND POOL THE MONEY ALL IN ONE BUNDLE!
ENOUGH FOR A NEST EGG, HUH? IN CASE YOU GET SICK--
OH, CARL CAN'T TAKE TIME TO BE SICK! HE'S TOO BUSY WORKING!
HEH! JUST LIKE MR. McDUCK! YOU AND HE DEVELOPED A LOT IN COMMON.
SURE DID!
THE MORE I KNEW HIM, THE MORE STRONGLY I REALIZED HE HAD A REDEEMING PERSONALITY. HE'S STILL RICH AND GREEDY...
OIL WELLS, RAILROADS, GOLD MINES, FARMS, FACTORIES, STEAMSHIPS, THEATRES–

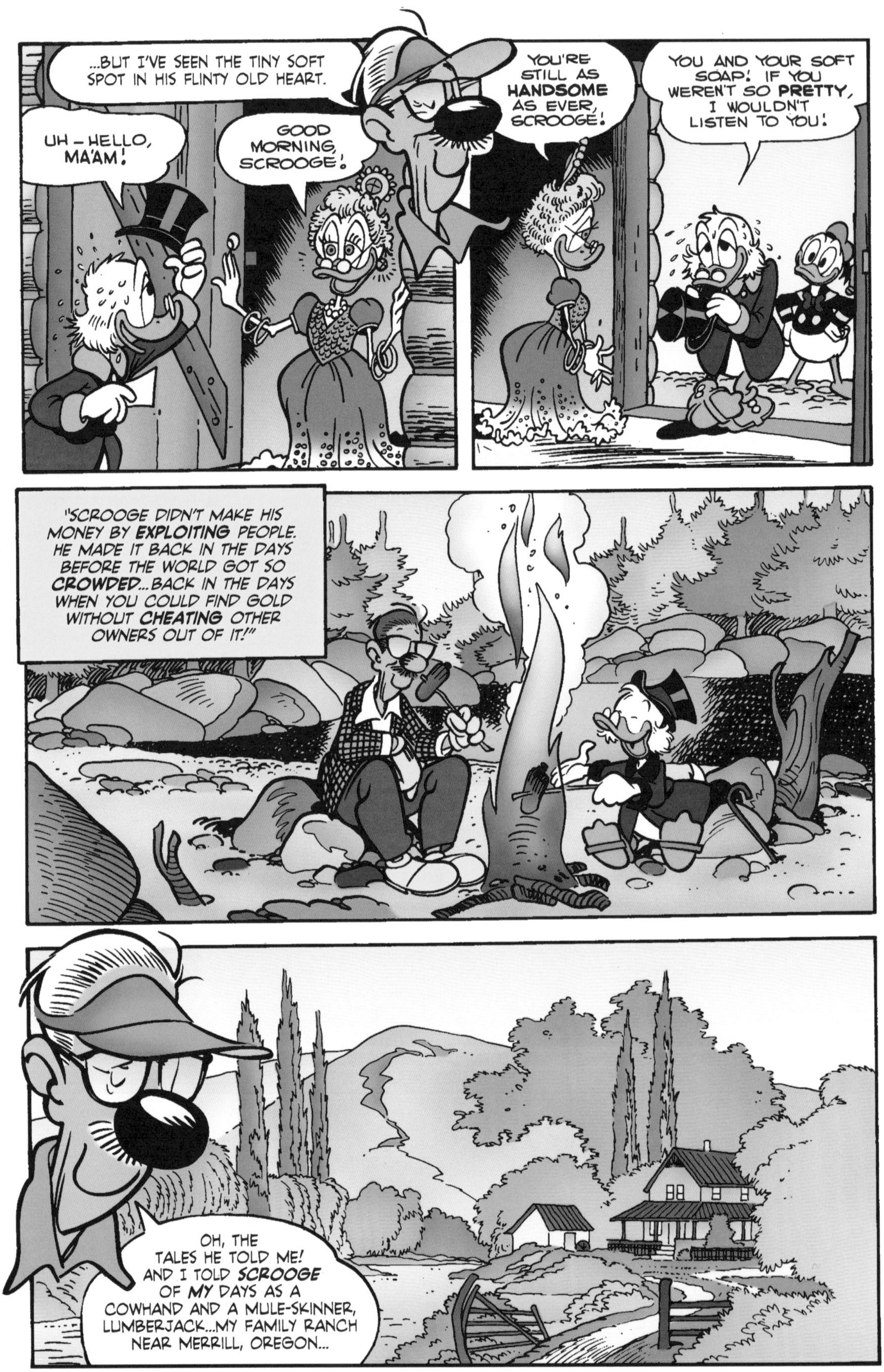
...BUT I'VE SEEN THE TINY SOFT SPOT IN HIS FLINTY OLD HEART.
UH – HELLO, MA'AM!
GOOD MORNING, SCROOGE!
YOU'RE STILL AS HANDSOME AS EVER, SCROOGE!
YOU AND YOUR SOFT SOAP! IF YOU WEREN'T SO PRETTY, I WOULDN'T LISTEN TO YOU!
"SCROOGE DIDN'T MAKE HIS MONEY BY EXPLOITING PEOPLE. HE MADE IT BACK IN THE DAYS BEFORE THE WORLD GOT SO CROWDED...BACK IN THE DAYS WHEN YOU COULD FIND GOLD WITHOUT CHEATING OTHER OWNERS OUT OF IT!"
OH, THE TALES HE TOLD ME! AND I TOLD SCROOGE OF MY DAYS AS A COWHAND AND A MULE-SKINNER, LUMBERJACK...MY FAMILY RANCH NEAR MERRILL, OREGON...

"AND HOW I DECIDED I COULD SELL GAG CARTOONS TO MAGAZINES! SURPRISINGLY, THEY *SOLD!*"

SOUNDS MORE *PROFITABLE* THAN MULE-SKINNING...ESPECIALLY FOR THE MULE!

NOPE! WAGES WERE GETTING SMALLER BY THE HOUR!

"I WAS REDUCED TO EATING *FIG BARS*. THEN I READ THAT *DISNEY'S* WAS LOOKING FOR CARTOONISTS. TWENTY DOLLARS A WEEK! SO I *DID* IT...I WENT OUT THERE ON A WILD GAMBLE THAT I COULD MAKE IT! FIRST AS AN ANIMATOR, THEN AS A STORY MAN..."

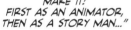

IF YOU COULD JUST *COME TO LIFE,* THIS WOULD BE *SO* MUCH EASIER!

"SINUS TROUBLE FORCED ME TO LEAVE THE STUDIO, BUT THE STORYTELLING WENT ON. IN *COMICS*...AND WITH *SCROOGE!*"

NOT TO MENTION SOME *OTHER* DUCKS.

HEY! GLADSTONE GANDER, THE WORLD'S LUCKIEST *PEST!*

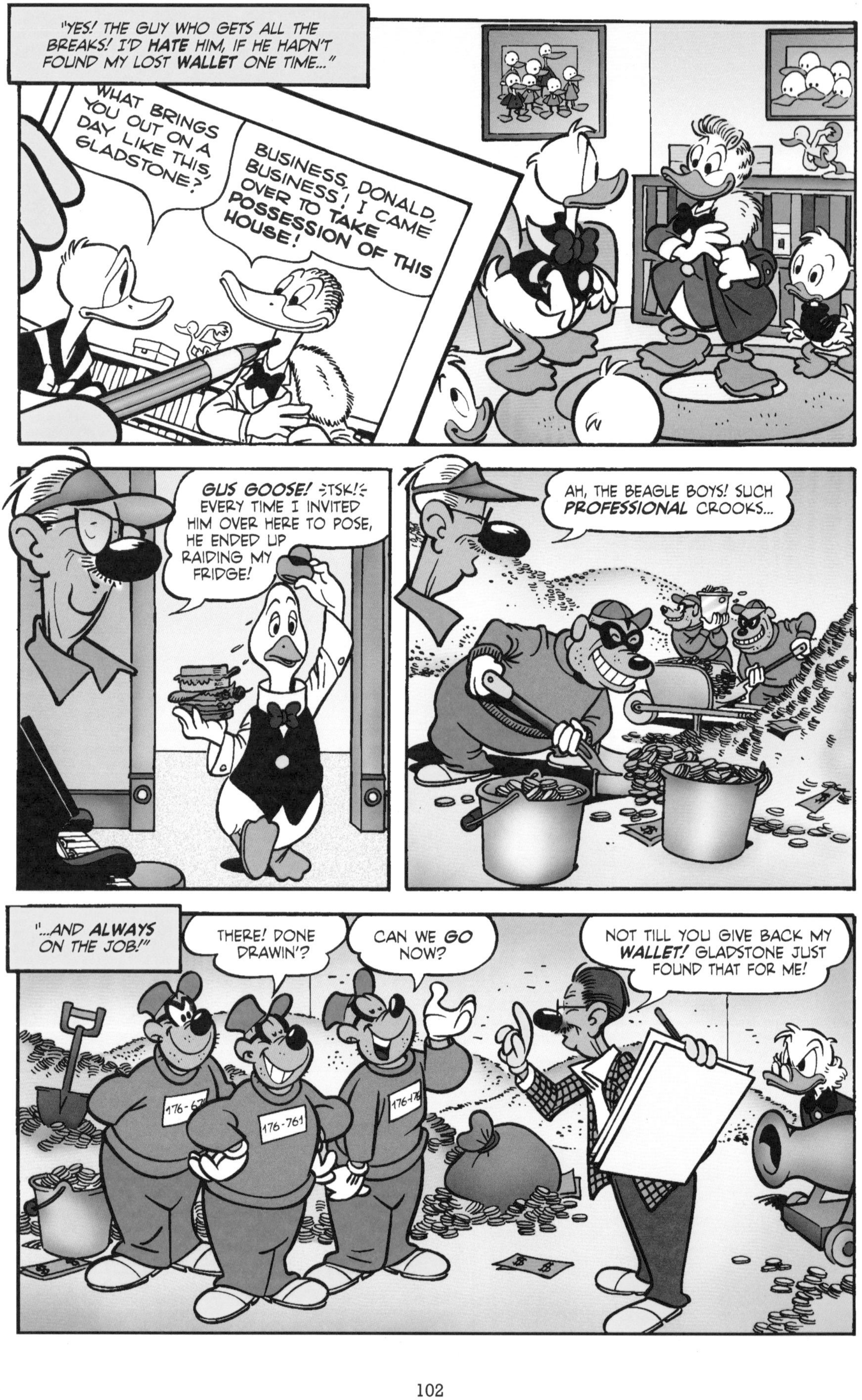

"YES! THE GUY WHO GETS ALL THE BREAKS! I'D HATE HIM, IF HE HADN'T FOUND MY LOST WALLET ONE TIME..."
WHAT BRINGS YOU OUT ON A DAY LIKE THIS, GLADSTONE?
BUSINESS, DONALD, BUSINESS! I CAME OVER TO TAKE POSSESSION OF THIS HOUSE!
GUS GOOSE! =TSK!= EVERY TIME I INVITED HIM OVER HERE TO POSE, HE ENDED UP RAIDING MY FRIDGE!
AH, THE BEAGLE BOYS! SUCH PROFESSIONAL CROOKS...
"...AND ALWAYS ON THE JOB!"
THERE! DONE DRAWIN'?
CAN WE GO NOW?
NOT TILL YOU GIVE BACK MY WALLET! GLADSTONE JUST FOUND THAT FOR ME!
176-761

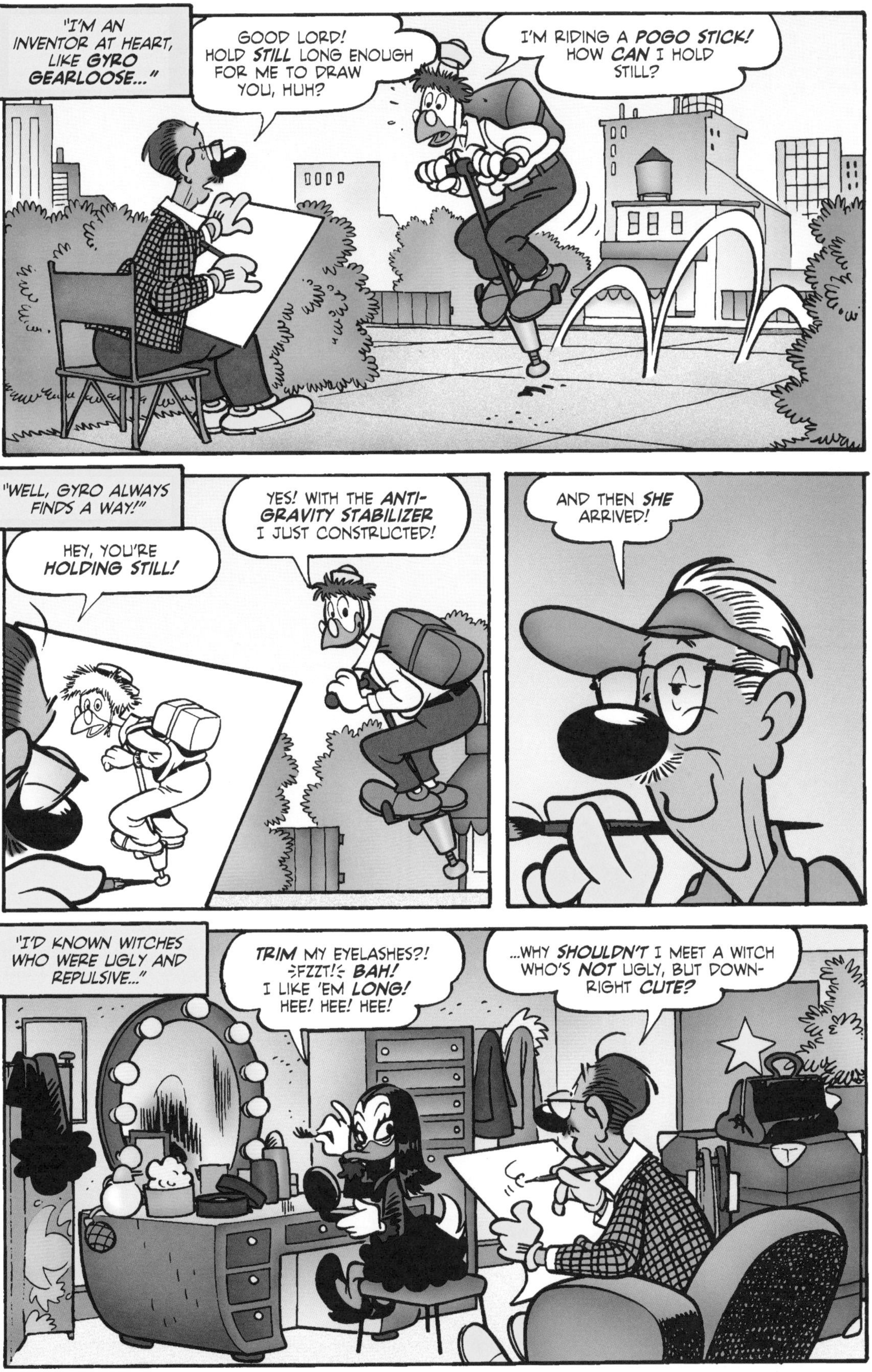
"I'M AN INVENTOR AT HEART, LIKE GYRO GEARLOOSE..."
GOOD LORD! HOLD STILL LONG ENOUGH FOR ME TO DRAW YOU, HUH?
I'M RIDING A POGO STICK! HOW CAN I HOLD STILL?
"WELL, GYRO ALWAYS FINDS A WAY!"
HEY, YOU'RE HOLDING STILL!
YES! WITH THE ANTI-GRAVITY STABILIZER I JUST CONSTRUCTED!
AND THEN SHE ARRIVED!
"I'D KNOWN WITCHES WHO WERE UGLY AND REPULSIVE..."
TRIM MY EYELASHES?! FZZT! BAH! I LIKE 'EM LONG! HEE! HEE! HEE!
...WHY SHOULDN'T I MEET A WITCH WHO'S NOT UGLY, BUT DOWN-RIGHT CUTE?

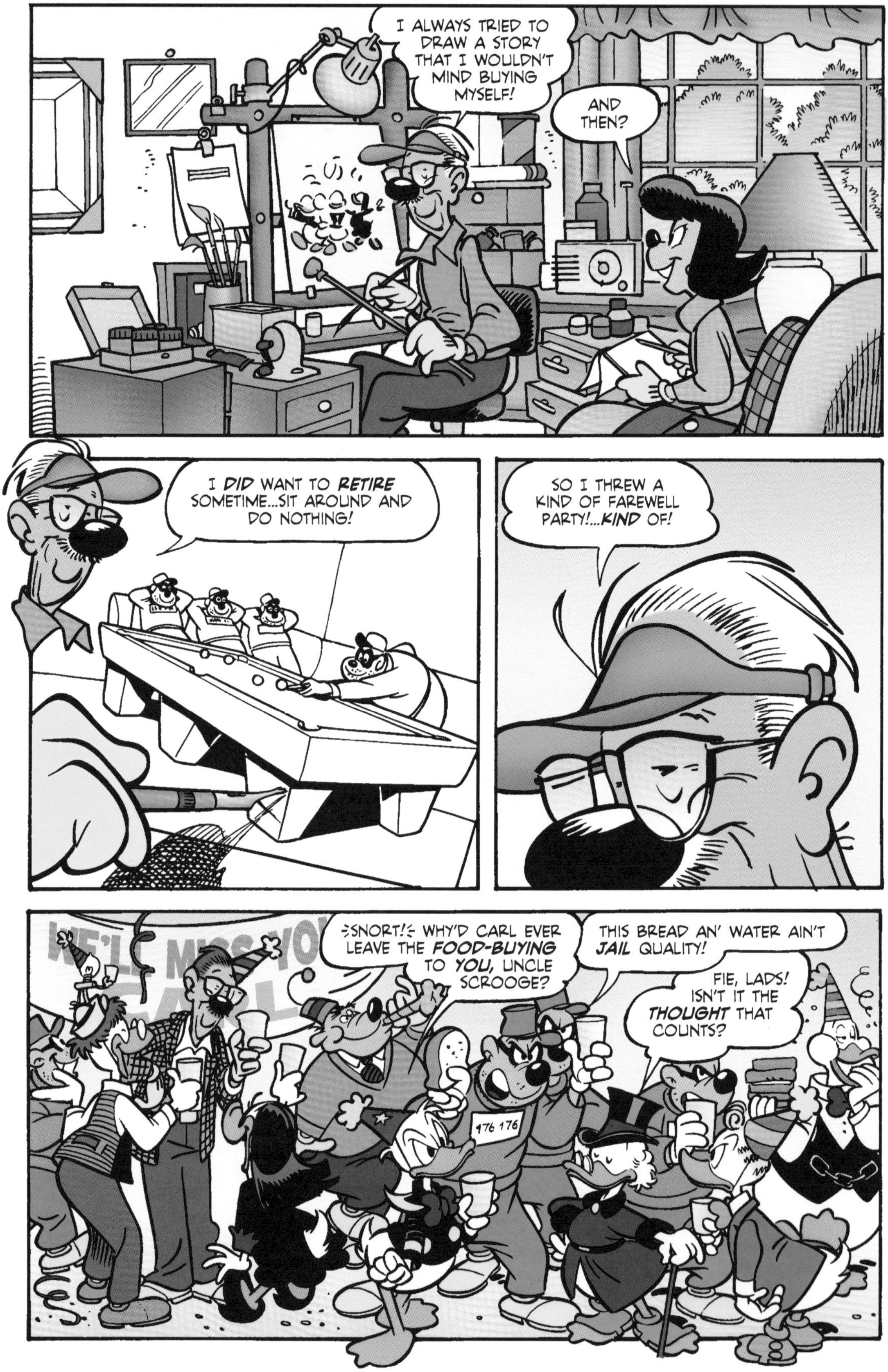
I ALWAYS TRIED TO DRAW A STORY THAT I WOULDN'T MIND BUYING MYSELF!
AND THEN?
I DID WANT TO RETIRE SOMETIME...SIT AROUND AND DO NOTHING!
SO I THREW A KIND OF FAREWELL PARTY!...KIND OF!
SNORT! WHY'D CARL EVER LEAVE THE FOOD-BUYING TO YOU, UNCLE SCROOGE?
THIS BREAD AN' WATER AIN'T JAIL QUALITY!
FIE, LADS! ISN'T IT THE THOUGHT THAT COUNTS?
176 176

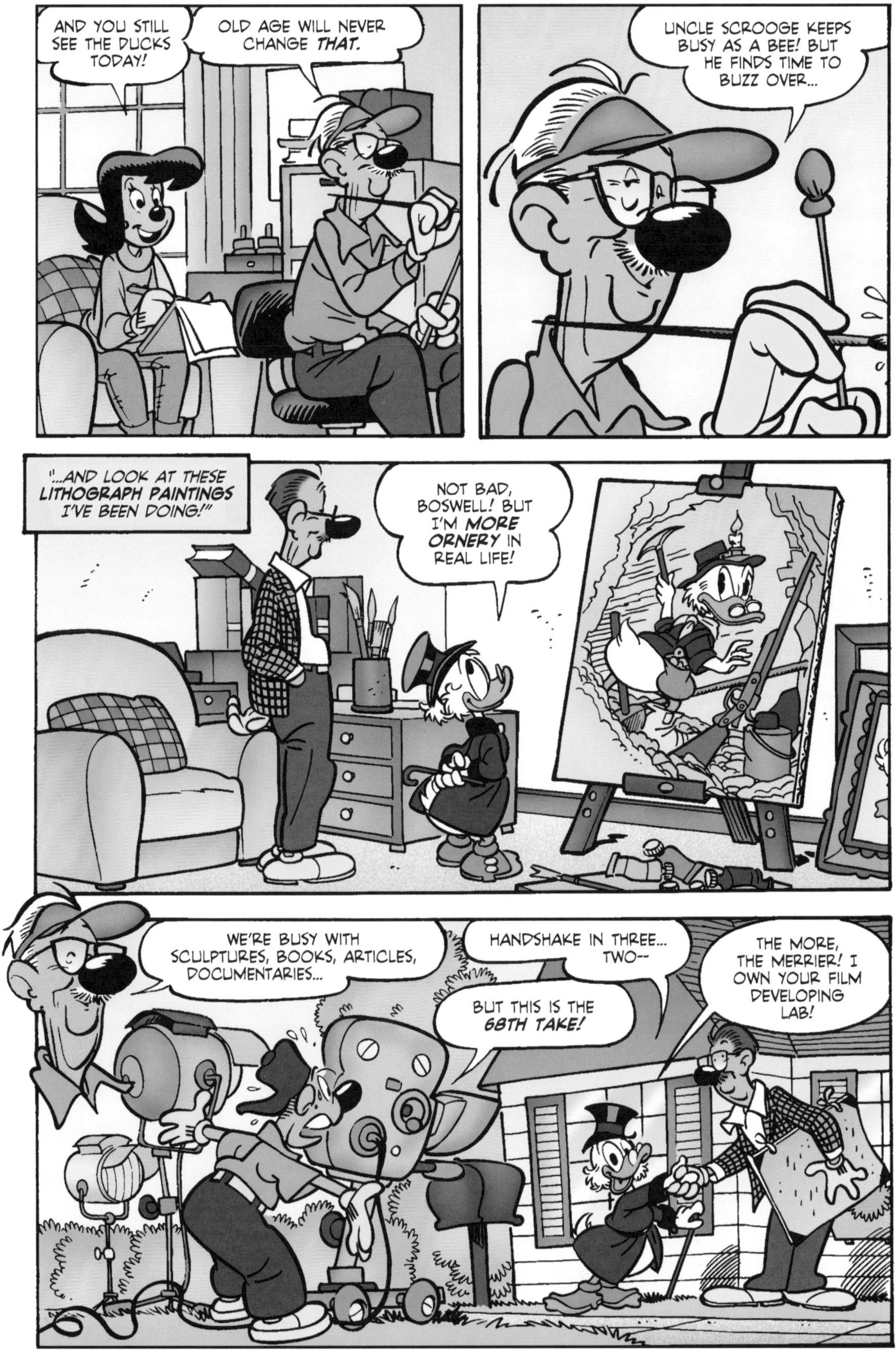

AND YOU STILL SEE THE DUCKS TODAY!
OLD AGE WILL NEVER CHANGE *THAT.*
UNCLE SCROOGE KEEPS BUSY AS A BEE! BUT HE FINDS TIME TO BUZZ OVER...
"...AND LOOK AT THESE **LITHOGRAPH PAINTINGS** I'VE BEEN DOING!"
NOT BAD, BOSWELL! BUT I'M **MORE ORNERY** IN REAL LIFE!
WE'RE BUSY WITH SCULPTURES, BOOKS, ARTICLES, DOCUMENTARIES...
HANDSHAKE IN THREE... TWO--
BUT THIS IS THE *68TH TAKE!*
THE MORE, THE MERRIER! I OWN YOUR FILM DEVELOPING LAB!

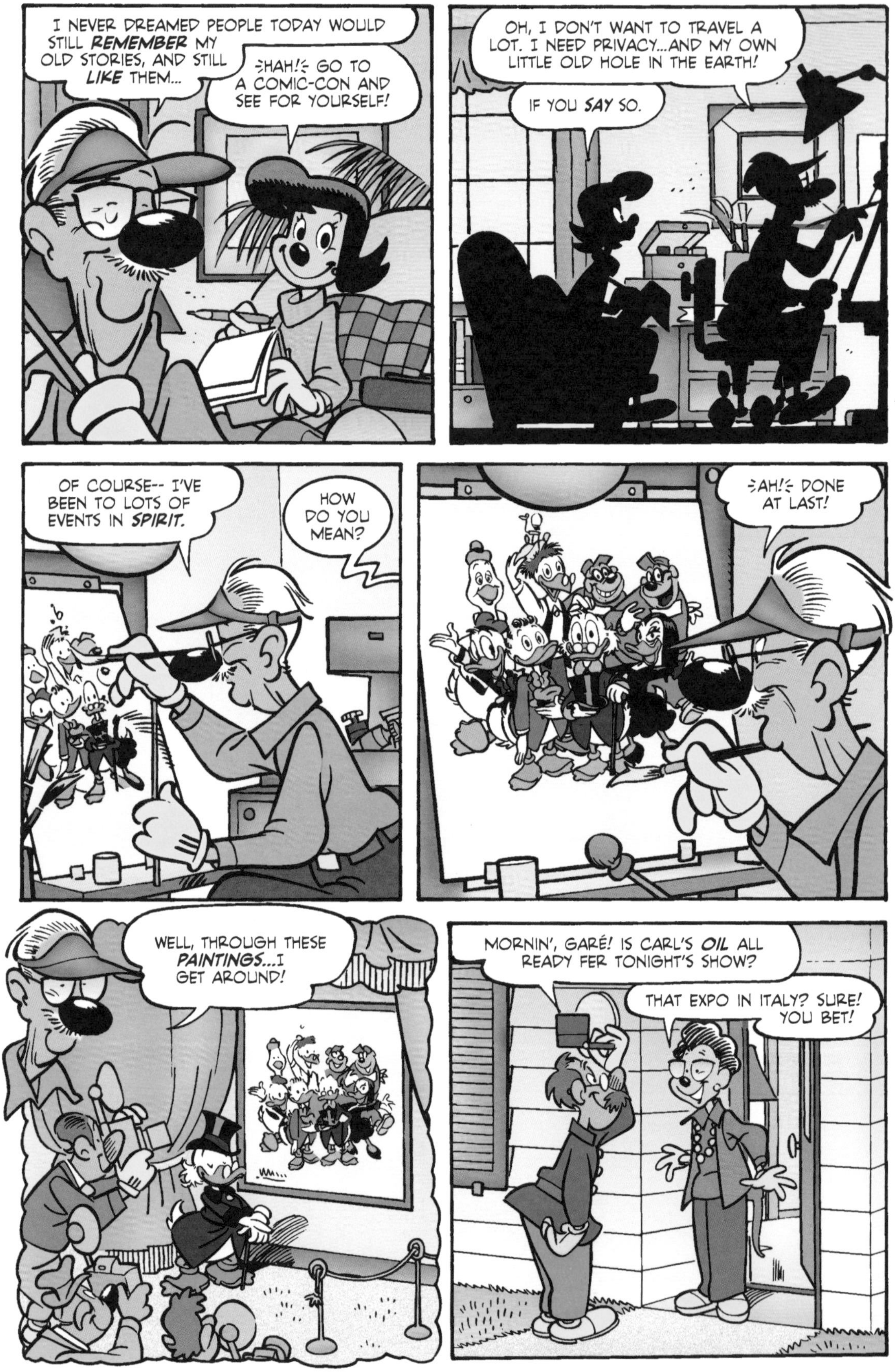
I NEVER DREAMED PEOPLE TODAY WOULD STILL REMEMBER MY OLD STORIES, AND STILL LIKE THEM...
HAH! GO TO A COMIC-CON AND SEE FOR YOURSELF!
OH, I DON'T WANT TO TRAVEL A LOT. I NEED PRIVACY...AND MY OWN LITTLE OLD HOLE IN THE EARTH!
IF YOU SAY SO.
OF COURSE-- I'VE BEEN TO LOTS OF EVENTS IN SPIRIT.
HOW DO YOU MEAN?
AH! DONE AT LAST!
WELL, THROUGH THESE PAINTINGS...I GET AROUND!
MORNIN', GARÉ! IS CARL'S OIL ALL READY FER TONIGHT'S SHOW?
THAT EXPO IN ITALY? SURE! YOU BET!

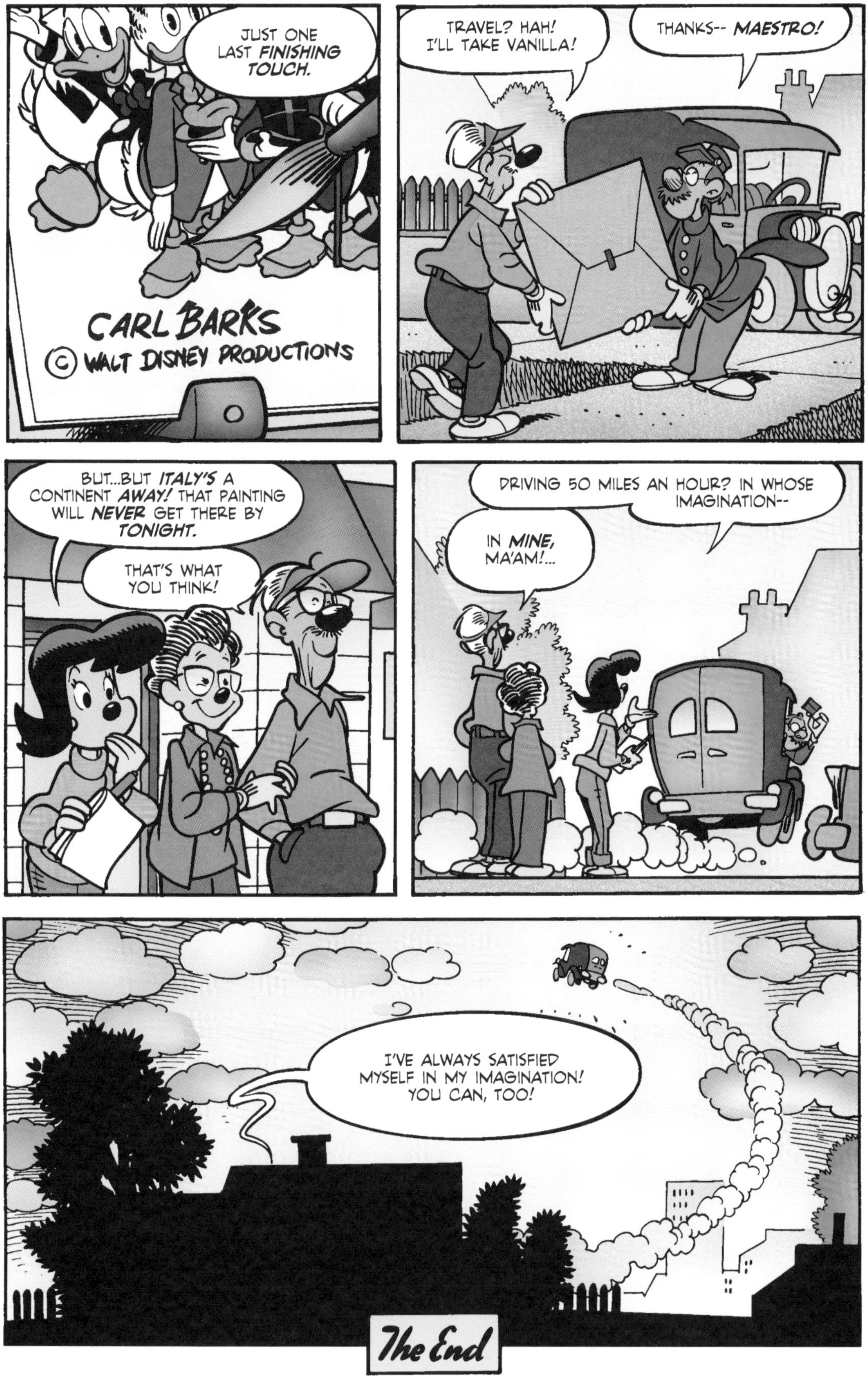
JUST ONE LAST FINISHING TOUCH.
CARL BARKS
© WALT DISNEY PRODUCTIONS
TRAVEL? HAH! I'LL TAKE VANILLA!
THANKS-- MAESTRO!
BUT...BUT ITALY'S A CONTINENT AWAY! THAT PAINTING WILL NEVER GET THERE BY TONIGHT.
THAT'S WHAT YOU THINK!
DRIVING 50 MILES AN HOUR? IN WHOSE IMAGINATION--
IN MINE, MA'AM!...
I'VE ALWAYS SATISFIED MYSELF IN MY IMAGINATION! YOU CAN, TOO!
The End

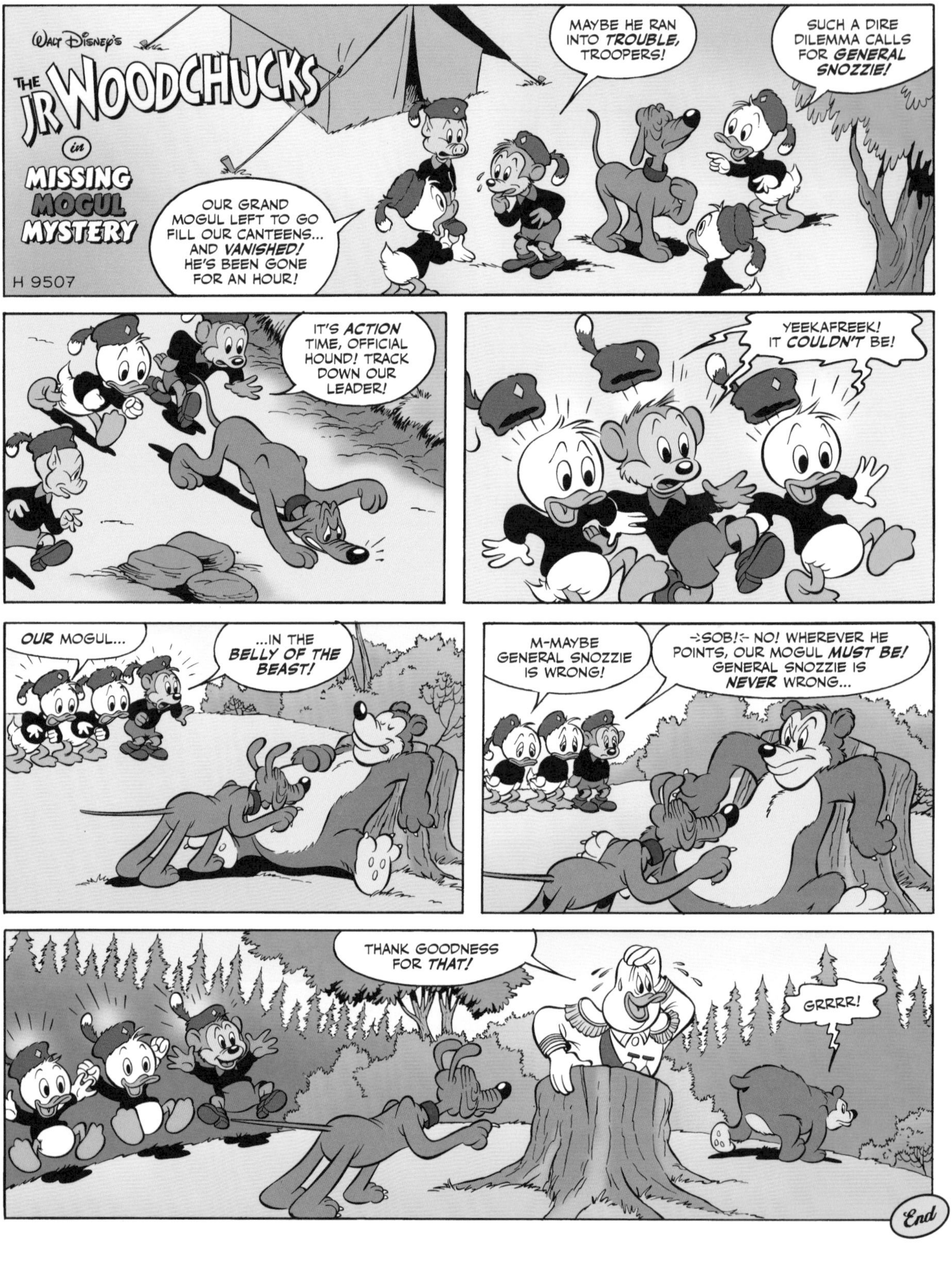

WALT DISNEY'S
THE JR WOODCHUCKS
in
MISSING MOGUL MYSTERY
H 9507
OUR GRAND MOGUL LEFT TO GO FILL OUR CANTEENS... AND VANISHED! HE'S BEEN GONE FOR AN HOUR!
MAYBE HE RAN INTO TROUBLE, TROOPERS!
SUCH A DIRE DILEMMA CALLS FOR GENERAL SNOZZIE!
IT'S ACTION TIME, OFFICIAL HOUND! TRACK DOWN OUR LEADER!
YEEKAFREEK! IT COULDN'T BE!
OUR MOGUL...
...IN THE BELLY OF THE BEAST!
M-MAYBE GENERAL SNOZZIE IS WRONG!
→SOB!← NO! WHEREVER HE POINTS, OUR MOGUL MUST BE! GENERAL SNOZZIE IS NEVER WRONG...
THANK GOODNESS FOR THAT!
GRRRR!
End

The Life and Times of $crooge McDuck

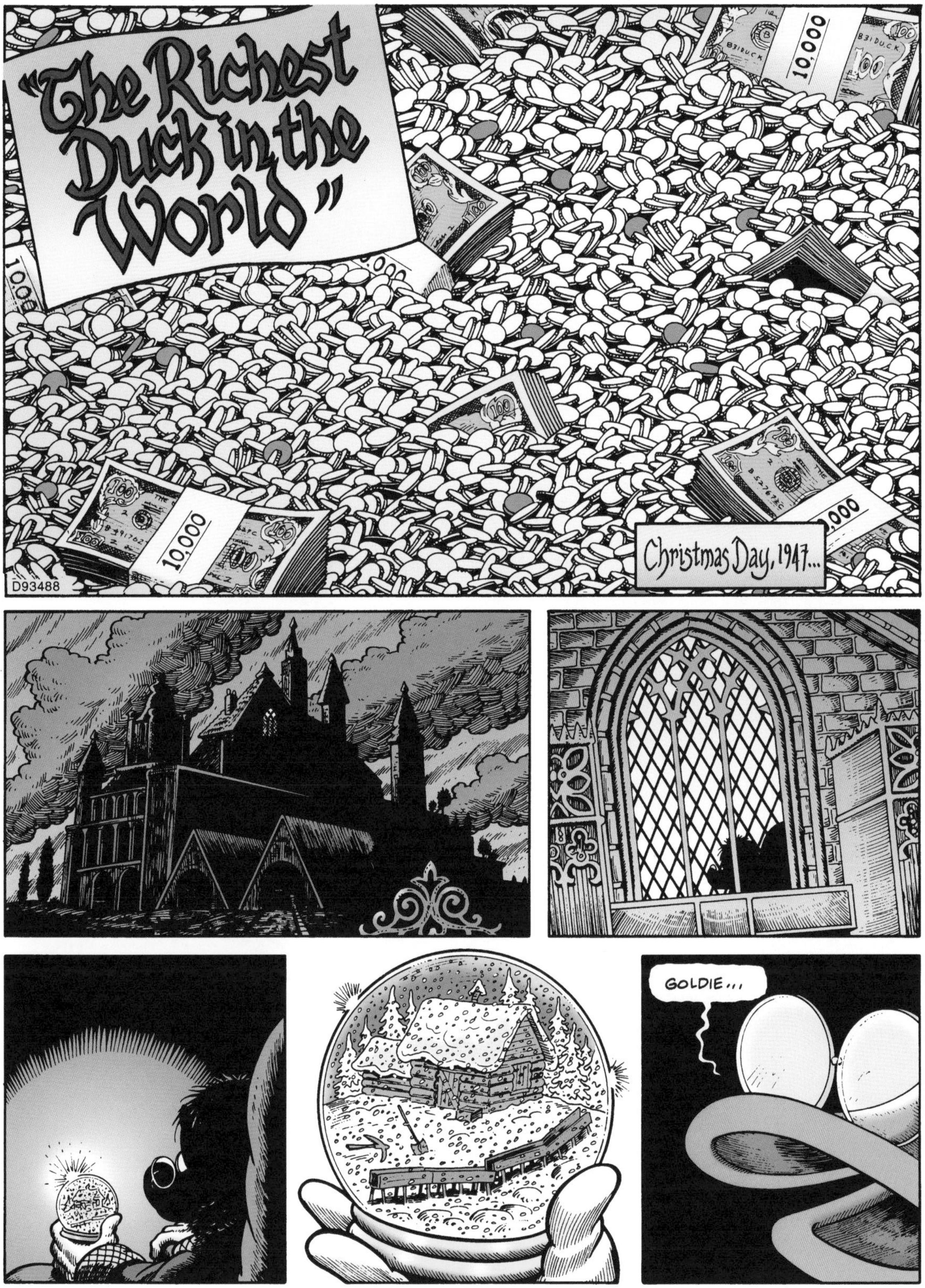
"The Richest Duck in the World"
10,000
10,000
Christmas Day, 1947...
D93488
GOLDIE...

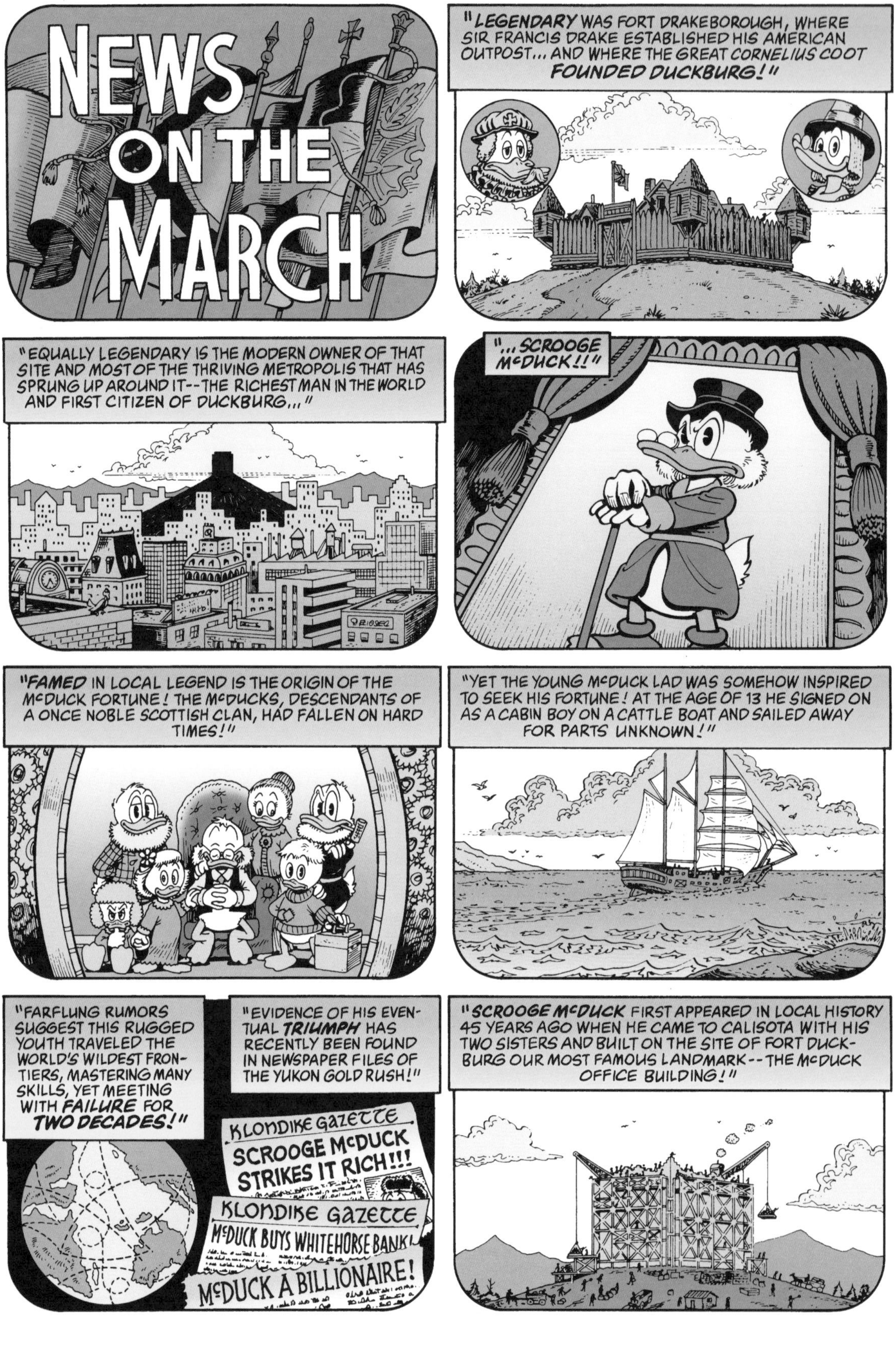
NEWS ON THE MARCH
"LEGENDARY WAS FORT DRAKEBOROUGH, WHERE SIR FRANCIS DRAKE ESTABLISHED HIS AMERICAN OUTPOST... AND WHERE THE GREAT CORNELIUS COOT FOUNDED DUCKBURG!"
"EQUALLY LEGENDARY IS THE MODERN OWNER OF THAT SITE AND MOST OF THE THRIVING METROPOLIS THAT HAS SPRUNG UP AROUND IT--THE RICHEST MAN IN THE WORLD AND FIRST CITIZEN OF DUCKBURG..."
"...SCROOGE McDUCK!!"
"FAMED IN LOCAL LEGEND IS THE ORIGIN OF THE McDUCK FORTUNE! THE McDUCKS, DESCENDANTS OF A ONCE NOBLE SCOTTISH CLAN, HAD FALLEN ON HARD TIMES!"
"YET THE YOUNG McDUCK LAD WAS SOMEHOW INSPIRED TO SEEK HIS FORTUNE! AT THE AGE OF 13 HE SIGNED ON AS A CABIN BOY ON A CATTLE BOAT AND SAILED AWAY FOR PARTS UNKNOWN!"
"FARFLUNG RUMORS SUGGEST THIS RUGGED YOUTH TRAVELED THE WORLD'S WILDEST FRONTIERS, MASTERING MANY SKILLS, YET MEETING WITH FAILURE FOR TWO DECADES!"
"EVIDENCE OF HIS EVENTUAL TRIUMPH HAS RECENTLY BEEN FOUND IN NEWSPAPER FILES OF THE YUKON GOLD RUSH!"
KLONDIKE GAZETTE
SCROOGE McDUCK STRIKES IT RICH!!!
KLONDIKE GAZETTE
McDUCK BUYS WHITEHORSE BANK!
McDUCK A BILLIONAIRE!
"SCROOGE McDUCK FIRST APPEARED IN LOCAL HISTORY 45 YEARS AGO WHEN HE CAME TO CALISOTA WITH HIS TWO SISTERS AND BUILT ON THE SITE OF FORT DUCKBURG OUR MOST FAMOUS LANDMARK--THE McDUCK OFFICE BUILDING!"

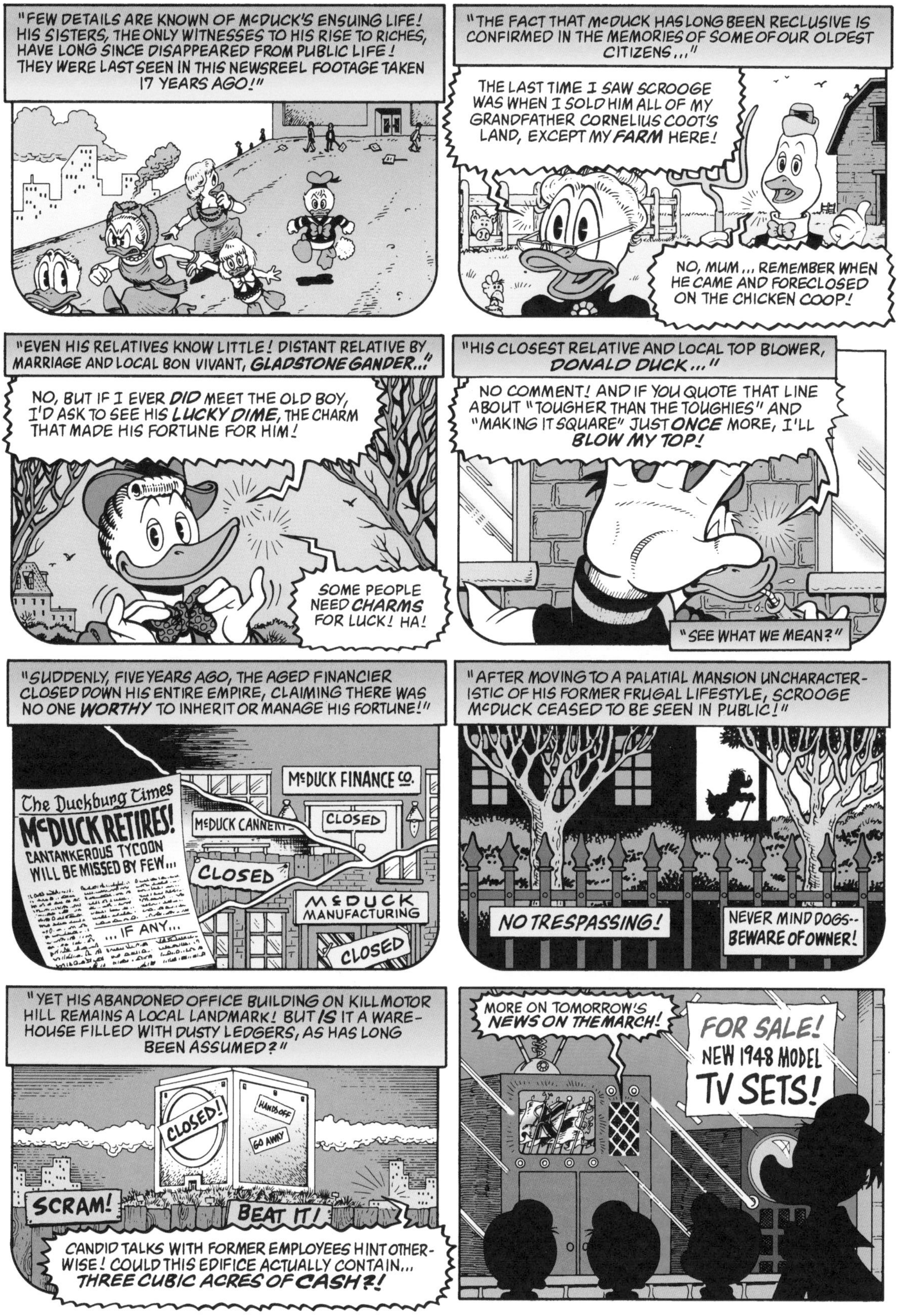
"FEW DETAILS ARE KNOWN OF McDUCK'S ENSUING LIFE! HIS SISTERS, THE ONLY WITNESSES TO HIS RISE TO RICHES, HAVE LONG SINCE DISAPPEARED FROM PUBLIC LIFE! THEY WERE LAST SEEN IN THIS NEWSREEL FOOTAGE TAKEN 17 YEARS AGO!"
"THE FACT THAT McDUCK HAS LONG BEEN RECLUSIVE IS CONFIRMED IN THE MEMORIES OF SOME OF OUR OLDEST CITIZENS..."
THE LAST TIME I SAW SCROOGE WAS WHEN I SOLD HIM ALL OF MY GRANDFATHER CORNELIUS COOT'S LAND, EXCEPT MY FARM HERE!
NO, MUM... REMEMBER WHEN HE CAME AND FORECLOSED ON THE CHICKEN COOP!
"EVEN HIS RELATIVES KNOW LITTLE! DISTANT RELATIVE BY MARRIAGE AND LOCAL BON VIVANT, GLADSTONE GANDER..."
NO, BUT IF I EVER DID MEET THE OLD BOY, I'D ASK TO SEE HIS LUCKY DIME, THE CHARM THAT MADE HIS FORTUNE FOR HIM!
SOME PEOPLE NEED CHARMS FOR LUCK! HA!
"HIS CLOSEST RELATIVE AND LOCAL TOP BLOWER, DONALD DUCK..."
NO COMMENT! AND IF YOU QUOTE THAT LINE ABOUT "TOUGHER THAN THE TOUGHIES" AND "MAKING IT SQUARE" JUST ONCE MORE, I'LL BLOW MY TOP!
"SEE WHAT WE MEAN?"
"SUDDENLY, FIVE YEARS AGO, THE AGED FINANCIER CLOSED DOWN HIS ENTIRE EMPIRE, CLAIMING THERE WAS NO ONE WORTHY TO INHERIT OR MANAGE HIS FORTUNE!"
The Duckburg Times
McDUCK RETIRES!
CANTANKEROUS TYCOON WILL BE MISSED BY FEW...
...IF ANY...
McDUCK FINANCE CO.
CLOSED
McDUCK CANNERY
CLOSED
McDUCK MANUFACTURING
CLOSED
"AFTER MOVING TO A PALATIAL MANSION UNCHARACTERISTIC OF HIS FORMER FRUGAL LIFESTYLE, SCROOGE McDUCK CEASED TO BE SEEN IN PUBLIC!"
NO TRESPASSING!
NEVER MIND DOGS-- BEWARE OF OWNER!
"YET HIS ABANDONED OFFICE BUILDING ON KILLMOTOR HILL REMAINS A LOCAL LANDMARK! BUT IS IT A WAREHOUSE FILLED WITH DUSTY LEDGERS, AS HAS LONG BEEN ASSUMED?"
CLOSED!
HANDS OFF
GO AWAY
SCRAM!
BEAT IT!
CANDID TALKS WITH FORMER EMPLOYEES HINT OTHERWISE! COULD THIS EDIFICE ACTUALLY CONTAIN... THREE CUBIC ACRES OF CASH?!
MORE ON TOMORROW'S NEWS ON THE MARCH!
FOR SALE! NEW 1948 MODEL TV SETS!

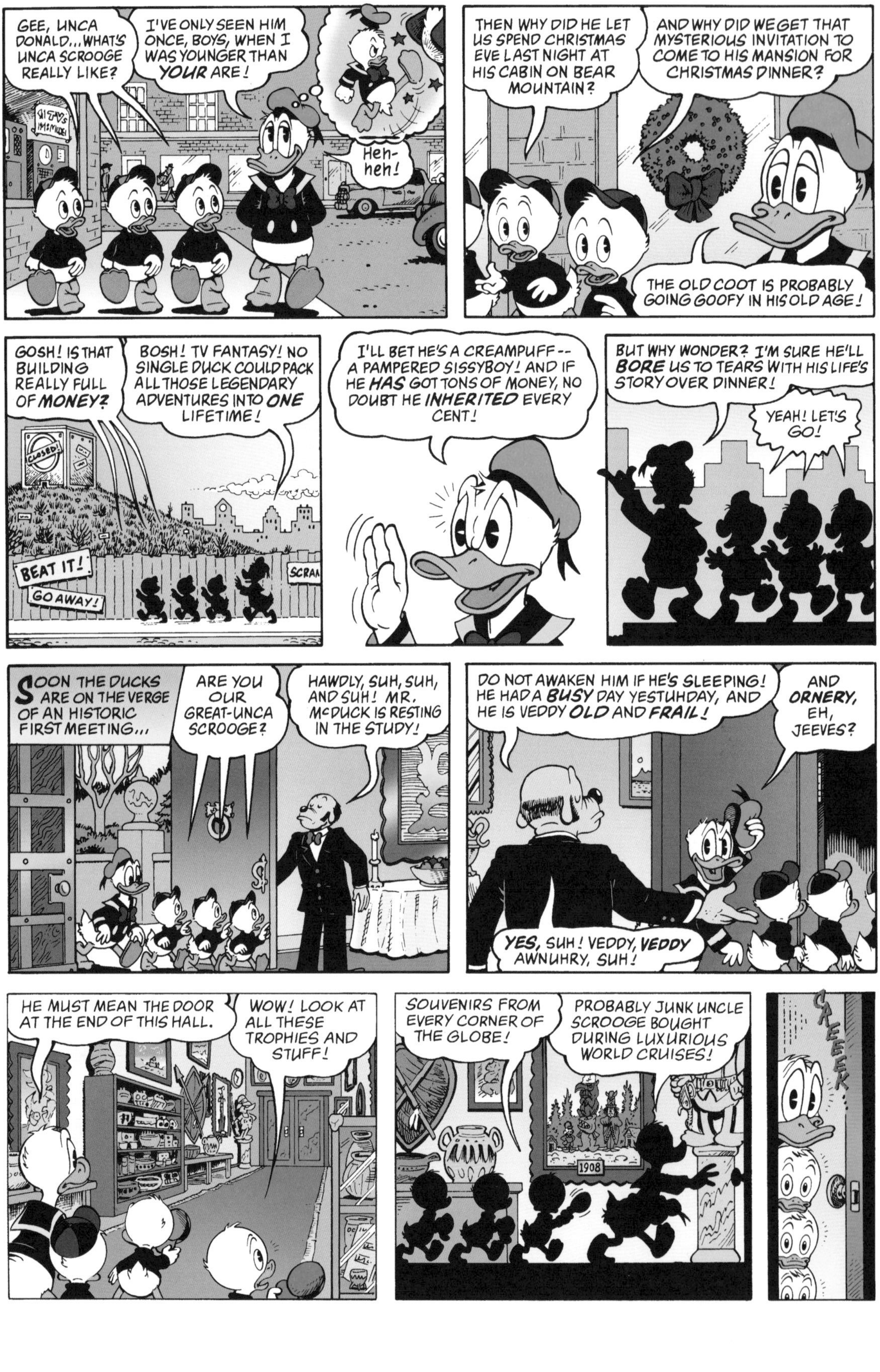
GEE, UNCA DONALD... WHAT'S UNCA SCROOGE REALLY LIKE?
I'VE ONLY SEEN HIM ONCE, BOYS, WHEN I WAS YOUNGER THAN YOUR ARE!
Heh-heh!
THEN WHY DID HE LET US SPEND CHRISTMAS EVE LAST NIGHT AT HIS CABIN ON BEAR MOUNTAIN?
AND WHY DID WE GET THAT MYSTERIOUS INVITATION TO COME TO HIS MANSION FOR CHRISTMAS DINNER?
THE OLD COOT IS PROBABLY GOING GOOFY IN HIS OLD AGE!
GOSH! IS THAT BUILDING REALLY FULL OF MONEY?
BOSH! TV FANTASY! NO SINGLE DUCK COULD PACK ALL THOSE LEGENDARY ADVENTURES INTO ONE LIFETIME!
CLOSED
BEAT IT!
GO AWAY!
I'LL BET HE'S A CREAMPUFF -- A PAMPERED SISSYBOY! AND IF HE HAS GOT TONS OF MONEY, NO DOUBT HE INHERITED EVERY CENT!
BUT WHY WONDER? I'M SURE HE'LL BORE US TO TEARS WITH HIS LIFE'S STORY OVER DINNER!
YEAH! LET'S GO!
SOON THE DUCKS ARE ON THE VERGE OF AN HISTORIC FIRST MEETING...
ARE YOU OUR GREAT-UNCA SCROOGE?
HAWDLY, SUH, SUH, AND SUH! MR. McDUCK IS RESTING IN THE STUDY!
DO NOT AWAKEN HIM IF HE'S SLEEPING! HE HAD A BUSY DAY YESTUHDAY, AND HE IS VEDDY OLD AND FRAIL!
AND ORNERY, EH, JEEVES?
YES, SUH! VEDDY, VEDDY AWNUHRY, SUH!
HE MUST MEAN THE DOOR AT THE END OF THIS HALL.
WOW! LOOK AT ALL THESE TROPHIES AND STUFF!
SOUVENIRS FROM EVERY CORNER OF THE GLOBE!
PROBABLY JUNK UNCLE SCROOGE BOUGHT DURING LUXURIOUS WORLD CRUISES!
1908
CREEEK

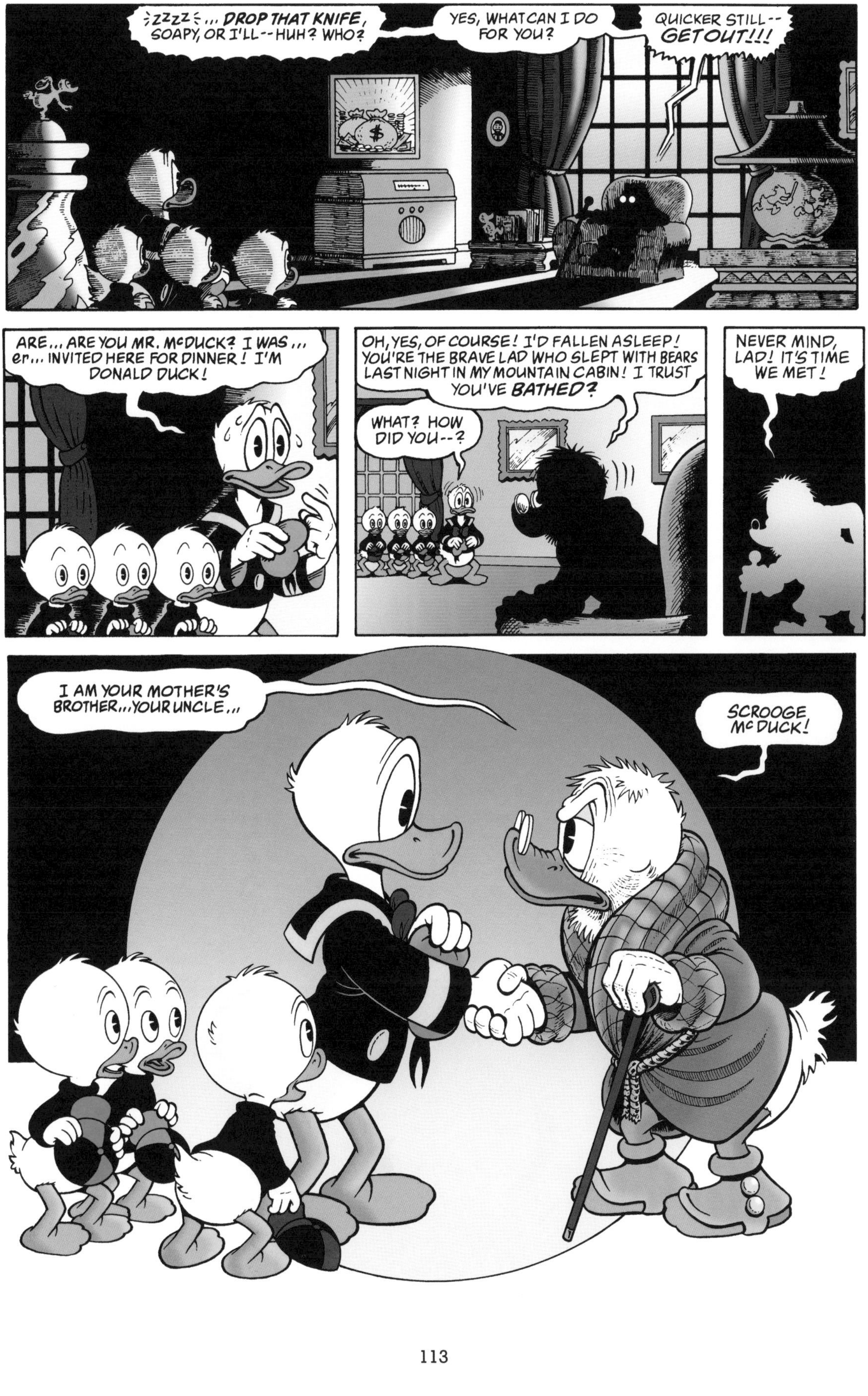
ZZZZ... DROP THAT KNIFE, SOAPY, OR I'LL--HUH? WHO?
YES, WHAT CAN I DO FOR YOU?
QUICKER STILL-- GET OUT!!!
ARE... ARE YOU MR. McDUCK? I WAS... er... INVITED HERE FOR DINNER! I'M DONALD DUCK!
OH, YES, OF COURSE! I'D FALLEN ASLEEP! YOU'RE THE BRAVE LAD WHO SLEPT WITH BEARS LAST NIGHT IN MY MOUNTAIN CABIN! I TRUST YOU'VE BATHED?
WHAT? HOW DID YOU--?
NEVER MIND, LAD! IT'S TIME WE MET!
I AM YOUR MOTHER'S BROTHER... YOUR UNCLE...
SCROOGE McDUCK!

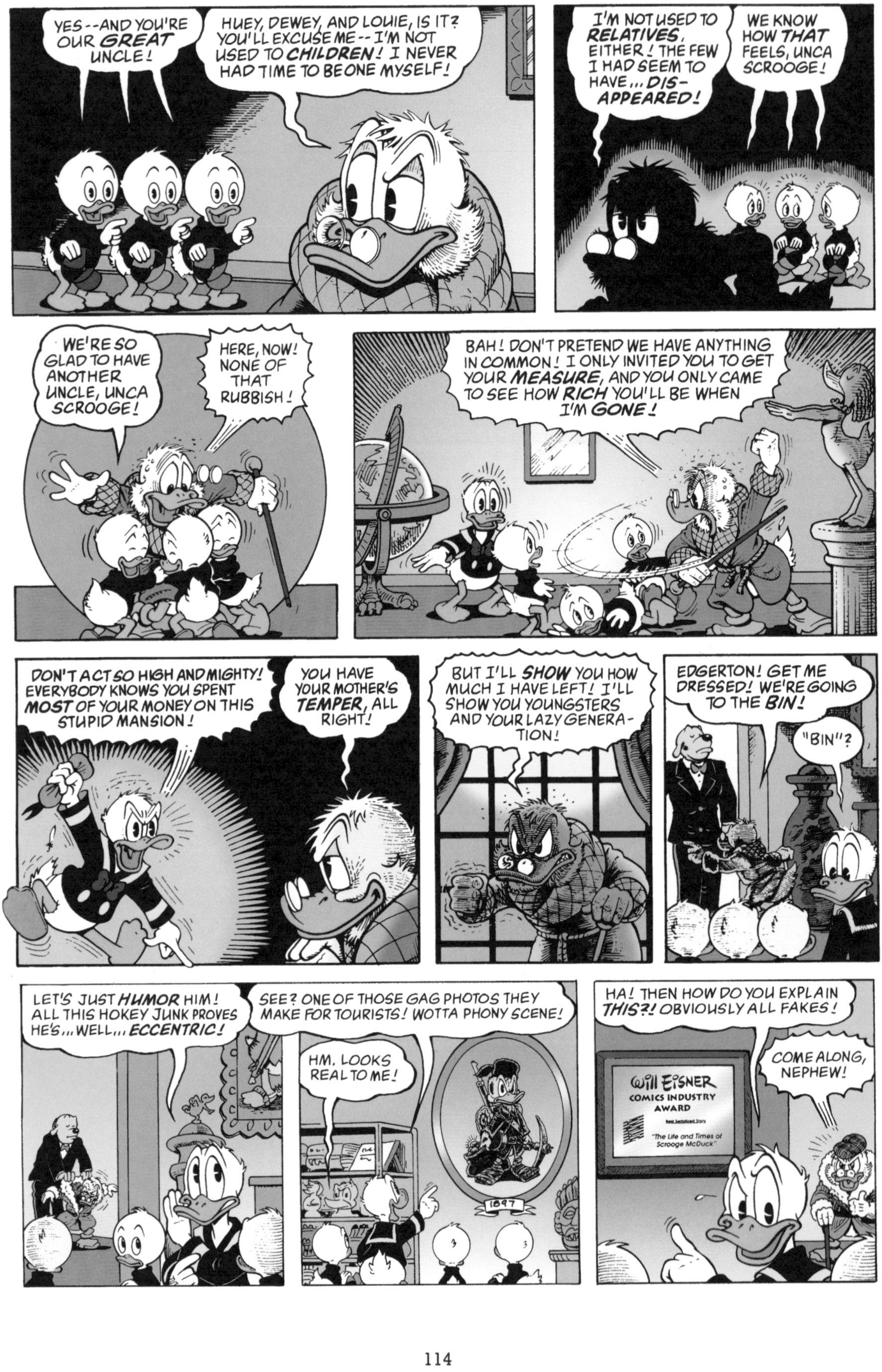
YES--AND YOU'RE OUR GREAT UNCLE!
HUEY, DEWEY, AND LOUIE, IS IT? YOU'LL EXCUSE ME--I'M NOT USED TO CHILDREN! I NEVER HAD TIME TO BE ONE MYSELF!
I'M NOT USED TO RELATIVES, EITHER! THE FEW I HAD SEEM TO HAVE... DIS-APPEARED!
WE KNOW HOW THAT FEELS, UNCA SCROOGE!
WE'RE SO GLAD TO HAVE ANOTHER UNCLE, UNCA SCROOGE!
HERE, NOW! NONE OF THAT RUBBISH!
BAH! DON'T PRETEND WE HAVE ANYTHING IN COMMON! I ONLY INVITED YOU TO GET YOUR MEASURE, AND YOU ONLY CAME TO SEE HOW RICH YOU'LL BE WHEN I'M GONE!
DON'T ACT SO HIGH AND MIGHTY! EVERYBODY KNOWS YOU SPENT MOST OF YOUR MONEY ON THIS STUPID MANSION!
YOU HAVE YOUR MOTHER'S TEMPER, ALL RIGHT!
BUT I'LL SHOW YOU HOW MUCH I HAVE LEFT! I'LL SHOW YOU YOUNGSTERS AND YOUR LAZY GENERA-TION!
EDGERTON! GET ME DRESSED! WE'RE GOING TO THE BIN!
"BIN"?
LET'S JUST HUMOR HIM! ALL THIS HOKEY JUNK PROVES HE'S... WELL... ECCENTRIC!
SEE? ONE OF THOSE GAG PHOTOS THEY MAKE FOR TOURISTS! WOTTA PHONY SCENE!
HM. LOOKS REAL TO ME!
1897
HA! THEN HOW DO YOU EXPLAIN THIS?! OBVIOUSLY ALL FAKES!
Will Eisner
COMICS INDUSTRY AWARD
"The Life and Times of Scrooge McDuck"
COME ALONG, NEPHEW!

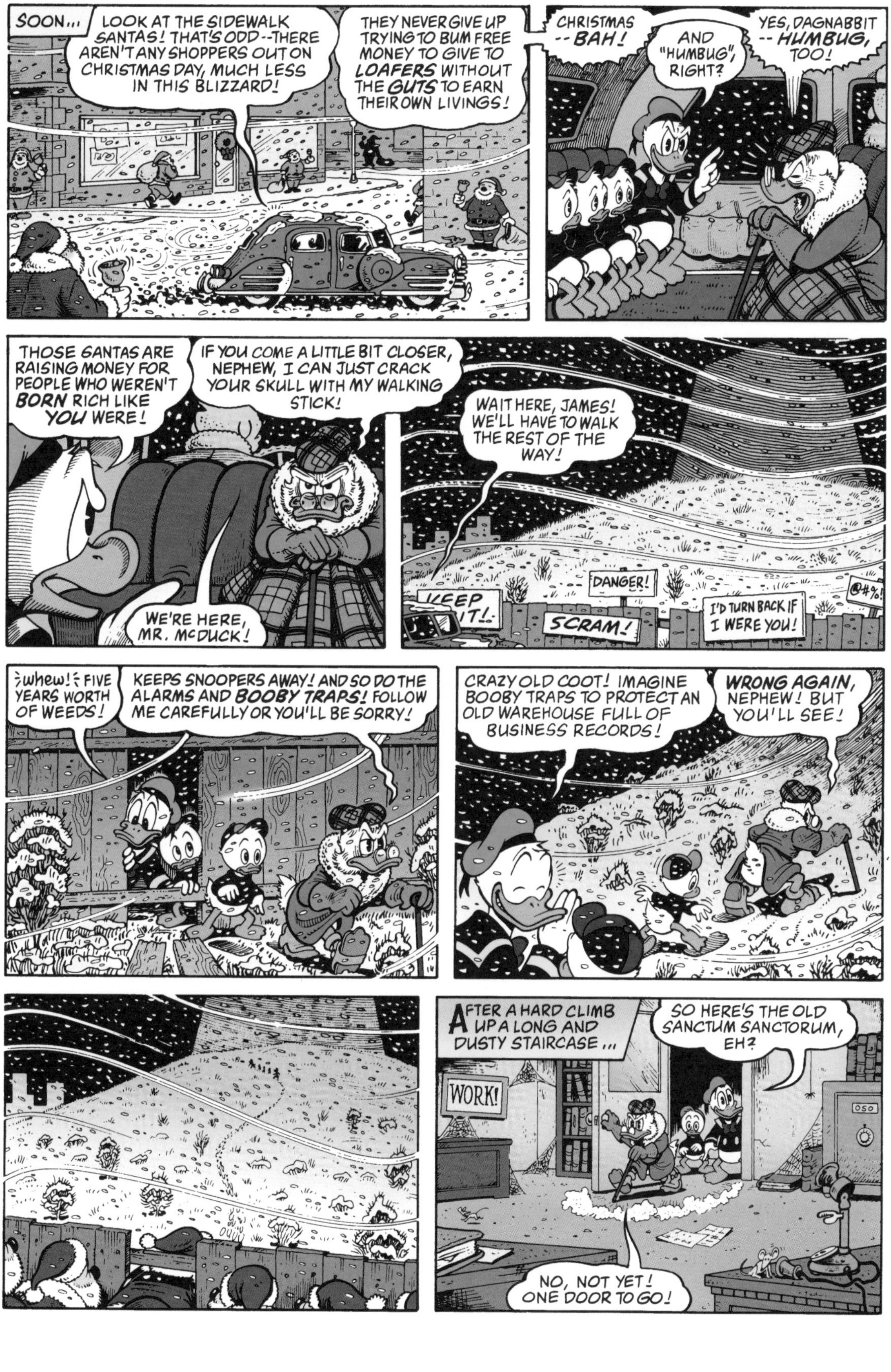

SOON...
LOOK AT THE SIDEWALK SANTAS! THAT'S ODD--THERE AREN'T ANY SHOPPERS OUT ON CHRISTMAS DAY, MUCH LESS IN THIS BLIZZARD!
THEY NEVER GIVE UP TRYING TO BUM FREE MONEY TO GIVE TO LOAFERS WITHOUT THE GUTS TO EARN THEIR OWN LIVINGS!
CHRISTMAS --BAH!
AND "HUMBUG", RIGHT?
YES, DAGNABBIT --HUMBUG, TOO!
THOSE SANTAS ARE RAISING MONEY FOR PEOPLE WHO WEREN'T BORN RICH LIKE YOU WERE!
IF YOU COME A LITTLE BIT CLOSER, NEPHEW, I CAN JUST CRACK YOUR SKULL WITH MY WALKING STICK!
WE'RE HERE, MR. McDUCK!
WAIT HERE, JAMES! WE'LL HAVE TO WALK THE REST OF THE WAY!
DANGER!
@#%!
SCRAM!
I'D TURN BACK IF I WERE YOU!
whew! FIVE YEARS WORTH OF WEEDS!
KEEPS SNOOPERS AWAY! AND SO DO THE ALARMS AND BOOBY TRAPS! FOLLOW ME CAREFULLY OR YOU'LL BE SORRY!
CRAZY OLD COOT! IMAGINE BOOBY TRAPS TO PROTECT AN OLD WAREHOUSE FULL OF BUSINESS RECORDS!
WRONG AGAIN, NEPHEW! BUT YOU'LL SEE!
AFTER A HARD CLIMB UP A LONG AND DUSTY STAIRCASE...
SO HERE'S THE OLD SANCTUM SANCTORUM, EH?
WORK!
NO, NOT YET! ONE DOOR TO GO!

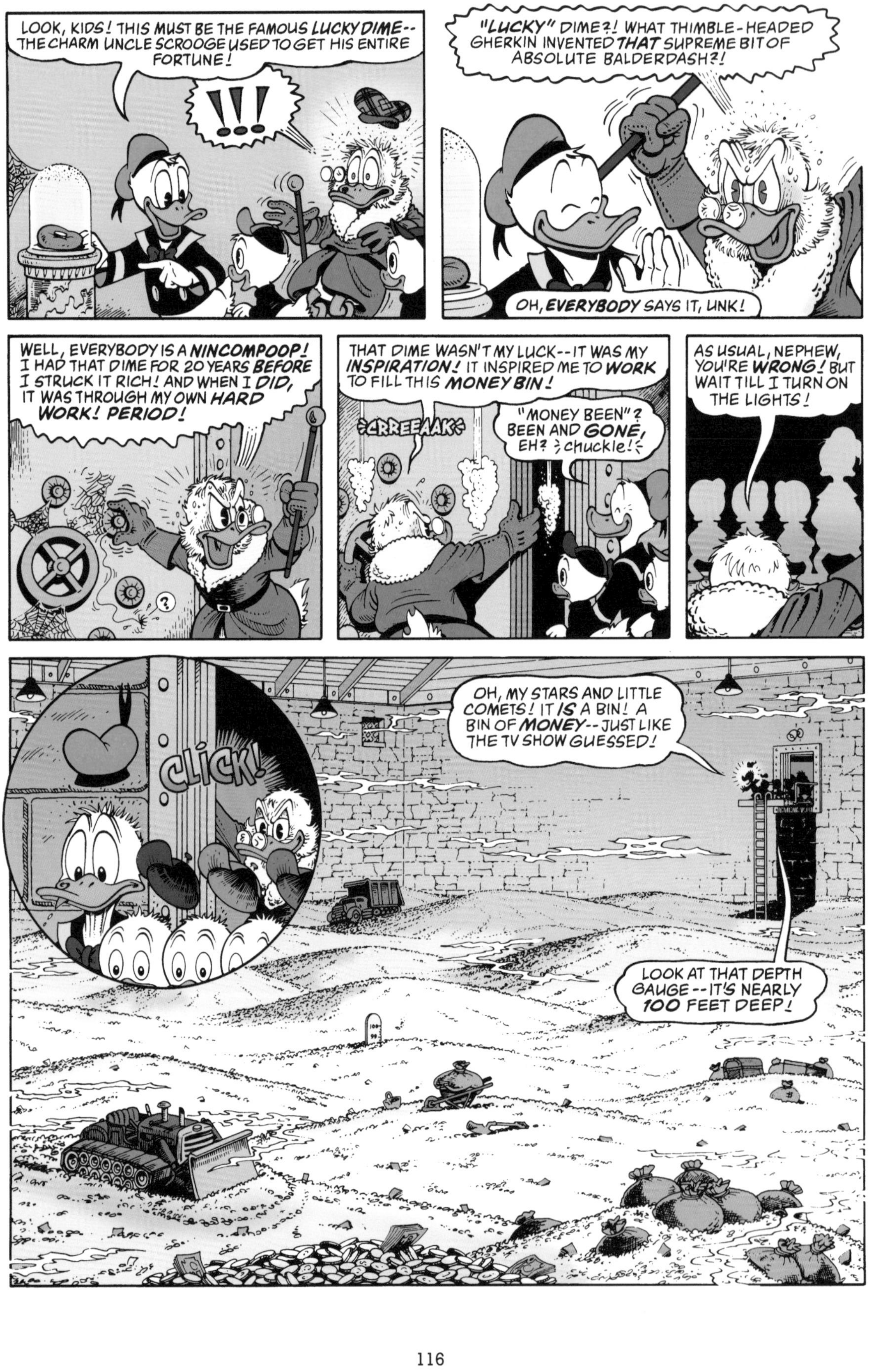
LOOK, KIDS! THIS MUST BE THE FAMOUS LUCKY DIME-- THE CHARM UNCLE SCROOGE USED TO GET HIS ENTIRE FORTUNE!
!!!
"LUCKY" DIME?! WHAT THIMBLE-HEADED GHERKIN INVENTED THAT SUPREME BIT OF ABSOLUTE BALDERDASH?!
OH, EVERYBODY SAYS IT, UNK!
WELL, EVERYBODY IS A NINCOMPOOP! I HAD THAT DIME FOR 20 YEARS BEFORE I STRUCK IT RICH! AND WHEN I DID, IT WAS THROUGH MY OWN HARD WORK! PERIOD!
?
THAT DIME WASN'T MY LUCK--IT WAS MY INSPIRATION! IT INSPIRED ME TO WORK TO FILL THIS MONEY BIN!
CRRREEAAK
"MONEY BEEN"? BEEN AND GONE, EH? chuckle!
AS USUAL, NEPHEW, YOU'RE WRONG! BUT WAIT TILL I TURN ON THE LIGHTS!
CLICK!
OH, MY STARS AND LITTLE COMETS! IT IS A BIN! A BIN OF MONEY--JUST LIKE THE TV SHOW GUESSED!
LOOK AT THAT DEPTH GAUGE--IT'S NEARLY 100 FEET DEEP!

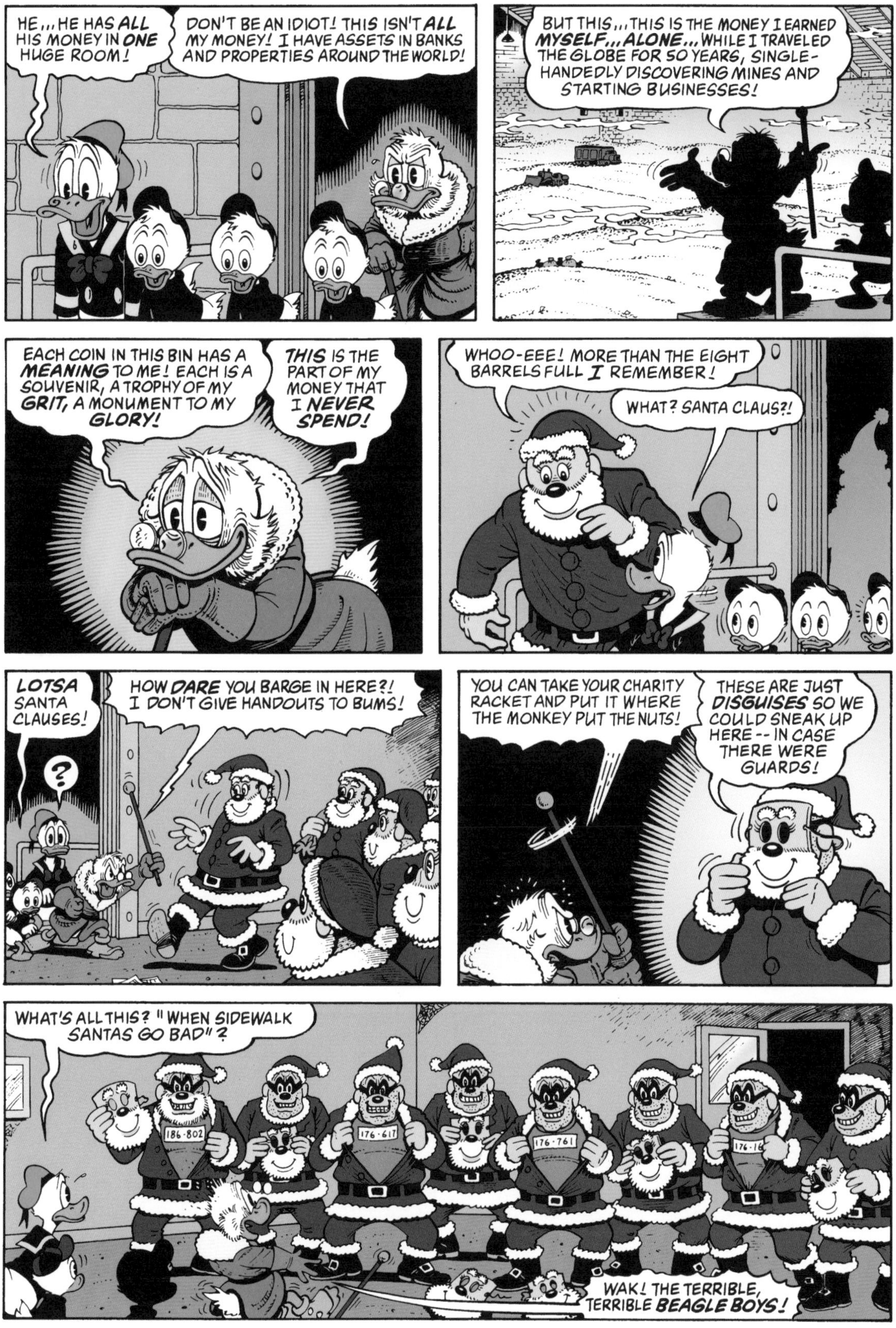
HE... HE HAS ALL HIS MONEY IN ONE HUGE ROOM!
DON'T BE AN IDIOT! THIS ISN'T ALL MY MONEY! I HAVE ASSETS IN BANKS AND PROPERTIES AROUND THE WORLD!
BUT THIS... THIS IS THE MONEY I EARNED MYSELF... ALONE... WHILE I TRAVELED THE GLOBE FOR 50 YEARS, SINGLE-HANDEDLY DISCOVERING MINES AND STARTING BUSINESSES!
EACH COIN IN THIS BIN HAS A MEANING TO ME! EACH IS A SOUVENIR, A TROPHY OF MY GRIT, A MONUMENT TO MY GLORY!
THIS IS THE PART OF MY MONEY THAT I NEVER SPEND!
WHOO-EEE! MORE THAN THE EIGHT BARRELS FULL I REMEMBER!
WHAT? SANTA CLAUS?!
LOTSA SANTA CLAUSES!
HOW DARE YOU BARGE IN HERE?! I DON'T GIVE HANDOUTS TO BUMS!
?
YOU CAN TAKE YOUR CHARITY RACKET AND PUT IT WHERE THE MONKEY PUT THE NUTS!
THESE ARE JUST DISGUISES SO WE COULD SNEAK UP HERE -- IN CASE THERE WERE GUARDS!
WHAT'S ALL THIS? "WHEN SIDEWALK SANTAS GO BAD"?
186-802
176-617
176-761
176-16
WAK! THE TERRIBLE, TERRIBLE BEAGLE BOYS!

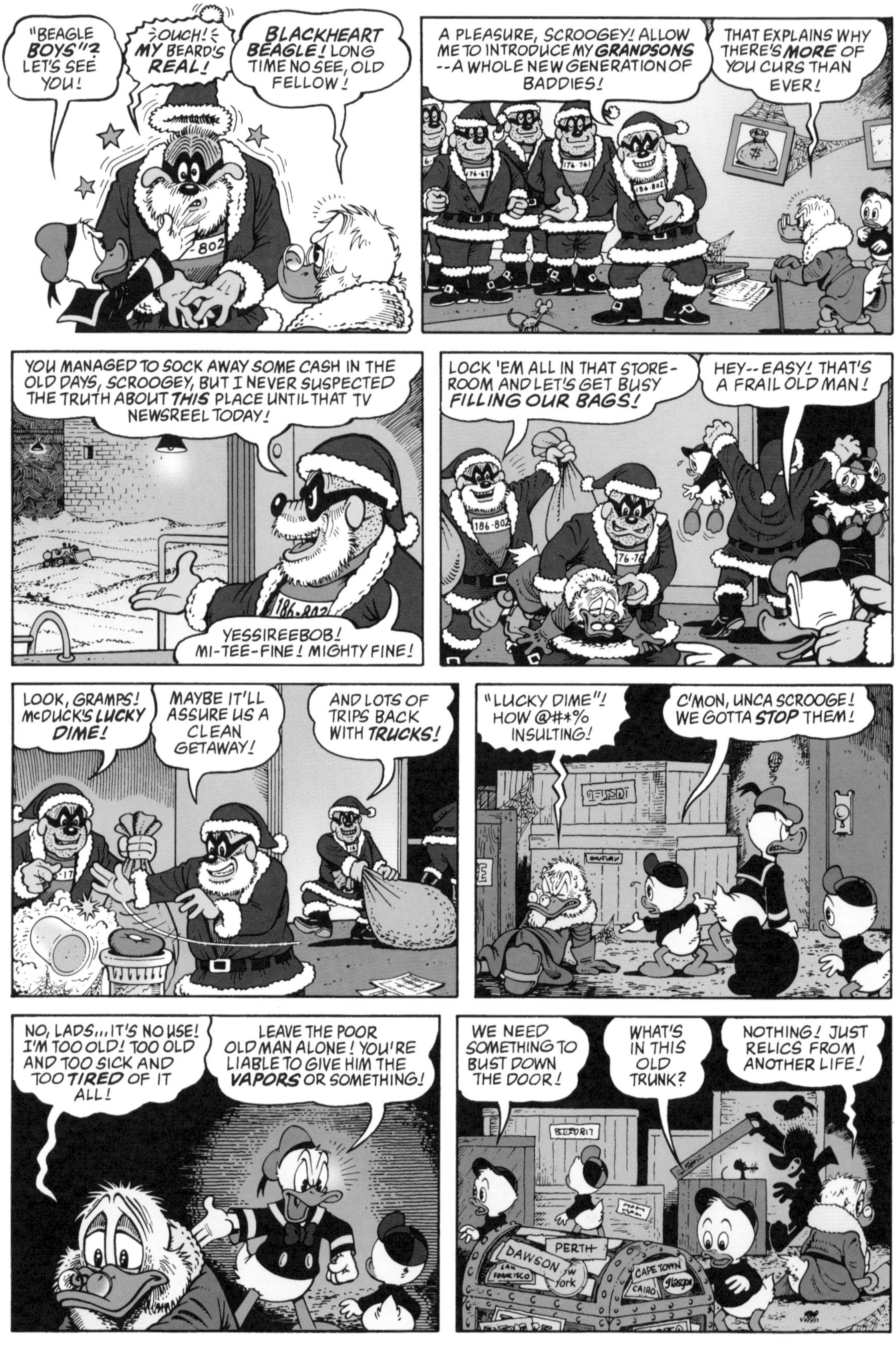
"BEAGLE BOYS"? LET'S SEE YOU!
OUCH! MY BEARD'S REAL!
BLACKHEART BEAGLE! LONG TIME NO SEE, OLD FELLOW!
A PLEASURE, SCROOGEY! ALLOW ME TO INTRODUCE MY GRANDSONS --A WHOLE NEW GENERATION OF BADDIES!
THAT EXPLAINS WHY THERE'S MORE OF YOU CURS THAN EVER!
YOU MANAGED TO SOCK AWAY SOME CASH IN THE OLD DAYS, SCROOGEY, BUT I NEVER SUSPECTED THE TRUTH ABOUT THIS PLACE UNTIL THAT TV NEWSREEL TODAY!
YESSIREEBOB! MI-TEE-FINE! MIGHTY FINE!
LOCK 'EM ALL IN THAT STORE-ROOM AND LET'S GET BUSY FILLING OUR BAGS!
HEY--EASY! THAT'S A FRAIL OLD MAN!
LOOK, GRAMPS! McDUCK'S LUCKY DIME!
MAYBE IT'LL ASSURE US A CLEAN GETAWAY!
AND LOTS OF TRIPS BACK WITH TRUCKS!
"LUCKY DIME"! HOW @#*% INSULTING!
C'MON, UNCA SCROOGE! WE GOTTA STOP THEM!
NO, LADS... IT'S NO USE! I'M TOO OLD! TOO OLD AND TOO SICK AND TOO TIRED OF IT ALL!
LEAVE THE POOR OLD MAN ALONE! YOU'RE LIABLE TO GIVE HIM THE VAPORS OR SOMETHING!
WE NEED SOMETHING TO BUST DOWN THE DOOR!
WHAT'S IN THIS OLD TRUNK?
NOTHING! JUST RELICS FROM ANOTHER LIFE!
DAWSON
PERTH
SAN FRANCISCO
NEW YORK
CAPE TOWN
CAIRO
glasgow

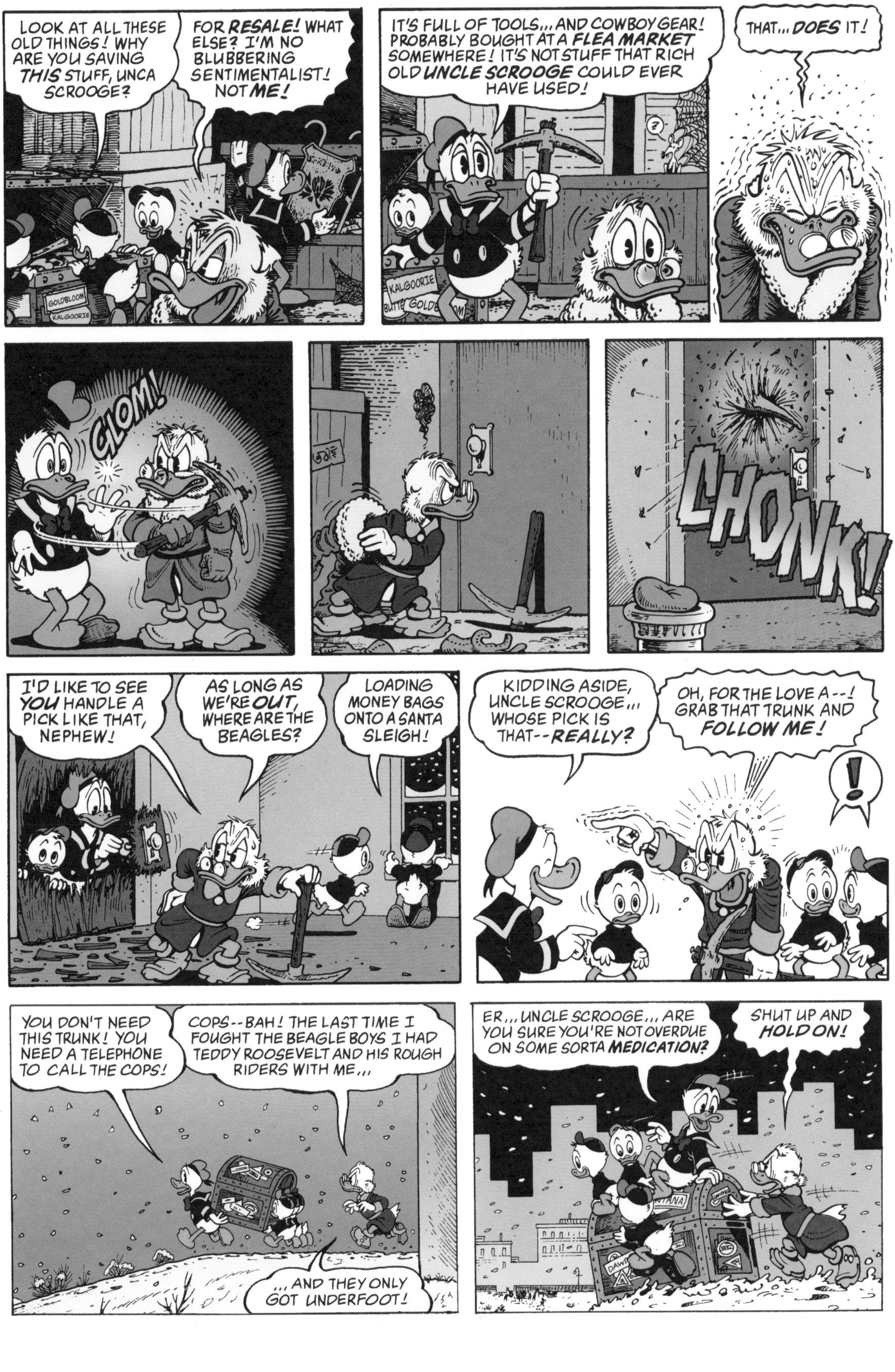
LOOK AT ALL THESE OLD THINGS! WHY ARE YOU SAVING THIS STUFF, UNCA SCROOGE?
FOR RESALE! WHAT ELSE? I'M NO BLUBBERING SENTIMENTALIST! NOT ME!
GOLDBLOOM
KALGOORIE
IT'S FULL OF TOOLS,,, AND COWBOY GEAR! PROBABLY BOUGHT AT A FLEA MARKET SOMEWHERE! IT'S NOT STUFF THAT RICH OLD UNCLE SCROOGE COULD EVER HAVE USED!
KALGOORIE
THAT,,, DOES IT!
GLOM!
CHONK!
I'D LIKE TO SEE YOU HANDLE A PICK LIKE THAT, NEPHEW!
AS LONG AS WE'RE OUT, WHERE ARE THE BEAGLES?
LOADING MONEY BAGS ONTO A SANTA SLEIGH!
KIDDING ASIDE, UNCLE SCROOGE,,, WHOSE PICK IS THAT--REALLY?
OH, FOR THE LOVE A--! GRAB THAT TRUNK AND FOLLOW ME!
!
YOU DON'T NEED THIS TRUNK! YOU NEED A TELEPHONE TO CALL THE COPS!
COPS--BAH! THE LAST TIME I FOUGHT THE BEAGLE BOYS I HAD TEDDY ROOSEVELT AND HIS ROUGH RIDERS WITH ME,,,
,,, AND THEY ONLY GOT UNDERFOOT!
ER,,, UNCLE SCROOGE,,, ARE YOU SURE YOU'RE NOT OVERDUE ON SOME SORTA MEDICATION?
SHUT UP AND HOLD ON!

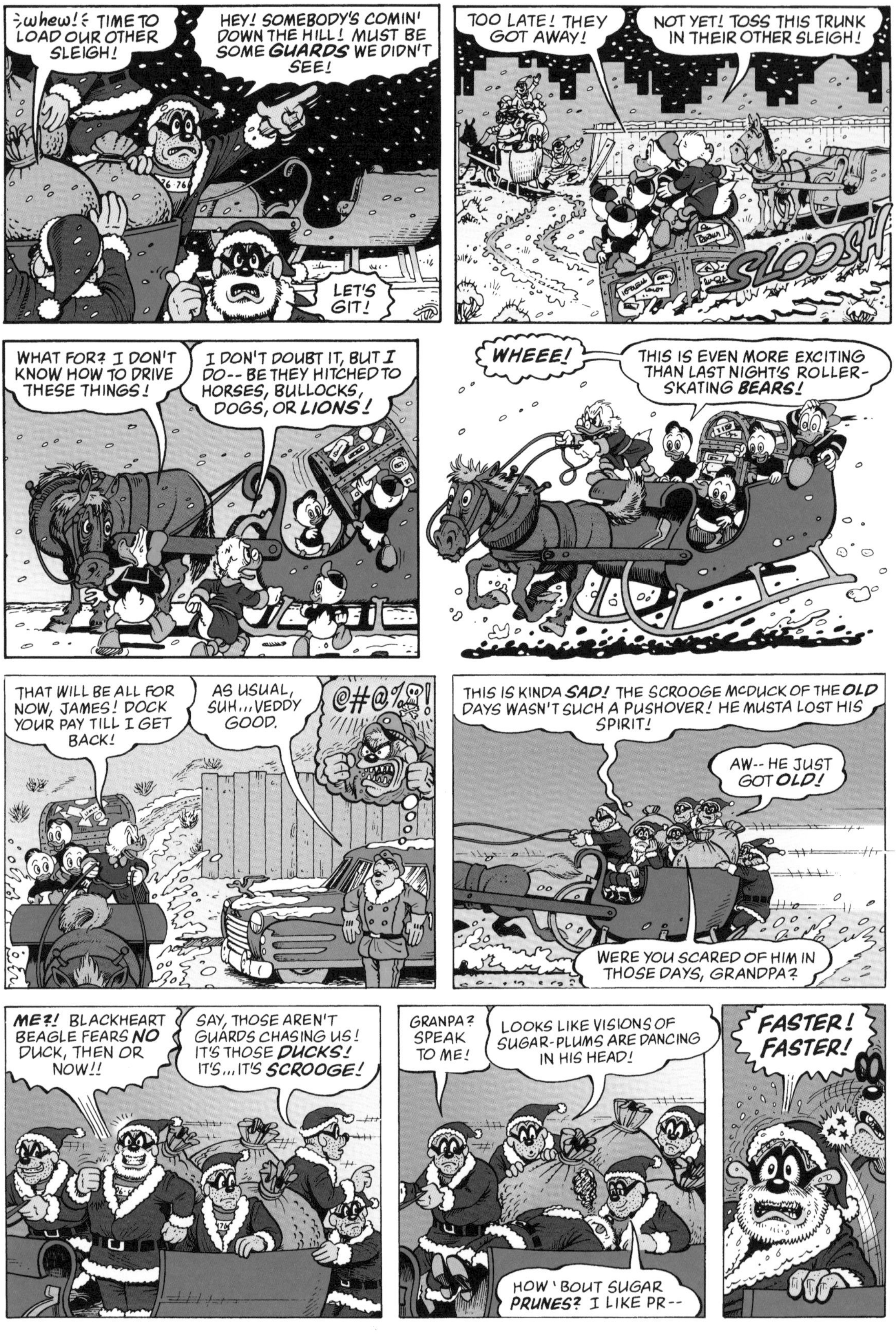

whew! TIME TO LOAD OUR OTHER SLEIGH!
HEY! SOMEBODY'S COMIN' DOWN THE HILL! MUST BE SOME GUARDS WE DIDN'T SEE!
LET'S GIT!
TOO LATE! THEY GOT AWAY!
NOT YET! TOSS THIS TRUNK IN THEIR OTHER SLEIGH!
SLOOSH
WHAT FOR? I DON'T KNOW HOW TO DRIVE THESE THINGS!
I DON'T DOUBT IT, BUT I DO-- BE THEY HITCHED TO HORSES, BULLOCKS, DOGS, OR LIONS!
WHEEE!
THIS IS EVEN MORE EXCITING THAN LAST NIGHT'S ROLLER-SKATING BEARS!
THAT WILL BE ALL FOR NOW, JAMES! DOCK YOUR PAY TILL I GET BACK!
AS USUAL, SUH... VEDDY GOOD.
@#@%!
THIS IS KINDA SAD! THE SCROOGE McDUCK OF THE OLD DAYS WASN'T SUCH A PUSHOVER! HE MUSTA LOST HIS SPIRIT!
AW-- HE JUST GOT OLD!
WERE YOU SCARED OF HIM IN THOSE DAYS, GRANDPA?
ME?! BLACKHEART BEAGLE FEARS NO DUCK, THEN OR NOW!!
SAY, THOSE AREN'T GUARDS CHASING US! IT'S THOSE DUCKS! IT'S... IT'S SCROOGE!
GRANPA? SPEAK TO ME!
LOOKS LIKE VISIONS OF SUGAR-PLUMS ARE DANCING IN HIS HEAD!
HOW 'BOUT SUGAR PRUNES? I LIKE PR--
FASTER! FASTER!

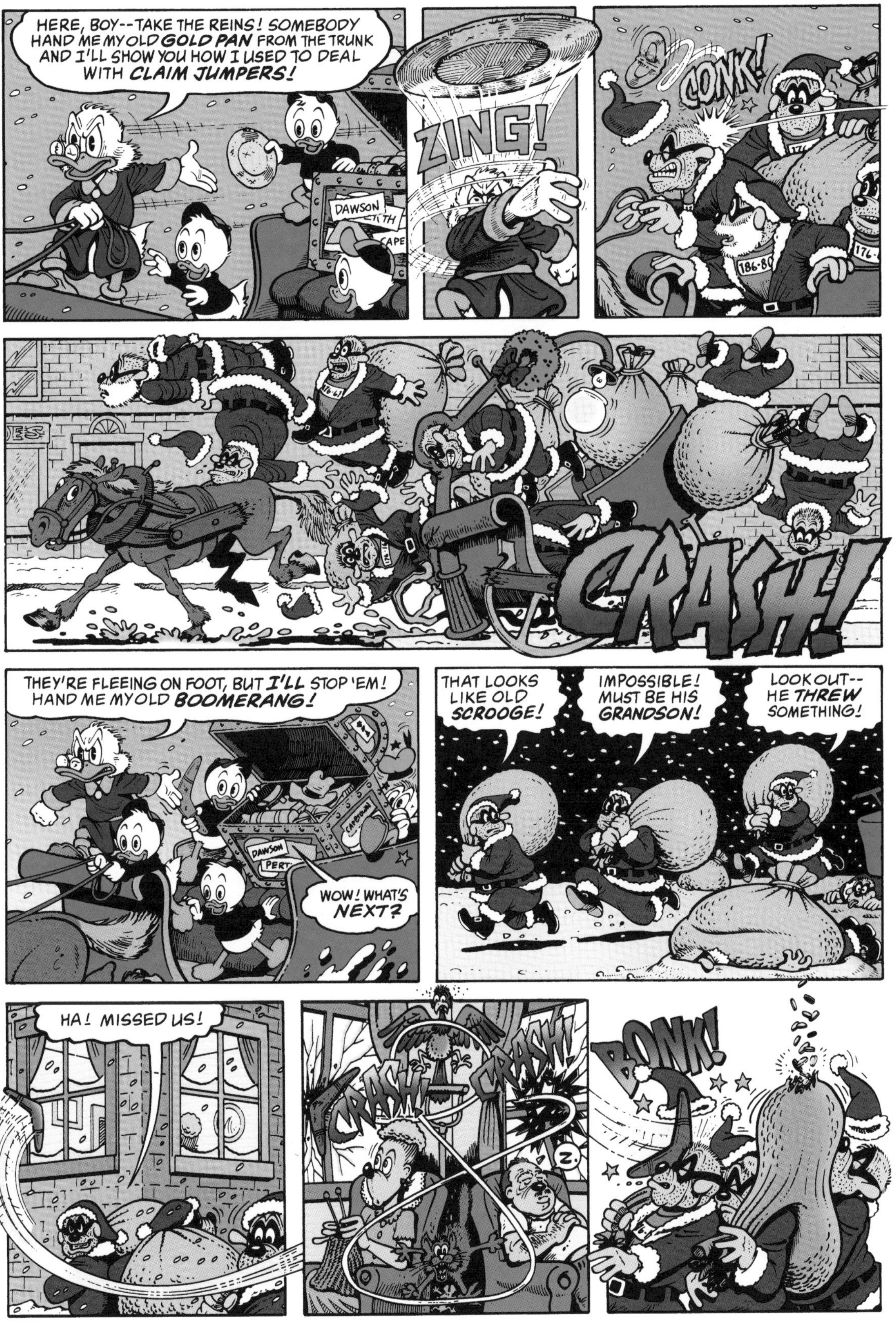
HERE, BOY--TAKE THE REINS! SOMEBODY HAND ME MY OLD GOLD PAN FROM THE TRUNK AND I'LL SHOW YOU HOW I USED TO DEAL WITH CLAIM JUMPERS!
DAWSON
ZING!
CONK!
CRASH!
THEY'RE FLEEING ON FOOT, BUT I'LL STOP 'EM! HAND ME MY OLD BOOMERANG!
DAWSON
WOW! WHAT'S NEXT?
THAT LOOKS LIKE OLD SCROOGE!
IMPOSSIBLE! MUST BE HIS GRANDSON!
LOOK OUT-- HE THREW SOMETHING!
HA! MISSED US!
CRASH!
CRASH!
BONK!

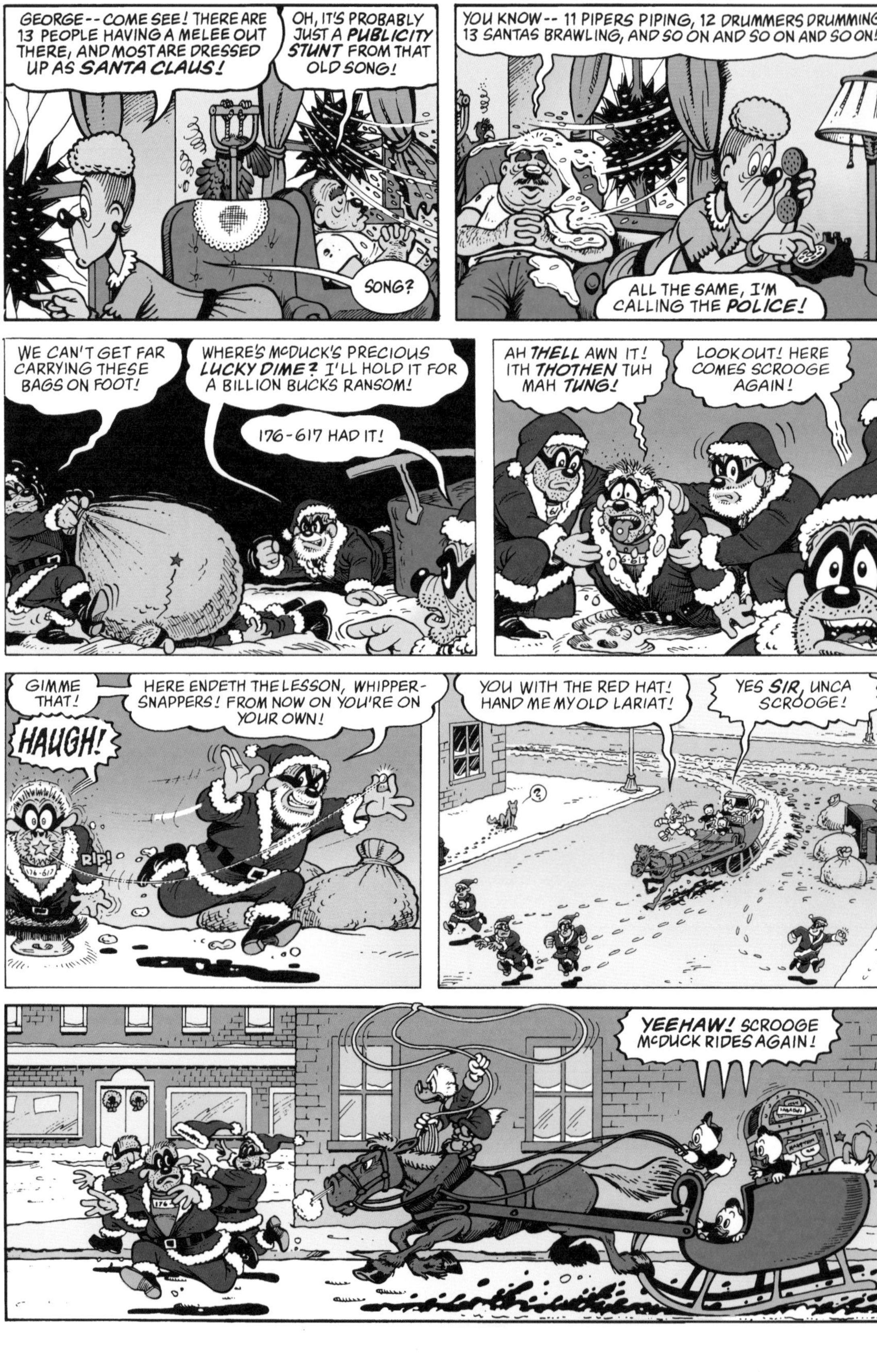
GEORGE--COME SEE! THERE ARE 13 PEOPLE HAVING A MELEE OUT THERE, AND MOST ARE DRESSED UP AS SANTA CLAUS!
OH, IT'S PROBABLY JUST A PUBLICITY STUNT FROM THAT OLD SONG!
SONG?
YOU KNOW-- 11 PIPERS PIPING, 12 DRUMMERS DRUMMING, 13 SANTAS BRAWLING, AND SO ON AND SO ON AND SO ON!
ALL THE SAME, I'M CALLING THE POLICE!
WE CAN'T GET FAR CARRYING THESE BAGS ON FOOT!
WHERE'S McDUCK'S PRECIOUS LUCKY DIME? I'LL HOLD IT FOR A BILLION BUCKS RANSOM!
176-617 HAD IT!
AH THELL AWN IT! ITH THOTHEN TUH MAH TUNG!
LOOKOUT! HERE COMES SCROOGE AGAIN!
GIMME THAT!
HAUGH!
HERE ENDETH THE LESSON, WHIPPER-SNAPPERS! FROM NOW ON YOU'RE ON YOUR OWN!
RIP!
YOU WITH THE RED HAT! HAND ME MY OLD LARIAT!
YES SIR, UNCA SCROOGE!
YEEHAW! SCROOGE McDUCK RIDES AGAIN!

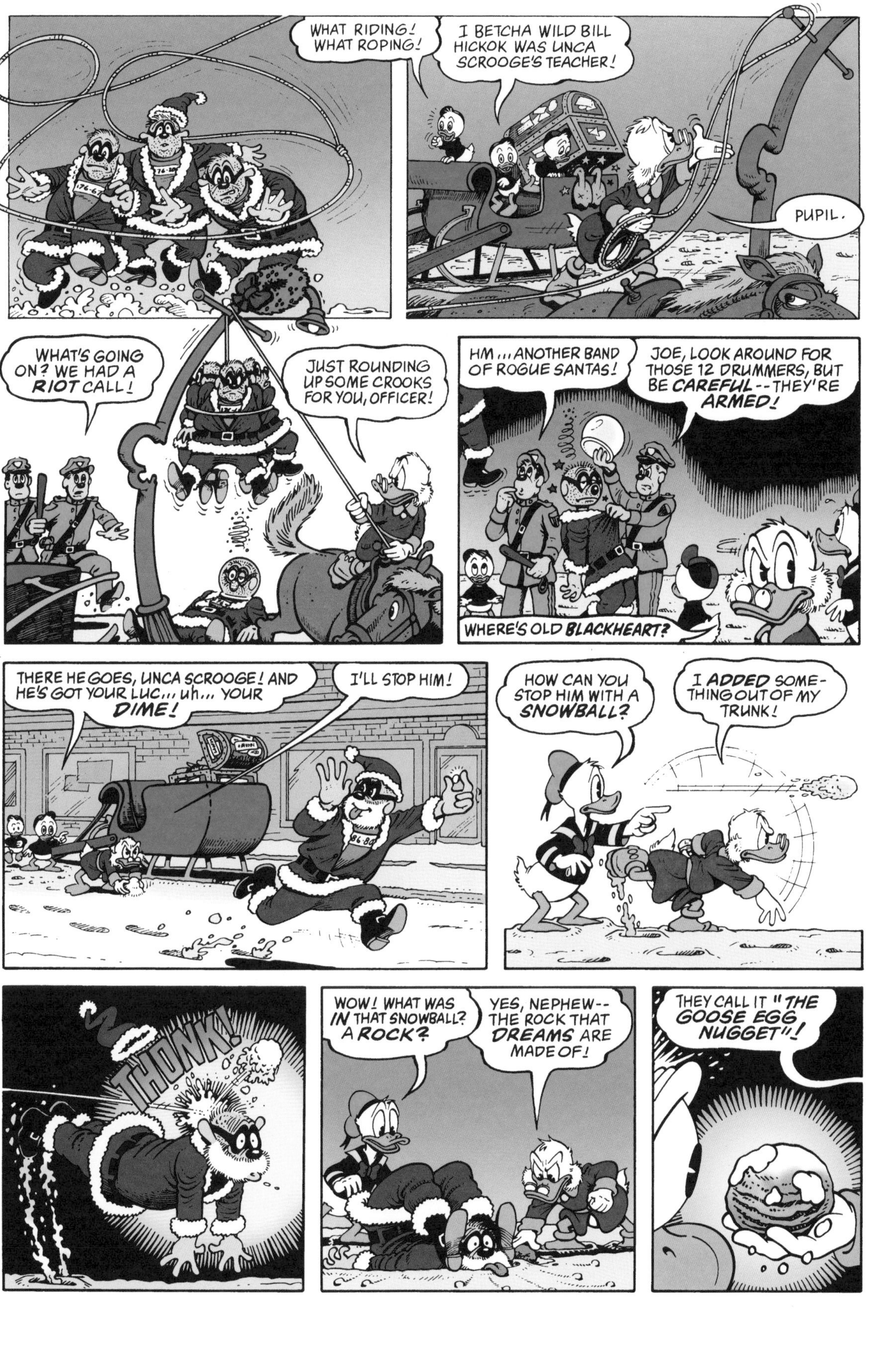
WHAT RIDING! WHAT ROPING!
I BETCHA WILD BILL HICKOK WAS UNCA SCROOGE'S TEACHER!
PUPIL.
WHAT'S GOING ON? WE HAD A RIOT CALL!
JUST ROUNDING UP SOME CROOKS FOR YOU, OFFICER!
HM... ANOTHER BAND OF ROGUE SANTAS!
JOE, LOOK AROUND FOR THOSE 12 DRUMMERS, BUT BE CAREFUL -- THEY'RE ARMED!
WHERE'S OLD BLACKHEART?
THERE HE GOES, UNCA SCROOGE! AND HE'S GOT YOUR LUC... uh... YOUR DIME!
I'LL STOP HIM!
HOW CAN YOU STOP HIM WITH A SNOWBALL?
I ADDED SOMETHING OUT OF MY TRUNK!
THONK!
WOW! WHAT WAS IN THAT SNOWBALL? A ROCK?
YES, NEPHEW -- THE ROCK THAT DREAMS ARE MADE OF!
THEY CALL IT "THE GOOSE EGG NUGGET"!

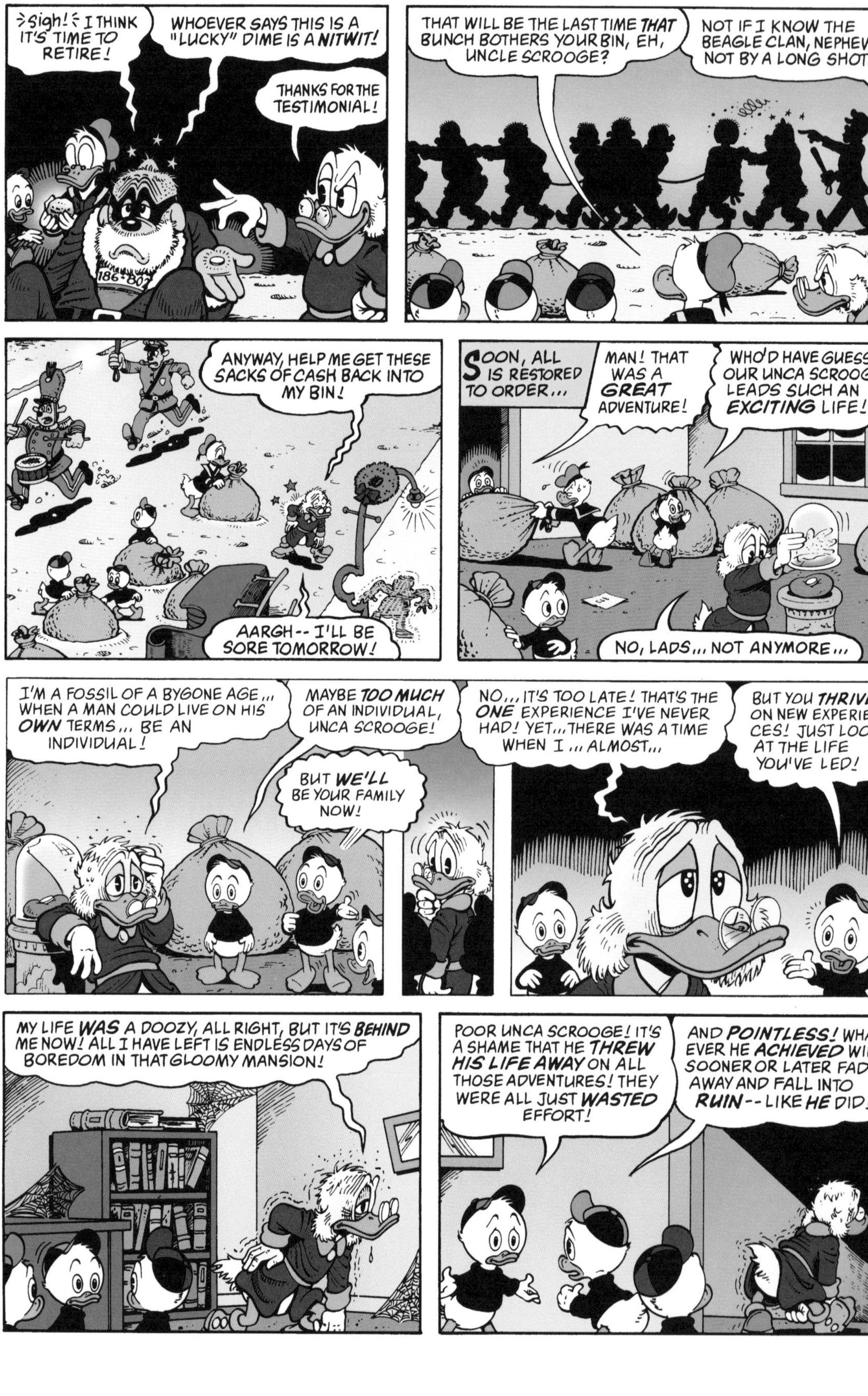

Sigh! I THINK IT'S TIME TO RETIRE!
WHOEVER SAYS THIS IS A "LUCKY" DIME IS A NITWIT!
THANKS FOR THE TESTIMONIAL!
186-802
THAT WILL BE THE LAST TIME THAT BUNCH BOTHERS YOUR BIN, EH, UNCLE SCROOGE?
NOT IF I KNOW THE BEAGLE CLAN, NEPHEW! NOT BY A LONG SHOT!
ANYWAY, HELP ME GET THESE SACKS OF CASH BACK INTO MY BIN!
AARGH -- I'LL BE SORE TOMORROW!
SOON, ALL IS RESTORED TO ORDER...
MAN! THAT WAS A GREAT ADVENTURE!
WHO'D HAVE GUESSED OUR UNCA SCROOGE LEADS SUCH AN EXCITING LIFE!
NO, LADS... NOT ANYMORE...
I'M A FOSSIL OF A BYGONE AGE... WHEN A MAN COULD LIVE ON HIS OWN TERMS... BE AN INDIVIDUAL!
MAYBE TOO MUCH OF AN INDIVIDUAL, UNCA SCROOGE!
BUT WE'LL BE YOUR FAMILY NOW!
NO... IT'S TOO LATE! THAT'S THE ONE EXPERIENCE I'VE NEVER HAD! YET... THERE WAS A TIME WHEN I... ALMOST...
BUT YOU THRIVE ON NEW EXPERIENCES! JUST LOOK AT THE LIFE YOU'VE LED!
MY LIFE WAS A DOOZY, ALL RIGHT, BUT IT'S BEHIND ME NOW! ALL I HAVE LEFT IS ENDLESS DAYS OF BOREDOM IN THAT GLOOMY MANSION!
POOR UNCA SCROOGE! IT'S A SHAME THAT HE THREW HIS LIFE AWAY ON ALL THOSE ADVENTURES! THEY WERE ALL JUST WASTED EFFORT!
AND POINTLESS! WHATEVER HE ACHIEVED WILL SOONER OR LATER FADE AWAY AND FALL INTO RUIN -- LIKE HE DID!

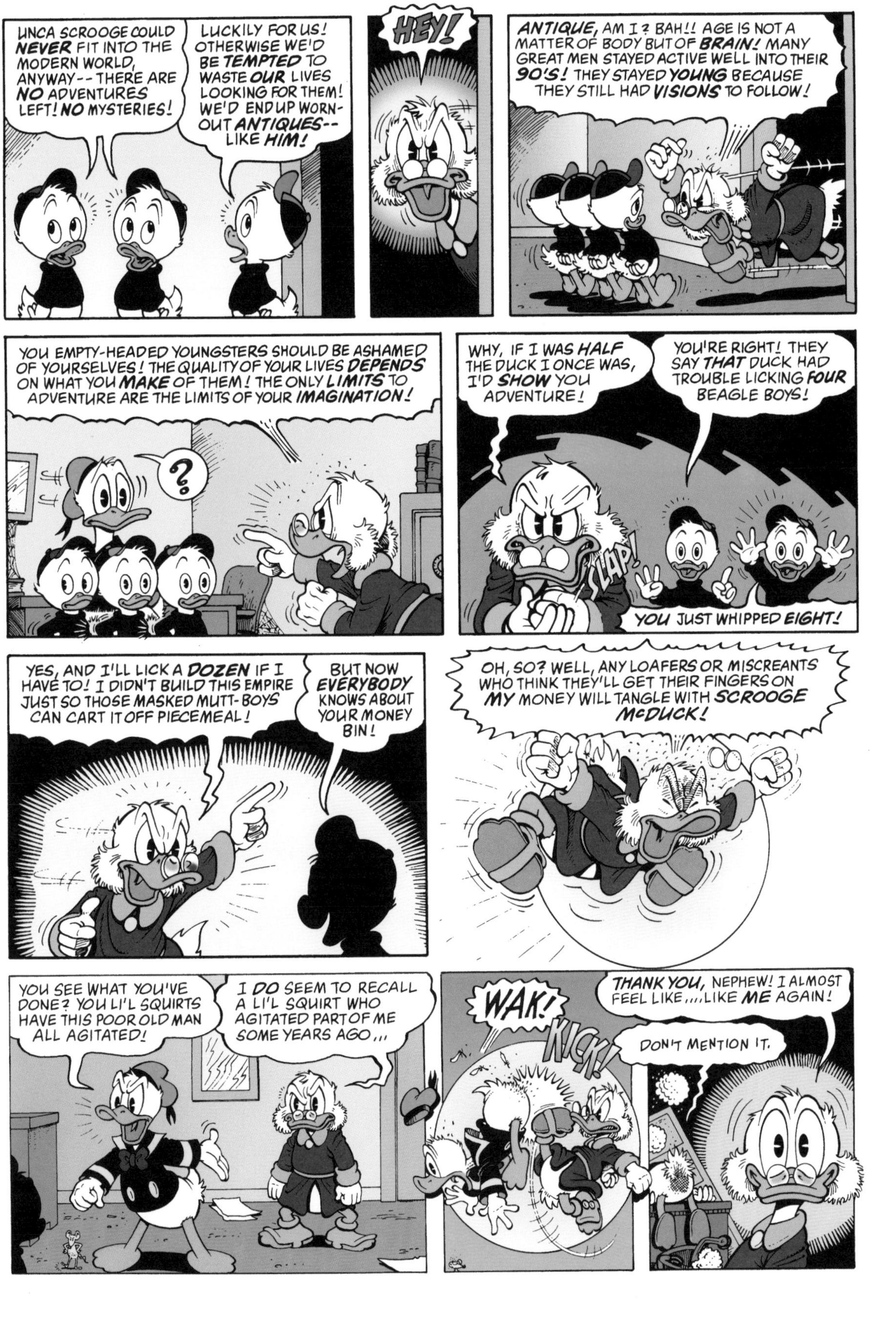
UNCA SCROOGE COULD NEVER FIT INTO THE MODERN WORLD, ANYWAY--THERE ARE NO ADVENTURES LEFT! NO MYSTERIES!
LUCKILY FOR US! OTHERWISE WE'D BE TEMPTED TO WASTE OUR LIVES LOOKING FOR THEM! WE'D END UP WORN-OUT ANTIQUES--LIKE HIM!
HEY!
ANTIQUE, AM I? BAH!! AGE IS NOT A MATTER OF BODY BUT OF BRAIN! MANY GREAT MEN STAYED ACTIVE WELL INTO THEIR 90'S! THEY STAYED YOUNG BECAUSE THEY STILL HAD VISIONS TO FOLLOW!
YOU EMPTY-HEADED YOUNGSTERS SHOULD BE ASHAMED OF YOURSELVES! THE QUALITY OF YOUR LIVES DEPENDS ON WHAT YOU MAKE OF THEM! THE ONLY LIMITS TO ADVENTURE ARE THE LIMITS OF YOUR IMAGINATION!
?
WHY, IF I WAS HALF THE DUCK I ONCE WAS, I'D SHOW YOU ADVENTURE!
YOU'RE RIGHT! THEY SAY THAT DUCK HAD TROUBLE LICKING FOUR BEAGLE BOYS!
SLAP!
YOU JUST WHIPPED EIGHT!
YES, AND I'LL LICK A DOZEN IF I HAVE TO! I DIDN'T BUILD THIS EMPIRE JUST SO THOSE MASKED MUTT-BOYS CAN CART IT OFF PIECEMEAL!
BUT NOW EVERYBODY KNOWS ABOUT YOUR MONEY BIN!
OH, SO? WELL, ANY LOAFERS OR MISCREANTS WHO THINK THEY'LL GET THEIR FINGERS ON MY MONEY WILL TANGLE WITH SCROOGE McDUCK!
YOU SEE WHAT YOU'VE DONE? YOU LI'L SQUIRTS HAVE THIS POOR OLD MAN ALL AGITATED!
I DO SEEM TO RECALL A LI'L SQUIRT WHO AGITATED PART OF ME SOME YEARS AGO...
WAK!
KICK!
THANK YOU, NEPHEW! I ALMOST FEEL LIKE....LIKE ME AGAIN!
DON'T MENTION IT.

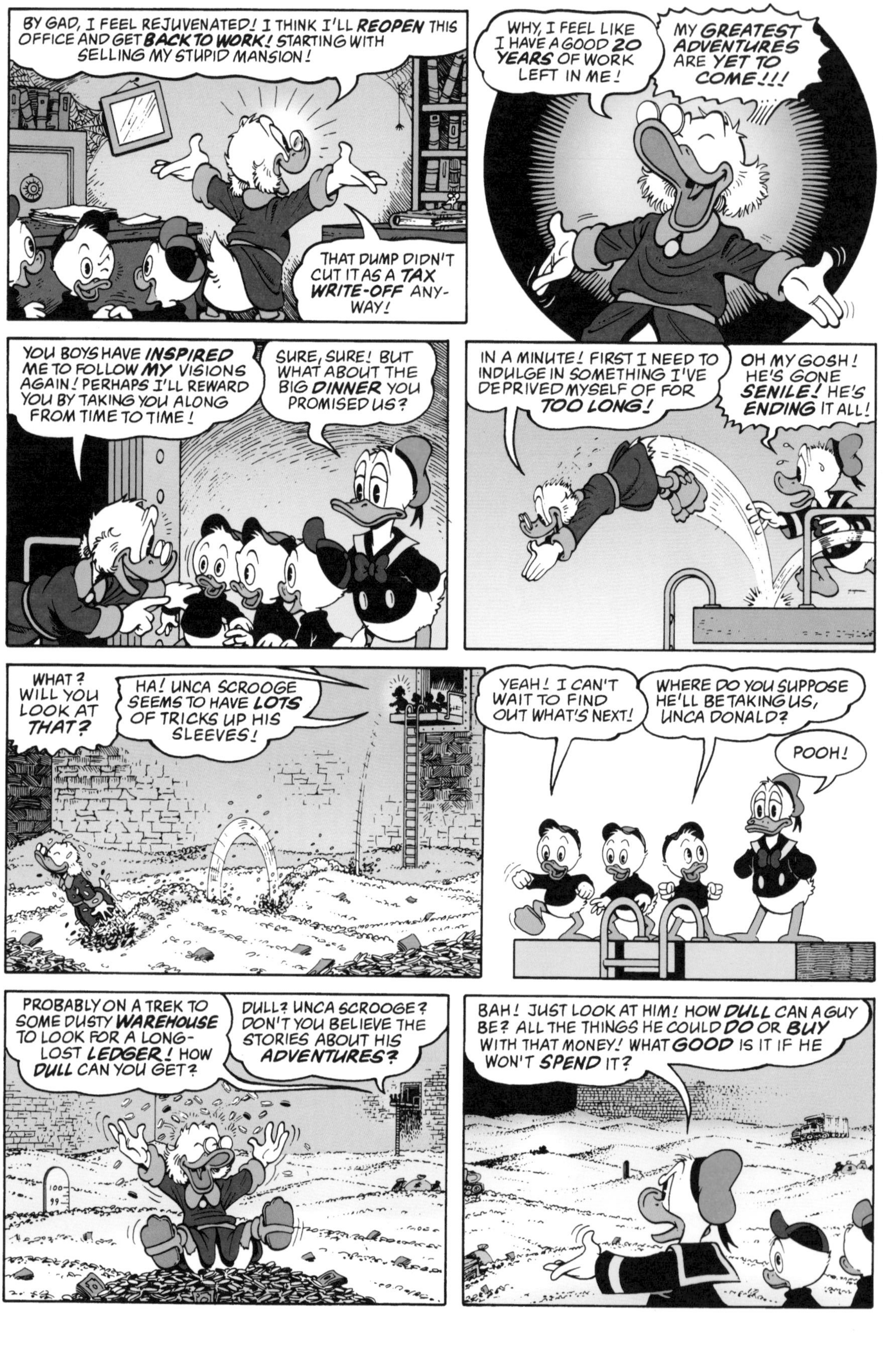
BY GAD, I FEEL REJUVENATED! I THINK I'LL REOPEN THIS OFFICE AND GET BACK TO WORK! STARTING WITH SELLING MY STUPID MANSION!
THAT DUMP DIDN'T CUT IT AS A TAX WRITE-OFF ANY-WAY!
WHY, I FEEL LIKE I HAVE A GOOD 20 YEARS OF WORK LEFT IN ME!
MY GREATEST ADVENTURES ARE YET TO COME!!!
YOU BOYS HAVE INSPIRED ME TO FOLLOW MY VISIONS AGAIN! PERHAPS I'LL REWARD YOU BY TAKING YOU ALONG FROM TIME TO TIME!
SURE, SURE! BUT WHAT ABOUT THE BIG DINNER YOU PROMISED US?
IN A MINUTE! FIRST I NEED TO INDULGE IN SOMETHING I'VE DEPRIVED MYSELF OF FOR TOO LONG!
OH MY GOSH! HE'S GONE SENILE! HE'S ENDING IT ALL!
WHAT? WILL YOU LOOK AT THAT?
HA! UNCA SCROOGE SEEMS TO HAVE LOTS OF TRICKS UP HIS SLEEVES!
YEAH! I CAN'T WAIT TO FIND OUT WHAT'S NEXT!
WHERE DO YOU SUPPOSE HE'LL BE TAKING US, UNCA DONALD?
POOH!
PROBABLY ON A TREK TO SOME DUSTY WAREHOUSE TO LOOK FOR A LONG-LOST LEDGER! HOW DULL CAN YOU GET?
DULL? UNCA SCROOGE? DON'T YOU BELIEVE THE STORIES ABOUT HIS ADVENTURES?
BAH! JUST LOOK AT HIM! HOW DULL CAN A GUY BE? ALL THE THINGS HE COULD DO OR BUY WITH THAT MONEY! WHAT GOOD IS IT IF HE WON'T SPEND IT?

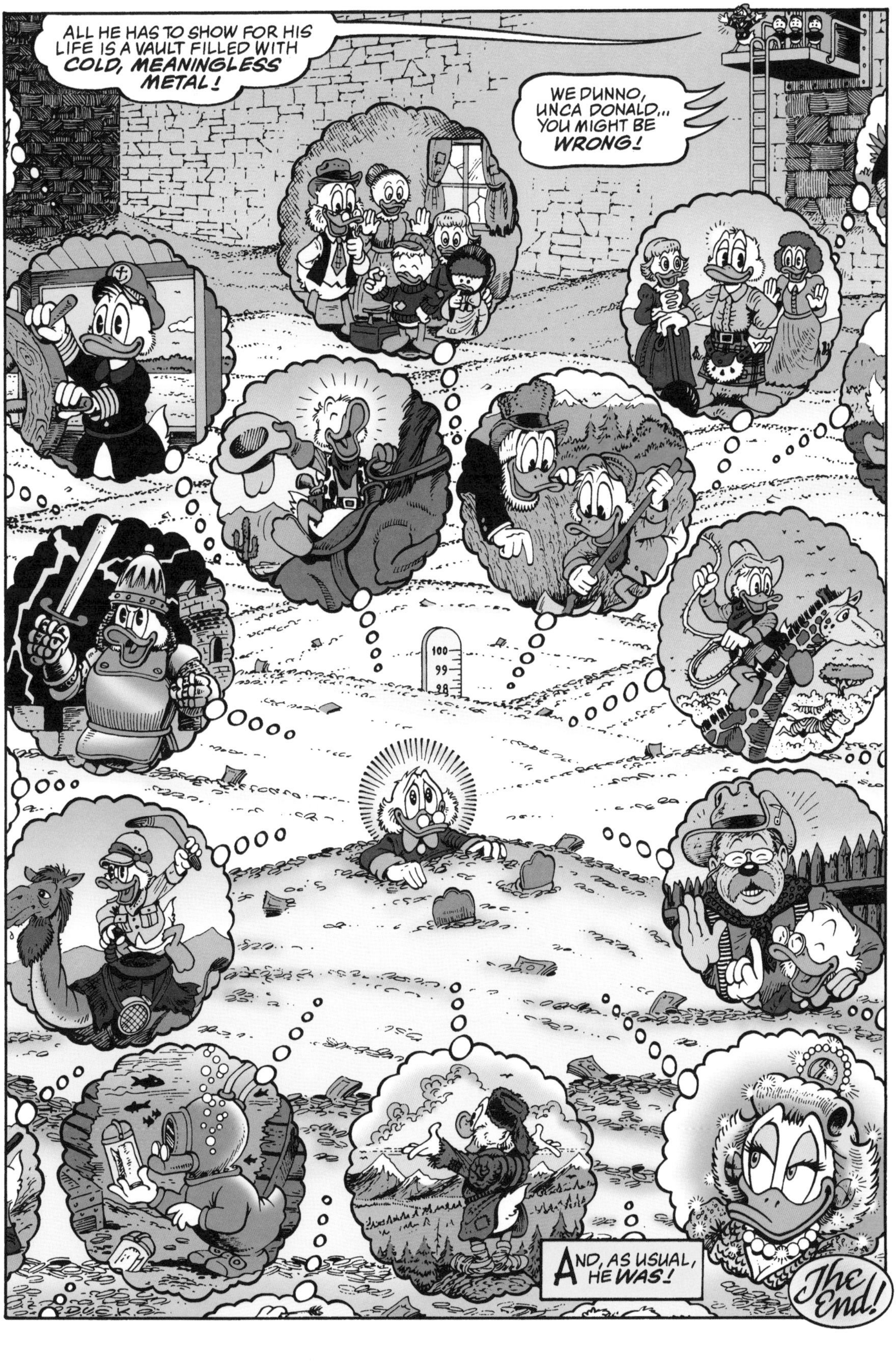
ALL HE HAS TO SHOW FOR HIS LIFE IS A VAULT FILLED WITH COLD, MEANINGLESS METAL!
WE DUNNO, UNCA DONALD... YOU MIGHT BE WRONG!
AND, AS USUAL, HE WAS!
The End!

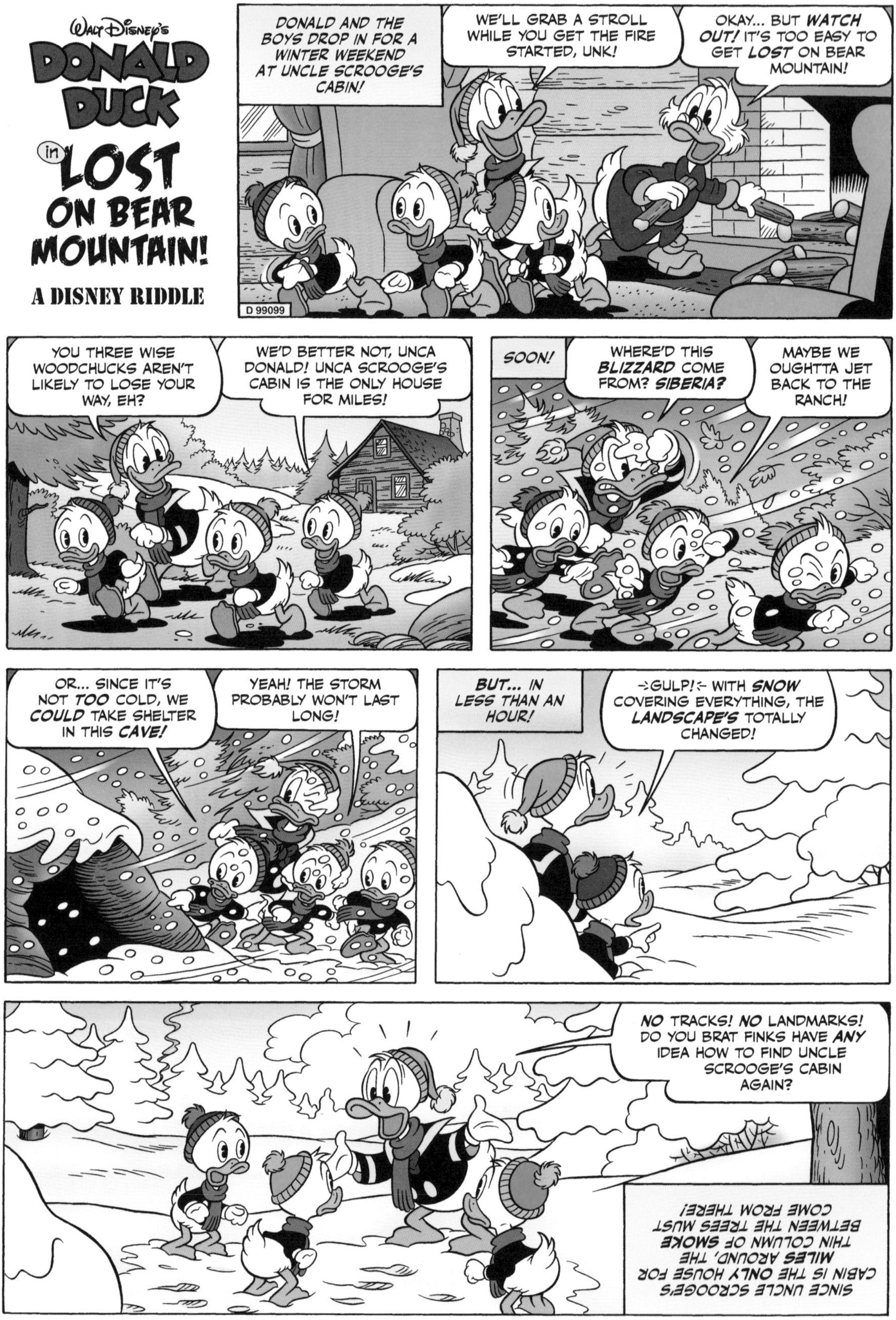
Walt Disney's
DONALD DUCK
in LOST ON BEAR MOUNTAIN!
A DISNEY RIDDLE
DONALD AND THE BOYS DROP IN FOR A WINTER WEEKEND AT UNCLE SCROOGE'S CABIN!
WE'LL GRAB A STROLL WHILE YOU GET THE FIRE STARTED, UNK!
OKAY... BUT WATCH OUT! IT'S TOO EASY TO GET LOST ON BEAR MOUNTAIN!
D 99099
YOU THREE WISE WOODCHUCKS AREN'T LIKELY TO LOSE YOUR WAY, EH?
WE'D BETTER NOT, UNCA DONALD! UNCA SCROOGE'S CABIN IS THE ONLY HOUSE FOR MILES!
SOON!
WHERE'D THIS BLIZZARD COME FROM? SIBERIA?
MAYBE WE OUGHTTA JET BACK TO THE RANCH!
OR... SINCE IT'S NOT TOO COLD, WE COULD TAKE SHELTER IN THIS CAVE!
YEAH! THE STORM PROBABLY WON'T LAST LONG!
BUT... IN LESS THAN AN HOUR!
-GULP!- WITH SNOW COVERING EVERYTHING, THE LANDSCAPE'S TOTALLY CHANGED!
NO TRACKS! NO LANDMARKS! DO YOU BRAT FINKS HAVE ANY IDEA HOW TO FIND UNCLE SCROOGE'S CABIN AGAIN?
SINCE UNCLE SCROOGE'S CABIN IS THE ONLY HOUSE FOR MILES AROUND, THE THIN COLUMN OF SMOKE BETWEEN THE TREES MUST COME FROM THERE!

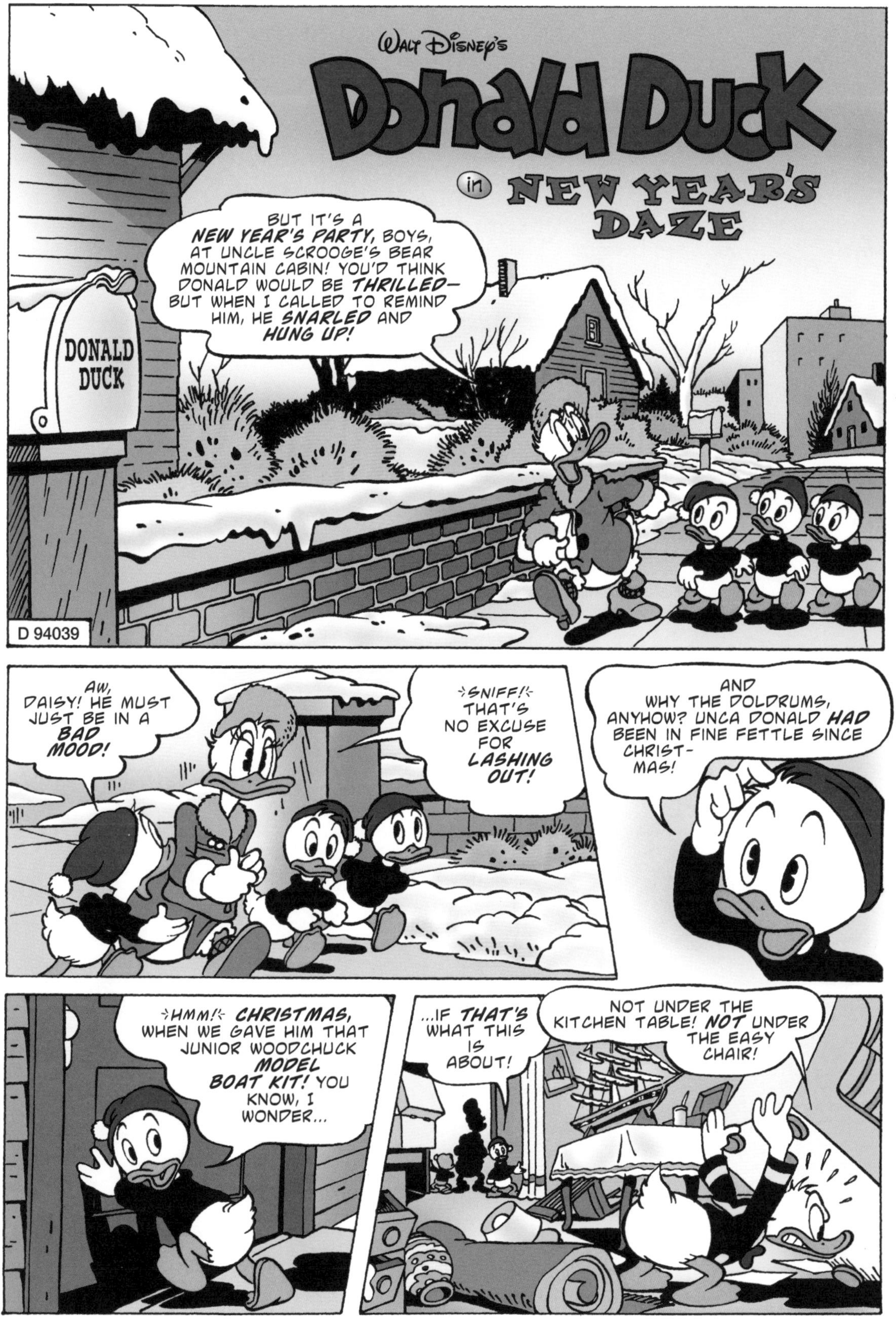
WALT DISNEY'S
Donald Duck
in NEW YEAR'S DAZE
BUT IT'S A NEW YEAR'S PARTY, BOYS, AT UNCLE SCROOGE'S BEAR MOUNTAIN CABIN! YOU'D THINK DONALD WOULD BE THRILLED— BUT WHEN I CALLED TO REMIND HIM, HE SNARLED AND HUNG UP!
DONALD DUCK
D 94039
AW, DAISY! HE MUST JUST BE IN A BAD MOOD!
SNIFF! THAT'S NO EXCUSE FOR LASHING OUT!
AND WHY THE DOLDRUMS, ANYHOW? UNCA DONALD HAD BEEN IN FINE FETTLE SINCE CHRIST-MAS!
HMM! CHRISTMAS, WHEN WE GAVE HIM THAT JUNIOR WOODCHUCK MODEL BOAT KIT! YOU KNOW, I WONDER...
...IF THAT'S WHAT THIS IS ABOUT!
NOT UNDER THE KITCHEN TABLE! NOT UNDER THE EASY CHAIR!

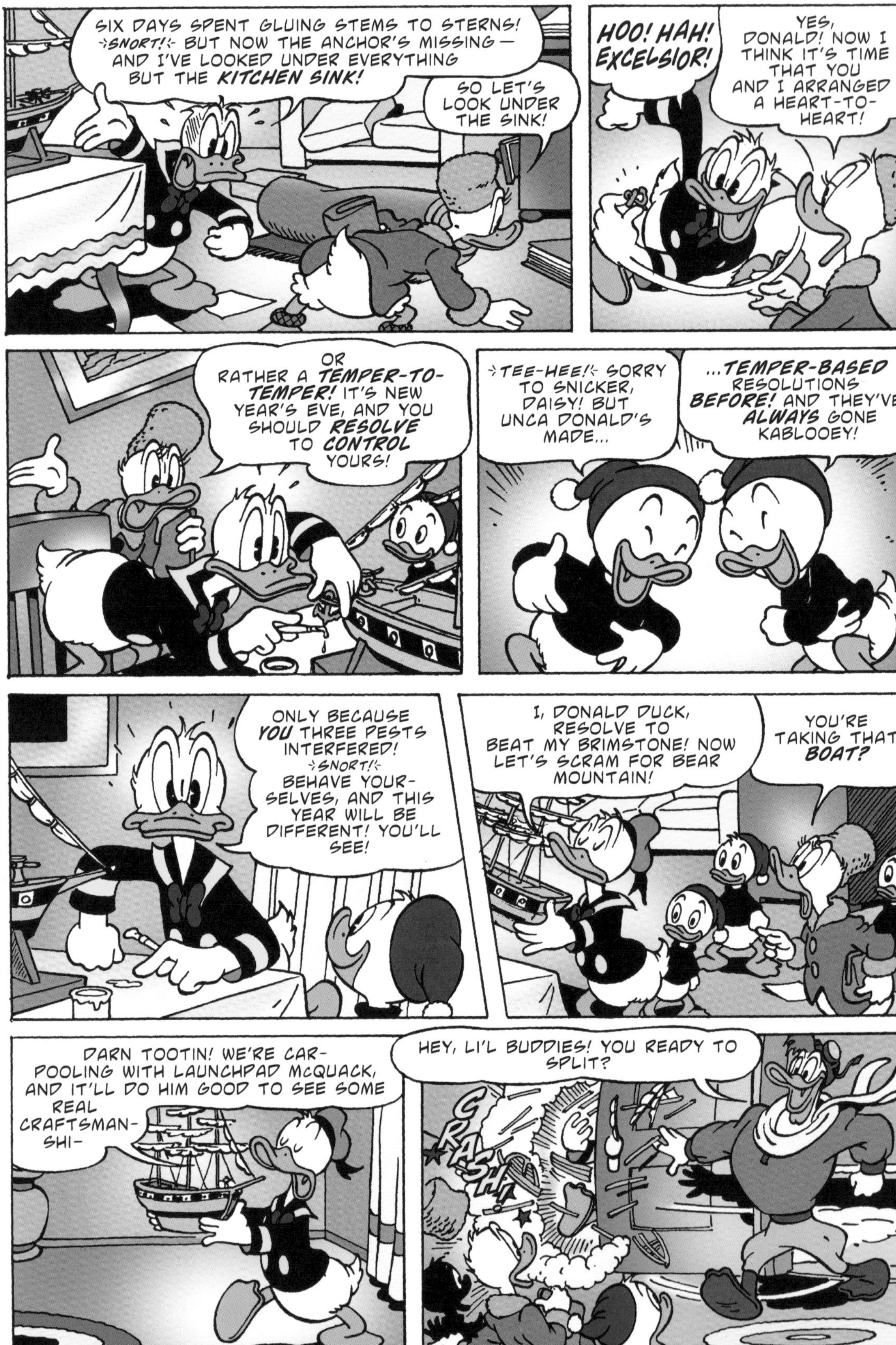
SIX DAYS SPENT GLUING STEMS TO STERNS! SNORT! BUT NOW THE ANCHOR'S MISSING — AND I'VE LOOKED UNDER EVERYTHING BUT THE KITCHEN SINK!
SO LET'S LOOK UNDER THE SINK!
HOO! HAH! EXCELSIOR!
YES, DONALD! NOW I THINK IT'S TIME THAT YOU AND I ARRANGED A HEART-TO-HEART!
OR RATHER A TEMPER-TO-TEMPER! IT'S NEW YEAR'S EVE, AND YOU SHOULD RESOLVE TO CONTROL YOURS!
TEE-HEE! SORRY TO SNICKER, DAISY! BUT UNCA DONALD'S MADE...
...TEMPER-BASED RESOLUTIONS BEFORE! AND THEY'VE ALWAYS GONE KABLOOEY!
ONLY BECAUSE YOU THREE PESTS INTERFERED! SNORT! BEHAVE YOURSELVES, AND THIS YEAR WILL BE DIFFERENT! YOU'LL SEE!
I, DONALD DUCK, RESOLVE TO BEAT MY BRIMSTONE! NOW LET'S SCRAM FOR BEAR MOUNTAIN!
YOU'RE TAKING THAT BOAT?
DARN TOOTIN! WE'RE CAR-POOLING WITH LAUNCHPAD McQUACK, AND IT'LL DO HIM GOOD TO SEE SOME REAL CRAFTSMANSHI-
HEY, LI'L BUDDIES! YOU READY TO SPLIT?
CRASH!

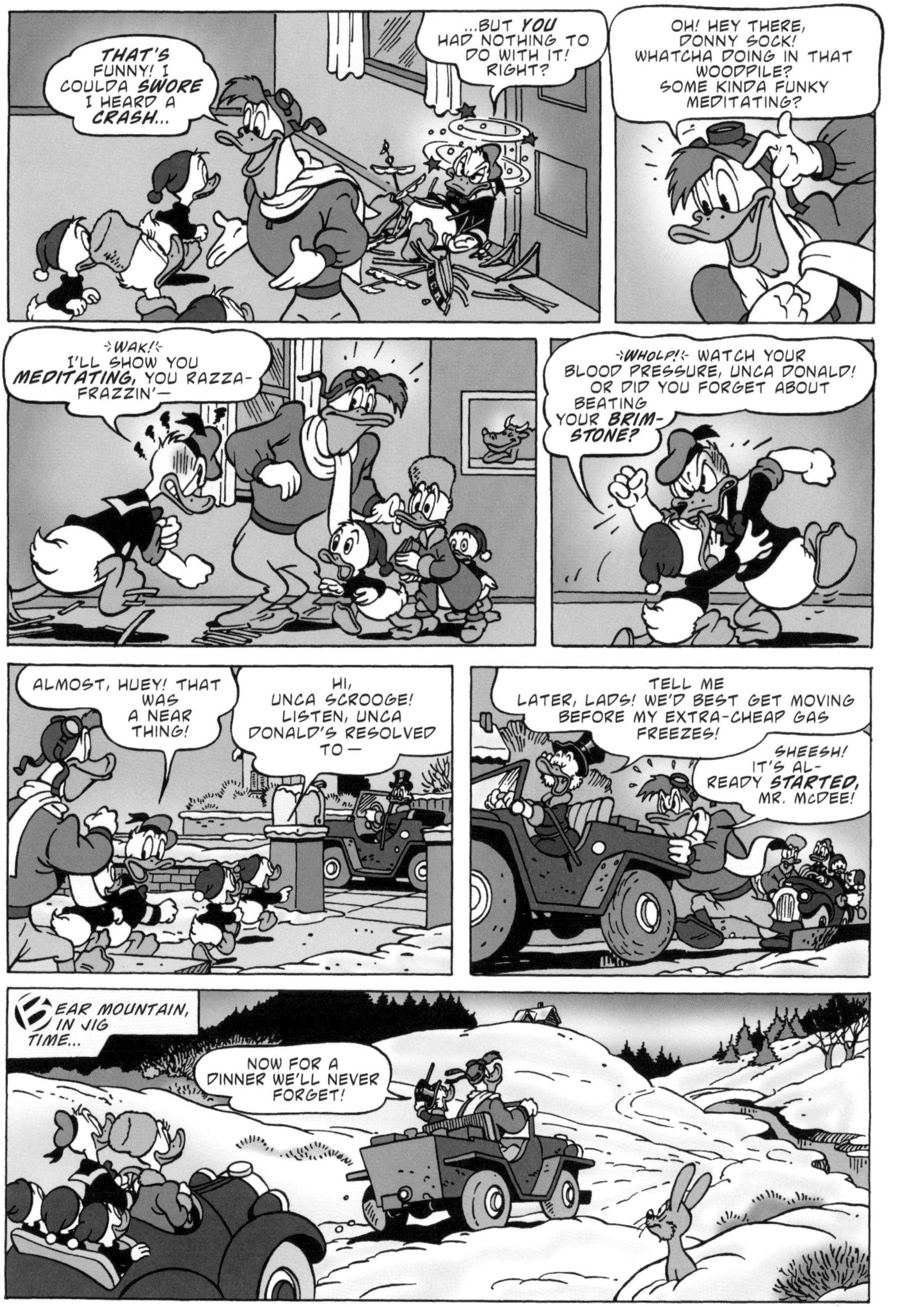
THAT'S FUNNY! I COULDA SWORE I HEARD A CRASH...
...BUT YOU HAD NOTHING TO DO WITH IT! RIGHT?
OH! HEY THERE, DONNY SOCK! WHATCHA DOING IN THAT WOODPILE? SOME KINDA FUNKY MEDITATING?
WAK! I'LL SHOW YOU MEDITATING, YOU RAZZA-FRAZZIN'—
WHOLP! WATCH YOUR BLOOD PRESSURE, UNCA DONALD! OR DID YOU FORGET ABOUT BEATING YOUR BRIMSTONE?
ALMOST, HUEY! THAT WAS A NEAR THING!
HI, UNCA SCROOGE! LISTEN, UNCA DONALD'S RESOLVED TO—
TELL ME LATER, LADS! WE'D BEST GET MOVING BEFORE MY EXTRA-CHEAP GAS FREEZES!
SHEESH! IT'S AL-READY STARTED, MR. McDEE!
BEAR MOUNTAIN, IN JIG TIME...
NOW FOR A DINNER WE'LL NEVER FORGET!

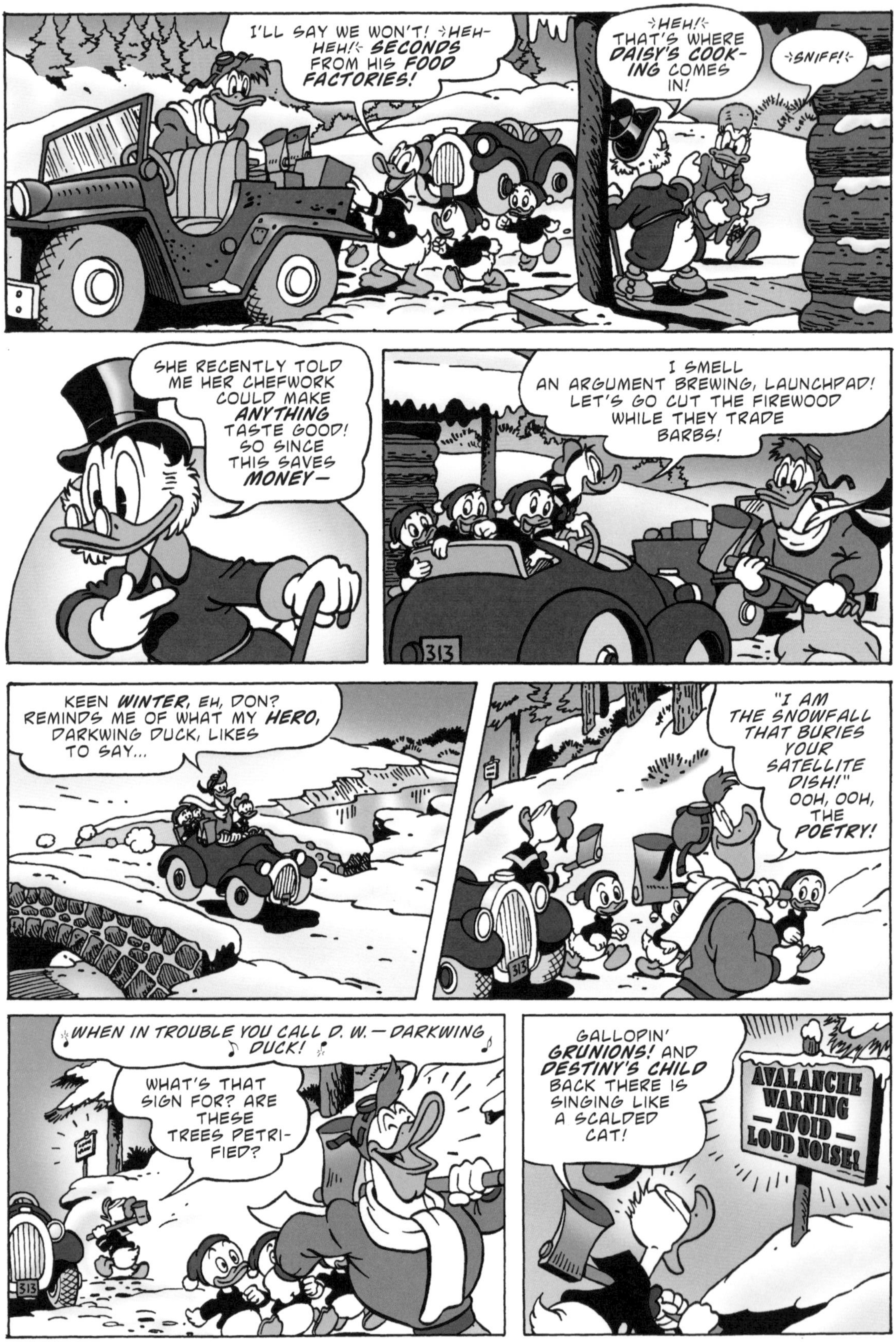
I'LL SAY WE WON'T! HEH-HEH! SECONDS FROM HIS FOOD FACTORIES!
HEH! THAT'S WHERE DAISY'S COOKING COMES IN!
SNIFF!
SHE RECENTLY TOLD ME HER CHEFWORK COULD MAKE ANYTHING TASTE GOOD! SO SINCE THIS SAVES MONEY—
I SMELL AN ARGUMENT BREWING, LAUNCHPAD! LET'S GO CUT THE FIREWOOD WHILE THEY TRADE BARBS!
313
KEEN WINTER, EH, DON? REMINDS ME OF WHAT MY HERO, DARKWING DUCK, LIKES TO SAY...
"I AM THE SNOWFALL THAT BURIES YOUR SATELLITE DISH!" OOH, OOH, THE POETRY!
313
WHEN IN TROUBLE YOU CALL D. W. — DARKWING DUCK!
WHAT'S THAT SIGN FOR? ARE THESE TREES PETRIFIED?
313
GALLOPIN' GRUNIONS! AND DESTINY'S CHILD BACK THERE IS SINGING LIKE A SCALDED CAT!
AVALANCHE WARNING — AVOID — LOUD NOISE!

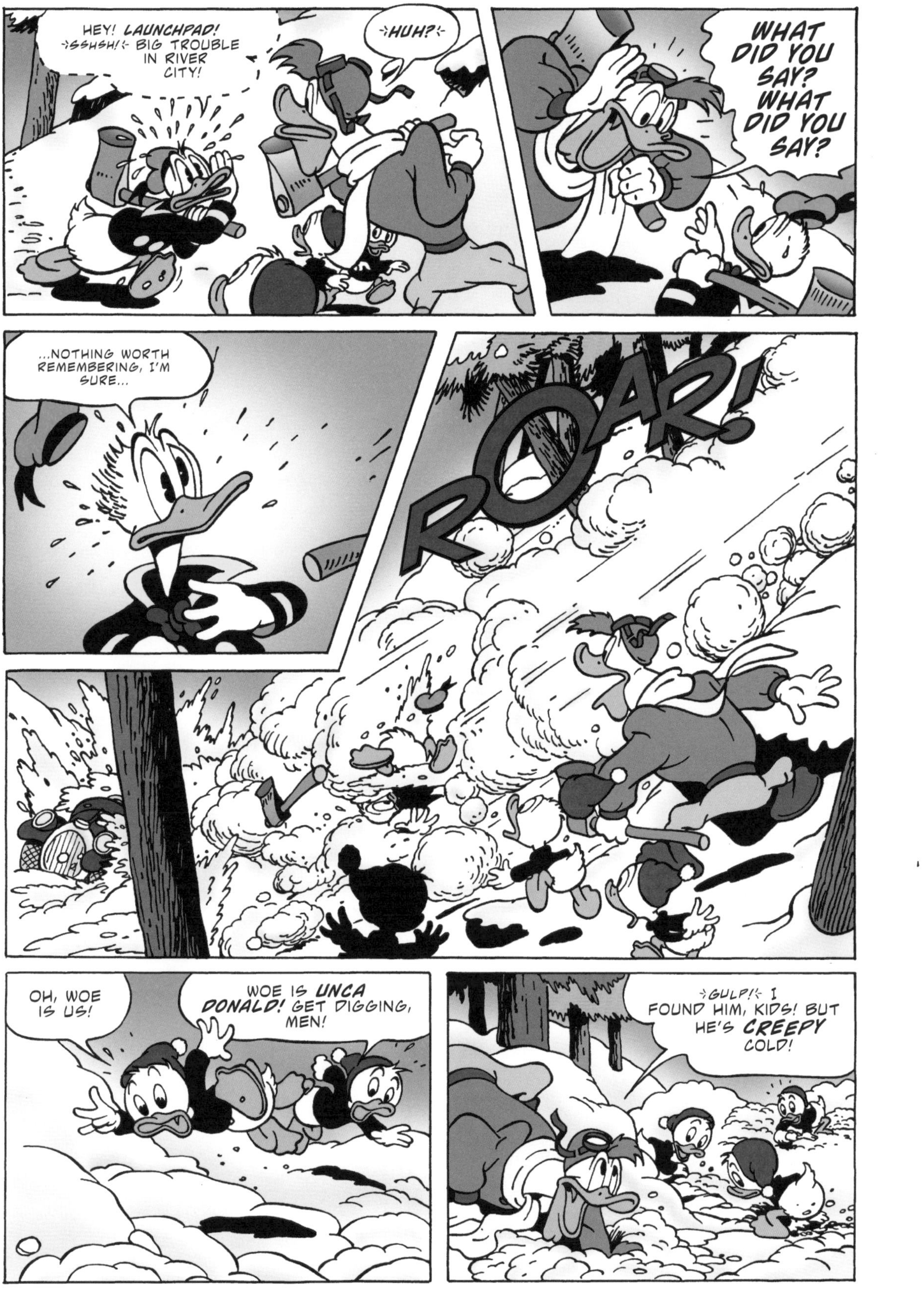
HEY! LAUNCHPAD! ~SSHSH!~ BIG TROUBLE IN RIVER CITY!
~HUH?~
WHAT DID YOU SAY? WHAT DID YOU SAY?
...NOTHING WORTH REMEMBERING, I'M SURE...
ROAR!
OH, WOE IS US!
WOE IS UNCA DONALD! GET DIGGING, MEN!
~GULP!~ I FOUND HIM, KIDS! BUT HE'S CREEPY COLD!

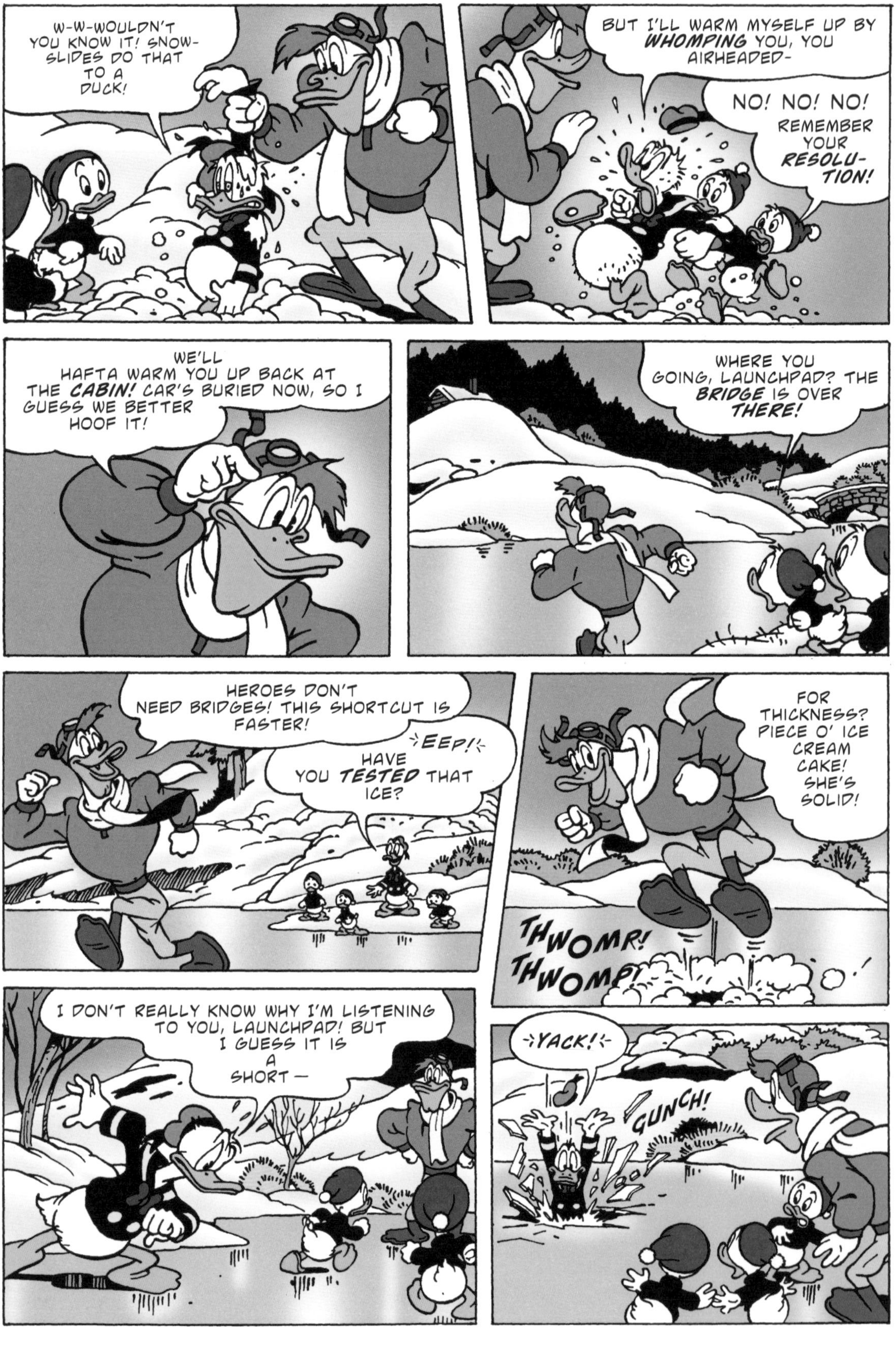
W-W-WOULDN'T YOU KNOW IT! SNOW-SLIDES DO THAT TO A DUCK!
BUT I'LL WARM MYSELF UP BY WHOMPING YOU, YOU AIRHEADED-
NO! NO! NO! REMEMBER YOUR RESOLU-TION!
WE'LL HAFTA WARM YOU UP BACK AT THE CABIN! CAR'S BURIED NOW, SO I GUESS WE BETTER HOOF IT!
WHERE YOU GOING, LAUNCHPAD? THE BRIDGE IS OVER THERE!
HEROES DON'T NEED BRIDGES! THIS SHORTCUT IS FASTER!
EEP!
HAVE YOU TESTED THAT ICE?
FOR THICKNESS? PIECE O' ICE CREAM CAKE! SHE'S SOLID!
THWOMP! THWOMP!
I DON'T REALLY KNOW WHY I'M LISTENING TO YOU, LAUNCHPAD! BUT I GUESS IT IS A SHORT —
YACK!
GUNCH!

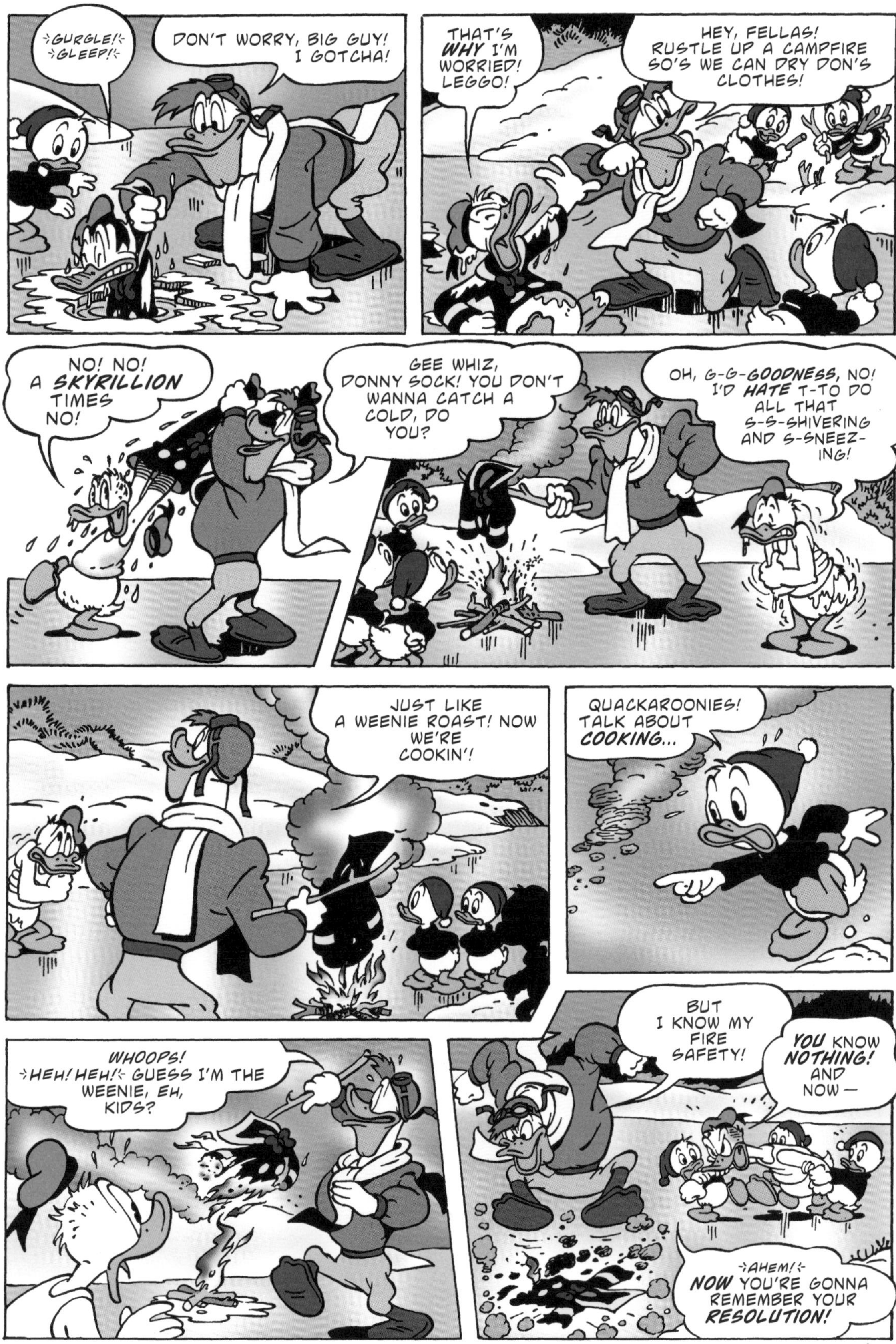

GURGLE! GLEEP!
DON'T WORRY, BIG GUY! I GOTCHA!
THAT'S WHY I'M WORRIED! LEGGO!
HEY, FELLAS! RUSTLE UP A CAMPFIRE SO'S WE CAN DRY DON'S CLOTHES!
NO! NO! A SKYRILLION TIMES NO!
GEE WHIZ, DONNY SOCK! YOU DON'T WANNA CATCH A COLD, DO YOU?
OH, G-G-GOODNESS, NO! I'D HATE T-TO DO ALL THAT S-S-SHIVERING AND S-SNEEZ-ING!
JUST LIKE A WEENIE ROAST! NOW WE'RE COOKIN'!
QUACKAROONIES! TALK ABOUT COOKING...
WHOOPS! HEH! HEH! GUESS I'M THE WEENIE, EH, KIDS?
BUT I KNOW MY FIRE SAFETY!
YOU KNOW NOTHING! AND NOW—
AHEM! NOW YOU'RE GONNA REMEMBER YOUR RESOLUTION!

OH, YES! MY RESOLUTION! HEAVEN FORBID I TEACH SOMEONE A *WELL-DESERVED* LESSON...

THOUGH THE MORE I SEE OF LAUNCHPAD, THE MORE I MISS THE NAVY!

SORRY, MR. MCDEE! BETTER DRIVE BACK TO TOWN! NO FIREWOOD!

NO SWEAT! GRANDMA AND GUS BROUGHT A BACKUP SUPPLY!

BUT WE STILL NEED TO LIGHT THE STOVE! YOU AND DONALD GO GET THE KEROSENE FROM THE TOOL SHED!

JUST LET ME DO THIS BY *MYSELF*, LAUNCHPAD!

BUT IT NEVER HURTS TO HELP!

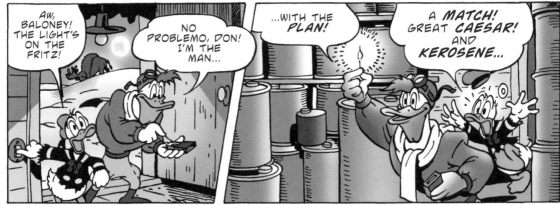

AW, BALONEY! THE LIGHT'S ON THE FRITZ!

NO PROBLEMO, DON! I'M THE MAN...

...WITH THE *PLAN!*

A *MATCH!* GREAT *CAESAR!* AND *KEROSENE*...

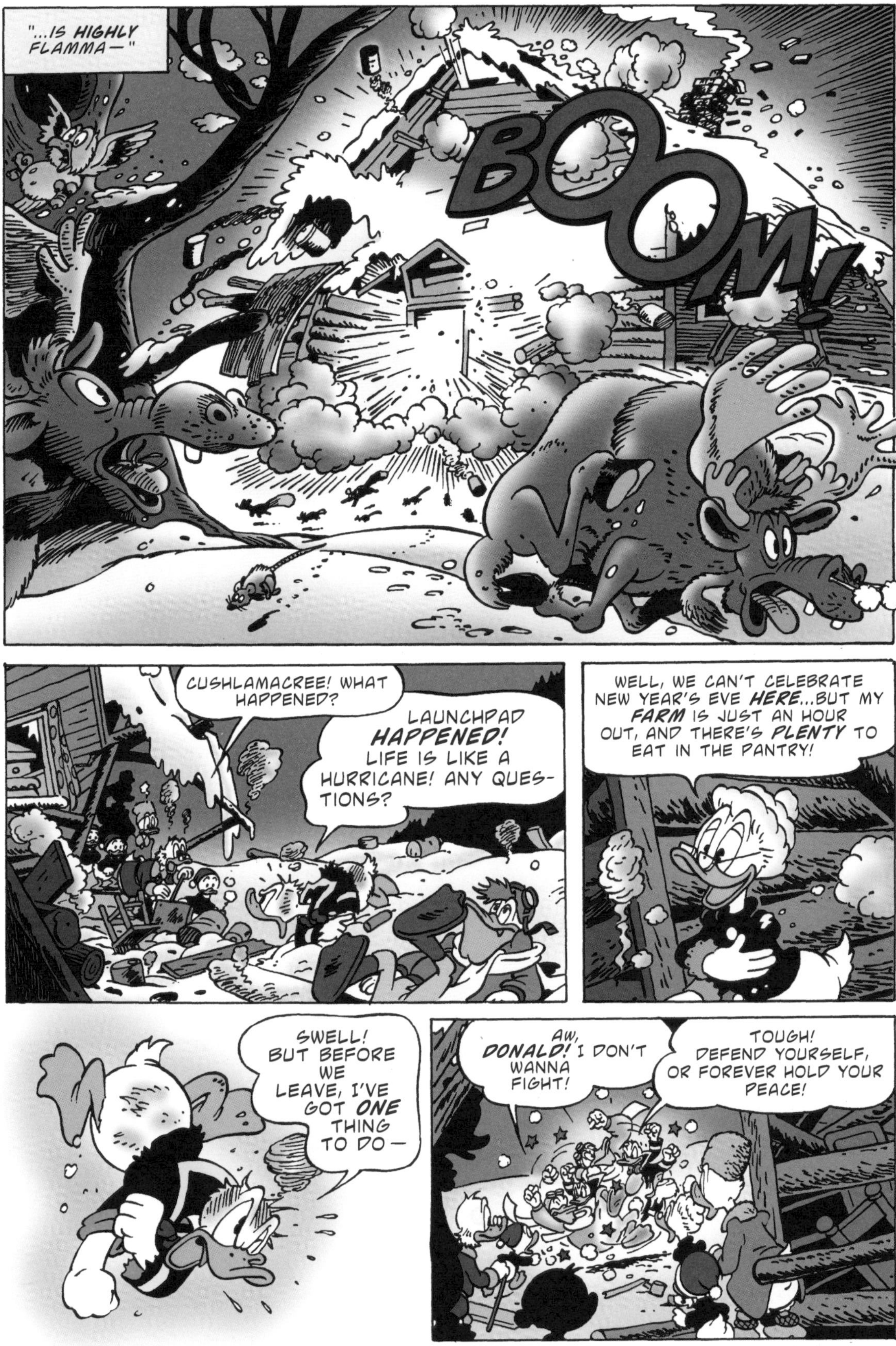
"...IS HIGHLY FLAMMA—"
BOOOM!
CUSHLAMACREE! WHAT HAPPENED?
LAUNCHPAD HAPPENED! LIFE IS LIKE A HURRICANE! ANY QUES- TIONS?
WELL, WE CAN'T CELEBRATE NEW YEAR'S EVE HERE...BUT MY FARM IS JUST AN HOUR OUT, AND THERE'S PLENTY TO EAT IN THE PANTRY!
SWELL! BUT BEFORE WE LEAVE, I'VE GOT ONE THING TO DO—
AW, DONALD! I DON'T WANNA FIGHT!
TOUGH! DEFEND YOURSELF, OR FOREVER HOLD YOUR PEACE!

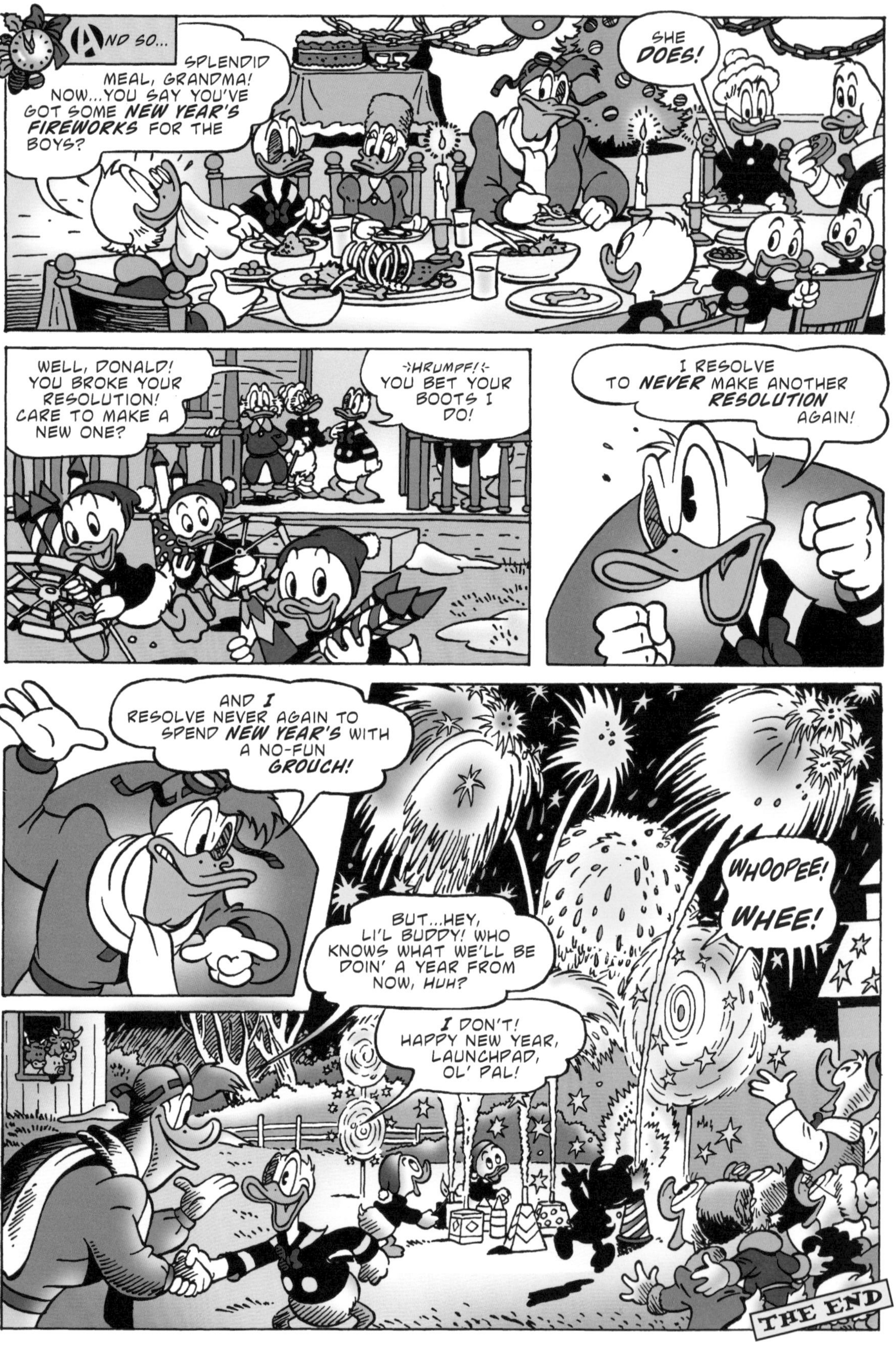
AND SO...
SPLENDID MEAL, GRANDMA! NOW...YOU SAY YOU'VE GOT SOME NEW YEAR'S FIREWORKS FOR THE BOYS?
SHE DOES!
WELL, DONALD! YOU BROKE YOUR RESOLUTION! CARE TO MAKE A NEW ONE?
HRUMPF! YOU BET YOUR BOOTS I DO!
I RESOLVE TO NEVER MAKE ANOTHER RESOLUTION AGAIN!
AND I RESOLVE NEVER AGAIN TO SPEND NEW YEAR'S WITH A NO-FUN GROUCH!
WHOOPEE!
WHEE!
BUT...HEY, LI'L BUDDY! WHO KNOWS WHAT WE'LL BE DOIN' A YEAR FROM NOW, HUH?
I DON'T! HAPPY NEW YEAR, LAUNCHPAD, OL' PAL!
THE END

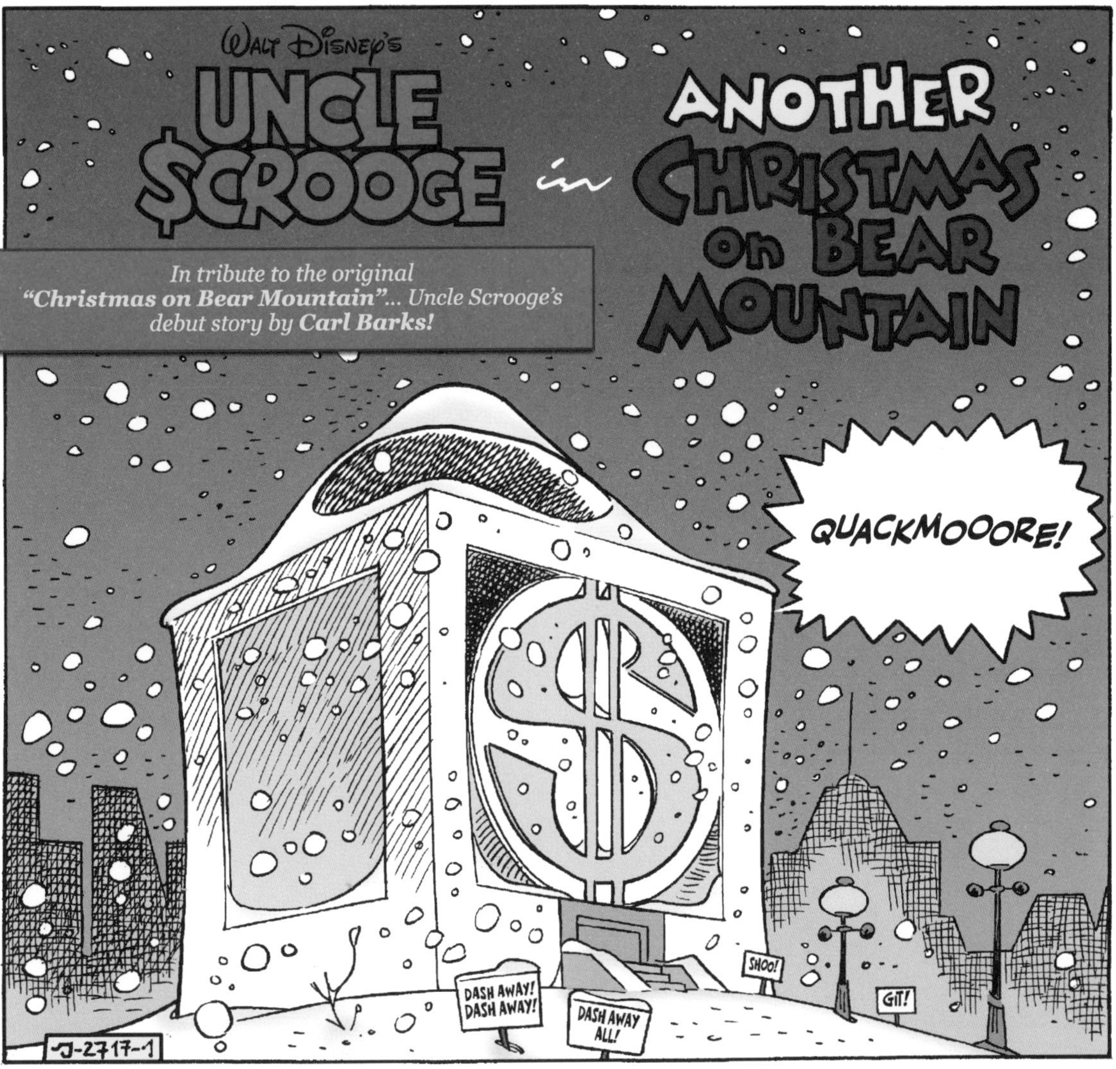
WALT DISNEY'S
UNCLE $CROOGE in ANOTHER CHRISTMAS on BEAR MOUNTAIN
In tribute to the original "Christmas on Bear Mountain"... Uncle Scrooge's debut story by Carl Barks!
QUACKMOOORE!
DASH AWAY! DASH AWAY!
DASH AWAY ALL!
SHOO!
GIT!
J-2717-1

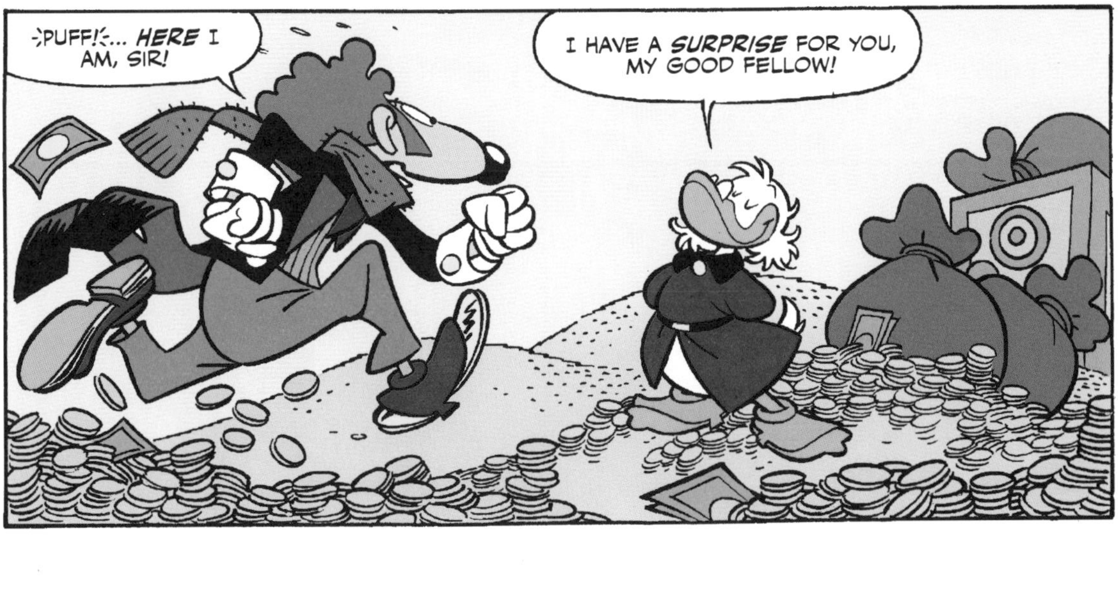
PUFF!... HERE I AM, SIR!
I HAVE A SURPRISE FOR YOU, MY GOOD FELLOW!

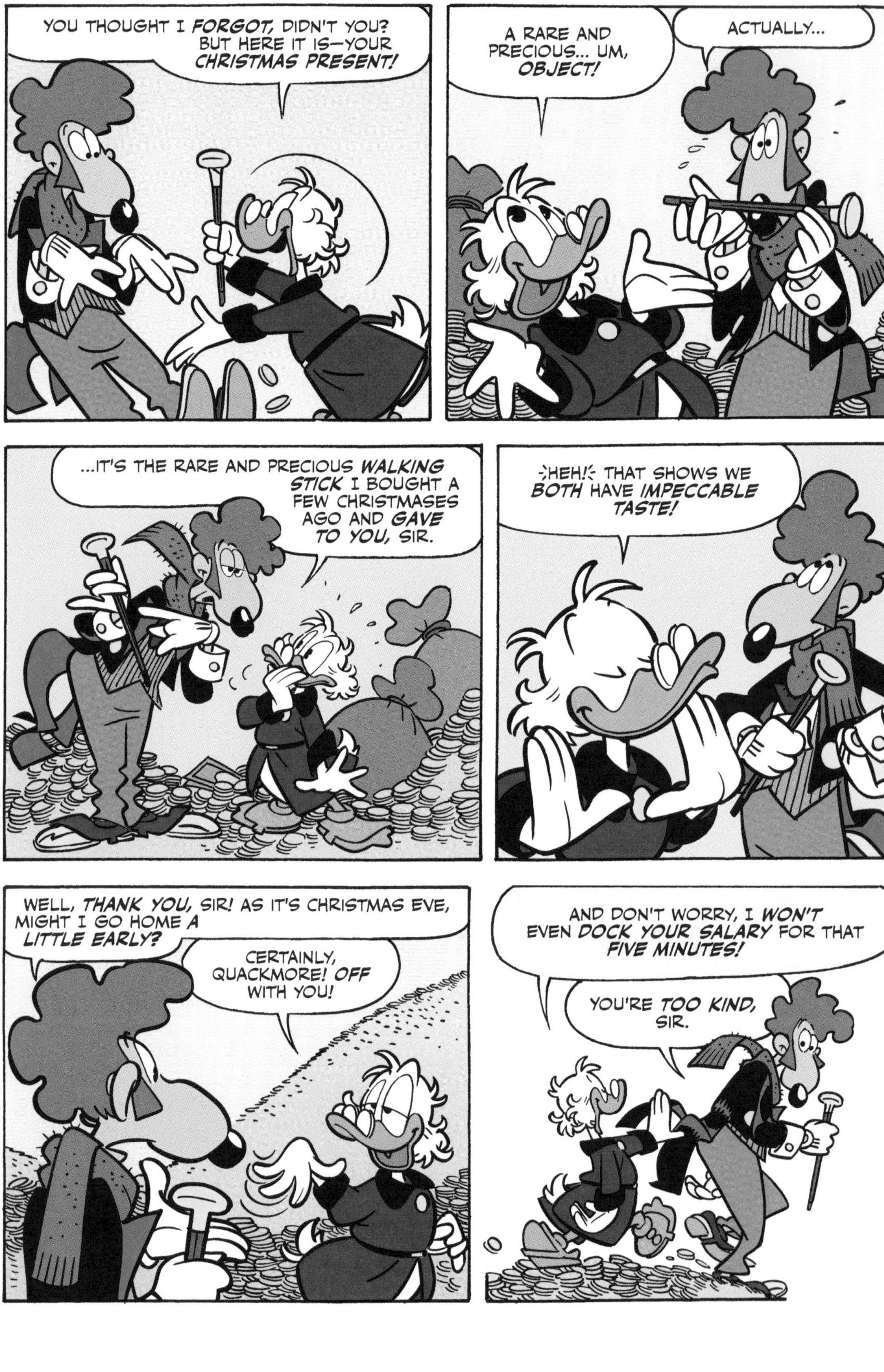
YOU THOUGHT I FORGOT, DIDN'T YOU? BUT HERE IT IS—YOUR CHRISTMAS PRESENT!
A RARE AND PRECIOUS... UM, OBJECT!
ACTUALLY...
...IT'S THE RARE AND PRECIOUS WALKING STICK I BOUGHT A FEW CHRISTMASES AGO AND GAVE TO YOU, SIR.
HEH! THAT SHOWS WE BOTH HAVE IMPECCABLE TASTE!
WELL, THANK YOU, SIR! AS IT'S CHRISTMAS EVE, MIGHT I GO HOME A LITTLE EARLY?
CERTAINLY, QUACKMORE! OFF WITH YOU!
AND DON'T WORRY, I WON'T EVEN DOCK YOUR SALARY FOR THAT FIVE MINUTES!
YOU'RE TOO KIND, SIR.

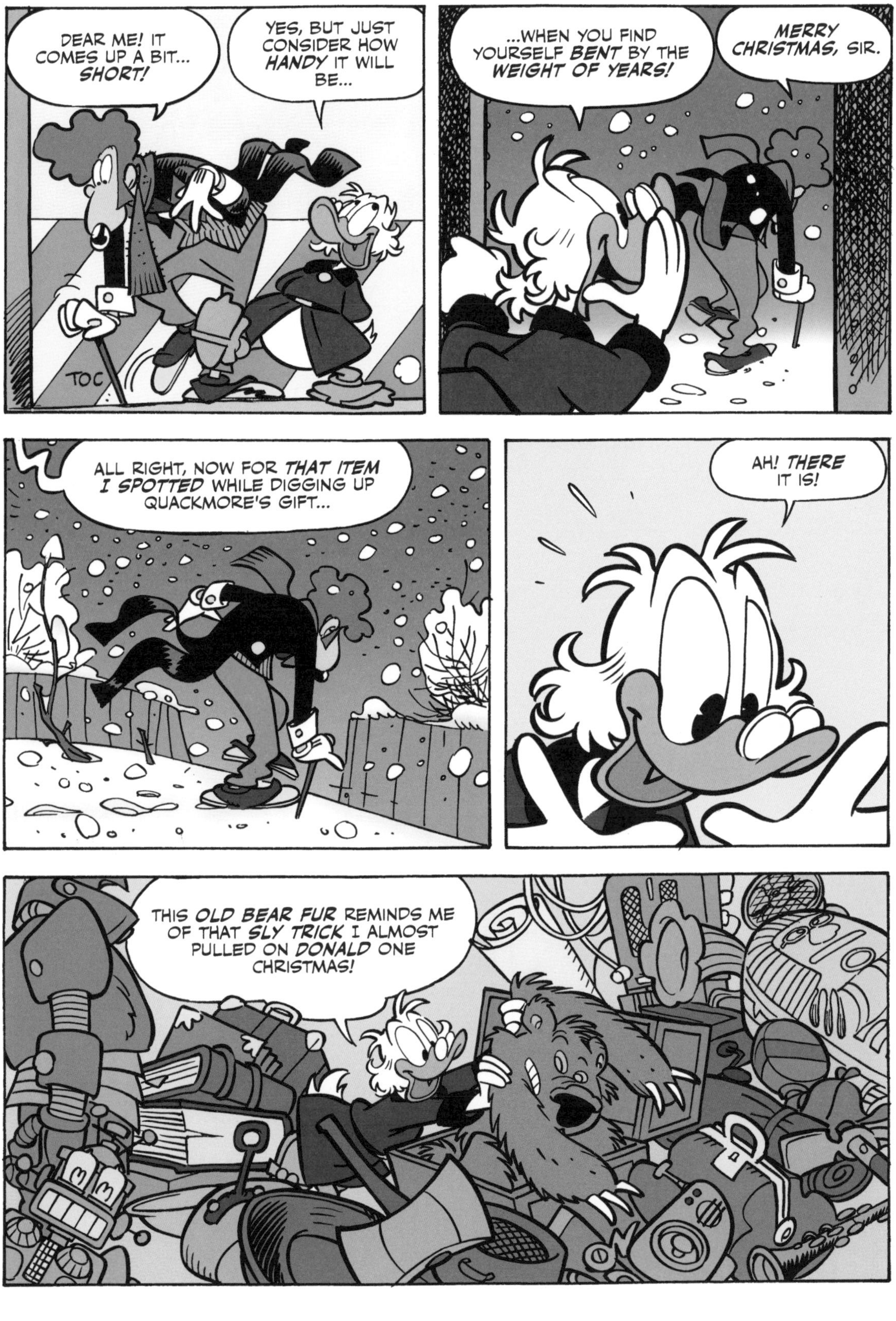
DEAR ME! IT COMES UP A BIT... SHORT!
YES, BUT JUST CONSIDER HOW HANDY IT WILL BE...
TOC
...WHEN YOU FIND YOURSELF BENT BY THE WEIGHT OF YEARS!
MERRY CHRISTMAS, SIR.
ALL RIGHT, NOW FOR THAT ITEM I SPOTTED WHILE DIGGING UP QUACKMORE'S GIFT...
AH! THERE IT IS!
THIS OLD BEAR FUR REMINDS ME OF THAT SLY TRICK I ALMOST PULLED ON DONALD ONE CHRISTMAS!

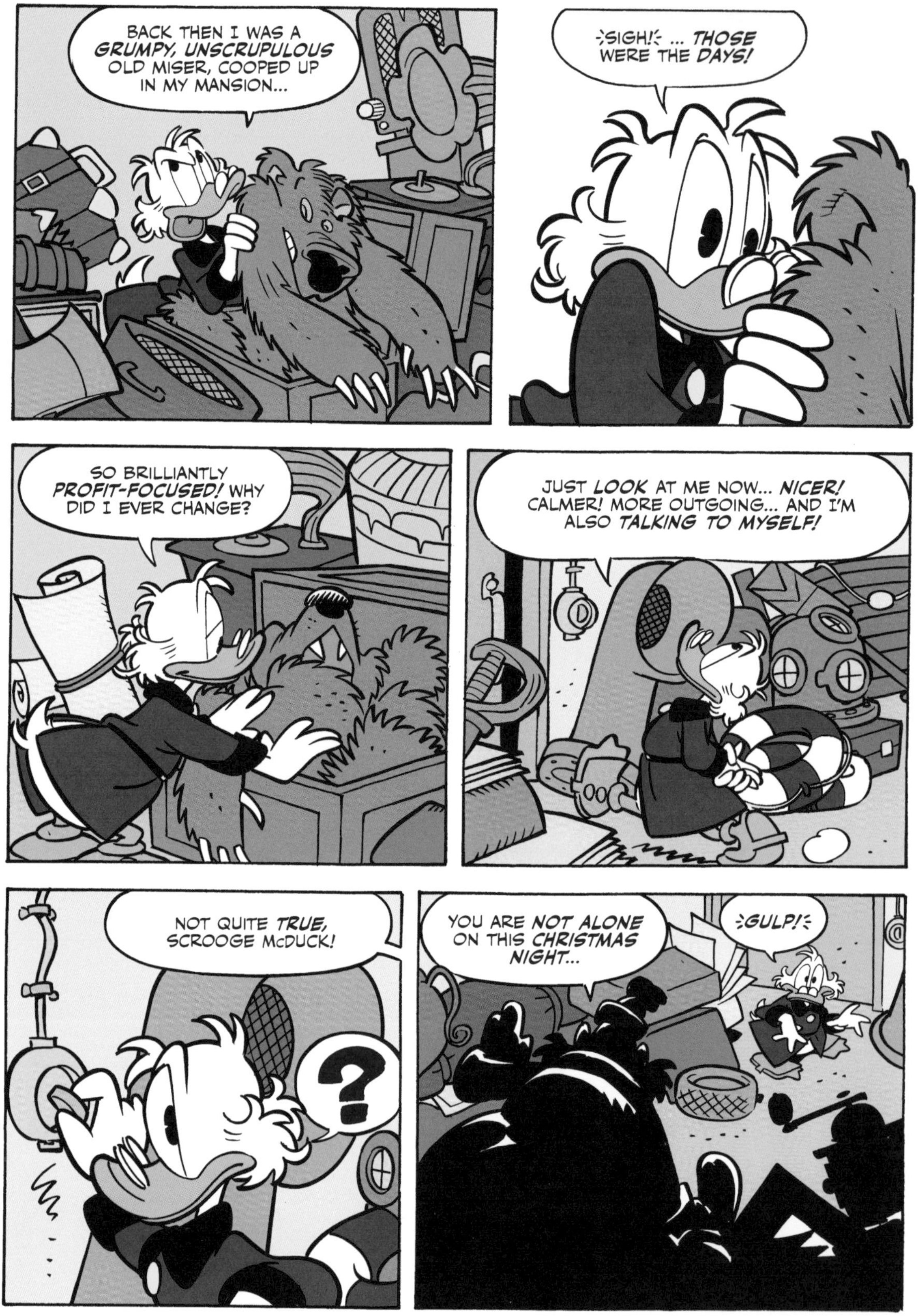
BACK THEN I WAS A GRUMPY, UNSCRUPULOUS OLD MISER, COOPED UP IN MY MANSION...
SIGH! ... THOSE WERE THE DAYS!
SO BRILLIANTLY PROFIT-FOCUSED! WHY DID I EVER CHANGE?
JUST LOOK AT ME NOW... NICER! CALMER! MORE OUTGOING... AND I'M ALSO TALKING TO MYSELF!
NOT QUITE TRUE, SCROOGE McDUCK!
?
YOU ARE NOT ALONE ON THIS CHRISTMAS NIGHT...
GULP!

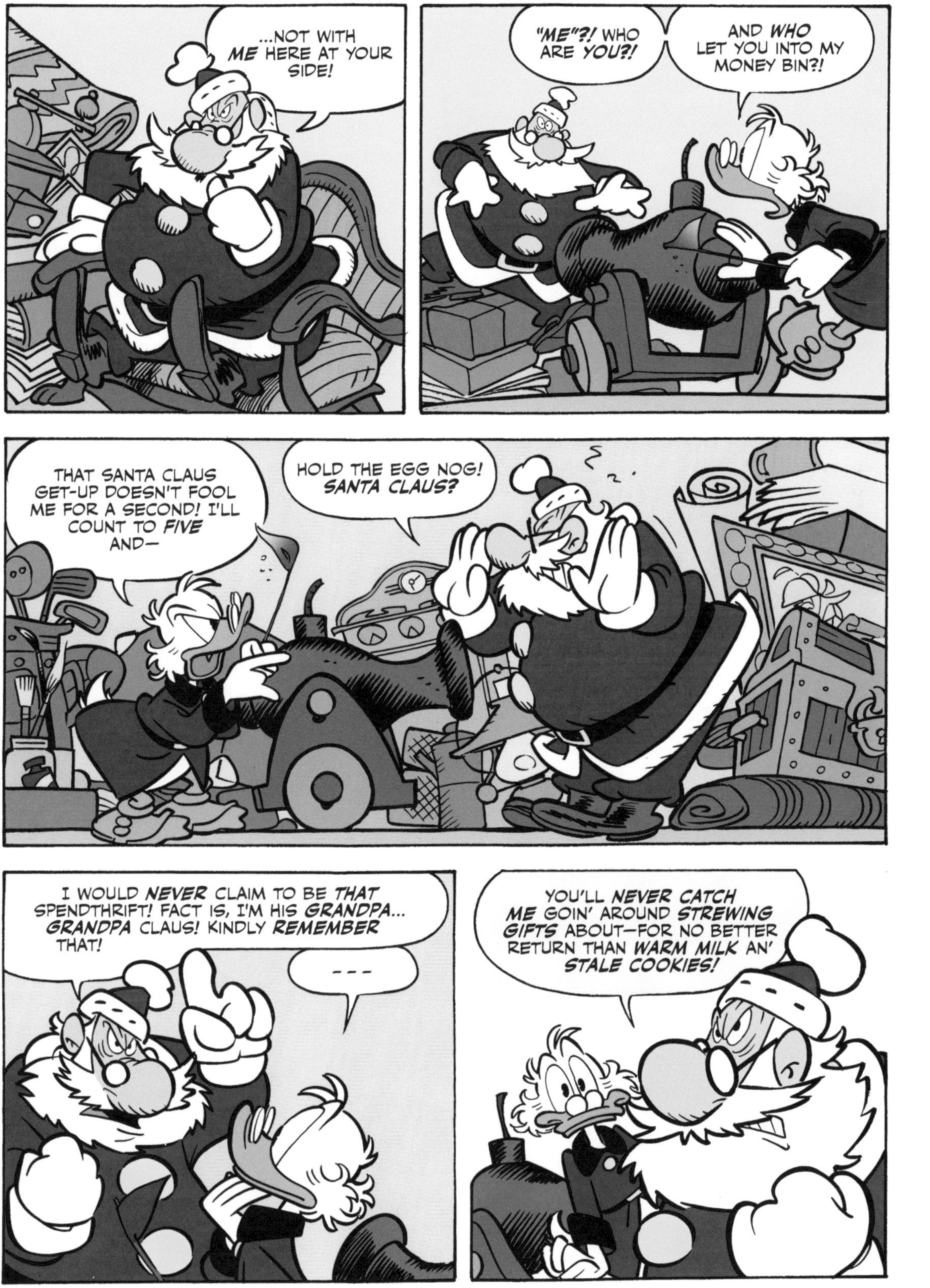
...NOT WITH ME HERE AT YOUR SIDE!
"ME"?! WHO ARE YOU?!
AND WHO LET YOU INTO MY MONEY BIN?!
THAT SANTA CLAUS GET-UP DOESN'T FOOL ME FOR A SECOND! I'LL COUNT TO FIVE AND—
HOLD THE EGG NOG! SANTA CLAUS?
I WOULD NEVER CLAIM TO BE THAT SPENDTHRIFT! FACT IS, I'M HIS GRANDPA... GRANDPA CLAUS! KINDLY REMEMBER THAT!
- - -
YOU'LL NEVER CATCH ME GOIN' AROUND STREWING GIFTS ABOUT—FOR NO BETTER RETURN THAN WARM MILK AN' STALE COOKIES!

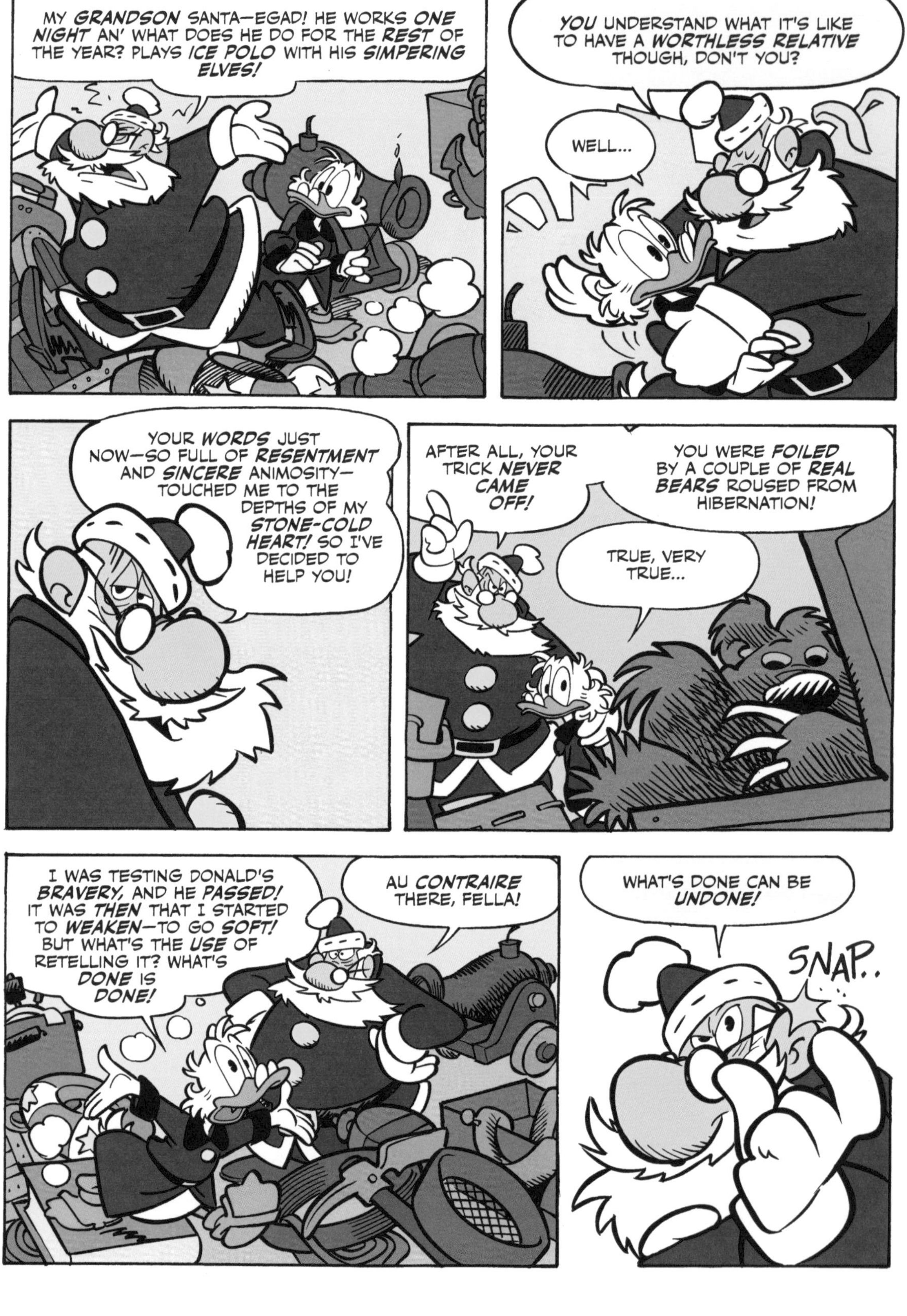
MY GRANDSON SANTA—EGAD! HE WORKS ONE NIGHT AN' WHAT DOES HE DO FOR THE REST OF THE YEAR? PLAYS ICE POLO WITH HIS SIMPERING ELVES!
YOU UNDERSTAND WHAT IT'S LIKE TO HAVE A WORTHLESS RELATIVE THOUGH, DON'T YOU?
WELL...
YOUR WORDS JUST NOW—SO FULL OF RESENTMENT AND SINCERE ANIMOSITY—TOUCHED ME TO THE DEPTHS OF MY STONE-COLD HEART! SO I'VE DECIDED TO HELP YOU!
AFTER ALL, YOUR TRICK NEVER CAME OFF!
YOU WERE FOILED BY A COUPLE OF REAL BEARS ROUSED FROM HIBERNATION!
TRUE, VERY TRUE...
I WAS TESTING DONALD'S BRAVERY, AND HE PASSED! IT WAS THEN THAT I STARTED TO WEAKEN—TO GO SOFT! BUT WHAT'S THE USE OF RETELLING IT? WHAT'S DONE IS DONE!
AU CONTRAIRE THERE, FELLA!
WHAT'S DONE CAN BE UNDONE!
SNAP..

YEEOW!

GLUB...!

THE *SNOW* MADE FOR A NICE, SOFT LANDING, EH?

IF YOU DON'T COUNT THE *ROCKS* UNDER IT...

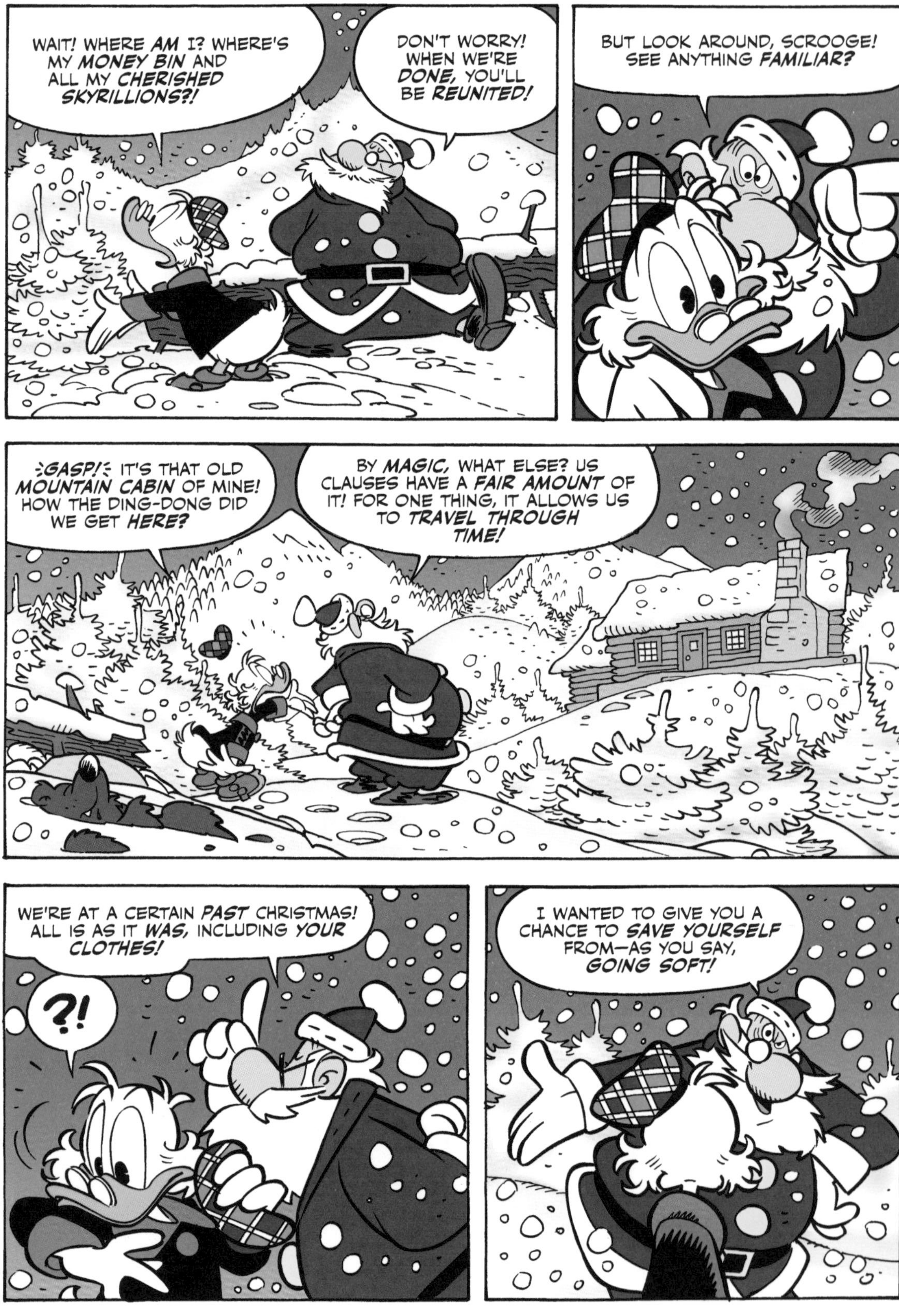
WAIT! WHERE AM I? WHERE'S MY MONEY BIN AND ALL MY CHERISHED SKYRILLIONS?!
DON'T WORRY! WHEN WE'RE DONE, YOU'LL BE REUNITED!
BUT LOOK AROUND, SCROOGE! SEE ANYTHING FAMILIAR?
GASP! IT'S THAT OLD MOUNTAIN CABIN OF MINE! HOW THE DING-DONG DID WE GET HERE?
BY MAGIC, WHAT ELSE? US CLAUSES HAVE A FAIR AMOUNT OF IT! FOR ONE THING, IT ALLOWS US TO TRAVEL THROUGH TIME!
WE'RE AT A CERTAIN PAST CHRISTMAS! ALL IS AS IT WAS, INCLUDING YOUR CLOTHES!
?!
I WANTED TO GIVE YOU A CHANCE TO SAVE YOURSELF FROM—AS YOU SAY, GOING SOFT!

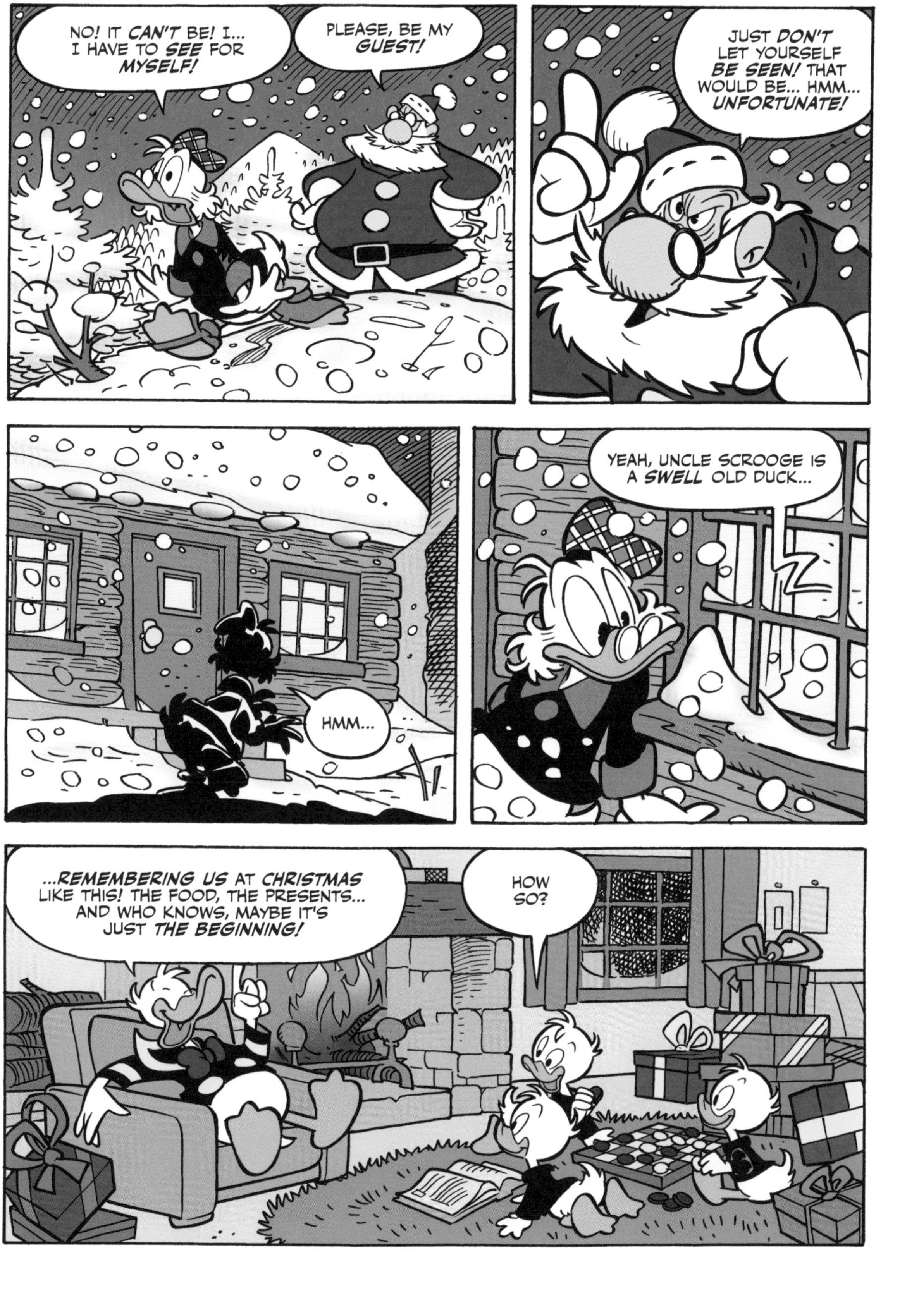
NO! IT CAN'T BE! I... I HAVE TO SEE FOR MYSELF!
PLEASE, BE MY GUEST!
JUST DON'T LET YOURSELF BE SEEN! THAT WOULD BE... HMM... UNFORTUNATE!
HMM...
YEAH, UNCLE SCROOGE IS A SWELL OLD DUCK...
...REMEMBERING US AT CHRISTMAS LIKE THIS! THE FOOD, THE PRESENTS... AND WHO KNOWS, MAYBE IT'S JUST THE BEGINNING!
HOW SO?

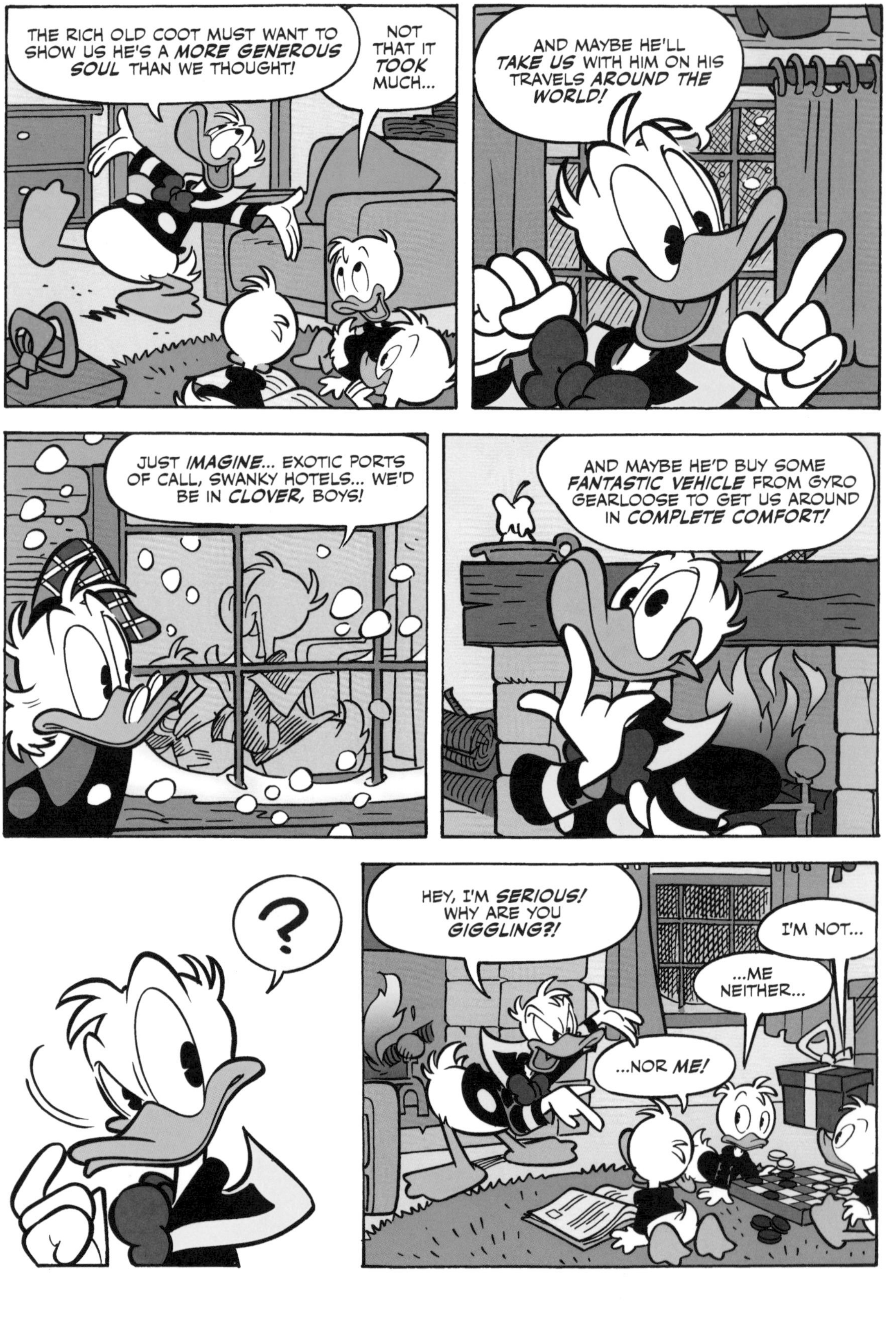
THE RICH OLD COOT MUST WANT TO SHOW US HE'S A MORE GENEROUS SOUL THAN WE THOUGHT!
NOT THAT IT TOOK MUCH...
AND MAYBE HE'LL TAKE US WITH HIM ON HIS TRAVELS AROUND THE WORLD!
JUST IMAGINE... EXOTIC PORTS OF CALL, SWANKY HOTELS... WE'D BE IN CLOVER, BOYS!
AND MAYBE HE'D BUY SOME FANTASTIC VEHICLE FROM GYRO GEARLOOSE TO GET US AROUND IN COMPLETE COMFORT!
?
HEY, I'M SERIOUS! WHY ARE YOU GIGGLING?!
I'M NOT...
...ME NEITHER...
...NOR ME!

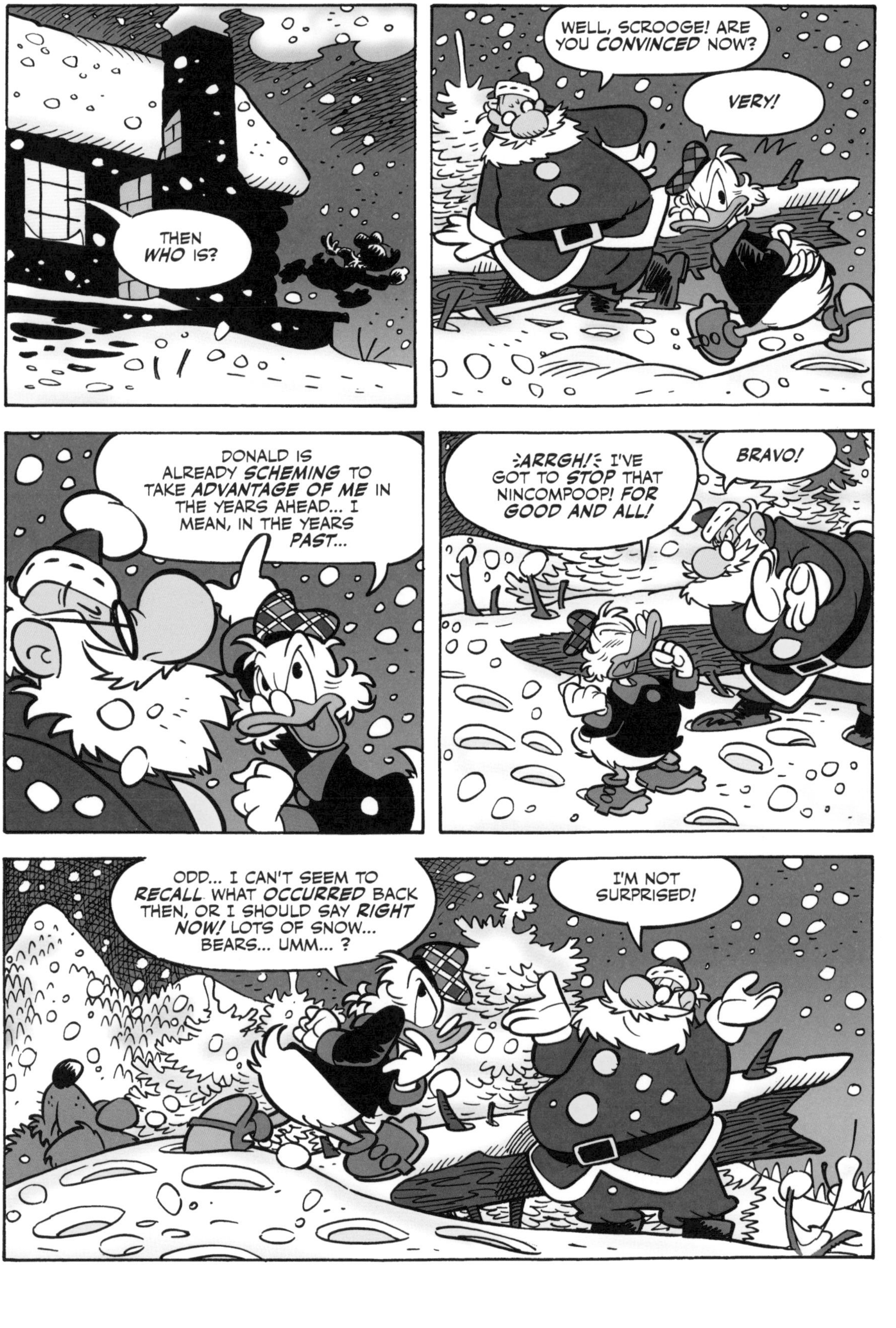
THEN WHO IS?
WELL, SCROOGE! ARE YOU CONVINCED NOW?
VERY!
DONALD IS ALREADY SCHEMING TO TAKE ADVANTAGE OF ME IN THE YEARS AHEAD... I MEAN, IN THE YEARS PAST...
ARRGH! I'VE GOT TO STOP THAT NINCOMPOOP! FOR GOOD AND ALL!
BRAVO!
ODD... I CAN'T SEEM TO RECALL WHAT OCCURRED BACK THEN, OR I SHOULD SAY RIGHT NOW! LOTS OF SNOW... BEARS... UMM... ?
I'M NOT SURPRISED!

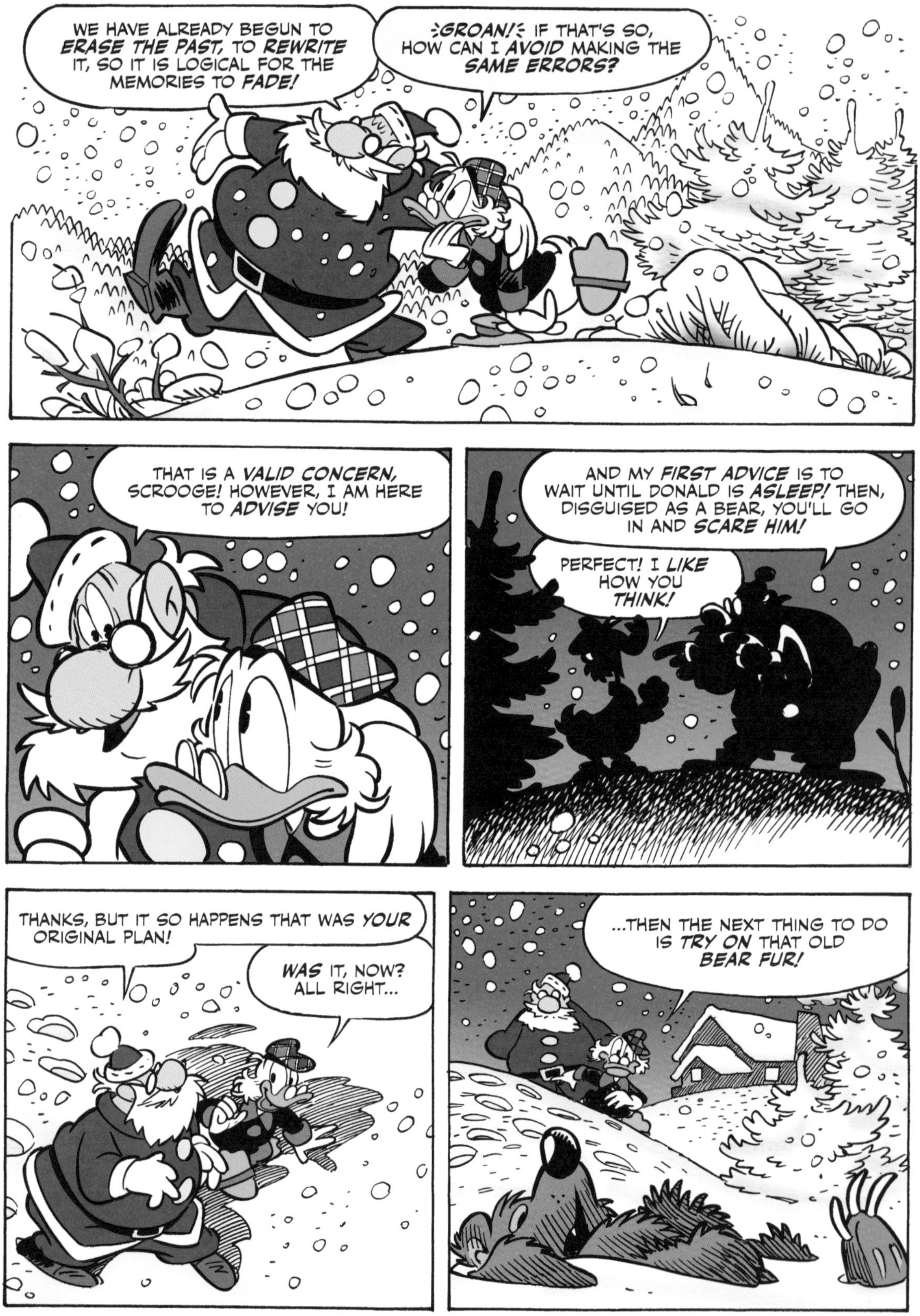
WE HAVE ALREADY BEGUN TO ERASE THE PAST, TO REWRITE IT, SO IT IS LOGICAL FOR THE MEMORIES TO FADE!
GROAN! IF THAT'S SO, HOW CAN I AVOID MAKING THE SAME ERRORS?
THAT IS A VALID CONCERN, SCROOGE! HOWEVER, I AM HERE TO ADVISE YOU!
AND MY FIRST ADVICE IS TO WAIT UNTIL DONALD IS ASLEEP! THEN, DISGUISED AS A BEAR, YOU'LL GO IN AND SCARE HIM!
PERFECT! I LIKE HOW YOU THINK!
THANKS, BUT IT SO HAPPENS THAT WAS YOUR ORIGINAL PLAN!
WAS IT, NOW? ALL RIGHT...
...THEN THE NEXT THING TO DO IS TRY ON THAT OLD BEAR FUR!

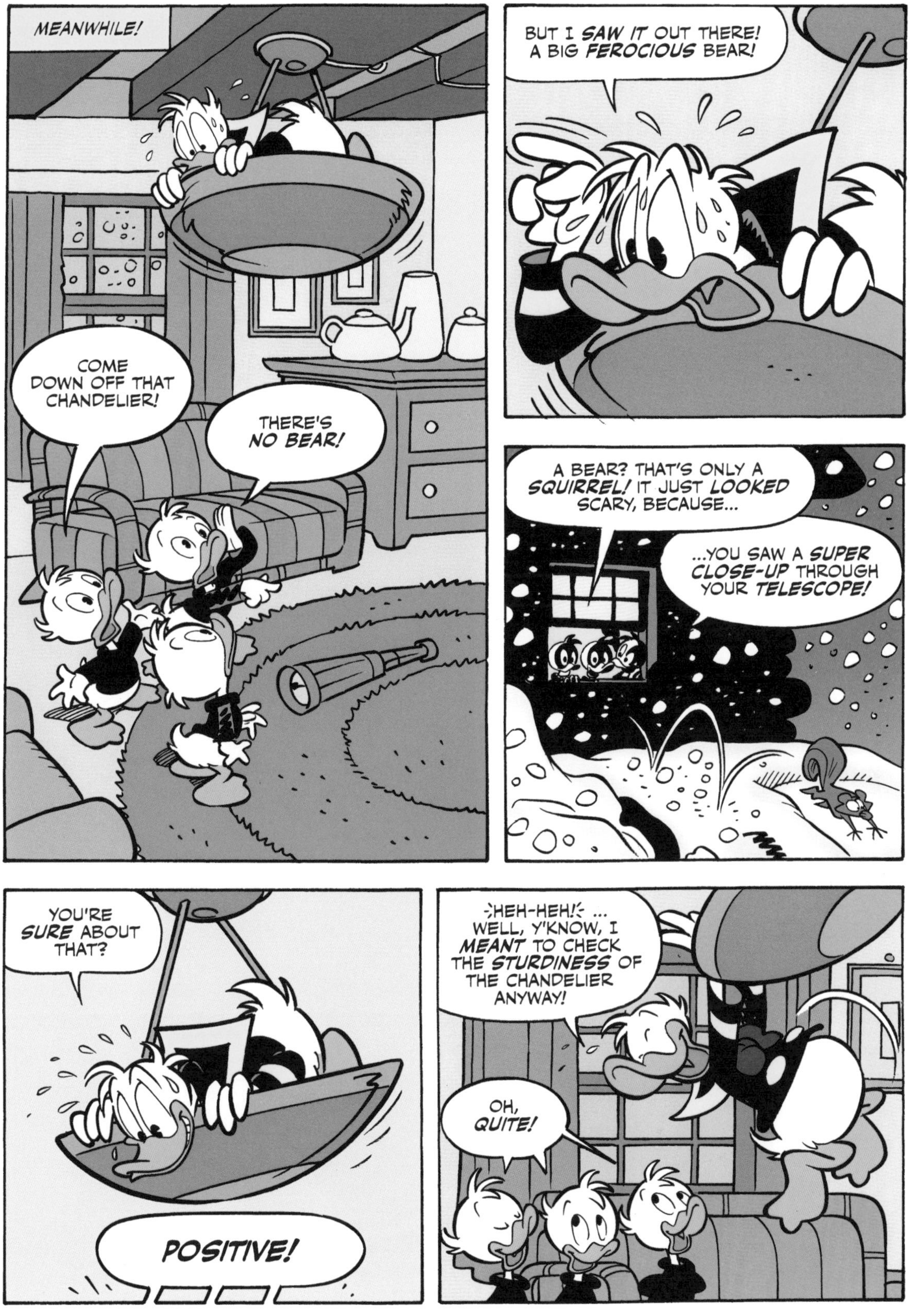
MEANWHILE!
COME DOWN OFF THAT CHANDELIER!
THERE'S NO BEAR!
BUT I SAW IT OUT THERE! A BIG FEROCIOUS BEAR!
A BEAR? THAT'S ONLY A SQUIRREL! IT JUST LOOKED SCARY, BECAUSE...
...YOU SAW A SUPER CLOSE-UP THROUGH YOUR TELESCOPE!
YOU'RE SURE ABOUT THAT?
POSITIVE!
HEH-HEH! ... WELL, Y'KNOW, I MEANT TO CHECK THE STURDINESS OF THE CHANDELIER ANYWAY!
OH, QUITE!

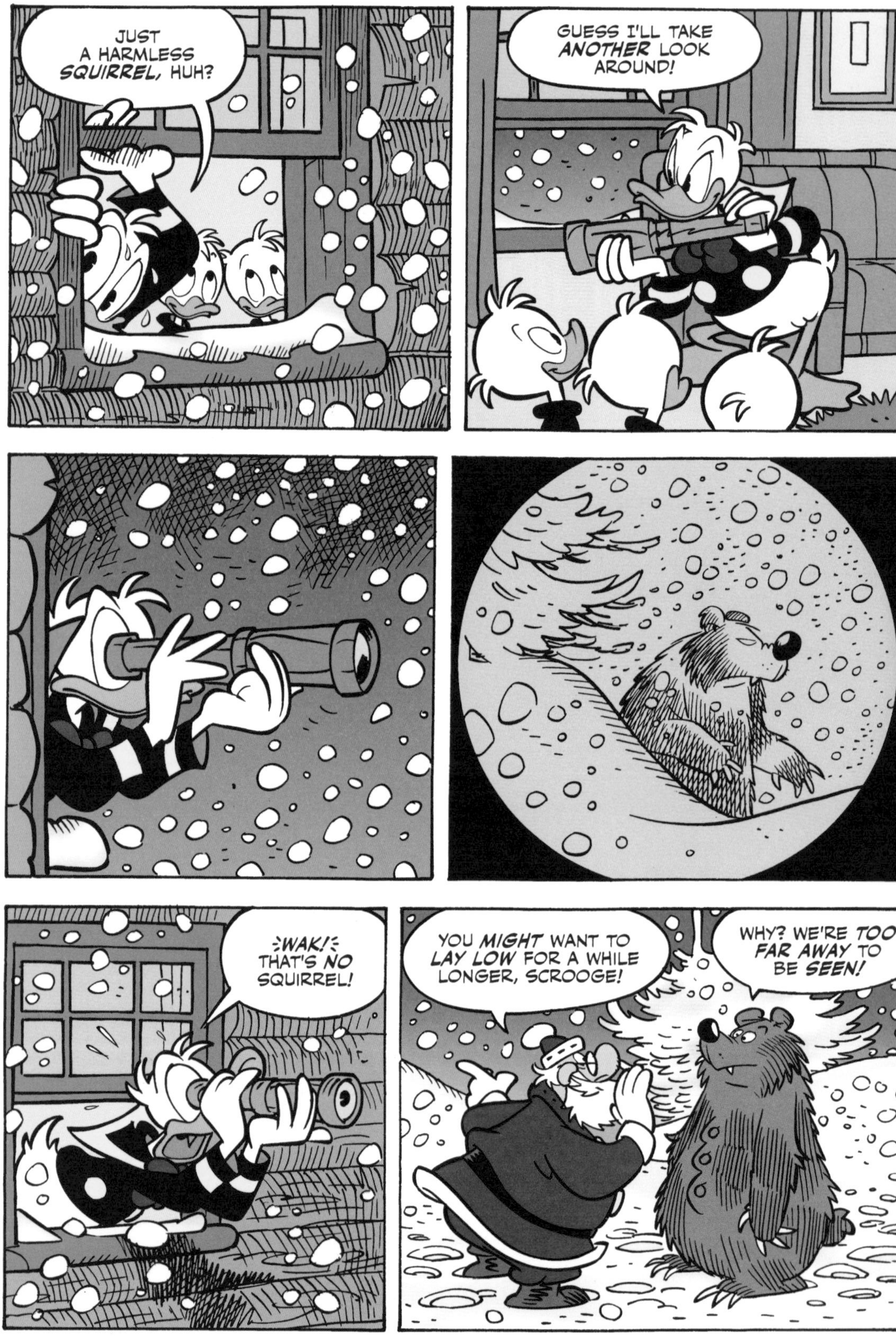
JUST A HARMLESS SQUIRREL, HUH?
GUESS I'LL TAKE ANOTHER LOOK AROUND!
WAK! THAT'S NO SQUIRREL!
YOU MIGHT WANT TO LAY LOW FOR A WHILE LONGER, SCROOGE!
WHY? WE'RE TOO FAR AWAY TO BE SEEN!

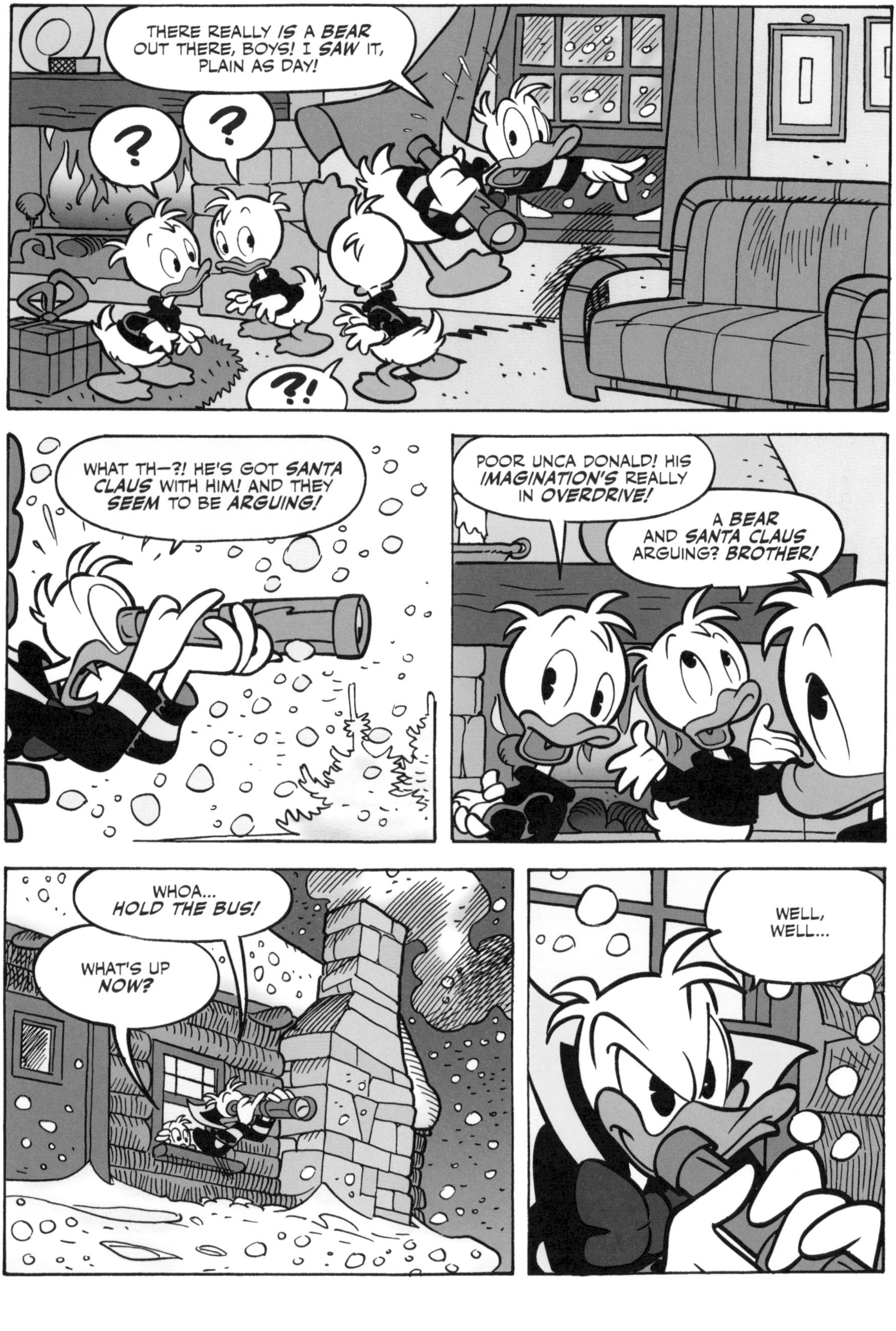
THERE REALLY IS A BEAR OUT THERE, BOYS! I SAW IT, PLAIN AS DAY!
?
?
?!
WHAT TH—?! HE'S GOT SANTA CLAUS WITH HIM! AND THEY SEEM TO BE ARGUING!
POOR UNCA DONALD! HIS IMAGINATION'S REALLY IN OVERDRIVE!
A BEAR AND SANTA CLAUS ARGUING? BROTHER!
WHOA... HOLD THE BUS!
WHAT'S UP NOW?
WELL, WELL...

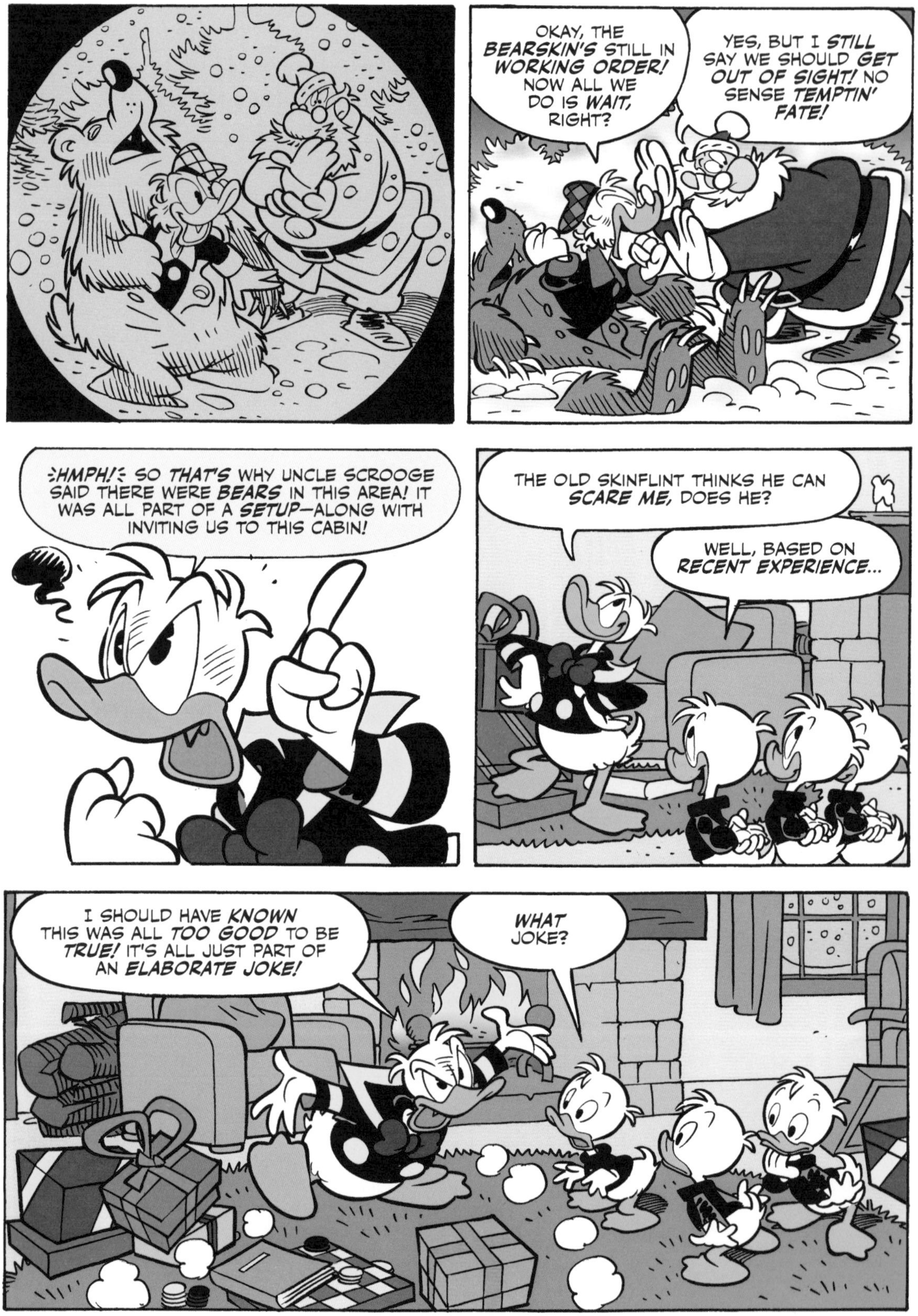
OKAY, THE BEARSKIN'S STILL IN WORKING ORDER! NOW ALL WE DO IS WAIT, RIGHT?
YES, BUT I STILL SAY WE SHOULD GET OUT OF SIGHT! NO SENSE TEMPTIN' FATE!
HMPH! SO THAT'S WHY UNCLE SCROOGE SAID THERE WERE BEARS IN THIS AREA! IT WAS ALL PART OF A SETUP—ALONG WITH INVITING US TO THIS CABIN!
THE OLD SKINFLINT THINKS HE CAN SCARE ME, DOES HE?
WELL, BASED ON RECENT EXPERIENCE...
I SHOULD HAVE KNOWN THIS WAS ALL TOO GOOD TO BE TRUE! IT'S ALL JUST PART OF AN ELABORATE JOKE!
WHAT JOKE?

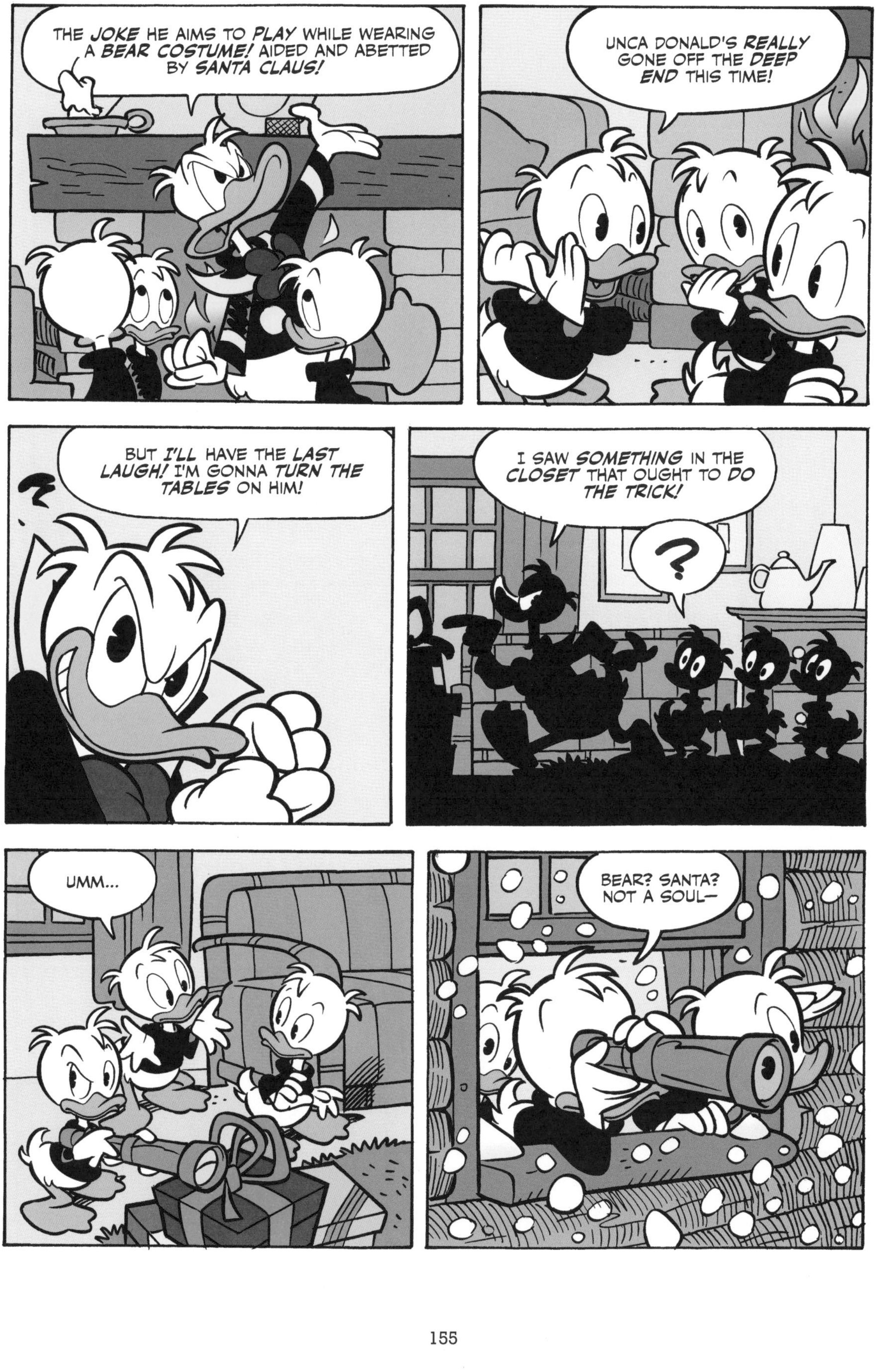
THE JOKE HE AIMS TO PLAY WHILE WEARING A BEAR COSTUME! AIDED AND ABETTED BY SANTA CLAUS!
UNCA DONALD'S REALLY GONE OFF THE DEEP END THIS TIME!
BUT I'LL HAVE THE LAST LAUGH! I'M GONNA TURN THE TABLES ON HIM!
I SAW SOMETHING IN THE CLOSET THAT OUGHT TO DO THE TRICK!
?
UMM...
BEAR? SANTA? NOT A SOUL—

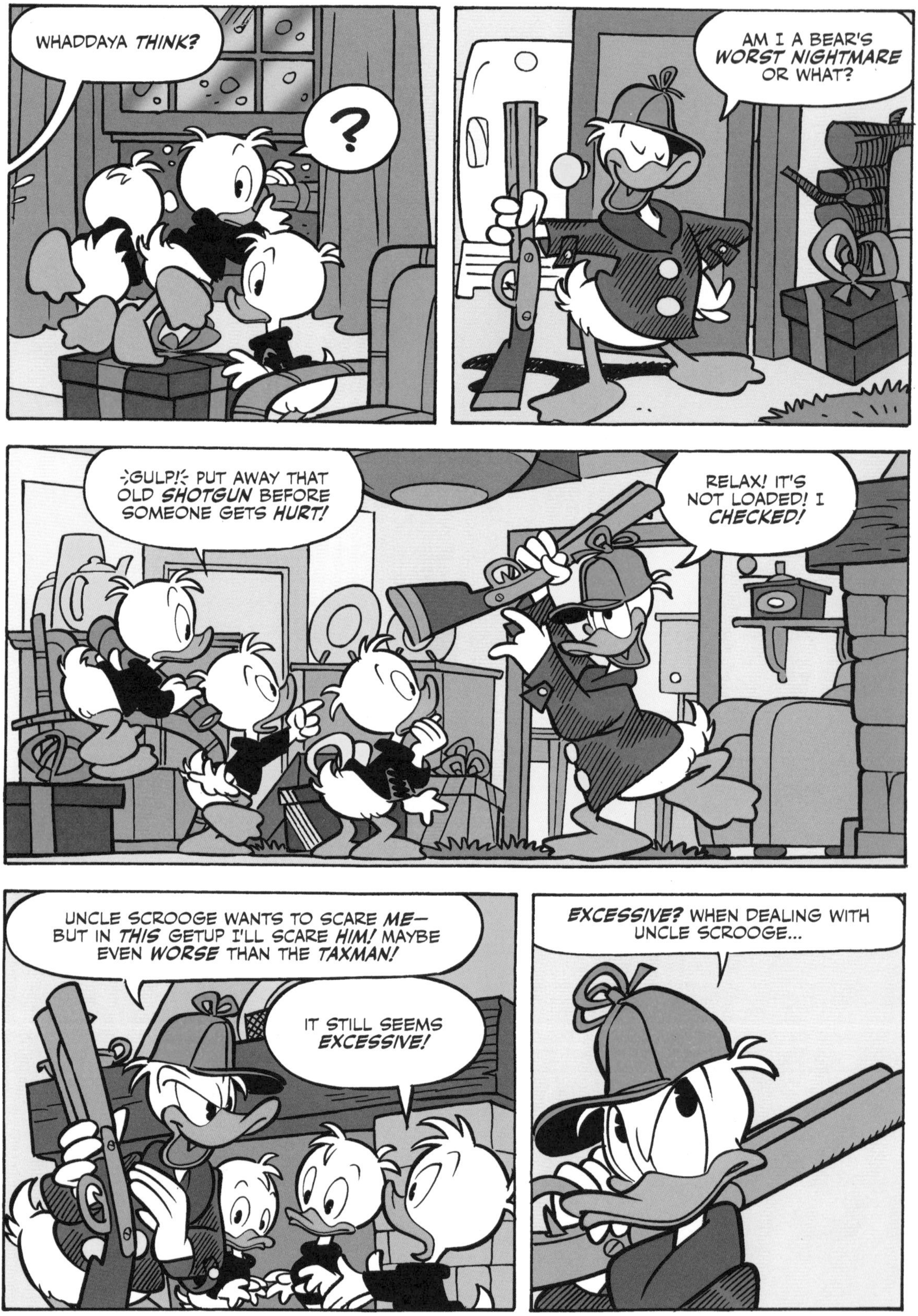
WHADDAYA THINK?
?
AM I A BEAR'S WORST NIGHTMARE OR WHAT?
GULP! PUT AWAY THAT OLD SHOTGUN BEFORE SOMEONE GETS HURT!
RELAX! IT'S NOT LOADED! I CHECKED!
UNCLE SCROOGE WANTS TO SCARE ME— BUT IN THIS GETUP I'LL SCARE HIM! MAYBE EVEN WORSE THAN THE TAXMAN!
IT STILL SEEMS EXCESSIVE!
EXCESSIVE? WHEN DEALING WITH UNCLE SCROOGE...

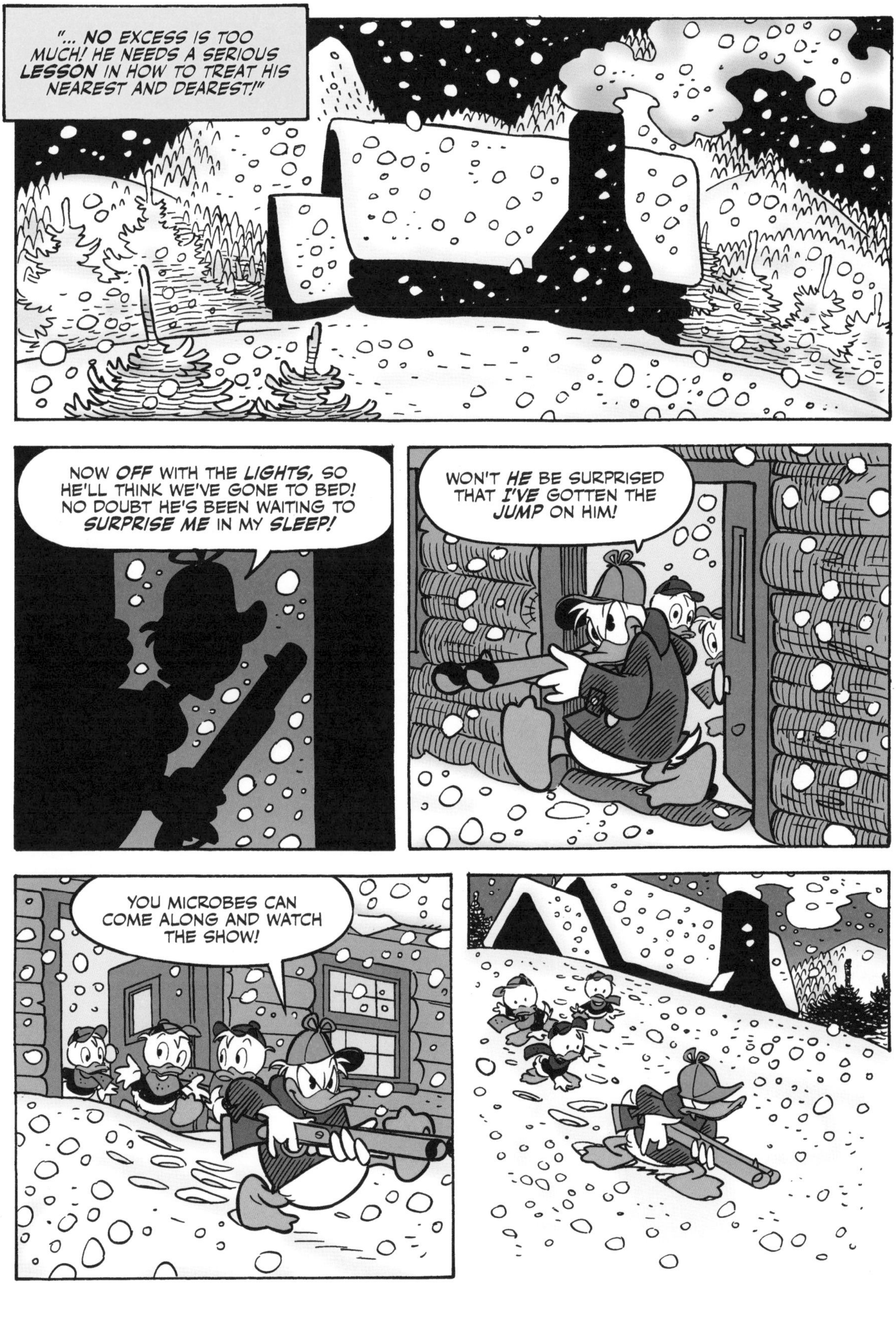
"... NO EXCESS IS TOO MUCH! HE NEEDS A SERIOUS LESSON IN HOW TO TREAT HIS NEAREST AND DEAREST!"
NOW OFF WITH THE LIGHTS, SO HE'LL THINK WE'VE GONE TO BED! NO DOUBT HE'S BEEN WAITING TO SURPRISE ME IN MY SLEEP!
WON'T HE BE SURPRISED THAT I'VE GOTTEN THE JUMP ON HIM!
YOU MICROBES CAN COME ALONG AND WATCH THE SHOW!

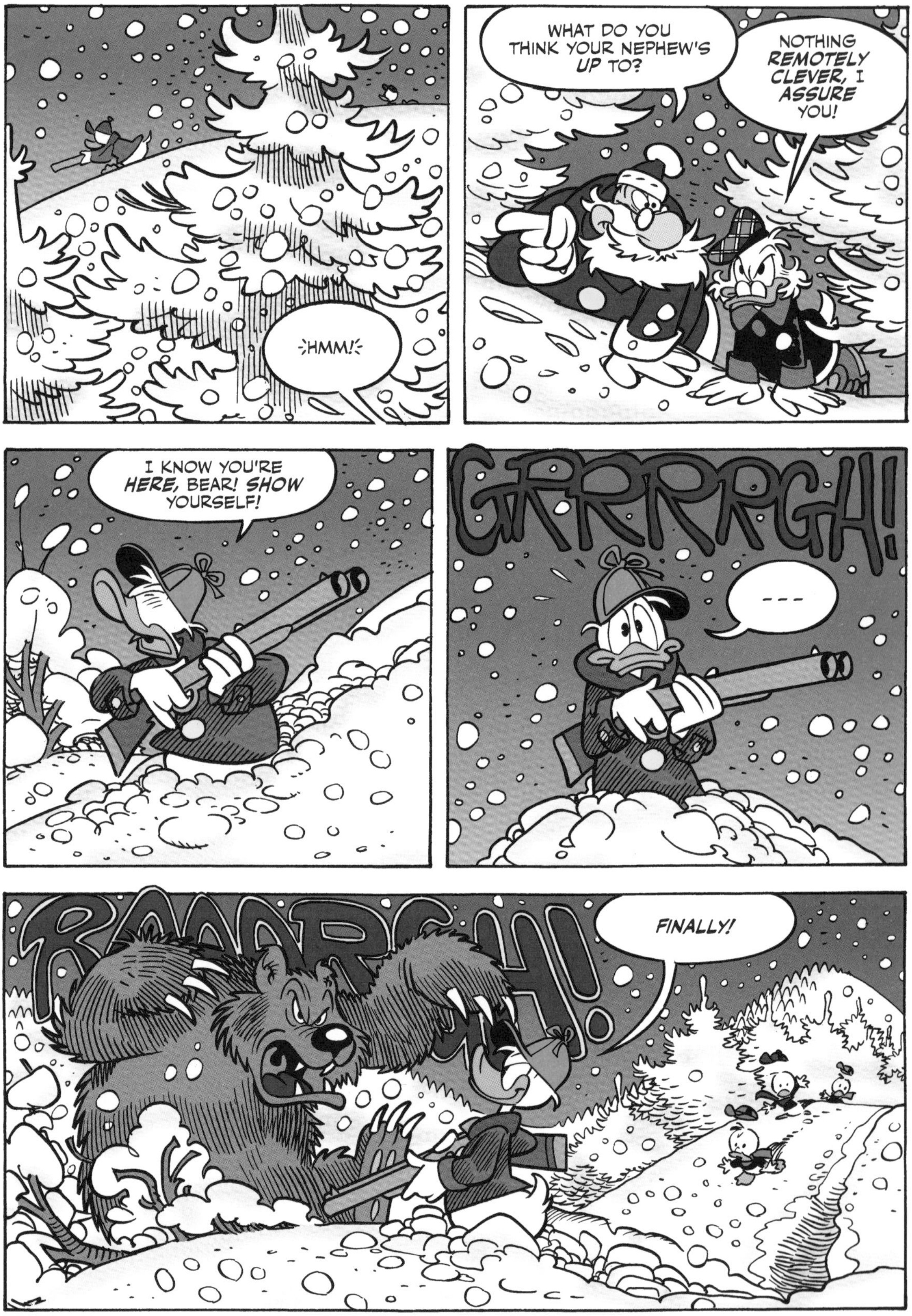
HMM!
WHAT DO YOU THINK YOUR NEPHEW'S UP TO?
NOTHING REMOTELY CLEVER, I ASSURE YOU!
I KNOW YOU'RE HERE, BEAR! SHOW YOURSELF!
GRRRRGH!

RAAARGH!
FINALLY!

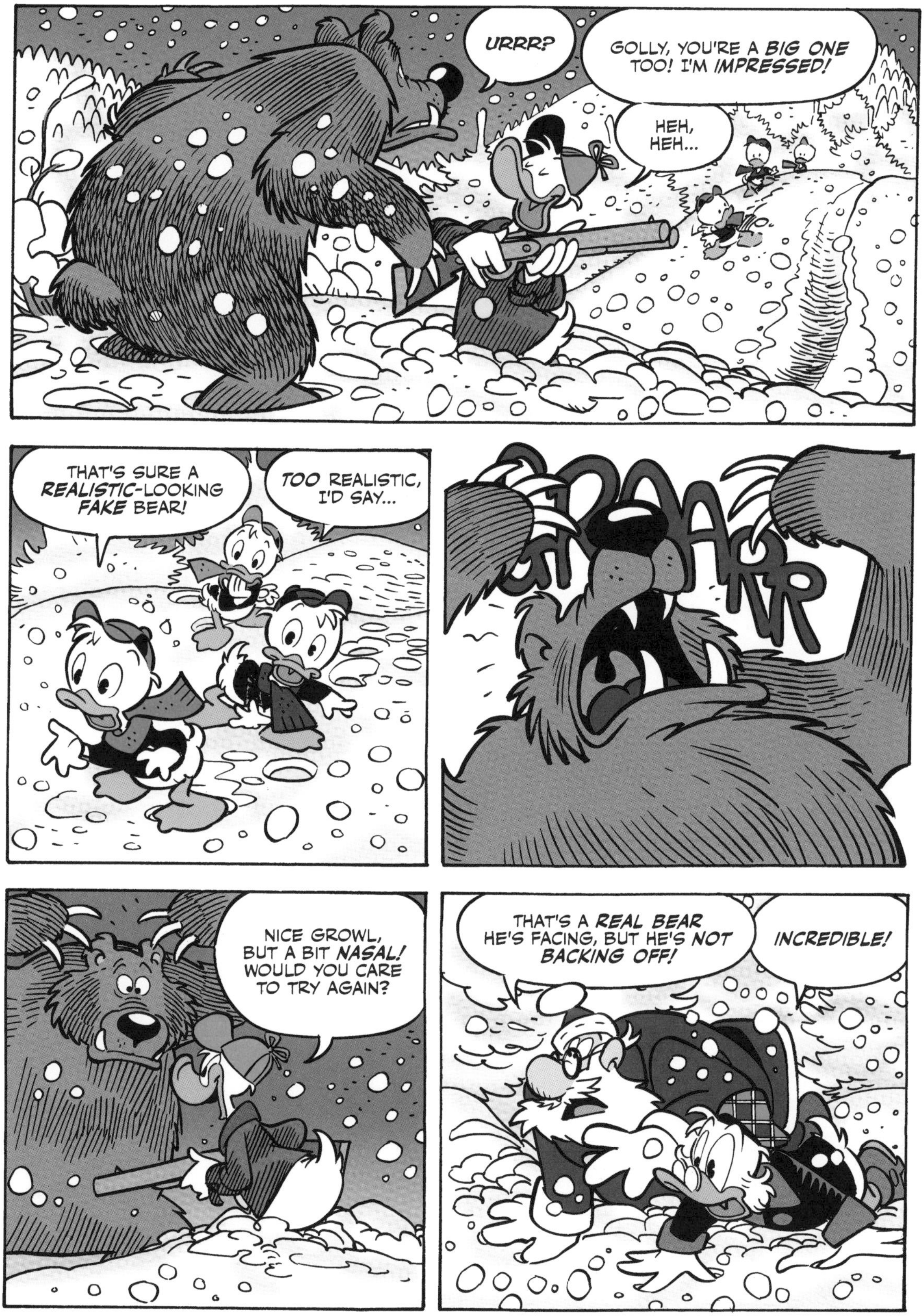
URRR?
GOLLY, YOU'RE A BIG ONE TOO! I'M IMPRESSED!
HEH, HEH...
THAT'S SURE A REALISTIC-LOOKING FAKE BEAR!
TOO REALISTIC, I'D SAY...
GROAARR
NICE GROWL, BUT A BIT NASAL! WOULD YOU CARE TO TRY AGAIN?
THAT'S A REAL BEAR HE'S FACING, BUT HE'S NOT BACKING OFF!
INCREDIBLE!

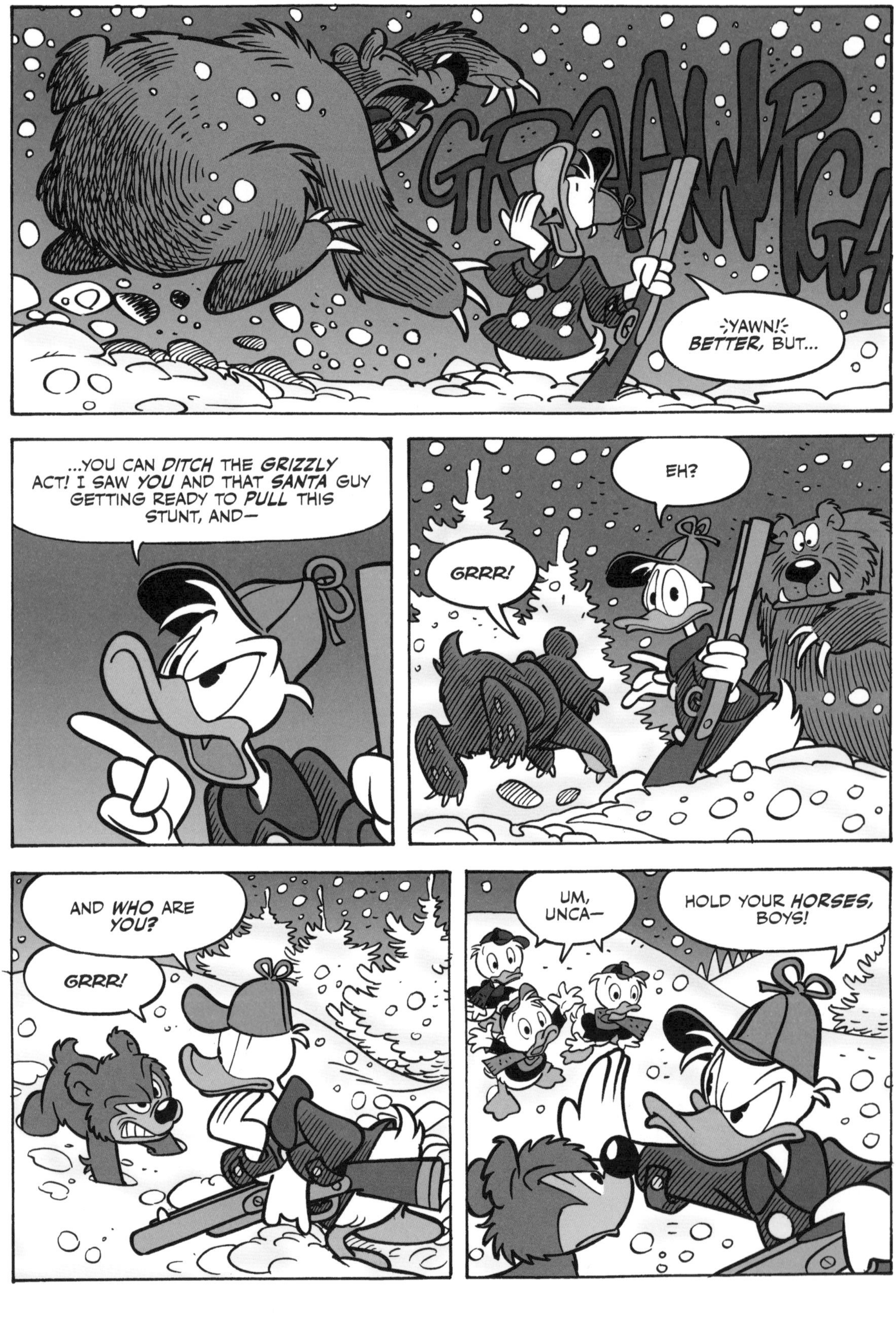

¡YAWN!¡ BETTER, BUT...
...YOU CAN DITCH THE GRIZZLY ACT! I SAW YOU AND THAT SANTA GUY GETTING READY TO PULL THIS STUNT, AND—
EH?
GRRR!
AND WHO ARE YOU?
GRRR!
UM, UNCA—
HOLD YOUR HORSES, BOYS!

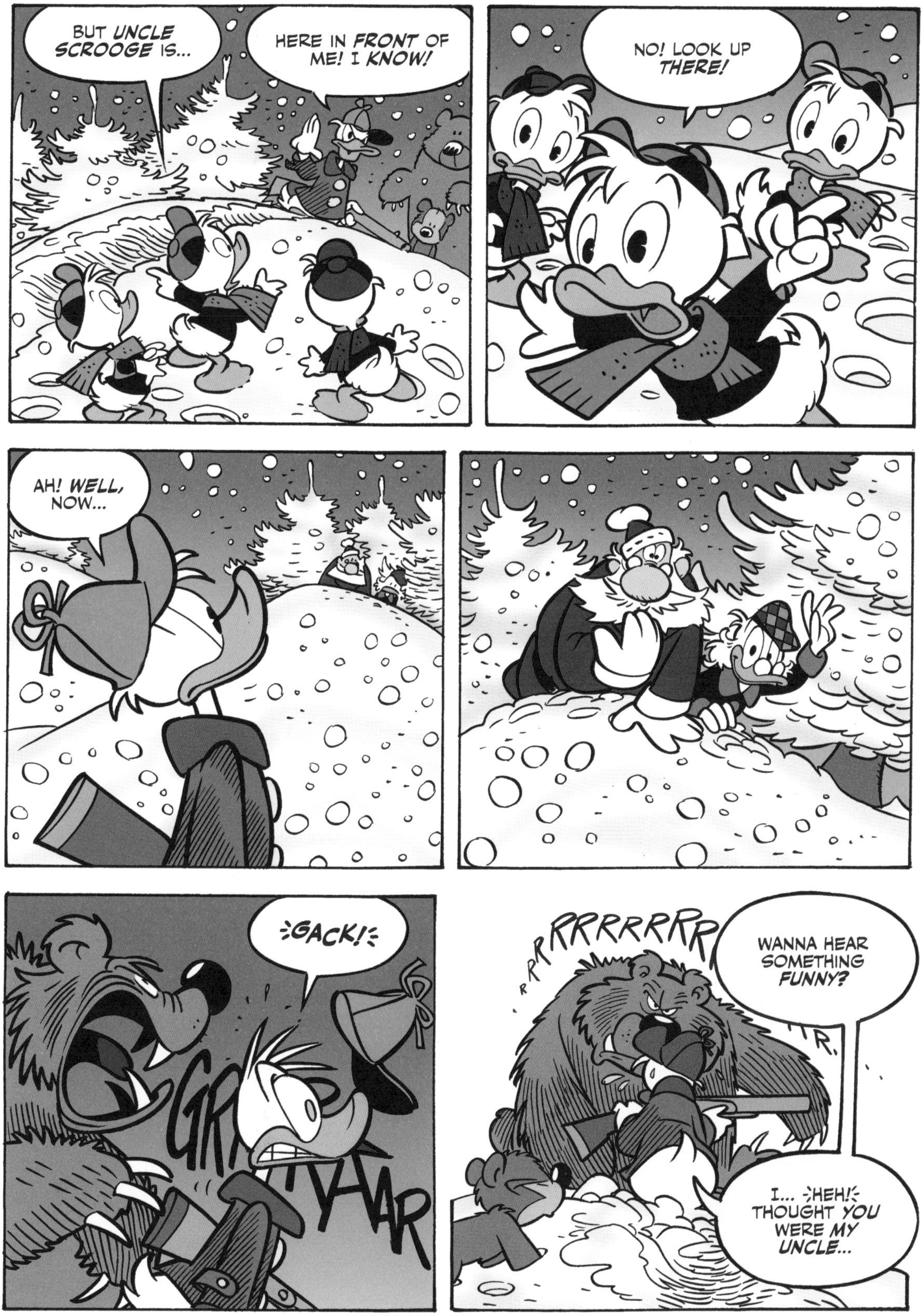
BUT UNCLE SCROOGE IS...
HERE IN FRONT OF ME! I KNOW!
NO! LOOK UP THERE!
AH! WELL, NOW...
GACK!
GRRYAHAR
RRRRRRRRR
WANNA HEAR SOMETHING FUNNY?
R.
I... HEH! THOUGHT YOU WERE MY UNCLE...

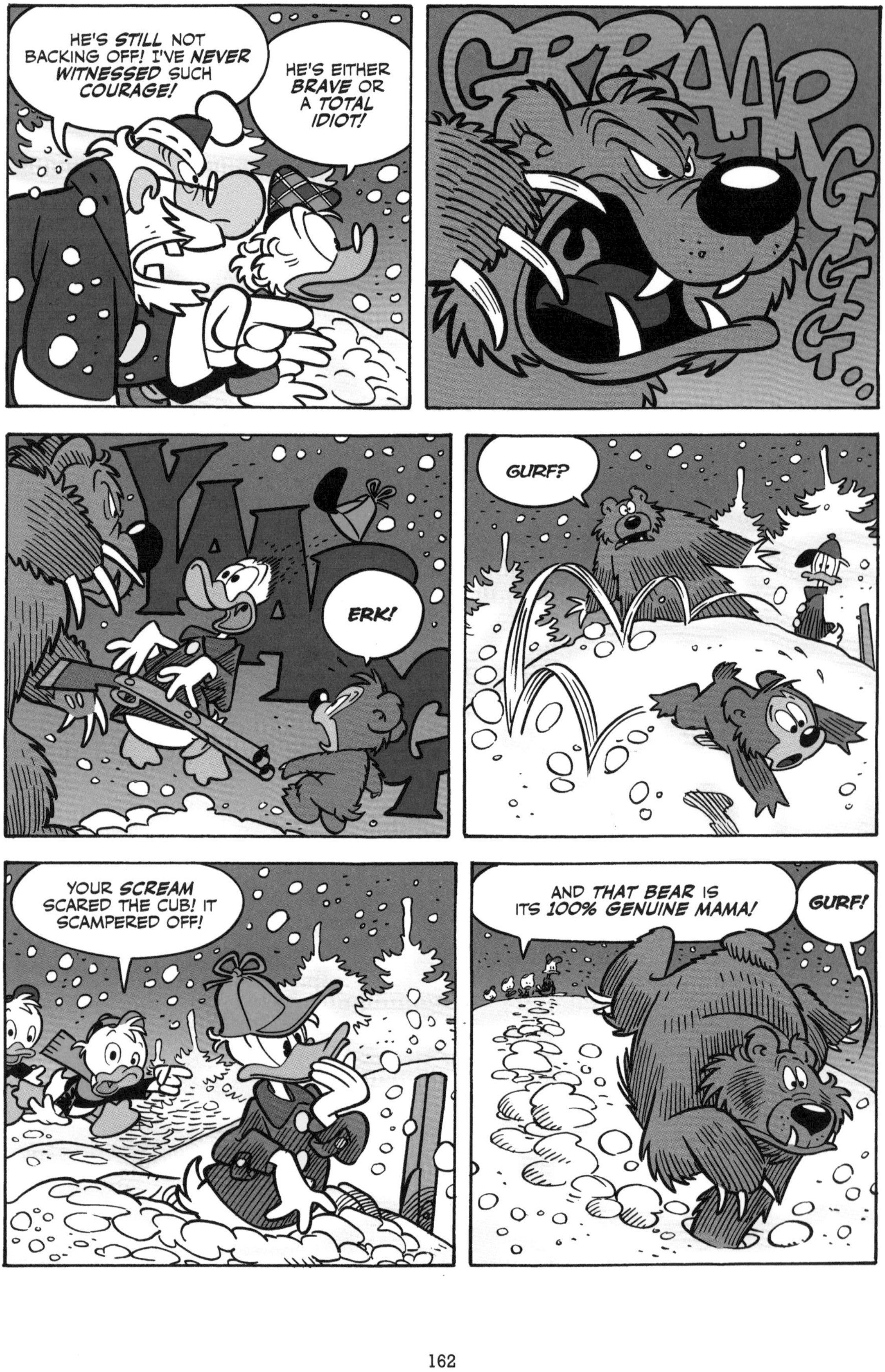
HE'S STILL NOT BACKING OFF! I'VE NEVER WITNESSED SUCH COURAGE!
HE'S EITHER BRAVE OR A TOTAL IDIOT!
GRRAARGGG...
YAAP
ERK!
GURF?
YOUR SCREAM SCARED THE CUB! IT SCAMPERED OFF!
AND THAT BEAR IS ITS 100% GENUINE MAMA!
GURF!

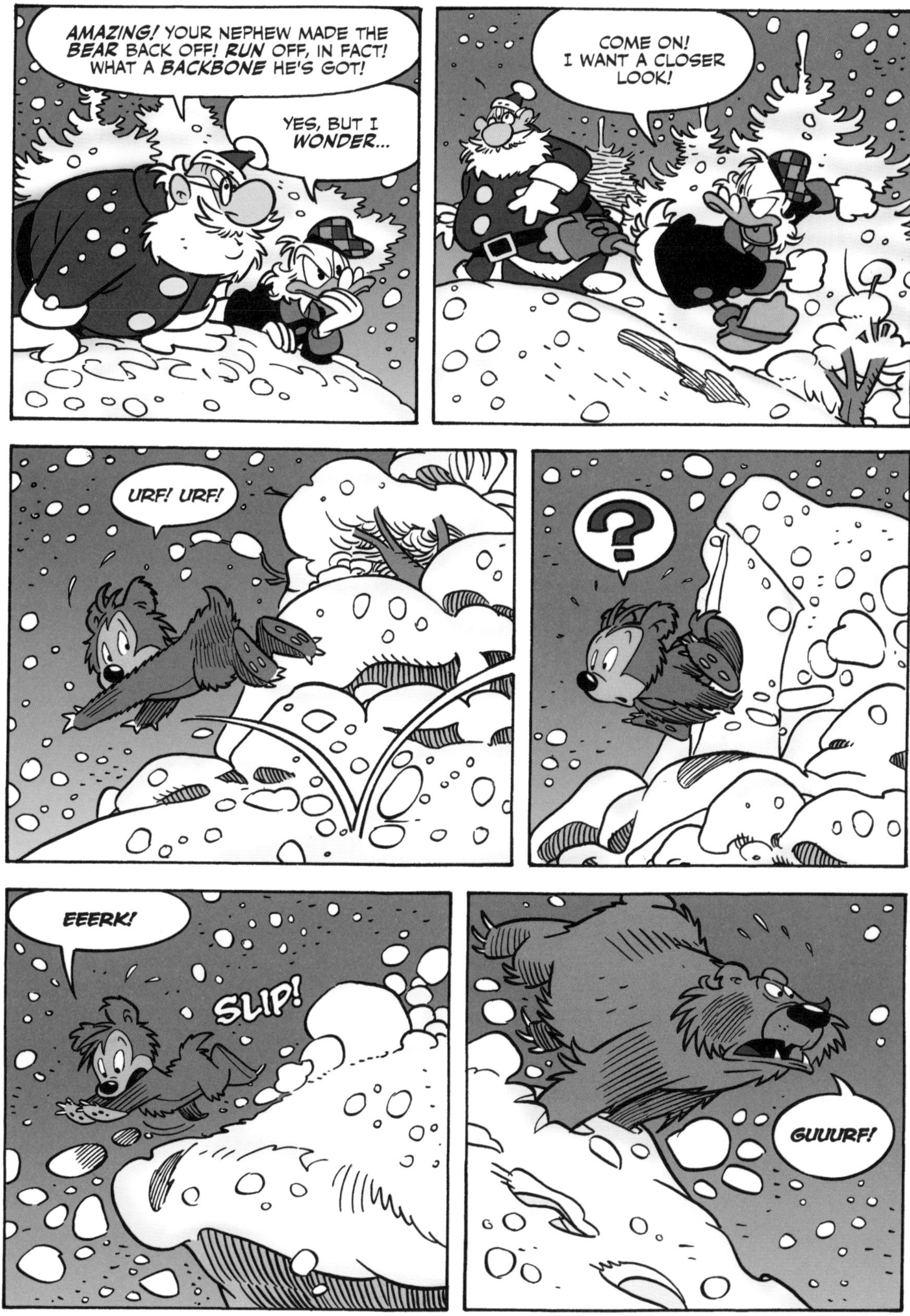
AMAZING! YOUR NEPHEW MADE THE BEAR BACK OFF! RUN OFF, IN FACT! WHAT A BACKBONE HE'S GOT!
YES, BUT I WONDER...
COME ON! I WANT A CLOSER LOOK!
URF! URF!
?
EEERK!
SLIP!
GUUURF!

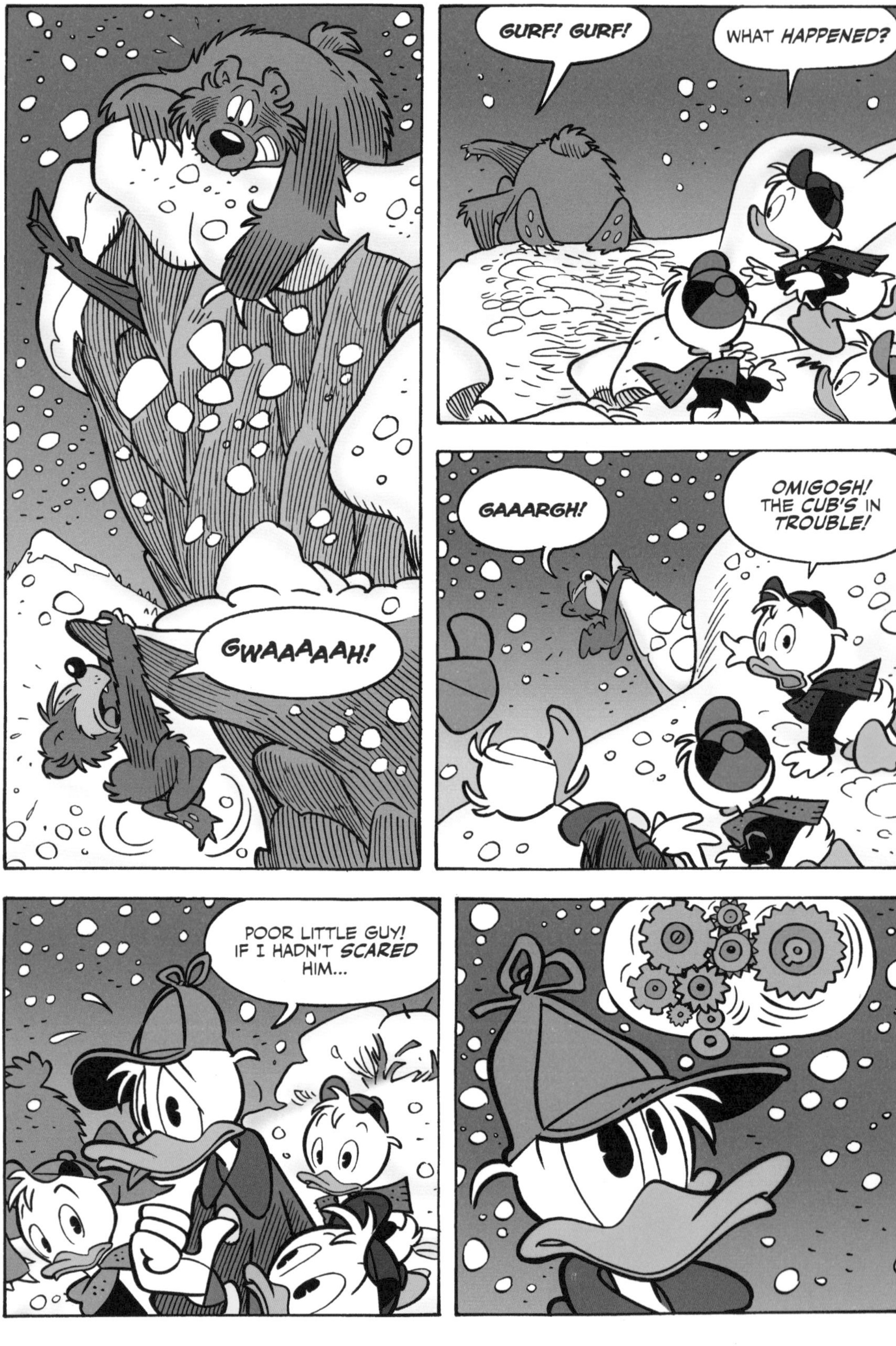
GWAAAAAH!
GURF! GURF!
WHAT HAPPENED?
GAAARGH!
OMIGOSH! THE CUB'S IN TROUBLE!
POOR LITTLE GUY! IF I HADN'T SCARED HIM...

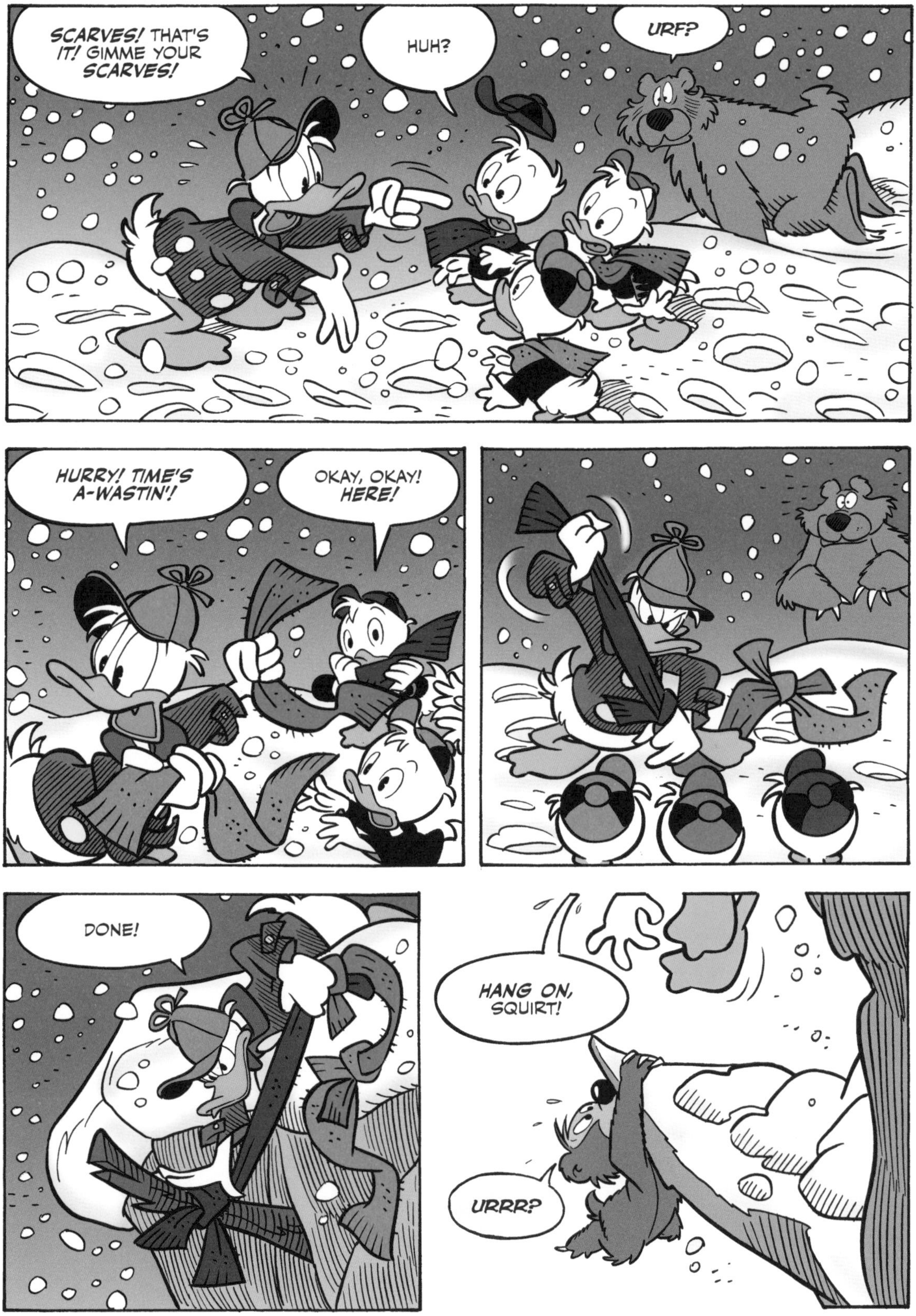
SCARVES! THAT'S IT! GIMME YOUR SCARVES!
HUH?
URF?
HURRY! TIME'S A-WASTIN'!
OKAY, OKAY! HERE!
DONE!
HANG ON, SQUIRT!
URRR?

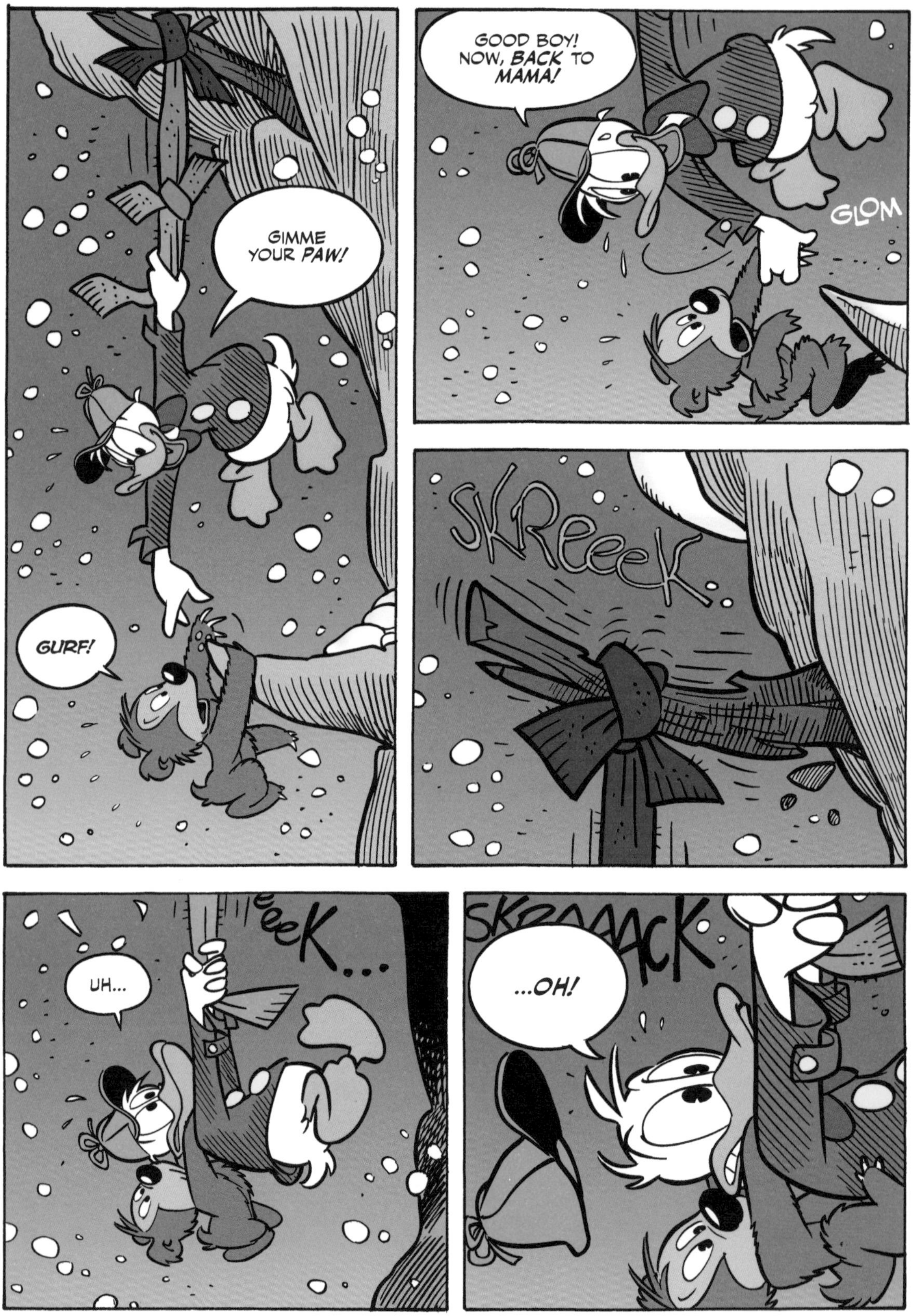
GIMME YOUR PAW!
GURF!
GOOD BOY! NOW, BACK TO MAMA!
GLOM
SKREEEK
UH...
EEEK...
SKRAAACK
...OH!

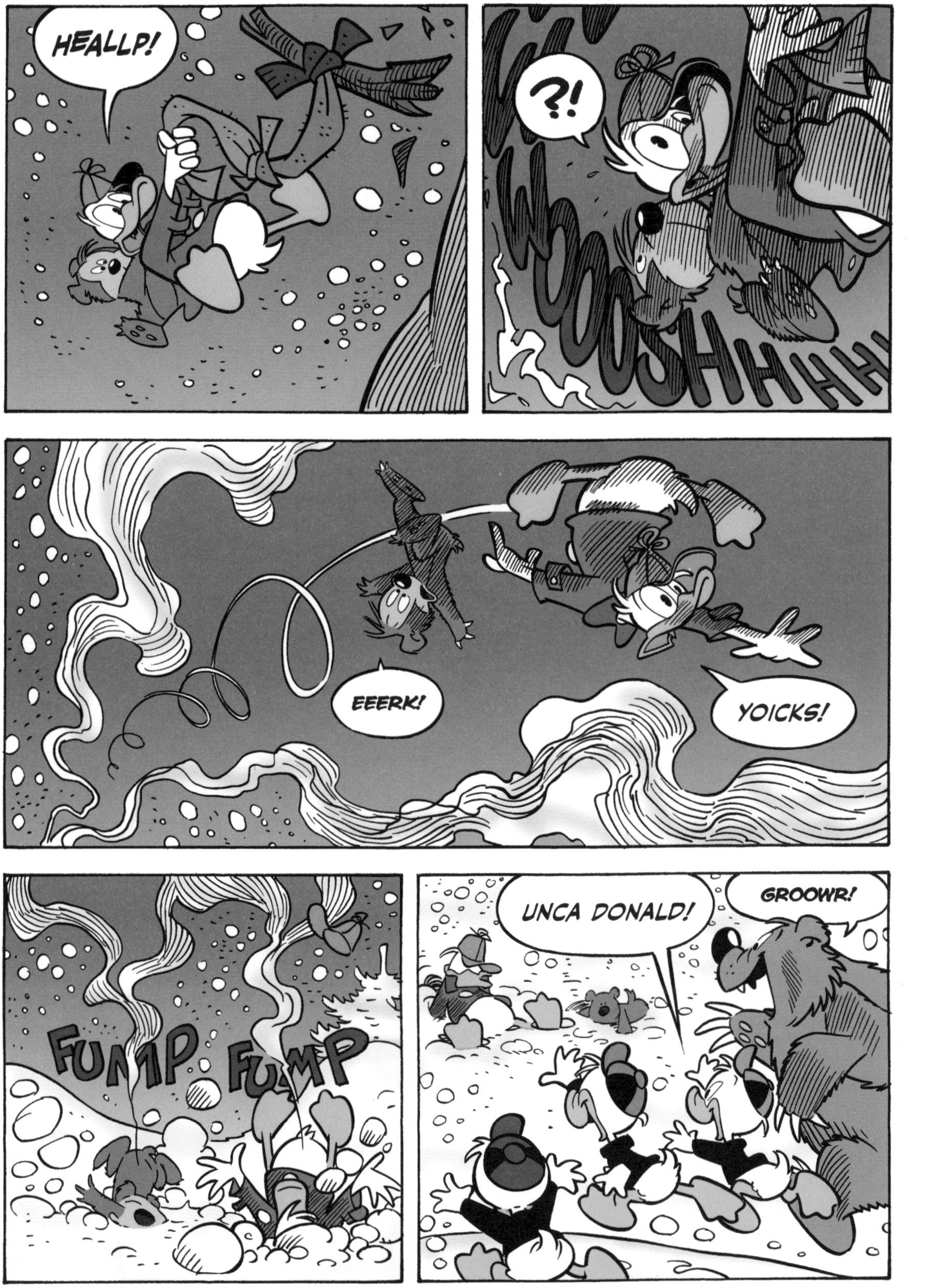
HEALLP!
?!
WHOOOSHHHH
EEERK!
YOICKS!
FUMP FUMP
UNCA DONALD!
GROOWR!

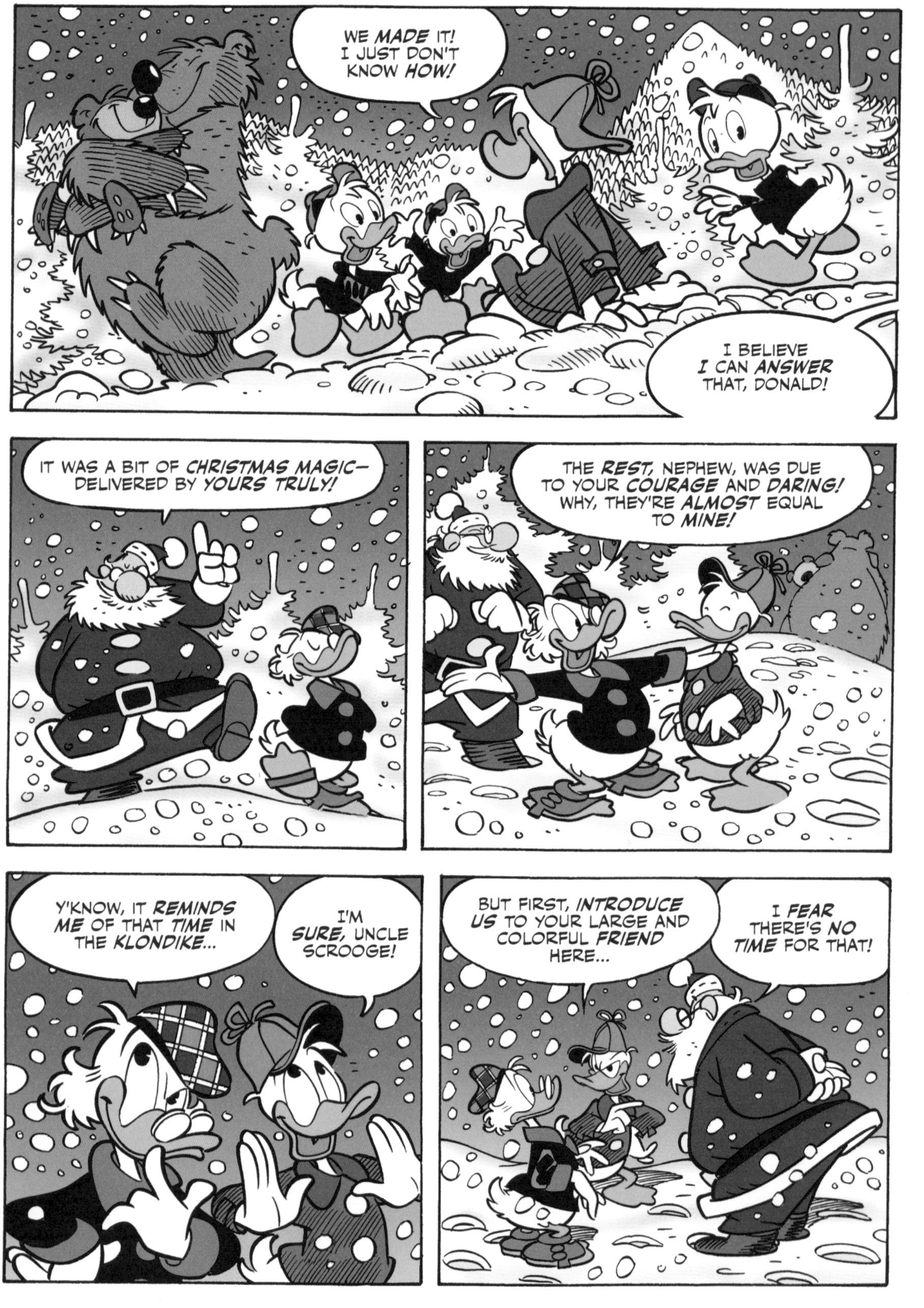

WE MADE IT! I JUST DON'T KNOW HOW!
I BELIEVE I CAN ANSWER THAT, DONALD!
IT WAS A BIT OF CHRISTMAS MAGIC— DELIVERED BY YOURS TRULY!
THE REST, NEPHEW, WAS DUE TO YOUR COURAGE AND DARING! WHY, THEY'RE ALMOST EQUAL TO MINE!
Y'KNOW, IT REMINDS ME OF THAT TIME IN THE KLONDIKE...
I'M SURE, UNCLE SCROOGE!
BUT FIRST, INTRODUCE US TO YOUR LARGE AND COLORFUL FRIEND HERE...
I FEAR THERE'S NO TIME FOR THAT!

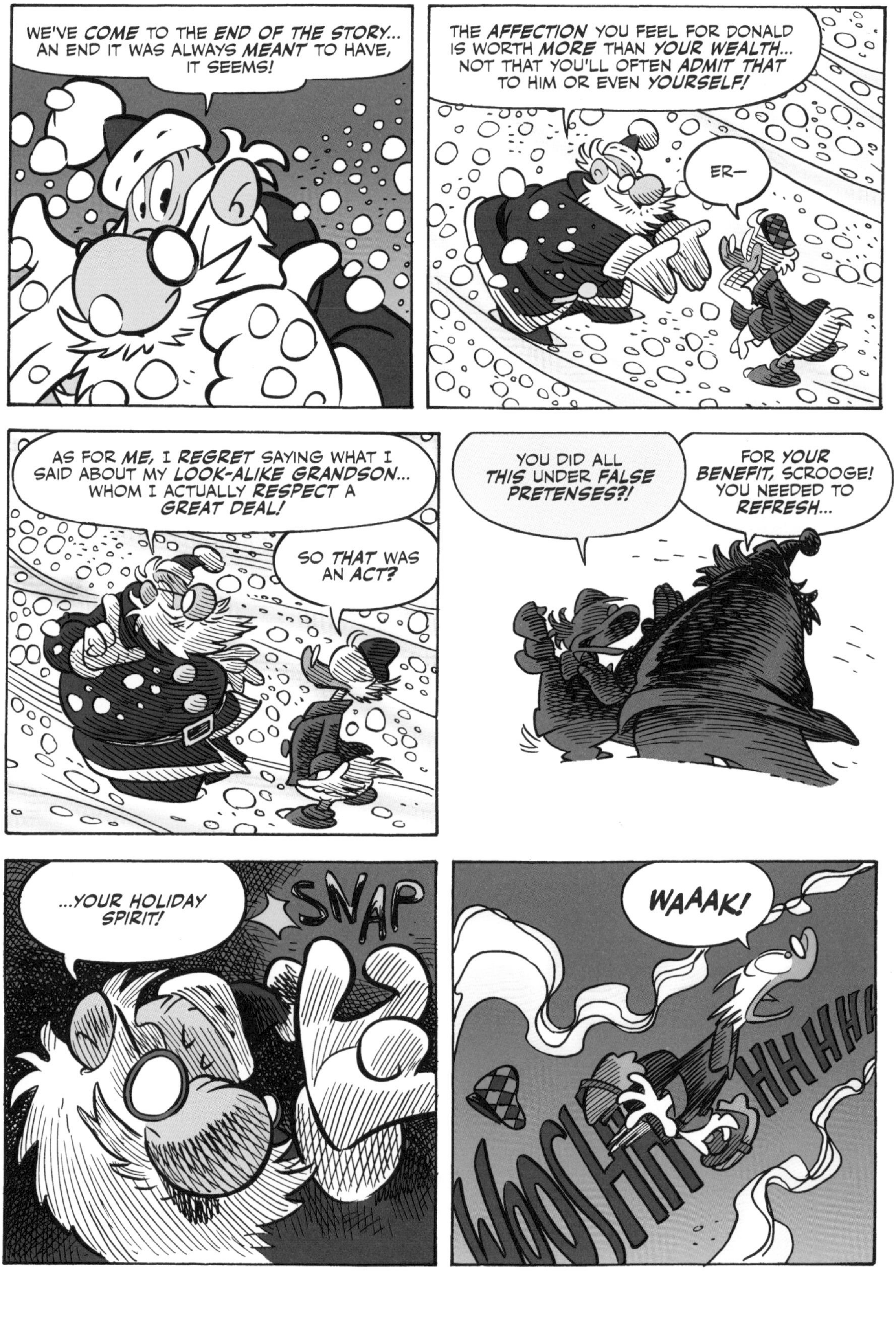
WE'VE COME TO THE END OF THE STORY... AN END IT WAS ALWAYS MEANT TO HAVE, IT SEEMS!
THE AFFECTION YOU FEEL FOR DONALD IS WORTH MORE THAN YOUR WEALTH... NOT THAT YOU'LL OFTEN ADMIT THAT TO HIM OR EVEN YOURSELF!
ER—
AS FOR ME, I REGRET SAYING WHAT I SAID ABOUT MY LOOK-ALIKE GRANDSON... WHOM I ACTUALLY RESPECT A GREAT DEAL!
SO THAT WAS AN ACT?
YOU DID ALL THIS UNDER FALSE PRETENSES?!
FOR YOUR BENEFIT, SCROOGE! YOU NEEDED TO REFRESH...
...YOUR HOLIDAY SPIRIT!
SNAP
WAAAK!
WOOSHHHHHHHHH

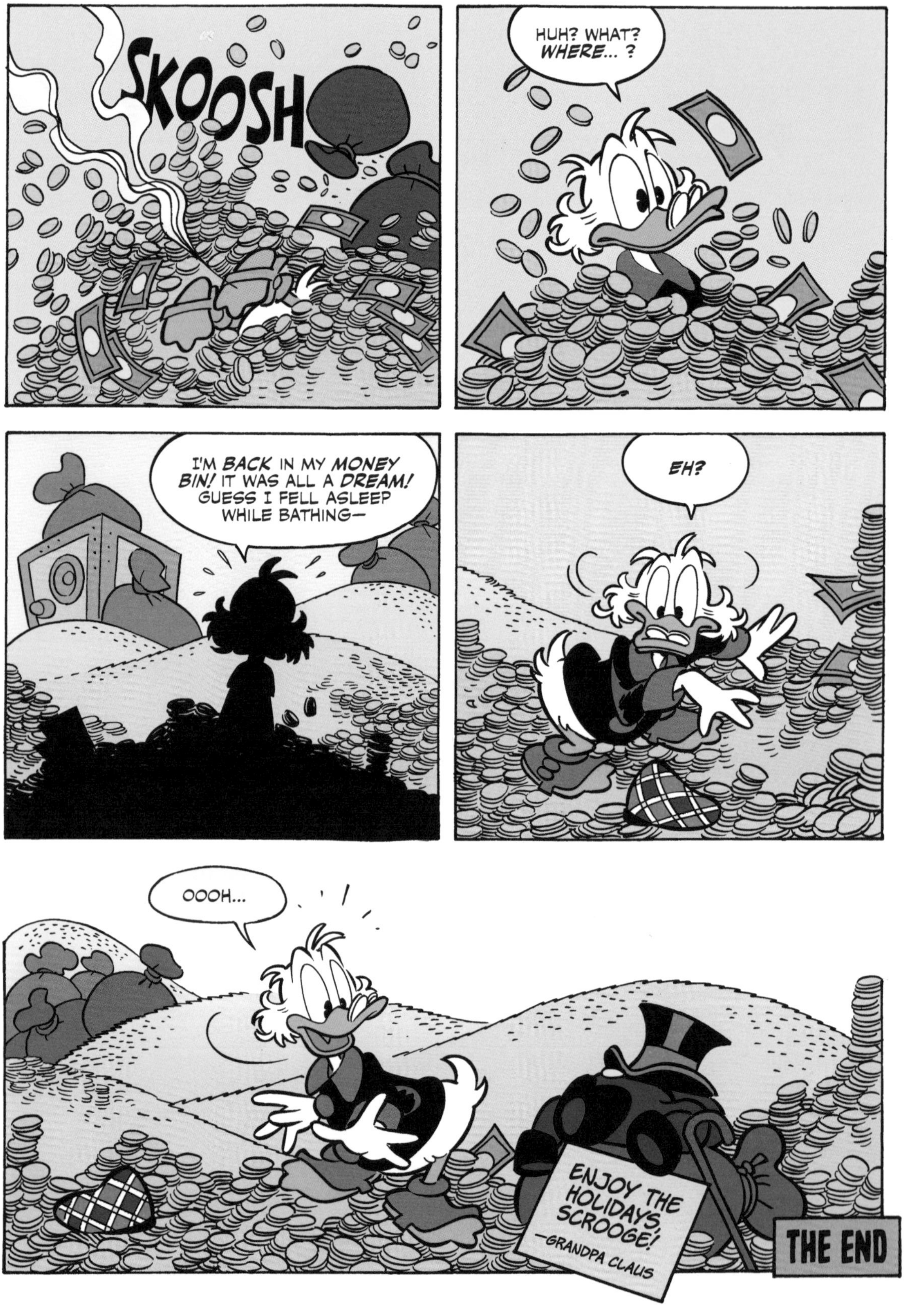
SKOOSH
HUH? WHAT? WHERE... ?
I'M BACK IN MY MONEY BIN! IT WAS ALL A DREAM! GUESS I FELL ASLEEP WHILE BATHING—
EH?
OOOH...
ENJOY THE HOLIDAYS, SCROOGE! —GRANDPA CLAUS
THE END

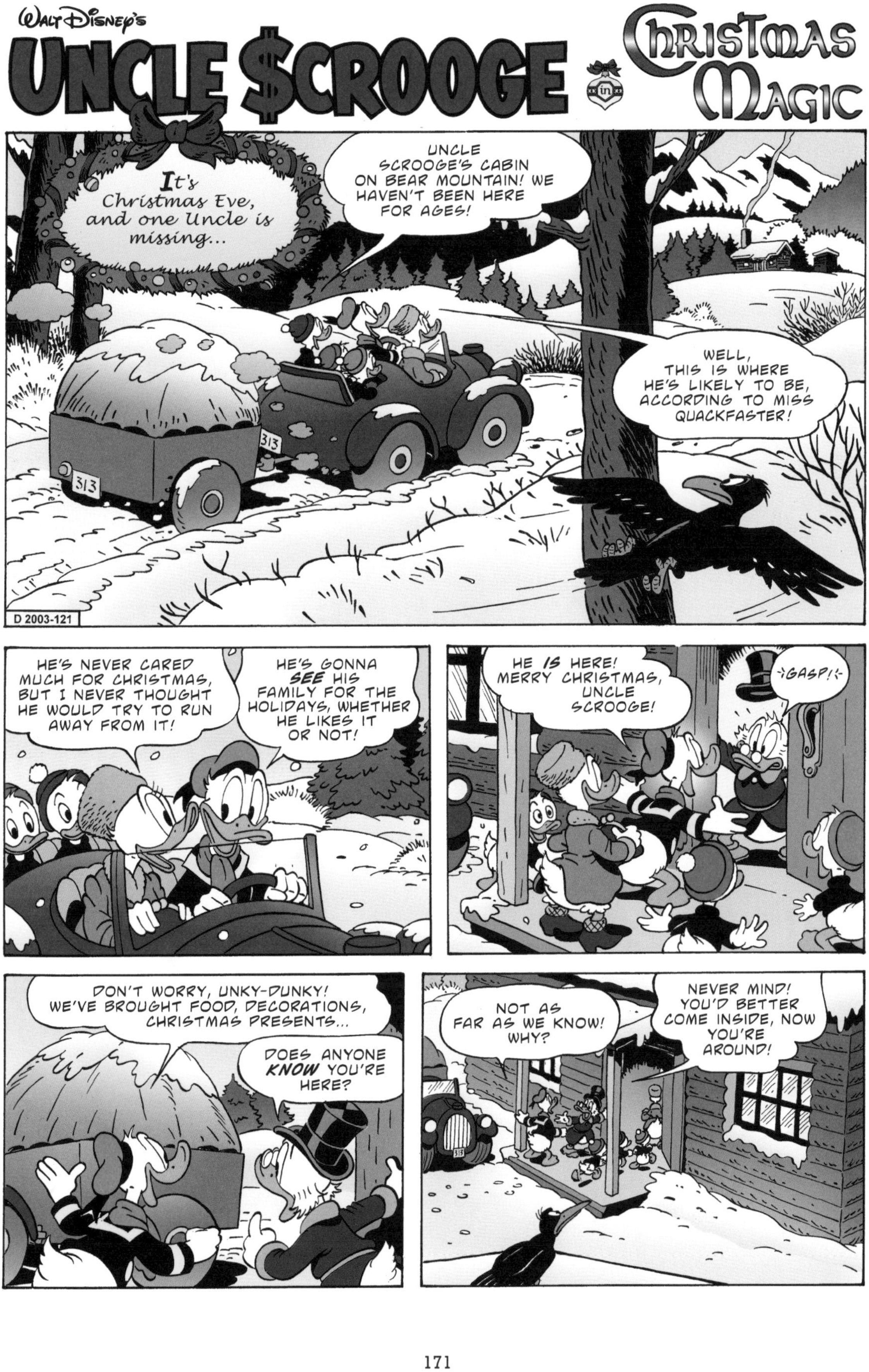
Walt Disney's
Uncle $crooge in Christmas Magic
It's Christmas Eve, and one Uncle is missing...
UNCLE SCROOGE'S CABIN ON BEAR MOUNTAIN! WE HAVEN'T BEEN HERE FOR AGES!
WELL, THIS IS WHERE HE'S LIKELY TO BE, ACCORDING TO MISS QUACKFASTER!
313
D 2003-121
HE'S NEVER CARED MUCH FOR CHRISTMAS, BUT I NEVER THOUGHT HE WOULD TRY TO RUN AWAY FROM IT!
HE'S GONNA SEE HIS FAMILY FOR THE HOLIDAYS, WHETHER HE LIKES IT OR NOT!
HE IS HERE! MERRY CHRISTMAS, UNCLE SCROOGE!
GASP!
DON'T WORRY, UNKY-DUNKY! WE'VE BROUGHT FOOD, DECORATIONS, CHRISTMAS PRESENTS...
DOES ANYONE KNOW YOU'RE HERE?
NOT AS FAR AS WE KNOW! WHY?
NEVER MIND! YOU'D BETTER COME INSIDE, NOW YOU'RE AROUND!

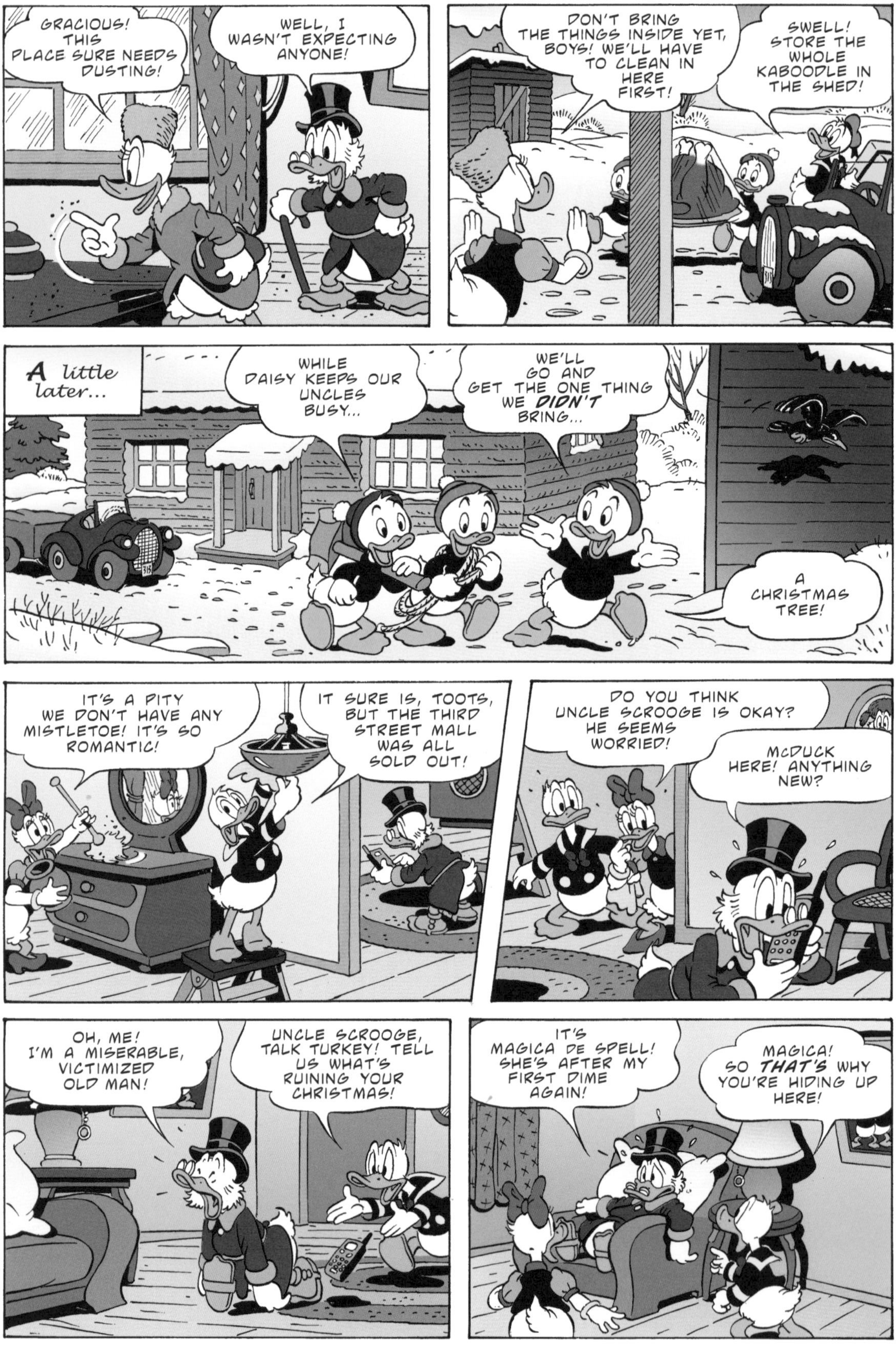
GRACIOUS! THIS PLACE SURE NEEDS DUSTING!
WELL, I WASN'T EXPECTING ANYONE!
DON'T BRING THE THINGS INSIDE YET, BOYS! WE'LL HAVE TO CLEAN IN HERE FIRST!
SWELL! STORE THE WHOLE KABOODLE IN THE SHED!
A little later...
WHILE DAISY KEEPS OUR UNCLES BUSY...
WE'LL GO AND GET THE ONE THING WE DIDN'T BRING...
A CHRISTMAS TREE!
IT'S A PITY WE DON'T HAVE ANY MISTLETOE! IT'S SO ROMANTIC!
IT SURE IS, TOOTS, BUT THE THIRD STREET MALL WAS ALL SOLD OUT!
DO YOU THINK UNCLE SCROOGE IS OKAY? HE SEEMS WORRIED!
McDUCK HERE! ANYTHING NEW?
OH, ME! I'M A MISERABLE, VICTIMIZED OLD MAN!
UNCLE SCROOGE, TALK TURKEY! TELL US WHAT'S RUINING YOUR CHRISTMAS!
IT'S MAGICA DE SPELL! SHE'S AFTER MY FIRST DIME AGAIN!
MAGICA! SO THAT'S WHY YOU'RE HIDING UP HERE!

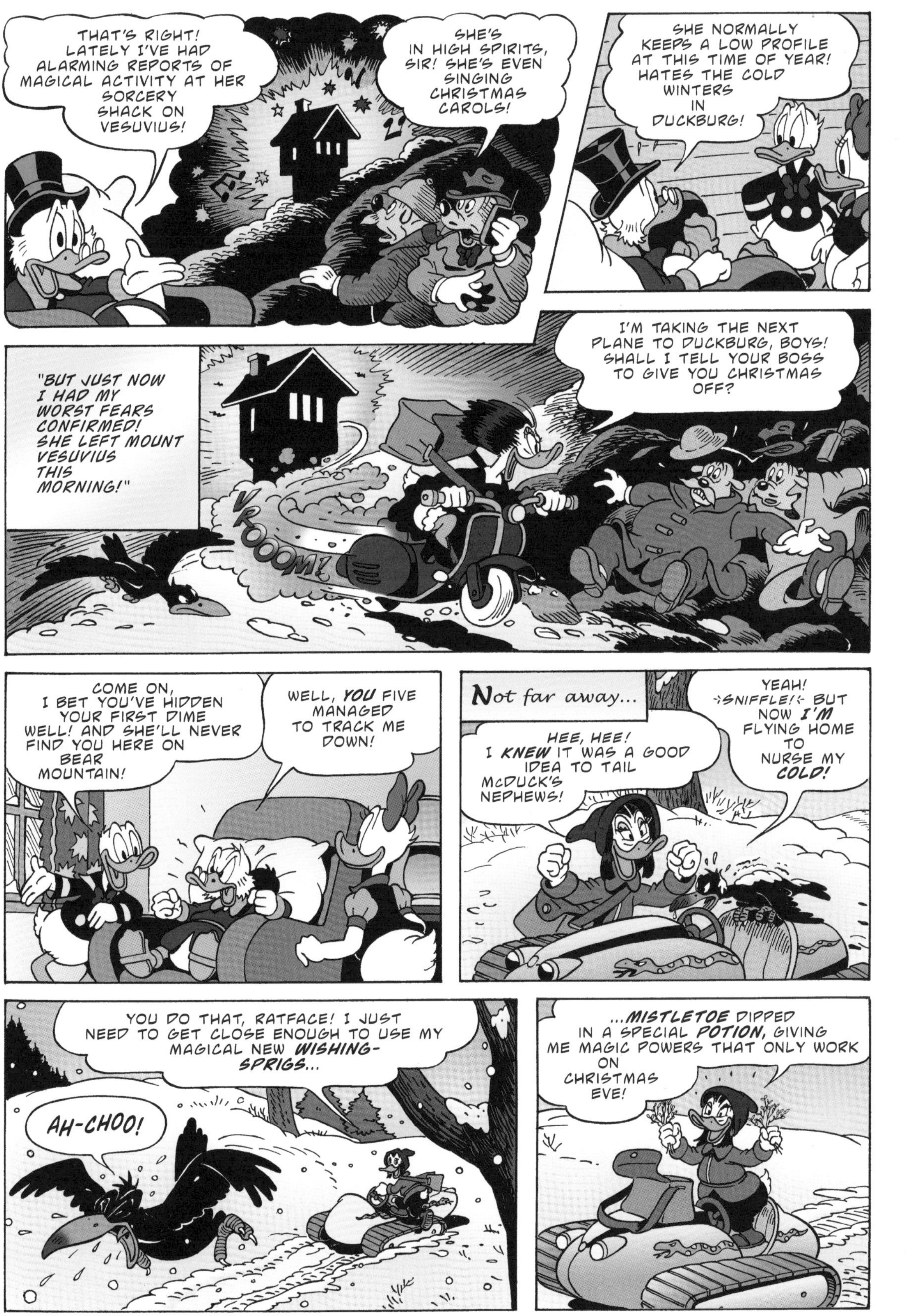
THAT'S RIGHT! LATELY I'VE HAD ALARMING REPORTS OF MAGICAL ACTIVITY AT HER SORCERY SHACK ON VESUVIUS!
SHE'S IN HIGH SPIRITS, SIR! SHE'S EVEN SINGING CHRISTMAS CAROLS!
SHE NORMALLY KEEPS A LOW PROFILE AT THIS TIME OF YEAR! HATES THE COLD WINTERS IN DUCKBURG!
"BUT JUST NOW I HAD MY WORST FEARS CONFIRMED! SHE LEFT MOUNT VESUVIUS THIS MORNING!"
I'M TAKING THE NEXT PLANE TO DUCKBURG, BOYS! SHALL I TELL YOUR BOSS TO GIVE YOU CHRISTMAS OFF?
VROOOOM!
COME ON, I BET YOU'VE HIDDEN YOUR FIRST DIME WELL! AND SHE'LL NEVER FIND YOU HERE ON BEAR MOUNTAIN!
WELL, YOU FIVE MANAGED TO TRACK ME DOWN!
Not far away...
HEE, HEE! I KNEW IT WAS A GOOD IDEA TO TAIL McDUCK'S NEPHEWS!
YEAH! -SNIFFLE!- BUT NOW I'M FLYING HOME TO NURSE MY COLD!
YOU DO THAT, RATFACE! I JUST NEED TO GET CLOSE ENOUGH TO USE MY MAGICAL NEW WISHING-SPRIGS...
AH-CHOO!
...MISTLETOE DIPPED IN A SPECIAL POTION, GIVING ME MAGIC POWERS THAT ONLY WORK ON CHRISTMAS EVE!

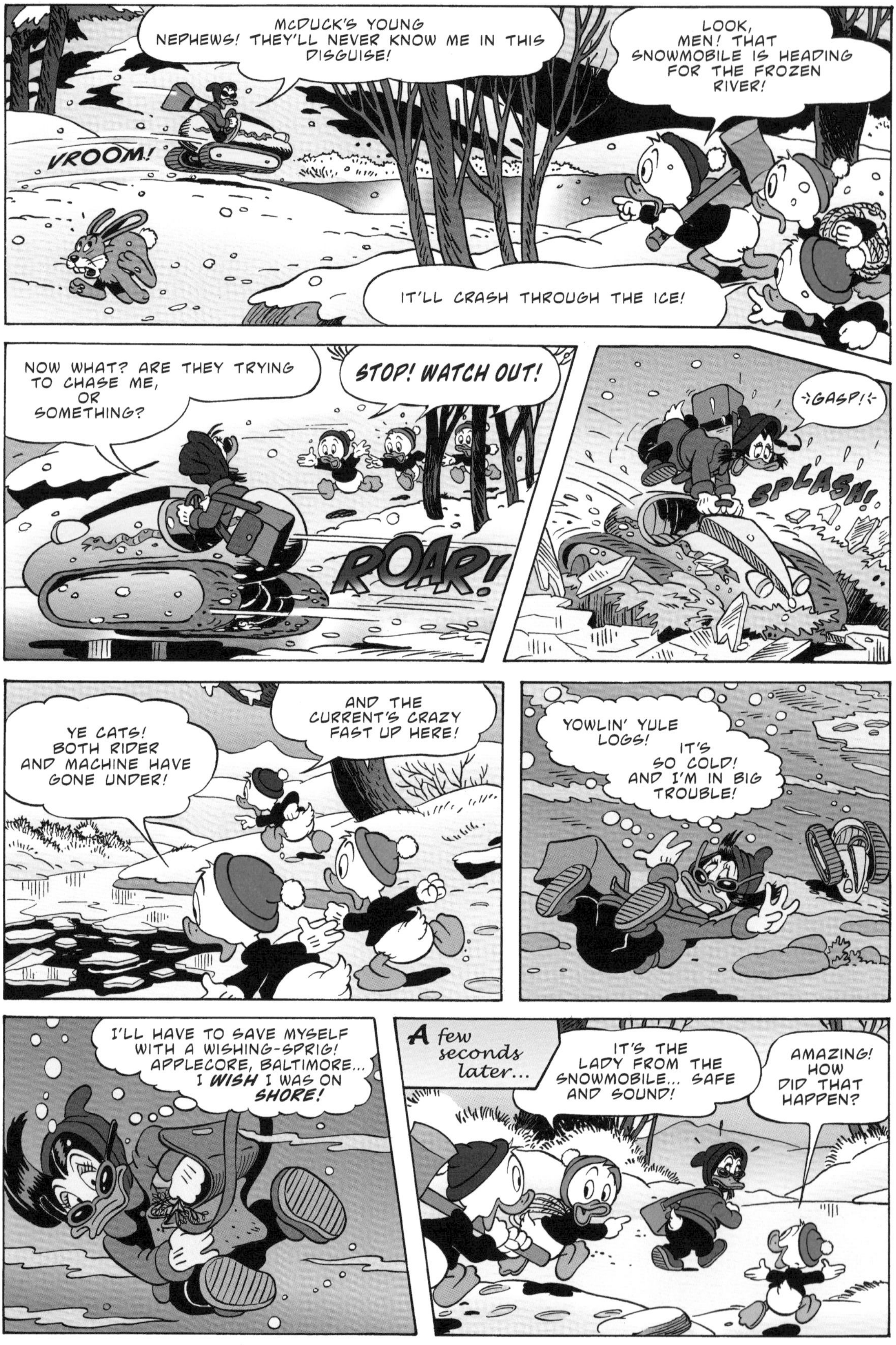
McDUCK'S YOUNG NEPHEWS! THEY'LL NEVER KNOW ME IN THIS DISGUISE!
VROOM!
LOOK, MEN! THAT SNOWMOBILE IS HEADING FOR THE FROZEN RIVER!
IT'LL CRASH THROUGH THE ICE!
NOW WHAT? ARE THEY TRYING TO CHASE ME, OR SOMETHING?
STOP! WATCH OUT!
ROAR!
GASP!
SPLASH!
YE CATS! BOTH RIDER AND MACHINE HAVE GONE UNDER!
AND THE CURRENT'S CRAZY FAST UP HERE!
YOWLIN' YULE LOGS! IT'S SO COLD! AND I'M IN BIG TROUBLE!
I'LL HAVE TO SAVE MYSELF WITH A WISHING-SPRIG! APPLECORE, BALTIMORE... I WISH I WAS ON SHORE!
A few seconds later...
IT'S THE LADY FROM THE SNOWMOBILE... SAFE AND SOUND!
AMAZING! HOW DID THAT HAPPEN?

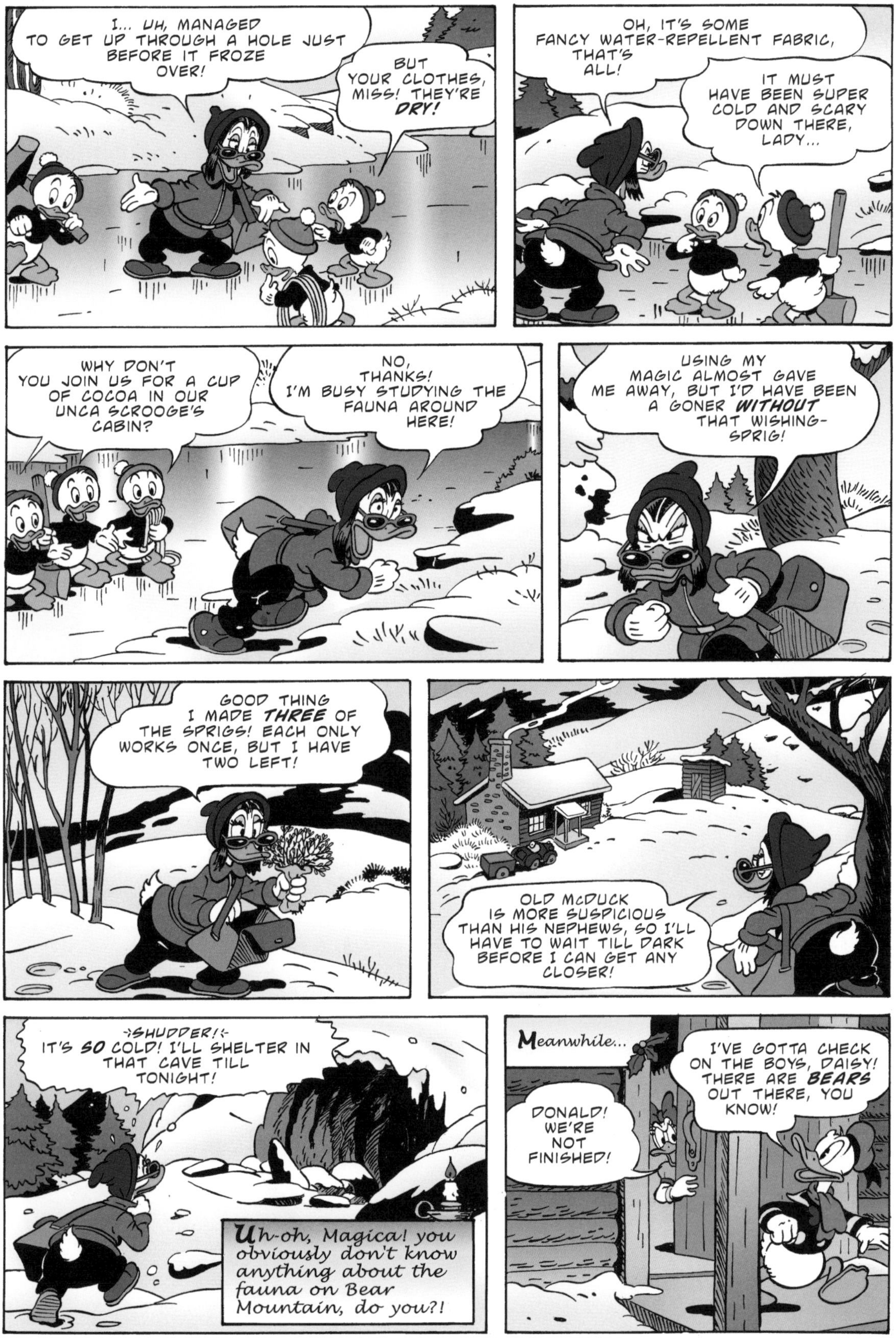
I... UH, MANAGED TO GET UP THROUGH A HOLE JUST BEFORE IT FROZE OVER!
BUT YOUR CLOTHES, MISS! THEY'RE DRY!
OH, IT'S SOME FANCY WATER-REPELLENT FABRIC, THAT'S ALL!
IT MUST HAVE BEEN SUPER COLD AND SCARY DOWN THERE, LADY...
WHY DON'T YOU JOIN US FOR A CUP OF COCOA IN OUR UNCA SCROOGE'S CABIN?
NO, THANKS! I'M BUSY STUDYING THE FAUNA AROUND HERE!
USING MY MAGIC ALMOST GAVE ME AWAY, BUT I'D HAVE BEEN A GONER WITHOUT THAT WISHING-SPRIG!
GOOD THING I MADE THREE OF THE SPRIGS! EACH ONLY WORKS ONCE, BUT I HAVE TWO LEFT!
OLD McDUCK IS MORE SUSPICIOUS THAN HIS NEPHEWS, SO I'LL HAVE TO WAIT TILL DARK BEFORE I CAN GET ANY CLOSER!
-SHUDDER!- IT'S SO COLD! I'LL SHELTER IN THAT CAVE TILL TONIGHT!
Uh-oh, Magica! you obviously don't know anything about the fauna on Bear Mountain, do you?!
Meanwhile...
I'VE GOTTA CHECK ON THE BOYS, DAISY! THERE ARE BEARS OUT THERE, YOU KNOW!
DONALD! WE'RE NOT FINISHED!

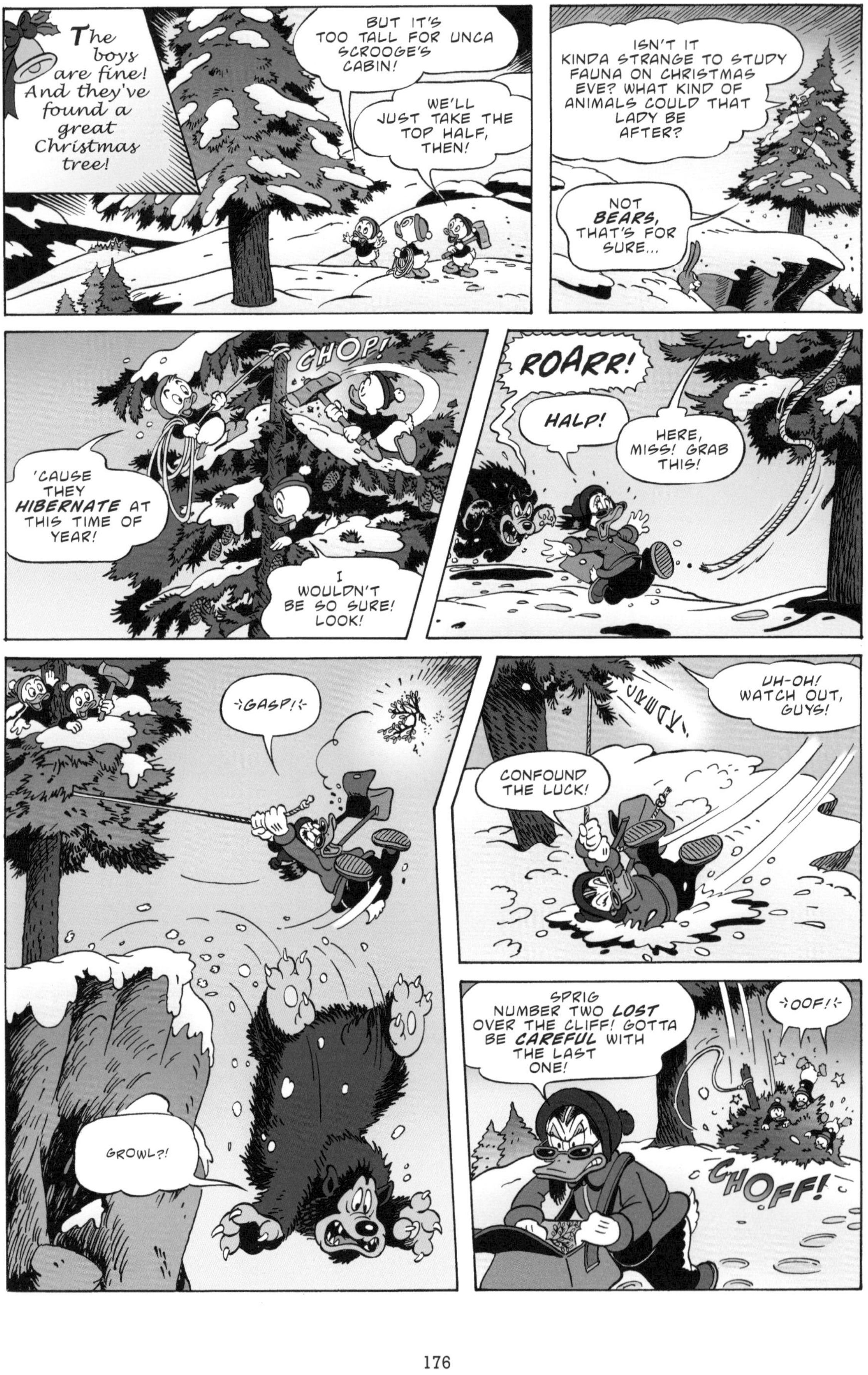
The boys are fine! And they've found a great Christmas tree!
BUT IT'S TOO TALL FOR UNCA SCROOGE'S CABIN!
WE'LL JUST TAKE THE TOP HALF, THEN!
ISN'T IT KINDA STRANGE TO STUDY FAUNA ON CHRISTMAS EVE? WHAT KIND OF ANIMALS COULD THAT LADY BE AFTER?
NOT **BEARS**, THAT'S FOR SURE...
CHOP!
'CAUSE THEY **HIBERNATE** AT THIS TIME OF YEAR!
I WOULDN'T BE SO SURE! LOOK!
ROARR!
HALP!
HERE, MISS! GRAB THIS!
GASP!
GROWL?!
CONFOUND THE LUCK!
UH-OH! WATCH OUT, GUYS!
SPRIG NUMBER TWO **LOST** OVER THE CLIFF! GOTTA BE **CAREFUL** WITH THE LAST ONE!
OOF!
CHOFF!

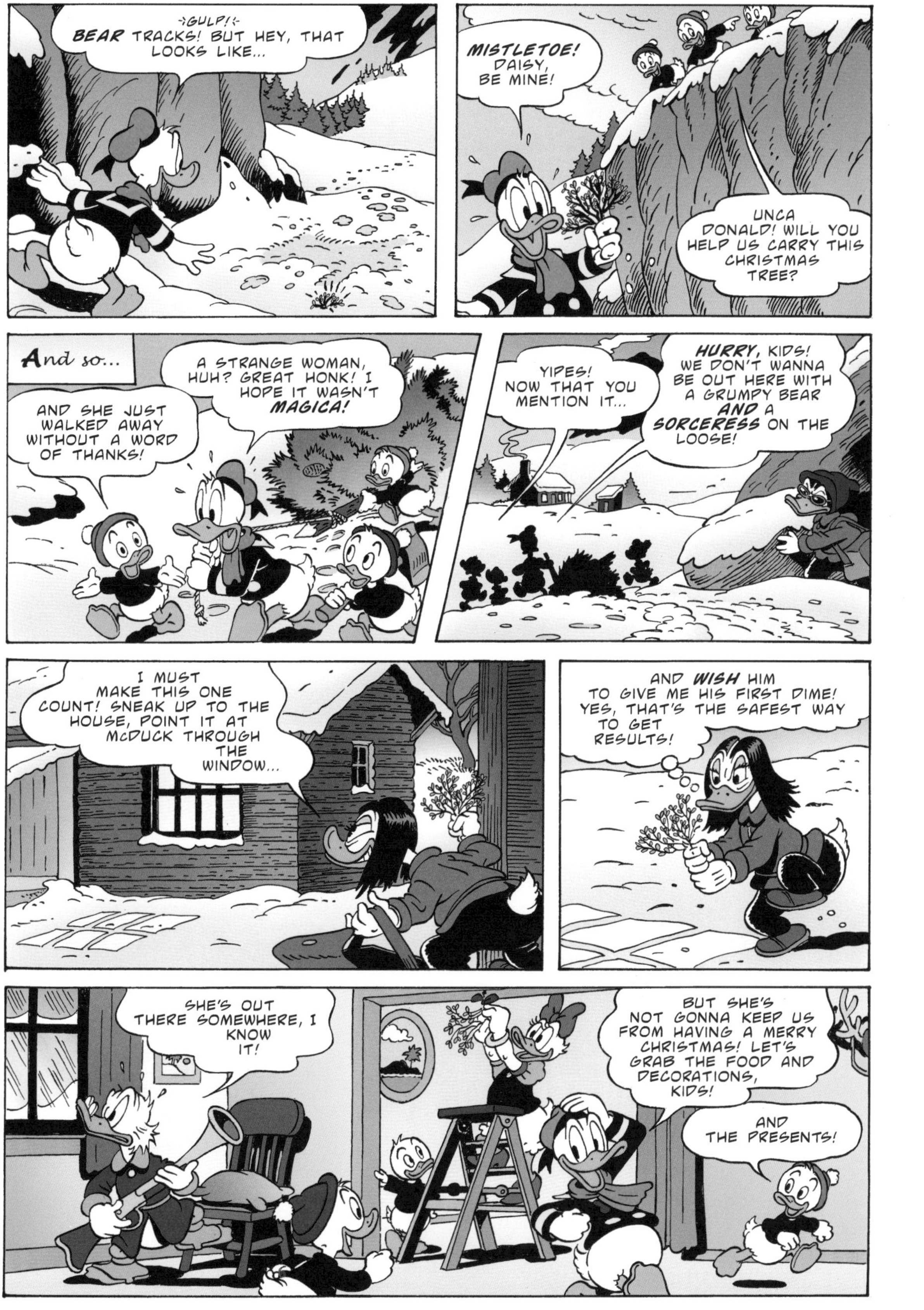
-GULP!-
BEAR TRACKS! BUT HEY, THAT LOOKS LIKE...
MISTLETOE! DAISY, BE MINE!
UNCA DONALD! WILL YOU HELP US CARRY THIS CHRISTMAS TREE?
And so...
AND SHE JUST WALKED AWAY WITHOUT A WORD OF THANKS!
A STRANGE WOMAN, HUH? GREAT HONK! I HOPE IT WASN'T MAGICA!
YIPES! NOW THAT YOU MENTION IT...
HURRY, KIDS! WE DON'T WANNA BE OUT HERE WITH A GRUMPY BEAR AND A SORCERESS ON THE LOOSE!
I MUST MAKE THIS ONE COUNT! SNEAK UP TO THE HOUSE, POINT IT AT McDUCK THROUGH THE WINDOW...
AND WISH HIM TO GIVE ME HIS FIRST DIME! YES, THAT'S THE SAFEST WAY TO GET RESULTS!
SHE'S OUT THERE SOMEWHERE, I KNOW IT!
BUT SHE'S NOT GONNA KEEP US FROM HAVING A MERRY CHRISTMAS! LET'S GRAB THE FOOD AND DECORATIONS, KIDS!
AND THE PRESENTS!

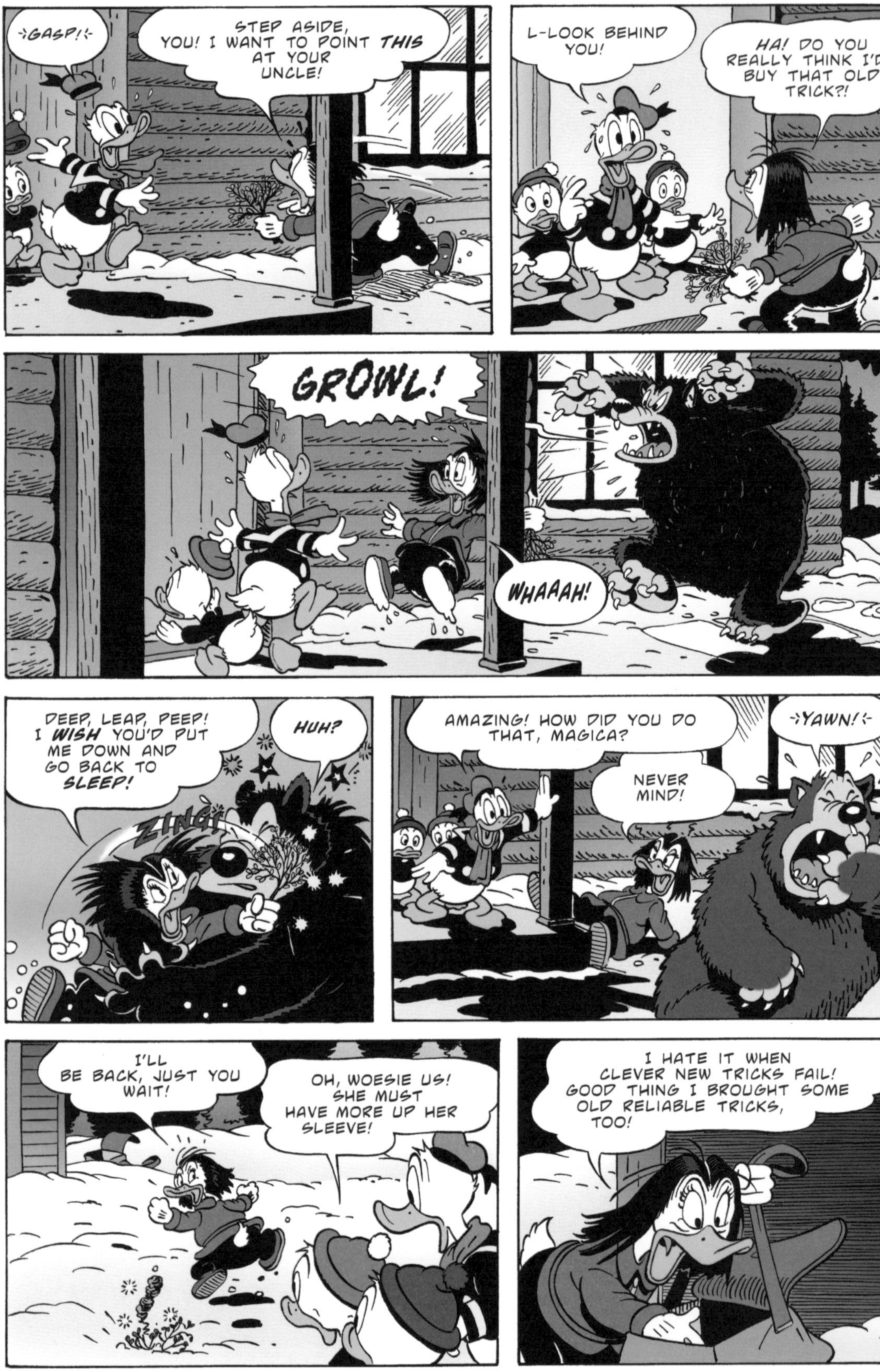

-GASP!-
STEP ASIDE, YOU! I WANT TO POINT THIS AT YOUR UNCLE!
L-LOOK BEHIND YOU!
HA! DO YOU REALLY THINK I'D BUY THAT OLD TRICK?!
GROWL!
WHAAAH!
DEEP, LEAP, PEEP! I WISH YOU'D PUT ME DOWN AND GO BACK TO SLEEP!
HUH?
ZING!
AMAZING! HOW DID YOU DO THAT, MAGICA?
-YAWN!-
NEVER MIND!
I'LL BE BACK, JUST YOU WAIT!
OH, WOESIE US! SHE MUST HAVE MORE UP HER SLEEVE!
I HATE IT WHEN CLEVER NEW TRICKS FAIL! GOOD THING I BROUGHT SOME OLD RELIABLE TRICKS, TOO!

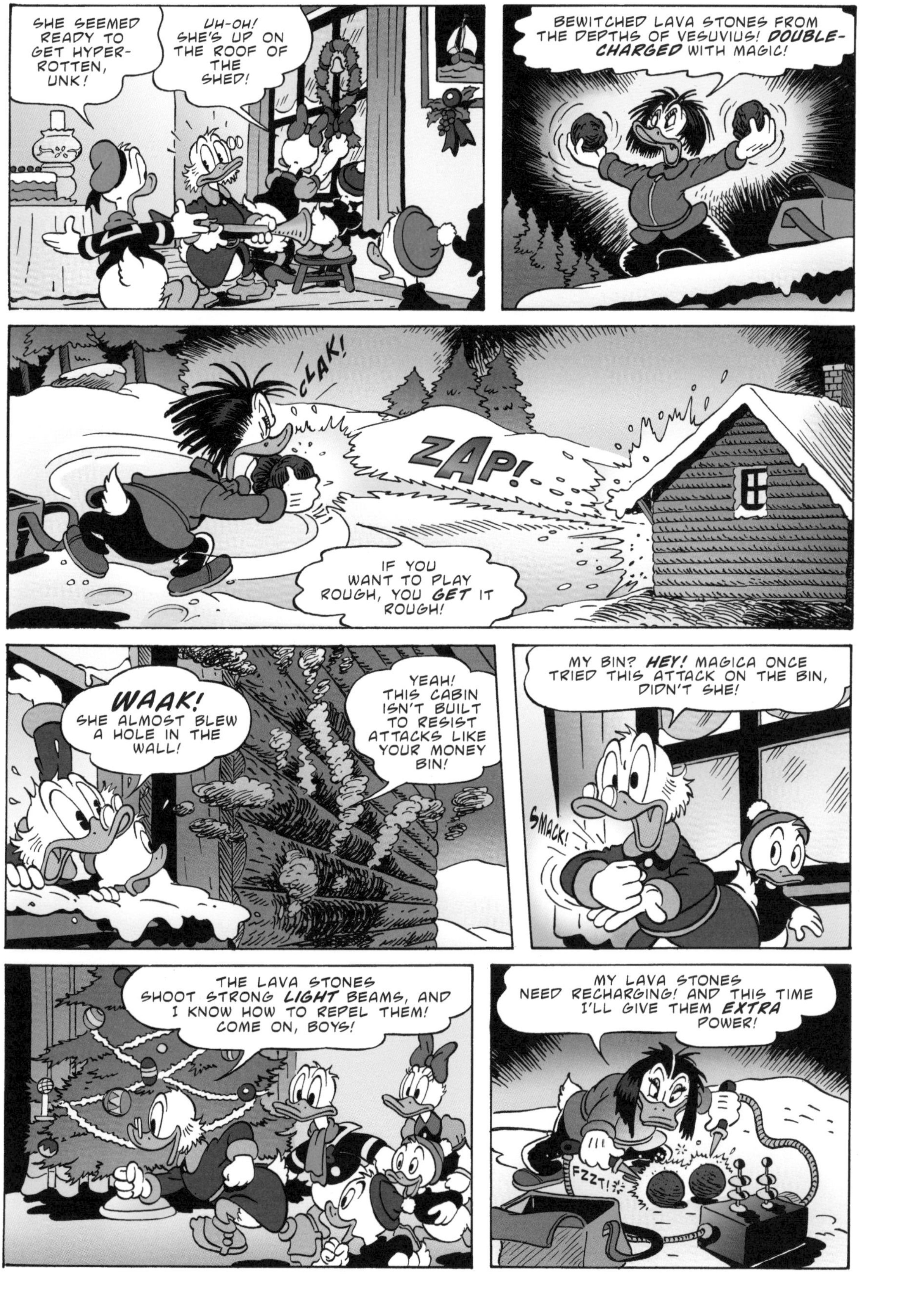

SHE SEEMED READY TO GET HYPER-ROTTEN, UNK!
UH-OH! SHE'S UP ON THE ROOF OF THE SHED!
BEWITCHED LAVA STONES FROM THE DEPTHS OF VESUVIUS! DOUBLE-CHARGED WITH MAGIC!
CLAK!
ZAP!
IF YOU WANT TO PLAY ROUGH, YOU GET IT ROUGH!
WAAK! SHE ALMOST BLEW A HOLE IN THE WALL!
YEAH! THIS CABIN ISN'T BUILT TO RESIST ATTACKS LIKE YOUR MONEY BIN!
MY BIN? HEY! MAGICA ONCE TRIED THIS ATTACK ON THE BIN, DIDN'T SHE!
SMACK!
THE LAVA STONES SHOOT STRONG LIGHT BEAMS, AND I KNOW HOW TO REPEL THEM! COME ON, BOYS!
MY LAVA STONES NEED RECHARGING! AND THIS TIME I'LL GIVE THEM EXTRA POWER!
FZZT!

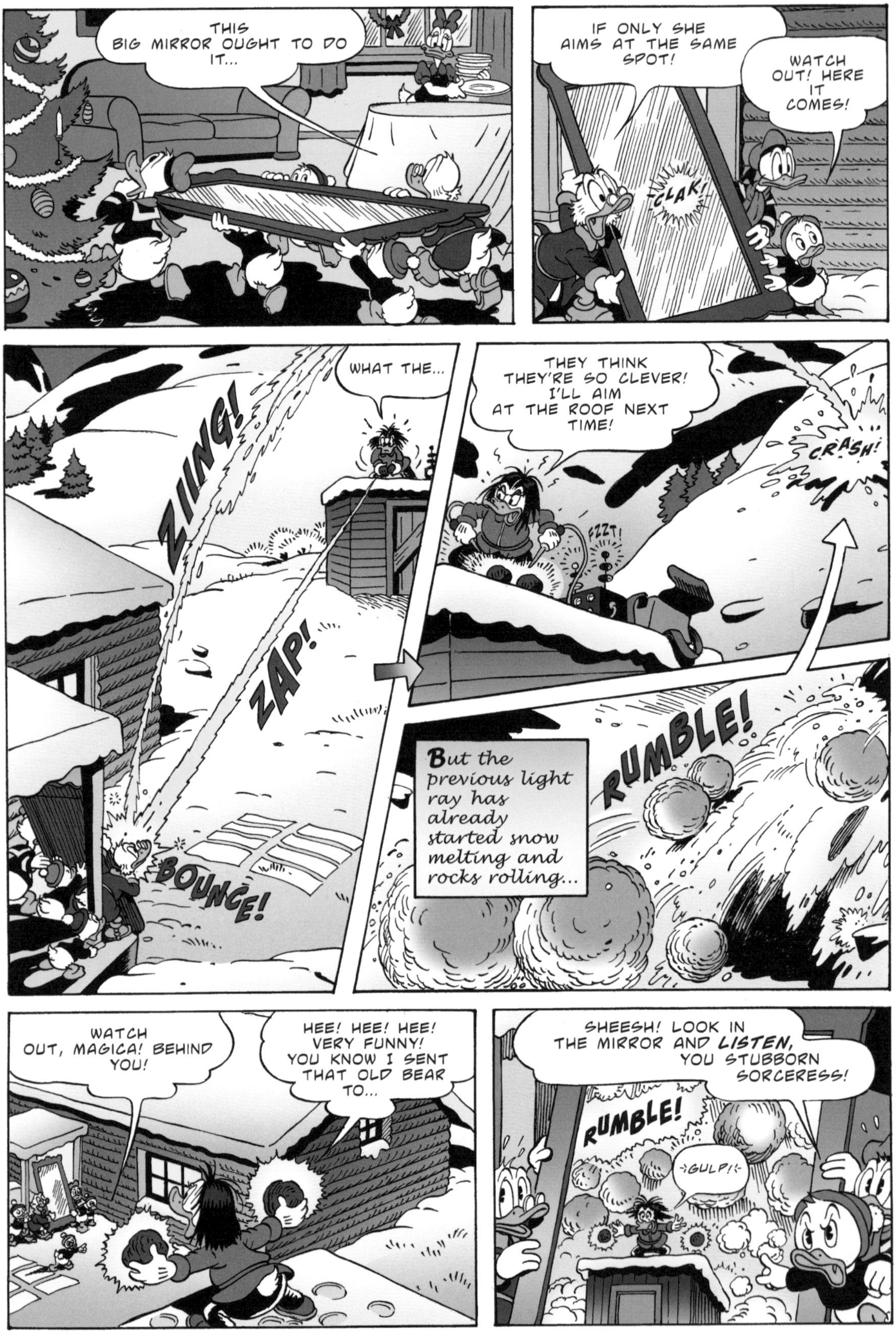
THIS BIG MIRROR OUGHT TO DO IT...
IF ONLY SHE AIMS AT THE SAME SPOT!
WATCH OUT! HERE IT COMES!
CLAK!
WHAT THE...
ZIING!
ZAP!
BOUNCE!
THEY THINK THEY'RE SO CLEVER! I'LL AIM AT THE ROOF NEXT TIME!
FZZT!
CRASH!
But the previous light ray has already started snow melting and rocks rolling...
RUMBLE!
WATCH OUT, MAGICA! BEHIND YOU!
HEE! HEE! HEE! VERY FUNNY! YOU KNOW I SENT THAT OLD BEAR TO...
SHEESH! LOOK IN THE MIRROR AND LISTEN, YOU STUBBORN SORCERESS!
RUMBLE!
GULP!

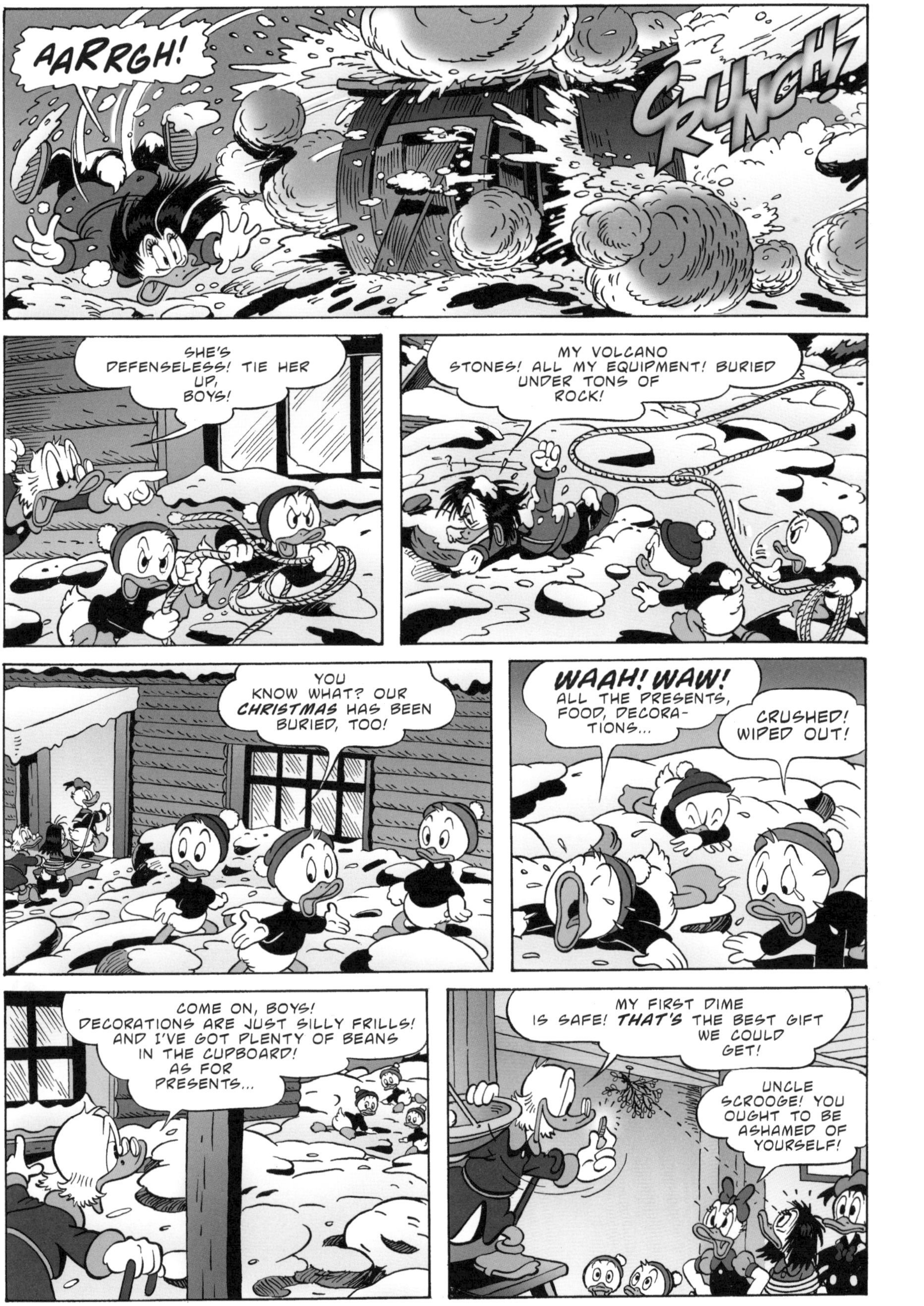
AARRGH!
CRUNCH!
SHE'S DEFENSELESS! TIE HER UP, BOYS!
MY VOLCANO STONES! ALL MY EQUIPMENT! BURIED UNDER TONS OF ROCK!
YOU KNOW WHAT? OUR CHRISTMAS HAS BEEN BURIED, TOO!
WAAH! WAW! ALL THE PRESENTS, FOOD, DECORATIONS...
CRUSHED! WIPED OUT!
COME ON, BOYS! DECORATIONS ARE JUST SILLY FRILLS! AND I'VE GOT PLENTY OF BEANS IN THE CUPBOARD! AS FOR PRESENTS...
MY FIRST DIME IS SAFE! THAT'S THE BEST GIFT WE COULD GET!
UNCLE SCROOGE! YOU OUGHT TO BE ASHAMED OF YOURSELF!

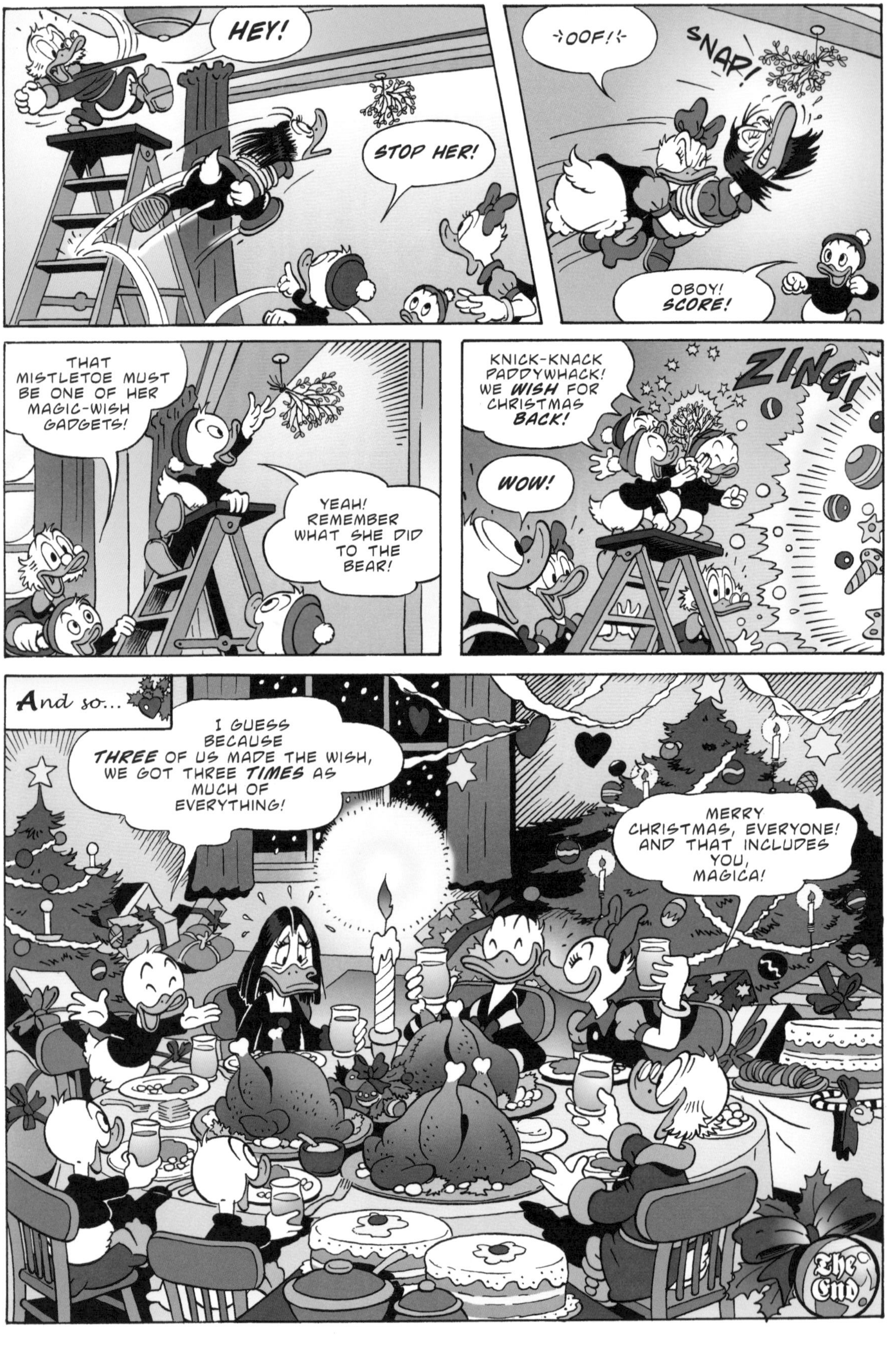
HEY!
STOP HER!
OOF!
SNAP!
OBOY! SCORE!
THAT MISTLETOE MUST BE ONE OF HER MAGIC-WISH GADGETS!
YEAH! REMEMBER WHAT SHE DID TO THE BEAR!
KNICK-KNACK PADDYWHACK! WE WISH FOR CHRISTMAS BACK!
WOW!
ZING!
And so...
I GUESS BECAUSE THREE OF US MADE THE WISH, WE GOT THREE TIMES AS MUCH OF EVERYTHING!
MERRY CHRISTMAS, EVERYONE! AND THAT INCLUDES YOU, MAGICA!
The End

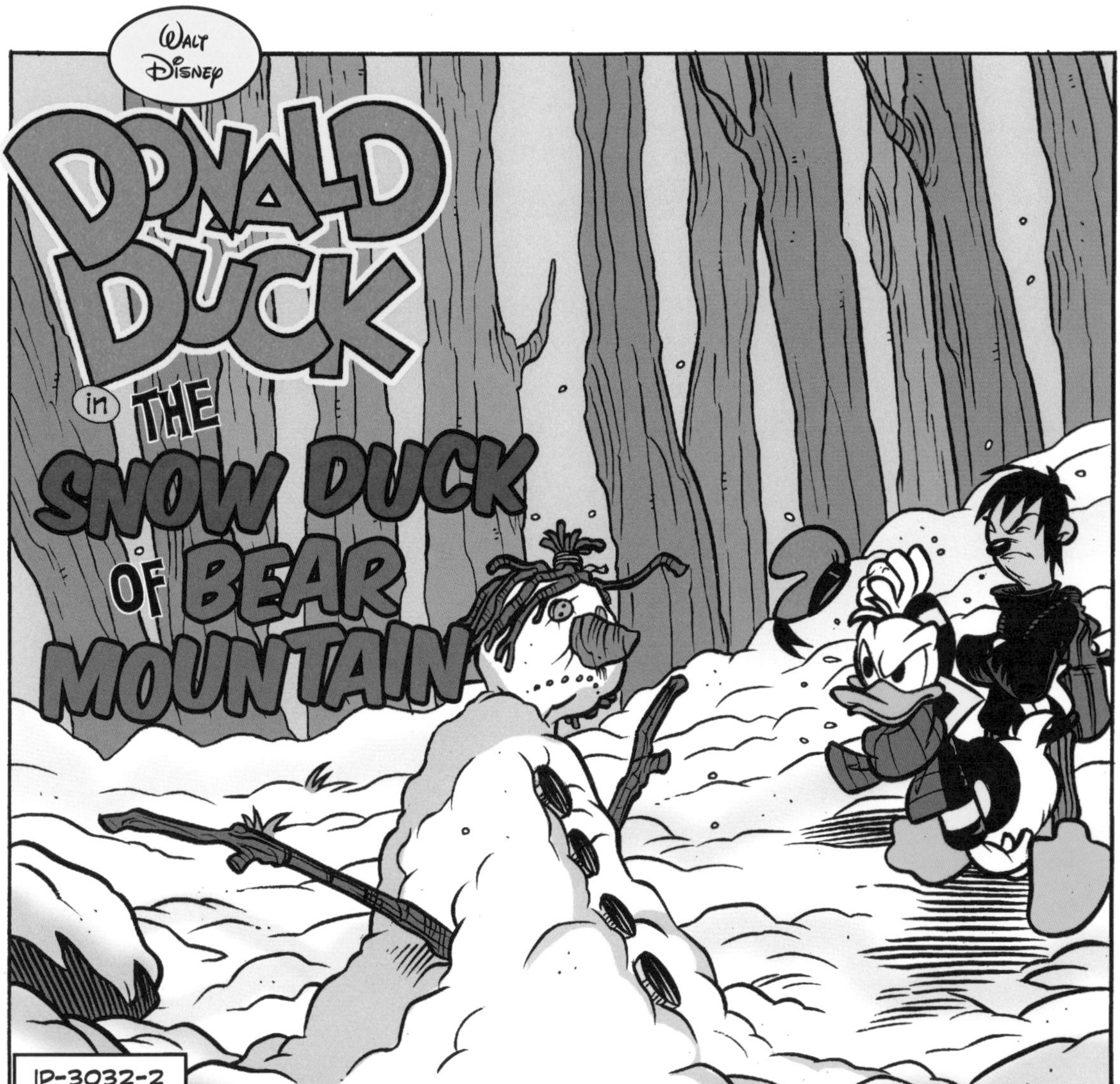
Walt Disney
Donald Duck
in The Snow Duck of Bear Mountain
IP-3032-2

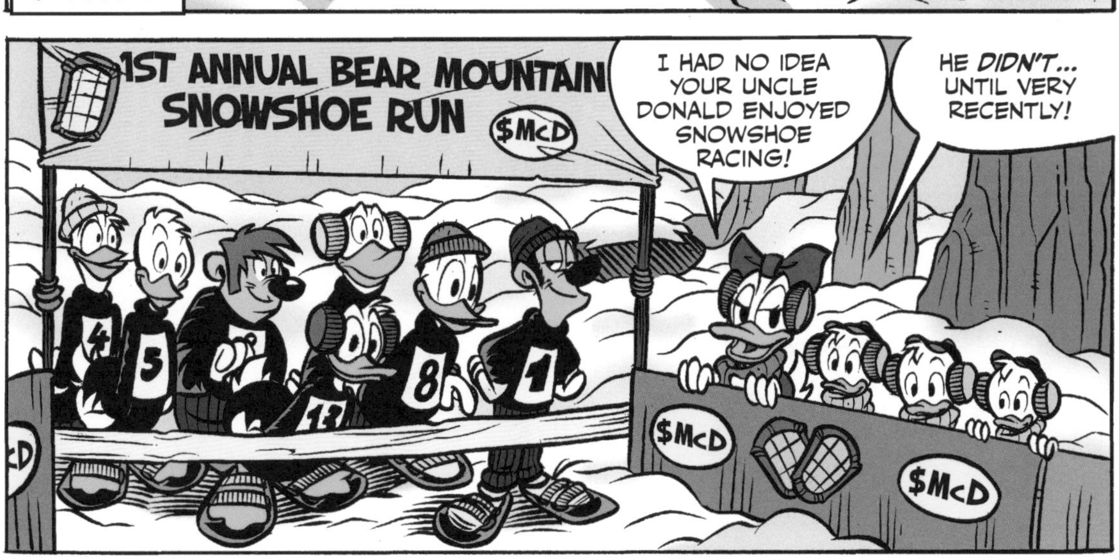
1ST ANNUAL BEAR MOUNTAIN SNOWSHOE RUN
$McD
I HAD NO IDEA YOUR UNCLE DONALD ENJOYED SNOWSHOE RACING!
HE *DIDN'T*... UNTIL VERY RECENTLY!
$McD
$McD

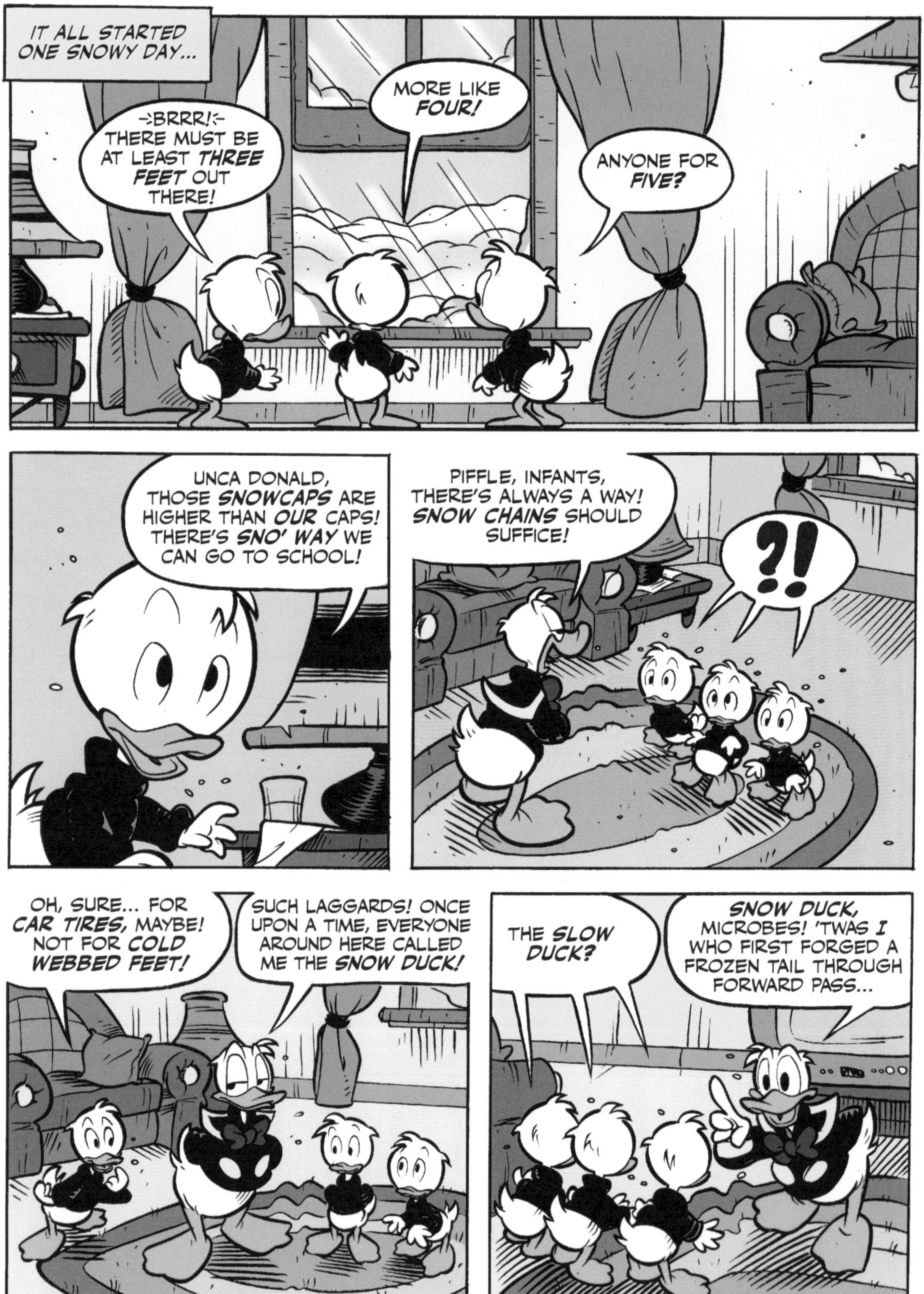
IT ALL STARTED ONE SNOWY DAY...
-BRRR!- THERE MUST BE AT LEAST THREE FEET OUT THERE!
MORE LIKE FOUR!
ANYONE FOR FIVE?
UNCA DONALD, THOSE SNOWCAPS ARE HIGHER THAN OUR CAPS! THERE'S SNO' WAY WE CAN GO TO SCHOOL!
PIFFLE, INFANTS, THERE'S ALWAYS A WAY! SNOW CHAINS SHOULD SUFFICE!
?!
OH, SURE... FOR CAR TIRES, MAYBE! NOT FOR COLD WEBBED FEET!
SUCH LAGGARDS! ONCE UPON A TIME, EVERYONE AROUND HERE CALLED ME THE SNOW DUCK!
THE SLOW DUCK?
SNOW DUCK, MICROBES! 'TWAS I WHO FIRST FORGED A FROZEN TAIL THROUGH FORWARD PASS...

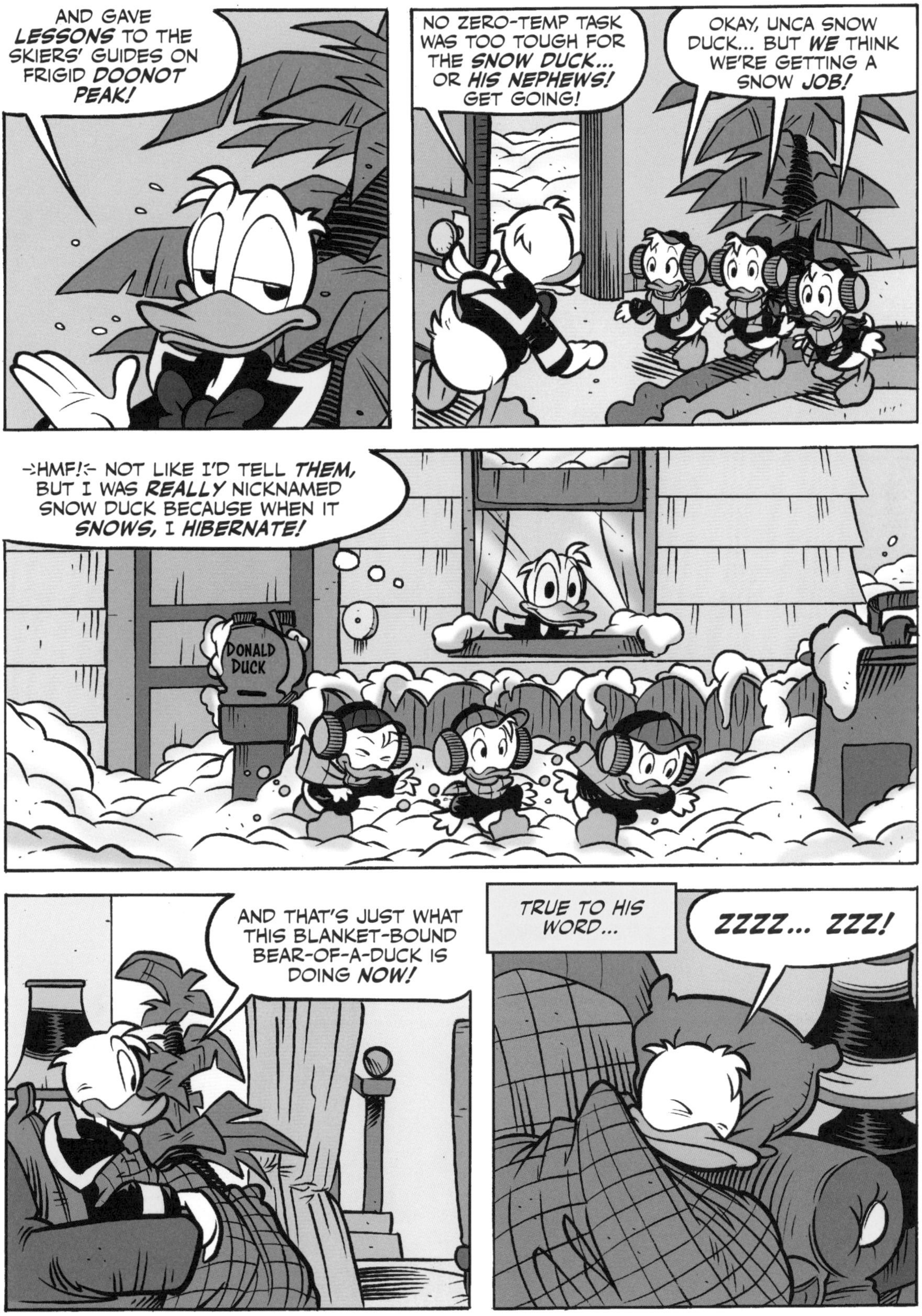
AND GAVE LESSONS TO THE SKIERS' GUIDES ON FRIGID DOONOT PEAK!
NO ZERO-TEMP TASK WAS TOO TOUGH FOR THE SNOW DUCK... OR HIS NEPHEWS! GET GOING!
OKAY, UNCA SNOW DUCK... BUT WE THINK WE'RE GETTING A SNOW JOB!
-HMF!- NOT LIKE I'D TELL THEM, BUT I WAS REALLY NICKNAMED SNOW DUCK BECAUSE WHEN IT SNOWS, I HIBERNATE!
DONALD DUCK
AND THAT'S JUST WHAT THIS BLANKET-BOUND BEAR-OF-A-DUCK IS DOING NOW!
TRUE TO HIS WORD...
ZZZZ... ZZZ!

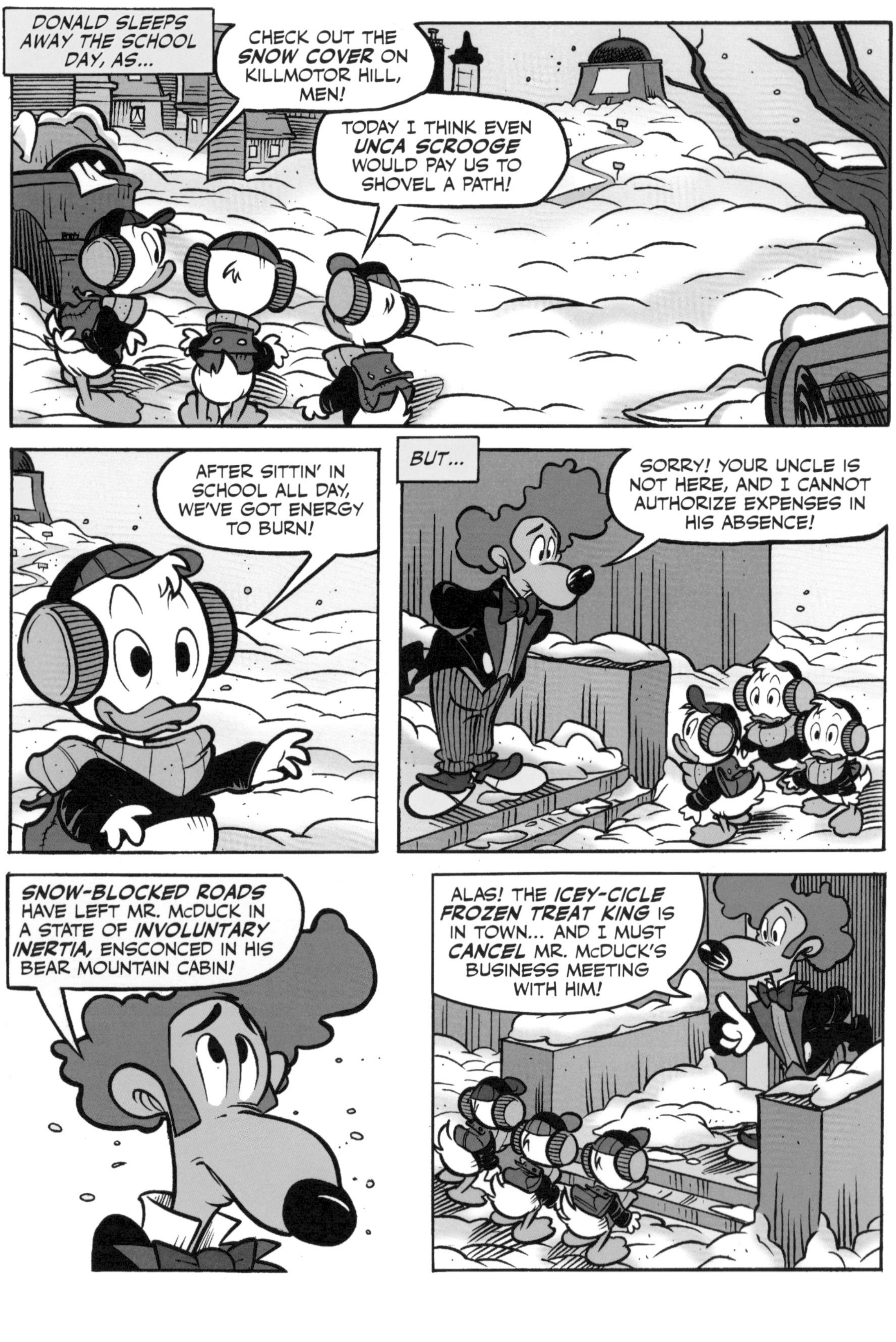
DONALD SLEEPS AWAY THE SCHOOL DAY, AS...
CHECK OUT THE SNOW COVER ON KILLMOTOR HILL, MEN!
TODAY I THINK EVEN UNCA SCROOGE WOULD PAY US TO SHOVEL A PATH!
AFTER SITTIN' IN SCHOOL ALL DAY, WE'VE GOT ENERGY TO BURN!
BUT...
SORRY! YOUR UNCLE IS NOT HERE, AND I CANNOT AUTHORIZE EXPENSES IN HIS ABSENCE!
SNOW-BLOCKED ROADS HAVE LEFT MR. McDUCK IN A STATE OF INVOLUNTARY INERTIA, ENSCONCED IN HIS BEAR MOUNTAIN CABIN!
ALAS! THE ICEY-CICLE FROZEN TREAT KING IS IN TOWN... AND I MUST CANCEL MR. McDUCK'S BUSINESS MEETING WITH HIM!

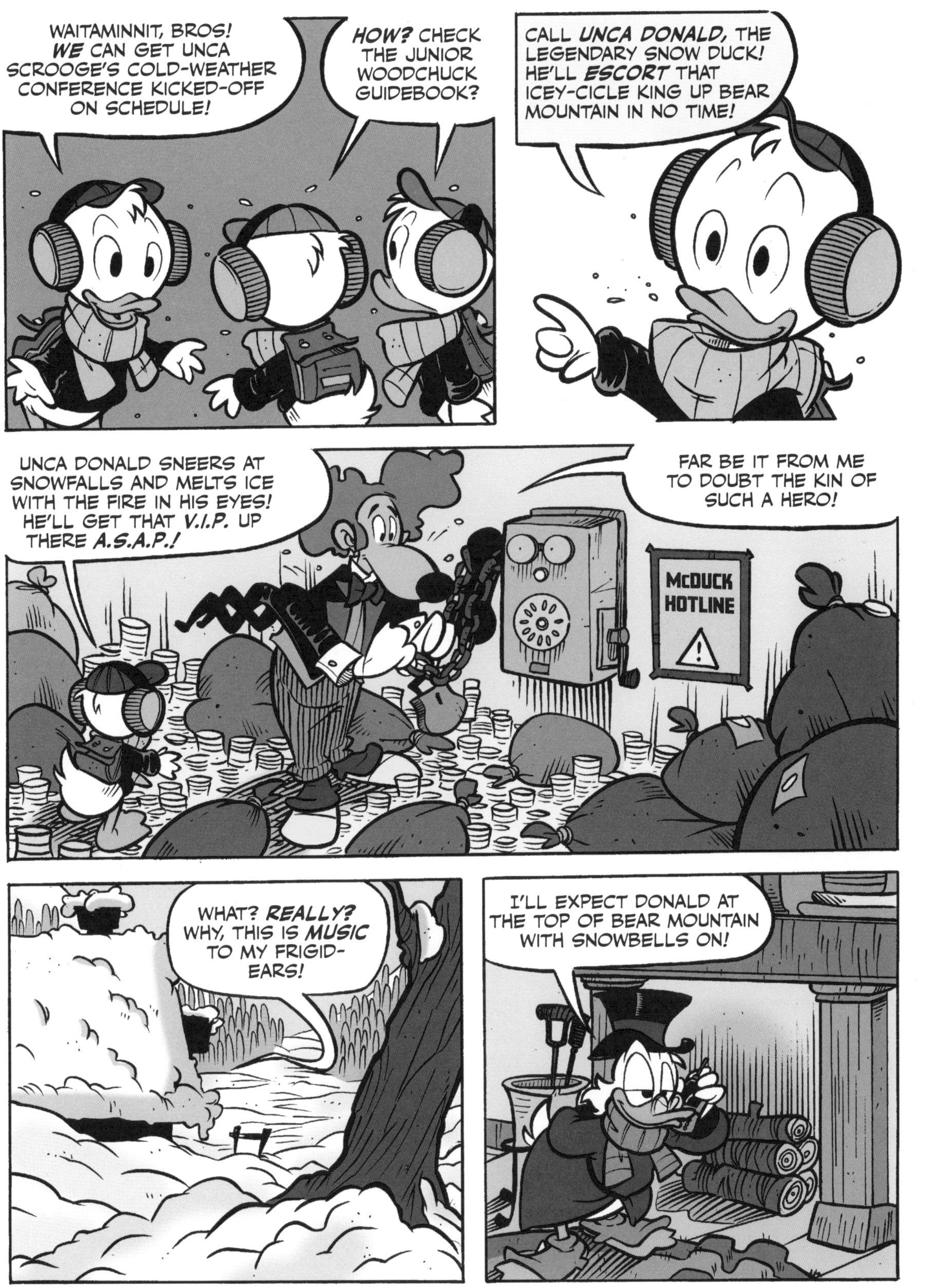
WAITAMINNIT, BROS! WE CAN GET UNCA SCROOGE'S COLD-WEATHER CONFERENCE KICKED-OFF ON SCHEDULE!
HOW? CHECK THE JUNIOR WOODCHUCK GUIDEBOOK?
CALL UNCA DONALD, THE LEGENDARY SNOW DUCK! HE'LL ESCORT THAT ICEY-CICLE KING UP BEAR MOUNTAIN IN NO TIME!
UNCA DONALD SNEERS AT SNOWFALLS AND MELTS ICE WITH THE FIRE IN HIS EYES! HE'LL GET THAT V.I.P. UP THERE A.S.A.P.!
FAR BE IT FROM ME TO DOUBT THE KIN OF SUCH A HERO!
McDUCK HOTLINE
WHAT? REALLY? WHY, THIS IS MUSIC TO MY FRIGID-EARS!
I'LL EXPECT DONALD AT THE TOP OF BEAR MOUNTAIN WITH SNOWBELLS ON!

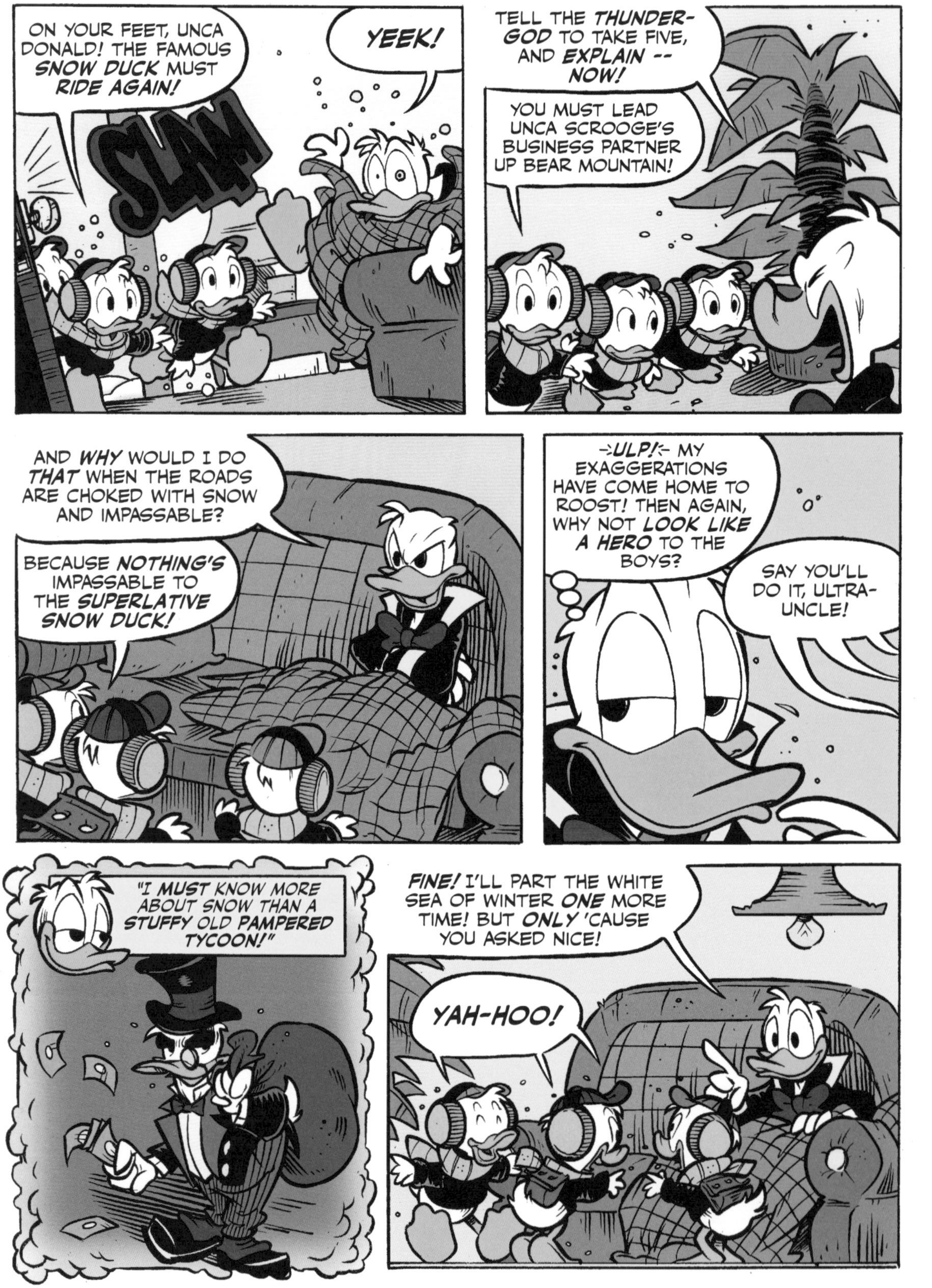
ON YOUR FEET, UNCA DONALD! THE FAMOUS SNOW DUCK MUST RIDE AGAIN!
SLAM
YEEK!
TELL THE THUNDER-GOD TO TAKE FIVE, AND EXPLAIN -- NOW!
YOU MUST LEAD UNCA SCROOGE'S BUSINESS PARTNER UP BEAR MOUNTAIN!
AND WHY WOULD I DO THAT WHEN THE ROADS ARE CHOKED WITH SNOW AND IMPASSABLE?
BECAUSE NOTHING'S IMPASSABLE TO THE SUPERLATIVE SNOW DUCK!
-ULP!- MY EXAGGERATIONS HAVE COME HOME TO ROOST! THEN AGAIN, WHY NOT LOOK LIKE A HERO TO THE BOYS?
SAY YOU'LL DO IT, ULTRA-UNCLE!
"I MUST KNOW MORE ABOUT SNOW THAN A STUFFY OLD PAMPERED TYCOON!"
FINE! I'LL PART THE WHITE SEA OF WINTER ONE MORE TIME! BUT ONLY 'CAUSE YOU ASKED NICE!
YAH-HOO!

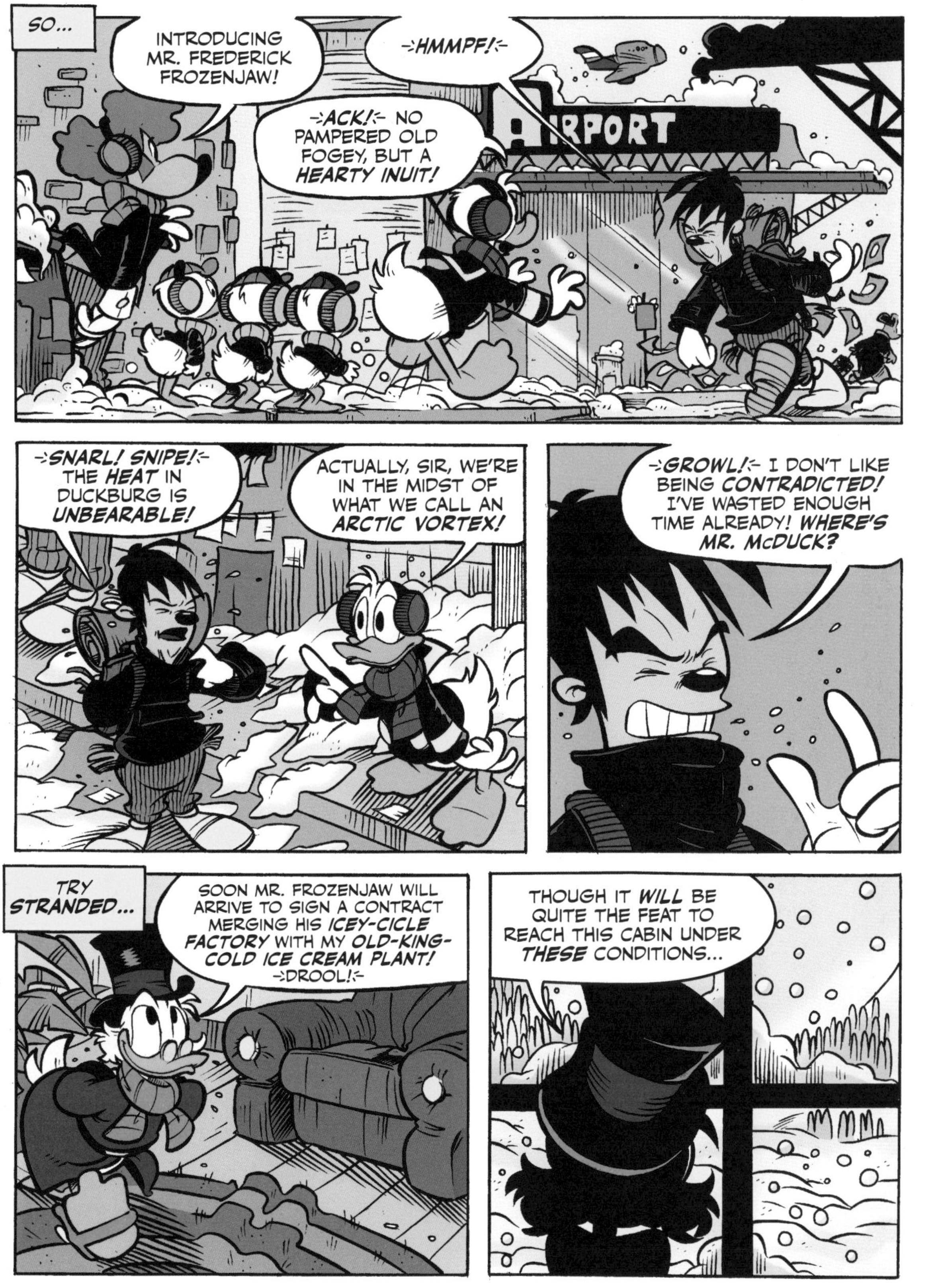
SO...
INTRODUCING MR. FREDERICK FROZENJAW!
-HMMPF!-
-ACK!- NO PAMPERED OLD FOGEY, BUT A HEARTY INUIT!
AIRPORT
-SNARL! SNIPE!- THE HEAT IN DUCKBURG IS UNBEARABLE!
ACTUALLY, SIR, WE'RE IN THE MIDST OF WHAT WE CALL AN ARCTIC VORTEX!
-GROWL!- I DON'T LIKE BEING CONTRADICTED! I'VE WASTED ENOUGH TIME ALREADY! WHERE'S MR. McDUCK?
TRY STRANDED...
SOON MR. FROZENJAW WILL ARRIVE TO SIGN A CONTRACT MERGING HIS ICEY-CICLE FACTORY WITH MY OLD-KING-COLD ICE CREAM PLANT! -DROOL!-
THOUGH IT WILL BE QUITE THE FEAT TO REACH THIS CABIN UNDER THESE CONDITIONS...

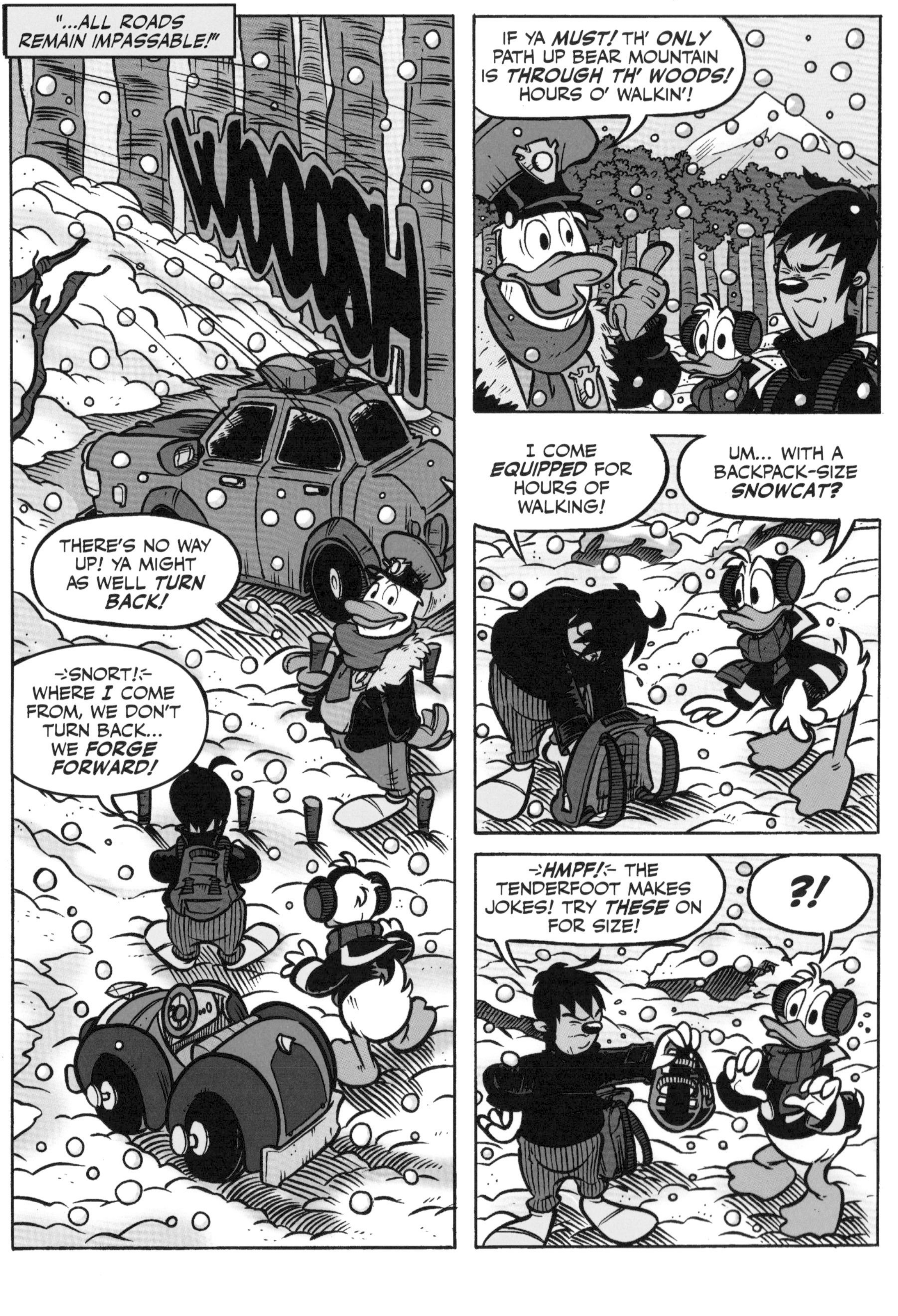
"...ALL ROADS REMAIN IMPASSABLE!"
WOOOSH
THERE'S NO WAY UP! YA MIGHT AS WELL TURN BACK!
-SNORT!- WHERE I COME FROM, WE DON'T TURN BACK... WE FORGE FORWARD!
IF YA MUST! TH' ONLY PATH UP BEAR MOUNTAIN IS THROUGH TH' WOODS! HOURS O' WALKIN'!
I COME EQUIPPED FOR HOURS OF WALKING!
UM... WITH A BACKPACK-SIZE SNOWCAT?
-HMPF!- THE TENDERFOOT MAKES JOKES! TRY THESE ON FOR SIZE!
?!

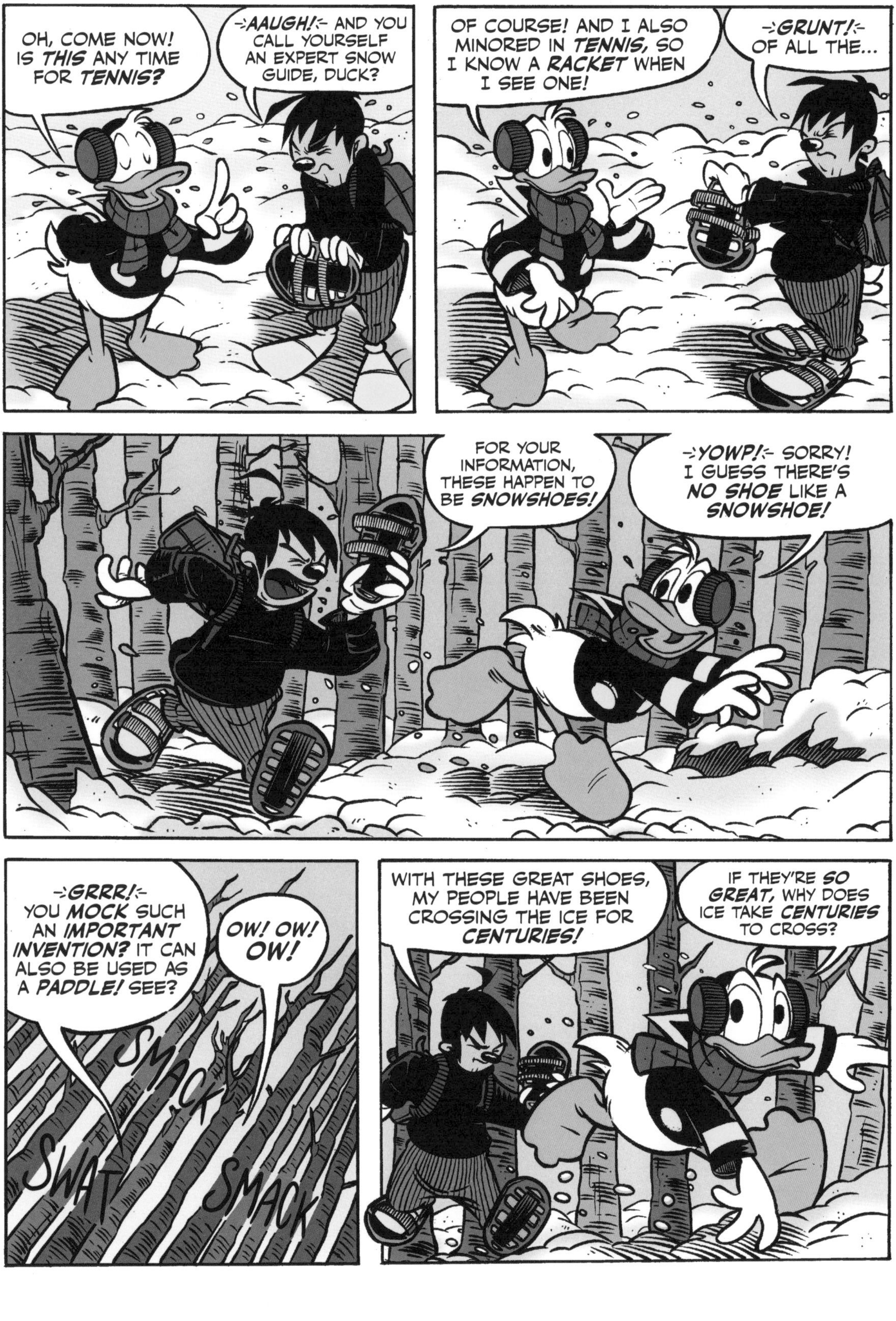
OH, COME NOW! IS THIS ANY TIME FOR TENNIS?
-AAUGH!- AND YOU CALL YOURSELF AN EXPERT SNOW GUIDE, DUCK?
OF COURSE! AND I ALSO MINORED IN TENNIS, SO I KNOW A RACKET WHEN I SEE ONE!
-GRUNT!- OF ALL THE...
FOR YOUR INFORMATION, THESE HAPPEN TO BE SNOWSHOES!
-YOWP!- SORRY! I GUESS THERE'S NO SHOE LIKE A SNOWSHOE!
-GRRR!- YOU MOCK SUCH AN IMPORTANT INVENTION? IT CAN ALSO BE USED AS A PADDLE! SEE?
OW! OW! OW!
SMACK
SWAT
SMACK
WITH THESE GREAT SHOES, MY PEOPLE HAVE BEEN CROSSING THE ICE FOR CENTURIES!
IF THEY'RE SO GREAT, WHY DOES ICE TAKE CENTURIES TO CROSS?

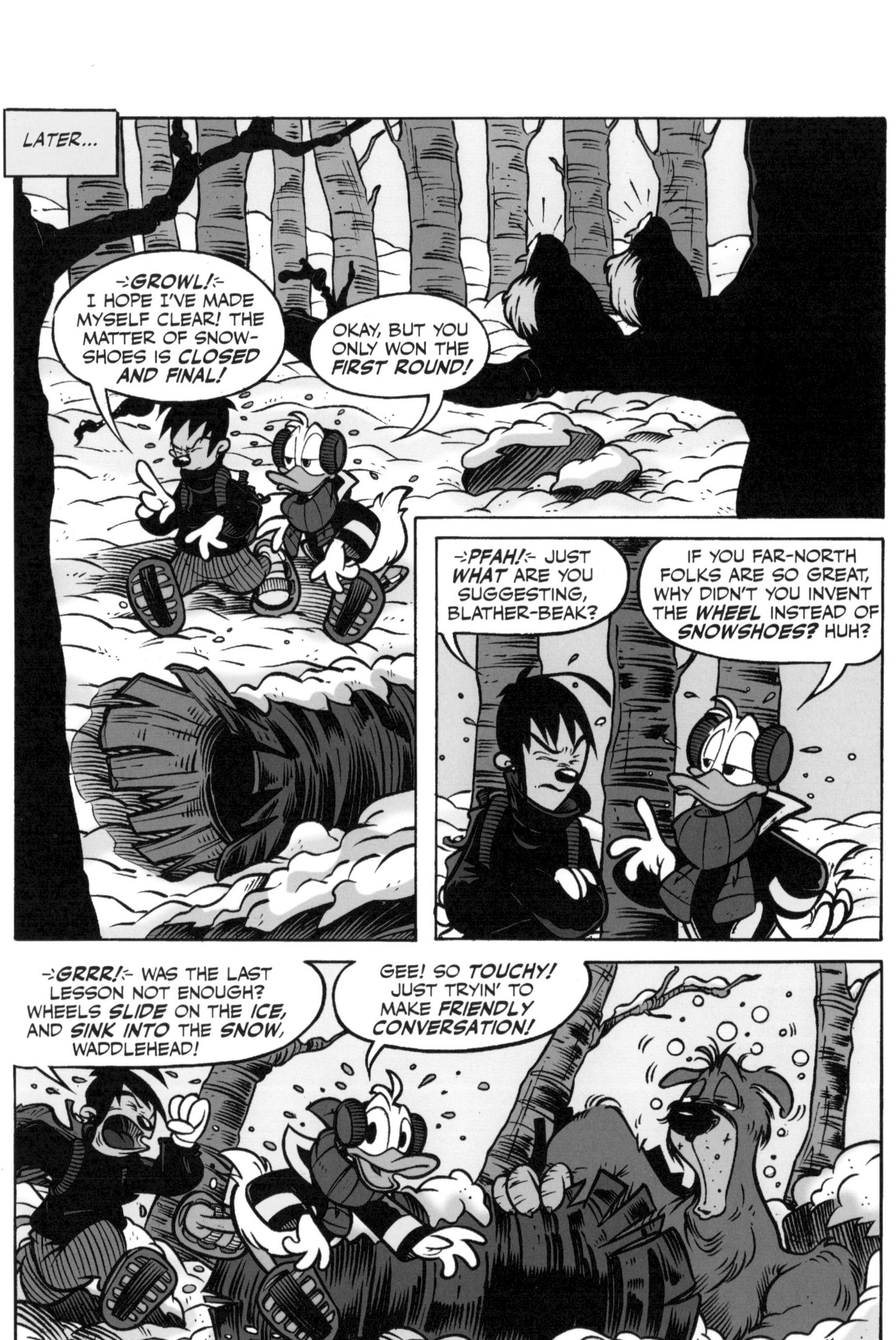
LATER...
-GROWL!- I HOPE I'VE MADE MYSELF CLEAR! THE MATTER OF SNOW-SHOES IS CLOSED AND FINAL!
OKAY, BUT YOU ONLY WON THE FIRST ROUND!
-PFAH!- JUST WHAT ARE YOU SUGGESTING, BLATHER-BEAK?
IF YOU FAR-NORTH FOLKS ARE SO GREAT, WHY DIDN'T YOU INVENT THE WHEEL INSTEAD OF SNOWSHOES? HUH?
-GRRR!- WAS THE LAST LESSON NOT ENOUGH? WHEELS SLIDE ON THE ICE, AND SINK INTO THE SNOW, WADDLEHEAD!
GEE! SO TOUCHY! JUST TRYIN' TO MAKE FRIENDLY CONVERSATION!

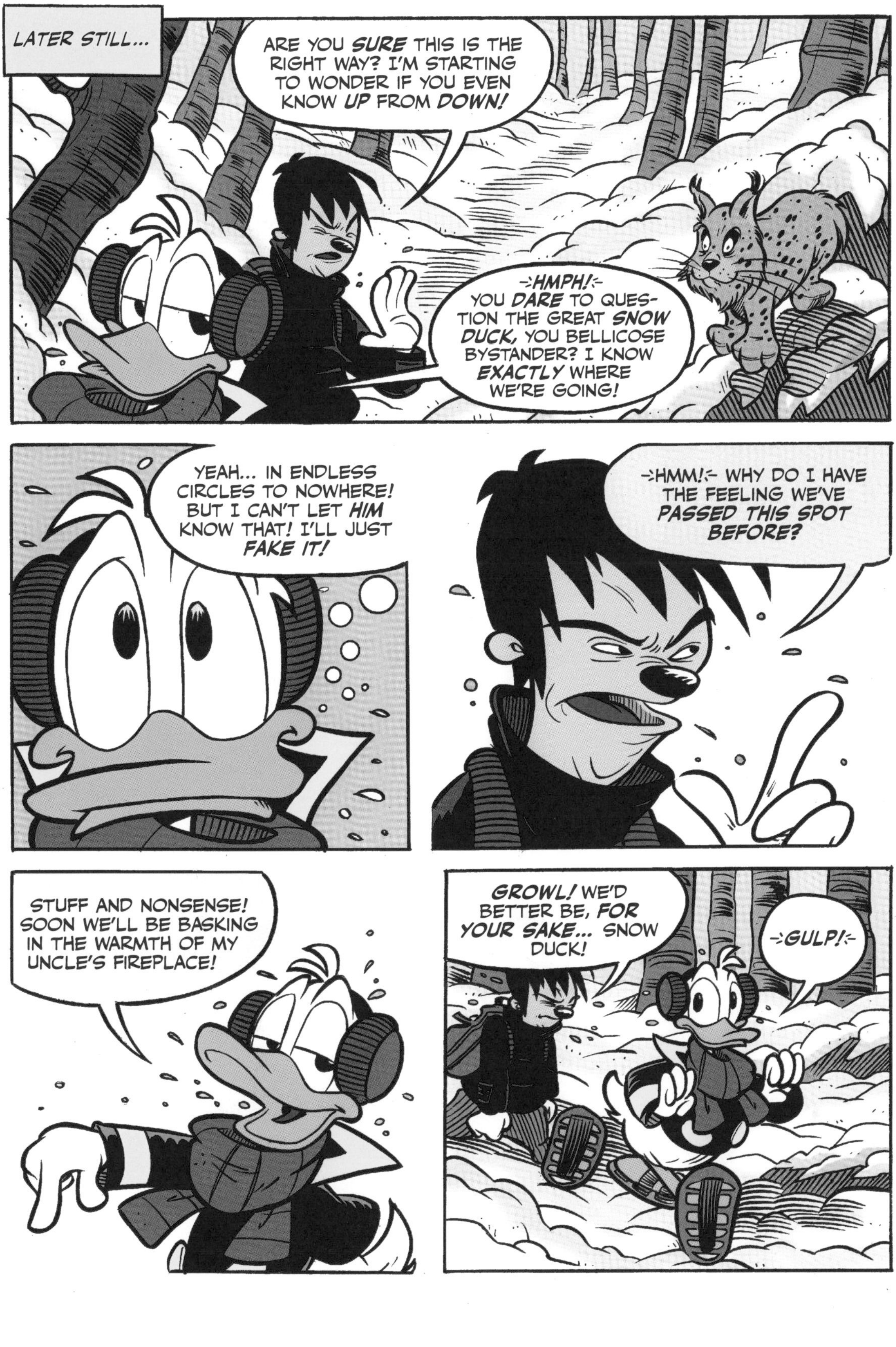
LATER STILL...
ARE YOU SURE THIS IS THE RIGHT WAY? I'M STARTING TO WONDER IF YOU EVEN KNOW UP FROM DOWN!
-HMPH!- YOU DARE TO QUESTION THE GREAT SNOW DUCK, YOU BELLICOSE BYSTANDER? I KNOW EXACTLY WHERE WE'RE GOING!
YEAH... IN ENDLESS CIRCLES TO NOWHERE! BUT I CAN'T LET HIM KNOW THAT! I'LL JUST FAKE IT!
-HMM!- WHY DO I HAVE THE FEELING WE'VE PASSED THIS SPOT BEFORE?
STUFF AND NONSENSE! SOON WE'LL BE BASKING IN THE WARMTH OF MY UNCLE'S FIREPLACE!
GROWL! WE'D BETTER BE, FOR YOUR SAKE... SNOW DUCK!
-GULP!-

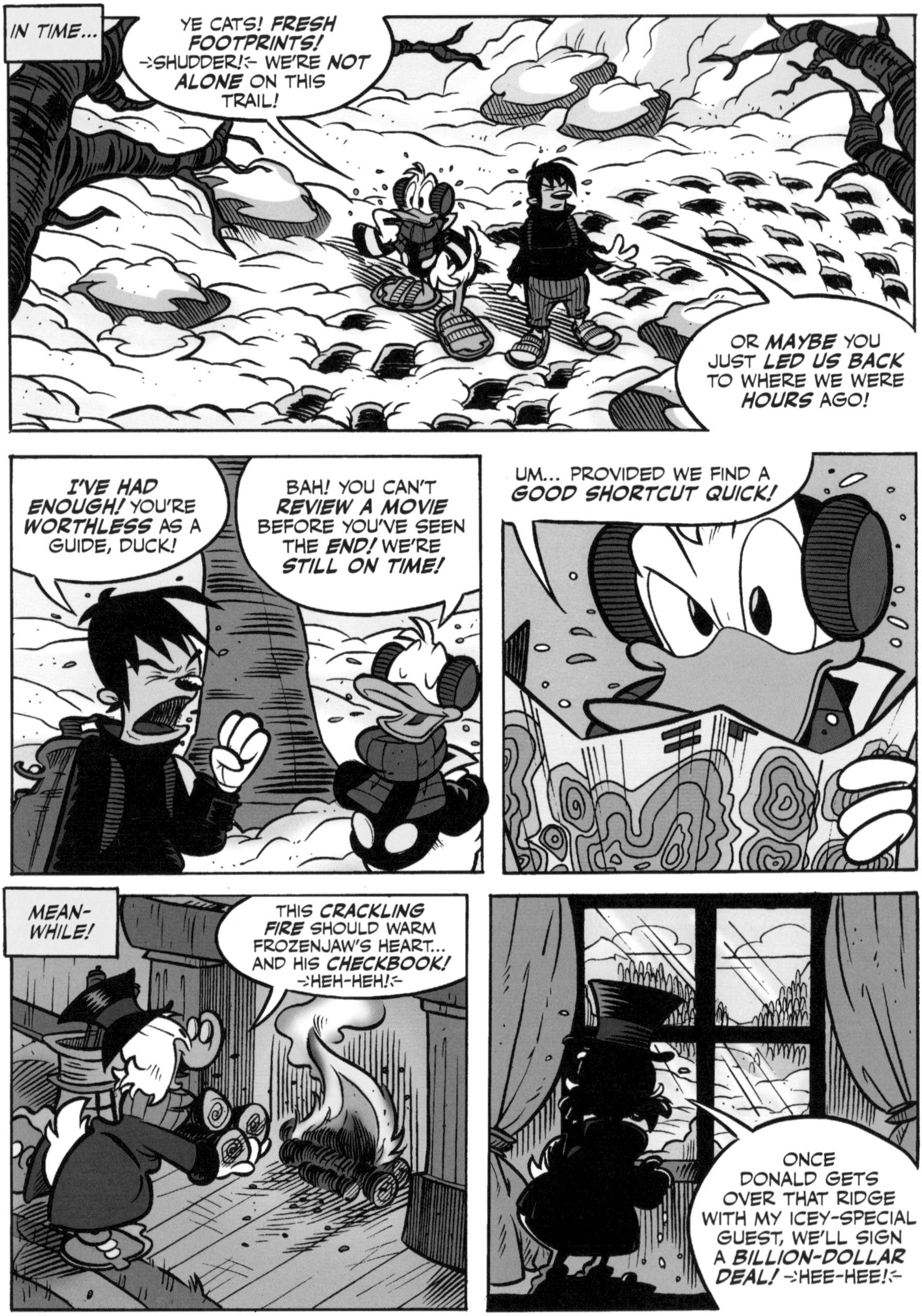

IN TIME...
YE CATS! FRESH FOOTPRINTS! -SHUDDER!- WE'RE NOT ALONE ON THIS TRAIL!
OR MAYBE YOU JUST LED US BACK TO WHERE WE WERE HOURS AGO!
I'VE HAD ENOUGH! YOU'RE WORTHLESS AS A GUIDE, DUCK!
BAH! YOU CAN'T REVIEW A MOVIE BEFORE YOU'VE SEEN THE END! WE'RE STILL ON TIME!
UM... PROVIDED WE FIND A GOOD SHORTCUT QUICK!
MEAN-WHILE!
THIS CRACKLING FIRE SHOULD WARM FROZENJAW'S HEART... AND HIS CHECKBOOK! -HEH-HEH!-
ONCE DONALD GETS OVER THAT RIDGE WITH MY ICEY-SPECIAL GUEST, WE'LL SIGN A BILLION-DOLLAR DEAL! -HEE-HEE!-

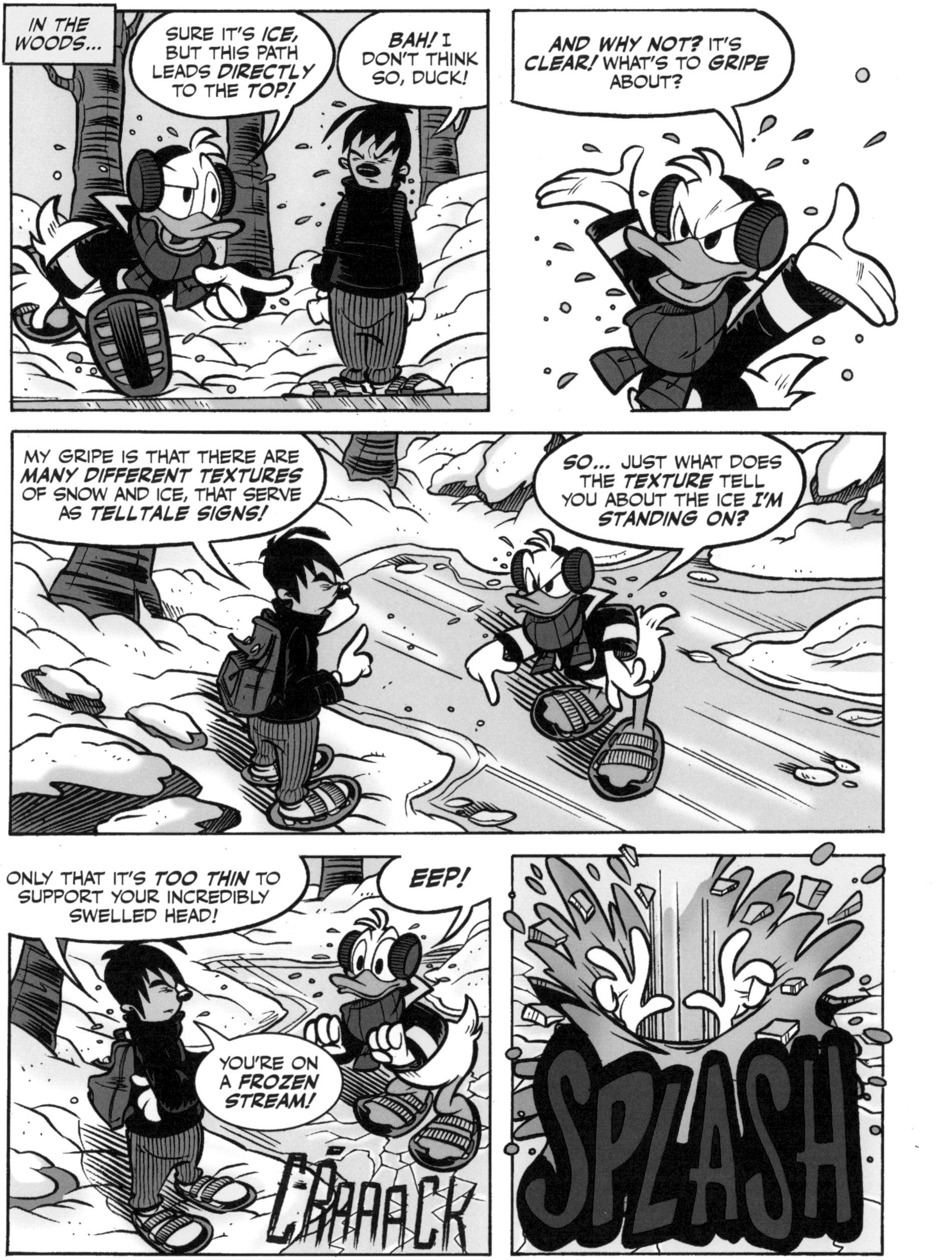
IN THE WOODS...
SURE IT'S ICE, BUT THIS PATH LEADS DIRECTLY TO THE TOP!
BAH! I DON'T THINK SO, DUCK!
AND WHY NOT? IT'S CLEAR! WHAT'S TO GRIPE ABOUT?
MY GRIPE IS THAT THERE ARE MANY DIFFERENT TEXTURES OF SNOW AND ICE, THAT SERVE AS TELLTALE SIGNS!
SO... JUST WHAT DOES THE TEXTURE TELL YOU ABOUT THE ICE I'M STANDING ON?
ONLY THAT IT'S TOO THIN TO SUPPORT YOUR INCREDIBLY SWELLED HEAD!
EEP!
YOU'RE ON A FROZEN STREAM!
CRAAACK
SPLASH

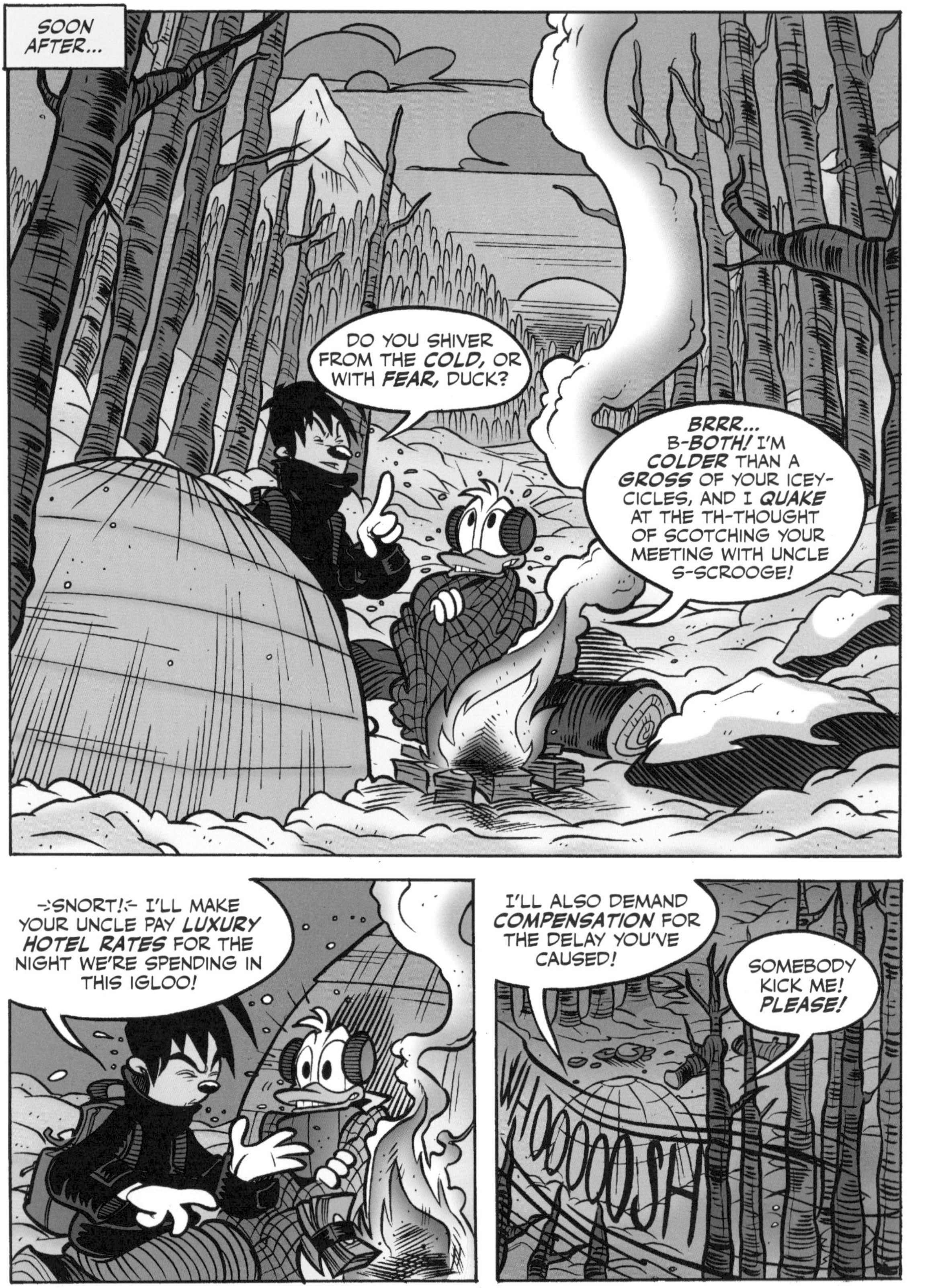
SOON AFTER...
DO YOU SHIVER FROM THE COLD, OR WITH FEAR, DUCK?
BRRR... B-BOTH! I'M COLDER THAN A GROSS OF YOUR ICEY-CICLES, AND I QUAKE AT THE TH-THOUGHT OF SCOTCHING YOUR MEETING WITH UNCLE S-SCROOGE!
-SNORT!- I'LL MAKE YOUR UNCLE PAY LUXURY HOTEL RATES FOR THE NIGHT WE'RE SPENDING IN THIS IGLOO!
I'LL ALSO DEMAND COMPENSATION FOR THE DELAY YOU'VE CAUSED!
SOMEBODY KICK ME! PLEASE!
WHOOOOOSH

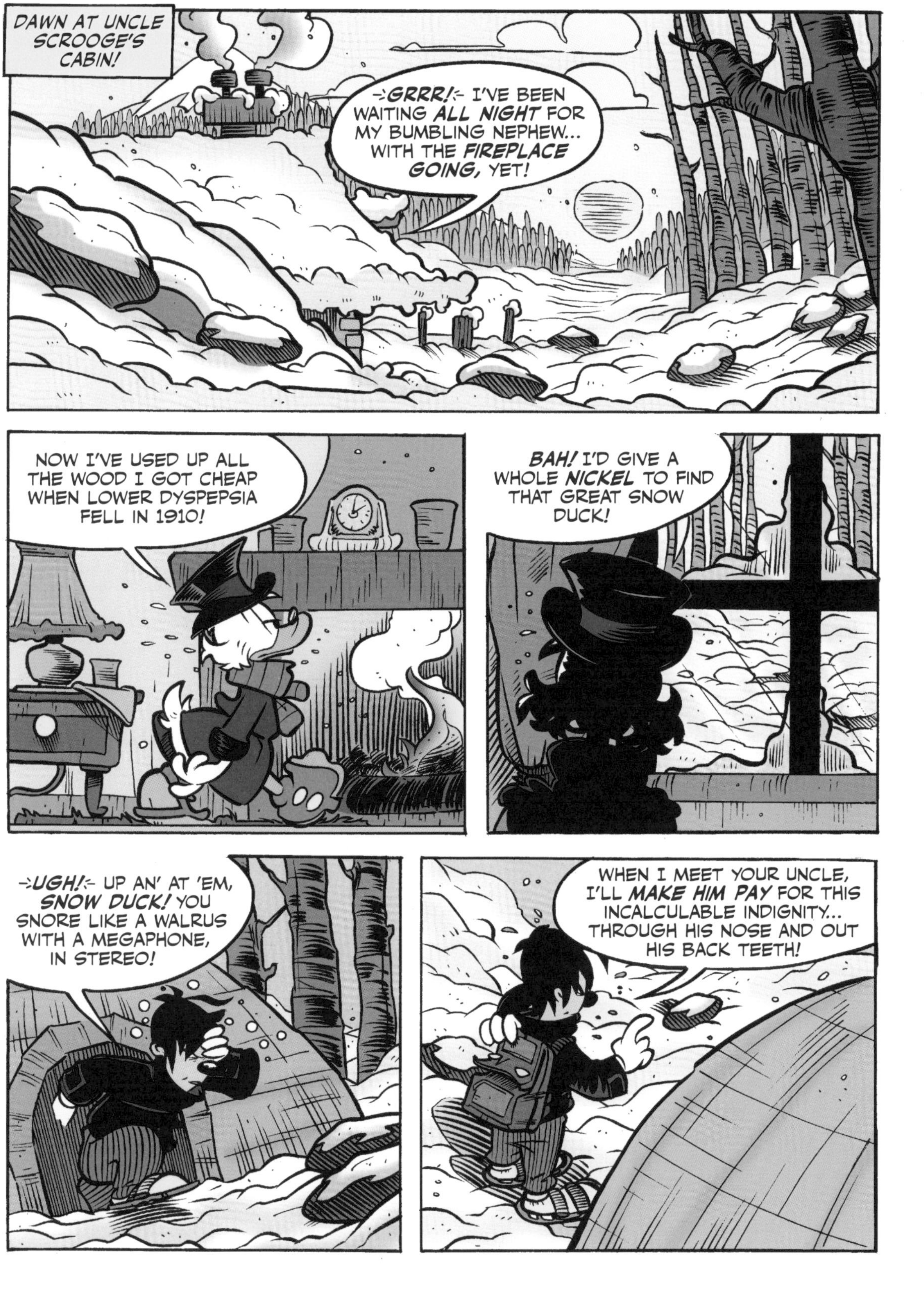
DAWN AT UNCLE SCROOGE'S CABIN!
–GRRR!– I'VE BEEN WAITING ALL NIGHT FOR MY BUMBLING NEPHEW... WITH THE FIREPLACE GOING, YET!
NOW I'VE USED UP ALL THE WOOD I GOT CHEAP WHEN LOWER DYSPEPSIA FELL IN 1910!
BAH! I'D GIVE A WHOLE NICKEL TO FIND THAT GREAT SNOW DUCK!
–UGH!– UP AN' AT 'EM, SNOW DUCK! YOU SNORE LIKE A WALRUS WITH A MEGAPHONE, IN STEREO!
WHEN I MEET YOUR UNCLE, I'LL MAKE HIM PAY FOR THIS INCALCULABLE INDIGNITY... THROUGH HIS NOSE AND OUT HIS BACK TEETH!

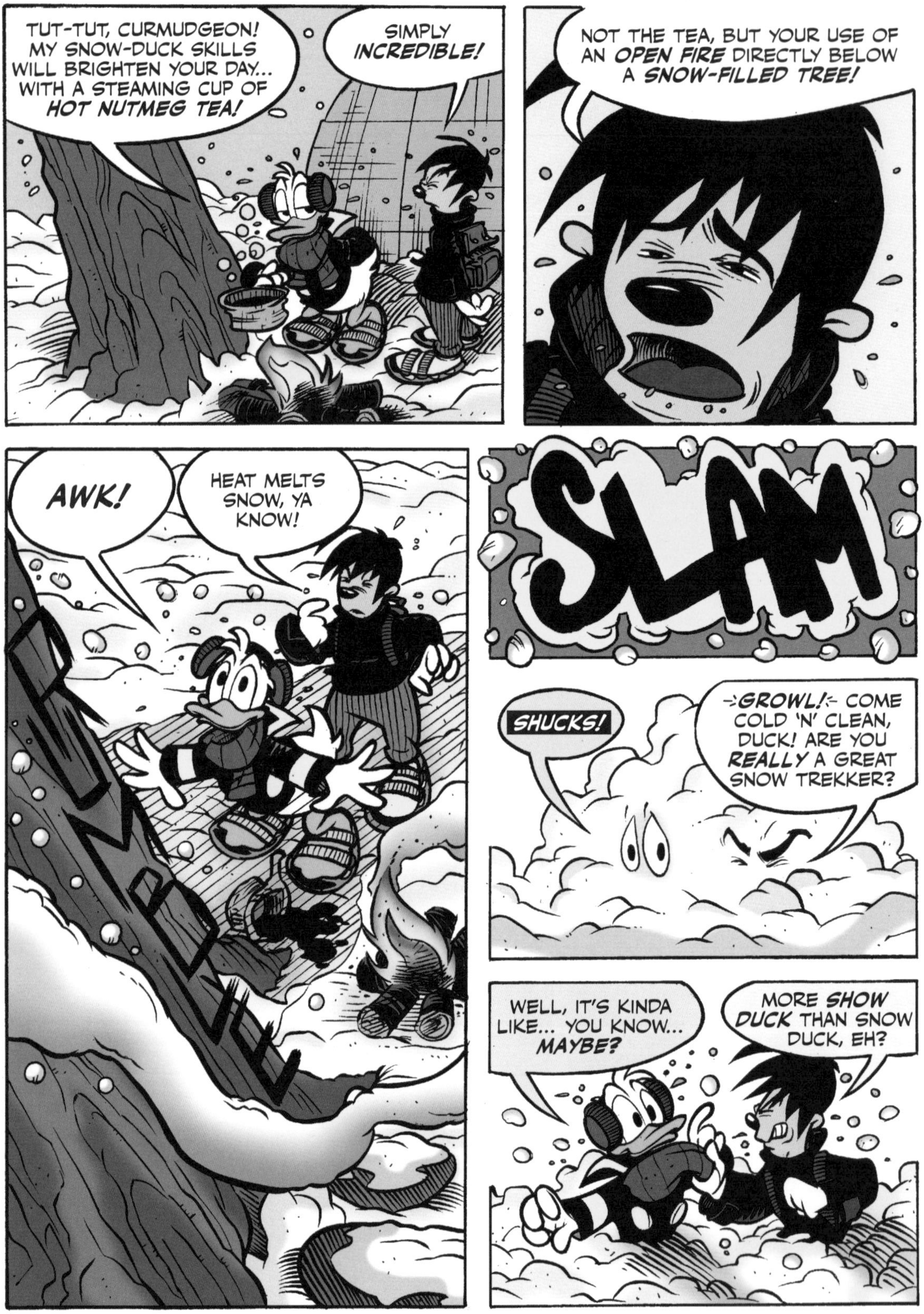
TUT-TUT, CURMUDGEON! MY SNOW-DUCK SKILLS WILL BRIGHTEN YOUR DAY... WITH A STEAMING CUP OF HOT NUTMEG TEA!
SIMPLY INCREDIBLE!
NOT THE TEA, BUT YOUR USE OF AN OPEN FIRE DIRECTLY BELOW A SNOW-FILLED TREE!
AWK!
HEAT MELTS SNOW, YA KNOW!
SLAM
SHUCKS!
-GROWL!- COME COLD 'N' CLEAN, DUCK! ARE YOU REALLY A GREAT SNOW TREKKER?
WELL, IT'S KINDA LIKE... YOU KNOW... MAYBE?
MORE SHOW DUCK THAN SNOW DUCK, EH?

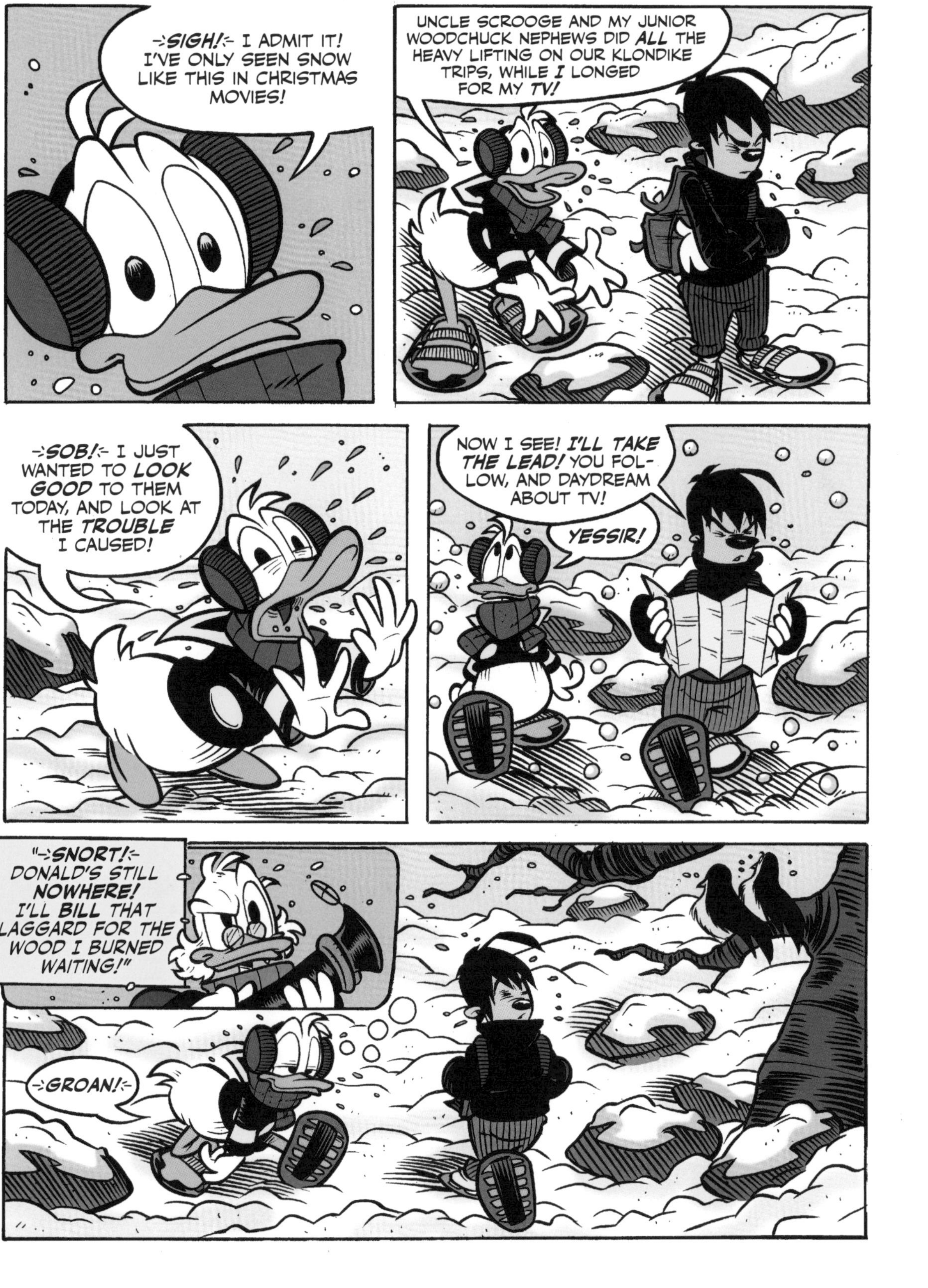
-SIGH!- I ADMIT IT! I'VE ONLY SEEN SNOW LIKE THIS IN CHRISTMAS MOVIES!
UNCLE SCROOGE AND MY JUNIOR WOODCHUCK NEPHEWS DID ALL THE HEAVY LIFTING ON OUR KLONDIKE TRIPS, WHILE I LONGED FOR MY TV!
-SOB!- I JUST WANTED TO LOOK GOOD TO THEM TODAY, AND LOOK AT THE TROUBLE I CAUSED!
NOW I SEE! I'LL TAKE THE LEAD! YOU FOLLOW, AND DAYDREAM ABOUT TV!
YESSIR!
"-SNORT!- DONALD'S STILL NOWHERE! I'LL BILL THAT LAGGARD FOR THE WOOD I BURNED WAITING!"
-GROAN!-

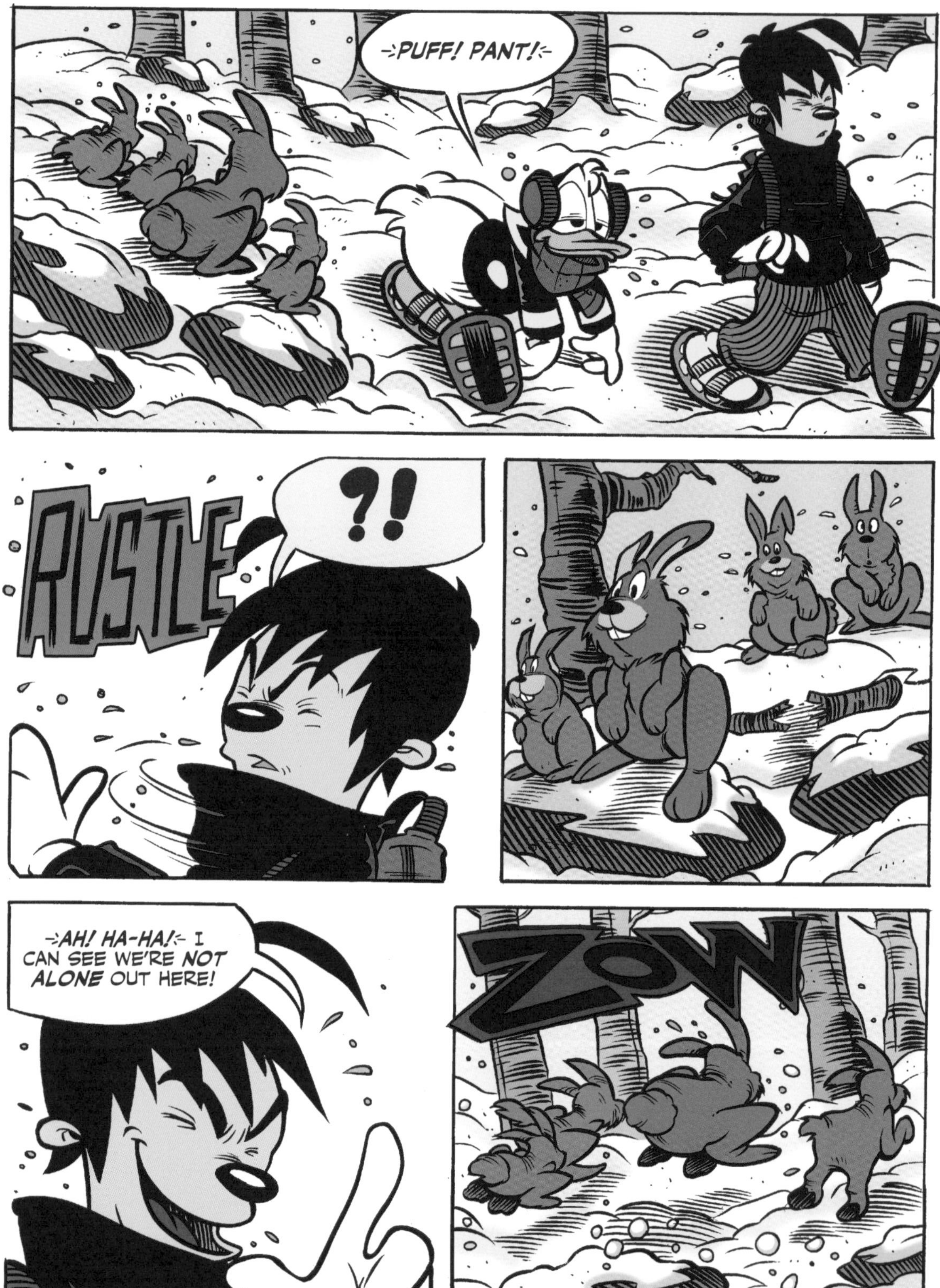
PUFF! PANT!
RUSTLE
?!
AH! HA-HA! I CAN SEE WE'RE NOT ALONE OUT HERE!
ZOW

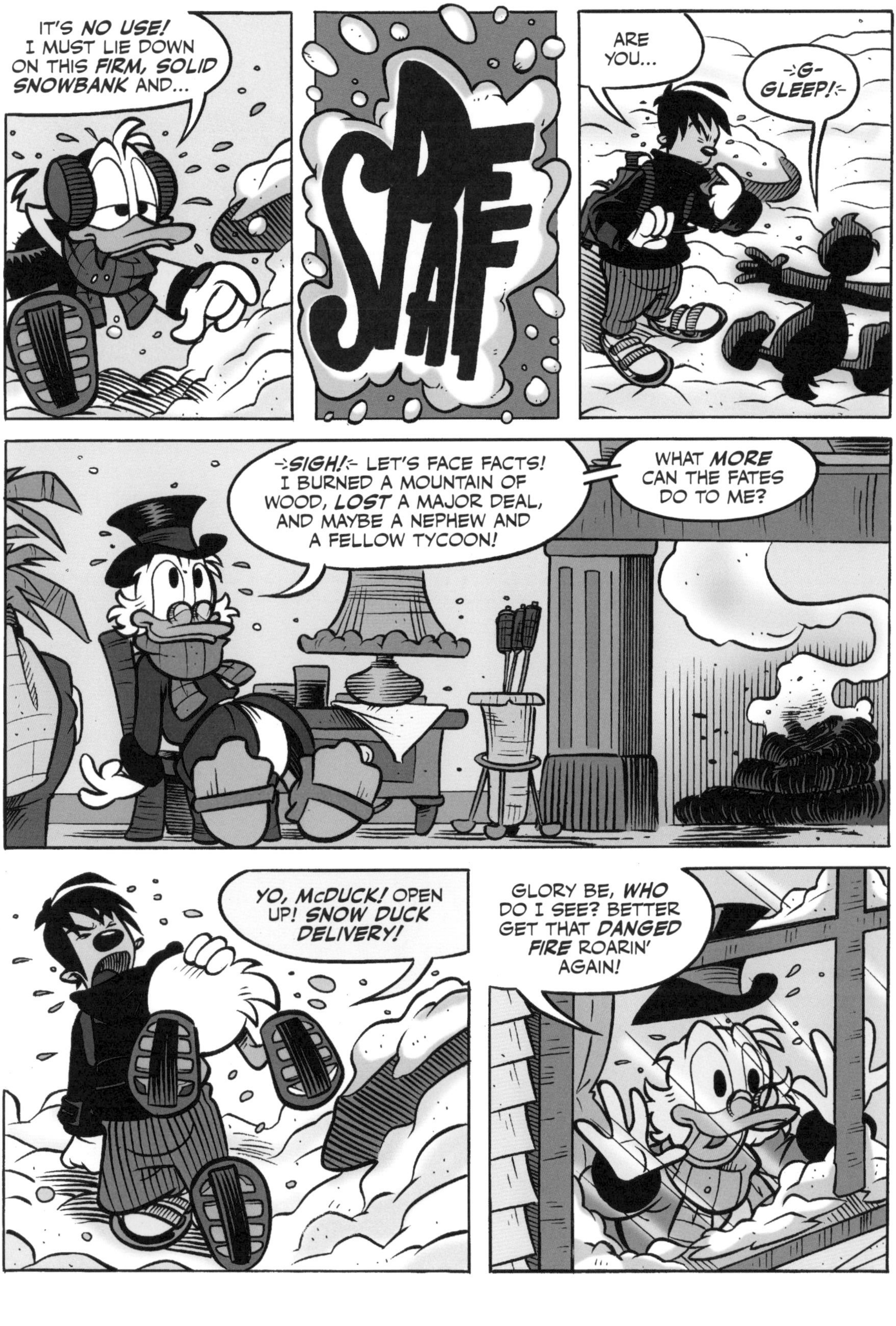
IT'S NO USE! I MUST LIE DOWN ON THIS FIRM, SOLID SNOWBANK AND...
SPAF
ARE YOU...
-G- GLEEP!-
-SIGH!- LET'S FACE FACTS! I BURNED A MOUNTAIN OF WOOD, LOST A MAJOR DEAL, AND MAYBE A NEPHEW AND A FELLOW TYCOON!
WHAT MORE CAN THE FATES DO TO ME?
YO, McDUCK! OPEN UP! SNOW DUCK DELIVERY!
GLORY BE, WHO DO I SEE? BETTER GET THAT DANGED FIRE ROARIN' AGAIN!

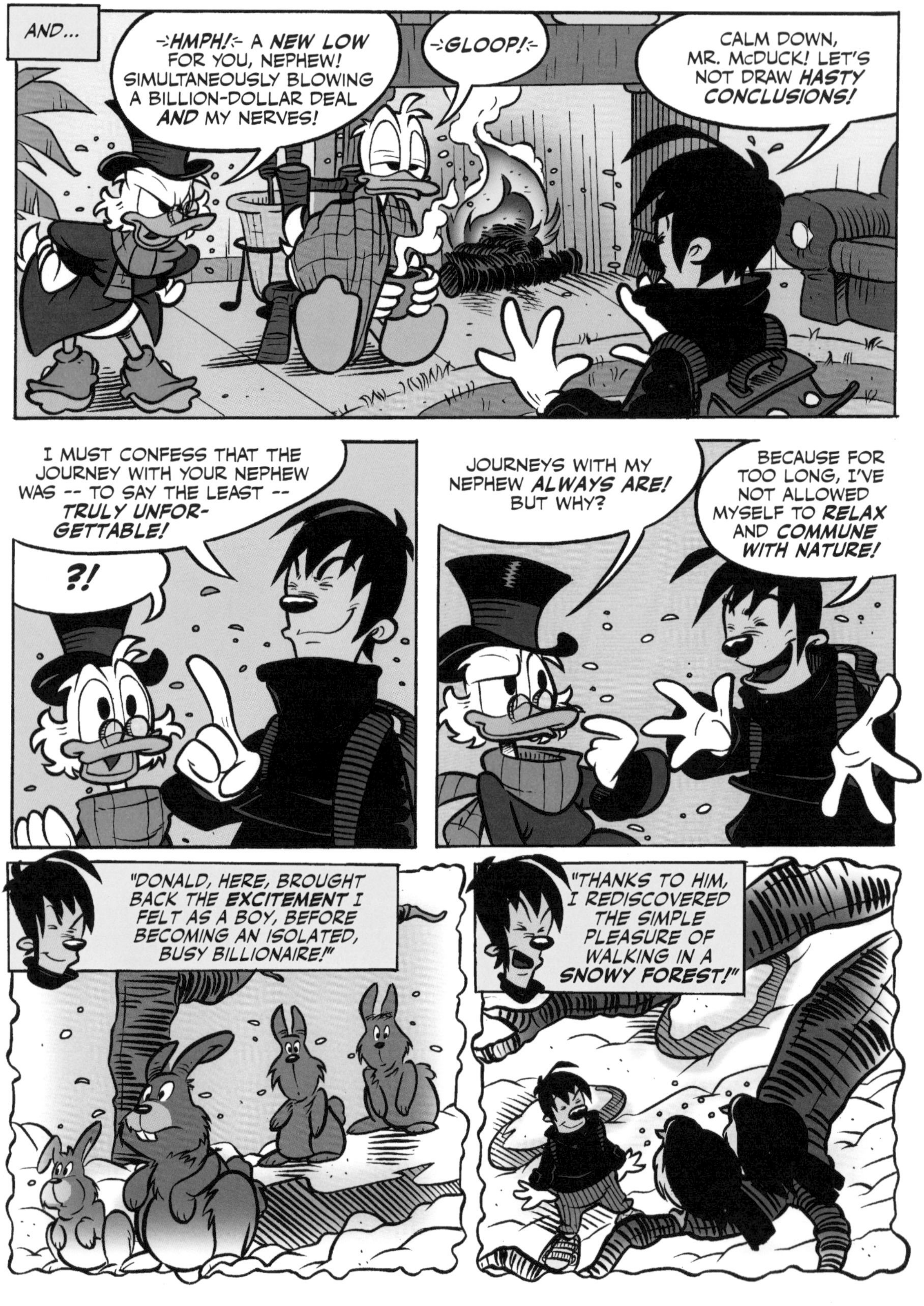
AND...
-HMPH!- A NEW LOW FOR YOU, NEPHEW! SIMULTANEOUSLY BLOWING A BILLION-DOLLAR DEAL AND MY NERVES!
-GLOOP!-
CALM DOWN, MR. McDUCK! LET'S NOT DRAW HASTY CONCLUSIONS!
I MUST CONFESS THAT THE JOURNEY WITH YOUR NEPHEW WAS -- TO SAY THE LEAST -- TRULY UNFOR-GETTABLE!
?!
JOURNEYS WITH MY NEPHEW ALWAYS ARE! BUT WHY?
BECAUSE FOR TOO LONG, I'VE NOT ALLOWED MYSELF TO RELAX AND COMMUNE WITH NATURE!
"DONALD, HERE, BROUGHT BACK THE EXCITEMENT I FELT AS A BOY, BEFORE BECOMING AN ISOLATED, BUSY BILLIONAIRE!"
"THANKS TO HIM, I REDISCOVERED THE SIMPLE PLEASURE OF WALKING IN A SNOWY FOREST!"

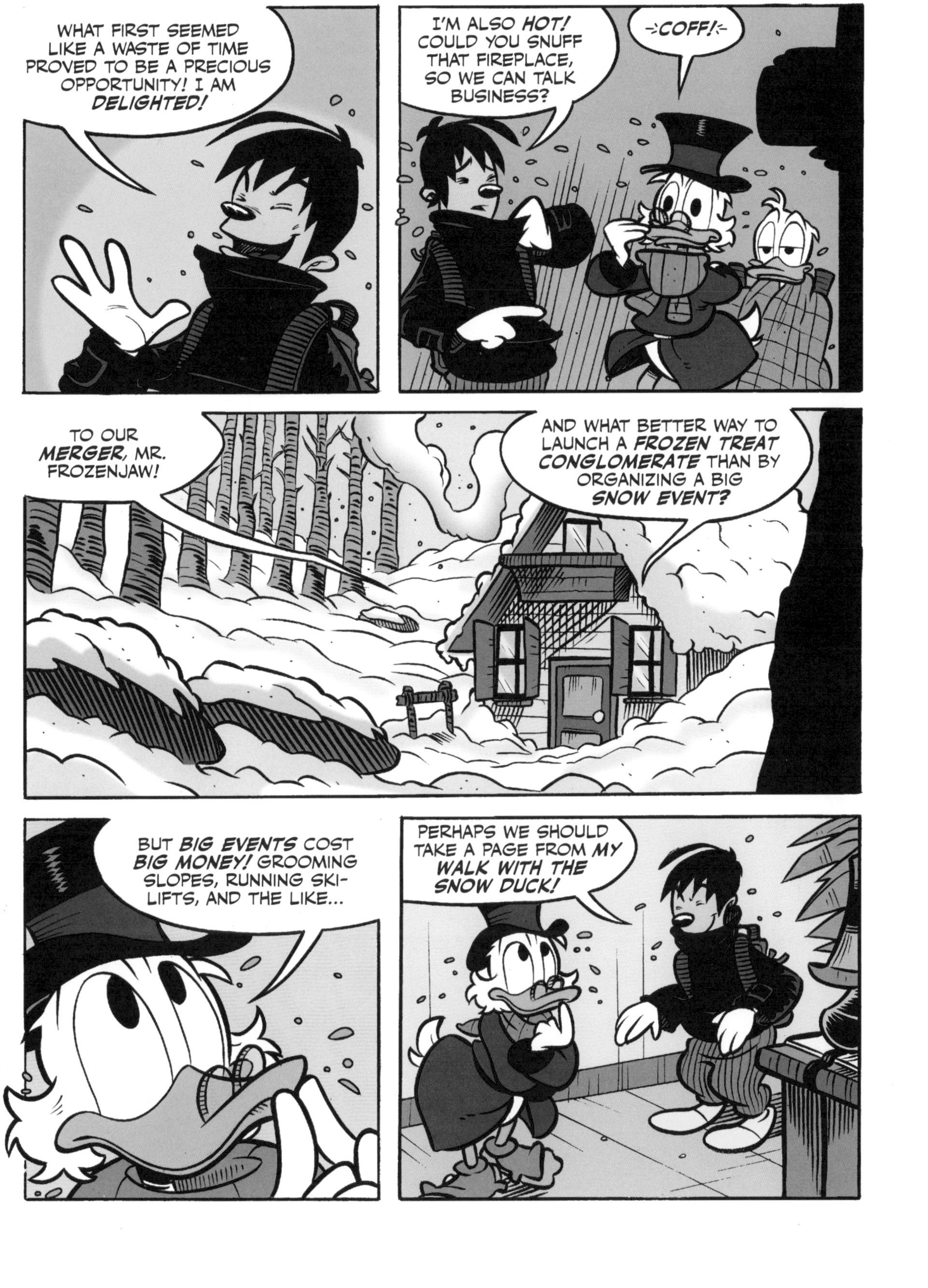
WHAT FIRST SEEMED LIKE A WASTE OF TIME PROVED TO BE A PRECIOUS OPPORTUNITY! I AM *DELIGHTED!*
I'M ALSO *HOT!* COULD YOU SNUFF THAT FIREPLACE, SO WE CAN TALK BUSINESS?
COFF!
TO OUR *MERGER*, MR. FROZENJAW!
AND WHAT BETTER WAY TO LAUNCH A *FROZEN TREAT CONGLOMERATE* THAN BY ORGANIZING A BIG *SNOW EVENT?*
BUT *BIG EVENTS* COST *BIG MONEY!* GROOMING SLOPES, RUNNING SKI-LIFTS, AND THE LIKE...
PERHAPS WE SHOULD TAKE A PAGE FROM *MY WALK WITH THE SNOW DUCK!*

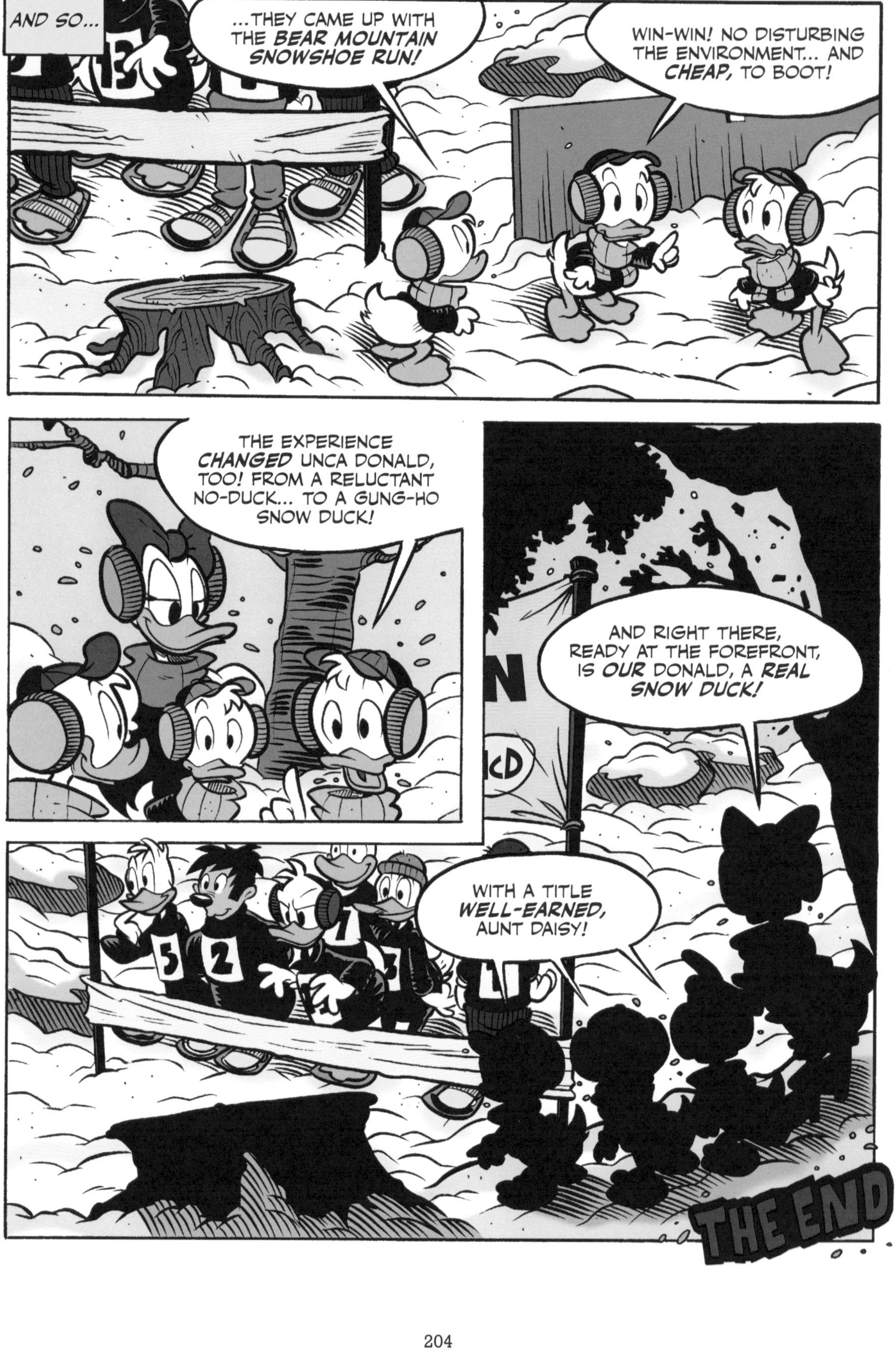
AND SO...
...THEY CAME UP WITH THE BEAR MOUNTAIN SNOWSHOE RUN!
WIN-WIN! NO DISTURBING THE ENVIRONMENT... AND CHEAP, TO BOOT!
THE EXPERIENCE CHANGED UNCA DONALD, TOO! FROM A RELUCTANT NO-DUCK... TO A GUNG-HO SNOW DUCK!
AND RIGHT THERE, READY AT THE FOREFRONT, IS OUR DONALD, A REAL SNOW DUCK!
WITH A TITLE WELL-EARNED, AUNT DAISY!
THE END

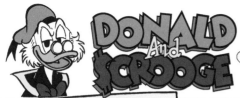

Donald And Scrooge in Holiday Hideaway on Bear Mountain

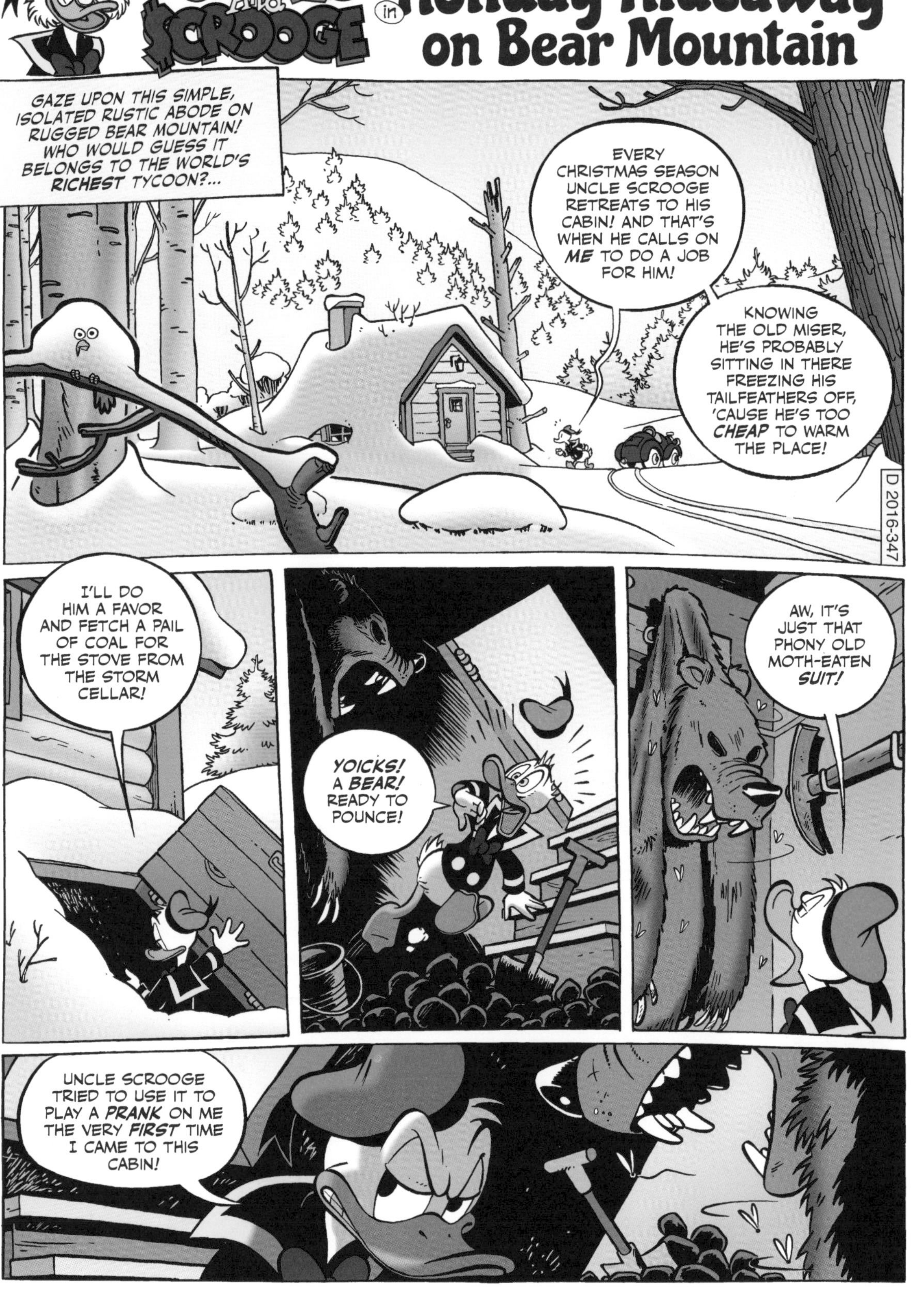
GAZE UPON THIS SIMPLE, ISOLATED RUSTIC ABODE ON RUGGED BEAR MOUNTAIN! WHO WOULD GUESS IT BELONGS TO THE WORLD'S RICHEST TYCOON?...
EVERY CHRISTMAS SEASON UNCLE SCROOGE RETREATS TO HIS CABIN! AND THAT'S WHEN HE CALLS ON ME TO DO A JOB FOR HIM!
KNOWING THE OLD MISER, HE'S PROBABLY SITTING IN THERE FREEZING HIS TAILFEATHERS OFF, 'CAUSE HE'S TOO CHEAP TO WARM THE PLACE!
D 2016-347
I'LL DO HIM A FAVOR AND FETCH A PAIL OF COAL FOR THE STOVE FROM THE STORM CELLAR!
YOICKS! A BEAR! READY TO POUNCE!
AW, IT'S JUST THAT PHONY OLD MOTH-EATEN SUIT!
UNCLE SCROOGE TRIED TO USE IT TO PLAY A PRANK ON ME THE VERY FIRST TIME I CAME TO THIS CABIN!

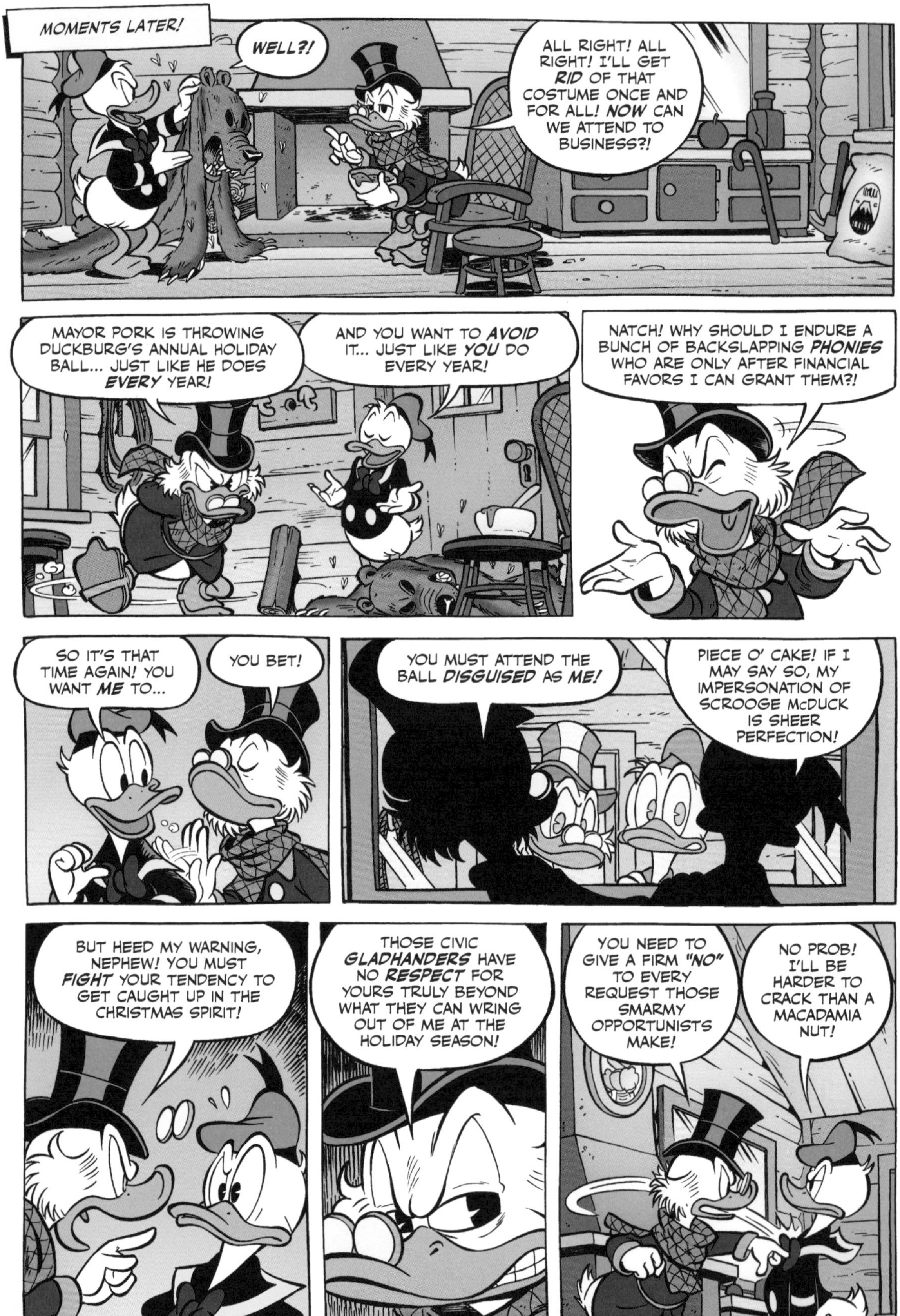
MOMENTS LATER!
WELL?!
ALL RIGHT! ALL RIGHT! I'LL GET RID OF THAT COSTUME ONCE AND FOR ALL! NOW CAN WE ATTEND TO BUSINESS?!
MAYOR PORK IS THROWING DUCKBURG'S ANNUAL HOLIDAY BALL... JUST LIKE HE DOES EVERY YEAR!
AND YOU WANT TO AVOID IT... JUST LIKE YOU DO EVERY YEAR!
NATCH! WHY SHOULD I ENDURE A BUNCH OF BACKSLAPPING PHONIES WHO ARE ONLY AFTER FINANCIAL FAVORS I CAN GRANT THEM?!
SO IT'S THAT TIME AGAIN! YOU WANT ME TO...
YOU BET!
YOU MUST ATTEND THE BALL DISGUISED AS ME!
PIECE O' CAKE! IF I MAY SAY SO, MY IMPERSONATION OF SCROOGE McDUCK IS SHEER PERFECTION!
BUT HEED MY WARNING, NEPHEW! YOU MUST FIGHT YOUR TENDENCY TO GET CAUGHT UP IN THE CHRISTMAS SPIRIT!
THOSE CIVIC GLADHANDERS HAVE NO RESPECT FOR YOURS TRULY BEYOND WHAT THEY CAN WRING OUT OF ME AT THE HOLIDAY SEASON!
YOU NEED TO GIVE A FIRM "NO" TO EVERY REQUEST THOSE SMARMY OPPORTUNISTS MAKE!
NO PROB! I'LL BE HARDER TO CRACK THAN A MACADAMIA NUT!

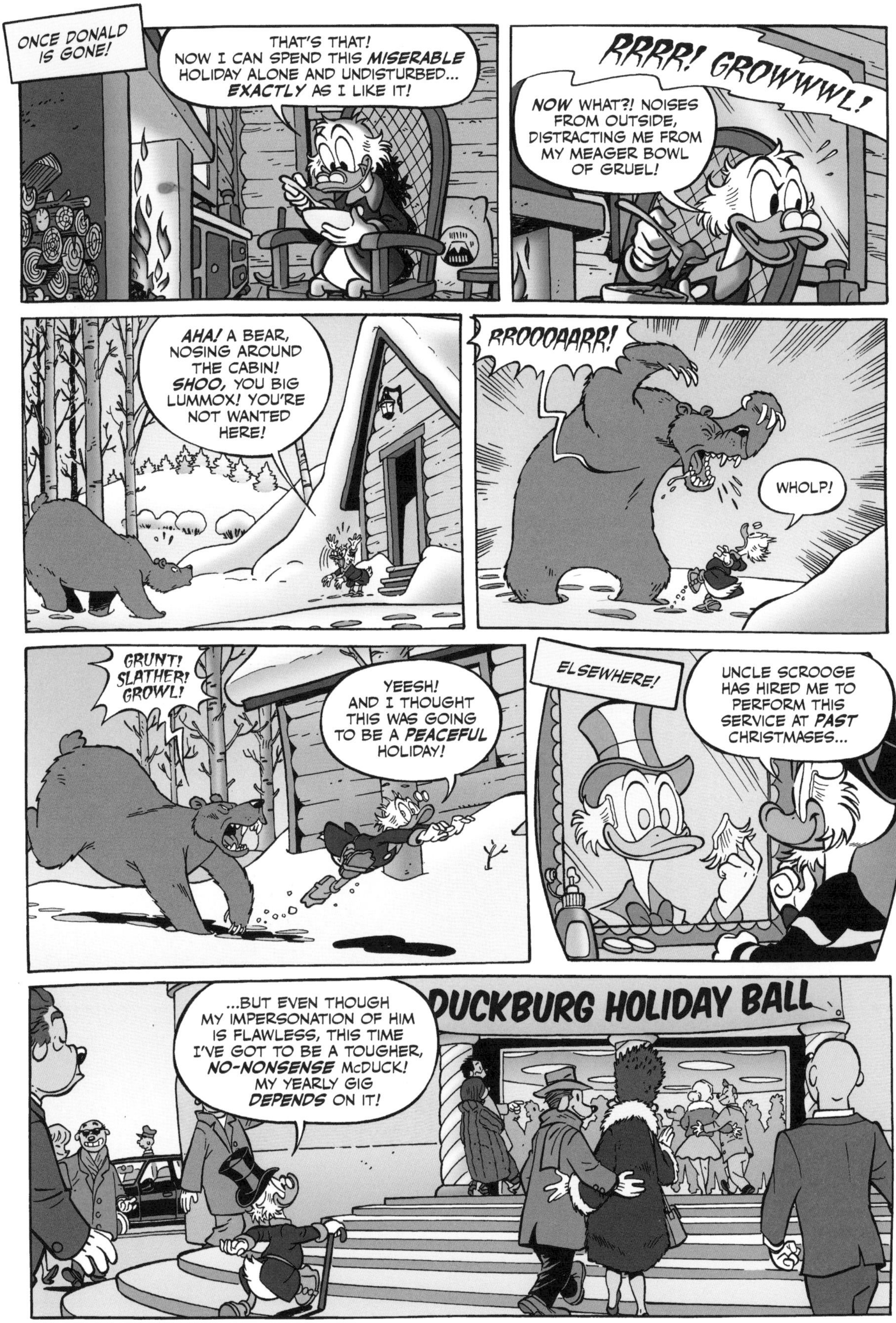
ONCE DONALD IS GONE!
THAT'S THAT! NOW I CAN SPEND THIS MISERABLE HOLIDAY ALONE AND UNDISTURBED... EXACTLY AS I LIKE IT!
RRRR! GROWWWL!
NOW WHAT?! NOISES FROM OUTSIDE, DISTRACTING ME FROM MY MEAGER BOWL OF GRUEL!
AHA! A BEAR, NOSING AROUND THE CABIN! SHOO, YOU BIG LUMMOX! YOU'RE NOT WANTED HERE!
RROOOAARR!
WHOLP!
GRUNT! SLATHER! GROWL!
YEESH! AND I THOUGHT THIS WAS GOING TO BE A PEACEFUL HOLIDAY!
ELSEWHERE!
UNCLE SCROOGE HAS HIRED ME TO PERFORM THIS SERVICE AT PAST CHRISTMASES...
DUCKBURG HOLIDAY BALL
...BUT EVEN THOUGH MY IMPERSONATION OF HIM IS FLAWLESS, THIS TIME I'VE GOT TO BE A TOUGHER, NO-NONSENSE McDUCK! MY YEARLY GIG DEPENDS ON IT!

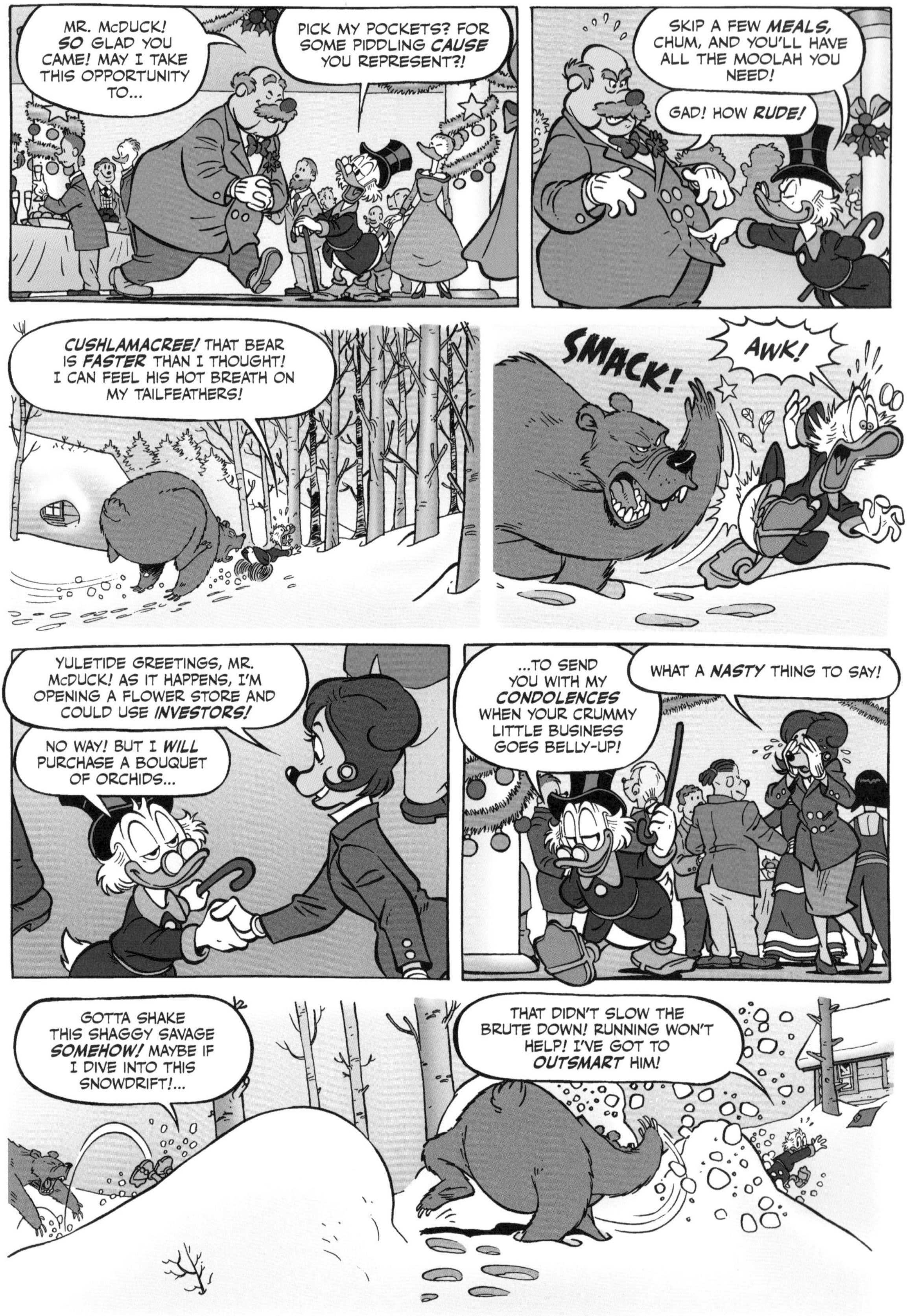

MR. McDUCK! SO GLAD YOU CAME! MAY I TAKE THIS OPPORTUNITY TO...
PICK MY POCKETS? FOR SOME PIDDLING CAUSE YOU REPRESENT?!
SKIP A FEW MEALS, CHUM, AND YOU'LL HAVE ALL THE MOOLAH YOU NEED!
GAD! HOW RUDE!
CUSHLAMACREE! THAT BEAR IS FASTER THAN I THOUGHT! I CAN FEEL HIS HOT BREATH ON MY TAILFEATHERS!
SMACK!
AWK!
YULETIDE GREETINGS, MR. McDUCK! AS IT HAPPENS, I'M OPENING A FLOWER STORE AND COULD USE INVESTORS!
NO WAY! BUT I WILL PURCHASE A BOUQUET OF ORCHIDS...
...TO SEND YOU WITH MY CONDOLENCES WHEN YOUR CRUMMY LITTLE BUSINESS GOES BELLY-UP!
WHAT A NASTY THING TO SAY!
GOTTA SHAKE THIS SHAGGY SAVAGE SOMEHOW! MAYBE IF I DIVE INTO THIS SNOWDRIFT!...
THAT DIDN'T SLOW THE BRUTE DOWN! RUNNING WON'T HELP! I'VE GOT TO OUTSMART HIM!

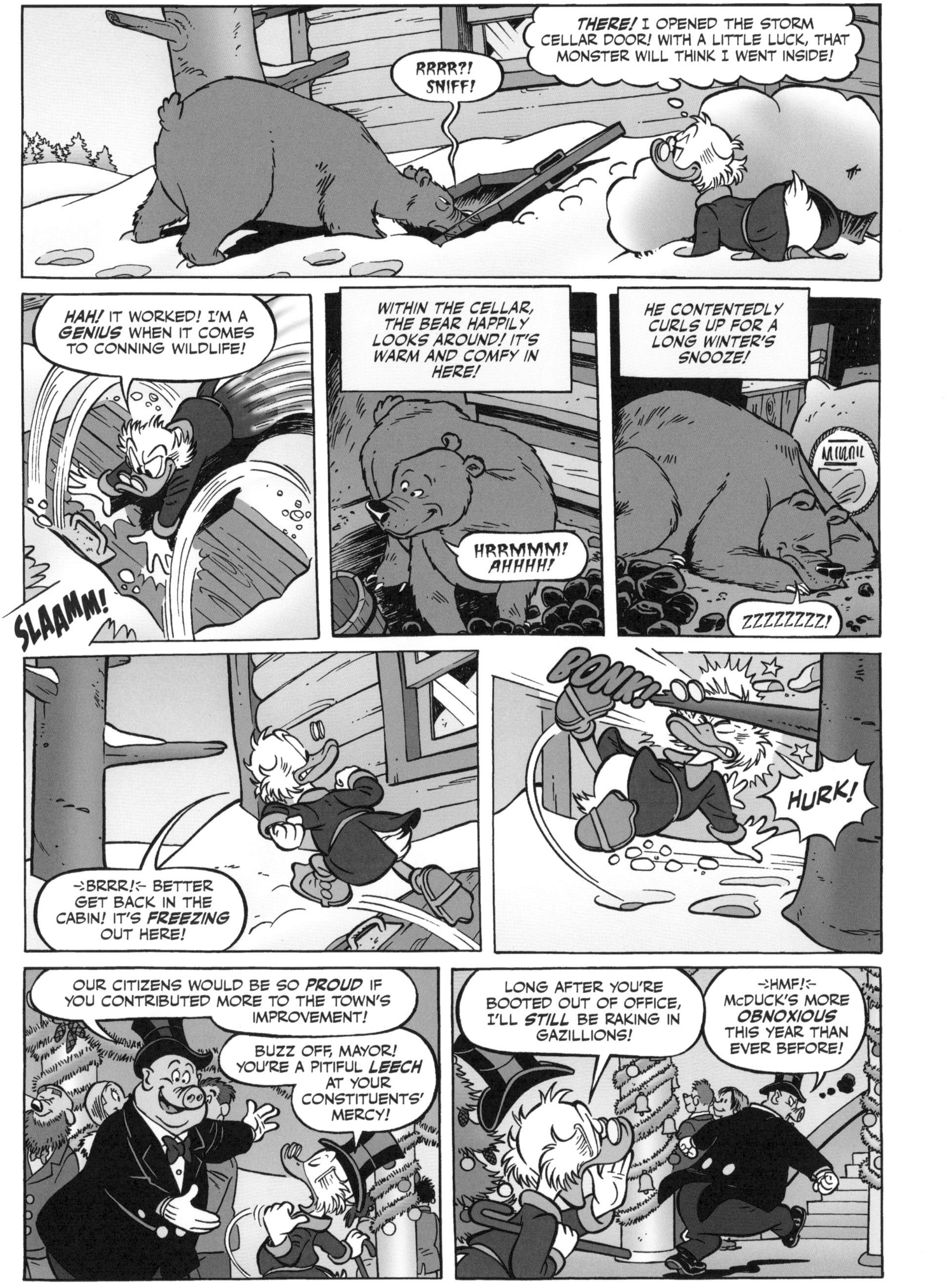
THERE! I OPENED THE STORM CELLAR DOOR! WITH A LITTLE LUCK, THAT MONSTER WILL THINK I WENT INSIDE!
RRRR?! SNIFF!
HAH! IT WORKED! I'M A GENIUS WHEN IT COMES TO CONNING WILDLIFE!
SLAAMM!
WITHIN THE CELLAR, THE BEAR HAPPILY LOOKS AROUND! IT'S WARM AND COMFY IN HERE!
HRRMMM! AHHHH!
HE CONTENTEDLY CURLS UP FOR A LONG WINTER'S SNOOZE!
ZZZZZZZZ!
-BRRR!- BETTER GET BACK IN THE CABIN! IT'S FREEZING OUT HERE!
BONK!
HURK!
OUR CITIZENS WOULD BE SO PROUD IF YOU CONTRIBUTED MORE TO THE TOWN'S IMPROVEMENT!
BUZZ OFF, MAYOR! YOU'RE A PITIFUL LEECH AT YOUR CONSTITUENTS' MERCY!
LONG AFTER YOU'RE BOOTED OUT OF OFFICE, I'LL STILL BE RAKING IN GAZILLIONS!
-HMF!- McDUCK'S MORE OBNOXIOUS THIS YEAR THAN EVER BEFORE!

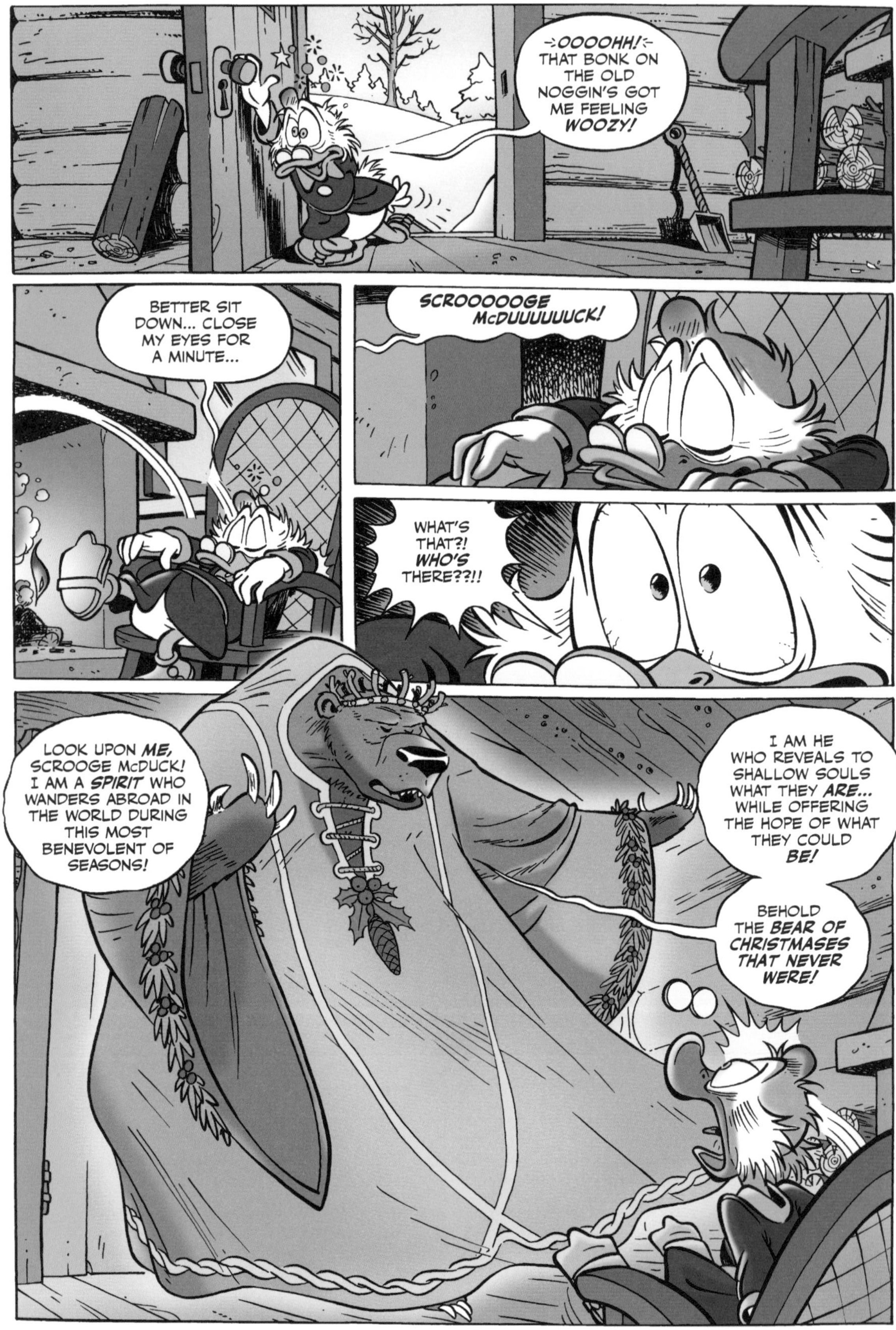
-OOOOHH!- THAT BONK ON THE OLD NOGGIN'S GOT ME FEELING WOOZY!
BETTER SIT DOWN... CLOSE MY EYES FOR A MINUTE...
SCROOOOOGE McDUUUUUUCK!
WHAT'S THAT?! WHO'S THERE??!!
LOOK UPON ME, SCROOGE McDUCK! I AM A SPIRIT WHO WANDERS ABROAD IN THE WORLD DURING THIS MOST BENEVOLENT OF SEASONS!
I AM HE WHO REVEALS TO SHALLOW SOULS WHAT THEY ARE... WHILE OFFERING THE HOPE OF WHAT THEY COULD BE!
BEHOLD THE BEAR OF CHRISTMASES THAT NEVER WERE!

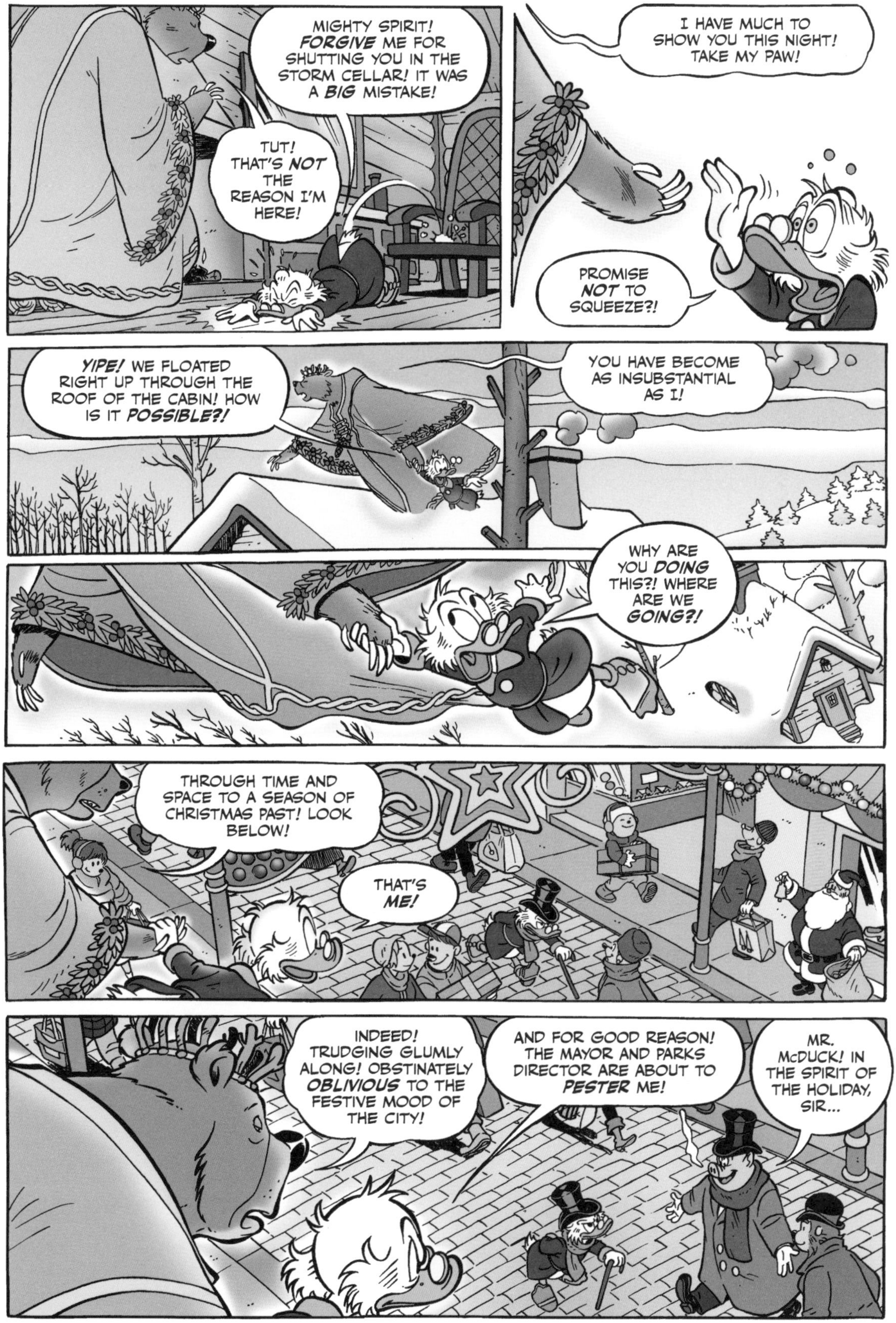
MIGHTY SPIRIT! FORGIVE ME FOR SHUTTING YOU IN THE STORM CELLAR! IT WAS A BIG MISTAKE!
TUT! THAT'S NOT THE REASON I'M HERE!
I HAVE MUCH TO SHOW YOU THIS NIGHT! TAKE MY PAW!
PROMISE NOT TO SQUEEZE?!
YIPE! WE FLOATED RIGHT UP THROUGH THE ROOF OF THE CABIN! HOW IS IT POSSIBLE?!
YOU HAVE BECOME AS INSUBSTANTIAL AS I!
WHY ARE YOU DOING THIS?! WHERE ARE WE GOING?!
THROUGH TIME AND SPACE TO A SEASON OF CHRISTMAS PAST! LOOK BELOW!
THAT'S ME!
INDEED! TRUDGING GLUMLY ALONG! OBSTINATELY OBLIVIOUS TO THE FESTIVE MOOD OF THE CITY!
AND FOR GOOD REASON! THE MAYOR AND PARKS DIRECTOR ARE ABOUT TO PESTER ME!
MR. McDUCK! IN THE SPIRIT OF THE HOLIDAY, SIR...

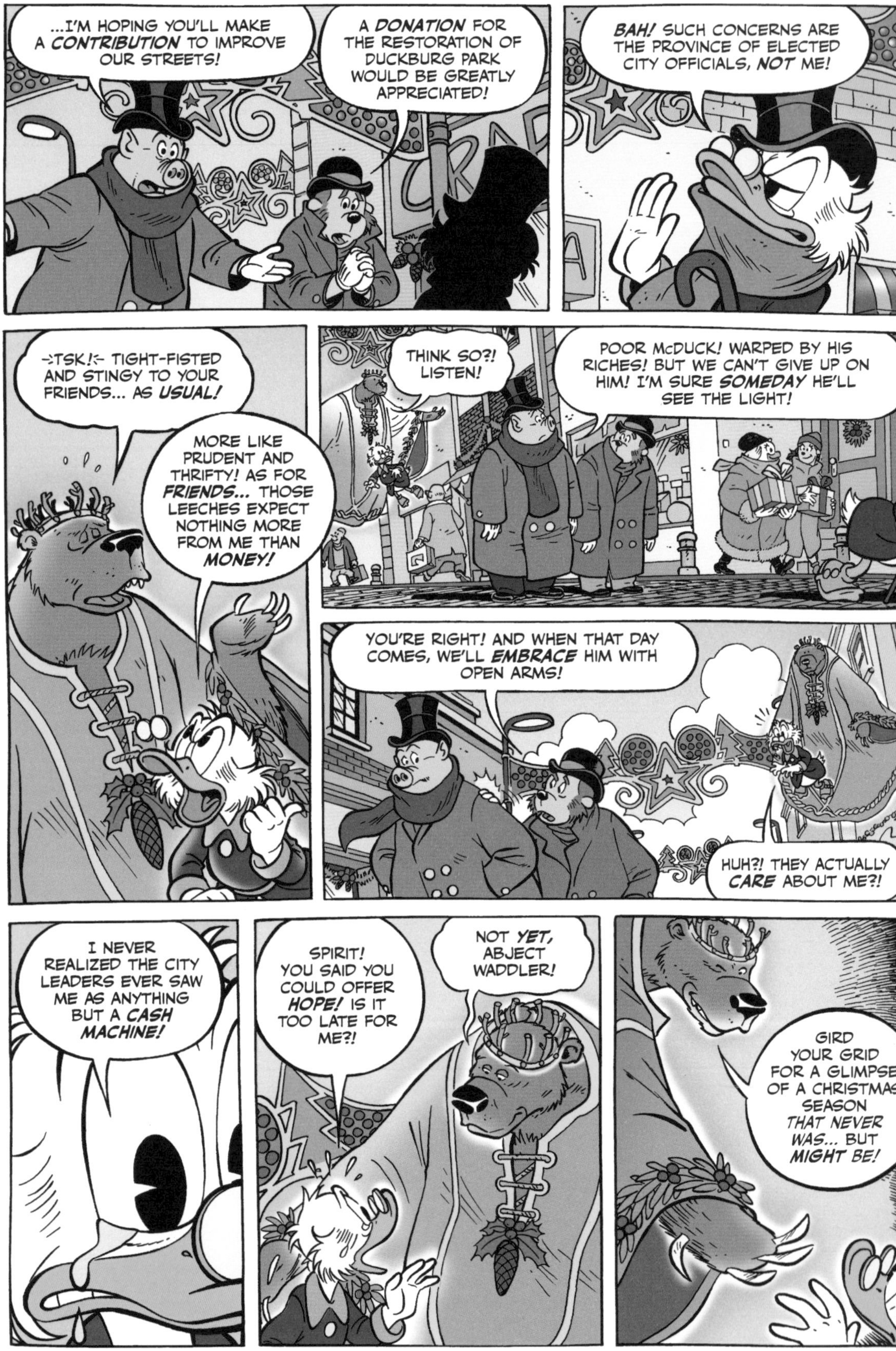

...I'M HOPING YOU'LL MAKE A CONTRIBUTION TO IMPROVE OUR STREETS!
A DONATION FOR THE RESTORATION OF DUCKBURG PARK WOULD BE GREATLY APPRECIATED!
BAH! SUCH CONCERNS ARE THE PROVINCE OF ELECTED CITY OFFICIALS, NOT ME!
-TSK!- TIGHT-FISTED AND STINGY TO YOUR FRIENDS... AS USUAL!
MORE LIKE PRUDENT AND THRIFTY! AS FOR FRIENDS... THOSE LEECHES EXPECT NOTHING MORE FROM ME THAN MONEY!
THINK SO?! LISTEN!
POOR McDUCK! WARPED BY HIS RICHES! BUT WE CAN'T GIVE UP ON HIM! I'M SURE SOMEDAY HE'LL SEE THE LIGHT!
YOU'RE RIGHT! AND WHEN THAT DAY COMES, WE'LL EMBRACE HIM WITH OPEN ARMS!
HUH?! THEY ACTUALLY CARE ABOUT ME?!
I NEVER REALIZED THE CITY LEADERS EVER SAW ME AS ANYTHING BUT A CASH MACHINE!
SPIRIT! YOU SAID YOU COULD OFFER HOPE! IS IT TOO LATE FOR ME?!
NOT YET, ABJECT WADDLER!
GIRD YOUR GRID FOR A GLIMPSE OF A CHRISTMAS SEASON THAT NEVER WAS... BUT MIGHT BE!

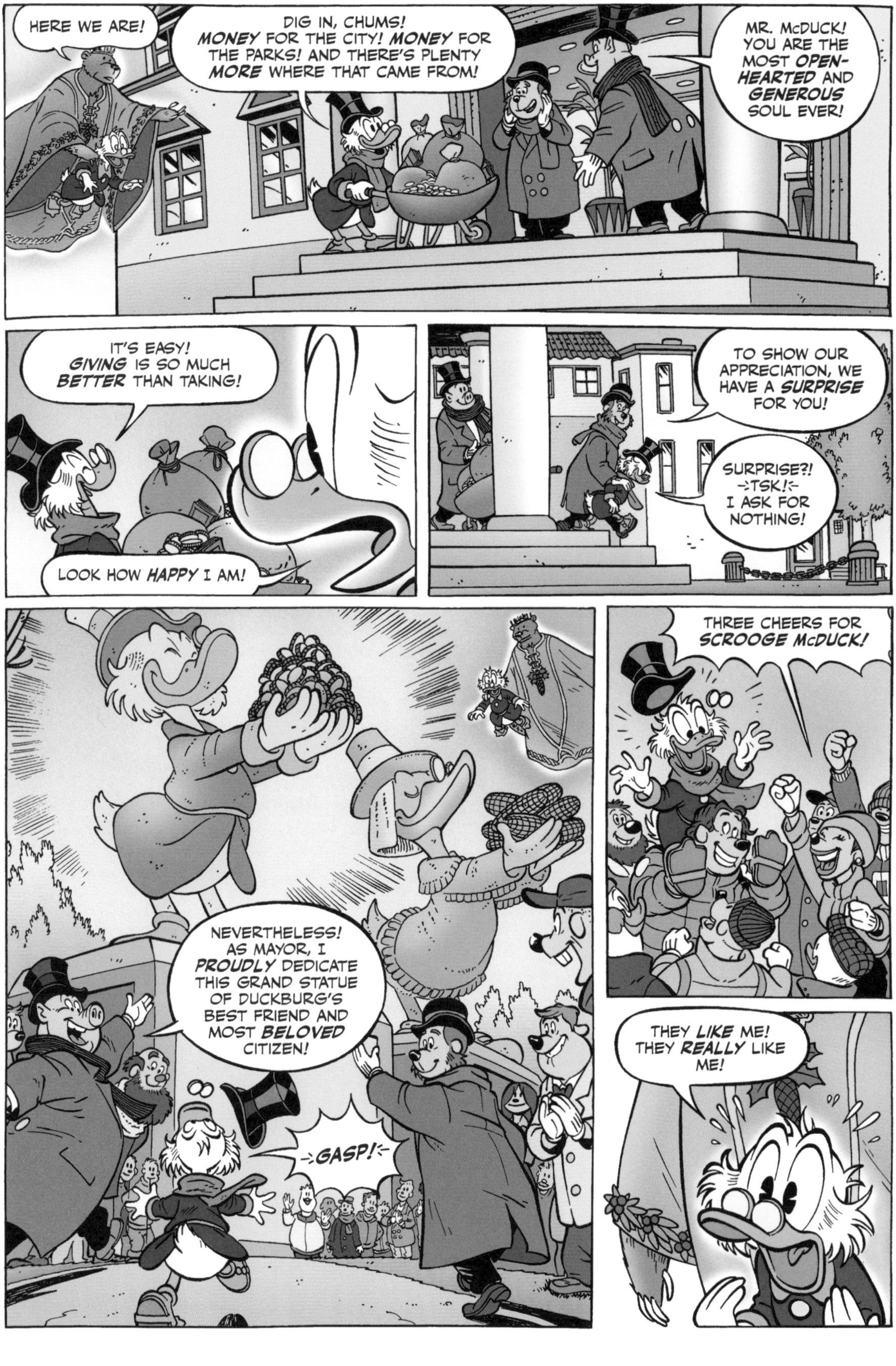
HERE WE ARE!
DIG IN, CHUMS! MONEY FOR THE CITY! MONEY FOR THE PARKS! AND THERE'S PLENTY MORE WHERE THAT CAME FROM!
MR. McDUCK! YOU ARE THE MOST OPEN-HEARTED AND GENEROUS SOUL EVER!
IT'S EASY! GIVING IS SO MUCH BETTER THAN TAKING!
LOOK HOW HAPPY I AM!
TO SHOW OUR APPRECIATION, WE HAVE A SURPRISE FOR YOU!
SURPRISE?! -TSK!- I ASK FOR NOTHING!
NEVERTHELESS! AS MAYOR, I PROUDLY DEDICATE THIS GRAND STATUE OF DUCKBURG'S BEST FRIEND AND MOST BELOVED CITIZEN!
-GASP!-
THREE CHEERS FOR SCROOGE McDUCK!
THEY LIKE ME! THEY REALLY LIKE ME!

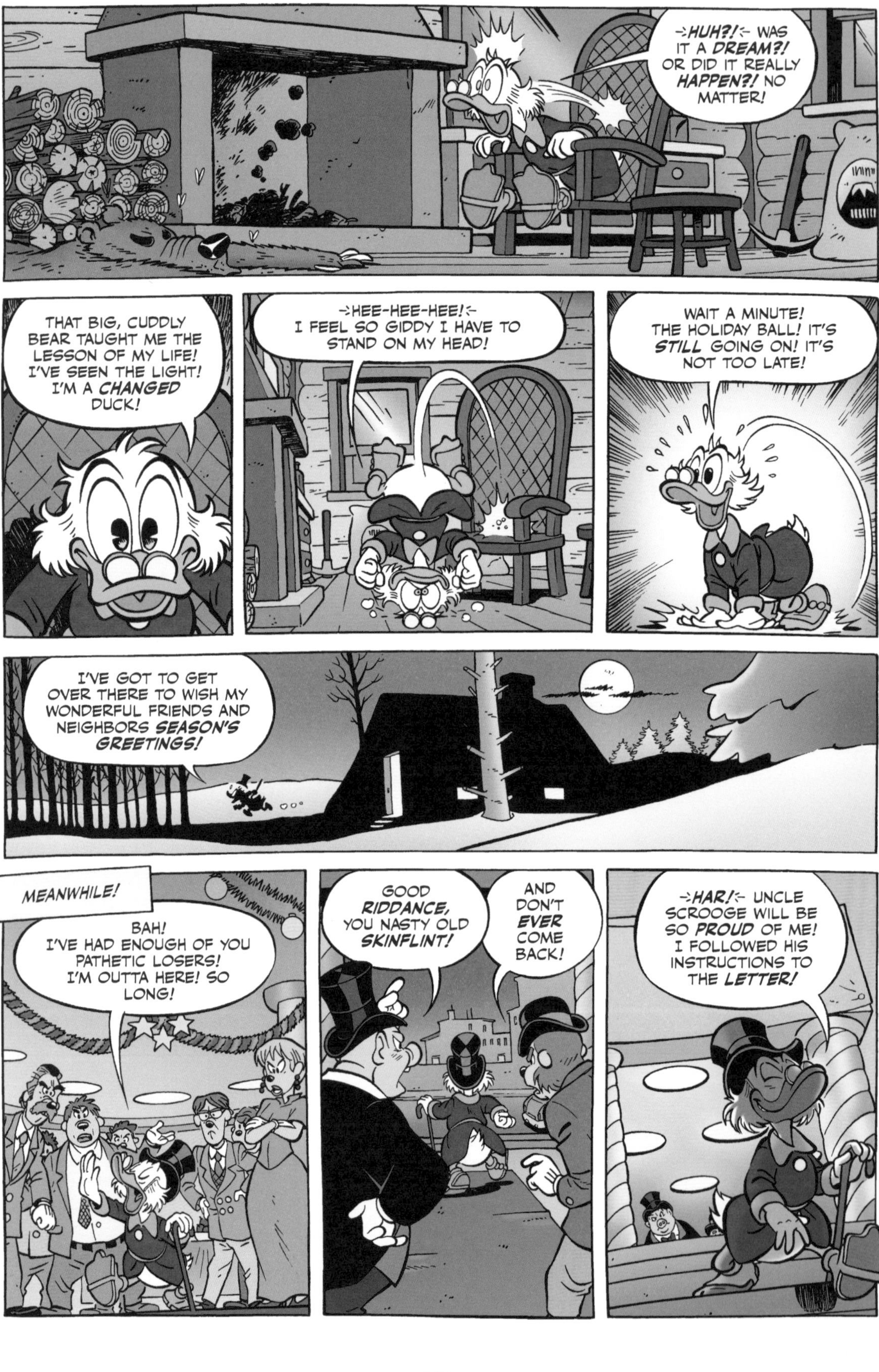
HUH?! WAS IT A DREAM?! OR DID IT REALLY HAPPEN?! NO MATTER!
THAT BIG, CUDDLY BEAR TAUGHT ME THE LESSON OF MY LIFE! I'VE SEEN THE LIGHT! I'M A CHANGED DUCK!
HEE-HEE-HEE! I FEEL SO GIDDY I HAVE TO STAND ON MY HEAD!
WAIT A MINUTE! THE HOLIDAY BALL! IT'S STILL GOING ON! IT'S NOT TOO LATE!
I'VE GOT TO GET OVER THERE TO WISH MY WONDERFUL FRIENDS AND NEIGHBORS SEASON'S GREETINGS!
MEANWHILE!
BAH! I'VE HAD ENOUGH OF YOU PATHETIC LOSERS! I'M OUTTA HERE! SO LONG!
GOOD RIDDANCE, YOU NASTY OLD SKINFLINT!
AND DON'T EVER COME BACK!
HAR! UNCLE SCROOGE WILL BE SO PROUD OF ME! I FOLLOWED HIS INSTRUCTIONS TO THE LETTER!

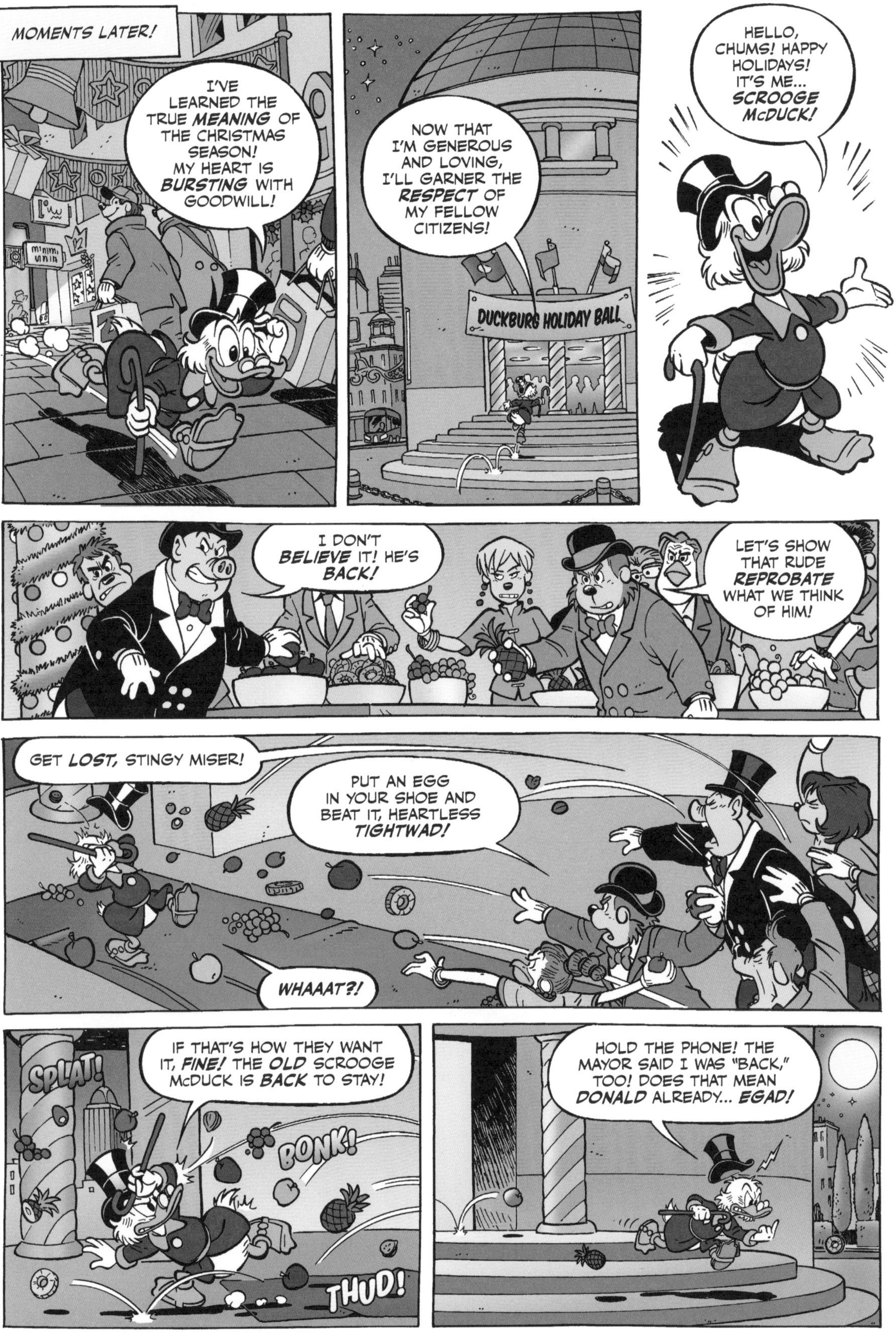
MOMENTS LATER!
I'VE LEARNED THE TRUE MEANING OF THE CHRISTMAS SEASON! MY HEART IS BURSTING WITH GOODWILL!
NOW THAT I'M GENEROUS AND LOVING, I'LL GARNER THE RESPECT OF MY FELLOW CITIZENS!
DUCKBURG HOLIDAY BALL
HELLO, CHUMS! HAPPY HOLIDAYS! IT'S ME... SCROOGE McDUCK!
I DON'T BELIEVE IT! HE'S BACK!
LET'S SHOW THAT RUDE REPROBATE WHAT WE THINK OF HIM!
GET LOST, STINGY MISER!
PUT AN EGG IN YOUR SHOE AND BEAT IT, HEARTLESS TIGHTWAD!
WHAAAT?!
IF THAT'S HOW THEY WANT IT, FINE! THE OLD SCROOGE McDUCK IS BACK TO STAY!
SPLAT!
BONK!
THUD!
HOLD THE PHONE! THE MAYOR SAID I WAS "BACK," TOO! DOES THAT MEAN DONALD ALREADY... EGAD!

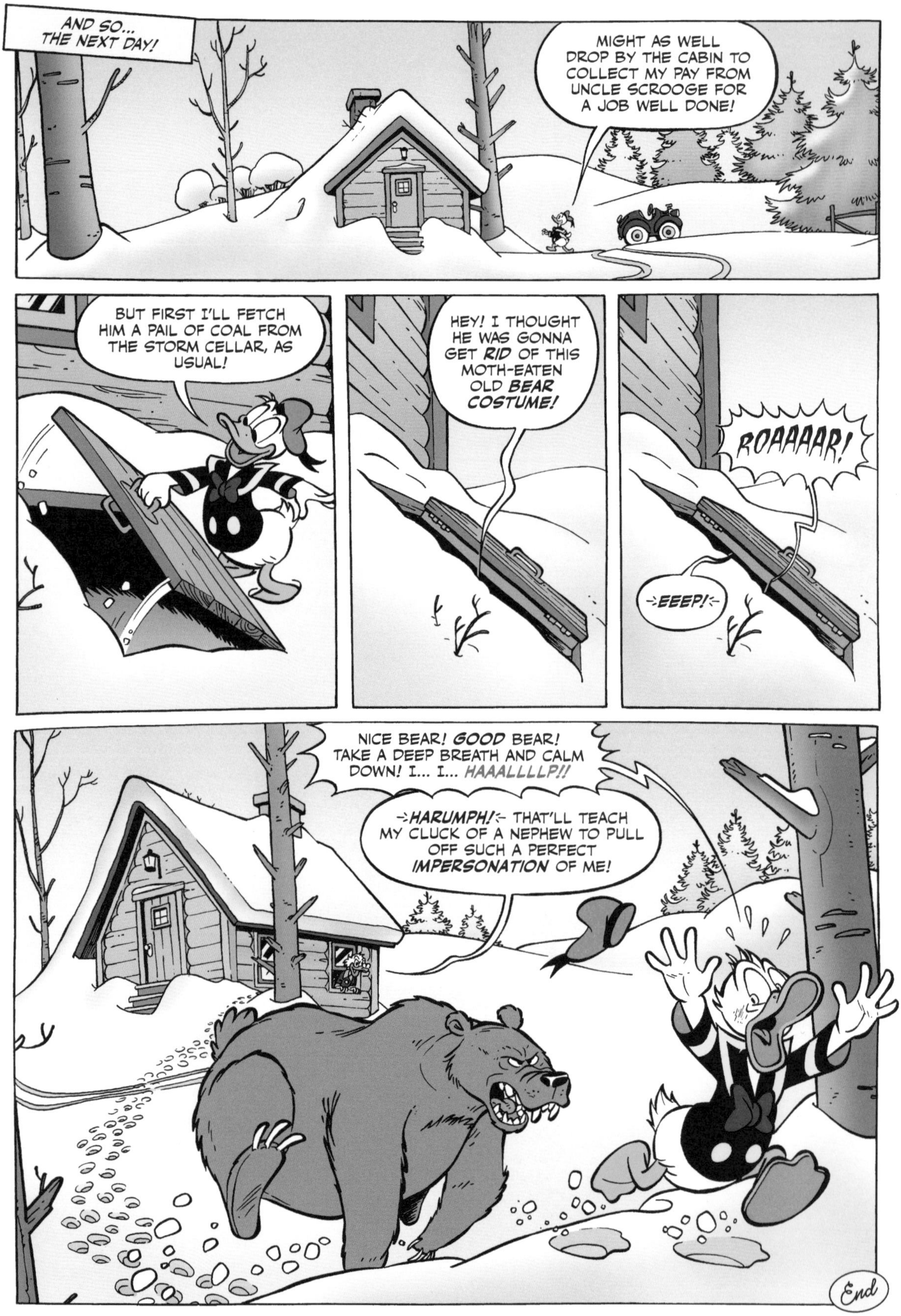

AND SO... THE NEXT DAY!
MIGHT AS WELL DROP BY THE CABIN TO COLLECT MY PAY FROM UNCLE SCROOGE FOR A JOB WELL DONE!
BUT FIRST I'LL FETCH HIM A PAIL OF COAL FROM THE STORM CELLAR, AS USUAL!
HEY! I THOUGHT HE WAS GONNA GET RID OF THIS MOTH-EATEN OLD BEAR COSTUME!
ROAAAAR!
EEEP!
NICE BEAR! GOOD BEAR! TAKE A DEEP BREATH AND CALM DOWN! I... I... HAAALLLLP!!
HARUMPH! THAT'LL TEACH MY CLUCK OF A NEPHEW TO PULL OFF SUCH A PERFECT IMPERSONATION OF ME!
End

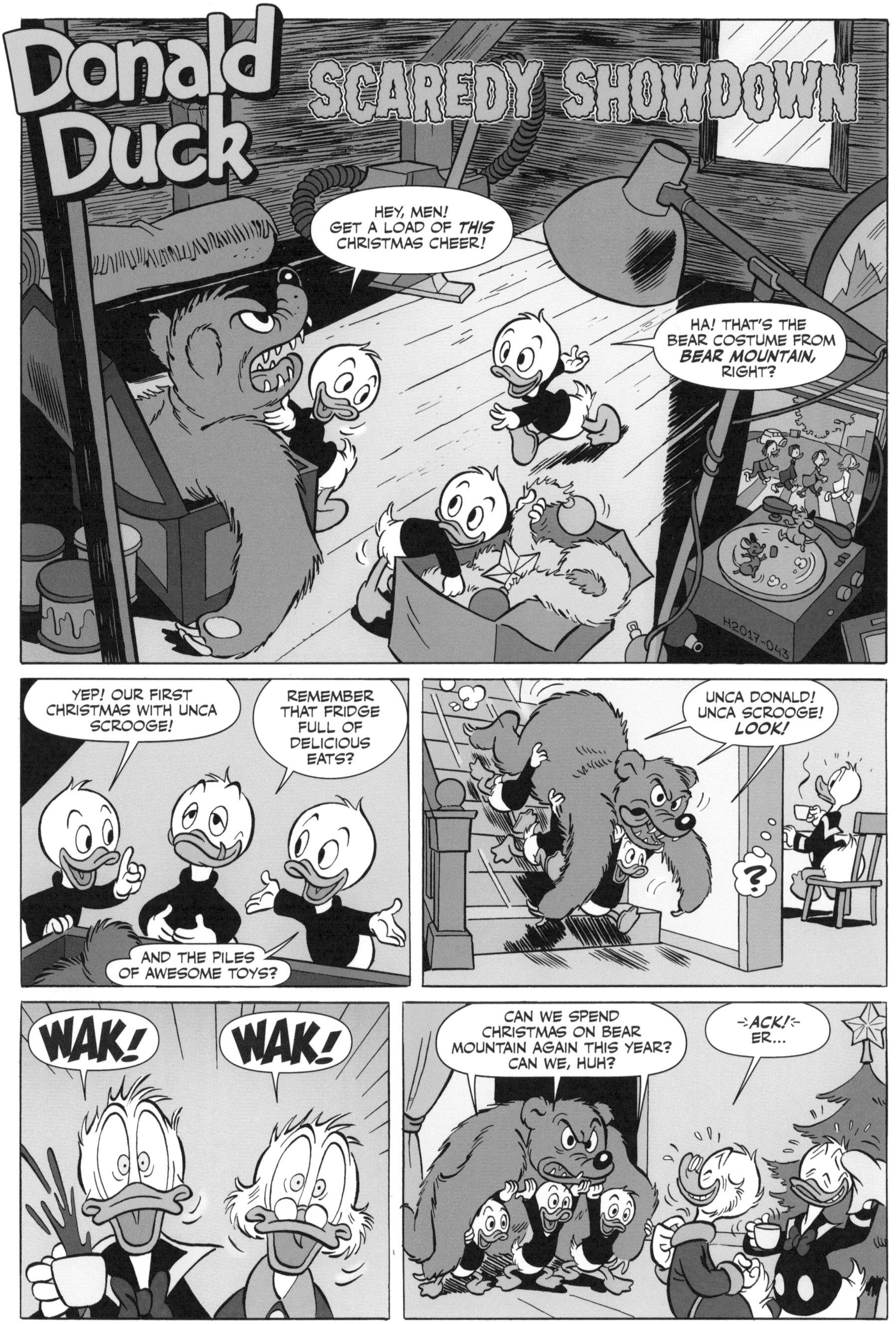

Donald Duck
SCAREDY SHOWDOWN
HEY, MEN! GET A LOAD OF *THIS* CHRISTMAS CHEER!
HA! THAT'S THE BEAR COSTUME FROM *BEAR MOUNTAIN,* RIGHT?
H2017-043
YEP! OUR FIRST CHRISTMAS WITH UNCA SCROOGE!
REMEMBER THAT FRIDGE FULL OF DELICIOUS EATS?
AND THE PILES OF AWESOME TOYS?
UNCA DONALD! UNCA SCROOGE! *LOOK!*
?
WAK!
WAK!
CAN WE SPEND CHRISTMAS ON BEAR MOUNTAIN AGAIN THIS YEAR? CAN WE, HUH?
ACK! ER...

NAY, LADS! IT'S CHEAPER -- UH, *CHUMMIER* TO HAVE CHRISTMAS AT HOME! IT'S TRADITION!

AND BESIDES, YOUR UNCLE DONALD IS TOO *SCARED* OF ALL THE *BEARS...*

SCARED? ⇥SNORT!⇤ *ME?!*

THE ONLY THING TO *FEAR* UP THERE IS *SCHEMIN' UNCLES* IN *COSTUMES!* REMEMBER?

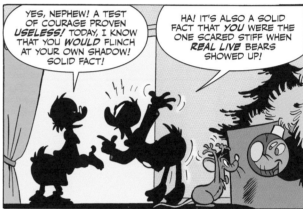

YES, NEPHEW! A TEST OF COURAGE PROVEN *USELESS!* TODAY, I KNOW THAT YOU *WOULD* FLINCH AT YOUR OWN SHADOW! SOLID FACT!

HA! IT'S ALSO A SOLID FACT THAT *YOU* WERE THE ONE SCARED STIFF WHEN *REAL LIVE* BEARS SHOWED UP!

SCARED STIFF, HUH? WHY -- BACK IN THE KLONDIKE, I FOUGHT BEARS ON *TOP* OF WOLVES AND BANDITS!

QUIT BLUFFIN'!

BONK!

WE *WILL* HAVE CHRISTMAS ON BEAR MOUNTAIN -- AND THE FIRST DUCK TO GET SCARED *PAYS FOR EVERYTHING!*

MY KIND OF CHALLENGE! START SCRIMPIN' AND SAVIN', NEPHEW!

HOORAY!

WE'RE OFF...

...TO BEAR MOUNTAIN!

PACK YOUR BAGS, BOYS!

AND BROTHER, WILL *I* PACK! I'LL MAKE *SURE* THAT OLD MISER FOOTS THE BILL!

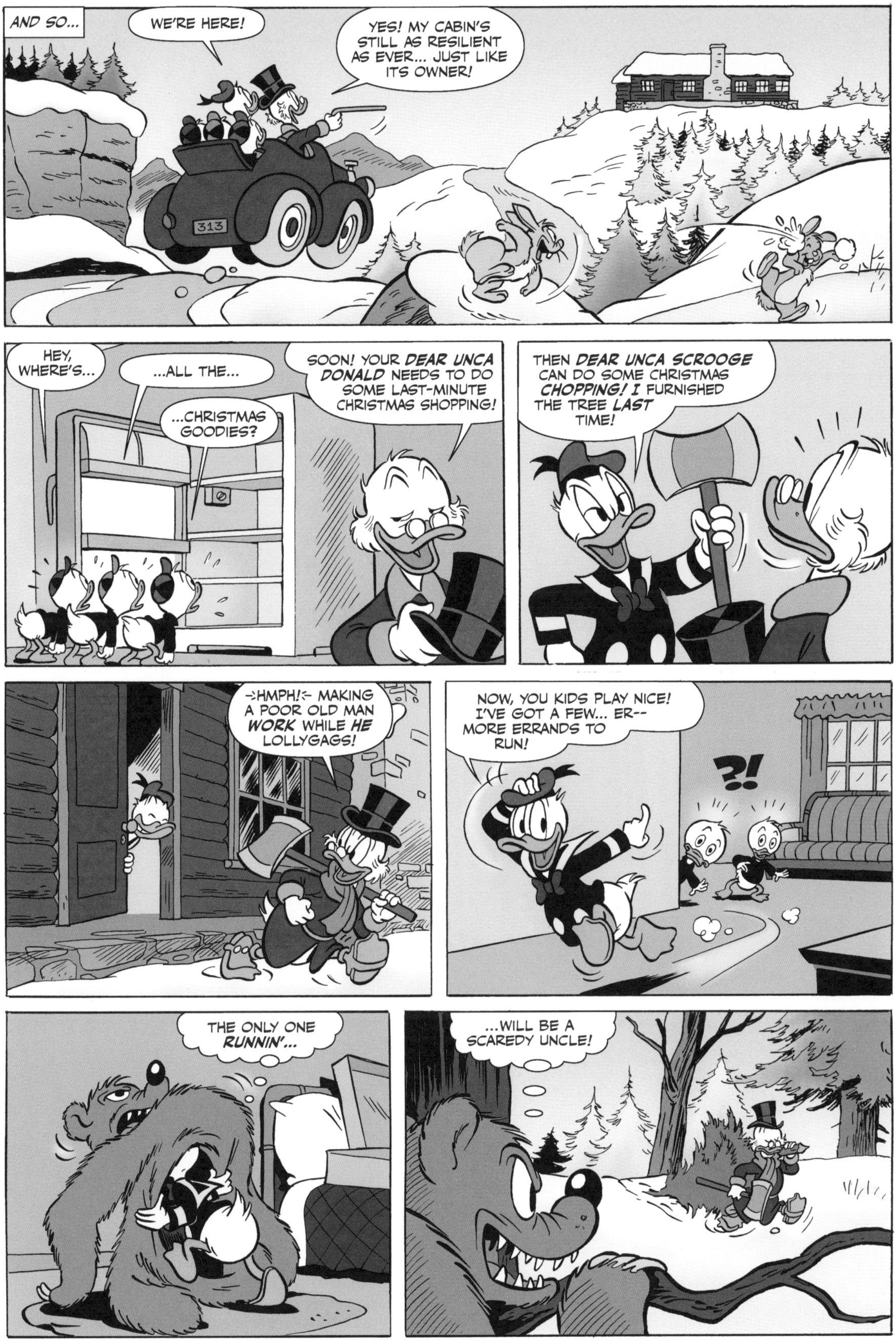
AND SO...
WE'RE HERE!
YES! MY CABIN'S STILL AS RESILIENT AS EVER... JUST LIKE ITS OWNER!
313
HEY, WHERE'S...
...ALL THE...
...CHRISTMAS GOODIES?
SOON! YOUR DEAR UNCA DONALD NEEDS TO DO SOME LAST-MINUTE CHRISTMAS SHOPPING!
THEN DEAR UNCA SCROOGE CAN DO SOME CHRISTMAS CHOPPING! I FURNISHED THE TREE LAST TIME!
-HMPH!- MAKING A POOR OLD MAN WORK WHILE HE LOLLYGAGS!
NOW, YOU KIDS PLAY NICE! I'VE GOT A FEW... ER-- MORE ERRANDS TO RUN!
?!
THE ONLY ONE RUNNIN'...
...WILL BE A SCAREDY UNCLE!

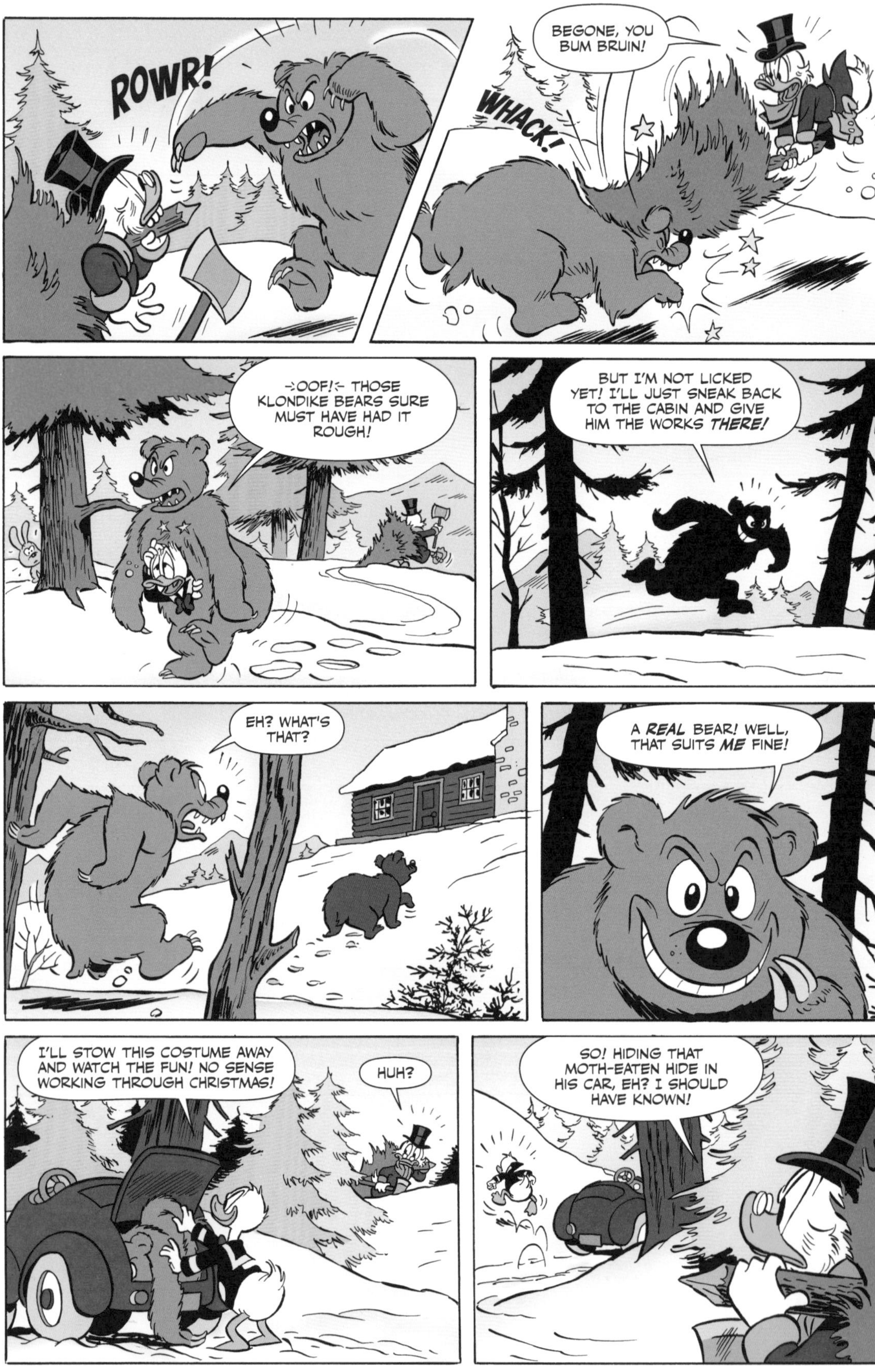
ROWR!
BEGONE, YOU BUM BRUIN!
WHACK!
-OOF!- THOSE KLONDIKE BEARS SURE MUST HAVE HAD IT ROUGH!
BUT I'M NOT LICKED YET! I'LL JUST SNEAK BACK TO THE CABIN AND GIVE HIM THE WORKS THERE!
EH? WHAT'S THAT?
A REAL BEAR! WELL, THAT SUITS ME FINE!
I'LL STOW THIS COSTUME AWAY AND WATCH THE FUN! NO SENSE WORKING THROUGH CHRISTMAS!
HUH?
SO! HIDING THAT MOTH-EATEN HIDE IN HIS CAR, EH? I SHOULD HAVE KNOWN!

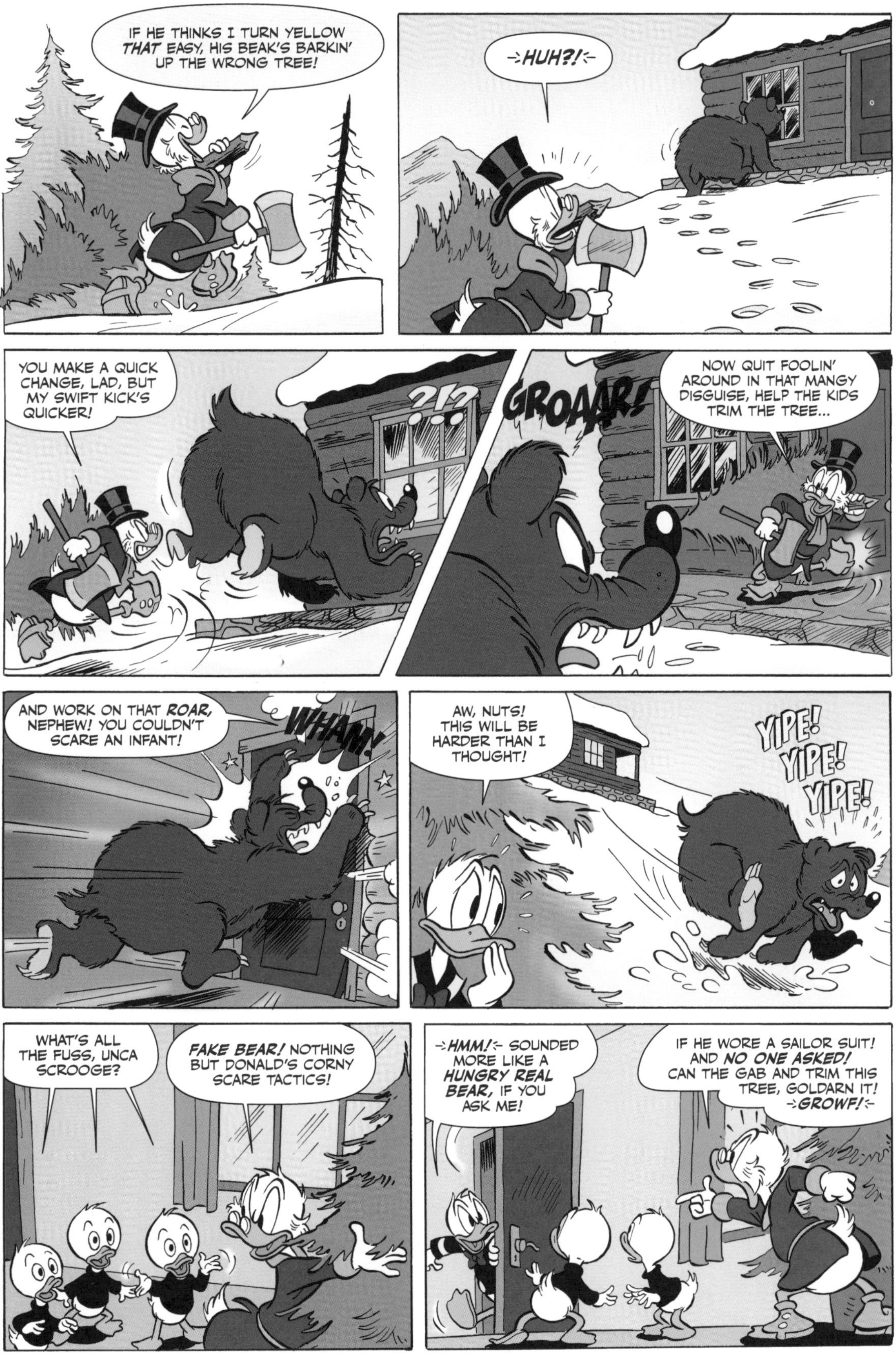
IF HE THINKS I TURN YELLOW THAT EASY, HIS BEAK'S BARKIN' UP THE WRONG TREE!
-HUH?!-
YOU MAKE A QUICK CHANGE, LAD, BUT MY SWIFT KICK'S QUICKER!
?!?
GROAAR!
NOW QUIT FOOLIN' AROUND IN THAT MANGY DISGUISE, HELP THE KIDS TRIM THE TREE...
AND WORK ON THAT ROAR, NEPHEW! YOU COULDN'T SCARE AN INFANT!
WHAM!
AW, NUTS! THIS WILL BE HARDER THAN I THOUGHT!
YIPE! YIPE! YIPE!
WHAT'S ALL THE FUSS, UNCA SCROOGE?
FAKE BEAR! NOTHING BUT DONALD'S CORNY SCARE TACTICS!
-HMM!- SOUNDED MORE LIKE A HUNGRY REAL BEAR, IF YOU ASK ME!
IF HE WORE A SAILOR SUIT! AND NO ONE ASKED! CAN THE GAB AND TRIM THIS TREE, GOLDARN IT! -GROWF!-

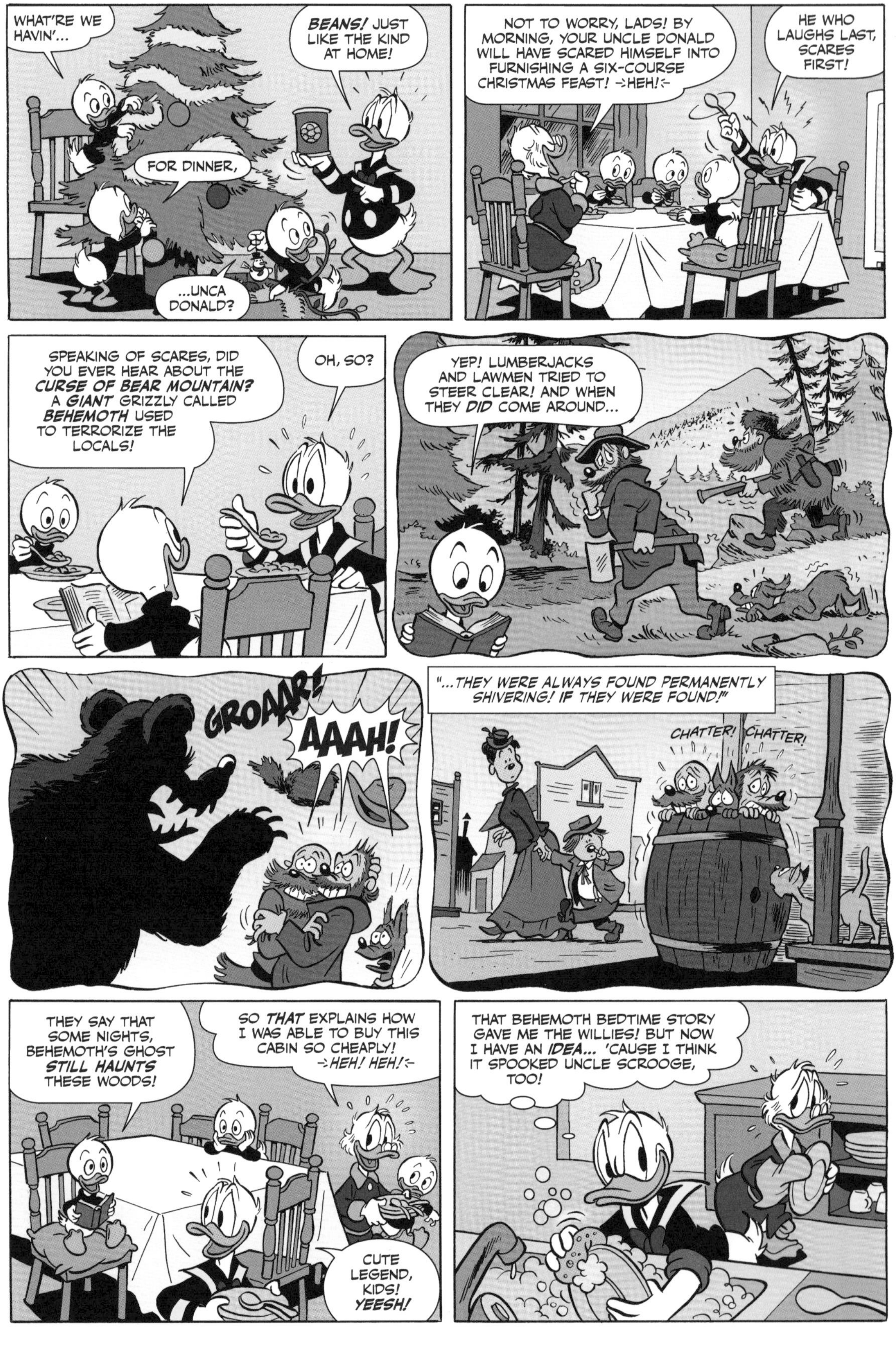
WHAT'RE WE HAVIN'...
FOR DINNER,
...UNCA DONALD?
BEANS! JUST LIKE THE KIND AT HOME!
NOT TO WORRY, LADS! BY MORNING, YOUR UNCLE DONALD WILL HAVE SCARED HIMSELF INTO FURNISHING A SIX-COURSE CHRISTMAS FEAST! -HEH!-
HE WHO LAUGHS LAST, SCARES FIRST!
SPEAKING OF SCARES, DID YOU EVER HEAR ABOUT THE CURSE OF BEAR MOUNTAIN? A GIANT GRIZZLY CALLED BEHEMOTH USED TO TERRORIZE THE LOCALS!
OH, SO?
YEP! LUMBERJACKS AND LAWMEN TRIED TO STEER CLEAR! AND WHEN THEY DID COME AROUND...
GROAAR!
AAAH!
"...THEY WERE ALWAYS FOUND PERMANENTLY SHIVERING! IF THEY WERE FOUND!"
CHATTER! CHATTER!
THEY SAY THAT SOME NIGHTS, BEHEMOTH'S GHOST STILL HAUNTS THESE WOODS!
SO THAT EXPLAINS HOW I WAS ABLE TO BUY THIS CABIN SO CHEAPLY! -HEH! HEH!-
CUTE LEGEND, KIDS! YEESH!
THAT BEHEMOTH BEDTIME STORY GAVE ME THE WILLIES! BUT NOW I HAVE AN IDEA... 'CAUSE I THINK IT SPOOKED UNCLE SCROOGE, TOO!

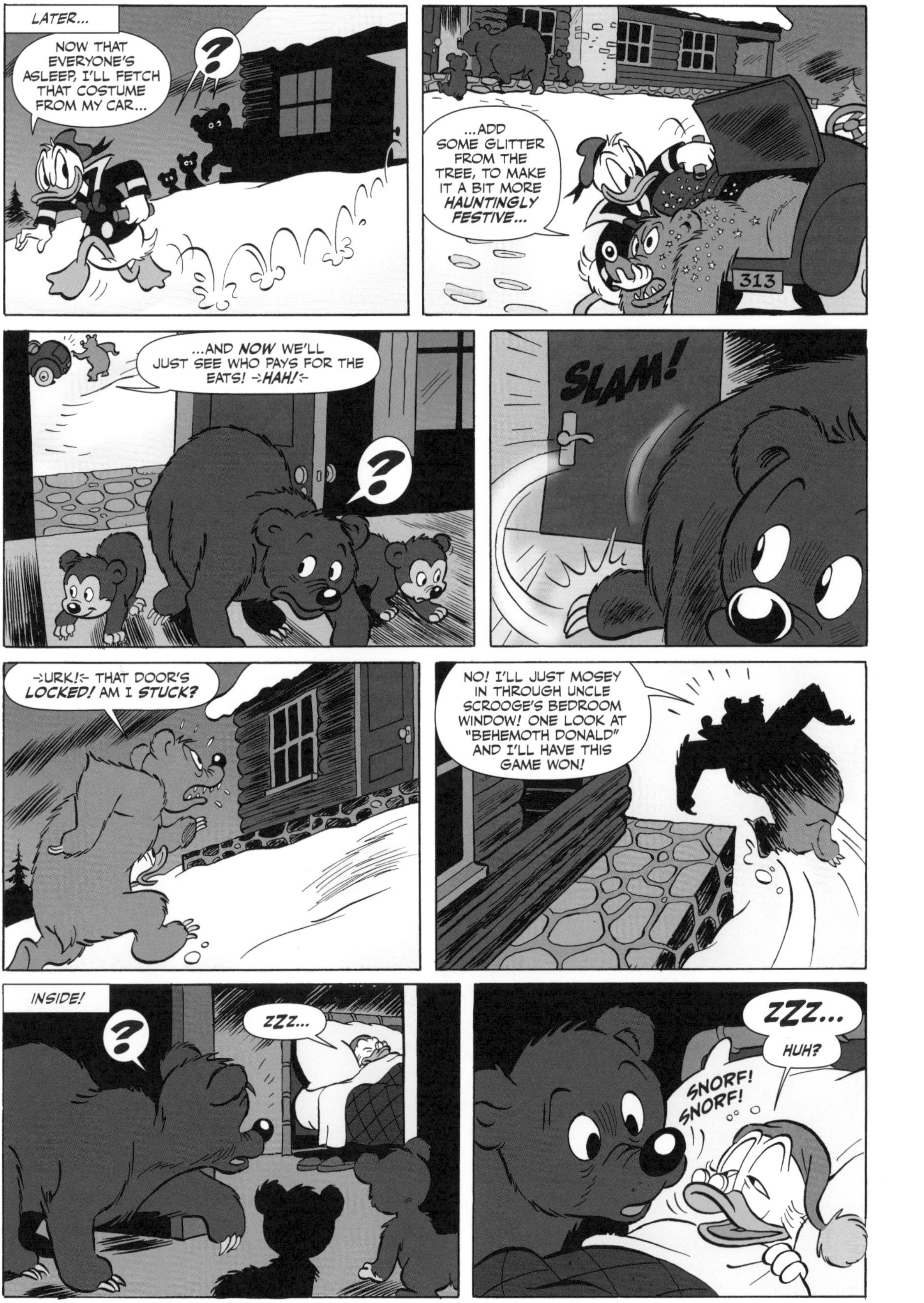
LATER...
NOW THAT EVERYONE'S ASLEEP, I'LL FETCH THAT COSTUME FROM MY CAR...
?
...ADD SOME GLITTER FROM THE TREE, TO MAKE IT A BIT MORE HAUNTINGLY FESTIVE...
313
...AND NOW WE'LL JUST SEE WHO PAYS FOR THE EATS! -HAH!-
?
SLAM!
-URK!- THAT DOOR'S LOCKED! AM I STUCK?
NO! I'LL JUST MOSEY IN THROUGH UNCLE SCROOGE'S BEDROOM WINDOW! ONE LOOK AT "BEHEMOTH DONALD" AND I'LL HAVE THIS GAME WON!
INSIDE!
?
ZZZ...
ZZZ...
HUH?
SNORF! SNORF!

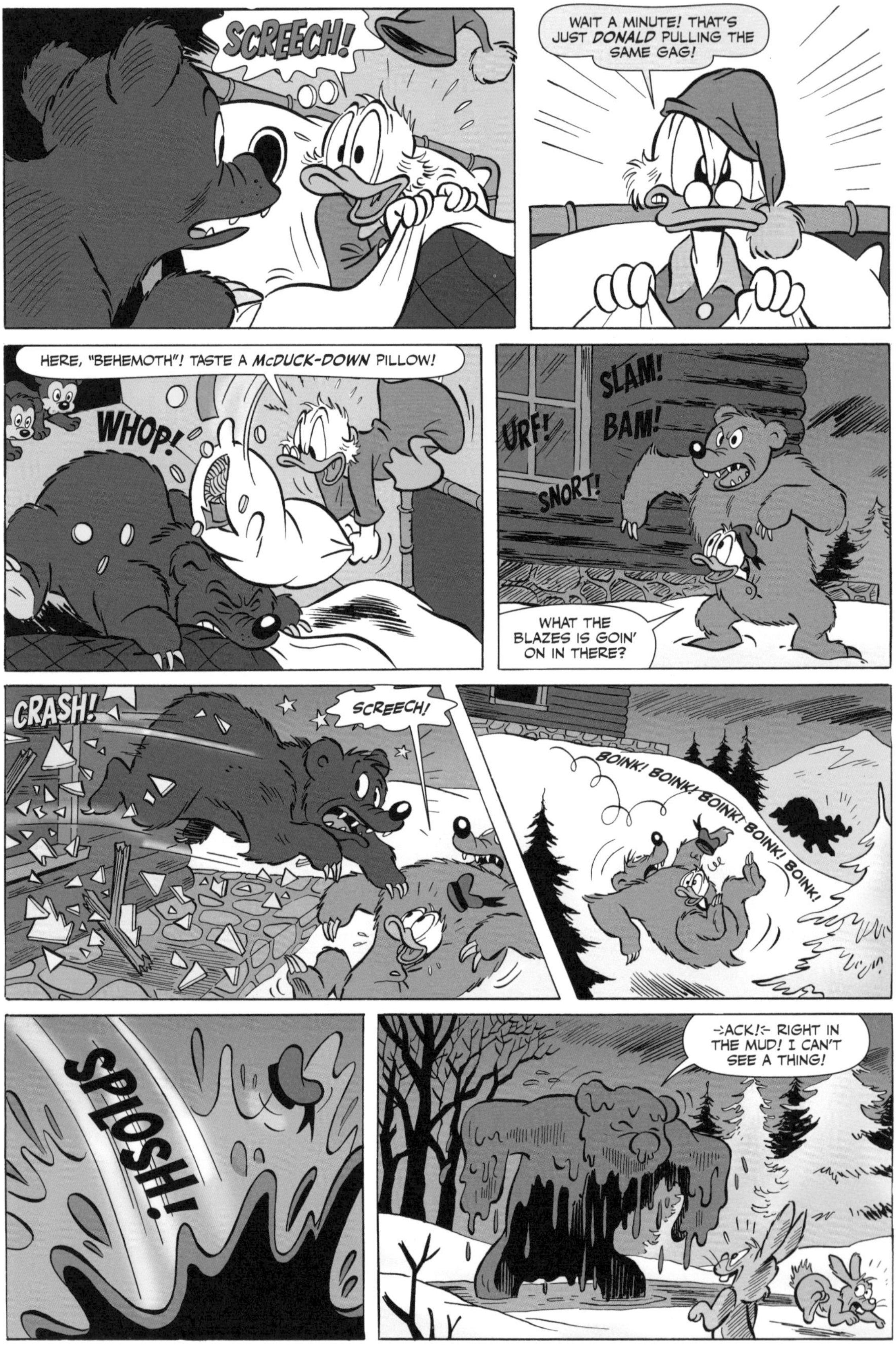
SCREECH!
WAIT A MINUTE! THAT'S JUST DONALD PULLING THE SAME GAG!
HERE, "BEHEMOTH"! TASTE A McDUCK-DOWN PILLOW!
WHOP!
SLAM!
URF!
BAM!
SNORT!
WHAT THE BLAZES IS GOIN' ON IN THERE?
CRASH!
SCREECH!
BOINK! BOINK! BOINK! BOINK! BOINK!
SPLOSH!
-ACK!- RIGHT IN THE MUD! I CAN'T SEE A THING!

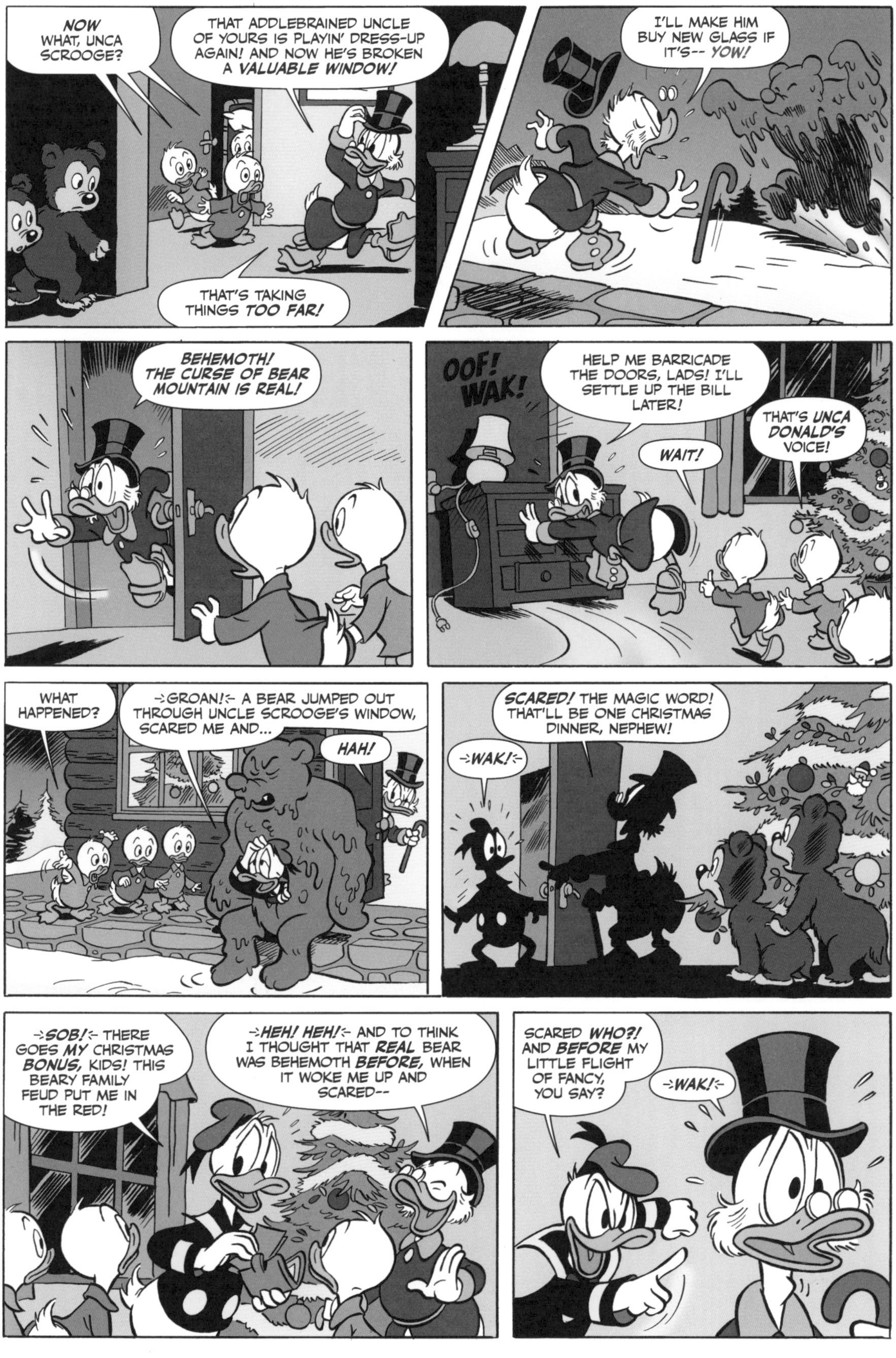
NOW WHAT, UNCA SCROOGE?
THAT ADDLEBRAINED UNCLE OF YOURS IS PLAYIN' DRESS-UP AGAIN! AND NOW HE'S BROKEN A VALUABLE WINDOW!
THAT'S TAKING THINGS TOO FAR!
I'LL MAKE HIM BUY NEW GLASS IF IT'S-- YOW!
BEHEMOTH! THE CURSE OF BEAR MOUNTAIN IS REAL!
OOF! WAK!
HELP ME BARRICADE THE DOORS, LADS! I'LL SETTLE UP THE BILL LATER!
WAIT!
THAT'S UNCA DONALD'S VOICE!
WHAT HAPPENED?
-GROAN!- A BEAR JUMPED OUT THROUGH UNCLE SCROOGE'S WINDOW, SCARED ME AND...
HAH!
SCARED! THE MAGIC WORD! THAT'LL BE ONE CHRISTMAS DINNER, NEPHEW!
-WAK!-
-SOB!- THERE GOES MY CHRISTMAS BONUS, KIDS! THIS BEARY FAMILY FEUD PUT ME IN THE RED!
-HEH! HEH!- AND TO THINK I THOUGHT THAT REAL BEAR WAS BEHEMOTH BEFORE, WHEN IT WOKE ME UP AND SCARED--
SCARED WHO?! AND BEFORE MY LITTLE FLIGHT OF FANCY, YOU SAY?
-WAK!-

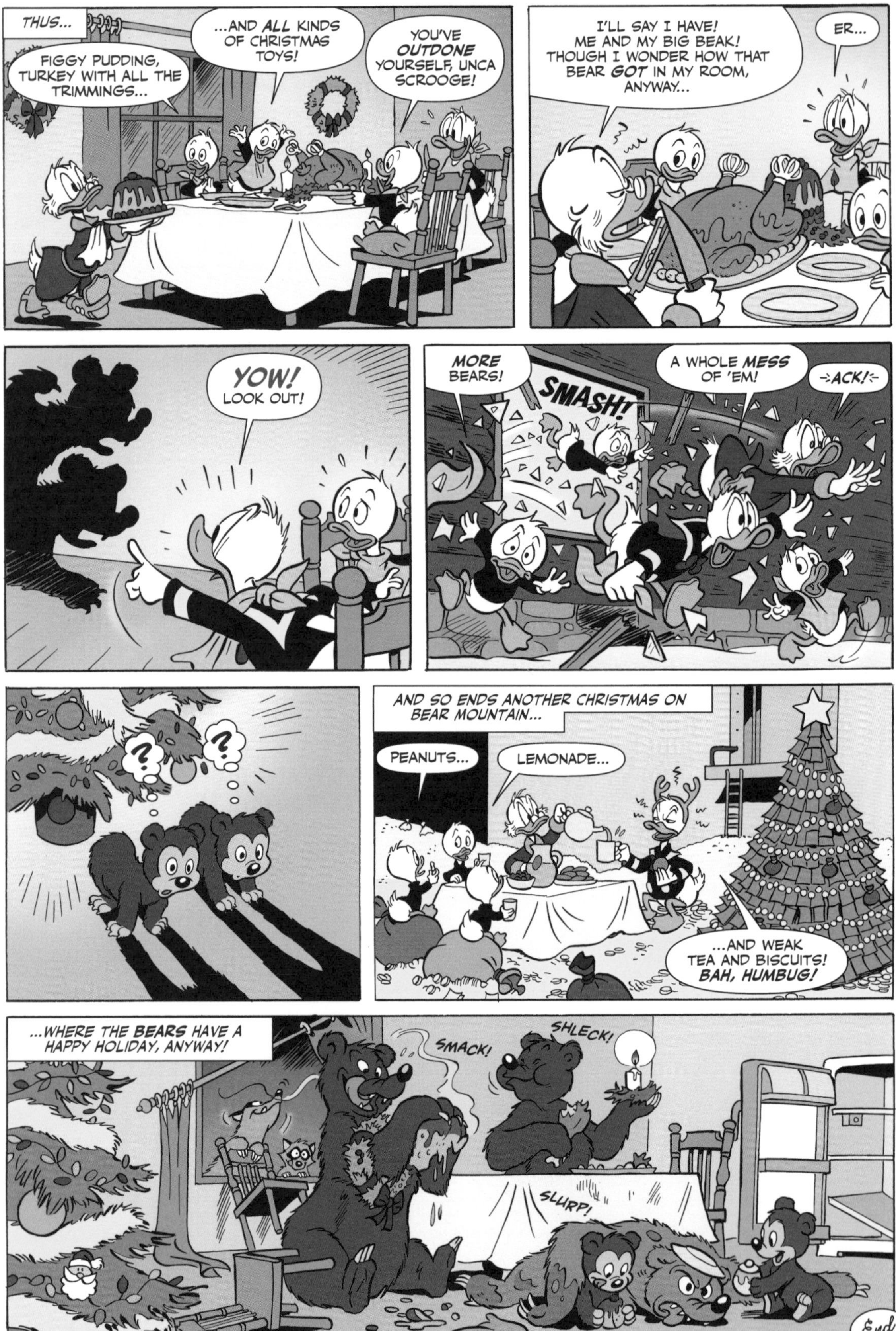
THUS...
FIGGY PUDDING, TURKEY WITH ALL THE TRIMMINGS...
...AND ALL KINDS OF CHRISTMAS TOYS!
YOU'VE OUTDONE YOURSELF, UNCA SCROOGE!
I'LL SAY I HAVE! ME AND MY BIG BEAK! THOUGH I WONDER HOW THAT BEAR GOT IN MY ROOM, ANYWAY...
ER...
YOW! LOOK OUT!
MORE BEARS!
SMASH!
A WHOLE MESS OF 'EM!
ACK!
AND SO ENDS ANOTHER CHRISTMAS ON BEAR MOUNTAIN...
PEANUTS...
LEMONADE...
...AND WEAK TEA AND BISCUITS! BAH, HUMBUG!
...WHERE THE BEARS HAVE A HAPPY HOLIDAY, ANYWAY!
SMACK!
SHLECK!
SLURP!
End

Disney

DuckTales

NIGHTMARE ON BEAR MOUNTAIN!

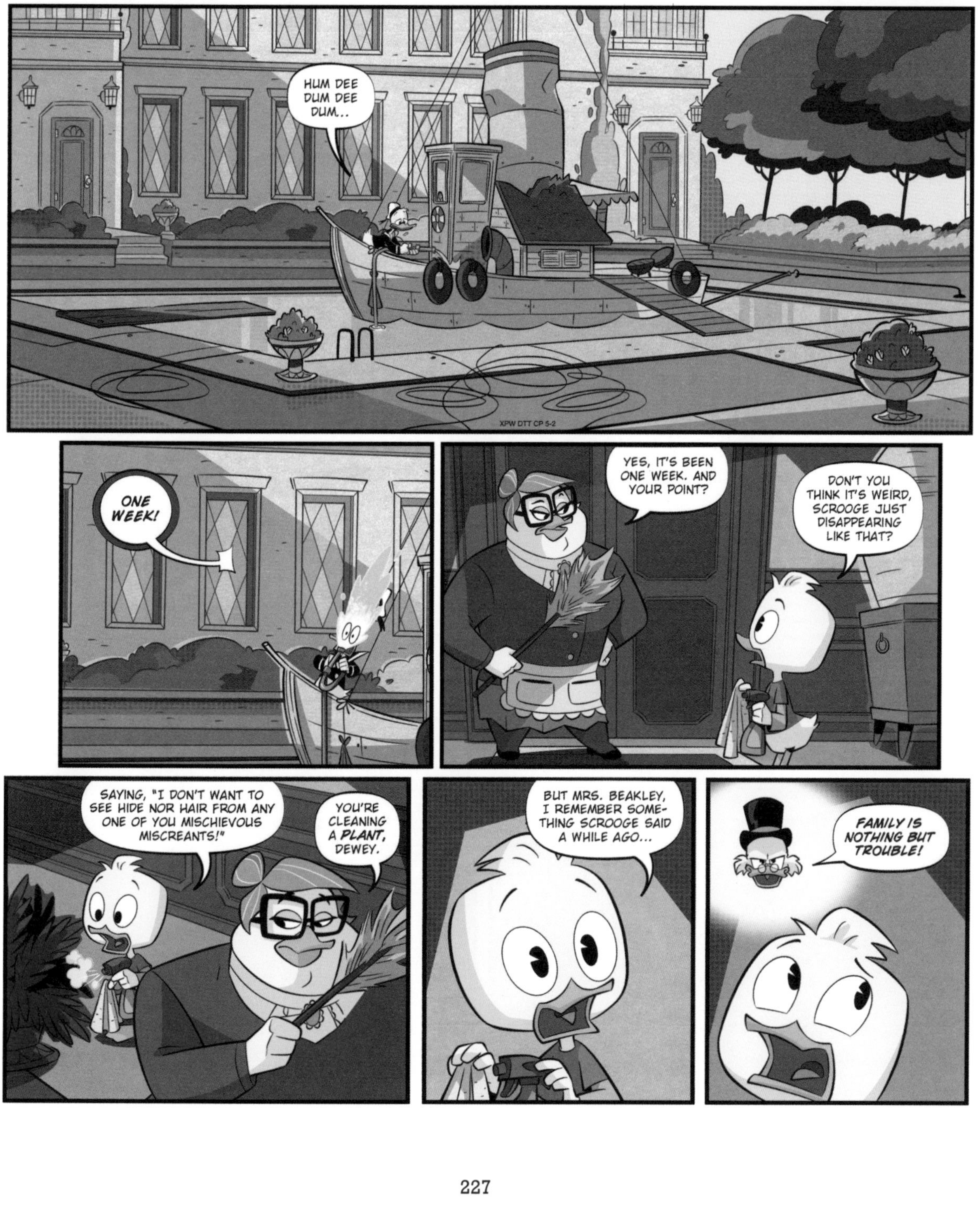
HUM DEE DUM DEE DUM...
XPW DTT CP 5-2
ONE WEEK!
YES, IT'S BEEN ONE WEEK. AND YOUR POINT?
DON'T YOU THINK IT'S WEIRD, SCROOGE JUST DISAPPEARING LIKE THAT?
SAYING, "I DON'T WANT TO SEE HIDE NOR HAIR FROM ANY ONE OF YOU MISCHIEVOUS MISCREANTS!"
YOU'RE CLEANING A *PLANT*, DEWEY.
BUT MRS. BEAKLEY, I REMEMBER SOME-THING SCROOGE SAID A WHILE AGO...
FAMILY IS NOTHING BUT TROUBLE!

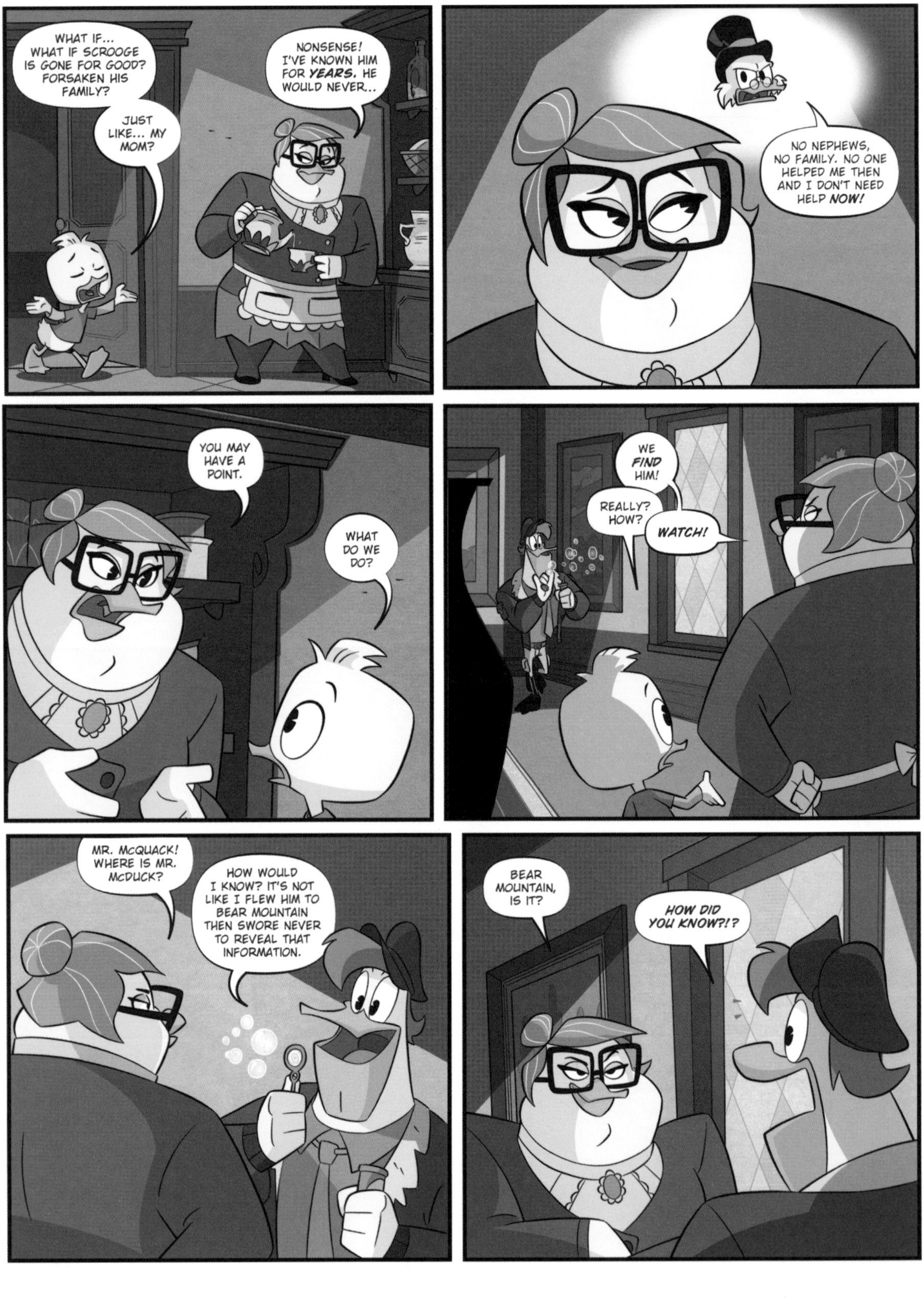
WHAT IF... WHAT IF SCROOGE IS GONE FOR GOOD? FORSAKEN HIS FAMILY?
JUST LIKE... MY MOM?
NONSENSE! I'VE KNOWN HIM FOR YEARS. HE WOULD NEVER...
NO NEPHEWS, NO FAMILY. NO ONE HELPED ME THEN AND I DON'T NEED HELP NOW!
YOU MAY HAVE A POINT.
WHAT DO WE DO?
WE FIND HIM!
REALLY? HOW?
WATCH!
MR. McQUACK! WHERE IS MR. McDUCK?
HOW WOULD I KNOW? IT'S NOT LIKE I FLEW HIM TO BEAR MOUNTAIN THEN SWORE NEVER TO REVEAL THAT INFORMATION.
BEAR MOUNTAIN, IS IT?
HOW DID YOU KNOW?!?

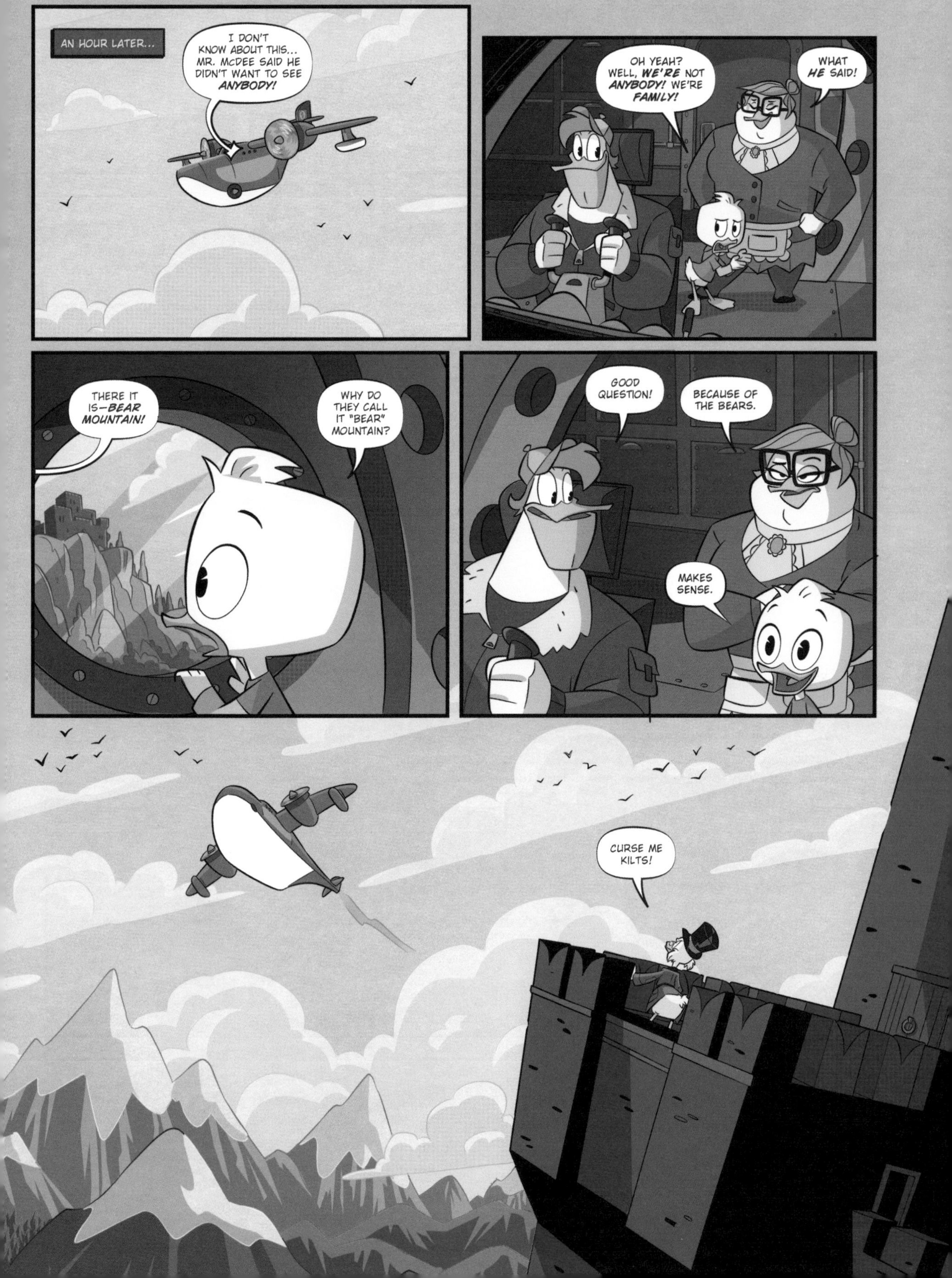

AN HOUR LATER...
I DON'T KNOW ABOUT THIS... MR. McDEE SAID HE DIDN'T WANT TO SEE ANYBODY!
OH YEAH? WELL, WE'RE NOT ANYBODY! WE'RE FAMILY!
WHAT HE SAID!
THERE IT IS—BEAR MOUNTAIN!
WHY DO THEY CALL IT "BEAR" MOUNTAIN?
GOOD QUESTION!
BECAUSE OF THE BEARS.
MAKES SENSE.
CURSE ME KILTS!

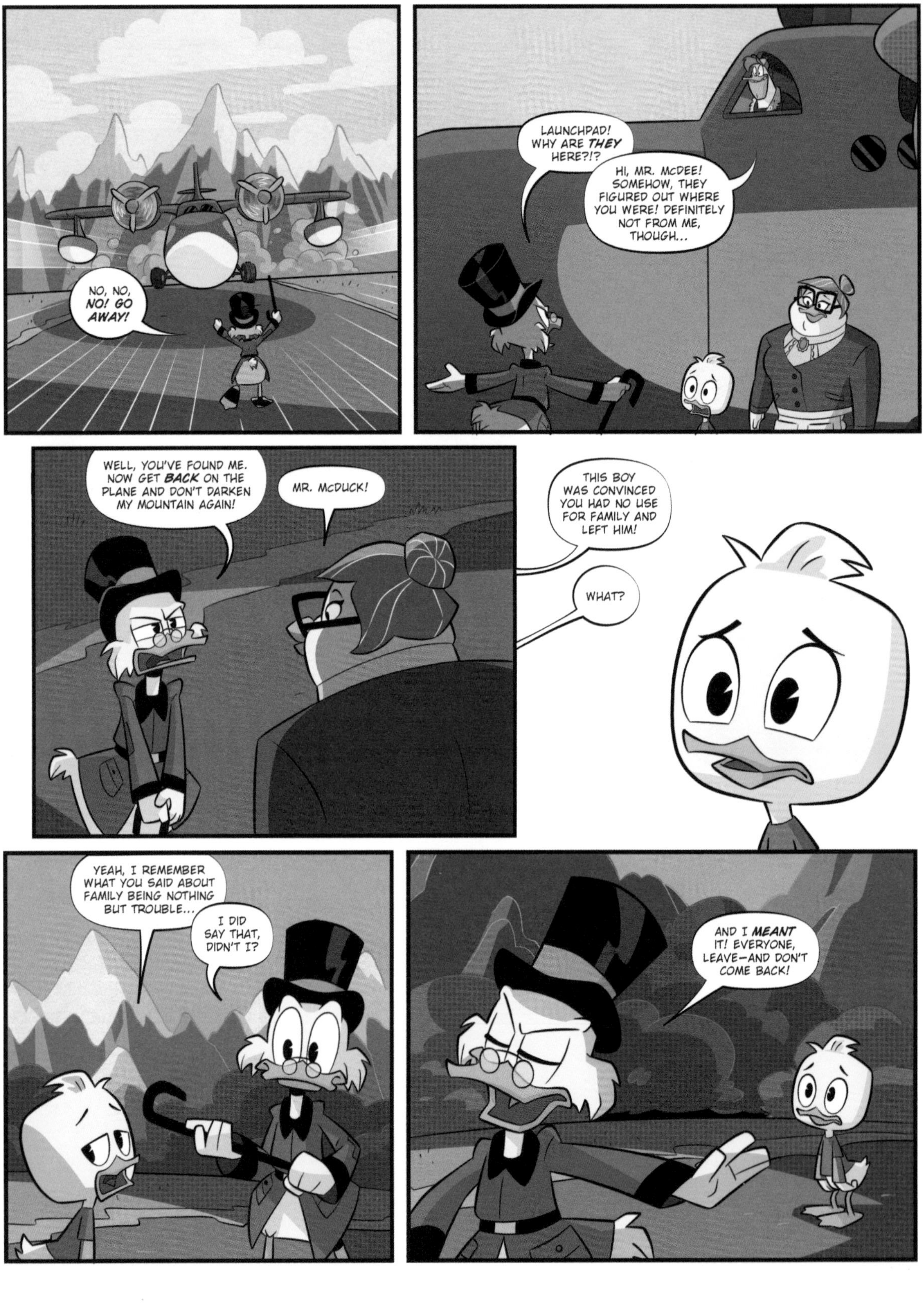
NO, NO, NO! GO AWAY!
LAUNCHPAD! WHY ARE THEY HERE?!?
HI, MR. MCDEE! SOMEHOW, THEY FIGURED OUT WHERE YOU WERE! DEFINITELY NOT FROM ME, THOUGH...
WELL, YOU'VE FOUND ME. NOW GET BACK ON THE PLANE AND DON'T DARKEN MY MOUNTAIN AGAIN!
MR. McDUCK!
THIS BOY WAS CONVINCED YOU HAD NO USE FOR FAMILY AND LEFT HIM!
WHAT?
YEAH, I REMEMBER WHAT YOU SAID ABOUT FAMILY BEING NOTHING BUT TROUBLE...
I DID SAY THAT, DIDN'T I?
AND I MEANT IT! EVERYONE, LEAVE—AND DON'T COME BACK!

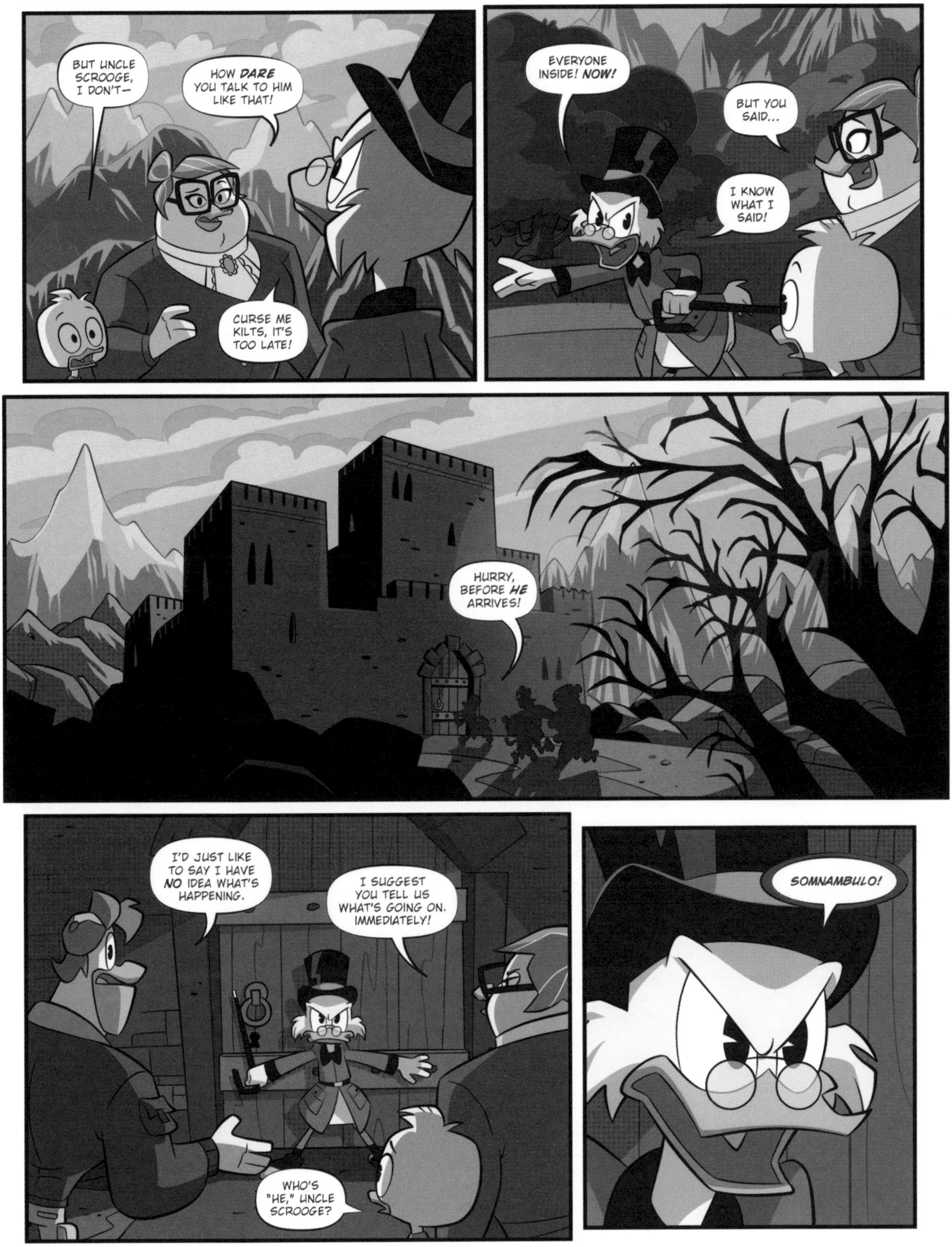
BUT UNCLE SCROOGE, I DON'T—
HOW DARE YOU TALK TO HIM LIKE THAT!
CURSE ME KILTS, IT'S TOO LATE!
EVERYONE INSIDE! NOW!
BUT YOU SAID...
I KNOW WHAT I SAID!
HURRY, BEFORE HE ARRIVES!
I'D JUST LIKE TO SAY I HAVE NO IDEA WHAT'S HAPPENING.
I SUGGEST YOU TELL US WHAT'S GOING ON. IMMEDIATELY!
WHO'S "HE," UNCLE SCROOGE?
SOMNAMBULO!

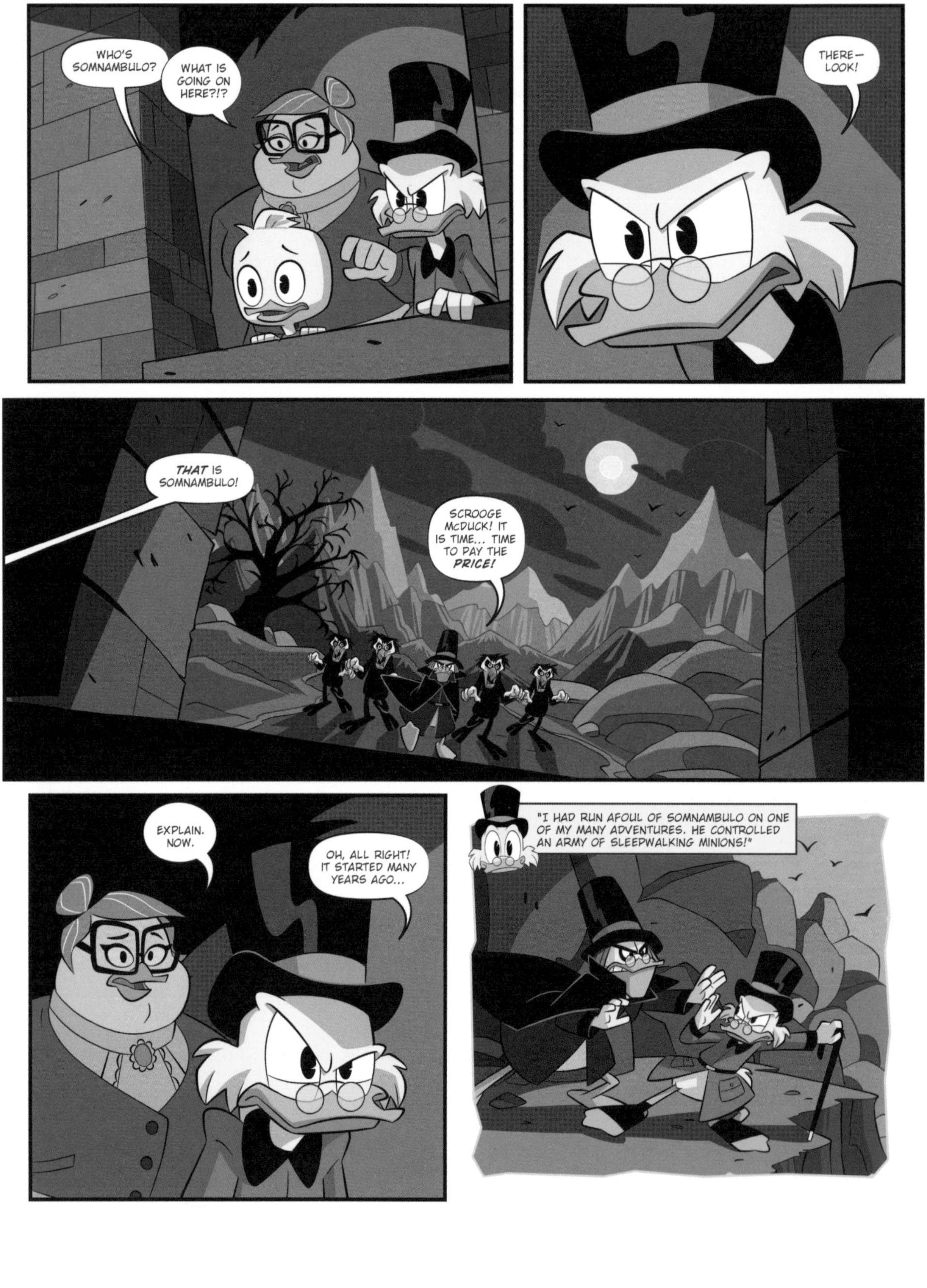
WHO'S SOMNAMBULO?
WHAT IS GOING ON HERE?!?
THERE— LOOK!
THAT IS SOMNAMBULO!
SCROOGE McDUCK! IT IS TIME... TIME TO PAY THE PRICE!
EXPLAIN. NOW.
OH, ALL RIGHT! IT STARTED MANY YEARS AGO...
"I HAD RUN AFOUL OF SOMNAMBULO ON ONE OF MY MANY ADVENTURES. HE CONTROLLED AN ARMY OF SLEEPWALKING MINIONS!"

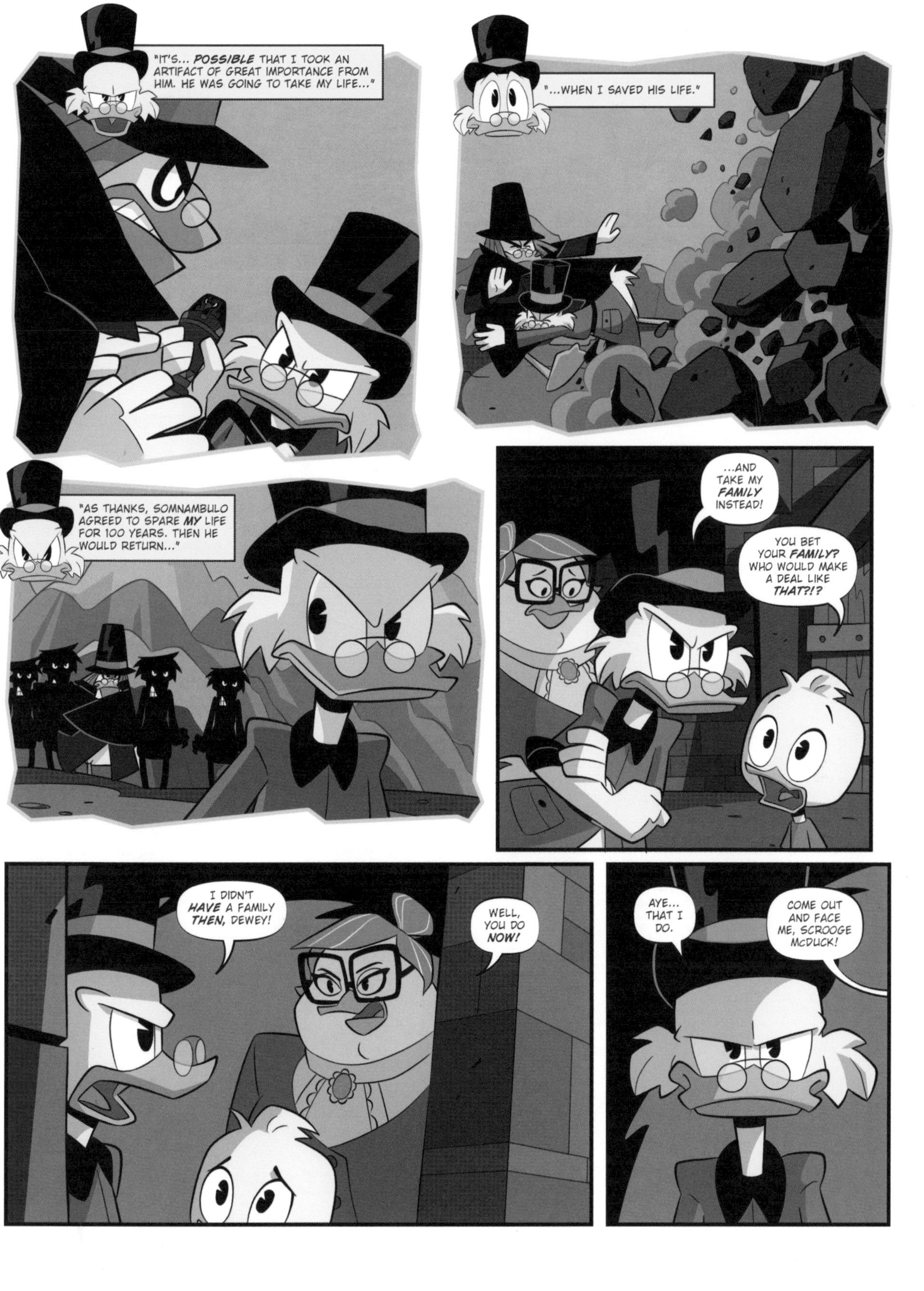
"IT'S... POSSIBLE THAT I TOOK AN ARTIFACT OF GREAT IMPORTANCE FROM HIM. HE WAS GOING TO TAKE MY LIFE..."
"...WHEN I SAVED HIS LIFE."
"AS THANKS, SOMNAMBULO AGREED TO SPARE MY LIFE FOR 100 YEARS. THEN HE WOULD RETURN..."
...AND TAKE MY FAMILY INSTEAD!
YOU BET YOUR FAMILY? WHO WOULD MAKE A DEAL LIKE THAT?!?
I DIDN'T HAVE A FAMILY THEN, DEWEY!
WELL, YOU DO NOW!
AYE... THAT I DO.
COME OUT AND FACE ME, SCROOGE McDUCK!

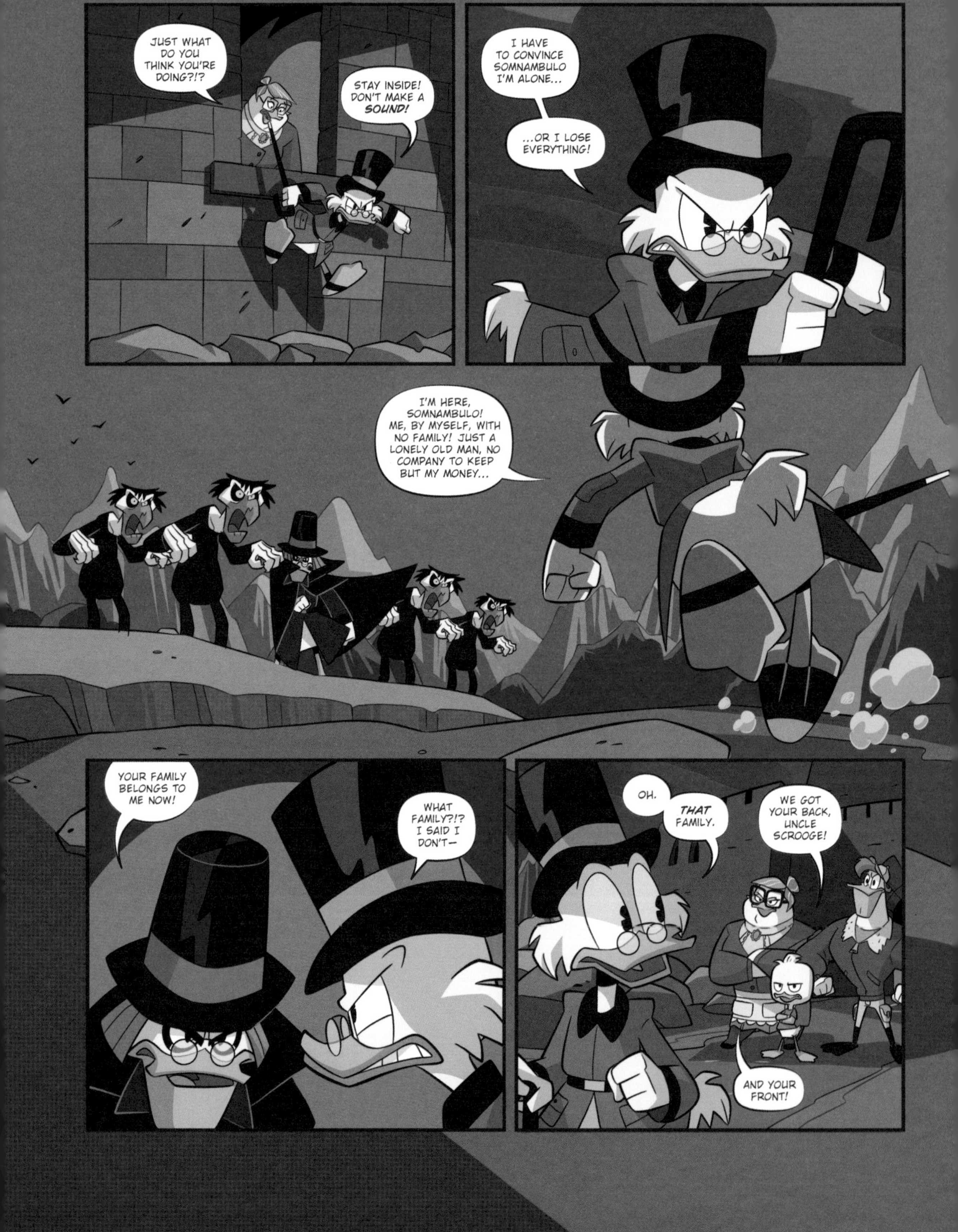
JUST WHAT DO YOU THINK YOU'RE DOING?!?
STAY INSIDE! DON'T MAKE A *SOUND!*
I HAVE TO CONVINCE SOMNAMBULO I'M ALONE...
...OR I LOSE EVERYTHING!
I'M HERE, SOMNAMBULO! ME, BY MYSELF, WITH NO FAMILY! JUST A LONELY OLD MAN, NO COMPANY TO KEEP BUT MY MONEY...
YOUR FAMILY BELONGS TO ME NOW!
WHAT FAMILY?!? I SAID I DON'T—
OH.
THAT FAMILY.
WE GOT YOUR BACK, UNCLE SCROOGE!
AND YOUR FRONT!

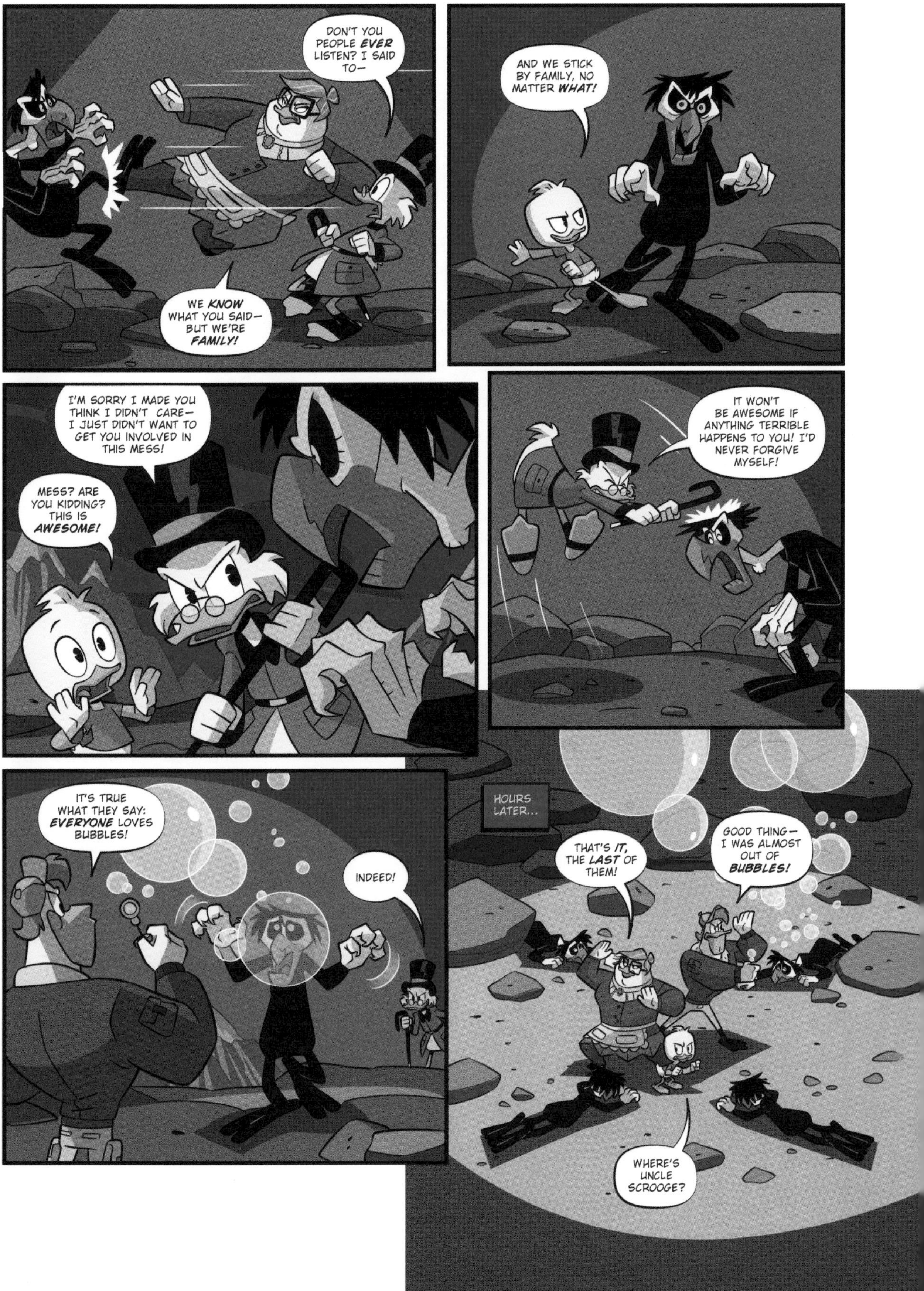

DON'T YOU PEOPLE EVER LISTEN? I SAID TO—
WE KNOW WHAT YOU SAID— BUT WE'RE FAMILY!
AND WE STICK BY FAMILY, NO MATTER WHAT!
I'M SORRY I MADE YOU THINK I DIDN'T CARE— I JUST DIDN'T WANT TO GET YOU INVOLVED IN THIS MESS!
MESS? ARE YOU KIDDING? THIS IS AWESOME!
IT WON'T BE AWESOME IF ANYTHING TERRIBLE HAPPENS TO YOU! I'D NEVER FORGIVE MYSELF!
IT'S TRUE WHAT THEY SAY: EVERYONE LOVES BUBBLES!
INDEED!
HOURS LATER...
THAT'S IT, THE LAST OF THEM!
GOOD THING— I WAS ALMOST OUT OF BUBBLES!
WHERE'S UNCLE SCROOGE?

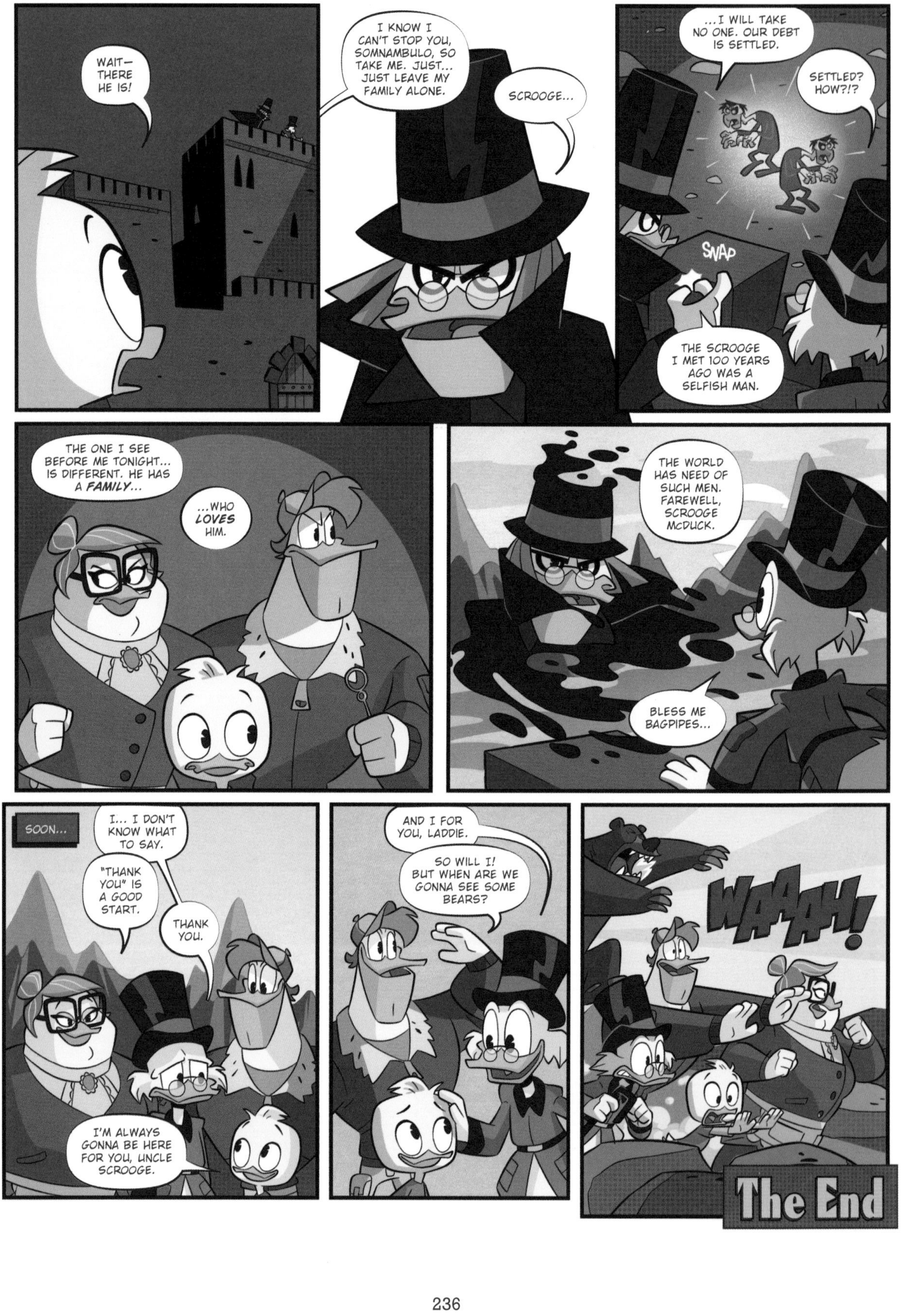
WAIT— THERE HE IS!
I KNOW I CAN'T STOP YOU, SOMNAMBULO, SO TAKE ME. JUST... JUST LEAVE MY FAMILY ALONE.
SCROOGE...
...I WILL TAKE NO ONE. OUR DEBT IS SETTLED.
SETTLED? HOW?!?
SNAP
THE SCROOGE I MET 100 YEARS AGO WAS A SELFISH MAN.
THE ONE I SEE BEFORE ME TONIGHT... IS DIFFERENT. HE HAS A *FAMILY*...
...WHO *LOVES* HIM.
THE WORLD HAS NEED OF SUCH MEN. FAREWELL, SCROOGE McDUCK.
BLESS ME BAGPIPES...
SOON...
I... I DON'T KNOW WHAT TO SAY.
"THANK YOU" IS A GOOD START.
THANK YOU.
I'M ALWAYS GONNA BE HERE FOR YOU, UNCLE SCROOGE.
AND I FOR YOU, LADDIE.
SO WILL I! BUT WHEN ARE WE GONNA SEE SOME BEARS?
WAAAH!
The End

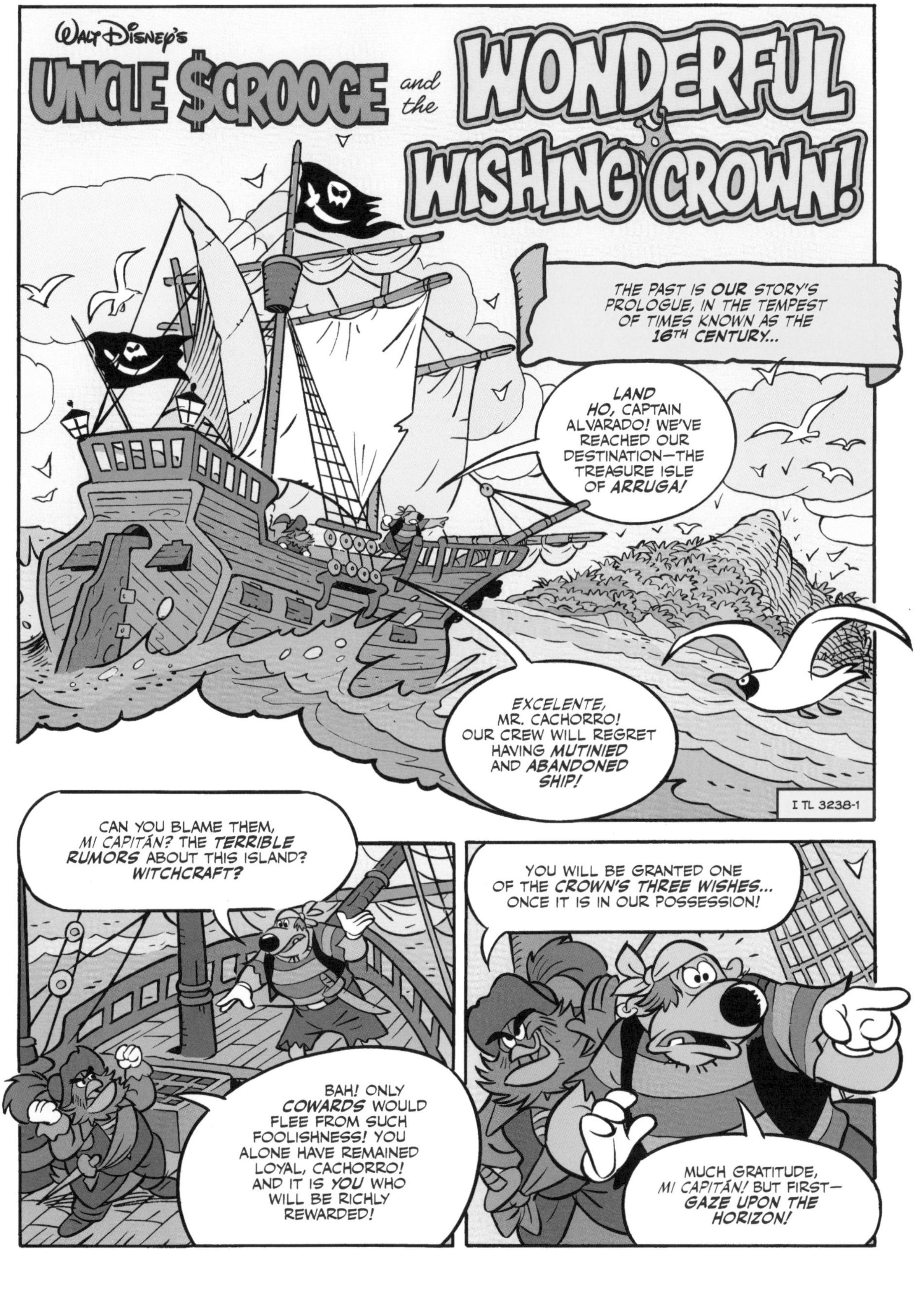

WALT DISNEY'S UNCLE $CROOGE and the WONDERFUL WISHING CROWN!
THE PAST IS OUR STORY'S PROLOGUE, IN THE TEMPEST OF TIMES KNOWN AS THE 16TH CENTURY...
LAND HO, CAPTAIN ALVARADO! WE'VE REACHED OUR DESTINATION—THE TREASURE ISLE OF ARRUGA!
EXCELENTE, MR. CACHORRO! OUR CREW WILL REGRET HAVING MUTINIED AND ABANDONED SHIP!
I TL 3238-1
CAN YOU BLAME THEM, MI CAPITÁN? THE TERRIBLE RUMORS ABOUT THIS ISLAND? WITCHCRAFT?
BAH! ONLY COWARDS WOULD FLEE FROM SUCH FOOLISHNESS! YOU ALONE HAVE REMAINED LOYAL, CACHORRO! AND IT IS YOU WHO WILL BE RICHLY REWARDED!
YOU WILL BE GRANTED ONE OF THE CROWN'S THREE WISHES... ONCE IT IS IN OUR POSSESSION!
MUCH GRATITUDE, MI CAPITÁN! BUT FIRST—GAZE UPON THE HORIZON!

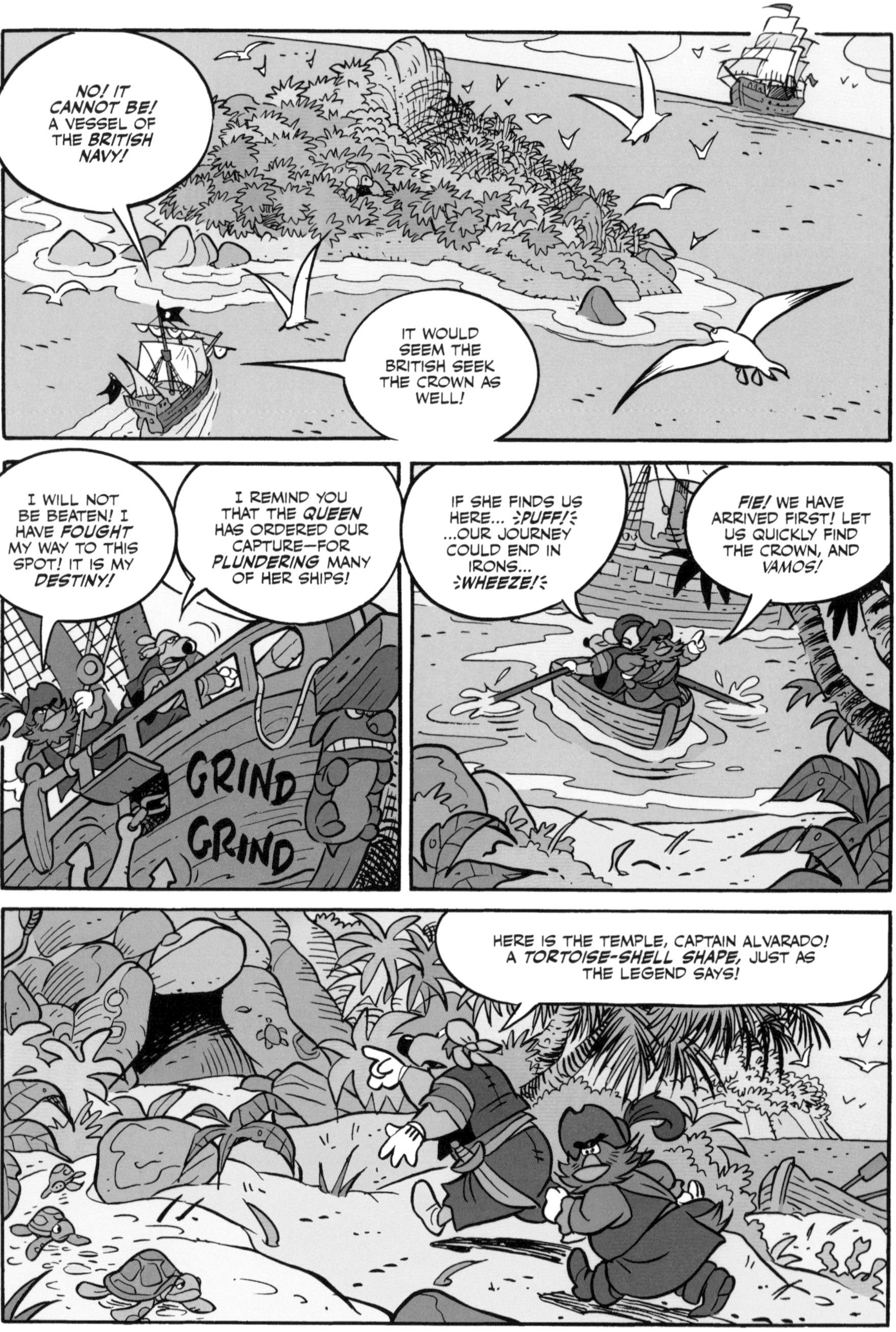
NO! IT CANNOT BE! A VESSEL OF THE BRITISH NAVY!
IT WOULD SEEM THE BRITISH SEEK THE CROWN AS WELL!
I WILL NOT BE BEATEN! I HAVE FOUGHT MY WAY TO THIS SPOT! IT IS MY DESTINY!
I REMIND YOU THAT THE QUEEN HAS ORDERED OUR CAPTURE—FOR PLUNDERING MANY OF HER SHIPS!
GRIND GRIND
IF SHE FINDS US HERE... PUFF! ...OUR JOURNEY COULD END IN IRONS... WHEEZE!
FIE! WE HAVE ARRIVED FIRST! LET US QUICKLY FIND THE CROWN, AND VAMOS!
HERE IS THE TEMPLE, CAPTAIN ALVARADO! A TORTOISE-SHELL SHAPE, JUST AS THE LEGEND SAYS!

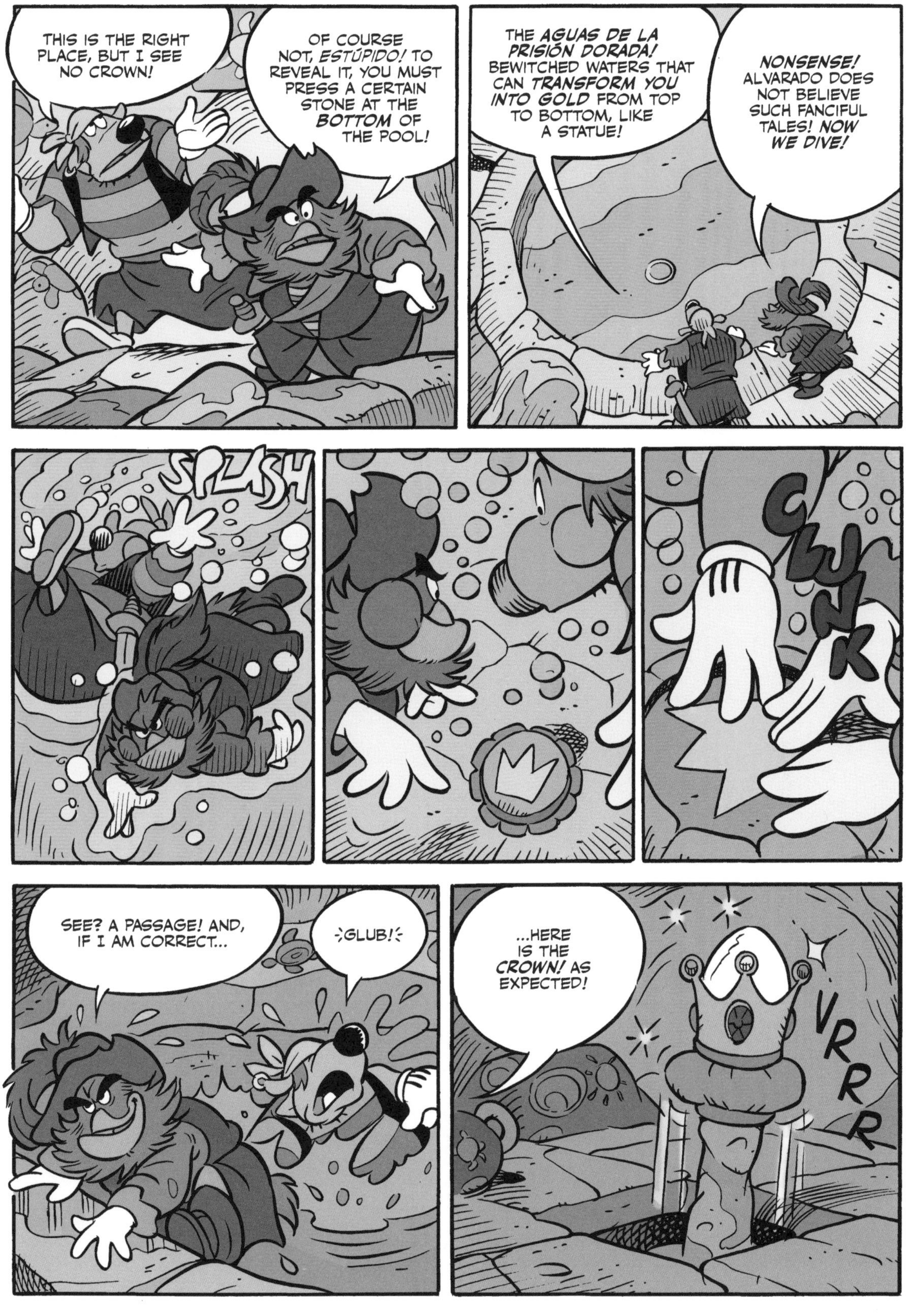
THIS IS THE RIGHT PLACE, BUT I SEE NO CROWN!
OF COURSE NOT, ESTÚPIDO! TO REVEAL IT, YOU MUST PRESS A CERTAIN STONE AT THE BOTTOM OF THE POOL!
THE AGUAS DE LA PRISIÓN DORADA! BEWITCHED WATERS THAT CAN TRANSFORM YOU INTO GOLD FROM TOP TO BOTTOM, LIKE A STATUE!
NONSENSE! ALVARADO DOES NOT BELIEVE SUCH FANCIFUL TALES! NOW WE DIVE!
SPLASH
CLUNK
SEE? A PASSAGE! AND, IF I AM CORRECT...
GLUB!
...HERE IS THE CROWN! AS EXPECTED!
VRRR

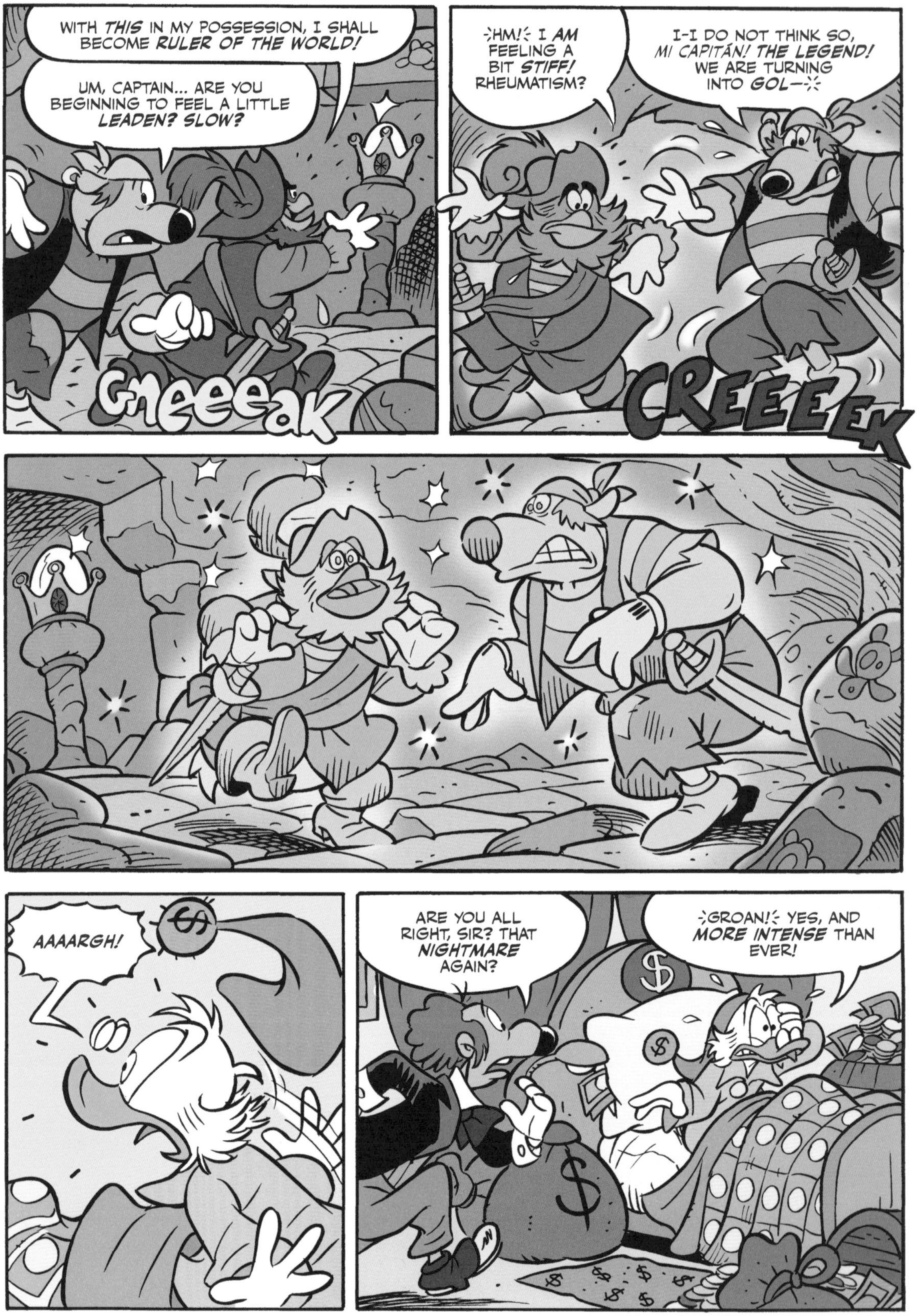

WITH *THIS* IN MY POSSESSION, I SHALL BECOME *RULER OF THE WORLD!*
UM, CAPTAIN... ARE YOU BEGINNING TO FEEL A LITTLE *LEADEN? SLOW?*
GNEEEAK
HM! I *AM* FEELING A BIT *STIFF!* RHEUMATISM?
I-I DO NOT THINK SO, *MI CAPITÁN! THE LEGEND!* WE ARE TURNING INTO *GOL—*
CREEEEK
AAAARGH!
ARE YOU ALL RIGHT, SIR? THAT *NIGHTMARE* AGAIN?
GROAN! YES, AND *MORE INTENSE* THAN EVER!

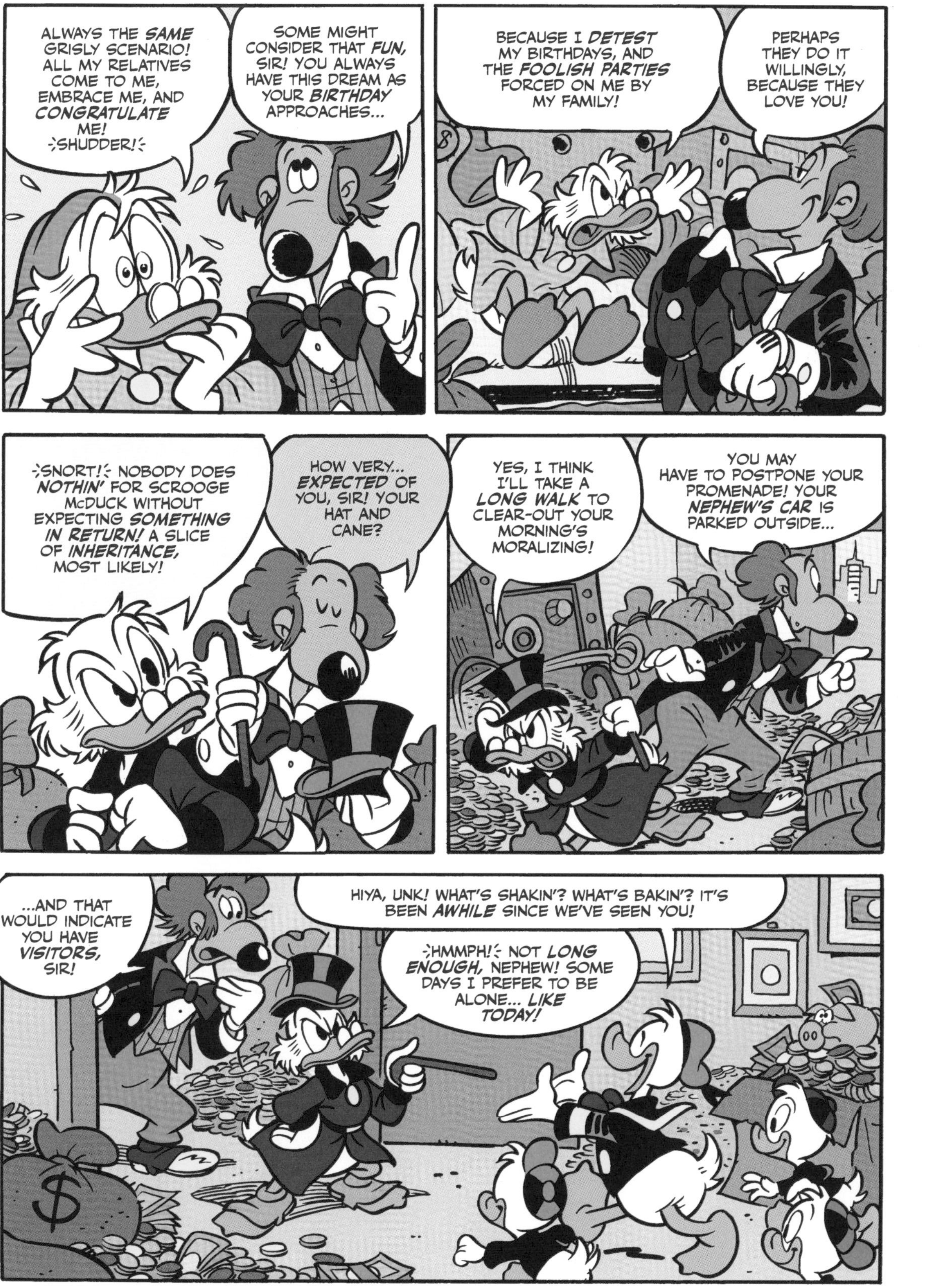
ALWAYS THE SAME GRISLY SCENARIO! ALL MY RELATIVES COME TO ME, EMBRACE ME, AND CONGRATULATE ME! -SHUDDER!-
SOME MIGHT CONSIDER THAT FUN, SIR! YOU ALWAYS HAVE THIS DREAM AS YOUR BIRTHDAY APPROACHES...
BECAUSE I DETEST MY BIRTHDAYS, AND THE FOOLISH PARTIES FORCED ON ME BY MY FAMILY!
PERHAPS THEY DO IT WILLINGLY, BECAUSE THEY LOVE YOU!
-SNORT!- NOBODY DOES NOTHIN' FOR SCROOGE McDUCK WITHOUT EXPECTING SOMETHING IN RETURN! A SLICE OF INHERITANCE, MOST LIKELY!
HOW VERY... EXPECTED OF YOU, SIR! YOUR HAT AND CANE?
YES, I THINK I'LL TAKE A LONG WALK TO CLEAR-OUT YOUR MORNING'S MORALIZING!
YOU MAY HAVE TO POSTPONE YOUR PROMENADE! YOUR NEPHEW'S CAR IS PARKED OUTSIDE...
...AND THAT WOULD INDICATE YOU HAVE VISITORS, SIR!
HIYA, UNK! WHAT'S SHAKIN'? WHAT'S BAKIN'? IT'S BEEN AWHILE SINCE WE'VE SEEN YOU!
-HMMPH!- NOT LONG ENOUGH, NEPHEW! SOME DAYS I PREFER TO BE ALONE... LIKE TODAY!

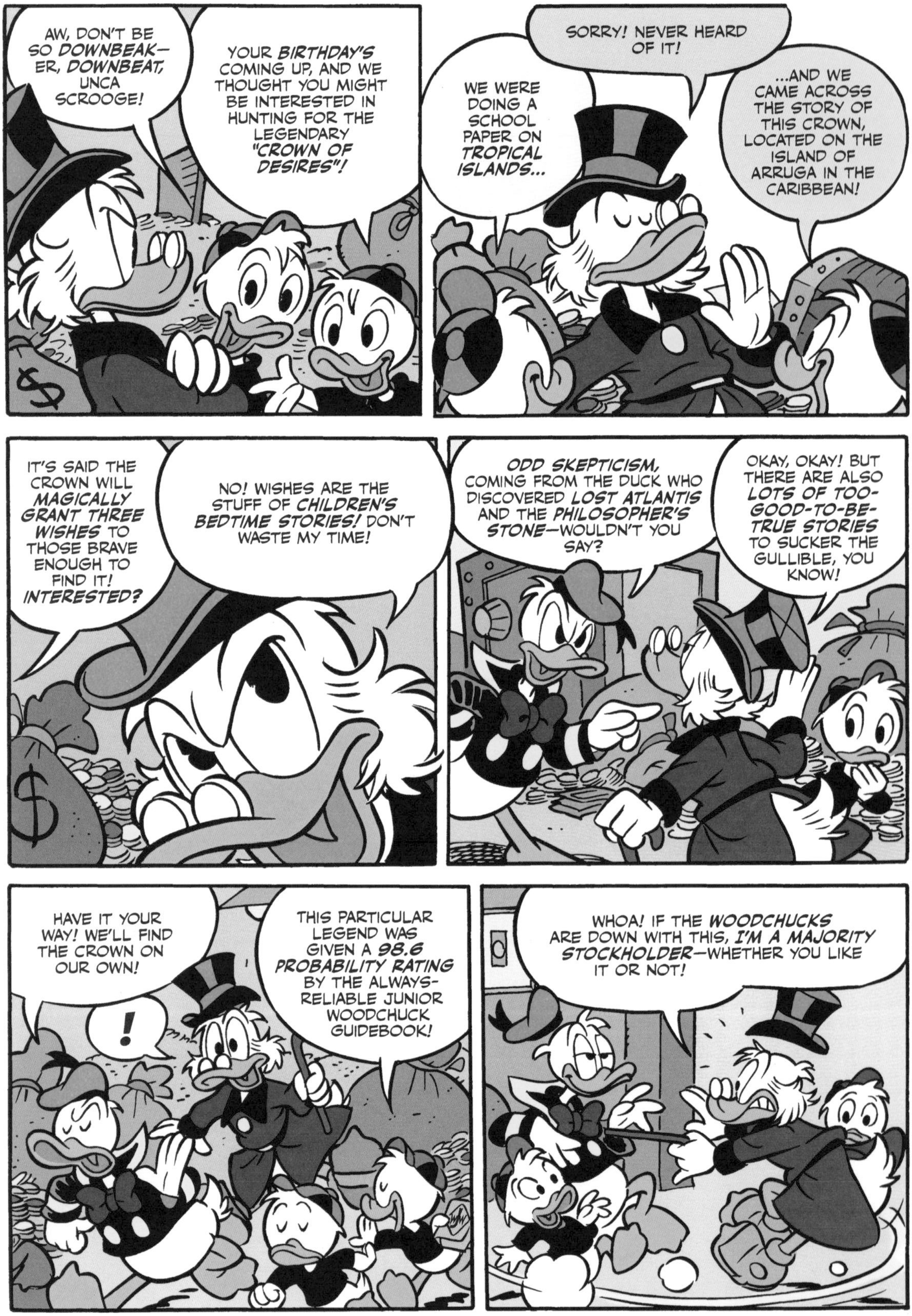
AW, DON'T BE SO DOWNBEAK-ER, DOWNBEAT, UNCA SCROOGE!
YOUR BIRTHDAY'S COMING UP, AND WE THOUGHT YOU MIGHT BE INTERESTED IN HUNTING FOR THE LEGENDARY "CROWN OF DESIRES"!
SORRY! NEVER HEARD OF IT!
WE WERE DOING A SCHOOL PAPER ON TROPICAL ISLANDS...
...AND WE CAME ACROSS THE STORY OF THIS CROWN, LOCATED ON THE ISLAND OF ARRUGA IN THE CARIBBEAN!
IT'S SAID THE CROWN WILL MAGICALLY GRANT THREE WISHES TO THOSE BRAVE ENOUGH TO FIND IT! INTERESTED?
NO! WISHES ARE THE STUFF OF CHILDREN'S BEDTIME STORIES! DON'T WASTE MY TIME!
ODD SKEPTICISM, COMING FROM THE DUCK WHO DISCOVERED LOST ATLANTIS AND THE PHILOSOPHER'S STONE—WOULDN'T YOU SAY?
OKAY, OKAY! BUT THERE ARE ALSO LOTS OF TOO-GOOD-TO-BE-TRUE STORIES TO SUCKER THE GULLIBLE, YOU KNOW!
HAVE IT YOUR WAY! WE'LL FIND THE CROWN ON OUR OWN!
THIS PARTICULAR LEGEND WAS GIVEN A 98.6 PROBABILITY RATING BY THE ALWAYS-RELIABLE JUNIOR WOODCHUCK GUIDEBOOK!
!
WHOA! IF THE WOODCHUCKS ARE DOWN WITH THIS, I'M A MAJORITY STOCKHOLDER—WHETHER YOU LIKE IT OR NOT!

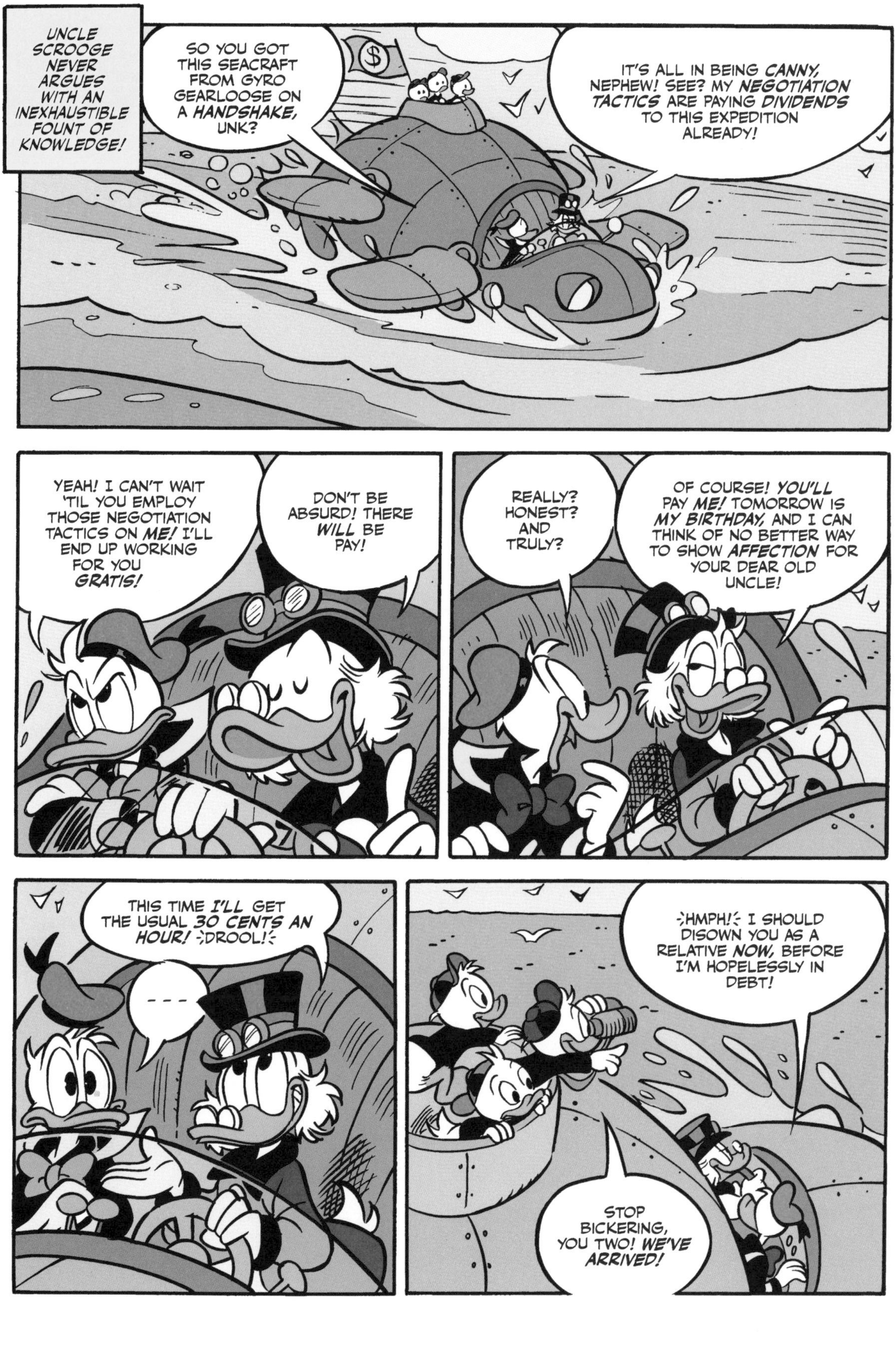

UNCLE SCROOGE NEVER ARGUES WITH AN INEXHAUSTIBLE FOUNT OF KNOWLEDGE!
SO YOU GOT THIS SEACRAFT FROM GYRO GEARLOOSE ON A HANDSHAKE, UNK?
IT'S ALL IN BEING CANNY, NEPHEW! SEE? MY NEGOTIATION TACTICS ARE PAYING DIVIDENDS TO THIS EXPEDITION ALREADY!
YEAH! I CAN'T WAIT 'TIL YOU EMPLOY THOSE NEGOTIATION TACTICS ON ME! I'LL END UP WORKING FOR YOU GRATIS!
DON'T BE ABSURD! THERE WILL BE PAY!
REALLY? HONEST? AND TRULY?
OF COURSE! YOU'LL PAY ME! TOMORROW IS MY BIRTHDAY, AND I CAN THINK OF NO BETTER WAY TO SHOW AFFECTION FOR YOUR DEAR OLD UNCLE!
THIS TIME I'LL GET THE USUAL 30 CENTS AN HOUR! DROOL!
- - -
HMPH! I SHOULD DISOWN YOU AS A RELATIVE NOW, BEFORE I'M HOPELESSLY IN DEBT!
STOP BICKERING, YOU TWO! WE'VE ARRIVED!

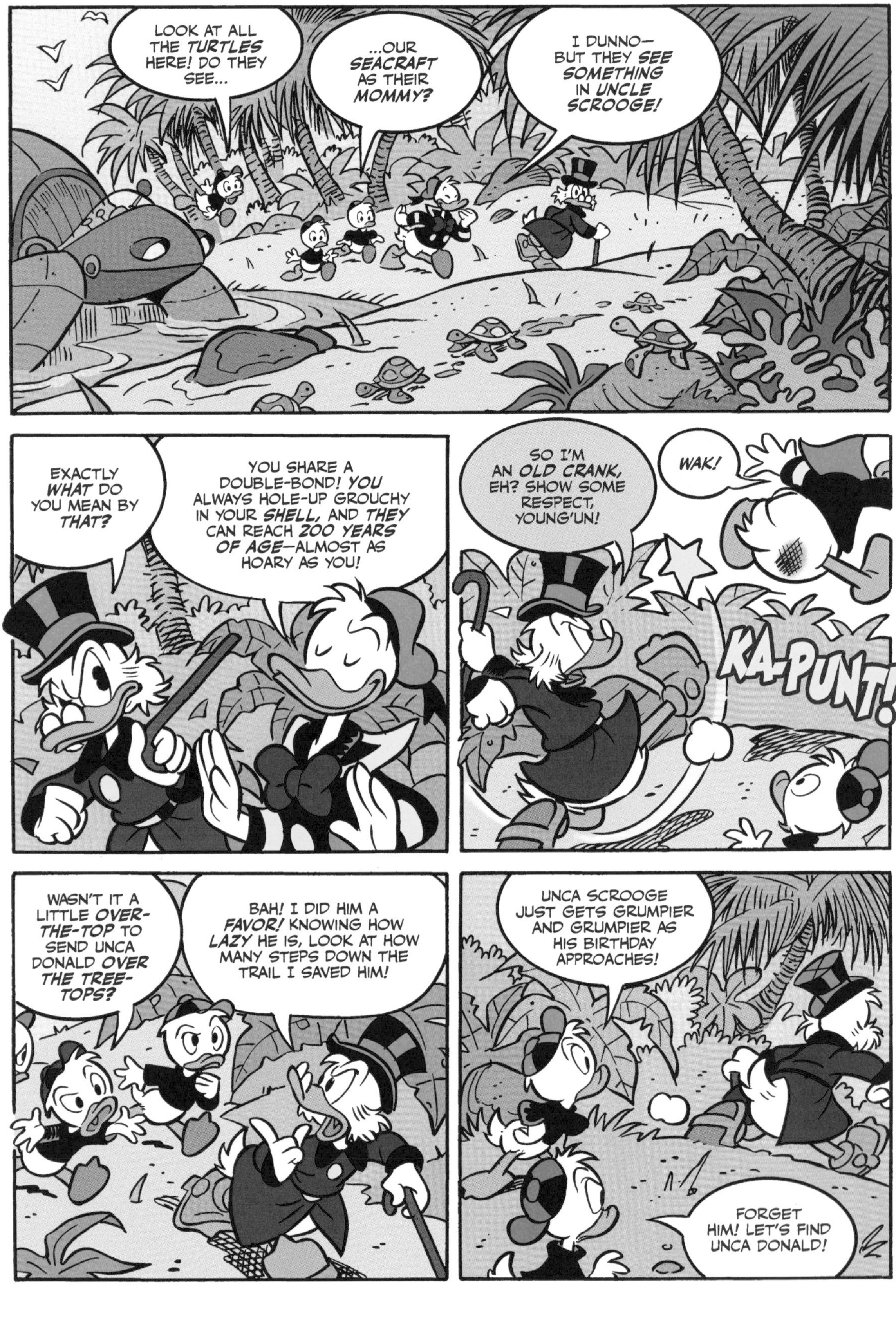
LOOK AT ALL THE TURTLES HERE! DO THEY SEE...
...OUR SEACRAFT AS THEIR MOMMY?
I DUNNO— BUT THEY SEE SOMETHING IN UNCLE SCROOGE!
EXACTLY WHAT DO YOU MEAN BY THAT?
YOU SHARE A DOUBLE-BOND! YOU ALWAYS HOLE-UP GROUCHY IN YOUR SHELL, AND THEY CAN REACH 200 YEARS OF AGE—ALMOST AS HOARY AS YOU!
SO I'M AN OLD CRANK, EH? SHOW SOME RESPECT, YOUNG'UN!
WAK!
KA-PUNT!
WASN'T IT A LITTLE OVER-THE-TOP TO SEND UNCA DONALD OVER THE TREE-TOPS?
BAH! I DID HIM A FAVOR! KNOWING HOW LAZY HE IS, LOOK AT HOW MANY STEPS DOWN THE TRAIL I SAVED HIM!
UNCA SCROOGE JUST GETS GRUMPIER AND GRUMPIER AS HIS BIRTHDAY APPROACHES!
FORGET HIM! LET'S FIND UNCA DONALD!

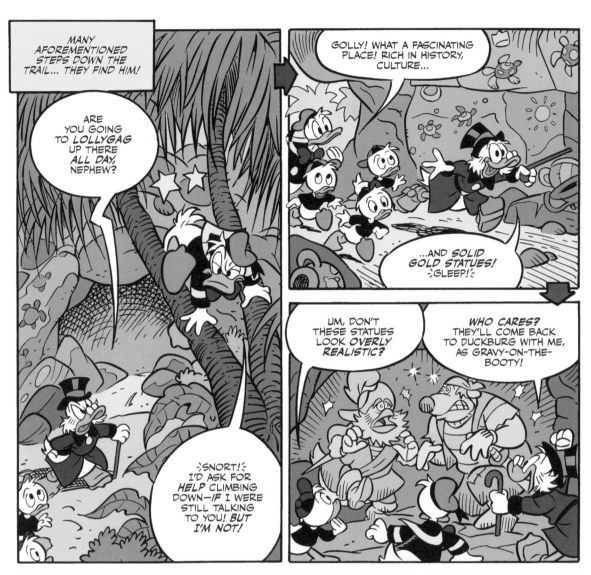

MANY AFOREMENTIONED STEPS DOWN THE TRAIL... THEY FIND HIM!

ARE YOU GOING TO *LOLLYGAG* UP THERE *ALL DAY*, NEPHEW?

÷SNORT!÷ I'D ASK FOR *HELP* CLIMBING DOWN—*IF* I WERE STILL TALKING TO YOU! *BUT I'M NOT!*

GOLLY! WHAT A FASCINATING PLACE! RICH IN HISTORY, CULTURE...

...AND *SOLID GOLD STATUES!* ÷GLEEP!÷

UM, DON'T THESE STATUES LOOK *OVERLY REALISTIC?*

WHO CARES? THEY'LL COME BACK TO DUCKBURG WITH ME, AS GRAVY-ON-THE-BOOTY!

SPEAKING OF THE BOOTY, WHERE'S THAT *CROWN?* LOST IN SOME LABYRINTH, PERHAPS?

OR MAYBE IT'S *RIGHT OVER THERE!*

MY STARS AND LITTLE COMETS! *HERE SHE IS*, IN ALL HER GLITTERING WONDER!

SOMEONE MUST HAVE *DISCOVERED* IT, BUT *WASN'T ABLE TO TAKE IT!* ...WHO?

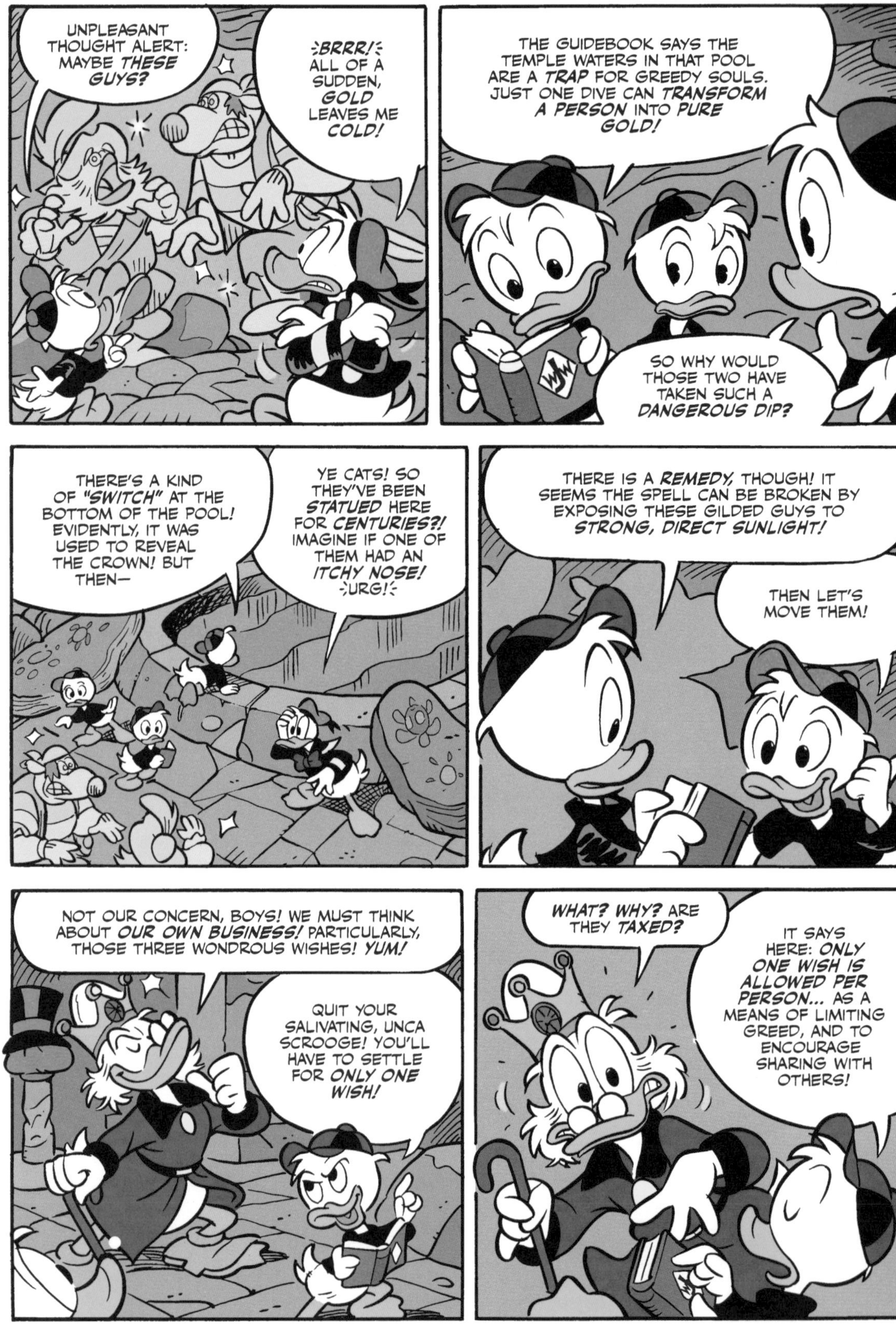
UNPLEASANT THOUGHT ALERT: MAYBE *THESE GUYS?*
BRRR! ALL OF A SUDDEN, *GOLD* LEAVES ME *COLD!*
THE GUIDEBOOK SAYS THE TEMPLE WATERS IN THAT POOL ARE A *TRAP* FOR GREEDY SOULS. JUST ONE DIVE CAN *TRANSFORM A PERSON* INTO *PURE GOLD!*
SO WHY WOULD THOSE TWO HAVE TAKEN SUCH A *DANGEROUS DIP?*
THERE'S A KIND OF *"SWITCH"* AT THE BOTTOM OF THE POOL! EVIDENTLY, IT WAS USED TO REVEAL THE CROWN! BUT THEN—
YE CATS! SO THEY'VE BEEN *STATUED* HERE FOR *CENTURIES?!* IMAGINE IF ONE OF THEM HAD AN *ITCHY NOSE!* URG!
THERE IS A *REMEDY,* THOUGH! IT SEEMS THE SPELL CAN BE BROKEN BY EXPOSING THESE GILDED GUYS TO *STRONG, DIRECT SUNLIGHT!*
THEN LET'S MOVE THEM!
NOT OUR CONCERN, BOYS! WE MUST THINK ABOUT *OUR OWN BUSINESS!* PARTICULARLY, THOSE THREE WONDROUS WISHES! *YUM!*
QUIT YOUR SALIVATING, UNCA SCROOGE! YOU'LL HAVE TO SETTLE FOR *ONLY ONE WISH!*
WHAT? WHY? ARE THEY *TAXED?*
IT SAYS HERE: *ONLY ONE WISH IS ALLOWED PER PERSON...* AS A MEANS OF LIMITING GREED, AND TO ENCOURAGE SHARING WITH OTHERS!

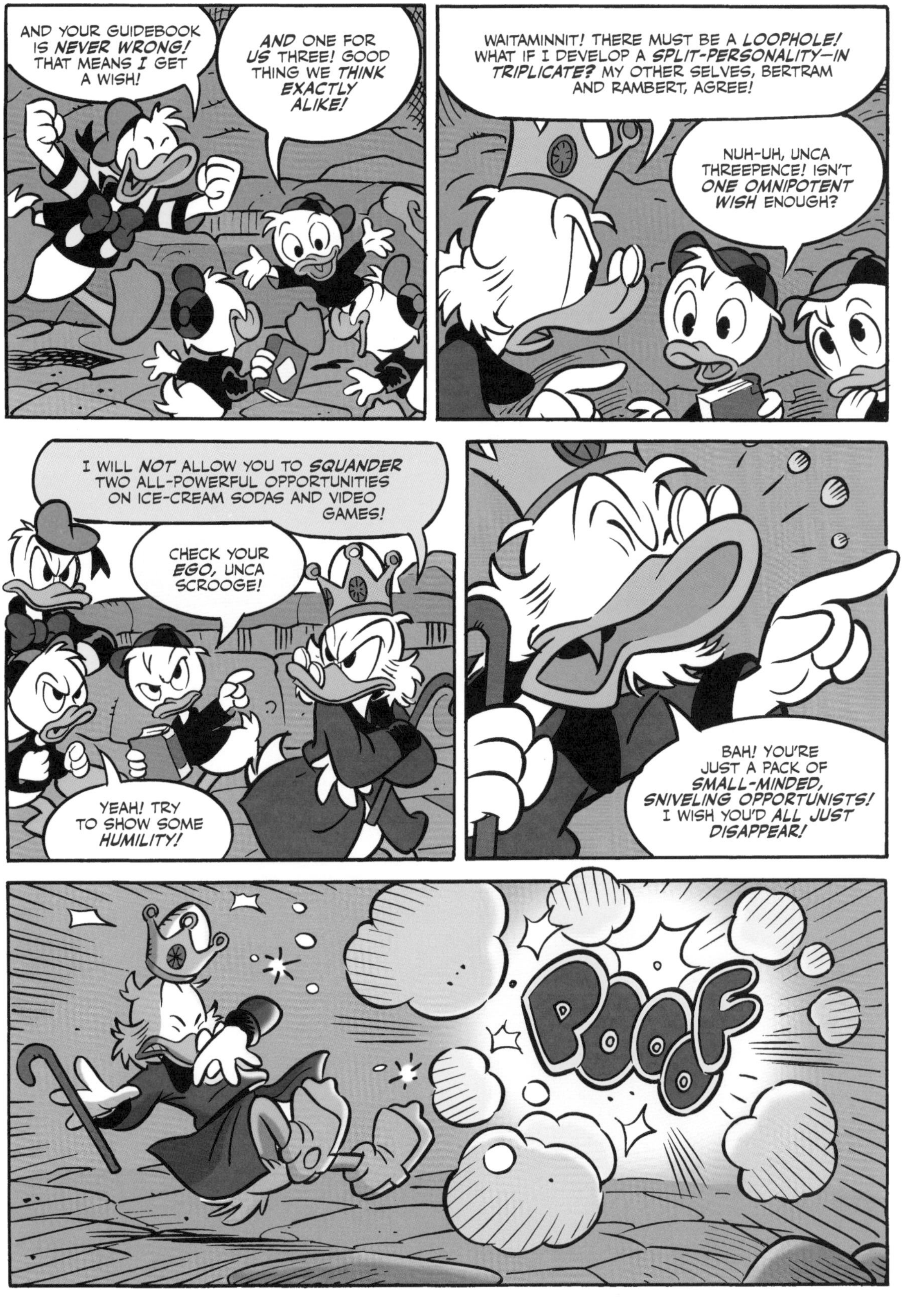
AND YOUR GUIDEBOOK IS NEVER WRONG! THAT MEANS I GET A WISH!
AND ONE FOR US THREE! GOOD THING WE THINK EXACTLY ALIKE!
WAITAMINNIT! THERE MUST BE A LOOPHOLE! WHAT IF I DEVELOP A SPLIT-PERSONALITY—IN TRIPLICATE? MY OTHER SELVES, BERTRAM AND RAMBERT, AGREE!
NUH-UH, UNCA THREEPENCE! ISN'T ONE OMNIPOTENT WISH ENOUGH?
I WILL NOT ALLOW YOU TO SQUANDER TWO ALL-POWERFUL OPPORTUNITIES ON ICE-CREAM SODAS AND VIDEO GAMES!
CHECK YOUR EGO, UNCA SCROOGE!
YEAH! TRY TO SHOW SOME HUMILITY!
BAH! YOU'RE JUST A PACK OF SMALL-MINDED, SNIVELING OPPORTUNISTS! I WISH YOU'D ALL JUST DISAPPEAR!
POOOF

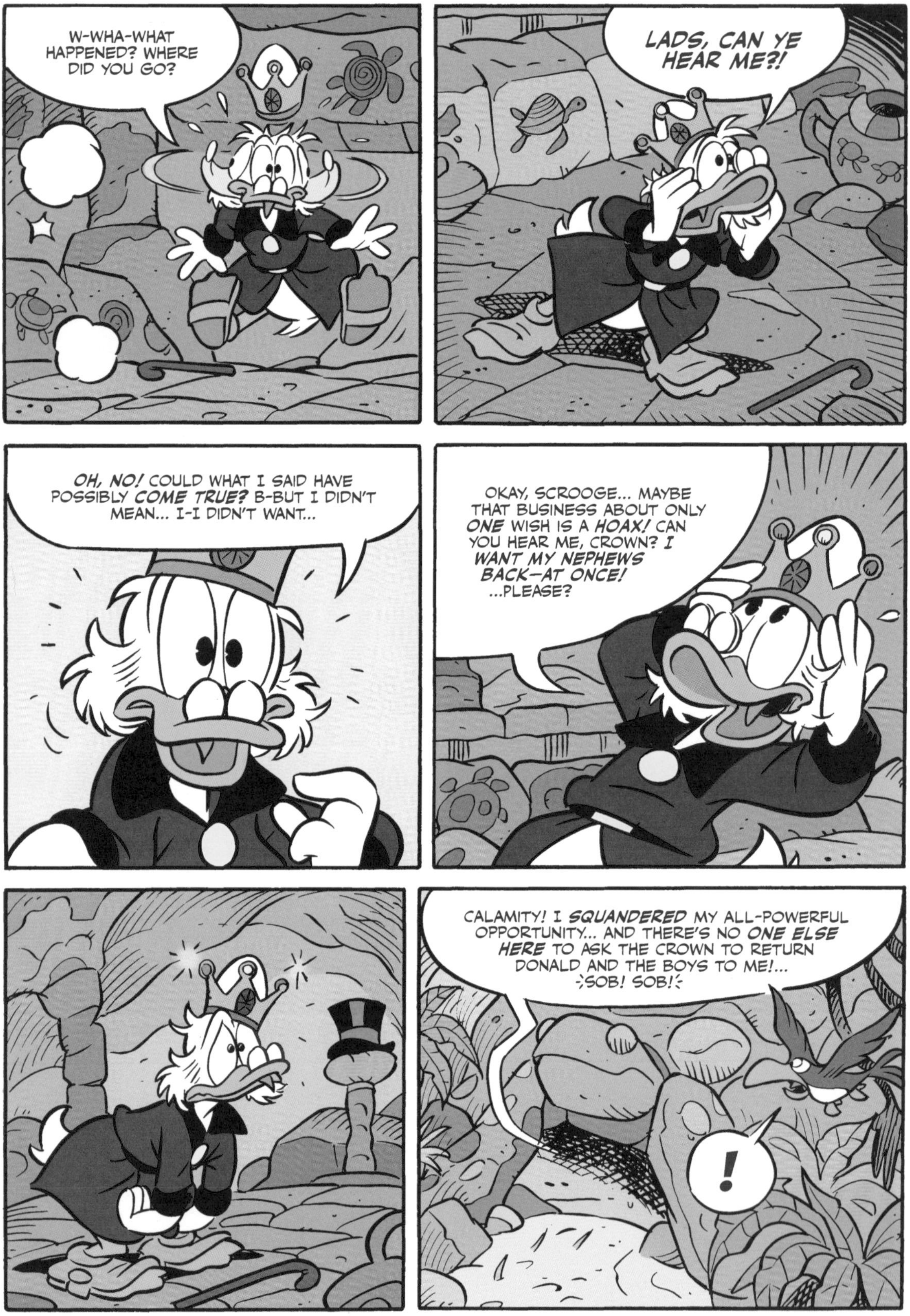
W-WHA-WHAT HAPPENED? WHERE DID YOU GO?
LADS, CAN YE HEAR ME?!
OH, NO! COULD WHAT I SAID HAVE POSSIBLY COME TRUE? B-BUT I DIDN'T MEAN... I-I DIDN'T WANT...
OKAY, SCROOGE... MAYBE THAT BUSINESS ABOUT ONLY ONE WISH IS A HOAX! CAN YOU HEAR ME, CROWN? I WANT MY NEPHEWS BACK—AT ONCE! ...PLEASE?
CALAMITY! I SQUANDERED MY ALL-POWERFUL OPPORTUNITY... AND THERE'S NO ONE ELSE HERE TO ASK THE CROWN TO RETURN DONALD AND THE BOYS TO ME!... SOB! SOB!
!

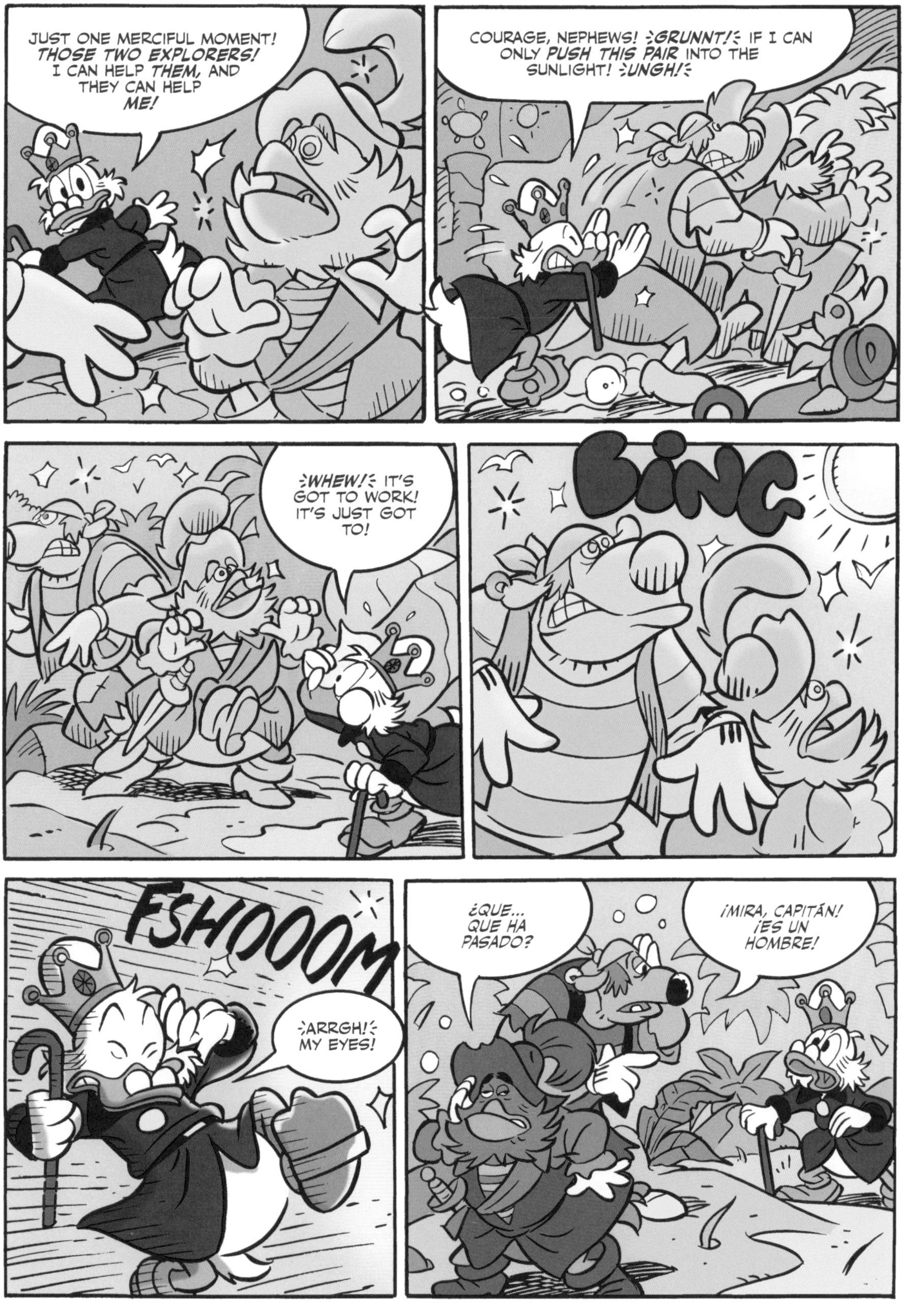
JUST ONE MERCIFUL MOMENT! THOSE TWO EXPLORERS! I CAN HELP THEM, AND THEY CAN HELP ME!
COURAGE, NEPHEWS! GRUNNT! IF I CAN ONLY PUSH THIS PAIR INTO THE SUNLIGHT! UNGH!
WHEW! IT'S GOT TO WORK! IT'S JUST GOT TO!
BING
FSHOOOM
ARRGH! MY EYES!
¿QUE... QUE HA PASADO?
¡MIRA, CAPITÁN! ¡ES UN HOMBRE!

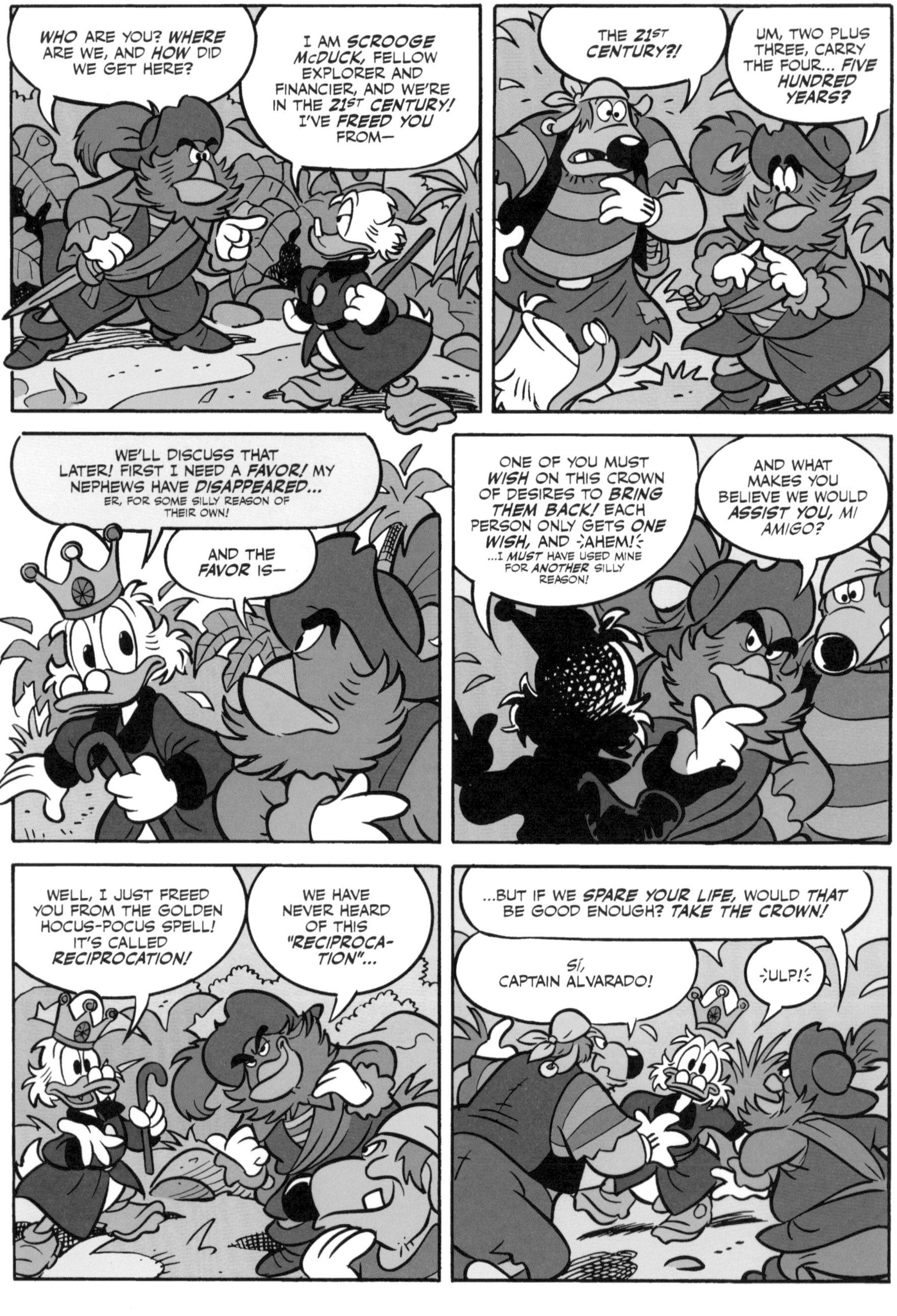
WHO ARE YOU? WHERE ARE WE, AND HOW DID WE GET HERE?
I AM SCROOGE McDUCK, FELLOW EXPLORER AND FINANCIER, AND WE'RE IN THE 21ST CENTURY! I'VE FREED YOU FROM—
THE 21ST CENTURY?!
UM, TWO PLUS THREE, CARRY THE FOUR... FIVE HUNDRED YEARS?
WE'LL DISCUSS THAT LATER! FIRST I NEED A FAVOR! MY NEPHEWS HAVE DISAPPEARED... ER, FOR SOME SILLY REASON OF THEIR OWN!
AND THE FAVOR IS—
ONE OF YOU MUST WISH ON THIS CROWN OF DESIRES TO BRING THEM BACK! EACH PERSON ONLY GETS ONE WISH, AND AHEM! ...I MUST HAVE USED MINE FOR ANOTHER SILLY REASON!
AND WHAT MAKES YOU BELIEVE WE WOULD ASSIST YOU, MI AMIGO?
WELL, I JUST FREED YOU FROM THE GOLDEN HOCUS-POCUS SPELL! IT'S CALLED RECIPROCATION!
WE HAVE NEVER HEARD OF THIS "RECIPROCATION"...
...BUT IF WE SPARE YOUR LIFE, WOULD THAT BE GOOD ENOUGH? TAKE THE CROWN!
SÍ, CAPTAIN ALVARADO!
ULP!

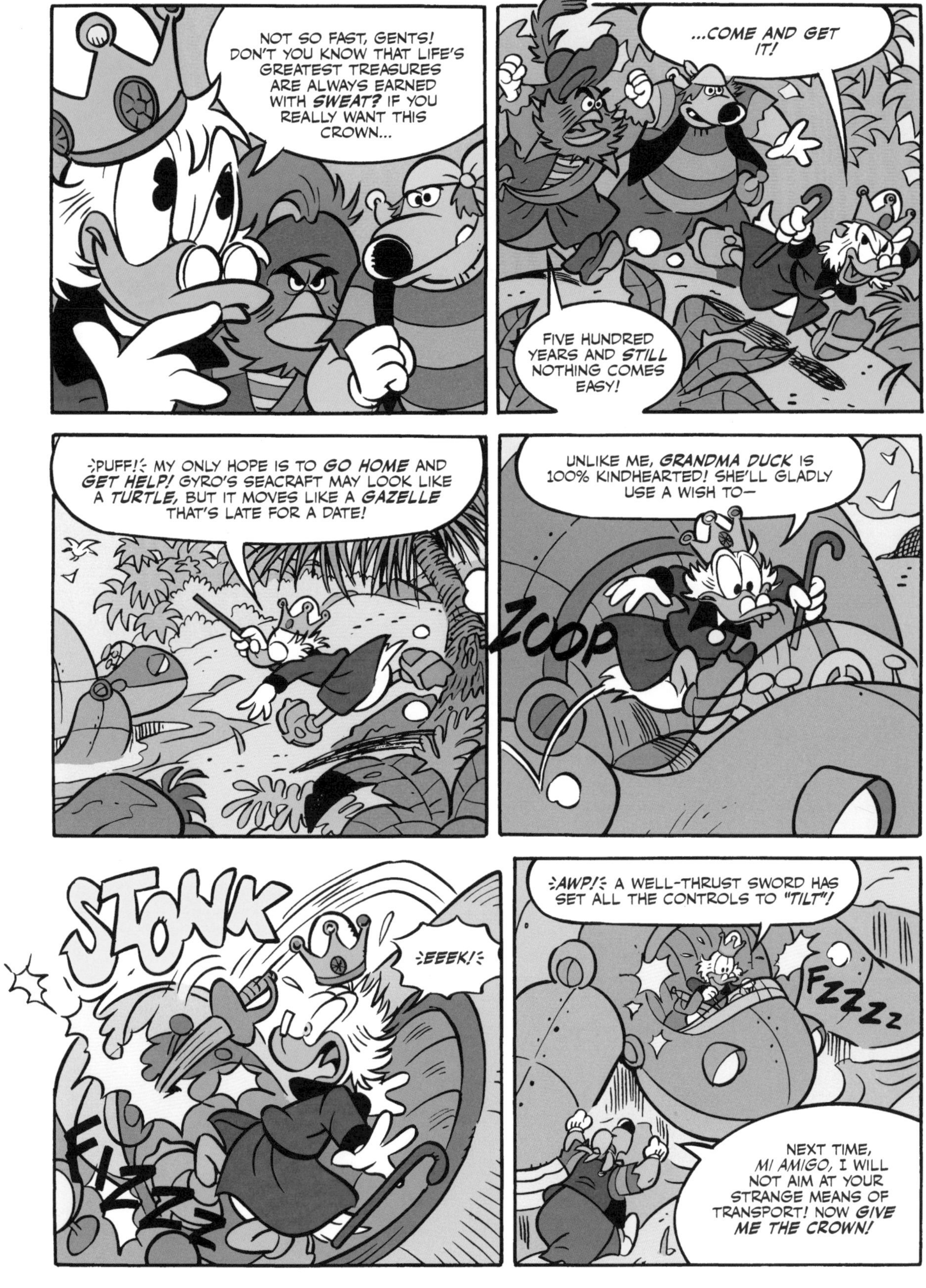
NOT SO FAST, GENTS! DON'T YOU KNOW THAT LIFE'S GREATEST TREASURES ARE ALWAYS EARNED WITH SWEAT? IF YOU REALLY WANT THIS CROWN...
...COME AND GET IT!
FIVE HUNDRED YEARS AND STILL NOTHING COMES EASY!
PUFF! MY ONLY HOPE IS TO GO HOME AND GET HELP! GYRO'S SEACRAFT MAY LOOK LIKE A TURTLE, BUT IT MOVES LIKE A GAZELLE THAT'S LATE FOR A DATE!
UNLIKE ME, GRANDMA DUCK IS 100% KINDHEARTED! SHE'LL GLADLY USE A WISH TO—
ZOOP
STONK
EEEK!
FIZZZZ
AWP! A WELL-THRUST SWORD HAS SET ALL THE CONTROLS TO "TILT"!
FZZZZZ
NEXT TIME, MI AMIGO, I WILL NOT AIM AT YOUR STRANGE MEANS OF TRANSPORT! NOW GIVE ME THE CROWN!

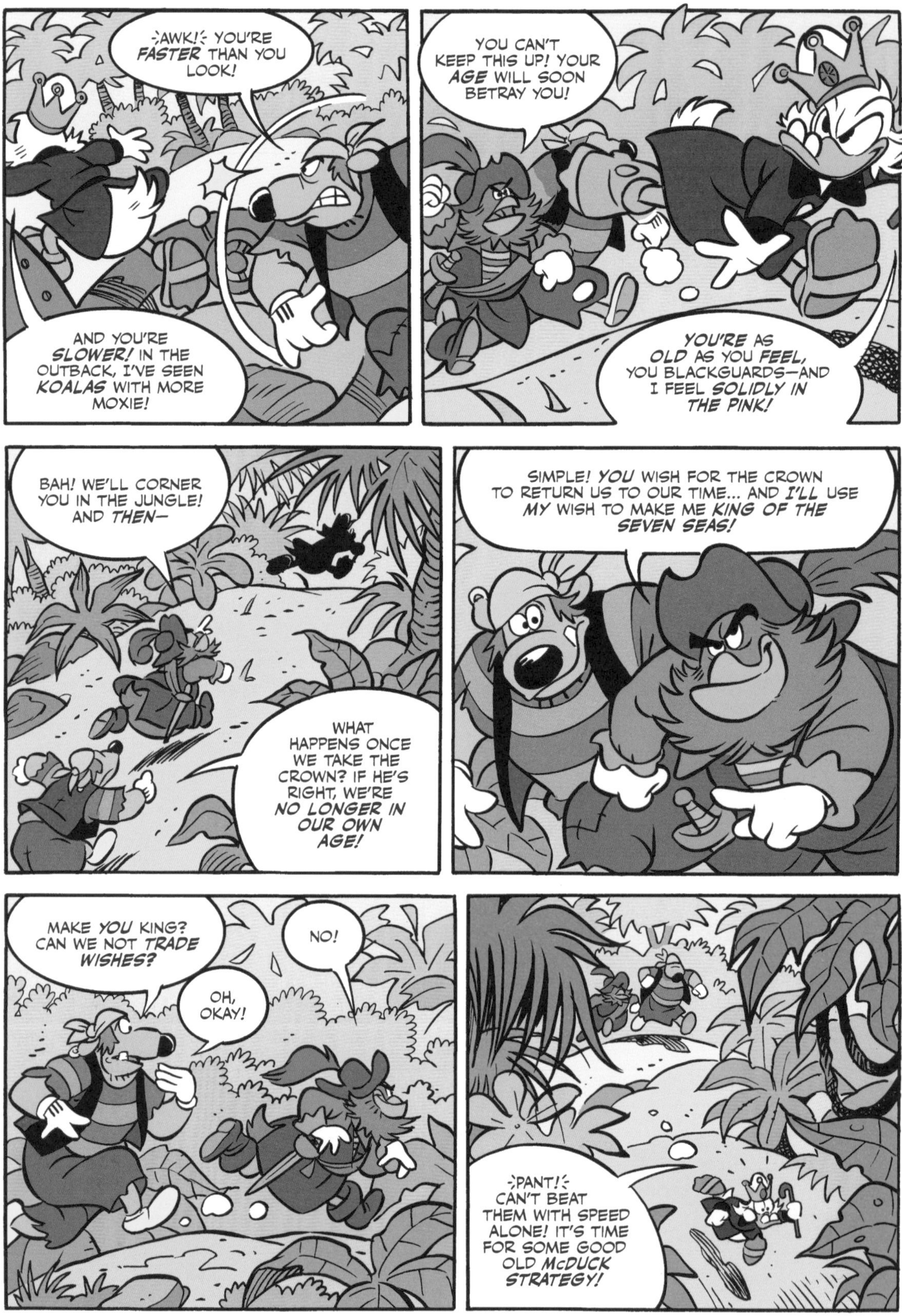

¦AWK!¦ YOU'RE FASTER THAN YOU LOOK!
AND YOU'RE SLOWER! IN THE OUTBACK, I'VE SEEN KOALAS WITH MORE MOXIE!
YOU CAN'T KEEP THIS UP! YOUR AGE WILL SOON BETRAY YOU!
YOU'RE AS OLD AS YOU FEEL, YOU BLACKGUARDS—AND I FEEL SOLIDLY IN THE PINK!
BAH! WE'LL CORNER YOU IN THE JUNGLE! AND THEN—
WHAT HAPPENS ONCE WE TAKE THE CROWN? IF HE'S RIGHT, WE'RE NO LONGER IN OUR OWN AGE!
SIMPLE! YOU WISH FOR THE CROWN TO RETURN US TO OUR TIME... AND I'LL USE MY WISH TO MAKE ME KING OF THE SEVEN SEAS!
MAKE YOU KING? CAN WE NOT TRADE WISHES?
NO!
OH, OKAY!
¦PANT!¦ CAN'T BEAT THEM WITH SPEED ALONE! IT'S TIME FOR SOME GOOD OLD McDUCK STRATEGY!

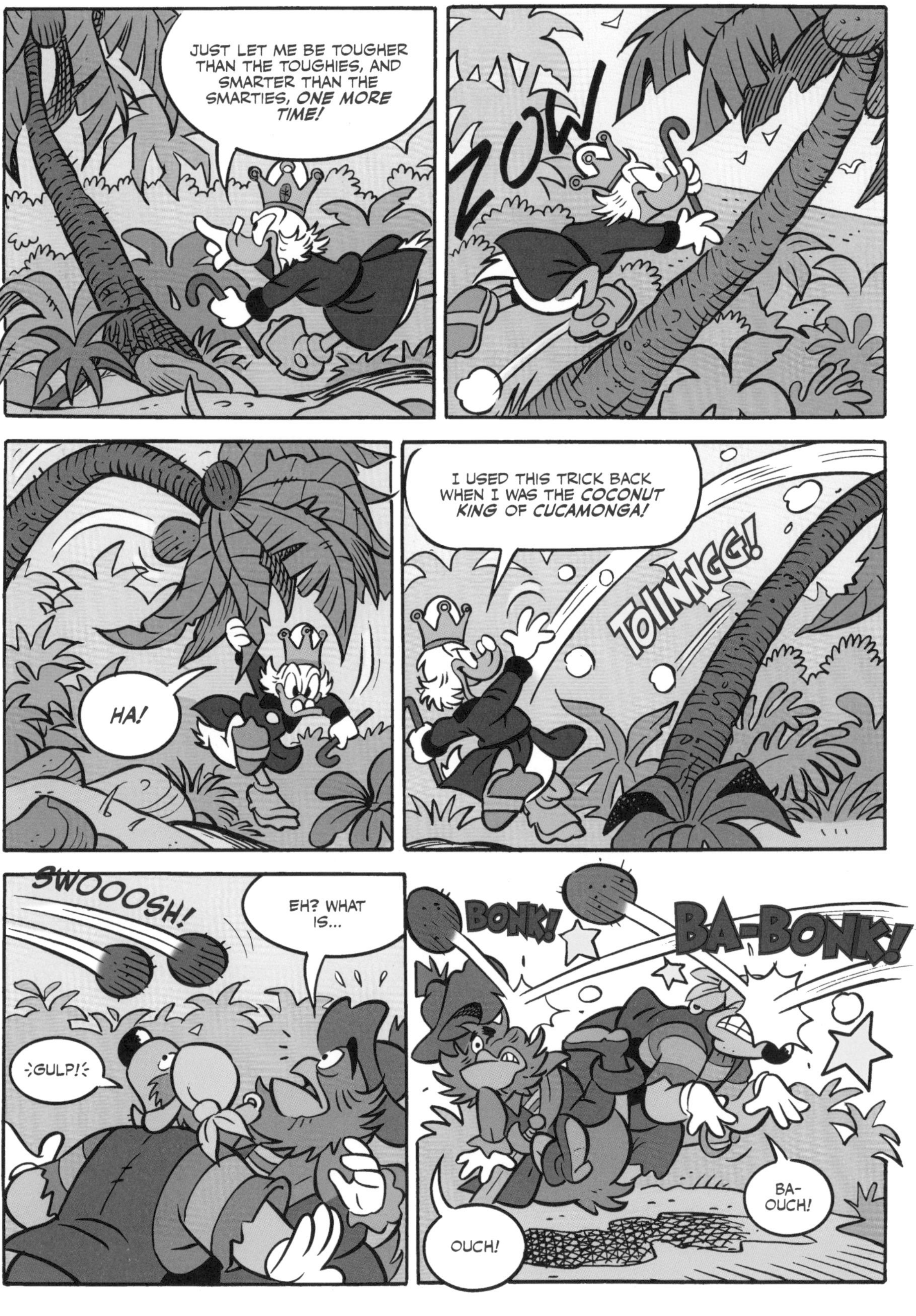
JUST LET ME BE TOUGHER THAN THE TOUGHIES, AND SMARTER THAN THE SMARTIES, ONE MORE TIME!
ZOW
I USED THIS TRICK BACK WHEN I WAS THE COCONUT KING OF CUCAMONGA!
HA!
TOINNGG!
SWOOOSH!
EH? WHAT IS...
GULP!
BONK!
BA-BONK!
BA-OUCH!
OUCH!

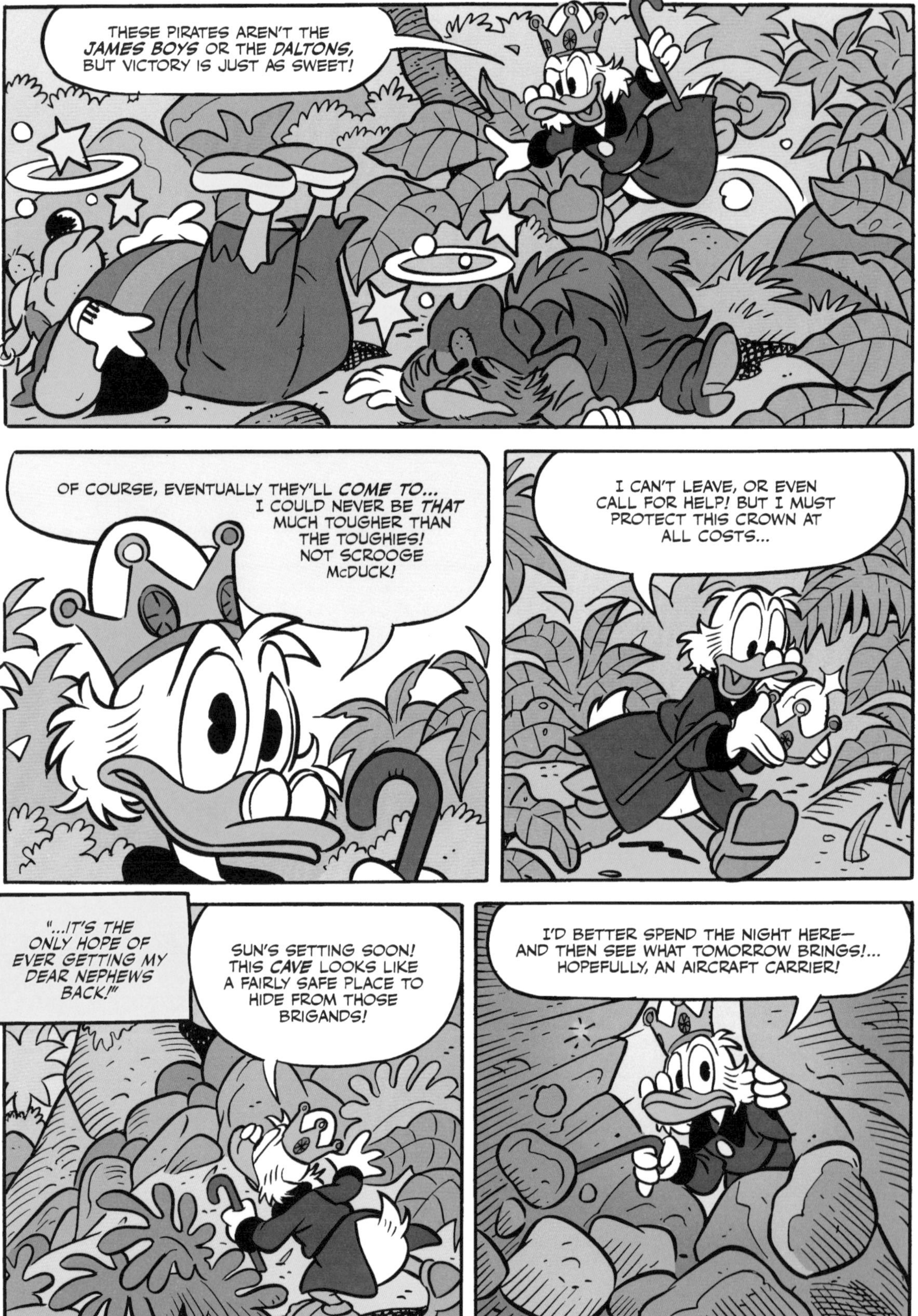

THESE PIRATES AREN'T THE *JAMES BOYS* OR THE *DALTONS,* BUT VICTORY IS JUST AS SWEET!
OF COURSE, EVENTUALLY THEY'LL *COME TO...* I COULD NEVER BE *THAT* MUCH TOUGHER THAN THE TOUGHIES! NOT SCROOGE McDUCK!
I CAN'T LEAVE, OR EVEN CALL FOR HELP! BUT I MUST PROTECT THIS CROWN AT ALL COSTS...
"...IT'S THE ONLY HOPE OF EVER GETTING MY DEAR NEPHEWS BACK!"
SUN'S SETTING SOON! THIS *CAVE* LOOKS LIKE A FAIRLY SAFE PLACE TO HIDE FROM THOSE BRIGANDS!
I'D BETTER SPEND THE NIGHT HERE— AND THEN SEE WHAT TOMORROW BRINGS!... HOPEFULLY, AN AIRCRAFT CARRIER!

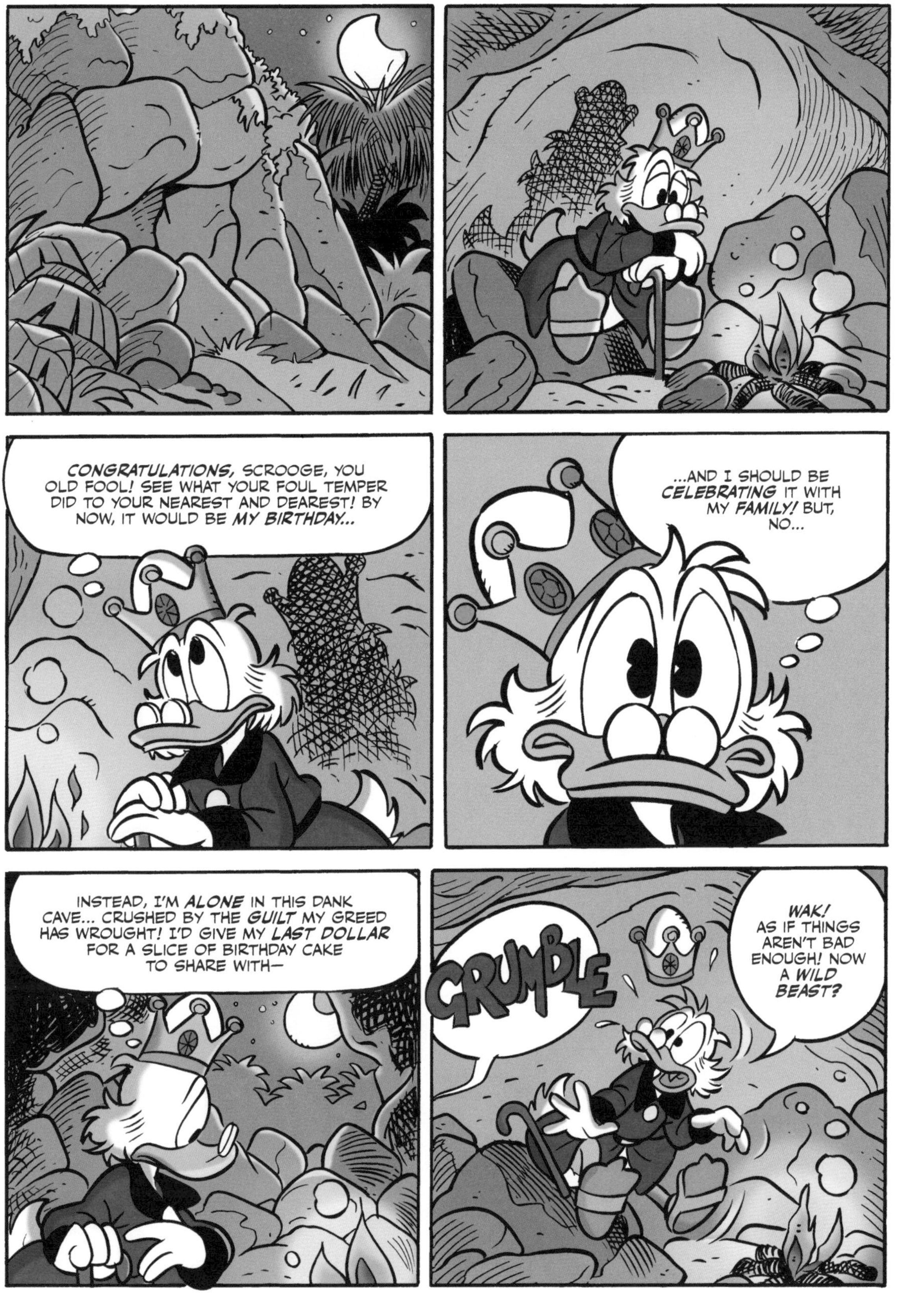
CONGRATULATIONS, SCROOGE, YOU OLD FOOL! SEE WHAT YOUR FOUL TEMPER DID TO YOUR NEAREST AND DEAREST! BY NOW, IT WOULD BE MY BIRTHDAY...
...AND I SHOULD BE CELEBRATING IT WITH MY FAMILY! BUT, NO...
INSTEAD, I'M ALONE IN THIS DANK CAVE... CRUSHED BY THE GUILT MY GREED HAS WROUGHT! I'D GIVE MY LAST DOLLAR FOR A SLICE OF BIRTHDAY CAKE TO SHARE WITH—
GRUMBLE
WAK! AS IF THINGS AREN'T BAD ENOUGH! NOW A WILD BEAST?

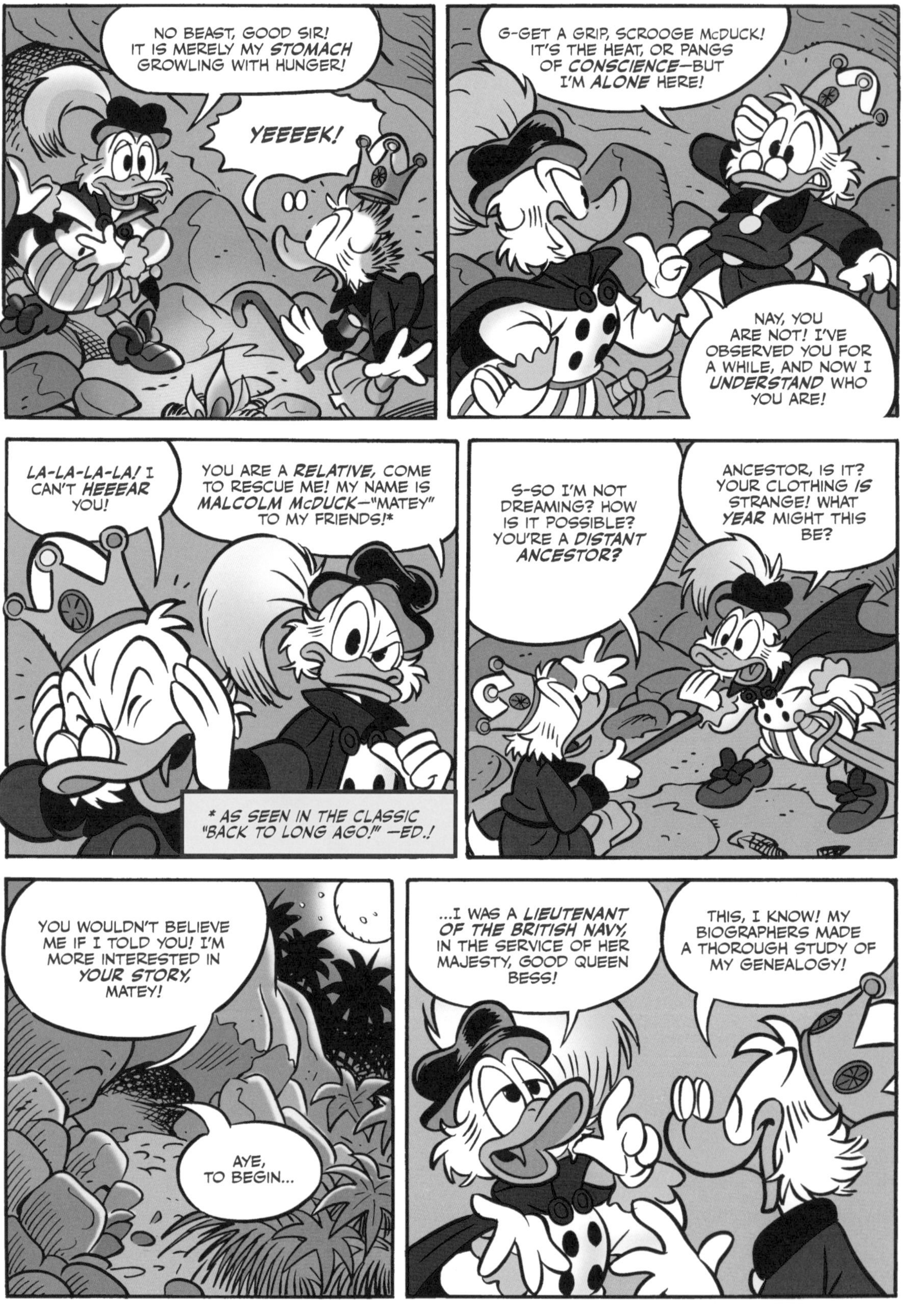

NO BEAST, GOOD SIR! IT IS MERELY MY *STOMACH* GROWLING WITH HUNGER!
YEEEEK!
G-GET A GRIP, SCROOGE McDUCK! IT'S THE HEAT, OR PANGS OF *CONSCIENCE*—BUT I'M *ALONE* HERE!
NAY, YOU ARE NOT! I'VE OBSERVED YOU FOR A WHILE, AND NOW I *UNDERSTAND* WHO YOU ARE!
LA-LA-LA-LA! I CAN'T *HEEEAR* YOU!
YOU ARE A *RELATIVE,* COME TO RESCUE ME! MY NAME IS *MALCOLM McDUCK*—"MATEY" TO MY FRIENDS!*
* AS SEEN IN THE CLASSIC "BACK TO LONG AGO!" —ED.!
S-SO I'M NOT DREAMING? HOW IS IT POSSIBLE? YOU'RE A *DISTANT ANCESTOR?*
ANCESTOR, IS IT? YOUR CLOTHING *IS* STRANGE! WHAT *YEAR* MIGHT THIS BE?
YOU WOULDN'T BELIEVE ME IF I TOLD YOU! I'M MORE INTERESTED IN *YOUR STORY,* MATEY!
AYE, TO BEGIN...
...I WAS A *LIEUTENANT OF THE BRITISH NAVY,* IN THE SERVICE OF HER MAJESTY, GOOD QUEEN BESS!
THIS, I KNOW! MY BIOGRAPHERS MADE A THOROUGH STUDY OF MY GENEALOGY!

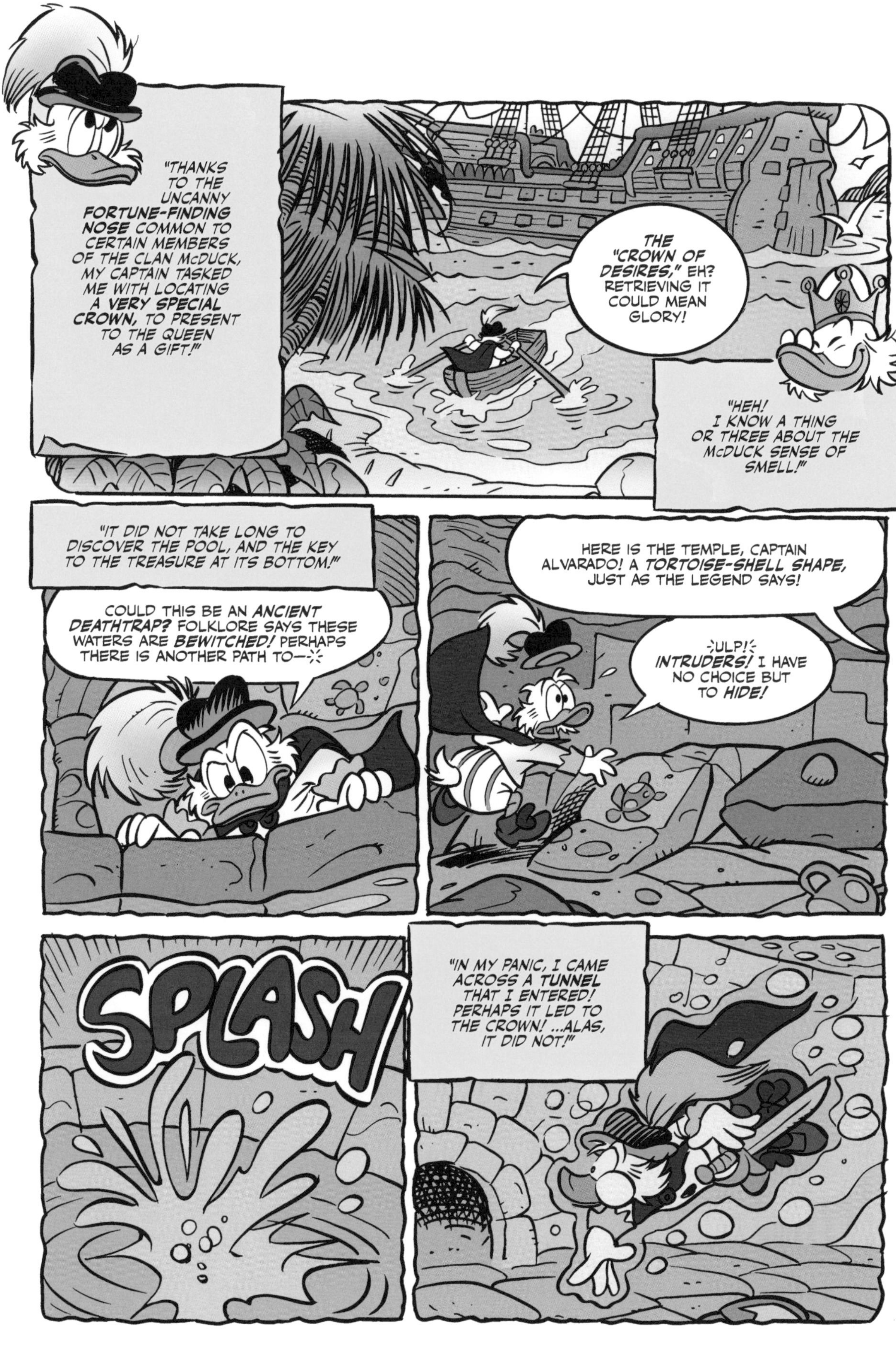
"THANKS TO THE UNCANNY FORTUNE-FINDING NOSE COMMON TO CERTAIN MEMBERS OF THE CLAN McDUCK, MY CAPTAIN TASKED ME WITH LOCATING A VERY SPECIAL CROWN, TO PRESENT TO THE QUEEN AS A GIFT!"
THE "CROWN OF DESIRES," EH? RETRIEVING IT COULD MEAN GLORY!
"HEH! I KNOW A THING OR THREE ABOUT THE McDUCK SENSE OF SMELL!"
"IT DID NOT TAKE LONG TO DISCOVER THE POOL, AND THE KEY TO THE TREASURE AT ITS BOTTOM!"
COULD THIS BE AN ANCIENT DEATHTRAP? FOLKLORE SAYS THESE WATERS ARE BEWITCHED! PERHAPS THERE IS ANOTHER PATH TO—
HERE IS THE TEMPLE, CAPTAIN ALVARADO! A TORTOISE-SHELL SHAPE, JUST AS THE LEGEND SAYS!
ULP! INTRUDERS! I HAVE NO CHOICE BUT TO HIDE!
SPLASH
"IN MY PANIC, I CAME ACROSS A TUNNEL THAT I ENTERED! PERHAPS IT LED TO THE CROWN! ...ALAS, IT DID NOT!"

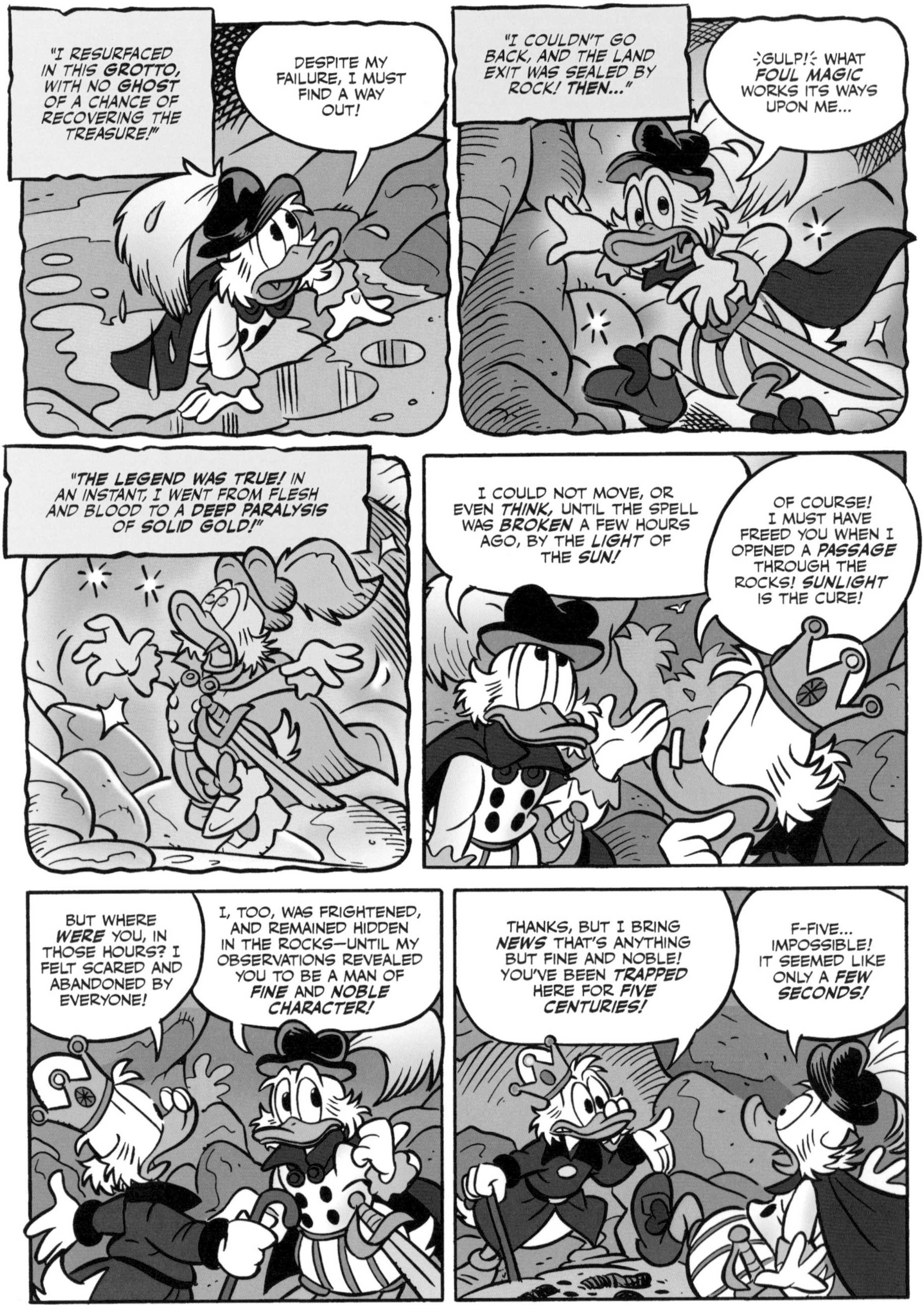
"I RESURFACED IN THIS GROTTO, WITH NO GHOST OF A CHANCE OF RECOVERING THE TREASURE!"
DESPITE MY FAILURE, I MUST FIND A WAY OUT!
"I COULDN'T GO BACK, AND THE LAND EXIT WAS SEALED BY ROCK! THEN..."
GULP! WHAT FOUL MAGIC WORKS ITS WAYS UPON ME...
"THE LEGEND WAS TRUE! IN AN INSTANT, I WENT FROM FLESH AND BLOOD TO A DEEP PARALYSIS OF SOLID GOLD!"
I COULD NOT MOVE, OR EVEN THINK, UNTIL THE SPELL WAS BROKEN A FEW HOURS AGO, BY THE LIGHT OF THE SUN!
OF COURSE! I MUST HAVE FREED YOU WHEN I OPENED A PASSAGE THROUGH THE ROCKS! SUNLIGHT IS THE CURE!
BUT WHERE WERE YOU, IN THOSE HOURS? I FELT SCARED AND ABANDONED BY EVERYONE!
I, TOO, WAS FRIGHTENED, AND REMAINED HIDDEN IN THE ROCKS—UNTIL MY OBSERVATIONS REVEALED YOU TO BE A MAN OF FINE AND NOBLE CHARACTER!
THANKS, BUT I BRING NEWS THAT'S ANYTHING BUT FINE AND NOBLE! YOU'VE BEEN TRAPPED HERE FOR FIVE CENTURIES!
F-FIVE... IMPOSSIBLE! IT SEEMED LIKE ONLY A FEW SECONDS!

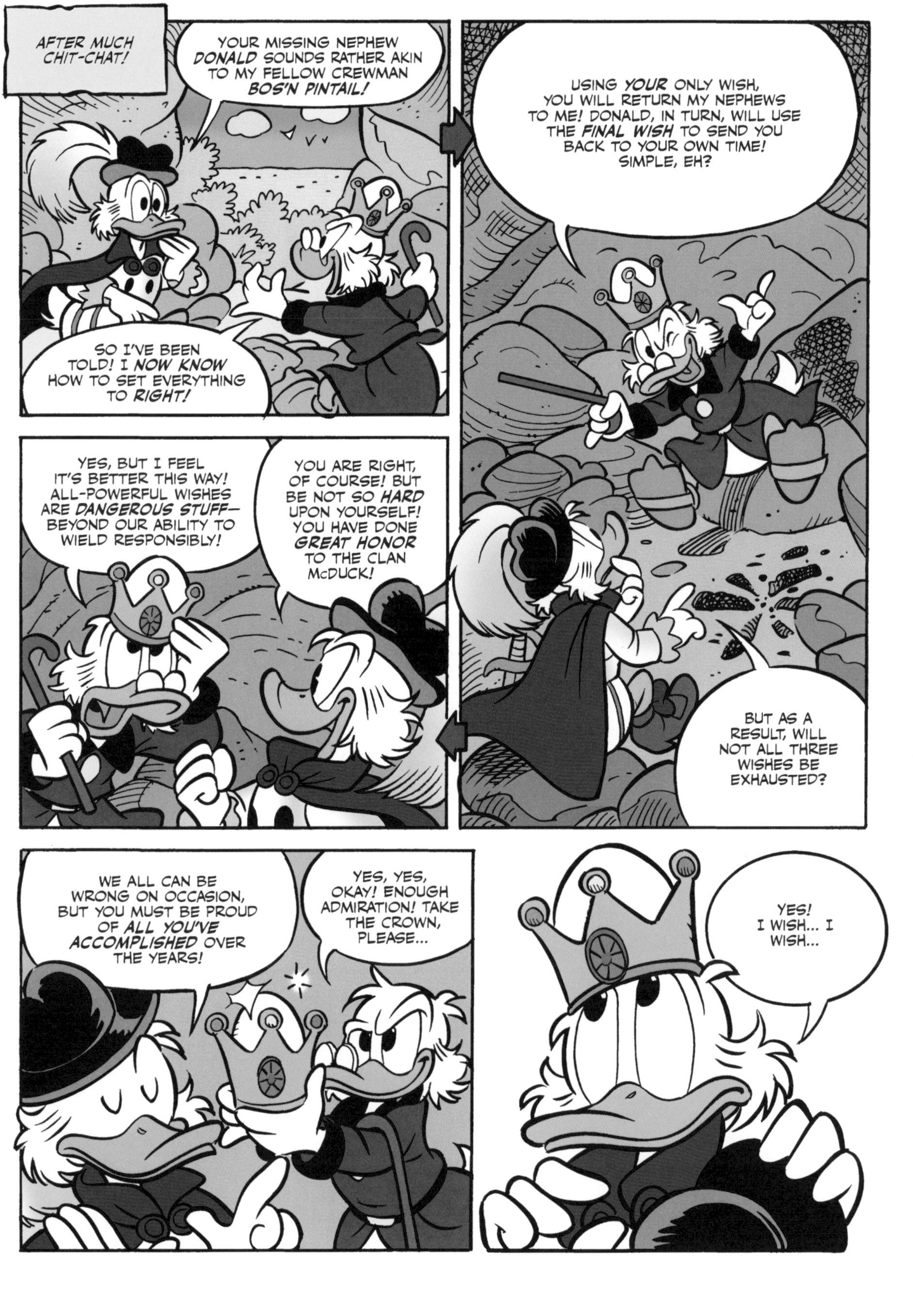
AFTER MUCH CHIT-CHAT!
YOUR MISSING NEPHEW DONALD SOUNDS RATHER AKIN TO MY FELLOW CREWMAN BOS'N PINTAIL!
SO I'VE BEEN TOLD! I NOW KNOW HOW TO SET EVERYTHING TO RIGHT!
USING YOUR ONLY WISH, YOU WILL RETURN MY NEPHEWS TO ME! DONALD, IN TURN, WILL USE THE FINAL WISH TO SEND YOU BACK TO YOUR OWN TIME! SIMPLE, EH?
BUT AS A RESULT, WILL NOT ALL THREE WISHES BE EXHAUSTED?
YES, BUT I FEEL IT'S BETTER THIS WAY! ALL-POWERFUL WISHES ARE DANGEROUS STUFF— BEYOND OUR ABILITY TO WIELD RESPONSIBLY!
YOU ARE RIGHT, OF COURSE! BUT BE NOT SO HARD UPON YOURSELF! YOU HAVE DONE GREAT HONOR TO THE CLAN McDUCK!
WE ALL CAN BE WRONG ON OCCASION, BUT YOU MUST BE PROUD OF ALL YOU'VE ACCOMPLISHED OVER THE YEARS!
YES, YES, OKAY! ENOUGH ADMIRATION! TAKE THE CROWN, PLEASE...
YES! I WISH... I WISH...

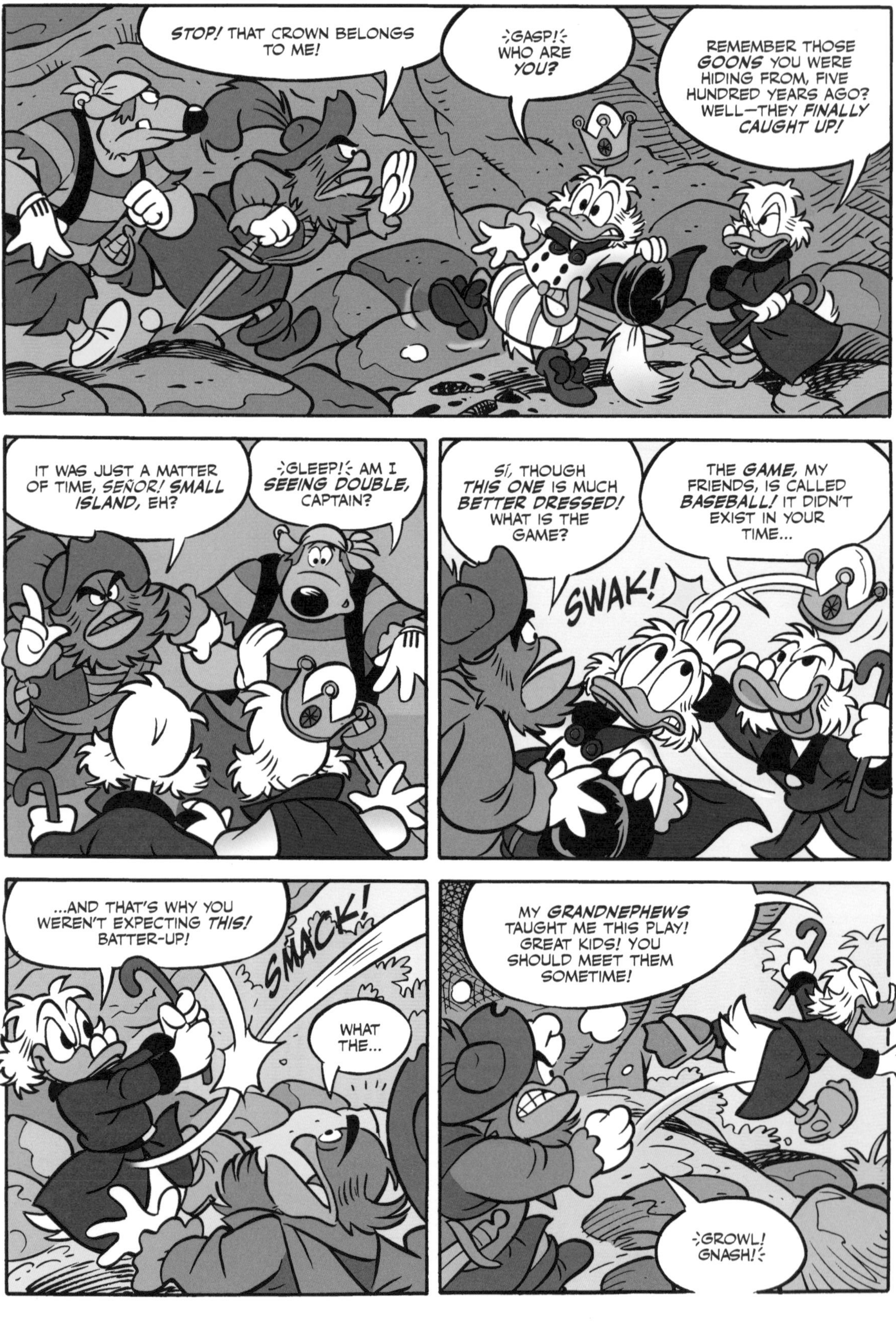
STOP! THAT CROWN BELONGS TO ME!
¡GASP!¡ WHO ARE YOU?
REMEMBER THOSE GOONS YOU WERE HIDING FROM, FIVE HUNDRED YEARS AGO? WELL—THEY FINALLY CAUGHT UP!
IT WAS JUST A MATTER OF TIME, SEÑOR! SMALL ISLAND, EH?
¡GLEEP!¡ AM I SEEING DOUBLE, CAPTAIN?
SÍ, THOUGH THIS ONE IS MUCH BETTER DRESSED! WHAT IS THE GAME?
THE GAME, MY FRIENDS, IS CALLED BASEBALL! IT DIDN'T EXIST IN YOUR TIME...
SWAK!
...AND THAT'S WHY YOU WEREN'T EXPECTING THIS! BATTER-UP!
SMACK!
WHAT THE...
MY GRANDNEPHEWS TAUGHT ME THIS PLAY! GREAT KIDS! YOU SHOULD MEET THEM SOMETIME!
¡GROWL! GNASH!¡

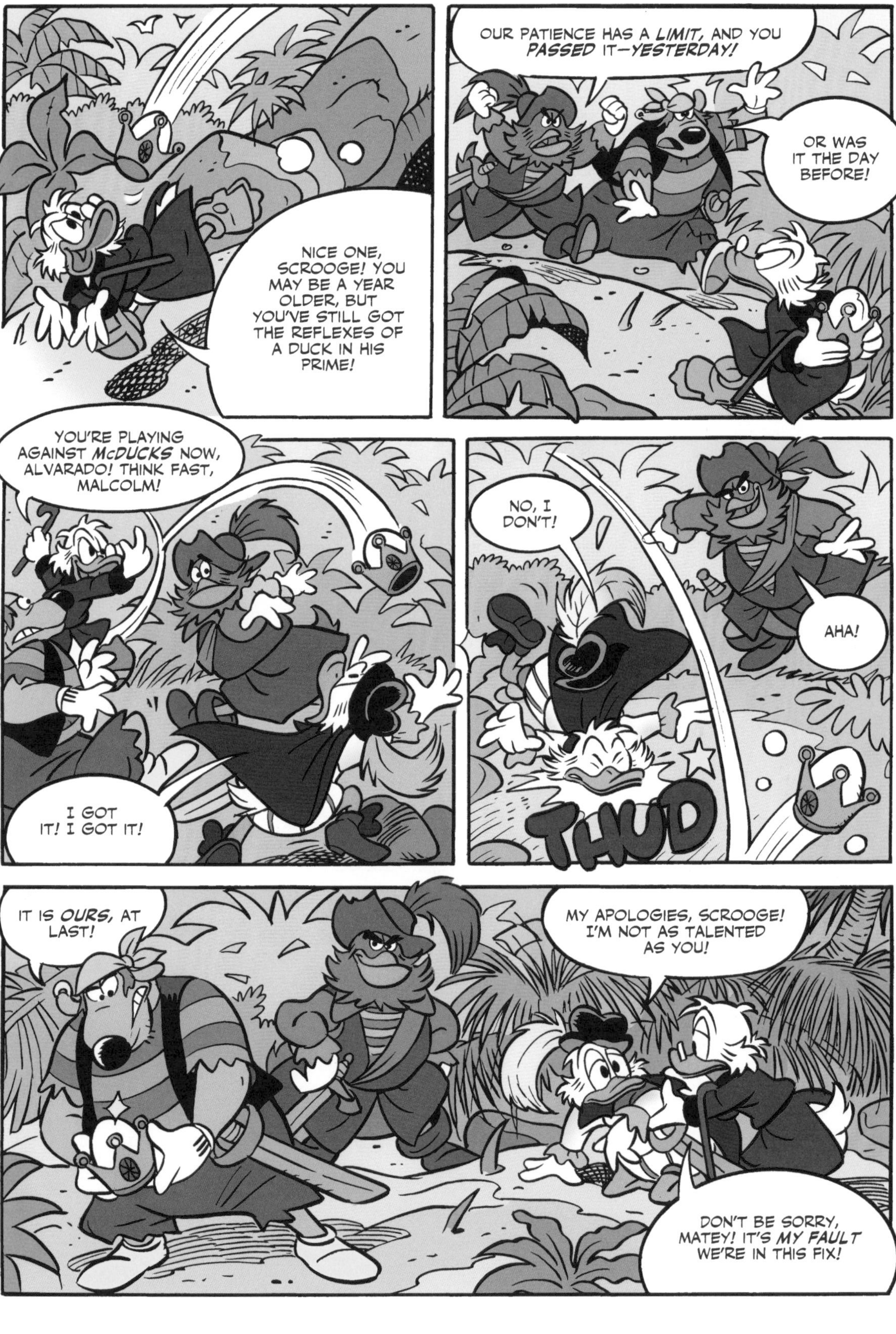
NICE ONE, SCROOGE! YOU MAY BE A YEAR OLDER, BUT YOU'VE STILL GOT THE REFLEXES OF A DUCK IN HIS PRIME!
OUR PATIENCE HAS A *LIMIT*, AND YOU *PASSED* IT—*YESTERDAY!*
OR WAS IT THE DAY BEFORE!
YOU'RE PLAYING AGAINST *McDUCKS* NOW, ALVARADO! THINK FAST, MALCOLM!
I GOT IT! I GOT IT!
NO, I DON'T!
AHA!
THUD
IT IS *OURS*, AT LAST!
MY APOLOGIES, SCROOGE! I'M NOT AS TALENTED AS YOU!
DON'T BE SORRY, MATEY! IT'S *MY FAULT* WE'RE IN THIS FIX!

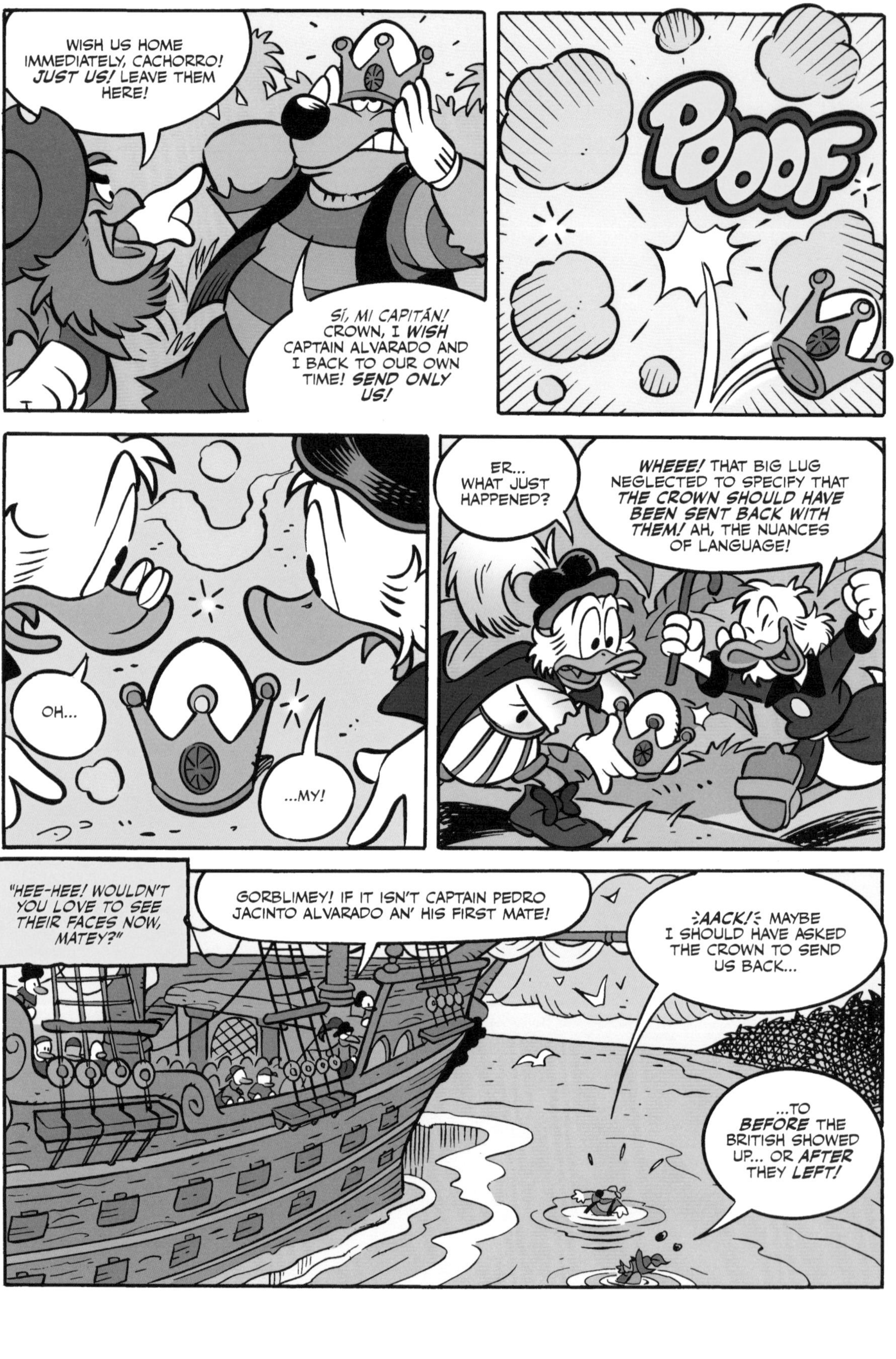
WISH US HOME IMMEDIATELY, CACHORRO! *JUST US!* LEAVE THEM HERE!
SÍ, MI CAPITÁN! CROWN, I *WISH* CAPTAIN ALVARADO AND I BACK TO OUR OWN TIME! *SEND ONLY US!*
POOOF
OH...
...MY!
ER... WHAT JUST HAPPENED?
WHEEE! THAT BIG LUG NEGLECTED TO SPECIFY THAT *THE CROWN SHOULD HAVE BEEN SENT BACK WITH THEM!* AH, THE NUANCES OF LANGUAGE!
"HEE-HEE! WOULDN'T YOU LOVE TO SEE THEIR FACES NOW, MATEY?"
GORBLIMEY! IF IT ISN'T CAPTAIN PEDRO JACINTO ALVARADO AN' HIS FIRST MATE!
AACK! MAYBE I SHOULD HAVE ASKED THE CROWN TO SEND US BACK...
...TO *BEFORE* THE BRITISH SHOWED UP... OR *AFTER* THEY *LEFT!*

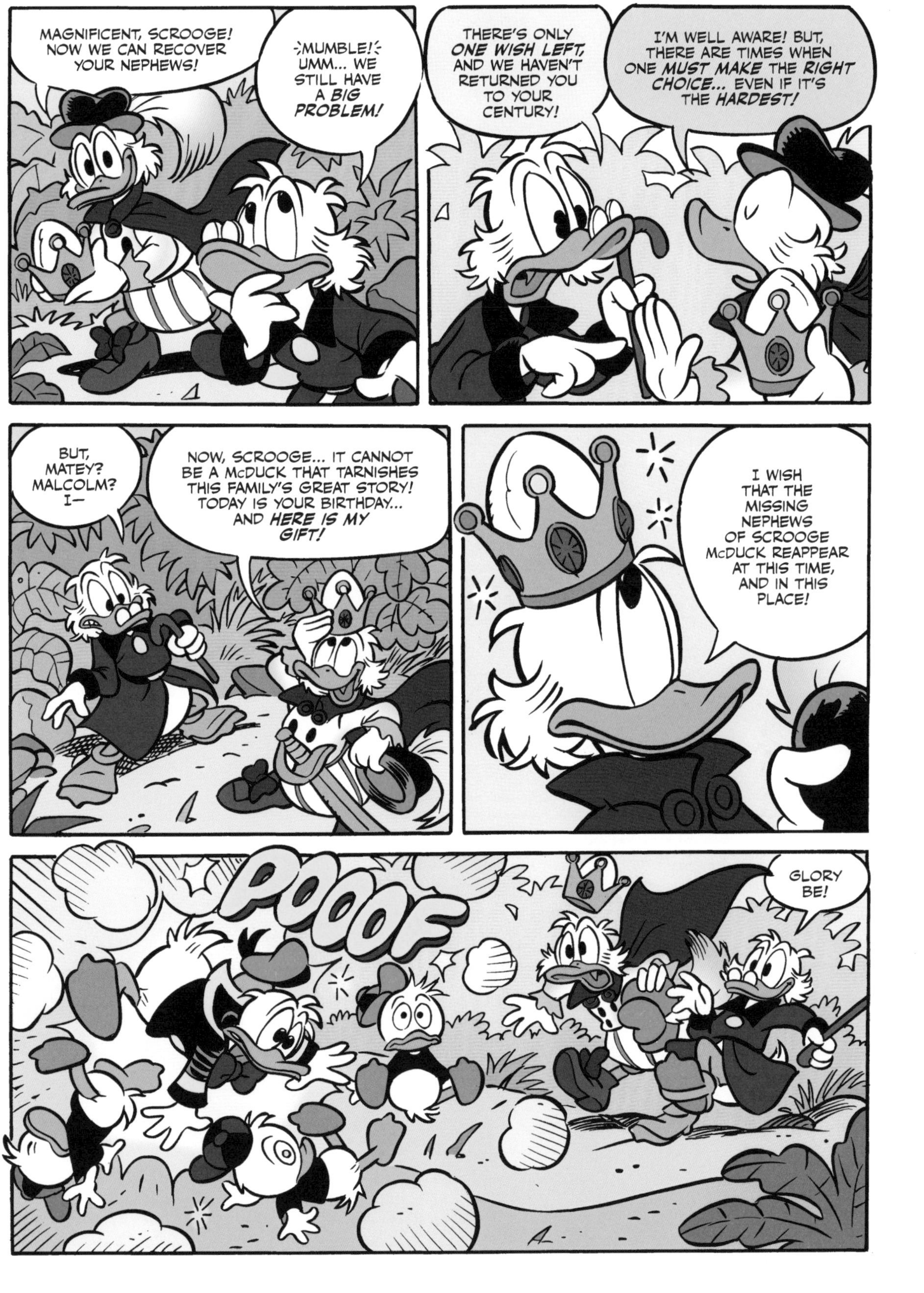
MAGNIFICENT, SCROOGE! NOW WE CAN RECOVER YOUR NEPHEWS!
MUMBLE! UMM... WE STILL HAVE A BIG PROBLEM!
THERE'S ONLY ONE WISH LEFT, AND WE HAVEN'T RETURNED YOU TO YOUR CENTURY!
I'M WELL AWARE! BUT, THERE ARE TIMES WHEN ONE MUST MAKE THE RIGHT CHOICE... EVEN IF IT'S THE HARDEST!
BUT, MATEY? MALCOLM? I—
NOW, SCROOGE... IT CANNOT BE A McDUCK THAT TARNISHES THIS FAMILY'S GREAT STORY! TODAY IS YOUR BIRTHDAY... AND HERE IS MY GIFT!
I WISH THAT THE MISSING NEPHEWS OF SCROOGE McDUCK REAPPEAR AT THIS TIME, AND IN THIS PLACE!
POOOF
GLORY BE!

WHA-WHA-WHA' HOPPEN'?

LAST I RECALL, WE WERE IN THE TEMPLE—

DONALD! BOYS! YOU'RE *BACK* AT LAST!

WHOA, NELLIE! SOMEONE HERE OWES US THE *EXPLANATION* OF THE *CENTURY*!

⸰SIGH!⸰ YOU'RE RIGHT...

"...AND THAT'S THE WAY IT HAPPENED, LADS! HONEST!"

I DON'T KNOW WHAT I COULD EVER DO TO MAKE YOU FORGIVE MY RASH AND SELFISH ACTIONS! NOW, YOU'LL NEVER HAVE YOUR TWO WISHES...

DON'T WORRY! SOME THINGS ARE *MORE IMPORTANT* THAN ALL-POWERFUL WISHES!

SO WE HAVE ONLY *ONE* THING TO SAY TO YOU, UNCA SCROOGE...

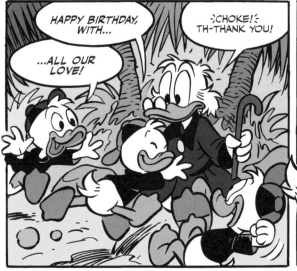

HAPPY BIRTHDAY, WITH...

...ALL OUR LOVE!

⸰CHOKE!⸰ TH-THANK YOU!

THAT'S ALL FINE AND DANDY ⸰CHOMP!⸰ BUT WE'RE STILL *STUCK* HERE WITH NO *BOAT*—OR SIGNAL ON MY *CELL*!

I WAS IN A *CELL* ONCE...

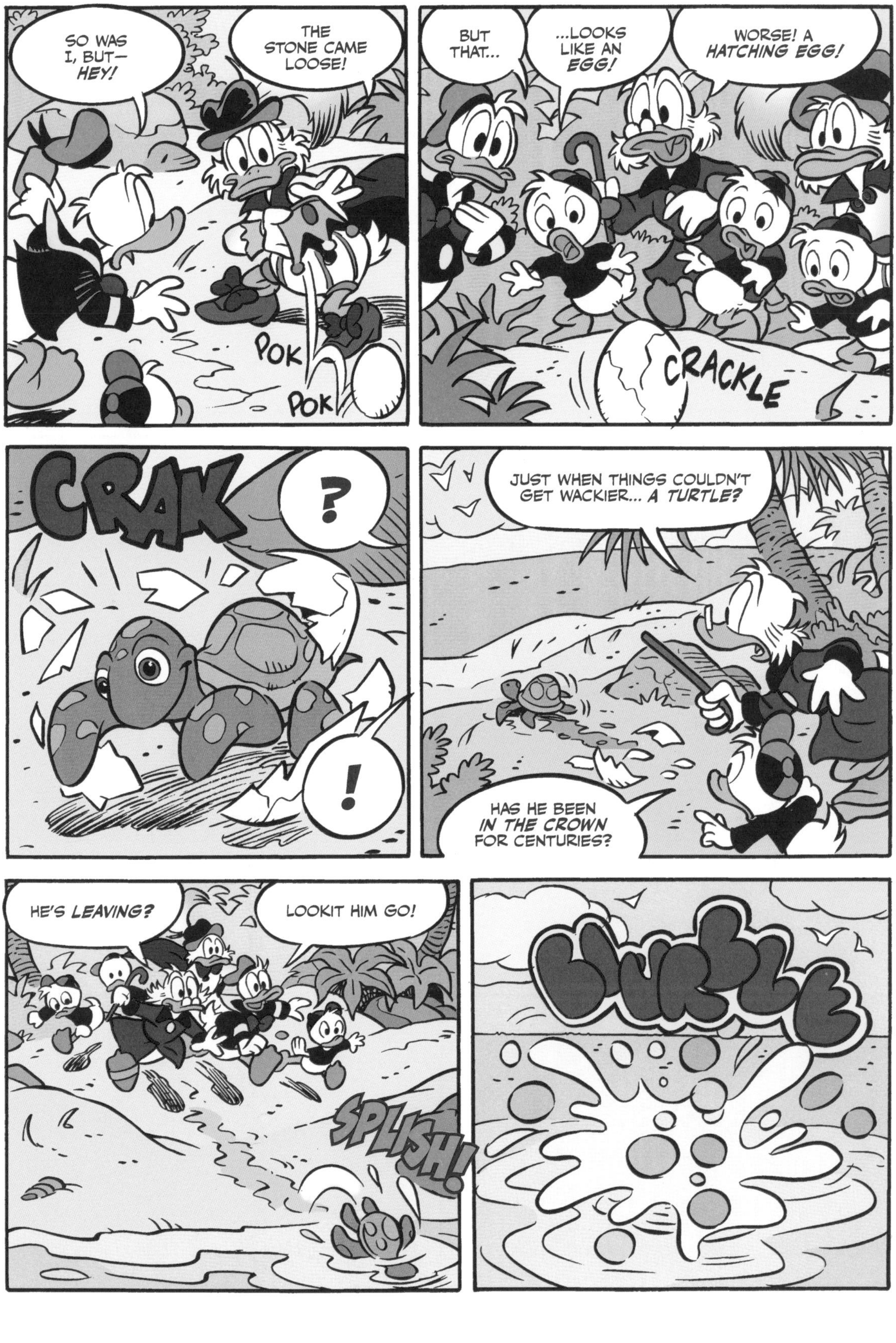
SO WAS I, BUT— HEY!
THE STONE CAME LOOSE!
POK
POK
BUT THAT...
...LOOKS LIKE AN EGG!
WORSE! A HATCHING EGG!
CRACKLE
CRAK
?
!
JUST WHEN THINGS COULDN'T GET WACKIER... A TURTLE?
HAS HE BEEN IN THE CROWN FOR CENTURIES?
HE'S LEAVING?
LOOKIT HIM GO!
SPLISH!
BLURBLE

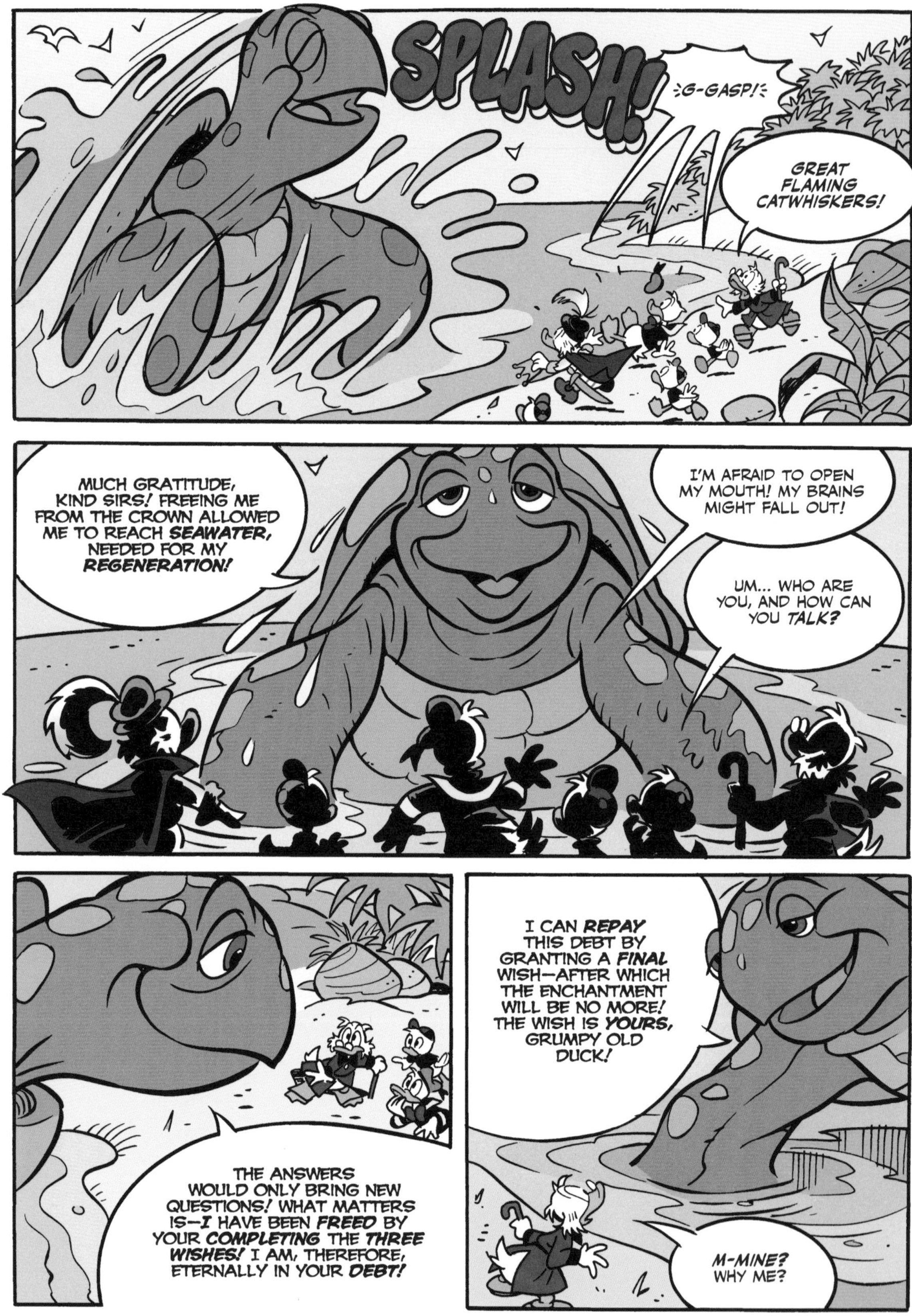
SPLASH!
G-GASP!
GREAT FLAMING CATWHISKERS!
MUCH GRATITUDE, KIND SIRS! FREEING ME FROM THE CROWN ALLOWED ME TO REACH SEAWATER, NEEDED FOR MY REGENERATION!
I'M AFRAID TO OPEN MY MOUTH! MY BRAINS MIGHT FALL OUT!
UM... WHO ARE YOU, AND HOW CAN YOU TALK?
THE ANSWERS WOULD ONLY BRING NEW QUESTIONS! WHAT MATTERS IS—I HAVE BEEN FREED BY YOUR COMPLETING THE THREE WISHES! I AM, THEREFORE, ETERNALLY IN YOUR DEBT!
I CAN REPAY THIS DEBT BY GRANTING A FINAL WISH—AFTER WHICH THE ENCHANTMENT WILL BE NO MORE! THE WISH IS YOURS, GRUMPY OLD DUCK!
M-MINE? WHY ME?

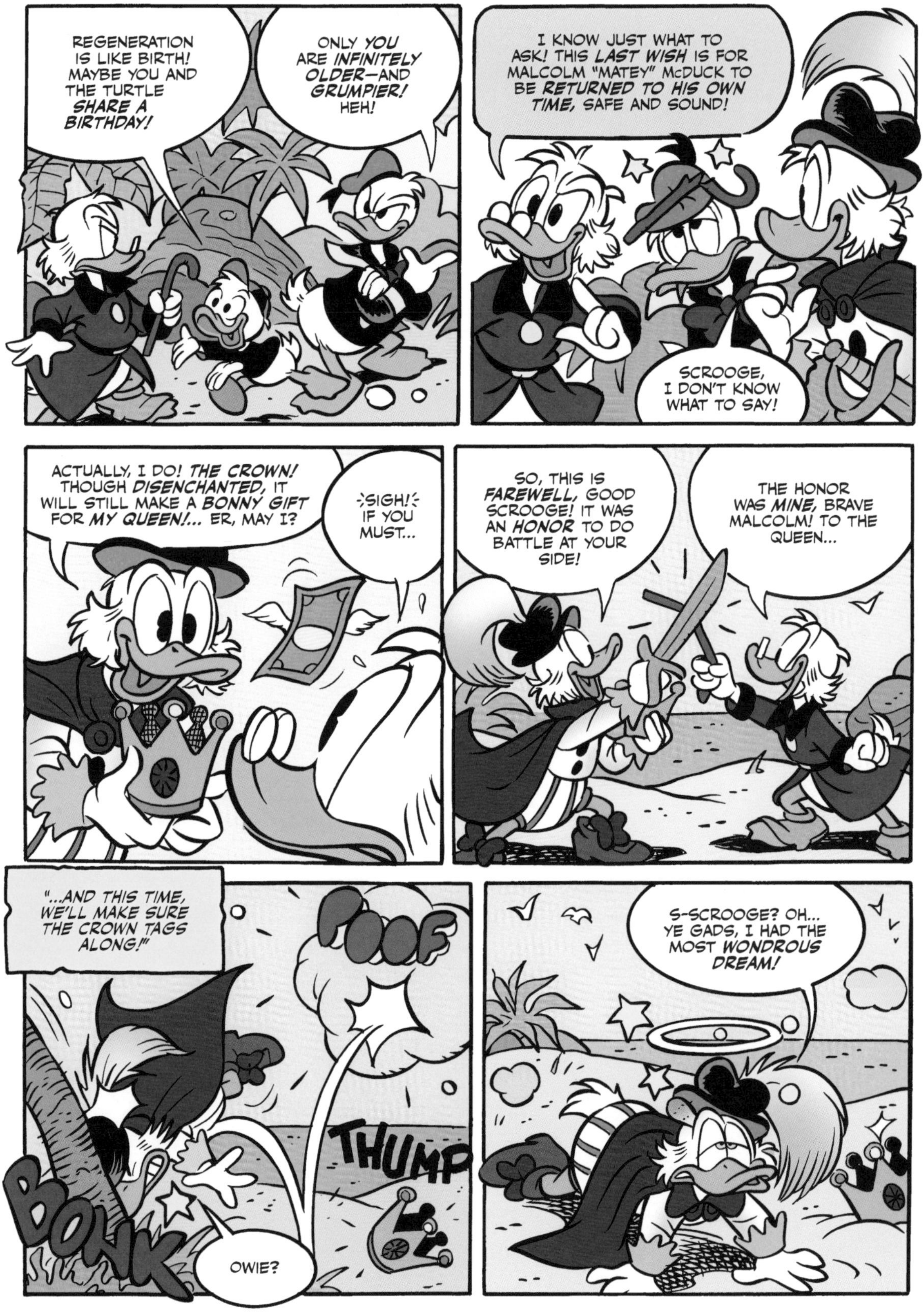
REGENERATION IS LIKE BIRTH! MAYBE YOU AND THE TURTLE SHARE A BIRTHDAY!
ONLY YOU ARE INFINITELY OLDER—AND GRUMPIER! HEH!
I KNOW JUST WHAT TO ASK! THIS LAST WISH IS FOR MALCOLM "MATEY" McDUCK TO BE RETURNED TO HIS OWN TIME, SAFE AND SOUND!
SCROOGE, I DON'T KNOW WHAT TO SAY!
ACTUALLY, I DO! THE CROWN! THOUGH DISENCHANTED, IT WILL STILL MAKE A BONNY GIFT FOR MY QUEEN!... ER, MAY I?
SIGH! IF YOU MUST...
SO, THIS IS FAREWELL, GOOD SCROOGE! IT WAS AN HONOR TO DO BATTLE AT YOUR SIDE!
THE HONOR WAS MINE, BRAVE MALCOLM! TO THE QUEEN...
"...AND THIS TIME, WE'LL MAKE SURE THE CROWN TAGS ALONG!"
POOF
THUMP
BONK
OWIE?
S-SCROOGE? OH... YE GADS, I HAD THE MOST WONDROUS DREAM!

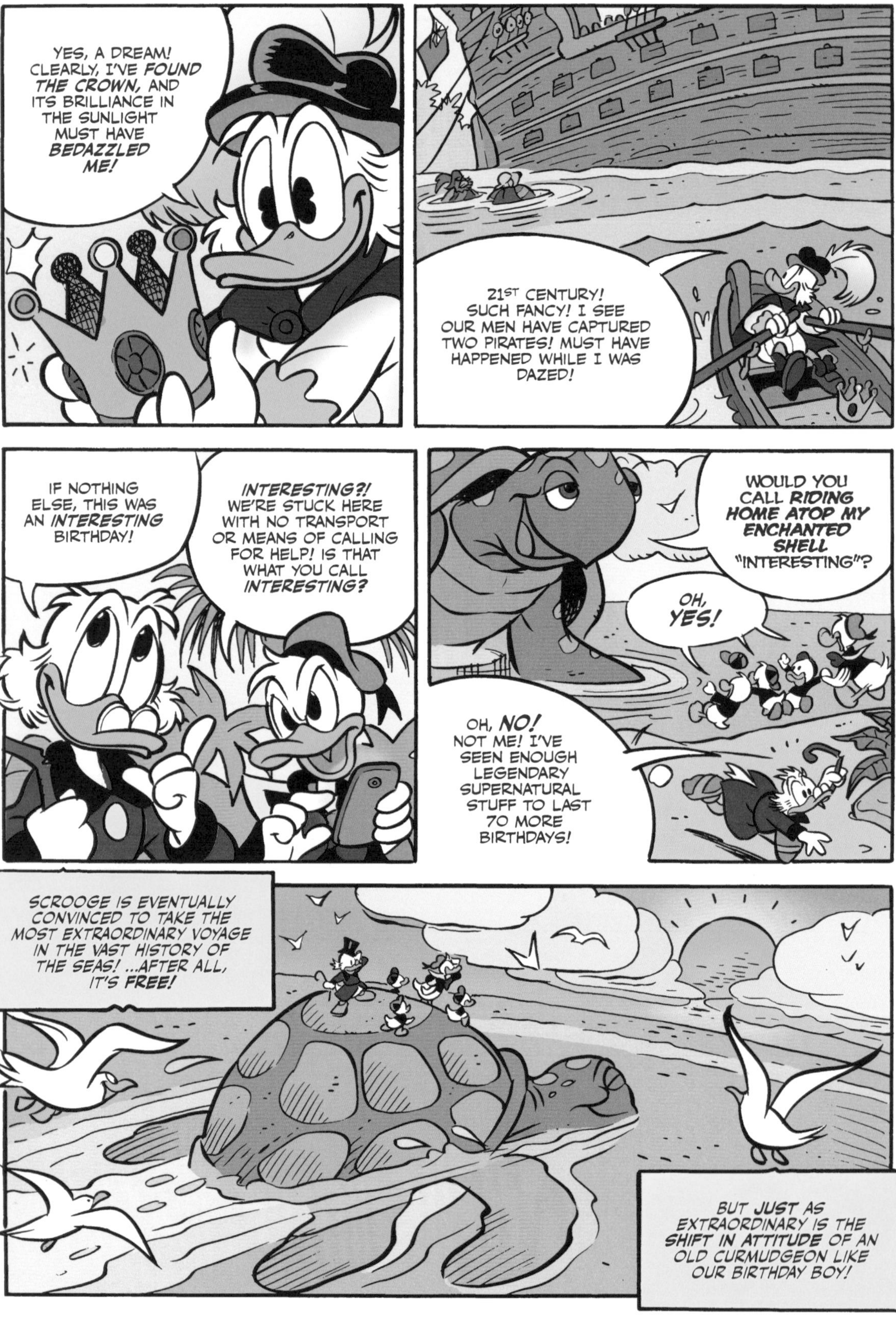
YES, A DREAM! CLEARLY, I'VE FOUND THE CROWN, AND ITS BRILLIANCE IN THE SUNLIGHT MUST HAVE BEDAZZLED ME!
21ST CENTURY! SUCH FANCY! I SEE OUR MEN HAVE CAPTURED TWO PIRATES! MUST HAVE HAPPENED WHILE I WAS DAZED!
IF NOTHING ELSE, THIS WAS AN INTERESTING BIRTHDAY!
INTERESTING?! WE'RE STUCK HERE WITH NO TRANSPORT OR MEANS OF CALLING FOR HELP! IS THAT WHAT YOU CALL INTERESTING?
WOULD YOU CALL RIDING HOME ATOP MY ENCHANTED SHELL "INTERESTING"?
OH, YES!
OH, NO! NOT ME! I'VE SEEN ENOUGH LEGENDARY SUPERNATURAL STUFF TO LAST 70 MORE BIRTHDAYS!
SCROOGE IS EVENTUALLY CONVINCED TO TAKE THE MOST EXTRAORDINARY VOYAGE IN THE VAST HISTORY OF THE SEAS! ...AFTER ALL, IT'S FREE!
BUT JUST AS EXTRAORDINARY IS THE SHIFT IN ATTITUDE OF AN OLD CURMUDGEON LIKE OUR BIRTHDAY BOY!

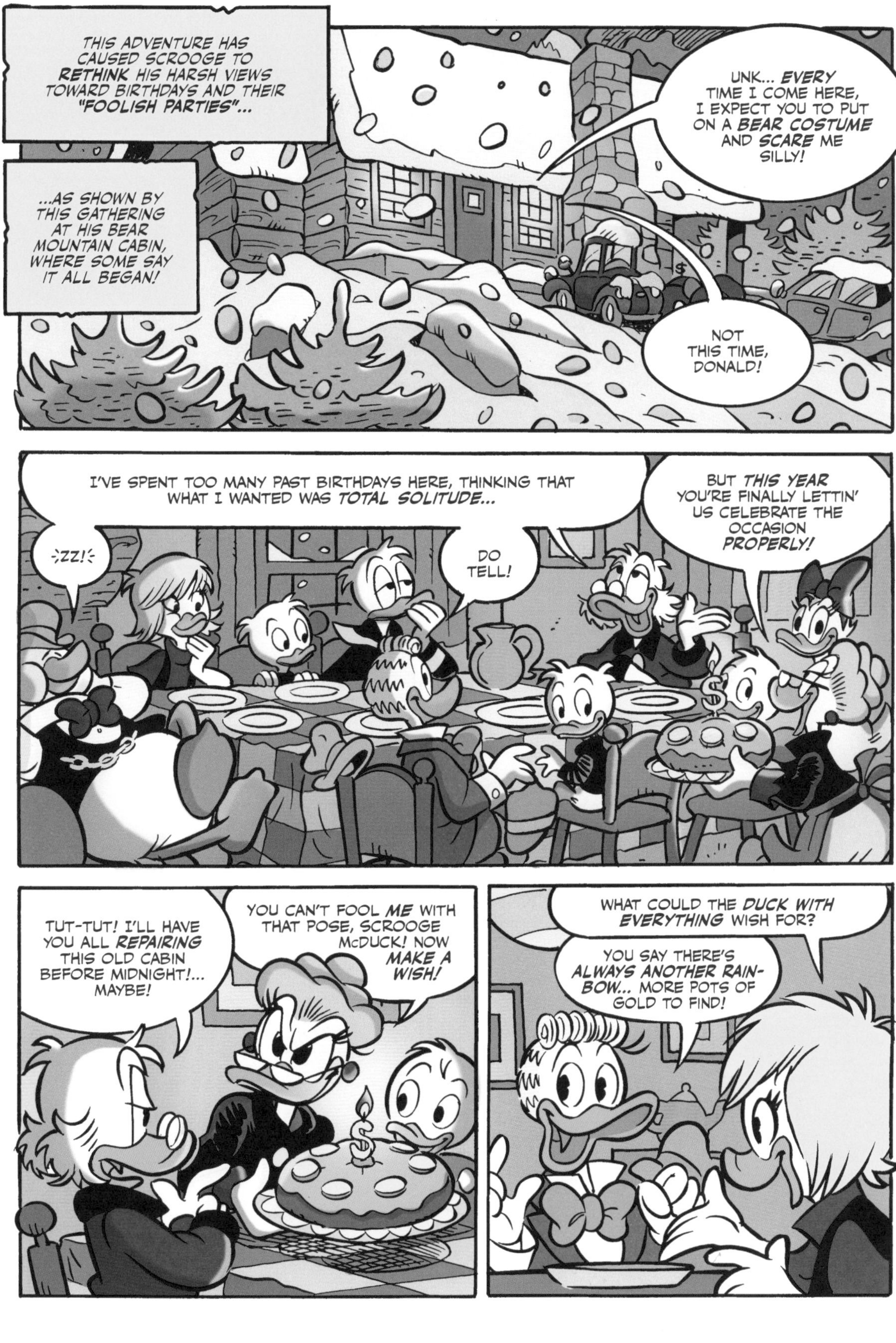

THIS ADVENTURE HAS CAUSED SCROOGE TO RETHINK HIS HARSH VIEWS TOWARD BIRTHDAYS AND THEIR "FOOLISH PARTIES"...
...AS SHOWN BY THIS GATHERING AT HIS BEAR MOUNTAIN CABIN, WHERE SOME SAY IT ALL BEGAN!
UNK... EVERY TIME I COME HERE, I EXPECT YOU TO PUT ON A BEAR COSTUME AND SCARE ME SILLY!
NOT THIS TIME, DONALD!
I'VE SPENT TOO MANY PAST BIRTHDAYS HERE, THINKING THAT WHAT I WANTED WAS TOTAL SOLITUDE...
ZZ!
DO TELL!
BUT THIS YEAR YOU'RE FINALLY LETTIN' US CELEBRATE THE OCCASION PROPERLY!
TUT-TUT! I'LL HAVE YOU ALL REPAIRING THIS OLD CABIN BEFORE MIDNIGHT!... MAYBE!
YOU CAN'T FOOL ME WITH THAT POSE, SCROOGE McDUCK! NOW MAKE A WISH!
WHAT COULD THE DUCK WITH EVERYTHING WISH FOR?
YOU SAY THERE'S ALWAYS ANOTHER RAIN-BOW... MORE POTS OF GOLD TO FIND!

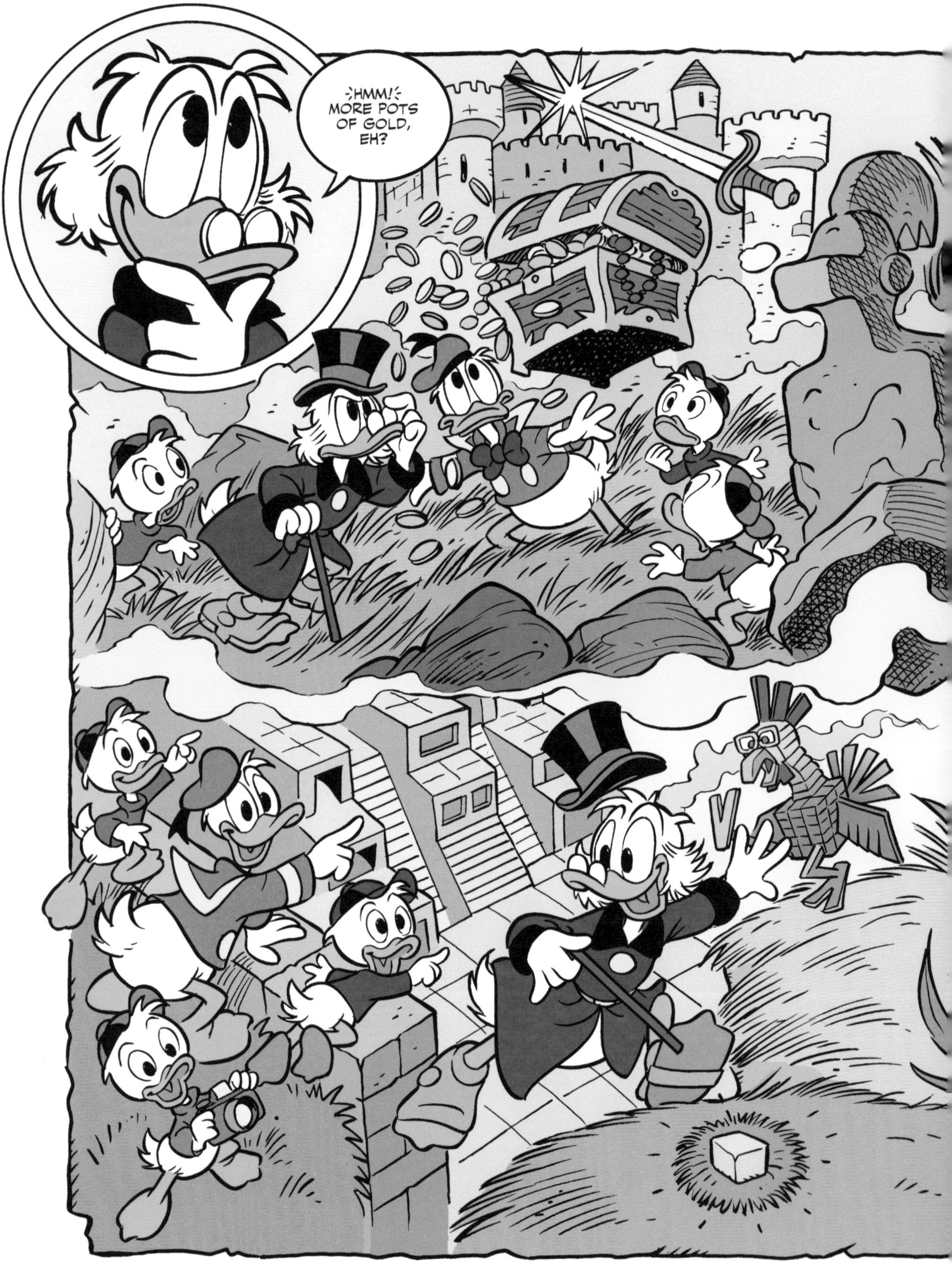
HMM! MORE POTS OF GOLD, EH?

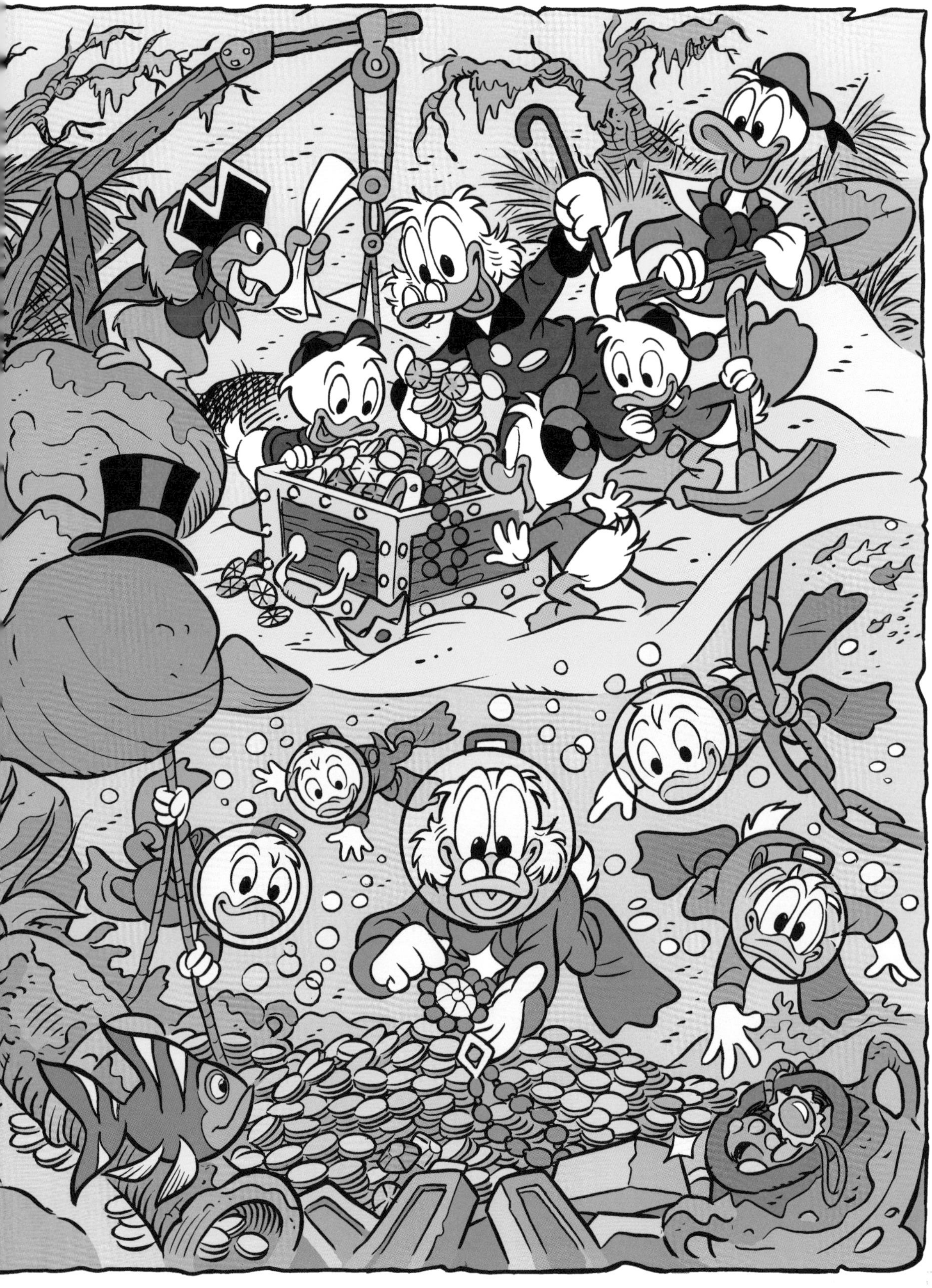

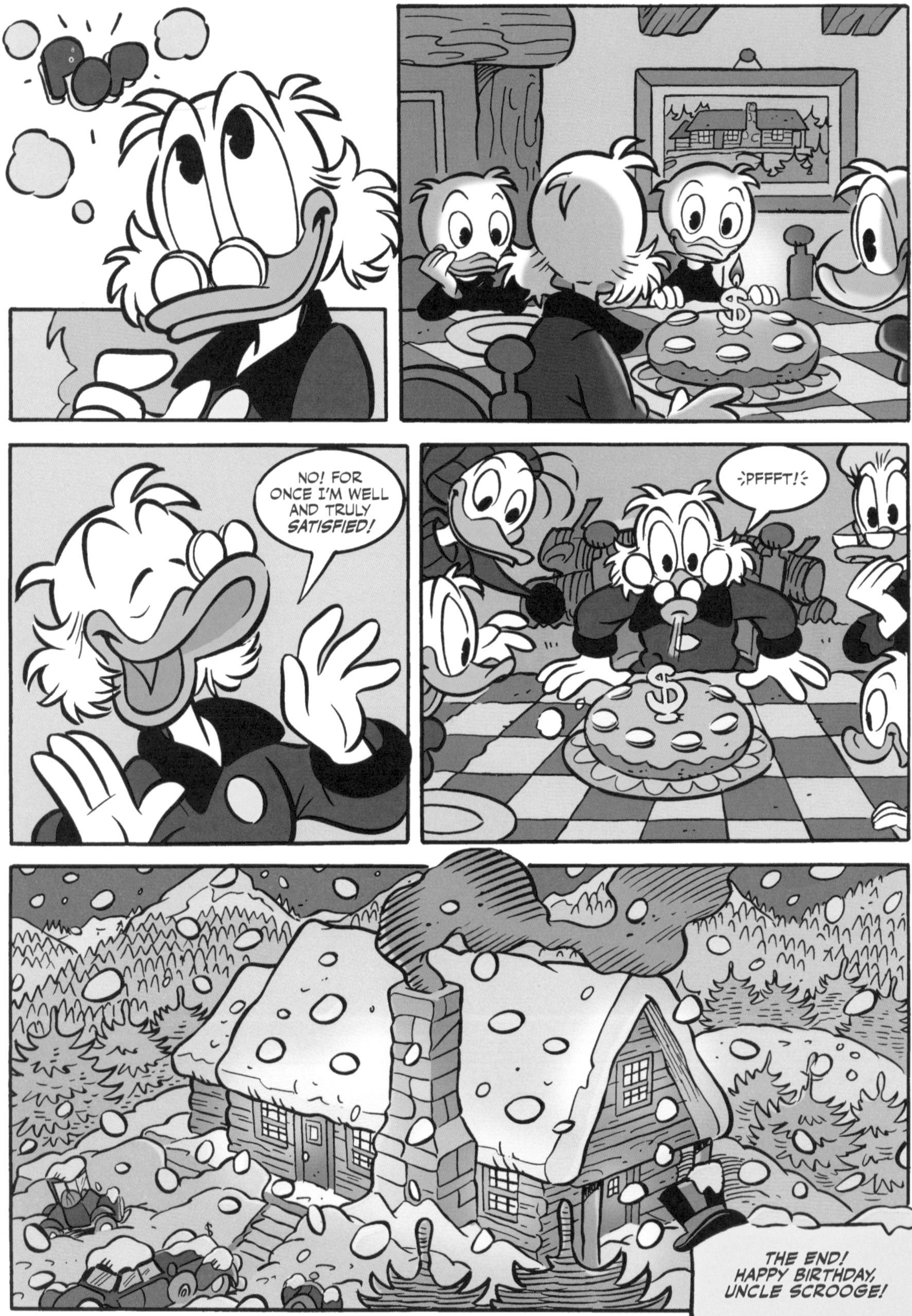
POP
NO! FOR ONCE I'M WELL AND TRULY SATISFIED!
PFFFT!
THE END! HAPPY BIRTHDAY, UNCLE SCROOGE!

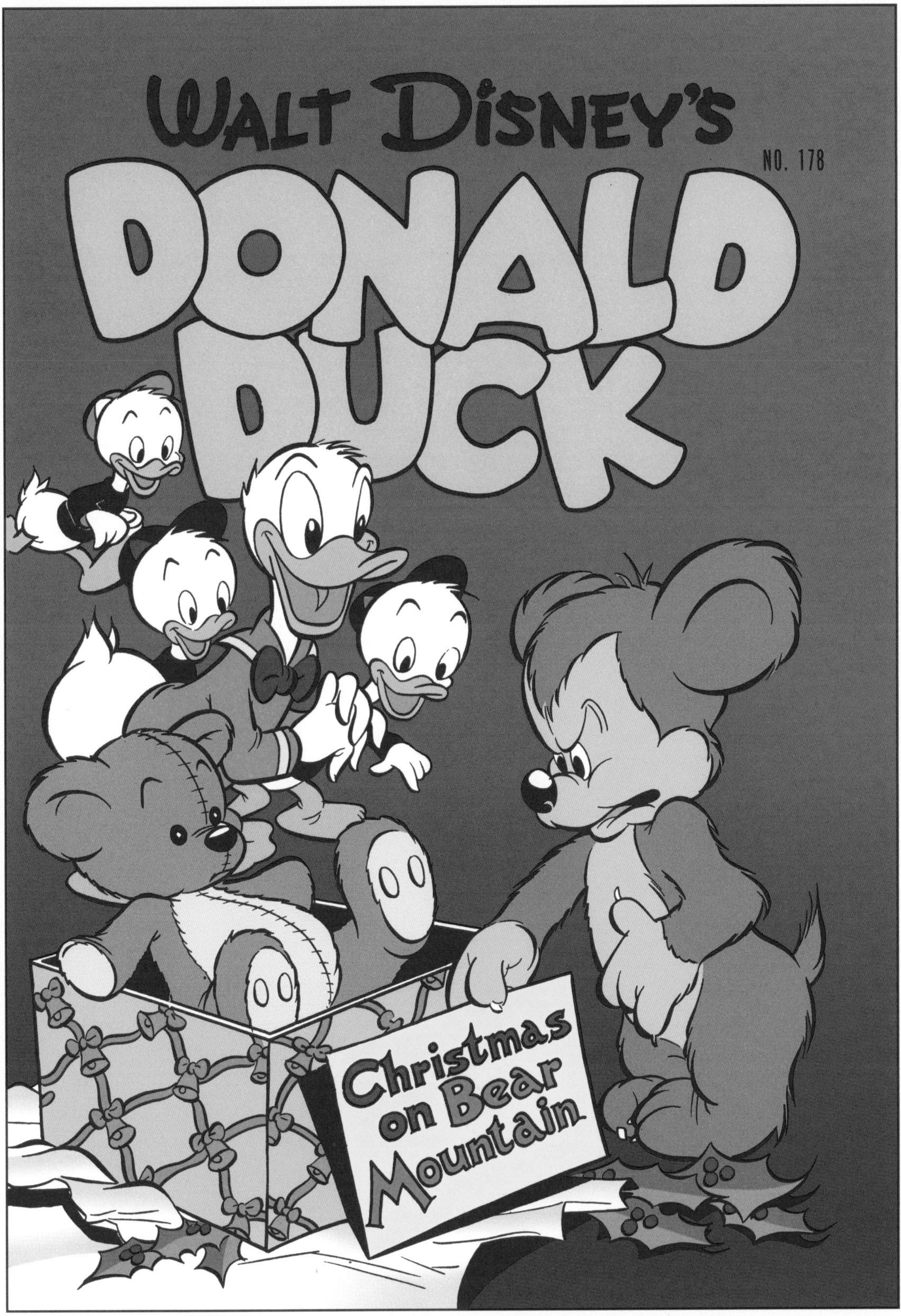
WALT DISNEY'S
NO. 178
DONALD DUCK
Christmas on Bear Mountain

CHRISTMAS ON BEAR MOUNTAIN

Cover to Donald Duck *Four Color* 178, December 1947: the first publication of "Christmas on Bear Mountain." Art by Dan Gormley; color restoration by David Gerstein.

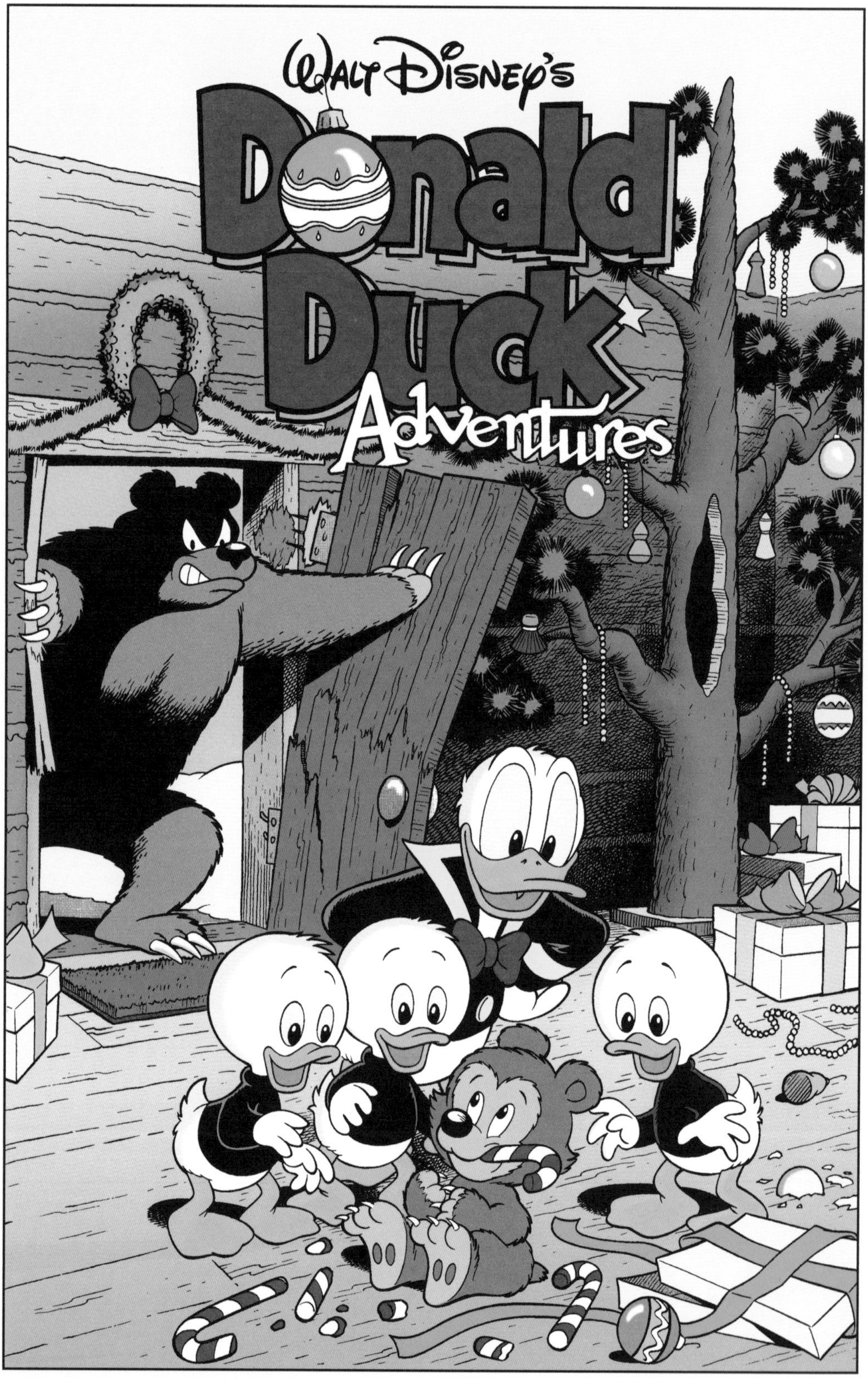
Walt Disney's
Donald Duck
Adventures

CHRISTMAS ON BEAR MOUNTAIN

Cover to *Donald Duck Adventures* [series II] 9, February 1991; layout by Bob Foster, art by Rick Hoover, color by Digikore Studios. This and other February-dated 1990s comic books actually went on sale three months earlier; the official issue date marked the *end* of the sales period.

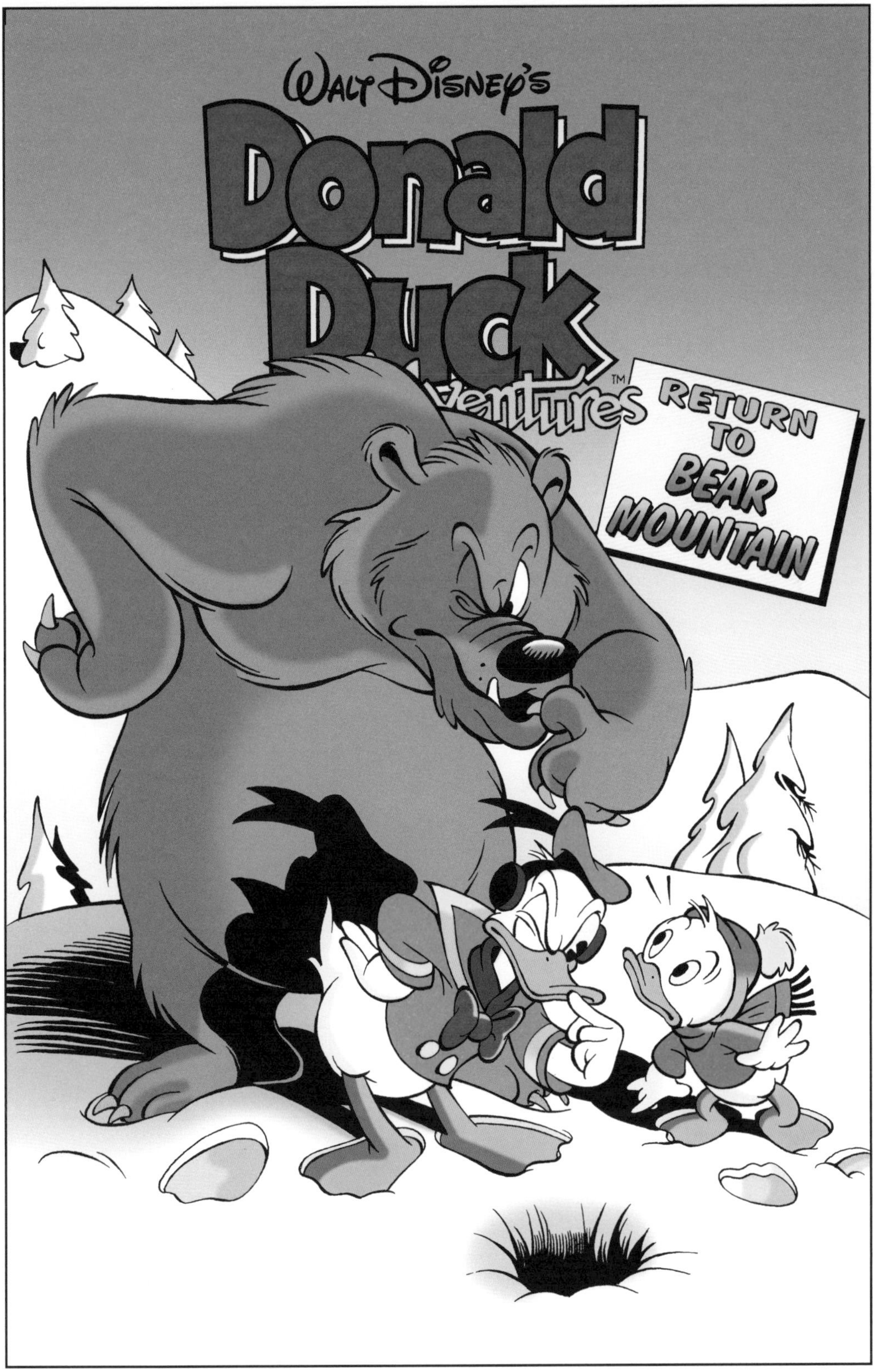
WALT DISNEY'S
Donald Duck
Adventures
TM
RETURN TO BEAR MOUNTAIN

RETURN TO BEAR MOUNTAIN

Cover to *Donald Duck Adventures* [series II] 33, February 1993; layout by Bob Foster, pencils by Jim Franzen, inks by Bruce Patterson, color by Susan Daigle-Leach and Digikore Studios.

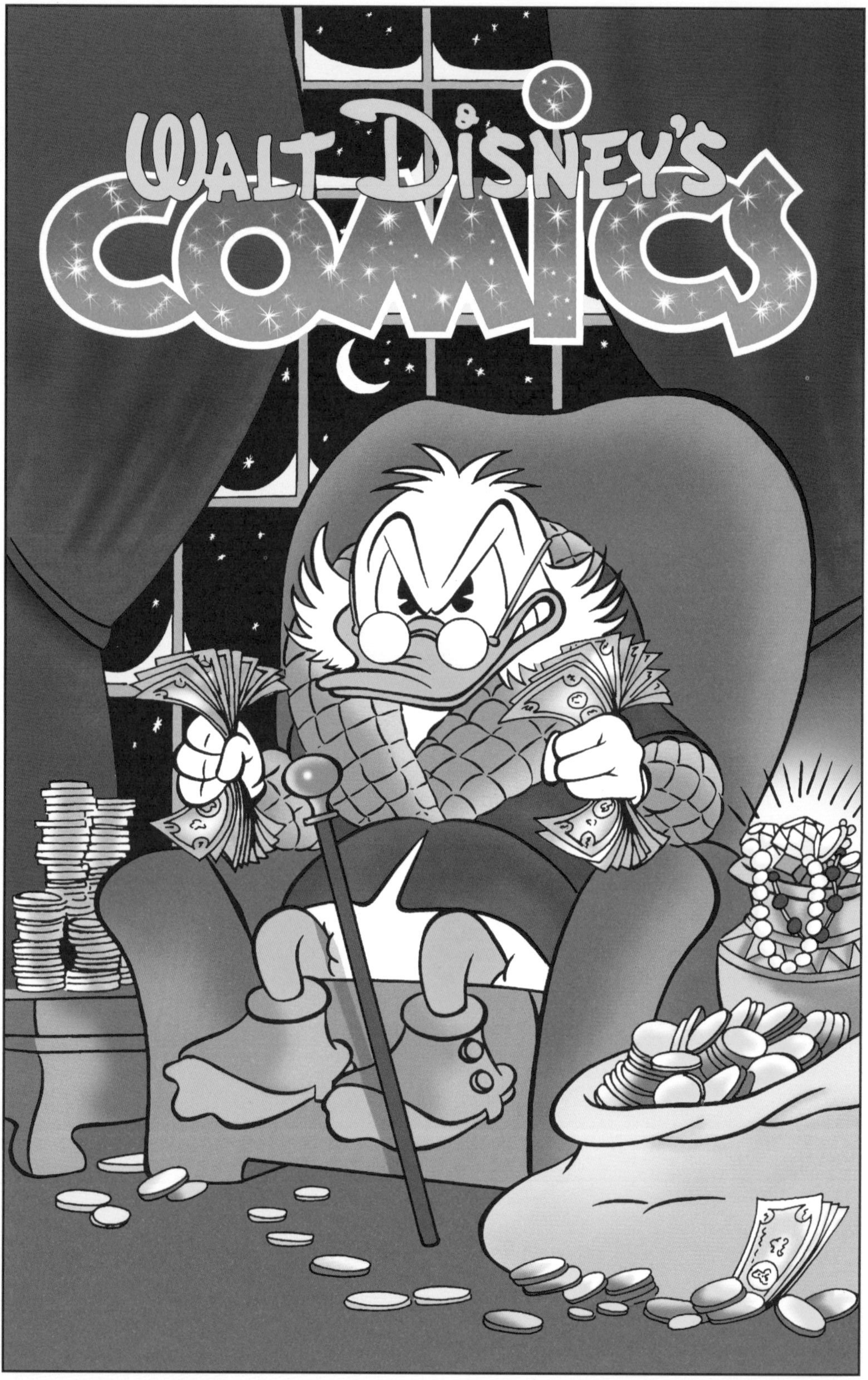
WALT DISNEY'S
COMICS

CHRISTMAS ON BEAR MOUNTAIN
Cover to *Walt Disney's Comics and Stories* 608, February 1998;
pencils by Carl Barks, inks by John Clark, color by Susan Daigle-Leach.

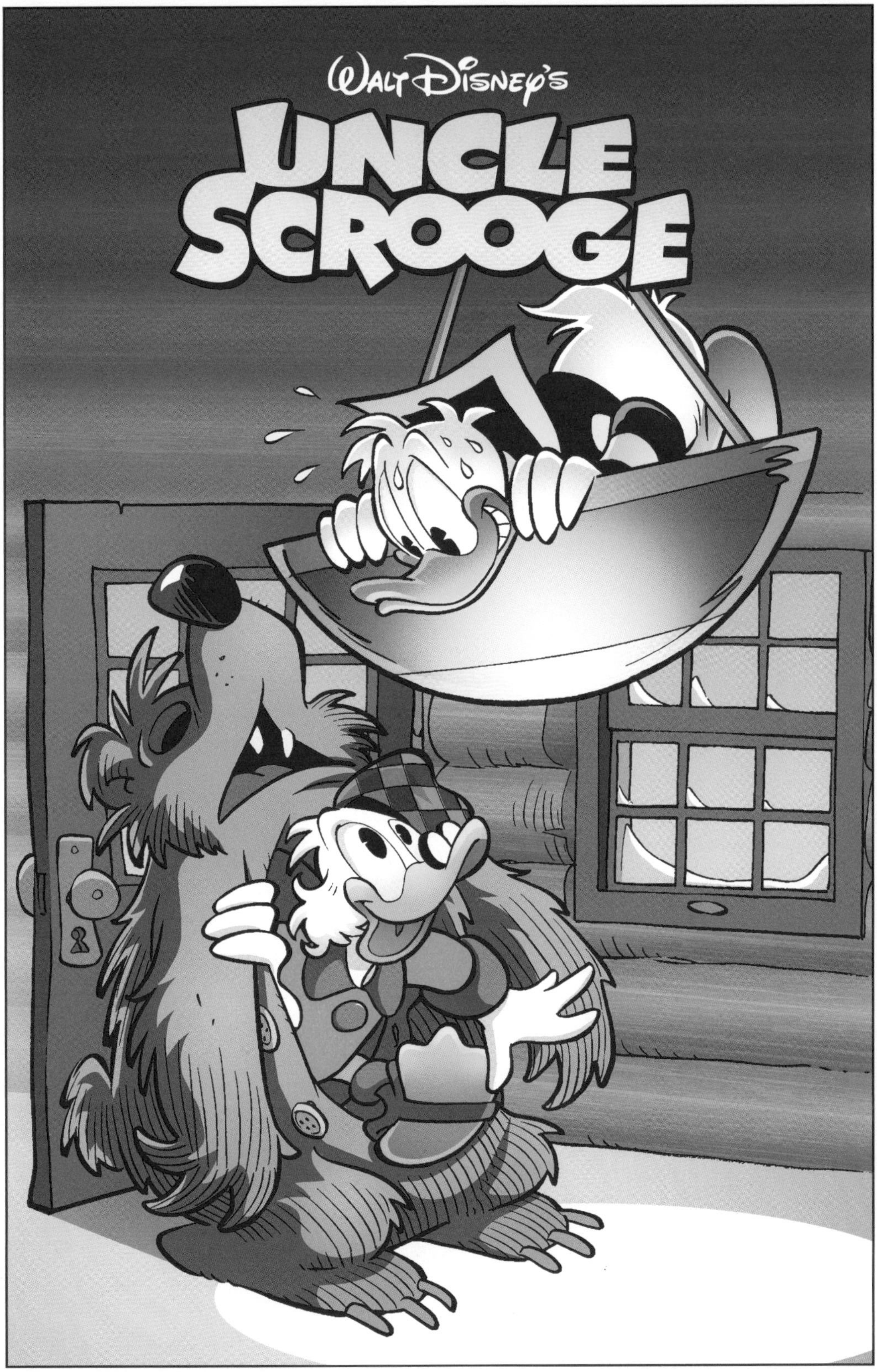
Walt Disney's
UNCLE SCROOGE

ANOTHER CHRISTMAS ON BEAR MOUNTAIN

Cover art for Danish *Walt Disney's Jumbobog* 343, December 23, 2008; first American printing on *Uncle Scrooge* 413, December 2015. Art by Giorgio Cavazzano; color by Ronda Pattison.

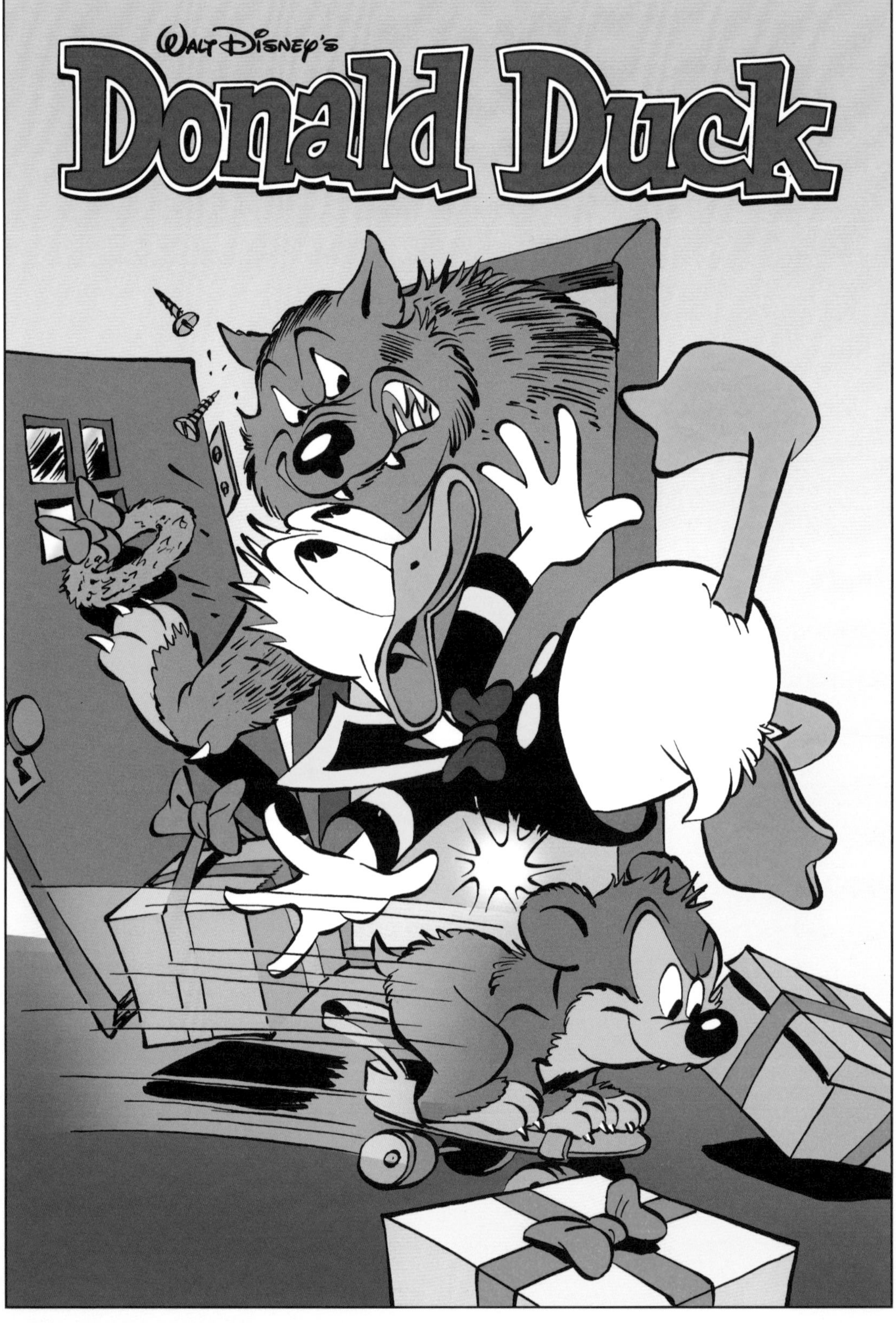
WALT DISNEY'S
Donald Duck

CHRISTMAS ON BEAR MOUNTAIN

Cover art for supplement to Danish *Anders And & Co.* 2012-50, December 10, 2012.

Art by Daan Jippes; colors by David Gerstein.

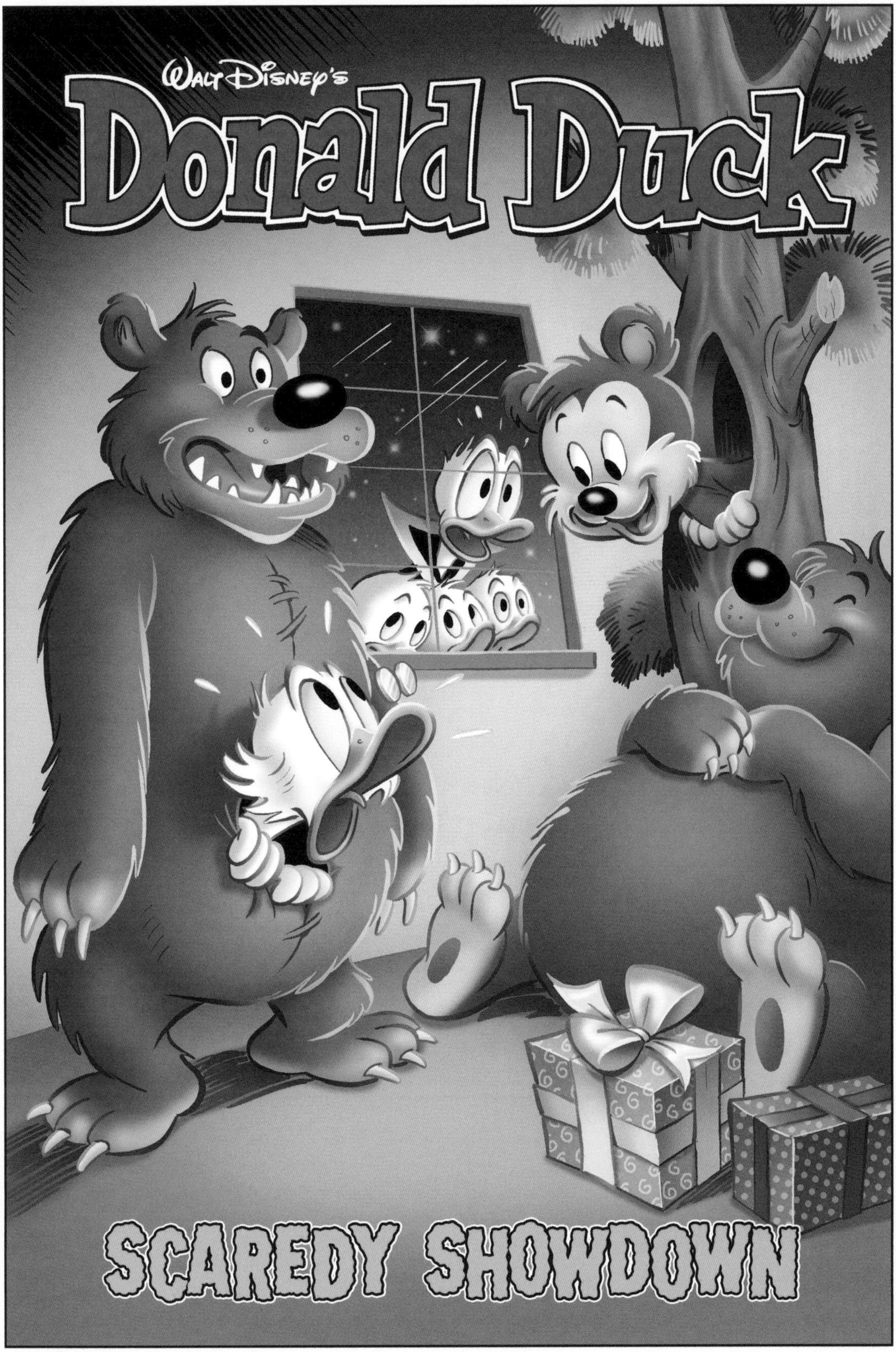
Walt Disney's
Donald Duck
SCAREDY SHOWDOWN

SCAREDY SHOWDOWN

Cover art for supplement to Dutch *Donald Duck Weekblad* 2017-52, December 21, 2017.
Pencils by Carmen Pérez and Michel Nadorp; inks and colors by Comicup Studio.

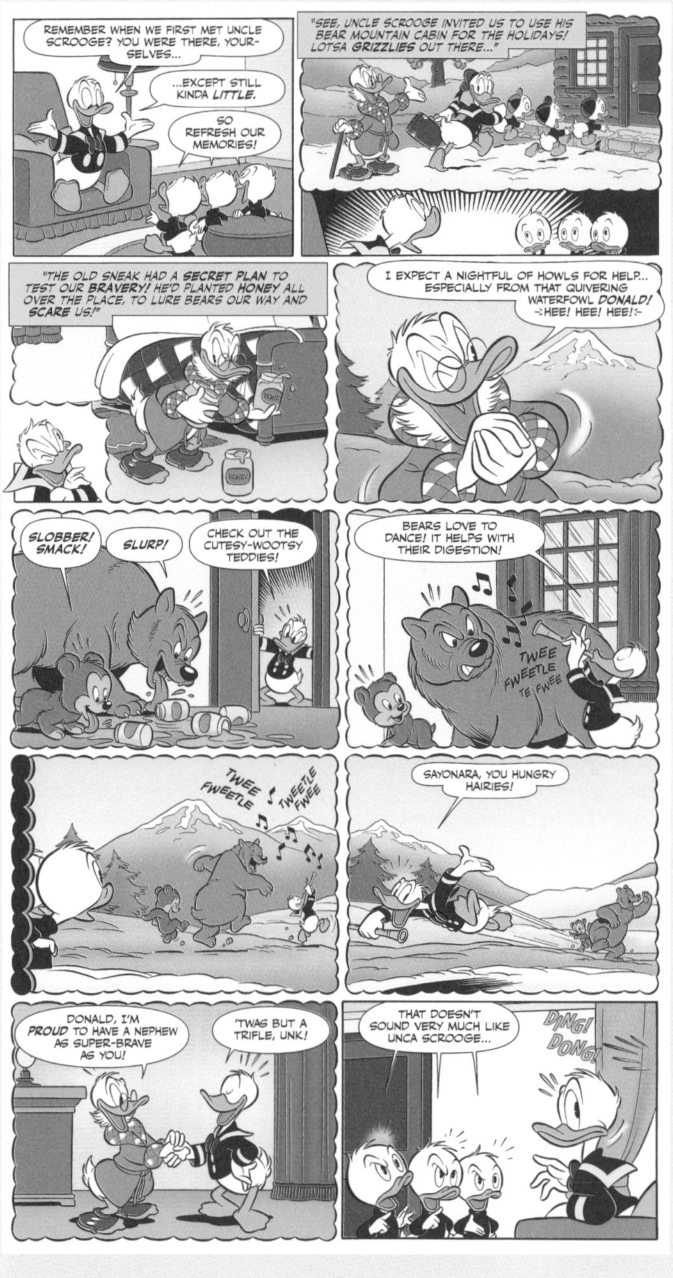
REMEMBER WHEN WE FIRST MET UNCLE SCROOGE? YOU WERE THERE, YOURSELVES...
...EXCEPT STILL KINDA LITTLE.
SO REFRESH OUR MEMORIES!
"SEE, UNCLE SCROOGE INVITED US TO USE HIS BEAR MOUNTAIN CABIN FOR THE HOLIDAYS! LOTSA GRIZZLIES OUT THERE..."
"THE OLD SNEAK HAD A SECRET PLAN TO TEST OUR BRAVERY! HE'D PLANTED HONEY ALL OVER THE PLACE, TO LURE BEARS OUR WAY AND SCARE US!"
I EXPECT A NIGHTFUL OF HOWLS FOR HELP... ESPECIALLY FROM THAT QUIVERING WATERFOWL DONALD! -HEE! HEE! HEE!-
SLOBBER! SMACK!
SLURP!
CHECK OUT THE CUTESY-WOOTSY TEDDIES!
BEARS LOVE TO DANCE! IT HELPS WITH THEIR DIGESTION!
TWEE FWEETLE TE FWEE
TWEE FWEETLE TWEETLE FWEE
SAYONARA, YOU HUNGRY HAIRIES!
DONALD, I'M PROUD TO HAVE A NEPHEW AS SUPER-BRAVE AS YOU!
'TWAS BUT A TRIFLE, UNK!
THAT DOESN'T SOUND VERY MUCH LIKE UNCA SCROOGE...
DING! DONG!

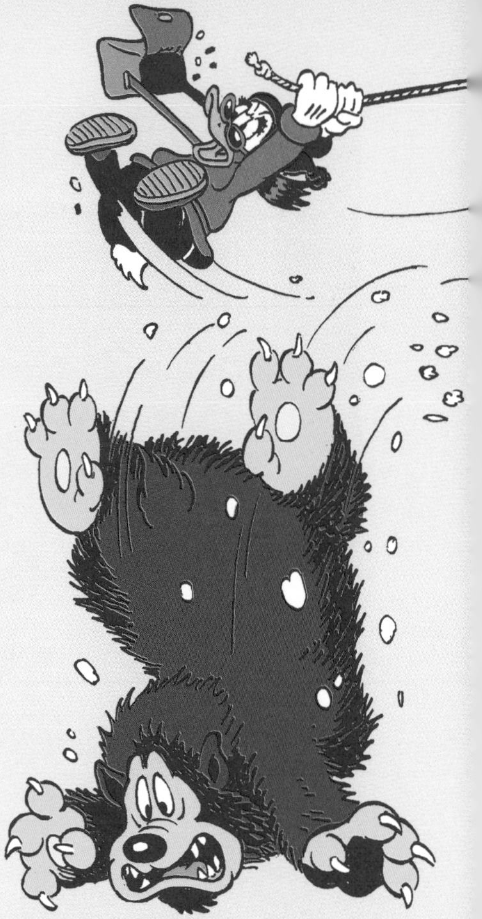

WHAT IF?

In an excerpt from the otherwise unrelated Donald Duck anniversary story "80 Amazing Years" (Dutch *Donald Duck Weekblad* 2014-24), our hero tells his disbelieving nephews this highly suspect version of the original Bear Mountain saga, with a more heroic Donald and a much meaner Scrooge. While this tall tale is windy even by Duckburg standards, it is—as of this writing—the only explanation ever given for how the Ducks got the bears *out* of Uncle Scrooge's cabin again. Story by Evert Geradts, pencils by Maximino Tortajada Aguilar, inks by Comicup Studio; translation, dialogue, and lettering by David Gerstein.

EDITORIAL STAFF

Editor **DAVID GERSTEIN** is an animation and comics researcher, writer, and editor best known for his work with The Walt Disney Company and its licensees. His published projects include *The Floyd Gottfredson Library of Walt Disney's Mickey Mouse* (Fantagraphics Books, 2011-2017), *The Don Rosa Library* (Fantagraphics Books, 2014-2018), and *Mickey Mouse: The Ultimate History* (with J.B. Kaufman; Taschen, 2018). Gerstein has also worked with Disney in efforts to locate lost Oswald the Lucky Rabbit cartoons and to preserve the Mickey Mouse newspaper strip.

Designer **KAYLA E.** is an award-winning artist, cartoonist, and designer of Mexican-American descent. She is the Art Director at Fantagraphics Books and Principal at Design Altar. *Precious Rubbish*, her experimental book-length autobiographical memoir, will be published by Fantagraphics Books in 2024.

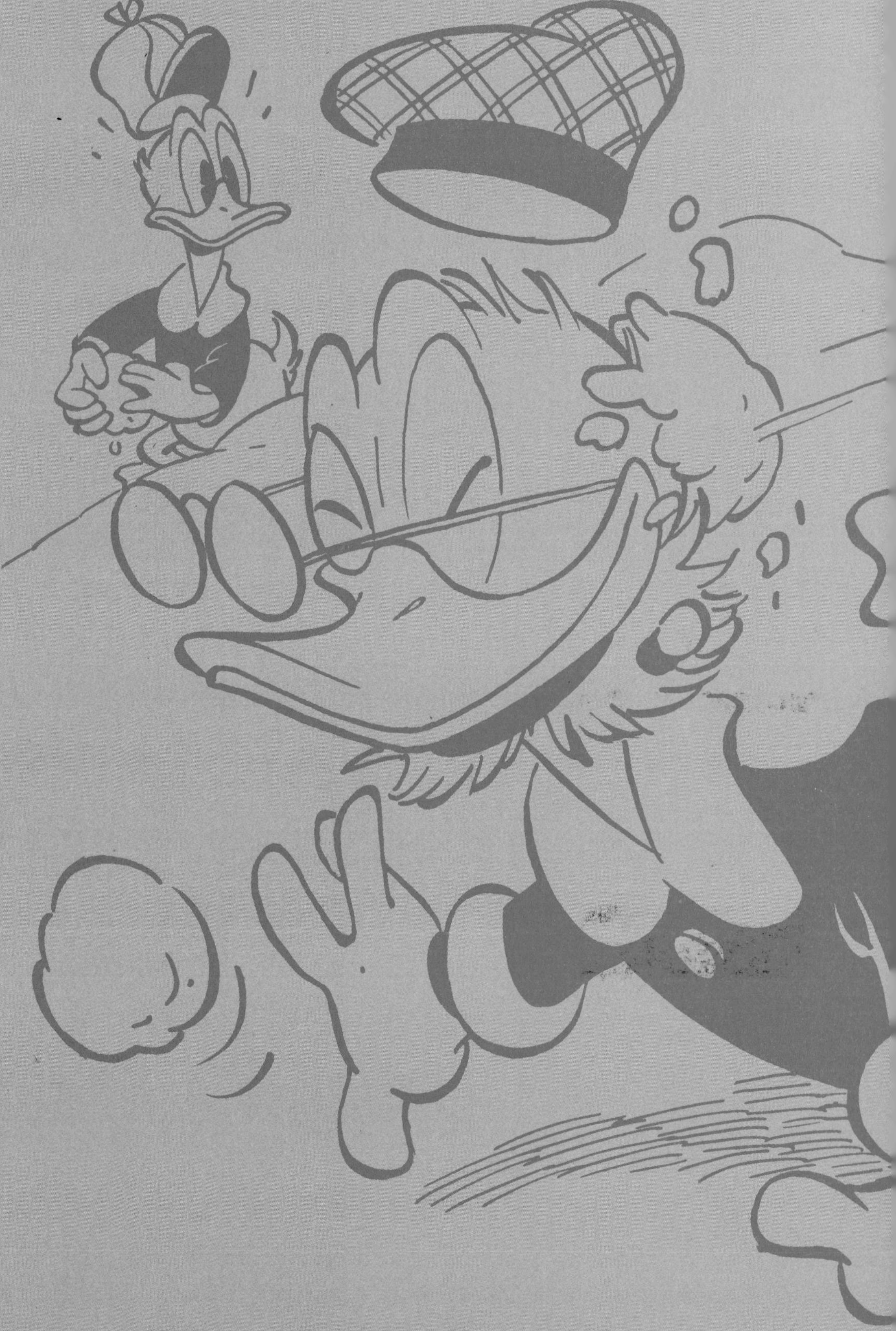